W9-BHI-068

A Practical Guide
to Autism

A Practical Guide to Autism

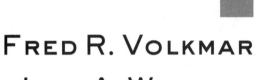

What Every Parent, Family Member, and Teacher Needs to Know

Fred R. Volkmar
Lisa A. Wiesner

WILEY

John Wiley & Sons, Inc.

This book is printed on acid-free paper. ♾

Copyright © 2009 by John Wiley & Sons, Inc. All rights reserved.
Published by John Wiley & Sons, Inc., Hoboken, New Jersey.

Published simultaneously in Canada.

No part of this publication may be reproduced, stored in a retrieval system, or transmitted in any form or by any means, electronic, mechanical, photocopying, recording, scanning, or otherwise, except as permitted under Section 107 or 108 of the 1976 United States Copyright Act, without either the prior written permission of the Publisher, or authorization through payment of the appropriate per-copy fee to the Copyright Clearance Center, Inc., 222 Rosewood Drive, Danvers, MA 01923, (978) 750-8400, fax (978) 646-8600, or on the web at www.copyright.com. Requests to the Publisher for permission should be addressed to the Permissions Department, John Wiley & Sons, Inc., 111 River Street, Hoboken, NJ 07030, (201) 748-6011, fax (201) 748-6008.

Limit of Liability/Disclaimer of Warranty: While the publisher and author have used their best efforts in preparing this book, they make no representations or warranties with respect to the accuracy or completeness of the contents of this book and specifically disclaim any implied warranties of merchantability or fitness for a particular purpose. No warranty may be created or extended by sales representatives or written sales materials. The advice and strategies contained herein may not be suitable for your situation. You should consult with a professional where appropriate. Neither the publisher nor author shall be liable for any loss of profit or any other commercial damages, including but not limited to special, incidental, consequential, or other damages.

This publication is designed to provide accurate and authoritative information in regard to the subject matter covered. It is sold with the understanding that the publisher is not engaged in rendering professional services. If legal, accounting, medical, psychological or any other expert assistance is required, the services of a competent professional person should be sought.

Designations used by companies to distinguish their products are often claimed as trademarks. In all instances where John Wiley & Sons, Inc. is aware of a claim, the product names appear in initial capital or all capital letters. Readers, however, should contact the appropriate companies for more complete information regarding trademarks and registration.

For general information on our other products and services please contact our Customer Care Department within the U.S. at (800) 762-2974, outside the United States at (317) 572-3993 or fax (317) 572-4002.

Wiley also publishes its books in a variety of electronic formats. Some content that appears in print may not be available in electronic books. For more information about Wiley products, visit our website at www.wiley.com.

Library of Congress Cataloging-in-Publication Data

Volkmar, Fred R.
  A practical guide to autism : what every parent, family member, and teacher needs to know / By Fred R. Volkmar, Lisa A. Wiesner.
      p. cm.
   Includes bibliographical references and index.
   ISBN 978-0-470-39473-1 (pbk.)
  1. Autism. I. Wiesner, Lisa A. II. Title.
   RC553.A88V65 2009
   616.85'88200835—dc22

                                                                                    2009021153

Printed in the United States of America
10 9 8 7 6 5 4 3 2 1

To Lucy and Emily,
who have taught us about being parents
and to the many children and their parents
who have taught us about being doctors

Contents

Foreword

Autism is in the public spotlight now more than ever as new research and information appears almost daily. Although in many ways this is a positive development it also presents challenges to families and practitioners who want to keep up with the latest developments and are left to sift through new information by themselves to see what is credible and relevant for them. Each of us needs a personal research assistant who can determine which information we need to pay attention to and let us know how it might affect our daily work and the children we are living with or serve.

Since we each don't have our own research assistants on staff, I am delighted to recommend this wonderful book by Fred Volkmar and Lisa Wiesner. Both of these talented professional leaders have combined their scientific skills and understanding of the field with great practical experience and ideas about how research can be translated into clinical practice. The result is a book that provides the best and most comprehensive information about recent scientific developments and a splendid practical guide for how they are being implemented and what we are learning in the process. The issues are presented in all of their complexity but translated into language that is clear, direct, and easy to follow. The format also lends itself to understanding the complex issues and their implications through excellent charts, question and answer sections, and chapters that vary from describing diagnostic issues to stating very specifically how to expand and evaluate the services one is receiving. The comprehensive references and lists of additional resources also add greatly to the overall package.

As a professional dedicated to understanding scientific advances and helping families and teachers to utilize them most effectively, I am very pleased to have an ally like this book available. I am very grateful to the authors for providing a very credible, practical, and relevant addition to our field to help the many advocates and family practitioners to better understand the exciting new developments and how they can be implemented in our day to day work. Those taking the time to read through this superb volume will find it time well spent that pays back dividends in many different ways.

Gary B. Mesibov, Ph.D.
Professor and Director of TEACCH
Treatment and Education of Autistic and Related Communication
Handicapped Children
University of North Carolina at Chapel Hill

Preface

We have written this book to provide parents and teachers with information that we hope will help them get the best possible care for their child or the children under their care. The two of us approach this from slightly different perspectives. One of us, Fred Volkmar, is a child psychiatrist whose main area of clinical work and research is in autism. The other, Lisa Wiesner, is a pediatrician who has seen children with autism and other disabilities in her pediatric practice. In addition to bringing our professional perspectives to the book, the two of us are married and parents of two children. We hope that this book will provide parents and teachers of individuals with autism and related disorders some practical and useful information.

Our aim is to provide an understandable guide to what we feel are the most important things for parents and teachers to know. We try, as much as possible, to refer readers to relevant materials—both books, chapters, and research papers. We have tried, as much as we can, to stick with resources that are readily available and written in ways that parents as well as professionals can understand. It is, in some ways, gratifying to be able to say that we are by no means exhaustive in this regard. There are many excellent resources not included here, although we've tried to give a reasonable sample of the best things available.

We have tried to think very broadly about the kinds of information that parents and teachers need to know. Accordingly, we have chapters focused on a wide range of topics. Given our interest in the medical as well as behavioral and educational aspects of autism, we've included chapters on medical issues, safety, and medications, as well as what would be the more usual chapters in a book of this kind.

We are very much aware that, for parents, the rewards of raising a child with an autism spectrum disorder are just as great as for any other parents. However, the challenges can be more daunting because parents have to take the child's difficulties into account in almost all decisions made about his or her education and health care. This book reviews basic information about autism and related conditions and how these disorders are diagnosed and treated. Keep in mind that in this book we are trying to provide important *general* information that will help parents and teachers provide good care. This book can't (and won't) substitute for having a good working relationship with the various professionals who can advise you about what is best for your child in particular. The information provided in this book should supplement but does not replace the need for the child and family to have an ongoing relationship with educators, health and mental health care providers, and legal professionals who know the child and specifics of the situation very well. Laws, for example, can vary significantly from state to state, and this knowledge may be important as parents and others think about long-term planning. Similarly, keep in mind that while we've made every effort to be accurate and up to date, knowledge changes over time, and with the increasing amount of research on autism, the pace of change has quickened considerably.

Over the past decade there have been important advances in understanding the syndrome and in treating its symptoms. We know now that we can recognize and reduce the negative effects of these conditions on the child's development and behavior. In considering any intervention, it is always important to weigh the risk against the possible benefit of the intervention. As the saying goes, "The perfect is sometimes the enemy of the good." That is, sometimes it is better not to strive for perfection but for reasonable care and quality of life. As discussed in this book, many new treatments for autism also periodically become available. Sometimes these are well evaluated scientifically. Unfortunately, much of the time they are not. In a later chapter in this book, we will review some of these treatments and discuss how parents and teachers can make informed decisions about using them.

In each chapter we include questions from parents and our answers. We hope that these are a helpful way for you to learn from the experience of others. Throughout the book, we also include some tables and boxed material with additional information. The final sections of the book include a glossary as well as a list of additional resources. A reading list is included at the end of every chapter. Again, remember that in reading this or any book, it is important to interpret the information with the specific child in mind. In this effort, various professionals can be important allies.

We are grateful to a number of our colleagues who have reviewed parts of this book in our efforts to make it helpful to parents. We have profited from their wisdom and comments. They include, in alphabetical order: Karyn Bailey, Leah Booth, Rebecca Carman, Kasia Chawarska, Mark Durand, Tina Goldsmith, Debbie Hilibrand, Ami Klin, Kathy Koenig, Andrés Martin, Prisca Marvin, Nancy Moss, Rhea Paul, Michael Powers, Brian Reichow, Terrell Reichow, Penn Rhodeen, Celine Saulnier, Larry Scahill, Alison Singer, Tristam Smith, Kathy Tsatsanis, and Sally Zanger. We also thank our various colleagues who kindly allowed us to reprint, sometimes with modifications, materials from other sources, particularly the *Handbook of Autism*. Gary Mesibov merits special thanks for his willingness to contribute a foreword. We also are grateful to our editor, Patricia Rossi, and the staff at Wiley for their unflagging support and help in making this book as parent friendly as possible. We also thank a dedicated staff of professionals who helped us assemble the final copy—Lori Klein and Rosemary Serra, and, in particular, Emily Deegan, who went above and beyond the call of duty in coping with the many demands of producing this book. Finally, we thank our children, who have taught us much about child development, and, of course, our patients and their families, who have taught us much about autism.

Fred Volkmar, MD
Lisa Wiesner, MD

CHAPTER 1

What Is Autism?

This chapter gives some background on **autism** and related **autism spectrum disorders (ASDs)**. The recognition of autism as a disorder is a relatively recent one, first described in 1943 but not "officially" used as a diagnosis until 1980. Other conditions such as Asperger's disorder were "officially" recognized even more recently. In this chapter we discuss these disorders and how our understanding of them has changed over the years. This is important for several reasons. One is that you may hear many different terms used to describe a child's difficulties. Second, because knowledge has changed over the years, there are some misconceptions about autism that you may encounter (particularly among people who haven't kept up with the field!). Finally, if you are looking at this book, you are probably wondering if a child you know has autism. We think it would be helpful for you to know something about autism!

Some Terms

The term *pervasive developmental disorder* **(PDD)** refers to the overarching group of conditions to which autism belongs. The term *PDD* refers to the *class* of disorder to which autism belongs—autism is a kind of PDD like apples are a kind of fruit. Within this class, several disorders are now officially recognized: Autism (also referred to as autistic disorder, infantile autism, or childhood autism), **Rett's disorder**, **childhood disintegrative disorder (CDD)** (also sometimes referred to as Heller's syndrome or disintegrative "psychosis"), **Asperger's** disorder (also sometimes called Asperger's syndrome or autistic psychopathy), and, finally, **pervasive developmental disorder not otherwise specified (PDD-NOS)** (sometimes termed *atypical PDD* or *atypical autism*). The terms *PDD* and *PDD-NOS* are sometimes confusing. The term *PDD* technically refers to all these disorders—that is, to the entire group of conditions. The term *PDD-NOS* is a specific diagnosis included within the PDD category; it refers to a condition in which the child has some troubles suggestive of autism, but these don't seem to fit the better defined diagnostic categories – it is essentially a term for conditions that are suggestive of autism but "not quite" autism. Paradoxically, this condition is probably the most common pervasive developmental disorder but is also the least studied. Although the term *ASD* is commonly used, it is not an "official" term but generally means the same thing as PDD, that is a disorder somewhere in the autism "ballpark." There are official guidelines for the diagnosis of each condition (see Appendix 1).

What Is an "Official" Diagnosis?

The most frequently used system for diagnosis in the United States is the American Psychiatric Association's ***Diagnostic and Statistical Manual of Mental Disorders***. It now exists in its fourth edition and is often referred to as **DSM-IV**. The diagnoses in the DSM-IV and the code numbers assigned to these diagnoses are used for many different purposes, such as record keeping, public health information, and insurance reimbursement. The DSM shares code numbers with the international diagnostic system (*International Classification of Diseases*, 10th ed. [**ICD**-10]). Fortunately, at present, the DSM and ICD approaches to the diagnosis of autism and related conditions are essentially the same. These give guidelines to physicians and other health care providers about diagnoses. As you can imagine, when there is a simple blood test or guideline (e.g., as there is for diabetes), the diagnostic part of things is pretty straightforward. For other conditions, particularly those involving development and behavior, we are not yet at the stage of having simple blood tests, so these guidelines focus more on the history of the child's development and observation of the child's behaviors. These guidelines are intended to particularly help people (including health care professionals) who aren't experts about the specific conditions. As we will discuss later in the book (Chapter 3), there are also some other good approaches to screening for conditions like autism—often, these are based on the official guidelines.

PERVASIVE DEVELOPMENTAL DISORDERS (PDDS) (SOMETIMES REFERRED TO AS AUTISM SPECTRUM DISORDERS [ASDS])	
Official Name	**Other names**
Autistic disorder	Childhood autism, infantile autism, early infantile autism
Rett's disorder	Rett's syndrome
Childhood disintegrative disorder	Heller's syndrome, disintegrative disorder, disintegrative psychosis
Asperger's disorder	Asperger's syndrome, autistic psychopathy, autistic personality disorder
Pervasive developmental disorder NOS	Atypical PDD, atypical personality, atypical autism

AUTISM

Leo Kanner and the First Description of Autism

The condition now known as **autistic disorder, childhood autism**, or **infantile autism** (all three names mean the same thing) was first described by Dr. Leo Kanner in 1943. Dr. Kanner, the first child psychiatrist in this country, reported on a group of 11 cases that appeared to exhibit what he called "an inborn disturbance of affective contact." By this he meant that, in contrast to normal babies, these children came into the world without the usual interest in other people. For normally developing babies, people are the single most interesting things in the environment. Kanner believed that the difficulty for children with autism in dealing with the social world was congenital in nature; that is, the children were born with it. Dr. Kanner gave a careful description of the unusual behaviors these first cases exhibited.

For example, he mentioned that these children exhibited "***resistance to change***." By this he meant that they literally were resistant to change, and also referred to this as "**insistence on sameness**." For example, a child might require that the parents take the same route to school or church every time they went and become very upset if there were any deviation from this routine. They might panic if anything in their living room was out of place. They might be very rigid about what kinds of clothes they would wear or foods they would eat. The term *resistance to change* also was used to refer to some of the unusual behaviors frequently seen in autism, for example, the apparently purposeless motor behaviors (stereotypies) such as body rocking, toe walking, and **hand flapping**. Dr. Kanner mentioned that when language developed at all, it was unusual. For example, the child with autism might fail to give the proper tone to his speech (i.e., might speak like a robot) or might echo language (**echolalia**) or confuse personal pronouns (**pronoun reversal**). For example, when asked if he wanted a cookie, the child might respond, "Wanna cookie, wanna cookie, wanna cookie." Sometimes the language that was echoed was from the distant past (delayed echolalia). Sometimes it happened at once (immediate echolalia). Sometimes part of it was echoed but part had been changed (mitigated echolalia). In his original report, Kanner stated that there were two things essential for a diagnosis of autism: (1) the autism or social isolation and (2) the unusual behaviors and insistence on sameness.

As time passed, it became clear that language/communication problems were also important in the diagnosis (when you think about it, of course, language is an important aspect of social development!). Including these problems along with the early onset of the condition that Kanner mentioned, we have what continue to be the four hallmarks of autism: (1) impaired social development of a type quite different from that in normal children; (2) impaired language and communication skills—again of a distinctive type; (3) resistance to change or insistence on sameness, as reflected in inflexible adherence to routines, motor mannerisms, stereotypies, and other behavioral oddities; and (4) an onset in the first years of life.

KANNER QUOTE

The outstanding, "pathognomonic," fundamental disorder is in the children's *inability to relate themselves* in the ordinary way to people and situations from the beginning of life. Their parents referred to them as having always been "self-sufficient"; "like in a shell"; "happiest when left alone"; "acting as if people weren't there"; "perfectly oblivious to everything about him"; "giving the impression of silent wisdom"; "failing to develop the usual amount of social awareness"; "acting almost as if hypnotized." This is not, as in schizophrenic children or adults, a departure from an initially present relationship; it is not a "withdrawal" from formerly existing participation. There is from the start an *extreme autistic aloneness* that, whenever possible, disregards, ignores, shuts out anything that comes into the child from outside. Direct physical contact or such motion or noise as threatens to disrupt the aloneness is either treated "as if it weren't there" . . . resented painfully as a distressing interference.

. . . This insistence on sameness led several children to become greatly disturbed upon the sight of anything broken or incomplete. A great part of the day was spent in demanding not only the sameness of the wording of a request but also the sameness of the sequence of events.

. . . The dread of change and incompleteness seems to be a major factor in the explanation of the monotonous repetitiousness and the resulting *limitation in the variety of spontaneous activity*. A situation, a performance, a sentence is not regarded as complete if it is not made up of exactly the same elements that were present at the time the child was first confronted with it. If the slighted ingredient is altered or removed the total situation is no longer the same. . . .

From Leo Kanner, "Autistic disturbances of affective contact," *Nervous Child*, 2, 217–250, 1943.

Some Early Mistakes About Autism

While Kanner's description remains a "classic," it was not, of course, the last word on the subject. Some aspects of his original report inadvertently served to mislead people. Some of these mistaken first impressions took many years to clarify. For example, Kanner originally thought that children with autism probably had normal **intelligence**. He thought this because they did rather well on some parts of **intelligence (IQ)** tests. On other parts, however, they did quite poorly or refused to cooperate at all. Kanner assumed that, if they did as well on all parts of the IQ test as they did on the one or two parts on which they seemed to do well, the child would not be retarded. Unfortunately, it turns out that often cognitive or intellectual skills are difficult to assess, in large part because they are very scattered. Put another way, children with autism often do some things well, such as solving puzzles, but they may have tremendous difficulty with more language-related tasks. The degree of discrepancy among different skill areas is very unusual in the typically developing population but very frequent in autism. We now appreciate that many, maybe about half, of children with strictly defined autism function in the range of **mental retardation (MR)** or **intellectual disability**[1] when you combine all of their sometimes quite variable scores. However, the pattern of performance in autism is very unusual and quite different from that usually seen in mental retardation without autism. You will see examples of this in Chapter 7, 8 and 9. Similarly, since the different abilities that go into estimating one's intelligence are often so different in autism, the use of a single score can be rather misleading; for example, sometimes a child with autism may have average or above-average abilities when it comes to tasks that are not verbal, whereas the same child's ability with verbal tasks can be very significantly delayed. In such cases, which score is the right one? Both are, in some sense, but this means that you have to understand this and avoid using a single score to represent how the child functions. Sometimes schools or agencies will want to use a single overall score to describe the child's cognitive abilities, but in fact the single score may be very misleading.

Fairly frequently (maybe 10% of the time), children with autism have some unusual ability, for example, to draw (see Figure 1.1), play music, or memorize things, or sometimes calculate days of the week for events in the past or future (calendar calculation). These abilities are usually isolated (the otherwise wonderful portrayal of the man with autism in the movie *Rain Man* is a bit misleading in this respect). These individuals, now usually referred to as *autistic savants*,

---

[1]Note that in some countries, such as England, people have started to refer to mental retardation as a learning disability; in the United States, the term *learning disability* generally refers to a very specific problem in learning (e.g., in reading). We will consistently use the term *intellectual disability* in this book to refer to the combination of significantly subaverage IQ (below 70) and similarly delayed adaptive skills as defined in the DSM-IV as mental retardation. We also use the term *developmentally delayed* to refer to children, especially young children, who seem to be at high risk for having intellectual disability/mental retardation.

FIGURE 1.1   ''Bim gets breakfast in the love kitchen.'' Drawing by a child with autism. Bim is the child's made-up cartoon character. We thank the child and his parents for permission to reproduce. Reprinted, with permission, from F. Volkmar and D. Pauls, Autism. *The Lancet, 2362, 1134, 2003.* Reprinted with permission.

sometimes lose their abilities as they get older. But it was just this kind of remarkable ability that led people to minimize the child's areas of difficulties.

FALSE LEADS FOR RESEARCH

- Impression of normal levels of intelligence because children did well on some parts of IQ tests:

  Implication: Bad performance due to lack of motivation of child (rather than variabilty in skills)

  Subsequent research: Significant scatter in abilities is often present, marked discrepancies between skills areas (e.g., verbal and nonverbal IQ) are common.

- Autism a form of schizophrenia:

Impression: Confusion with schizophrenia given the use of the word *autism* (earlier used to describe self-centered thinking in schizophrenia).

Implication: Autism might be the earliest manifestation of schizophrenia.

Subsequent research: Autism and schizophrenia are not related; rarely (no more than expected by chance) children with autism develop schizophrenia.

- Increased rate in more families with higher levels of education in Kanner's original paper:

  Implication: Effects of experience.

  Subsequent research: There is no increase in autism among parents with more education (more educated parents likely to get to the one child psychiatrist in the country).

- No associated medical conditions (children had an attractive appearance):

  Implication: Exclusion of "organic" cases (if medical condition present) from having autism.

  Subsequent research: High rates of seizures, higher than expected rates of some disorders—especially some genetic disorders.

Another source of confusion came because Dr. Kanner originally suggested that autism was not associated with other medical conditions. We now know this is not true. Over the years, hundreds of conditions have been reported to be related to autism; it now seems that really only a few are especially frequent with autism. For example, we now know that sometimes autism is seen with conditions like **fragile X syndrome** or **tuberous sclerosis** (both of which will be discussed in Chapter 10).

When we look at all the different medical conditions that might be involved in causing or contributing to the child's autism, probably no more than 10% of autistic individuals have them. Most importantly, as children with autism were followed over time, it became apparent that 20–25% of them would develop **seizures (epilepsy)**, as we discuss in Chapter 12.

Dr. Kanner originally guessed that autism was a very distinctive condition, and we now know that this is true. At the same time, he used the word *autism*— a word that previously had been used to describe the unusual, self-centered, and self-contained thinking seen in a major mental disorder called **schizophrenia**. Thus, his use of the word *autism* suggested to many that perhaps autism was the earliest form of schizophrenia. It took many years for this to be clarified. We now know that autism and schizophrenia are not related. Very occasionally, but not more than would be expected by chance, individuals with autism may, as adolescents or adults, develop an illness like schizophrenia. Autism differs from schizophrenia, however, in many different ways, including its clinical features, course, associated difficulties, and family history.

Finally, Kanner mentioned that in 10 of 11 families, the parent or parents were highly educated and successful. It also appeared that parents and children interacted somewhat unusually at times. This led to the idea, particularly in the 1950s, that highly successful parents somehow ignored or otherwise ill treated their child to cause autism and that, as a result, autistic children might be well served by isolating them from their families. This view was taken by a man named Bruno Bettelheim at his school at the University of Chicago. It is now very clear that this is not true. Instead, it is clear that Kanner's original sample was a highly selected one; that is, individuals who were very educated and successful in the 1940s would be just the kinds of people who could find the one person and only child psychiatrist in the country who was doing research on the kinds of problems their children had. It also became clear that unusual aspects of parent–child interaction were just as likely to come from the child, rather than the parent. In contrast to the 1950s, where often the emphasis was on putting the child in an institution, we now believe that children with autism are best served by remaining in their families and communities and that other children, parents, and family members are their best and strongest advocates.

Services for Children with Autism

Until the passage of the Education for All Handicapped Children Act in 1975, parents of children with autism often were at a loss as to how to educate them. Research began to suggest that structured educational programs were more effective than unstructured ones—that is, programs in which the adult had an agenda for teaching the child were better than ones in which the child was left to her own devices to learn. Before 1975, parents often were told by schools that there was no way their child could be educated. Often, parents were advised to place their child in a residential or large state institution where the child got little in the way of intervention. Indeed only a small proportion of children with autism were educted in public schools before passage of this law.

Now schools in the United States are mandated to provide a free and appropriate education for all individuals with disabilities. This is a radically different approach. As programs have become increasingly sophisticated, schools have done an increasingly better job of providing education for children with autism. This means that schools often are now the major place for **intervention** for children with autism. As a result, it appears that more children are being identified in schools and receiving services and, importantly, it also seems that, as a group, children with autism are doing better. As we'll talk about in Chapter 9 many are now able to go to college.

ASPERGER'S DISORDER

In understanding Asperger's disorder, it is important to know where the concept came from in the first place, how it has been used over the years to refer to very different kinds of problems in children, and how it is used now. Hans Asperger was a medical student working at the University of Vienna during World War II. He had to write a paper on some aspect of research, and he chose to write his paper on boys who had trouble forming groups. These boys had marked social problems, but their language and communication was, in some ways, very good. Asperger described them as being rather pedantic "little professors" who tended to intellectualize everything. Asperger also mentioned that they had unusual interests. For example, the child would know all the train or bus schedules into and out of Vienna. These unusual and what are termed **circumscribed interests** continue to be an important feature of the condition. They are unusual in that they are indeed highly circumscribed but, more importantly, they interfere with other aspects of the child's life. This is what changes something from being a personality quirk into a disorder that merits intervention. In addition, Asperger mentioned that the boys were clumsy and awkward in terms of motor skills. He also mentioned that in several cases it appeared that other family members, particularly fathers, had similar kinds of problems.

ASPERGER'S DISORDER

- Asperger (1944) medical student in Vienna wrote his medical school thesis on boys who couldn't form groups.
- Described a series of boys with marked social and motor problems, unusual circumscribed interests (that interfered with getting skills in other areas), but good language and cognitive abilities. Family history was often positive for similar problems in fathers.
- Modifications in original description over time. Cases seen in girls, in lower IQ individuals, some individuals with language problems.

Asperger thought of the condition he described as something more like a personality trait, rather than a developmental disorder. He speculated that the condition was not usually recognized until after about age 3. Asperger originally chose a name that has been translated from the German as either *autistic psychopathy* or *autistic personality disorder* for the condition; that is, he used the word *autistic* in the same way that Leo Kanner, just a year before, had used the word *autism*. However, because of the war, neither Asperger nor Kanner knew of each other's work for some time. Asperger used the word *psychopathy* because he also noted that these boys had difficulties with being compliant and had some behavior problems. In recent years, the practice has been to refer to this condition as *Asperger's disorder* or *Asperger's syndrome* (AS). Asperger, who lived for many years after describing this condition, saw many cases in his lifetime. And even until the end of his life, he felt that the condition was different from infantile autism.

Although Asperger had been working on his condition for many years following World War II, it received little recognition until the 1980s in English-speaking countries when Dr. Lorna Wing published a paper on it. She said that some aspects of Asperger's original report had to be modified. For example, she felt AS could be seen in girls and children with mild mental retardation. She also pointed out that the family histories could be more complicated than Asperger originally thought. As time went on, several different views of Asperger's disorder came into being. Some people were confused about the relationship of Asperger's disorder and autism; that is, whether Asperger's disorder was just the same thing as autism in smarter people. Another set of investigators and clinicians equated the term with adults with autism. Yet another set of clinicians would use the term *Asperger's disorder* interchangeably with the term *pervasive developmental disorder not otherwise specified* or *atypical pervasive developmental disorder* (this is a concept discussed subsequently in this chapter). Finally, some continued to use the term *Asperger's disorder* to refer to a specific set of symptoms that would deserve a special category in a book like the DSM-IV.

Additional problems arose because researchers outside the field of psychiatry also began to see very socially odd children who did not quite seem to have autism. A number of terms came into use that had some degree of overlap with AS. For example, some **neurologists** described something they called the *right hemisphere learning disability syndrome*; from within the speech/language literature came the concept of *semantic–pragmatic processing disorder*, and from psychology a profile of disabilities called the **nonverbal learning disability** (NLD) syndrome was described. Within the field of psychiatry itself, there have been some attempts to describe children with problems similar to those described by Asperger, notably the notion of **"schizoid personality"** as described by Sula Wolf and her colleagues (1995). It is perhaps not surprising, given all these factors, that there has been much controversy about Asperger's disorder.

As currently defined, AS shares some features with autism—notably, the social interaction problems—but early language and cognitive skills are relatively preserved. In contrast to autism, the child's difficulties usually are not recognized for some years, and usually the child has a very intense and all-absorbing interest. Figure 1.2 provides an autobiographical statement (name changed, of course) and drawing illustrating this 10-year-old boy's area of obsessive interest—in his case, time in the universal sense. He was interested in fitting together the various

My name is Robert Edwards. I am an intelligent, unsociable but adaptable person. I would like to dispel any untrue rumors about me. I cannot fly. I cannot use telekinesis. My brain is not large enough to destroy the entire world when unfolded. I did not teach my long-haired guinea pig, Chronos, to eat everything in sight (that is the nature of the long-haired guinea pig).

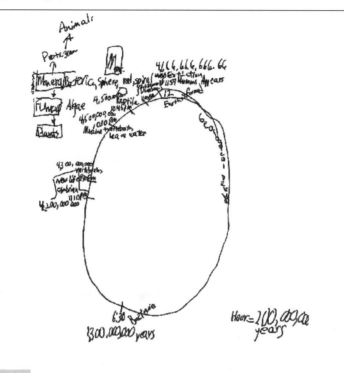

FIGURE 1.2   **Autobiographical statement and drawing of area of special interest, 10-year-old boy with Asperger's disorder.**

Volkmar et al. *American Journal of Psychiatry, 157*(2), 262–267. Reprinted with permission.

periods of recorded and prerecorded history and would spend his free time researching these issues and trying to talk to peers about them.

Sometimes it is difficult to distinguish AS from high-functioning autism. Regardless of which is the better term, the important thing here is to highlight that the child's difficulties are not simply willful bad behavior, but have come from a developmental problem—this is particularly true when a child has good verbal skills. Often, children with AS have a particular kind of learning disability, NLD where nonverbal skills can be quite impaired even when verbal skills are good. Documenting the child's profile of strengths and weaknesses can be very helpful to schools. One important treatment difference from more typical autism is that since children with AS have better verbal skills, we can sometimes use language-based treatments such as very structured and problem-oriented **psychotherapy** and counseling. If verbal skills are much better than nonverbal ones, we can also try to use this in teaching. Other implications of AS may have to do with other aspects of planning, for example, vocational planning. Patients with AS may not have good motor skills, and it is important to realize this in helping them plan for adult work.

NONVERBAL LEARNING DISABILITY (NLD)

- A *profile* (pattern of strengths and weaknesses) on psychological testing.
- Both *assets* AND *deficits* are present.

Strengths	Weaknesses
Auditory perception	Tactile perception
Rote verbal capacities	Motor coordination
Verbal memory skills	Visual-spatial skills
Verbal output	Nonverbal problem solving

- NLD has a deleterious impact on the person's capacity for socialization.
- NLD is not an official diagnosis.
- NLD does seem to be frequently associated with Asperger's disorder and sometimes PDD-NOS but NOT with autism (in autism a different profile is usually seen with nonverbal skills being a relative strength for the child, not an area of weakness).
- Important implications of NLD profile for research on brain mechanisms.

CHILDHOOD DISINTEGRATIVE DISORDER

Although it is, fortunately, rather rare, CDD is important for several reasons. It first was described almost 100 years ago by a specialist in special education, Theodore Heller, who was working in Vienna. He noticed that several children had developed normally for some years and then had a marked and profound loss of skills. They did not regain skills to previous levels. Originally, Heller termed this condition *dementia infantilis*. Subsequently, it has been called other things: **disintegrative psychosis**, **Heller's syndrome**, or now childhood disintegrative disorder. The term *disintegrative psychosis* captured the child's loss of skills, but the word **psychosis** implied some loss of reality testing, which we no longer believe exists. The term *childhood disintegrative disorder* has the advantage of describing the condition without prejudging its cause. This condition clearly is quite rare, although it is also the case that many times children with the condition probably have not been adequately diagnosed or studied. Consistent with what Heller said in the first place, children with this condition develop normally for several years of life. Typically, they talk on time, walk on time, acquire the capacity to speak in sentences, are normally socially related, and have achieved bladder and bowel control. Usually between the ages of 3 and 4 years, the child experiences a marked and enduring regression in skills. Many behaviors that resemble those in autism develop, such as the motor mannerisms (stereotypies) and the profound lack of interest in other people. One of the interesting questions for present research is whether children with autism who have a major regression in their **development** are exhibiting something like this condition. We talk more about these issues and regression in Chapter 13.

CHILDHOOD DISINTEGRATIVE DISORDER (CDD)

- First described by Theodore Heller in 1908.
- Child has a period of normal development.
  Usually 3–4 years, normal language and self-care skills.
  By definition, the child has the capacity for speech.
- Either rapid or more gradual regression in multiple areas.
  Child comes to exhibit many features of autism.
- Sometimes a brain-based disorder is found that accounts for the regression.
- Usually minimal recovery (outcome in general is worse than autism).
- Condition is rare but of much interest given potential for finding a specific cause.

RETT'S DISORDER

In 1966, a Viennese physician, Andreas Rett, described a group of girls with an unusual history. They were apparently normal at birth and developed normally for the first months of life. However, usually within the first year or so of life, their head growth began to decrease in rate. In addition, they started to lose developmental skills they had acquired. As time went on, they lost purposeful hand movements, and various unusual symptoms began to develop. They seemed to lose interest in other people in the preschool years, which is why there was the potential to misdiagnose the girls as having autism. As they became somewhat older, the developmental losses became more progressive and quite different from those in autism. Unusual hand-washing or hand-wringing stereotypies developed. Purposeful hand movements were lost (see Figure 1.3).

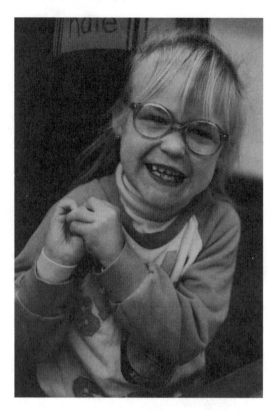

FIGURE 1.3   **Stereotypic hand movements in Rett's syndrome**

Reprinted, with permission, from R. Van Acker, J. Loncola, and E. Y. Van Acker. Rett's syndrome: A pervasive developmental disorders. In F. Volkmar, R. Paul, A. Klin, & D. Cohen (Eds.), *Handbook of autism and pervasive developmental disorders*, (3rd ed., chap. 7, p. 127).Hoboken, NJ: Wiley, 2005.

Additionally, the girls developed other unusual respiratory symptoms, such as breath-holding spells or air swallowing (aerophagia). Seizure disorders sometimes developed as well. Problems in walking and in posture were seen and, over time, **scoliosis** (curvature of the spine) often developed. By adulthood, the girls had become severely retarded young women. However, their course was different from that seen in autism. The degree of problems in breathing, loss of hand movements and other motor difficulties, curvature of the spine, and so on suggested that this was a very distinct condition. We discuss Rett's disorder in much more detail in Chapter 12.

RETT'S DISORDER

- First described by Andreas Rett (1966).
- All cases were female in his original report.
- Early development was normal.

- Head growth slowed (relative to rest of body).
- Purposeful hand movements lost.
- Some "autistic-like" features which tended to lessen over time.
- Various associated problems.
  - Scoliosis (curvature of the spine) and movement problems.
  - Unusual breathing patterns/breath-holding spells.
- Characteristic course.
- A gene has recently been identified that seems to be responsible for Rett's in at least some cases.

PERVASIVE DEVELOPMENTAL DISORDER NOT OTHERWISE SPECIFIED

PDD-NOS is the so-called subthreshold pervasive developmental disorder. That is, this is the category that is used when a child, adolescent, or adult exhibits some features of a PDD but does not meet all the criteria for a diagnosis of one of the very specifically defined PDDs. This diagnosis is problematic in that it is a matter of clinical judgment on the part of clinicians as to whether to use it. Probably not surprisingly, given the essentially "nondefinition" definition, the term is used very inconsistently. Furthermore, the nature of this definition means that it is hard for researchers to have funding to study the condition. Somewhat paradoxically, it almost certainly is the case that this condition is several times more common than autism, affecting perhaps one in several hundred children. When you hear on the radio or television that the rate of autism is 1 in 150 children, it actually is more accurate to say that the rate of autism *spectrum* disorder is 1 in 150; this number includes all of the disorders within the PDD class.

PDD-NOS

- Historic interest in children with some but not all features of autism ("autistic like").
- By definition, the definition is a "negative" one—that is, children who do not meet criteria for autism, Asperger's, etc.
- The child must have problems in the social area of the type seen in autism and at least one in either communication/play or odd behavior.

- The relationship of PDD-NOS to autism remains unclear—is this best seen as part of a "broad autism phenotype" or something different from autism?
- There may be several subtypes of PDD-NOS—some children with PDD-NOS have major problems with attention, others with emotional overreactivity.

Although research on PDD-NOS is relatively sparse, some studies have appeared in recent years. Moreover, clinicians often have more experience from a clinical point of view with it because it seems to be more common than strictly defined autism. Children with PDD-NOS have problems in social interaction, but these are not as severe and pervasive as those in autism. These may include sometimes more overt and sometimes more subtle problems, for example, in initiating conversation, in playing with other children, in relating to parents or siblings. Unusual sensitivities are relatively common, although again usually not as severe as in autism. The term *PDD-NOS* is sometimes also used for children with very severe intellectual deficiency, who often have some features of autism, particularly stereotyped motor movements. With the exception of very retarded children, the outcome in PDD-NOS generally appears to be better than in most if not all of the other PDDs.

For a diagnosis of PDD-NOS to be made, the child should exhibit some problem in social interaction of the type usually seen in autism or other PDDs and at least some problem either in language and communication skills or in unusual behavioral responses to the environment and restricted interests. A single symptom of autism is, by itself, *not* sufficient for a diagnosis of PDD-NOS; rather, there have to be troubles in both the social area and either the language/communication or unusual behaviors category. As a practical matter, the diagnosis of PDD-NOS is used in several rather different situations. Sometimes very young children have many, but not all, of the features of autism. For example, at age 30 months the child may have marked social and communicative difficulties but does not exhibit the unusual behaviors usually associated with autism. This child might be given a diagnosis of PDD-NOS but then go on to develop unusual mannerisms or movements or other unusual responses to the environment; in this case, the diagnosis of autistic disorder would then be made. Occasionally, the term is used rather loosely; for example, someone may talk to you about PDD or mild autism when they mean PDD-NOS. In such situations, it is important to explicitly ask what is meant. Keep in mind that it is perfectly appropriate for a clinician to say that he or she isn't absolutely certain about the diagnosis particularly for younger children where the issue may become clarified only with certainty over time. What is important is getting appropriate services for the child.

How Common Are Autism and Related Conditions?

The first studies of the frequency or epidemiology of autism were conducted in the 1960s. Since that time, many studies have been conducted, mostly in Great Britain and countries other than the United States. Given what we know about autism, there is no reason to suppose that the frequency of autism is vastly different here, although there has been concern, as we'll discuss in a moment, that the frequency of autism may be increasing in this country. The lack of many good studies in the United States complicates the answer to this question, as we'll see shortly; it also makes it harder for educators and others to plan for the care of children with autism.

The various studies around the world have involved over 4 million children. Estimates of the rate of autism vary somewhat from study to study. If you lump all the studies together, a reasonable estimate of the rate is around 1.3 cases per 1,000 if you focus on autism strictly defined; if you broaden the group to include all individuals with a PDD or ASD, the number of cases is somewhere between 3 and 6 per 1,000 children.

Is the Rate of Autism Increasing?

There is some concern that the rate of autism may be increasing. However, we really don't know if this is true for several reasons. First, it is clear that awareness of autism has increased dramatically so that cases are more likely to be noticed. When one of us (FV) moved to New Haven in 1980 to work on autism at the Yale Child Study Center with Donald Cohen, people would ask what my research was about and when I said, "Autism," they would frequently say something like, "Isn't that wonderful—we need more artistic children"; people didn't even know what the word meant! Today, there are ads on radio and television from the Ad Council about autism and posted in the background of TV shows advertising autism-related groups. Another possible reason for an apparent (but not real) increase is changes in the diagnostic guidelines for autism—the current systems (both DSM and ICD) were designed to do a better job of detecting autism in more able children. Another problem has been the tendency to equate autism (strictly defined) with the much broader (and much less well defined) autism "spectrum." Finally, there is an unusual problem with autism. Since the label often gets children more services than other labels, parents may push to get an autism label for educational purposes even if the child doesn't have autism strictly defined (this is a problem called **diagnostic substitution** and one of the reasons we have to be skeptical about state-reported data based on school services). This is a real problem since states, and sometimes regions within states, vary widely (and wildly) in terms of how they provide services—in some states, only the label of autism really gets needed services. There is an excellent and very readable review of these issues in *Unstrange Minds*, a book by Roy Grinker, a professor who is also a parent (the book is listed in the reading list at the end of this chapter).

Sex Differences

It is clear that autism appears to be at least 3 to 5 times more frequent in boys. However, when girls have autism, they are more likely to have intellectual

TABLE 1.1	DIFFERENTIAL DIAGNOSTIC FEATURES OF AUTISM AND NONAUTISTIC PERVASIVE DEVELOPMENTAL DISORDERS				
Feature	Autistic Disorder	Asperger's Disorder	Rett's Disorder	Childhood Disintegrative Disorder	Pervasive Developmental Disorder-NOS
Age at recognition (months)	0–36	Usually >36	5–30	>24	Variable
Sex ratio	M>F	M>F	F (?M)	M>F	M>F
Loss of skills	Variable	Usually not	Marked	Marked	Usually not
Social skills	Very poor	Poor	Varies with age	Very poor	Variable
Communication skills	Usually poor	Fair	Very poor	Very poor	Fair to good
Circumscribed interests	Variable (mechanical)	Marked (facts)	NA	NA	Variable
Family history— similar problems	Sometimes	Frequent	Not usually	No	Sometimes
Seizure disorder	Common	Uncommon	Frequent	Common	Uncommon
Head growth decelerates	No	No.	Yes	No	No
IQ range	Severe MR to normal	Mild MR to normal	Severe MR	Severe MR	Severe MR to normal
Outcome	Poor to good	Fair to good	Very poor	Very poor	Fair to good

M = male, F = female, MR = mental retardation, NA = not applicable.
SOURCE: Adapted, with permission, from F. R. Volkmar & D. Cohen, Nonautistic pervasive developmental disorders. In R. Michaels et al. (Eds.), *Psychiatry* (chap. 27.2, p. 4). Philadelphia, PA: Lippincott-Raven, 1985.

deficiency. We do not yet understand the basis for these differences. One theory is that, perhaps on a genetic basis, girls are generally somewhat less vulnerable to autism (hence the greater frequency in boys) and that for girls to have autism they must have greater genetic or central nervous system damage (hence the higher rate of intellectual deficiency in girls). Asperger's disorder and CDD are more common in males, and Rett's is usually found only in females. There does not appear to be as marked a sex difference in PDD-NOS.

Rates of Other Disorders

Information on the frequency of other PDDs is not nearly as good as that for autism. Fortunately, both Rett's disorder and CDD are much less common than autism. AS estimates have ranged widely, from 1 in 500 children to 1 in 10,000; the condition is clearly less common if one uses a strict definition for it.

PDD-NOS is almost certainly the most common form of pervasive developmental disorder. Some have estimated the frequency of PDD-NOS as frequent as 1 in about 200, but again solid research data are lacking. Clearly, at least one in several hundred have some form of serious social disability consistent with autism or a related condition; this means that these conditions are a major public health problem. Table 1.1 summarizes the similarities and differences of the various PDDs.

SUMMARY

This chapter has given some background information on autism and other PDDs. Relatively speaking, these are all fairly new diagnostic concepts, and in some ways it is surprising that we know as much as we already do about them. All these conditions share impairment in social interaction as a major feature although in Rett's the social problems are most notably early in life and then dramatically lessen. They differ from each other in various ways. The most well known of these disorders, autism, is seen in between 1 in 800 to 1 in 1,000 children. With the exception of PDD-NOS, the other conditions, such as Rett's disorder, CDD, and Asperger's disorder, are probably less common. We know that autism is often, but not always, associated with intellectual deficiency and is more common in boys than in girls. We also know that autism is frequently associated with evidence of brain impairment, such as seizure disorders, and parents (and doctors) should be alert to the possibility of a child's developing seizures. Fragile X is clearly seen in some children with autism, and routine testing for this condition makes sense. It makes sense to be particularly thorough when first evaluating a child for possible autism and in situations where the presentation is unusual and something "does not quite fit."

■ READING LIST

American Psychiatric Association. (2000). *Diagnostic and Statistical Manual of Mental Disorders* (4th ed., text revision). American Psychiatric Press.

Asperger, H. (1944). Die "autistichen Psychopathen" im Kindersalter. *Archive fur psychiatrie und Nervenkrankheiten, 117,* 76–136. Reprinted (in part) in Frith, U. (Ed.) (1991). *Autism and Asperger syndrome.* Cambridge: Cambridge University Press, 1991.

Attwood, T. (2006). *The complete guide to Asperger's syndrome.* Philadelphia, PA: Jessica Kingsley.

Baron-Cohen, S. (2004). *The essential difference: Male and female brains and the truth about autism.* New York: Basic Books.

Bashe, P. R., Kirby, B. L., Baron-Cohen, S., & Attwood, T. (2005). *The OASIS guide to Asperger syndrome: Completely revised and updated: Advice, support, insight, and inspiration.* New York: Crown.

Exkorn, K. (2005). *The autism sourcebook: Everything you need to know about diagnosis, treatment, coping, and healing.* New York: Regan Books.

Fombonne, E. (2005). *Epidemiological studies of pervasive developmental disorders.* In F. R. Volkmar, R. Paul, A. Klin, & D. Cohen (Eds.), *Handbook of autism and pervasive developmental disorders* (3rd ed., pp. 42–69). Hoboken, NJ: Wiley.

Frith, U., & Hill, E. (Eds.). (2004). *Autism: Mind and brain.* New York: Oxford University Press.

Grinker, R. R. (2007). *Unstrange minds: Remapping the world of autism.* New York: Basic Books.

Howlin, P. (1998). *Children with autism and Asperger syndrome: A guide for practicitioners and careers.* New York: Wiley.

Kanner, L. (1943). Autistic disturbances of affective contact. *Nervous Child, 2,* 217–250.

Klin, A., McPartland, J., & Volkmar, F. R. (2005). *Asperger syndrome.* In F. R. Volkmar, R. Paul, A. Klin, & D. Cohen (Eds.), *Handbook of autism and pervasive developmental disorders* (3rd ed., pp. 88–125). New York: Wiley.

Klin, A., Sparrow, S. S., & Volkmar, F. R. (Eds.). (2000). *Asperger syndrome.* New York: Guilford Press.

Mesibov, G. B., Shea, V., & Adams, L. W. (2001). *Understanding Asperger syndrome and high functioning autism.* New York: Kluwer Academic/Plenum Publishers.

Neisworth, J. T., Wolfe, P. S. (2005). *The Autism Encyclopedia.* Baltimore, MD: Brookes.

Powers, M. D. (2000). *Children with autism: A parent's guide* (2nd ed.), Bethesda, MD: Woodbine House.

Powers, M. D., & Poland, J. (2003). *Asperger syndrome and your child: A parent's guide.* New York: HarperCollins.

Romanowski-Bashe, P., Kirby, B. L., Baron-Cohen, S., & Attwood, T. (2005). *The OASIS guide to Asperger syndrome: Completely revised and updated: Advice, support, insight, and inspiration.* New York: Crown.

Schreibman, L. (2005). *The science and fiction of autism.* Cambridge, MA: Harvard University Press.

Siegel, B. (1998). *The world of the autistic child: Understanding and treating autism spectrum disorders.* New York: Oxford University Press.

Thompson, T. (2007). *Making sense of autism.* Baltimore, MD: Brookes.

Towbin, K. (2005). *Pervasive developmental disorder not otherwise specified.* In F. R. Volkmar, R. Paul, A. Klin, & D. Cohen (Eds.), *Handbook of autism and pervasive developmental disorders,* (3rd ed., pp. 165–200). Hoboken, NJ: Wiley.

Van Acker, R., Loncola, J. A., & Van Acker, E. Y. (2005). Rett syndrome: A pervasive developmental disorder. In F. R. Volkmar, R. Paul, A. Klin, & D. Cohen (Eds.), *Handbook of autism and pervasive developmental disorders*, (3rd ed., pp. 126–164). Hoboken, NJ: Wiley.

Volkmar, F. R.(Ed.). (2007). *Autism and pervasive developmental disorders* (rev. ed.). New York: Cambridge University Press.

Volkmar, F., Klin, A., & Pauls, D. (1998). Nosological and genetic aspects of Asperger's syndrome. *Journal of Autism and Developmental Disorders, 28,* 457–463.

Volkmar, F. R., Koenig, K., & State, M. (2005). Childhood disintegrative disorder. In F. R. Volkmar, R. Paul, A. Klin, & D. Cohen (Eds.), *Handbook of autism and pervasive developmental disorders* (3rd ed., pp. 70–86). Hoboken, NJ: Wiley.

Volkmar, F. R., Paul, R., Klin, A., & Cohen, D. (Eds.). (2005). *Handbook of autism and pervasive developmental disorders* (3rd ed.) Hoboken, NJ: Wiley.

Wetherby, A. M., & Prizant, B. M. (2000). *Autism spectrum disorders: A transactional developmental perspective.* Baltimore, MD: Brookes.

Whitman, T. L. (2004). *The development of autism: A self-regulatory perspective.* London: Jessica Kingsley.

Wing, L. (1981). Asperger's syndrome: A clinical account. *Psychological Medicine, 11*(1), 115–129.

Wing, L. (2001). *The autistic spectrum: A parent's guide to understanding and helping your child.* Berkeley, CA: Ulysses Press.

Wolff, S. (1995). *Loners: The life path of unusual children.* London: Routledge.

▪ QUESTIONS AND ANSWERS

1. **Is there a "typical" child with autism?**

    We have information, particularly from epidemiological studies, that tells us about *groups* of children with autism. In this sense, we have information on the typical or "average" child with autism, but it is important to realize that this is not a real individual; rather, it gives a sense of what can be. It is the *range* of what we see in autism, which is very unusual. As a diagnostic term, *autism* can be applied to the angelic-appearing, mute 2-year-old who is sitting in a corner playing with a piece of string; it can also apply to a college graduate who does computer ordering for a small company. If we had a large group of people with autism in a room together, we most likely would be struck initially by the differences and not the similarities. If, however, we spent more time, the similarities would begin to be seen. These would include major problems in negotiating through the social world, in communicating with others, and in responding to the nonsocial environment. These three commonalities are what are seen in every person with autism.

2. **Did autism exist before Leo Kanner described it?**

    Undoubtedly, there were cases of autism before Kanner first described the condition. For example, some people have argued that cases of so-called "wild" or "feral" children like Victor the Wild Boy, who was reported in France in the early 1800s, were really children with autism. It is possible that before the improvements in childhood mortality in the 20th century and before the increased concern with children, cases of autism had not been noticed. It was Kanner's genius to be a very careful observer and become aware of what we now know as autism.

3. **Does the diagnosis really matter?**

This is a good question—the answer is yes and a qualified no. The complication is that diagnosis is used for many different things—for research, for teaching people about commonalities in illnesses and disorders, for communicating rapidly, and for getting educational services. All these are legitimate goals, and the needs for diagnosis will vary somewhat depending on what the goal is. Essentially, the diagnosis grounds us in the general territory we are dealing with, but, of course, in terms of coming up with a program or treatment, we need to take the needs of the individual child into account. There are some people who would advocate against giving a diagnosis to avoid giving premature or stigmatizing labels; however, it is just these labels that sometimes help a child get services. For purposes of research, again depending on what is being studied, often rather strict diagnostic labels are needed, that is, to avoid what would be a confounding or complicating issue in interpreting the results of a research study.

4. **Is the frequency of autism increasing?**

The short answer is that we don't really know for sure. It is the case that *schools* and *departments of education* have seen increased numbers of children with autism presenting for special services. One problem, however, is that labels for educational purposes may be more concerned with getting services than with precise diagnosis. Many educators understandably (from the point of view of giving services) lump autism and all related disorders together—this means that some of the "data" cited as indicating an increase in autism is really about the broader spectrum of autism and related conditions. Often, when one hears about the explosion of "autism," one is really hearing about this. Another problem is that methods of diagnosis have changed over time and there has been a real (and in many ways successful) effort to expand the awareness of teachers, health care professionals, day care providers, and others about autism; that is, part of the reported increase may be more apparent than real in that the cases were already there but had been overlooked. Finally, the lack of good epidemiological data on autism, particularly in this country, makes it very difficult to answer the question in a way we could feel confident in. All this being said, it is concerning that estimates of autism around the world seem to have increased over time—it remains to be seen how much this is a "real" increase.

5. **What are the differences between girls and boys with autism?**

There are several differences. In the first place, boys are much more likely to have autism than girls (about 3 to 5 times more likely). But when girls have autism, they tend to have more severe cognitive problems. It is probably the case that, for whatever reason, girls are less vulnerable than boys and, accordingly, for a girl to get autism a bigger genetic "hit" is needed (presumably accounting for the greater degree of cognitive impairment). In Asperger's disorder (and in individuals with autism who function in the normal cognitive range), the ratio of boys to girls is much higher. In Rett's disorder, females are most commonly affected.

6. **Is childhood disintegrative disorder the same thing as disintegrative psychosis? If so, does that mean it is like schizophrenia?**

An old term for childhood disintegrative disorder was *disintegrative psychosis*. This term came to be used at a time when science wasn't as advanced as it is today; the word *psychosis* was used in a very broad way. Today, the term *psychosis* has a very specific meaning; it implies a loss of reality testing and the presence of problems in thinking, such as delusions and hallucinations. Children with CDD do not exhibit these.

7. **Someone told me that Asperger's disorder is the same as autism. Is this true?**

There is much disagreement about the relationship of the two disorders. Clearly, there is *some* relationship in terms of severe social difficulties. Several different problems complicate this issue. One problem is that the term *Asperger's disorder* has come to be used for many different things; another is that various terms for disorders have come through other sources and these concepts overlap (at least in part) with Asperger's. Terms like semantic–pragmatic processing disorder, right hemisphere syndrome, semantic–pragmatic disorder have all been used—along with nonverbal learning disability. Our own view, and that of the DSM, is that these are separate disorders. Major differences have to do with the fact that language is so very good (in some ways) in Asperger's. Also, in Asperger's, unusual preoccupations with fact-based knowledge about some topic is usually present. Finally, in contrast to autism, parents of children with Asperger's disorder tend not to be worried until the child enters preschool.

8. **Can Rett's coexist with autism?**

No; by definition the two disorders are distinctive. There is a relatively brief "autistic-like" phase in Rett's (usually in the preschool years), but after that the conditions are quite different.

9. **My child has been diagnosed with PDD-NOS but the school has given him the label of autism. Is this okay?**

Labels used by schools often differ somewhat from those used by medical professionals. These labels also vary considerably from state to state and sometimes within states! Often, for purposes of getting appropriate services, the label *autism* is used very broadly, so in this case it may be perfectly fine for your child. Keep in mind that you need to evaluate this in the context of your child's particular needs and that you can always ask to discuss the label and change or drop it.

10. **My daughter had a diagnosis of PDD-NOS when she was younger. Now she is 10 years old and has been mainstreamed for 2 years. She no longer needs special services. Can we now drop the label that used to get her special services that she no longer needs?**

Yes, you can indeed drop the label. If it turns out, for whatever reason, that in the future she needs some special services, you can revisit this issue with the school.

11. **One of the teacher's in my child's Sunday school made some comment to me about parents causing autism. She said she was taught that "refrigerator mothers" did this. Is there any truth to this?**

No, there is no truth to it. In the 1950s, there was some thought that perhaps parental care might cause autism, but it has become apparent that this is not true. A whole generation of professionals (and parents) heard about this, and sometimes you will still find someone who was taught this. Give your friend a copy of this book or another recent one on autism!

CHAPTER 2

What Causes Autism?

The earliest descriptions and discussions of autism, not surprisingly, focused on today what we might call "classical" autism—that is, autism as strictly defined and much less on what we would now think of as autism spectrum disorders or the broader autism phenotype, as it is sometimes called. As we mentioned in the first chapter, Kanner's first paper on autism was very influential in several different ways although some of his first observations have been modified over time. His description of autism was unusually clear about what he saw as the central features present in autism (problems in social interaction and unusual responses to the environment). He also was clear in suggesting that autism was congenital; that is, children were born with it although we now know that sometimes children seem to develop autism in the first years of life. Kanner speculated that autism was not associated with intellectual disability (mental retardation) because children did well on some parts of intelligence quotient (IQ) tests. Some aspects of his report misled people, for example, into thinking parents of children with autism might somehow cause the disorder. The early (and mistaken) notion that autism was more common in families where parents were more successful indirectly contributed to a very unfortunate development in the 1950s: blaming the parent (usually the mother) for the child's troubles. Bruno Bettleheim of the University of Chicago advocated removing children from the home in an attempt to address what he saw as the fundamental problem. The idea that parents somehow caused autism damaged a generation of parents who felt responsible for their child's difficulties. However, beginning in the 1960s, and particularly in the 1970s, research began to show that autism was a brain-based disorder.

As children with autism were followed over time, it was clear that many of them—perhaps 20% or so—would develop seizures. Other children exhibited unusual features on neurological examination such as persistent "primitive" **reflexes** (which are present at birth but typically disappear in children after a few months). Some studies reported that children with autism were more likely to have had complications either before or during birth. Still other studies reported associations of autism with a number of medical conditions that were known to affect brain development. Most importantly, it became clear that autism has a strong **genetic** aspect. Although we still don't know the absolute cause of autism, the best evidence suggests that autism is a brain-based disorder with a very strong genetic component. Although the exact genetic cause (or causes) is not known, we are much closer to finding genes than we were even a few years ago.

GENETIC CAUSES OF AUTISM

In the 1970s, an article written by some prominent **geneticists** suggested that there was no genetic contribution in autism. However, autism was relatively rare and the data was very limited. Shortly thereafter, a very important paper by Susan Folstein and Michael Rutter (1977) appeared, which suggested that rates of autism in identical (or monozygotic) twins were much higher than rates in same-sex fraternal (or dizygotic) twins.[1] Identical twins have identical genes, while fraternal twins share only some genes. The implication of this finding was that there was potentially a very strong genetic contribution in autism. A number of studies have now shown that this is the case (see Rutter, 2005 for a detailed discussion). Several different additional findings have emerged.

As scientists began to look into the issue of the genetics of autism, it became apparent that rates of autism were increased in the brothers and sisters of children with autism. Rates reported vary between 1 in 10 and 1 in 50. This does not seem like a very high rate *unless* one realizes that the rate of classical or strictly defined autism in the general population is between 1 in 800 and 1,000 or so and that, although autism is by no means common in siblings of autistic children the rate is clearly increased— relative to the general population.

GENETICS OF AUTISM

Strong role for genetic factors suggested by:

- High rates of concordance in identical twins (if one twin has it, the other one is very likely to have it).
- Increased risk for autism in siblings (2–10%) (this is significantly greater than the population rate).

---

[1]Monozygotic or identical twins are always same sex of course but genetic studies of fraternal twins with autism have generally focused on same-sex twin pairs because of the gender difference in autism, or, put another way, these studies have typically not used boy-girl fraternal twin pairs because of this sex difference.

What genes are involved?

- It appears that multiple genes contribute to autism.
- Attempts are under way to identify these genes.

What happens once genes are identified?

- It will be possible to develop animal models.
- We will better understand how the genes work in the brain.
- There may be implications for diagnosis and screening.

Other work also began to look at associated problems in siblings and suggested that even when siblings did not have autism, they did seem to have an increase in other problems, including language and learning difficulties. It still is not exactly clear what is inherited in autism. It is possible that what is inherited is a more general predisposition to difficulties rather than to autism as such. Recent work on family members also suggests that there may be higher rates of mood and anxiety problems in family members as well as, perhaps, more social difficulties.

Although research has increasingly highlighted the importance of genetic factors in autism, final answers are not yet in. The genetics of autism is not straightforward or very simple, and it appears that multiple genes are probably involved; estimates of the number of genes range from 4 to 20 or even more. To make life more complicated, it may also be the case that not all forms of autism have the same genetic basis but might come about in other ways; for example, there might be a specific problem at the moment of conception when some genetic material might be lost or a genetic change (**mutation**) might occur. It might be that other things are involved, for example early birth difficulties might interact with a genetic predisposition to cause autism. Major efforts are now under way to identify potential genes in autism. Genes that may be involved (known as "candidate genes") are presently being investigated. It seems likely that some genetic cause (or causes) of autism will be identified over the next few years.

SEIZURE DISORDERS AND ELECTROENCEPHALOGRAPHIC ABNORMALITIES

One of the important things that helped doctors realize parents weren't to blame for autism was an increasing awareness of the higher-than-expected risk autistic children had for developing seizures. Seizure disorders (also referred to as **epilepsy** or **convulsions**) are a group of conditions that result from abnormal electrical activity in the brain. The symptoms of seizure disorders are quite varied. They can range from brief episodes where the child seems to "tune out" to

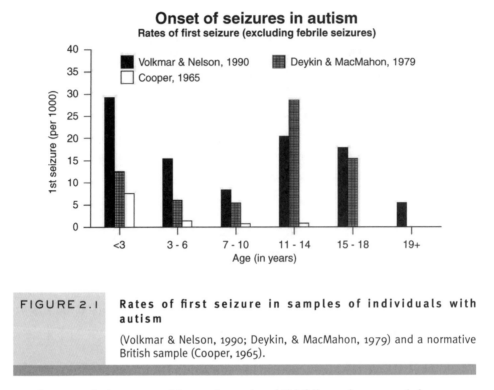

Onset of seizures in autism
Rates of first seizure (excluding febrile seizures)

FIGURE 2.1 **Rates of first seizure in samples of individuals with autism**

(Volkmar & Nelson, 1990; Deykin, & MacMahon, 1979) and a normative British sample (Cooper, 1965).

much more obvious convulsions where the child falls to the ground, loses consciousness, and has alternating periods of muscle contraction and relaxation. There are many different kinds of epilepsy (see Chapter 12).

One of the ways doctors look for seizure activity is through the **electroencephalogram** (or **EEG**), which measures electrical activity in the brain. Both early and more recent studies suggest that as many of 50% of individuals with autism have abnormalities in their EEGs; findings on the EEG are diverse and not specific to autism, but the higher rates of abnormality are, of course, suggestive of some basic problem with the way the brain is "wired." In the "normal" population of children, rates of first seizure are highest around the time of birth and then greatly decrease over time. Figure 2.1 presents information from two studies of children with autism or autism and pervasive developmental disorder not otherwise specified (PDD-NOS), as well as data from a large normative sample of British children. The rates for developing seizures are higher in children with classical autism.

OTHER NEUROLOGICAL PROBLEMS

A number of other neurological problems are observed in autism. Again, these are of many different types; not every child has every problem, and some children will have none. Some children with autism have delays in the development of hand dominance (preference for right or left hand) later than typically developing children. They can also have general decreases in muscle tone in the body and be somewhat "floppy" as babies (technically called **hypotonia**). Sometimes individuals with autism have unusual reflexes; often, these are reflexes that are usually seen only in very young babies but can persist into adulthood in individuals with autism. For example, if the doctor brings a reflex hammer toward the baby's mouth, she may start to suck as if anticipating the bottle or breast; this *visual rooting reflex* is sometimes seen even in adults with autism, whereas in most people it disappears very early in childhood. Other problems may be seen in the way that individuals with autism walk or with their posture.

Neuroanatomy and Brain Imaging Studies

Various methods can be used to study the brain, ranging from actual studies of brain tissues obtained at the time of death (postmortem studies) to studies of the living and active brain through **functional magnetic resonance imaging (fMRI)**. A number of findings deserve mention. Both autopsy and brain imaging studies have suggested that at least some individuals with autism have increased brain size and that this develops in the first year or so of life. Several studies have suggested the possibility that there are some alterations in brain structure, particularly in those parts of the brain that process more emotional or social information (the limbic system) and possibly in the cerebellum. The **cerebellum** is the part of the brain that, among other things, helps coordinate and control movement. One investigator has, in particular, noted specific changes in the cerebellum in individuals with autism; unfortunately, other investigators have generally not been able to find this.

AREAS OF POSSIBLE BRAIN INVOLVEMENT IN AUTISM	
Areas of Possible Difficulty	**Functions**
Prefrontal cerebral cortex	Social thinking
Hypothalamus	Attachment behaviors
Amygdala	Social orientation, emotional learning
Fusiform gyrus	Face recognition
Middle temporal gyrus	Recognition of facial expression
Pulvinar	Emotional relevance

In the last few years, several interesting findings have emerged from studies of functional neuroimaging in autism. A paper from our (Yale) group documented that children with autism and Asperger's syndrome seem to process the information in faces differently in the brain; basically, they use the object processing areas, whereas most of us use a very specialized face processing center in the brain. This may be one of the reasons that faces don't seem to have the same "specialness" for people with autism that they do for typically developing people. It might also account for an interesting finding in autism—people with autism do just as well identifying faces upside down as opposed to right side up. After about 6 months of age, typically developing babies (and people in general—try this with your driver's license the next time you go through the airport screener!) have real trouble identifying upside-down faces (known as the *facial inversion effect*).

Another, possibly related finding is that higher functioning individuals with autism—and, for that matter, many babies with autism—tend to look at mouths rather than eyes and the upper parts of the face when watching very intense social interactions. Our group originally demonstrated this by having very able people with autism and typically developing viewers watch clips from the movie classic *Who's Afraid of Virginia Woolf* and discovered great differences in how the very cognitively able viewers with autism watched the movie. In contrast to typically developing viewers, who spend more time looking at the eyes and top half of the face, the viewers with autism tended to focus on mouths and objects (the latter usually more or less totally extraneous to the plot of the movie). This is demonstrated visually in Figures 2.2 and 2.3. Figure 2.2 shows the differences in visual

FIGURE 2.2   **Visual focus of an autistic man and a normal comparison subject showing a film clip of a conversation.**

Typically developing person (top line) goes back and forth between the eyes in viewing a social scene; a high-functioning person with autism goes back and forth between the mouths of the speakers.

Reprinted, with permission, from Klin, A., Jones, W., Schultz, R., Volkmar, F., & Cohen, D. (2002). Defining and quantifying the social phenotype in autism. *American Journal of Psychiatry, 159,* 895–908.

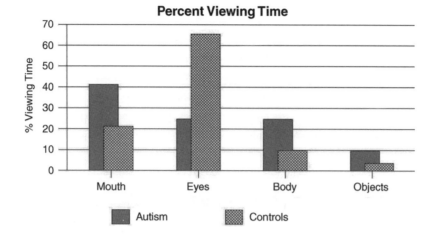

Percent Viewing Time

FIGURE 2.3   **Percent viewing time spent focused on mouth, eye, object, and body regions in viewers with autism and typically developing persons.**

All differences are significant.

Data adapted, with permission, from A. Klin, W. Jones, R. Schultz, F. Volkmar, & D. Cohen. (2002). Visual fixation patterns during viewing naturalistic social situations as predictors of social competence in individuals with autism. *Archives of General Psychiatry, 39*(9), 809–816.

scanning of a viewer with autism (bottom line), who focuses on mouths (and then only on the person speaking), versus the typical viewer, who focuses on the eyes. Figure 2.3 shows the data for groups of cases—there is little overlap of the groups in terms of where they watch. Given that most (maybe about 90%) of the important social information is conveyed in the top half of the face, it is probably not such a surprise that viewers with autism are missing most of the relevant action. These differences in visual tracking seem to develop very early (see Chapter 7) and may be a reflection of different brain mechanisms used to process social information. This is a very active area of research right now.

NEUROCHEMISTRY

Nerve cells use different kinds of chemicals to communicate with each other. A number of these systems have been studied in autism, and there is some suggestion of alterations in these systems. Most of the work has centered on the chemical **serotonin** (also sometimes referred to as 5-HT or 5-hydroxytryptamine). A number of studies have shown that levels of serotonin in the blood are often increased in individuals with autism. Unfortunately, the relationship between blood levels and brain levels of this chemical are not always clear. Other studies have focused on the chemical **dopamine**, which is involved in parts of the brain that control movement and is part of a broader system that relates to levels of alertness and what is technically called *arousal*. Many of the drugs used to treat symptoms of autism affect these chemicals (see Chapter 15).

NEUROCHEMISTRY OF AUTISM	
Neural transmitter	**Function, relevance to autism**
Serotonin	Regulates sleep, mood, body temperature High levels in blood of many individuals with autism Affected by some medications
Dopamine	Control of motor functions One class of medicines used in autism (neuroleptics) block dopamine function
Norepinephrine	Involved in states of arousal, stress response, memory, and anxiety; affected by some medications

RISKS DURING PREGNANCY AND CHILDBIRTH

Could autism be caused by problems during pregnancy, labor, and delivery? A number of studies have looked at this question. Generally, they have employed some rating scale that looks at the degree of risk during the pregnancy and/or during labor and delivery. Early studies seemed to show that there was an increased risk based on the use of these rating scales. Factors that seemed to be associated with increased risk for autism included older age in the mother, prematurity, and some other problems during labor and delivery. Several studies have also suggested that doctors or nurses may be more likely to notice something wrong with the newborn, even if it is very minor. This suggests an important point and a major problem in understanding whether problems during pregnancy or labor and delivery might cause autism; that is, it would be reasonable to assume that if there were something wrong with the child from the moment of conception that was picked up at birth, we might be seeing problems at birth that may result from some vulnerability in the child. Thus, it would be just as reasonable to assume that problems in the child cause difficulties in the pregnancy. The growing body of work on genetic factors in autism, which is discussed shortly, would be most consistent with this idea.

At the same time, it is reasonably clear that horrendous difficulties during labor and delivery, particularly when associated with severe fetal distress, won't *help* any child and have the potential to further cause trouble for a child who was going to have autism.

ENVIRONMENTAL CAUSES OF AUTISM

Interest in the possibility that environmental factors contribute to autism stems from several sources, including reports of "cluster" cases, an assumption that the rate of autism has risen over time, and associations with potential environmental toxins like mercury (or thimerosal in vaccines). It is indeed clear that even in identical twins, while the rate of concordance for autism is high, it is not 100%.

However, as we discussed in Chapter 1, it is not so clear that the rate of autism is increasing. It is reasonably clear that we are doing a better job of finding cases, that there is much more awareness of autism, and that we've changed the ways we diagnose autism and have expanded the number of children diagnosed. As we discuss in Chapter 10, the vast majority of serious scientific studies have not supported the idea that vaccines (or thimerosal) cause autism. Furthermore, some of the evidence proposed for environmental factors is based on case reports, which are often difficult to interpret. For example, there was an early impression that autism was associated with congenital rubella infection, but, over time, these usually very delayed children looked less and less autistic. At present, there is not particularly strong evidence for specific environmental etiologies, although clearly more work is needed in this area. Some good summaries of work in this area are included in the reading list at the end of this chapter.

MEDICAL CONDITIONS AND AUTISM

It took many years before people considered the possibility that autism was associated with some medical conditions, such as seizures. As autism came to be better recognized, it became associated with a number of other medical conditions, and there was interest in the possibility that some of these conditions *caused* autism. However, much of this work was based on **case reports**, wherein a doctor sends a letter or a short paper to a professional journal, which reports that autism is associated with_____syndrome (you can fill in the blank with essentially any known medical condition). Case reports have some value but also have many limitations since there is a bias for only positive reports to be published (similar to the situation with the regular media!). The issue is not whether you *ever* see autism and condition X, but whether in larger groups of individuals the frequency of condition X is significantly greater in autism than you would expect, given how common condition X is in the general population.

Another problem relates to the diagnosis of autism in the first place. Some researchers take a very broad view of autism; others, a more narrow one. If a broad view is taken, estimates of the rate of autism will naturally tend to be higher and there will be the impression that autism is more likely associated with other medical conditions. In other words, if a broader definition of autism is used, there will be more diagnoses of autism among people with severe and profound intellectual disability, in part because levels of repetitive movements and unusual behaviors are higher in this group of cases. Also in this group of cases, with lower IQs, about half the time there is an associated medical condition, and thus a condition that might contribute to the person's handicap is much more likely to be found, regardless of whether they have autism! Two rather different views emerge from the published research on medical conditions associated with autism. If a very broad view of autism is taken, perhaps one-third of cases of autism might be related to some condition; however, if a narrow view is taken, probably only 10% of cases are.

Various conditions have been identified as possibly being associated with autism, including **phenylketonuria**, **congenital rubella**, **tuberous sclerosis**, and **fragile X syndrome**. However, careful research has led us to rethink how strong these relationships are, and at present the strongest associations are with fragile X and tuberous sclerosis.

Fragile X Syndrome

Fragile X syndrome is a common syndrome associated with intellectual disability and, sometimes, with autism. It is probably second only to Down syndrome as the most identified genetic source of mental retardation. Fragile X syndrome particularly affects boys and has sometimes been associated with autism. All of us have 23 pairs of **chromosomes**. Boys have an X chromosome (from their mothers) and a Y chromosome (from their fathers). It is called fragile X syndrome because the X chromosome was noted to sometimes break or be "fragile" when examined. Because boys have only one X chromosome, they are more likely to have the disorder (i.e., there is no extra X to make up the difference). In girls, who have two X chromosomes, the disorder may be expressed in a somewhat milder form. Fragile X is one of the more common causes of intellectual disability/mental retardation, perhaps affecting 1 in 800 to 1,000 children.

Associated problems in fragile X syndrome include mild intellectual disability/mental retardation (although sometimes IQ is in the normal range). In addition, language problems, attentional difficulties, and symptoms suggestive of autism (problems with eye contact and self-stimulatory behaviors) may be observed. Boys with the disorder may have some unusual body features, such as large ears and genitals; the face may be long and narrow, and the palate (the roof of the mouth) may be unusually high and arched. Motor and learning problems are relatively common. Low muscle tone as well as dental and eye problems may be observed. Sometimes individuals with this condition have seizures.

FRAGILE X SYNDROME

- Symptoms: social anxiety, "autistic-like" symptoms, and sometimes autism.
- About 1–2% of individuals with autism have fragile X.
- A simple blood test can be used to determine whether fragile X is present.
- Syndrome can be seen in boys and girls.
- The genetic basis of this condition has been well described.

Early reports suggested a very strong association between autism and fragile X syndrome, with claims that as many as 60% of individuals with autism had fragile X. There was much optimism that a genetic cause of autism had been found. However, subsequent (and better) studies have suggested that the association between fragile X syndrome and autism is not nearly as strong as it first appeared. In the early studies there was not careful attention to appropriate controls or to diagnosis of autism. Recent research indicates that between 1% and 2% of individuals with autism have fragile X; this rate is not much different from what would be expected from any sample of children with mild intellectual disability—that about 1% of individuals with fragile X have autism. Thus, although it remains important to consider testing for fragile X, the rate of the condition in autism is relatively small and accounts for only a very small subgroup of children with autism.

At the present time, the main impact of diagnosing fragile X relates to the implications for genetic counseling of parents and sisters of affected individuals; that is, the treatment of the child with autism and fragile X is no different than that for the autistic child without fragile X. However, for parents who know that they have a risk for subsequent children with fragile X, prenatal testing and termination of pregnancy (if that is an option for the parents) is available. In the past, the diagnosis of fragile X syndrome was made on the basis of an actual examination of the child's chromosomes, obtained through a blood sample and grown in a laboratory. This time-consuming and costly procedure has now been replaced in many centers by a more direct DNA test for the fragile X abnormality. The genetic cause of fragile X has now been identified.

Tuberous Sclerosis

Tuberous sclerosis affects about 1 in 10,000 people and, although rare, has been noted to be significantly associated with autism. It is seen equally as frequently in boys and in girls. Symptoms include the growth of unusual tissue or benign tumors in the skin, eye, brain, and other organs. Over half of infants with the disorder will have white patches on their skin at birth. The tubers may be seen in the brain and can be detected by **computed tomography (CT)** or **magnetic resonance imaging (MRI)** scan. The tumors associated with this disorder are often seen in the preschool years and may increase in frequency during **puberty**. These growths are "benign" in the sense that, unlike cancer, they do not spread, but their effect on growth and development can be very serious. Individuals with this condition often have **developmental delay** and intellectual disability and seizures.

The disorder is inherited as an *autosomal dominant* trait, meaning that it is on the autosomes (i.e., not on the sex chromosomes) and that if you get one copy of this gene from either parent, you are likely to have the disorder. A gene for the disorder has been located on chromosome 9.

Although the effects of the disorder can be severe, the degree of severity in tuberous sclerosis is variable. Children with tuberous sclerosis may have speech delays and learning problems. They often have motor problems as well. Sometimes the first symptoms are seen in infancy or early childhood, often with the onset of seizures. Between 50% and 60% of affected individuals show intellectual disability, and about 80% have seizures. Sometimes the findings include a specific abnormality in brain wave (EEG) testing. The seizures may include a specific kind of muscle spasm (myoclonic jerks). Sometimes individuals seem to be much less severely affected; it seems likely that this happens in some special circumstances, for example, as a result of spontaneous genetic change not inherited from the parents.

Interestingly, early reports on tuberous sclerosis appeared in the 1930s and described some problems suggestive of autism (which was not described until the 1940s!). These problems included stereotyped movement, abnormal speech, and social problems. Hyperactivity, aggression, and other behavior difficulties have also been reported.

In studies of individuals with autism, about 1–2% also have tuberous sclerosis; this figure is higher only if individuals with autism *and* seizures are included (about 8–12% of such cases may have tuberous sclerosis). But not every child with tuberous sclerosis has autism. The ratio of boys to girls in autism associated with tuberous sclerosis is about the same; this is in contrast to autism in general, where the rate of autism is clearly several times higher in boys than in girls. Sometimes tuberous sclerosis is not associated with intellectual disability; studies of this small subgroup do not seem to suggest high rates of autism or similar problems, but the final answers are not yet in. Promising work on the genetic causes of tuberous sclerosis is now under way.

Disorders of Metabolism: Phenylketonuria (PKU)

PKU is caused by a problem in the body's use of the amino acid phenylalanine. As a result, levels of this amino acid build up in the body and eventually are excreted in the urine. This disorder is rather rare, affecting about 1 in 10,000 babies. If it is not treated, PKU can cause severe intellectual disability, growth problems, and seizures. Although the baby may otherwise appear normal at birth, symptoms gradually develop, including problems in feeding and development. Fortunately, with the recognition of the cause of the disorder, doctors realized that the condition could be treated with a special diet that eliminates phenylalanine. This is one of a handful of dietary treatments medically proven to have a major role in preventing/treating developmental problems. PKU is now screened for at birth in this country, since prompt treatment allows children with PKU to have normal and productive lives.

Early papers suggested that PKU was a risk factor for autism. However, more recent research has questioned this view. Well-controlled studies do not seem to suggest that there are higher-than-expected rates of PKU or other disorders of metabolism in autism. It seems likely that early reports of such associations probably equated "autistic features" (usually meaning stereotyped, self-stimulatory behaviors) with autism. It is still appropriate to consider screening children with severe developmental difficulties for inborn errors of metabolism, but there is not a clear relationship of these disorders to autism.

Congenital Infections

There have been some reports associating autism with infections either before or at the time of birth or shortly thereafter. The kinds of infections for which this have been claimed are quite varied and include congenital rubella, cytomegalovirus, herpes simplex, and human immunodeficiency virus (HIV—the AIDS virus). A few papers have also reported that there might be some association of autism with the time of year when children are born that might suggest some fluctuation in association with the prevalence of other infections. However, other studies have not seen such associations. Probably the most interest in terms of infection has centered around congenital rubella.

Congenital rubella occurs when a baby still in its mother's womb is infected with the rubella (German measles) virus. Women who have not had rubella or who have not had the immunization for it are at very high risk for having a baby with congenital rubella if they develop rubella while they are pregnant. The risk is greatest during the first 8 weeks or so of the pregnancy (a time when sometimes women may not realize they are pregnant).

The virus often does severe damage to the developing baby. The baby may be born with problems in the heart, eyes, and ears. The head may be small, and there may be problems with other parts of the body. Hearing loss may develop; deafness and blindness are relatively common. Intellectual disability and various behavior problems may be observed. While a few children do not have symptoms, most do. Fortunately, greater awareness of the seriousness of this condition and the development of a vaccine have reduced the frequency of this condition. The vaccination of young children has been very helpful in this effort.

Early reports on congenital rubella suggested that these children often seemed to have autism. As we mentioned earlier in the chapter, there were a number of issues with this conclusion since these children had multiple problems—they were often deaf or had impaired vision and severe learning difficulties so being sure of the diagnosis was complicated. As with other conditions, the presence of **autistic-like** features was taken as suggestive of autism; however, follow-up studies have shown that over time the social and other problems of these children seem to improve in ways that would not be typical of autism.

PSYCHOLOGICAL MODELS OF AUTISM

Following the error of the early "blame the parent" notion, speculation about how autism might be understood through psychology was held back in some important ways. Over the last two decades, new theoretical models have been proposed that try to understand the developmental and behavioral aspects of autism from the point of view of psychological development; it must be emphasized that this is an attempt to understand brain-based difficulties and *not* to blame the parents. These attempts are of some interest in terms of research and may, perhaps, lead to some treatment advances. It is important to realize that several rather different approaches have been used. One attempts to view the social problems in autism as one of many different difficulties caused by the same factor (or factors). The other view emphasizes the social difficulties as primary in some basic way, that is, as leading to other problems. These all have their pros and cons and none has, at least as yet, emerged as the "winner." At present, they all have something to offer in terms of alternative models of how we might understand autism.

The **Theory of Mind** approach has emphasized the idea that there is a basic problem for children with autism in empathizing with others, that is, having a "theory of mind," or theory of what motivations, intention, and so on, impact on the behavior of others. This approach, first proposed by Simon Baron-Cohen (see reading list) has been remarkably productive in terms of research. The simplicity and elegance of this theory have added to its attractiveness. There are, however, two problems with this model. One is that the severe difficulties in social interaction impact behaviors seen in very, very young children—children of a few weeks of age. This is a time well before the ability to "put yourself into the other's place" has really developed. Another problem is that many higher functioning individuals on the autism spectrum can do "theory of mind" tasks just fine, and yet these individuals are still very socially disabled.

Another approach, termed the **executive dysfunction hypothesis**, emphasizes deficits in "executive functions" (a topic we discuss in greater detail in Chapter 6). The notion of executive functions refers, basically, to the whole range of abilities involved in planning and organization. For example, seeing the multiple steps involved in a complicated task, plotting a solution in terms of getting to the desired result, keeping the desired result in mind, and being able to work out alternatives when this is needed (Pennington & Ozonoff, 1996). Within this view, autism is related to difficulties in dealing with change and a tendency to engage in repetitive behavior and **perseveration** as well as to problems in developing planning and problem-solving abilities due to a lack of coordinated reasoning and ongoing adjustment to feedback (Ozonoff, 1997). As we discuss later in this book, there is no question that children with autism spectrum disorders often have severe problems in this area. From the point of view of a more general theory, however, there are some difficulties. Probably most importantly, difficulties in this area are not unique and specific to autism; that is, children with attention deficit hyperactivity disorder also have problems with organization (but don't have social troubles of the same type seen in autism).

A somewhat different theory proposes that the difficulties in autism relate to **"weak central coherence."** The idea here is that people with autism have trouble getting the "big picture" (Happé, Briskman, & Frith, 2001); they don't see the interconnections of things—a "not seeing the forest for the trees" problem. This theory would account for some of the people with autism who are gifted in one area but very deficient in another area. Although very attractive in many ways, the experimental evidence has been somewhat weak and contradictory. Other approaches, for example, Klin and colleagues (2003) focus more on the social difficulties being a primary cause of autism, with many of the symptoms arising from the limited interest in people and the negative consequences of brain and psychological development.

UNDERSTANDING THE CAUSES OF PDDs OTHER THAN AUTISM

Our understanding of the causes of PDDs other than autism is not generally as far advanced as in autism, with the major exception of Rett's disorder. Again, we understand that all these conditions have a basis in problems in the brain. This is suggested by such things as rates of seizure disorder and, occasionally, other abnormalities as well. The role of genetic factors in Rett's syndrome is now clearly established, as a gene has been found to be involved in most cases (see Chapter 13). Compared to Rett's syndrome, childhood disintegrative disorder is apparently less common and has been even less frequently studied. For many years doctors presumed that there was some specific medical process that could always be identified to explain why children developed normally for several years and then had a major deterioration. It is clear that this is the exception rather than the rule. Occasionally, such a process is identified that is similar, in some ways, to the dementias of adults (such as Alzheimer's disease, where there is progressive loss of functioning). Interestingly, however, in CDD behavior and developmental skills usually deteriorate and then stay at the same, relatively low, level. This kind of plateau is not usually observed when a progressive medical condition is present. As in autism, the involvement of the brain is suggested by the high rates of EEG abnormality and seizure disorder. Information on brain structure and functioning is very limited, although research on this aspect of CDD is now under way. It is possible that the condition might develop in several different ways.

CHILDHOOD DISINTEGRATIVE DISORDER

Causes of Childhood Disintegrative Disorder

- Early impression of possible psychological causes seems wrong.
- The distinctive and unusual pattern of onset suggests some specific disease process.
- Most of the time, despite intensive searching, no specific medical cause is found.
- Occasionally the condition is associated with some neurological disorder similar in some ways to adult dementia, but this is not usually the case.

In Asperger's syndrome (AS) there have been several reports of associated abnormalities, but these are mostly based on reports of single cases rather than group studies. One interesting finding has been that Asperger's is frequently associated with **nonverbal learning disability** (NLD) and the difficulties in AS have been taken by some to suggest difficulties in the right part of the brain (in contrast to autism, where the presence of **language** problems has often been taken to suggest problems in the left part of the brain). Although research on the issue of genetic contributions in Asperger's is not as well advanced as that in autism there is already some evidence for a strong genetic component with high rates of social difficulty in members of the immediate family.

ASPERGER'S DISORDER

Causes of Asperger's Disorder

- Genetics:
  - Asperger commented on high rate of similar conditions in fathers.

- Recent research does suggest higher rates of social problems in male relatives.
- Female relatives tend to have higher rates of anxiety and depression.
- It is possible that this is even more strongly genetic than autism.
- Brain functioning:
- Association with Nonverbal Learning Disability Profile.
- Suggestion that problems are more likely in the right cerebral cortex.

Research on the causes of PDD-NOS is the least advanced of all the PDD conditions. There is a strong suggestion of a possible genetic component, since many individuals with autism have relatives with language, learning, or social difficulties. It is possible that what we now see as PDD-NOS may, some day, be identified as a variant of autism—for example, one which comes about when some, but not all, the **genes** that cause autism are present. It is also likely that there really may be important distinctions within the broad group of PDD-NOS cases. For example, some cases may have a more genetic basis and may be more closely related to autism; others may have a different basis and might be close to other conditions (e.g., language or attentional problems). It is also possible that some combination of factors might cause PDD-NOS.

SUMMARY

We have now come to appreciate that genetic factors are very much involved in autism. In some ways this has been a surprise, since early work did not seem to suggest a strong genetic basis. This early work was very limited, and only when the first studies of twins were done was the possible genetic basis of autism recognized. Studies of twins showed that if the twins were identical (with exactly the same genetic makeup) and if one had autism, there was a very high chance the other twin would as well; if the twins were fraternal (not exactly the same genetic makeup but sharing as many genes as any siblings would), the rate was much lower. As time went on, it also became clear that a range of other problems—in language and learning and social interaction—might be inherited. Active research around the world is being conducted to look for the genes that cause autism.

■ READING LIST

Altevogt, B. M., Hanson, S. L., & Leshner, A. I. (2008). Autism and the environment: Challenges and opportunities for research. *Pediatrics*, *121*, 1225–3000.

Anderson, G. M., & Y. Hoshino (2005). Neurochemical studies of autism. In F. R. Volkmar, A. Klin, R. Paul, & D. J. Cohen (Eds.), *Handbook of autism and pervasive developmental disorders* (vol. 1, pp. 453–472). Hoboken, NJ: Wiley.

Baron-Cohen, S. (1995) *Mindblindness*. Cambridge, MA: MIT Press.

Baron-Cohen, S. (2003). *The essential difference: The truth about the male and female brain*. New York: Basic Books.

Baron-Cohen, S., Tager-Flusberg, H., & Cohen, D. (Eds.). (2000). *Understanding other minds: Perspectives from developmental neuroscience* (2nd ed., pp. 357–388). Oxford: Oxford University Press.

Cooper, J. E. (1975). Epilepsy in a longitudinal survey of 5000 children. *British Medical Journal*, 1: 1020–1022.

Folstein, S. E., & Rutter, M. (1977) Genetic influences in infantile autism. *Nature, 265*, 726–728.

Fombonne, E. (2005). Epidemiological studies of pervasive developmental disorders. In F. R. Volkmar, A. Klin, R. Paul, & D. J. Cohen (Eds.), *Handbook of autism and pervasive developmental disorders* (vol. 1, pp. 42–69). Hoboken, NJ: Wiley.

Happé, F. (2005). The weak central coherence account of autism. In F. R. Volkmar, A. Klin, R. Paul, & D. J. Cohen (Eds.), *Handbook of autism and pervasive developmental disorders* (vol. 1, pp. 640–649). Hoboken, NJ: Wiley.

Happé, F., Briskman, J., & Frith, U. (2001). Exploring the cognitive phenotype of autism: Weak "central coherence" in parents and siblings of children with autism: I. Experimental tests. *Journal of Child Psychology and Psychiatry, 42*(3), 299–307.

Hermelin, B. (2001). *Bright splinters of the mind: A personal story of research with autistic savants*. Philadelphia, PA: Jessica Kingsley.

Klin, A., Jones, W., Schultz, R., Volkmar, F., & Cohen, D. J. (2002). Defining and quantifying the social phenotype in autism. *American Journal of Psychiatry, 159*(6), 895–908.

Klin, A., Jones, W., Schultz, R., & Volkmar F. (2003). The enactive mind—from actions to cognition: Lessons from autism. *Philosophical Transactions of the Royal Society, Biological Sciences, 358*, 345–360.

Klin, A., McPartland, J., & Volkmar, F. (2005). Asperger syndrome. In F. R. Volkmar, A. Klin, R. Paul, & D. J. Cohen (Eds.), *Handbook of autism and pervasive developmental disorders* (vol. 1, pp. 88–125). Hoboken, NJ: Wley.

Minshew, N. J., Sweeney, J. A., Bauman, M. L., & Webb, S. J. (2005). Neurologic aspects of autism. In F. R. Volkmar, A. Klin, R. Paul, & D. J. Cohen (Eds.), *Handbook of autism and pervasive developmental disorders* (vol. 1, pp. 453–472). Hoboken, NJ: Wiley.

Mesibov, G. B., Adams, L. W., & Klinger, L. G. (1997). *Autism: Understanding the disorder*. New York: Kluwer Academic/Plenum Publishers.

Ozonoff, S., Rogers, S. J., & Hendren R. O. (2003). *Autism spectrum disorders: A research review for practioners*. Washington, DC: American Psychiatric Press.

Ozonoff, S., South, M., & Provencal, S. (2005). Executive functions. In F. R. Volkmar, A. Klin, R. Paul, & D. J. Cohen (Eds.), *Handbook of autism and pervasive developmental disorders* (vol. 1, 606–627). Hoboken, NJ: Wiley.

Pennington, B. F., & Ozonoff, S. (1996). Executive functions and developmental psychopathology. *Journal of Child Psychology and Psychiatry, 37*, 51–87.

Russell, J. (1997). *Autism as an executive disorder*. New York: Oxford University Press.

Rutter, M. (2005). Aetiology of autism: Findings and questions. *Journal of Intellectual Disability Research, 49*(4), 231–238.

Rutter, M. (2005). Genetic influences and autism. In F. R. Volkmar, A. Klin, R. Paul, & D. J. Cohen (Eds.), *Handbook of autism and pervasive developmental disorders* (vol. 1, pp. 425–452). Hoboken, NJ: Wiley.

Schultz, R. T., & Robbins, D. L. (2005). Functional neuroimaging studies of autism spectrum disorders. In F. R. Volkmar, A. Klin, R. Paul, & D. J. Cohen (Eds.), *Handbook of autism and pervasive developmental disorders* (vol. 1, pp. 515–533). Hoboken, NJ: Wiley.

Szatmari, P. (2004). *A mind apart: Understanding children with autism and Asperger syndrome.* New York: Guilford Press.

Van Acker, R., Loncola, J. A., & VanAcker, E. Y. (2005). Rett syndrome: A pervasive developmental disorder. In F. R. Volkmar, A. Klin, R. Paul, & D. J. Cohen (Eds.), *Handbook of autism and pervasive developmental disorders* (vol. 1, pp. 126–164). Hoboken, NJ: Wiley.

Volkmar, F. R., Koenig, K., & State, M. (2005). Childhood disintegrative disorder. In F. R. Volkmar, A. Klin, R. Paul, & D. J. Cohen (Eds.), *Handbook of autism and pervasive developmental disorders* (vol. 1, pp. 70–78). Hoboken, NJ: Wiley.

Weber, J. (2000). *Children with fragile X syndrome: A parents' guide.* Bethesda, MD: Woodbine House.

Wing, L., & Potter, D. (2002, August). The epidemiology of autistic spectrum disorders: Is the prevalence rising?. *Mental Retardation & Developmental Disabilities Research Reviews, 8*(3), 151–161.

■ QUESTIONS AND ANSWERS

1. **I have one child with autism and am thinking about having a second. What are the chances my second child could have autism?**

   In general, having had one child with autism increases your risk of having another by probably between 2% and 10%. This does not sound like much of a risk until you think that roughly 1 child in a 800 to 1,000 in the general population has autism, which means your chances are substantially increased. We have seen families with three and four children with autism. Keep in mind that this is a question we can answer in general terms—for a specific answer relevant to you, speak with a genetic counselor, who can take into account all the special factors in your situation, such as family history.

2. **Are a brain scan and an EEG always necessary in evaluating a child with autism?**

   In general without a specific clinical reason to do it, the likelihood of finding something is small. If there are specific clinical reasons to do these tests, for example, if you suspect seizures or if the child's history and behavior are highly unusual, then they should be done.

3. **Are there any lab tests that diagnose autism?**

   At present, the answer is no. When genes for autism are found, there may be some such tests in the future. At the moment, the only additional lab test that makes sense is the test for fragile X (a blood test). Special genetic tests are now able to look for missing genes. Other tests may be needed, given the child's history and examination.

4. **Can autism be diagnosed from an EEG?**

    No. Autism is diagnosed based on history and clinical examination. The EEG is useful in the diagnosis of seizure disorders, which are sometimes associated with autism.

5. **What will it mean if genes are found for autism?**

    A number of things will have to happen before the findings can translate into new treatments. These include discovering how the gene works and how it operates in development and in the brain, and development of an animal model. Developing an animal model is important, since this would help with understanding what is happening in the brain and give us more potential for testing possible treatments. There *may* be some important implications quickly for screening. There also *may* be some possibility of understanding the broader spectrum of autism and related conditions. Keep in mind that this is a very active area of research and that the answer to this question may change dramatically in the next several years.

CHAPTER 3

Getting a Diagnosis

A diagnosis is a label that serves as a shorthand way for professionals and others to communicate with each other very quickly. You might think getting a diagnosis would be a simple business, but, unfortunately, for autism there is not (at least at the time this chapter is written and probably not for some time) a simple blood or laboratory test to determine who is autistic. There now are blood tests for a few conditions that are associated with autism, such as fragile X syndrome and Rett's disorder. In autism, we have to rely on the judgment of (hopefully) experienced clinicians, who may do any of several things to help them arrive at a diagnosis. Usually, getting a diagnosis is one part of getting an **assessment**. The goals of the assessment often include things in addition to the diagnosis, for example, clarifying the child's strengths and weaknesses, challenges the child has in learning, and so forth. In this chapter, we review some important aspects of getting a diagnosis and doing an assessment. In subsequent chapters, we'll talk in more detail about some of the assessment **instruments**, for example, as they are relevant to younger children (Chapter 7), school-age children (Chapter 8), or adolescents and adults (Chapter 9). We also devote some discussion to testing and assessment issues in discussing building skills (Chapter 6).

You may well ask, "Does a diagnosis make a difference?" For some purposes (e.g., for getting early intervention services), providers may not be so concerned about a precise diagnosis but rather about the child's need for services. In part, this reflects an awareness, particularly in very young children, that diagnoses can sometimes be hard to make. However, a diagnosis can be helpful. A diagnosis may help to "frame" the child's needs, for example, for educational and speech and language services. It is important to realize that diagnosis helps us to know only the general kinds of problems or issues presented; it does not tell us a lot about the specifics of an individual child because there is such a range of abilities and needs among children with autism spectrum disorders. Sometimes parents want the label (for educational purposes) that may get their child the most services.

As with many other things, life is lived in the details, and it is the specifics about autism that are very important. For example, is the child verbal or nonverbal? Does he have any motor difficulties? How socially related is the child? Does he have behavior problems that interfere with programming for him? These issues are particularly important for autism and related disorders, given the wide range of disabilities we see in children with these conditions. Since we don't yet know the exact cause of autism, we presently rely on observation and history to make the diagnosis. Various guidelines, rating scales, and checklists have been developed, and they may help in making a diagnosis, but they never replace the importance of a skilled clinician's observations and assessment.

This chapter covers aspects related to getting a diagnosis of autism and autism spectrum disorders (ASDs). We discuss some of the more common ways that parents and professionals become concerned about the child and the kinds of behaviors that very young children with autism exhibit. We discuss the uses and limitations of diagnosis, as well as what a good diagnostic **evaluation** consists of. We also address some of the more frequent sources of disagreement on diagnosis and, finally, what should happen after a diagnosis is made. As with other chapters in this book, it is important to realize that when we give examples, not every child will behave or develop in the same way and that the examples are just that. This chapter will be of greatest interest to parents of younger children, as well as to parents who are trying to understand what goes into an assessment of their child. In the next chapters, we talk about the critical issue of translating the diagnostic assessment into services, and the chapters following that discuss age-related aspects of ASDs.

FIRST CONCERNS

There are many ways that parents become aware that something is wrong with how their child is developing:

- Sometimes parents gradually become aware that there is something about their child that is different—maybe she seems less interested in her parents than they expect or has some unusual reaction to sounds or noise.

- Other parents trace their concerns to a very specific event, such as seeing their child with other children of about the same age.

- Occasionally, a grandparent or friend, or sometimes a day care provider or the child's doctor, may mention that they are worried about how the child is doing.

- Sometimes parents will say that, as they think about it, maybe there were some signs of trouble even earlier than they first thought.

- Sometimes parents will say that their child was, as an infant, "too good," making few demands on them.

- At other times parents will tell us that the child had difficulties from shortly after birth, for example, being difficult to console or being very demanding.

- Somewhat less commonly, parents will feel as if their child was doing reasonably well until, say, 18 months of age, when either he lost ground or seemed to stop moving forward developmentally.

- Parents who have already had one child may make comparisons and realize that their new child is developing in a very different way.

Probably the most common cause of concern is speech delay. Concerns that the child may be deaf are also very frequent, although usually, unlike deaf children, the child with autism seems to respond to some sounds. The child with autism may use pointing to get things or may pull a parent by the hand (often with no or limited eye contact) to get something, but does not seem interested in sharing attention. For example, he rarely points to show things to parents. Some parents, especially, first-time parents, may not have realized that there was anything unusual about this behavior and do not ask their doctor about it until 18 or 20 months, when their child is still not speaking.

In other cases, parents may be worried about their child's development even earlier. When this happens, it is often the child's lack of social relatedness, that is, his lack of interest in parents and other people, that causes concern. In our experience, parents are more likely to be concerned about this when they have had experience with children. Occasionally, parents will be worried because their child does not seem to enjoy contact with them, but she is interested in odd or unusual aspects of the environment, such as rocking by herself in a corner. Or parents may be concerned that their child has chosen an unusual transitional object to comfort herself. Rather than choosing something soft (and typical) such as a blanket or toy, she may choose something hard (and unusual). The child may also be less interested in the actual object than in the "kind" of object (e.g., carrying a specific magazine around and taking it to bed with her but not caring which issue of the magazine it is). Sometimes the child will have dreadful and almost "catastrophic" responses to certain events in the environment. For example, when the vacuum cleaner is used, he runs upstairs crying and cannot be consoled for hours. Other children may have unusual aversions to food or certain smells. Some of the early warning signs for autism are listed in Table 3.1.

When parents of children with autism are asked when they were first worried about their child, it is clear that many are concerned by a year and most by 16 to

TABLE 3.1	WARNING SIGNS OF AUTISM IN THE FIRST AND SECOND YEARS OF LIFE*

Birth to 12 months:

Social interaction problems: Doesn't anticipate social routines, doesn't look much at other people, not interested in social games, little affection for family members, happy to be left alone

Communication problems: Poor response to own name, doesn't look much at objects held by others

Unusual responses/interests: Doesn't like to be touched, excessive mouthing of objects

After 12 months (and before age 3):

Social interaction problems: Eye contact abnormal, limited looking at other people, limited range of expression, limited pleasure in games, little motor imitation, poor play skills (no pretend, limited use of materials for play)

Communication: Low rates of verbal/nonverbal communication, doesn't share an interest with people (e.g., showing things), poor response to name, doesn't respond to gestures, uses other person's body as a tool (e.g., takes hand of parent to get a desired object without eye contact), unusual sounds

Unusual responses/interests: Objects used inappropriately, play repetitive and limited, repetitive interests, unusual sensory responses, hand/finger mannerisms

Adapted with permission, from table 8.1 Autism in infancy and early childhood, by K. Chawarska and F. Volkmar (2005), *Handbook of Autism* (3rd ed., pp. 230).

20 months. By age 2, about three-fourths of parents will be concerned, and by age three, essentially all parents, even those of more cognitively able children with autism will be worried.

With other ASDs such as Asperger's disorder, children are often even older before parents are first worried. Asperger himself pointed out that parents are more commonly concerned as the child enters nursery school and is exposed to typically developing peers. Usually, the child will have, if anything, seemed to the parents rather gifted and precocious (e.g., with an early interest in reading). However, the child's good verbal abilities may stand in contrast to difficulties with motor activities and social problems.

In pervasive developmental disorders not otherwise specified (PDD-NOS), the symptoms, at least early on, are usually not as dramatic as those of children with autism and, as a result, parents may wonder for some time about the child before expressing concern. The fact that a child with PDD-NOS often seems to do well in some situations may mislead educators and other professionals, and they may fail to appreciate the child's difficulties. This may also reflect the fact that the child's problems may be most apparent at home rather than in the doctor's office or at nursery school.

In the past, parents often had to fight to convince health care providers that something was wrong with their child. Fortunately, health care providers are now usually much more alert to developmental problems, although occasionally a physician may still reassure worried parents that their child is "just language delayed." Children who have only language delay are, however, socially related and don't have the unusual behaviors we see in autism.

SCREENING AND INITIAL ASSESSMENTS

Although Dr. Leo Kanner first described several characteristics that were central for a diagnosis of autism in 1943, it was not until 1980 that enough work on autism had been done for autism to be included, for the first time, as an "official" psychiatric diagnosis in the United States. These diagnostic criteria were published in the third edition of the American Psychiatric Association's *Diagnostic and Statistical Manual of Mental Disorders* (also referred to as DSM-III). The current guidelines to the "official" diagnosis of autism in DSM-IV and the International guide (ICD-10) to diagnosis (see appendix 1) are intended to help doctors and educators by giving some *general* guidance about the features that ought to be observed. They do *not* replace the need for a careful examination. While a diagnosis of autism or other PDD may help parents and teachers think about general issues that may be relevant to the child, the diagnostic label is not a substitute for a careful and comprehensive evaluation, which can serve as the basis for developing a detailed and individualized program of intervention.

Typically, parents talk to their health care provider about obtaining an initial assessment. This person should know local resources and may be able to tell parents how to arrange for an initial assessment through a state or local program fairly quickly; depending on the child's age, this may be through a birth-to-three program or through a public school. The purposes of this assessment usually include getting some basic information on the child's development and behavior and hopefully coming up with a provisional diagnosis or "working" diagnosis and establishing the child's eligibility for services. This initial assessment may be relatively brief; often, parents will want to obtain an assessment at a more specialized center that has much experience in working with children with autism. It will probably take a while to get an appointment in such a center, and it is a good idea to start services while waiting for this more extensive evaluation.

For children under 3 years of age, there are specific agencies and often teams of people who can evaluate children suspected of having a disability. The names of these agencies vary from state to state; they may be called early intervention programs, or birth-to-three programs. In some states, these services are run by departments of education; in other states, they may be part of the departments of developmental disabilities or health. These organizations usually will provide a team of people to establish a need for intervention services for the child under 3. Children over 3 are usually cared for within the public school system (we talk more about age-related issues and services in the subsequent chapters).

Screening Tests

Evaluation teams often vary considerably in terms of how much they know about autism. Typically, the team will establish the child's levels of functioning and potential needs by doing some initial assessment of the child, talking to you and getting a history, and, sometimes, completing special checklists or rating scales. Table 3.2 provides a list of some of these—you will see that often they depend on parent report rather than on testing the child. Sometimes these teams feel confident about making a diagnosis; other teams may specifically wish to avoid giving a diagnostic label. Usually, the focus of these early assessments is establishing that the child is eligible for services. If a child is delayed in development, he may be eligible for services even without a diagnosis. However, for autism in particular, it makes sense to start intervention as soon as possible, since it is clear that for many (although not all) children with autism, early intervention can make an important difference in the child's outcome. If the child will receive appropriate services only if he has a diagnosis of autism, PDD, or ASD, it may be appropriate for you to make a fuss about the importance of an appropriate diagnosis in getting a good intervention program.

As we mentioned, Asperger's disorder is not usually recognized until after age 3. Diagnosis of the much rarer conditions of Rett's syndrome and childhood disintegrative disorder (CDD) is discussed in much greater detail later in this book. We talk more about the kinds of behaviors that are seen in very young children in Chapter 7.

In the United States, once the child reaches age 3, responsibility for evaluating for disabilities falls upon the school system. Like early intervention programs, school systems employ teams of evaluators whose job it is to determine which children require **special educational** and therapeutic services to learn. Parents can start the evaluation process by calling the special education department at their local public school and asking how to refer their child for an evaluation. The evaluators there can include special educators, school **psychologists**, **speech–language pathologists**, and **occupational** and **physical therapists**.

You should realize that school systems may use different labels than medical ones. These sometimes, but not always, correspond to the more typical medical ones. Increasingly, schools and state departments of education are recognizing autism (or sometimes PDD or ASD) as an acceptable label to get special services. Other states or school districts may not and may use other labels such as "other health impaired," "neurological impaired," and so on. Occasionally, particularly for higher functioning and somewhat older children, the school may want to use a label such as *social–emotional maladjustment* (SEM). This can be very problematic, since it is a general term that refers to a range of children

TABLE 3.2   FREQUENTLY USED SCREENING INSTRUMENTS FOR
AUTISM

Name	Format and Comments
Autism Behavior Checklist (ABC) (Krug, Arick, Almond, 1980)	Teacher- or parent-completed checklist; useful for screening; 57 yes/no items (items are weighted), score >67 indicates autism. Parents' scores may be higher than teachers. May work less well in more cognitively able students.
Checklist for Autism in Toddlers (CHAT) (Baron-Cohen, Allen, Gillberg, 1992)	Screening instrument. Small number of parent reported items and even fewer observational items. When positive, very suggestive of autism but may miss cases. Problems with original sample.
Modified Checklist for Autism in Toddlers (M-CHAT) (Robbins, Fein, Barton, & Green, 2001)	Modification of CHAT with additional items; 23 yes/no items for parent ratings, focus on behaviors relevant to early diagnosis. Used 18–30 months of age. Scoring a bit complicated, with some items more critical than others. Early studies suggest good reliability and ability to screen efficiently.
Childhood Autism Rating Scale (CARS) (Schopler, Reicher, and Rennner, 1988)	Assessment of the child. Looks at severity of autistic behaviors; useful for screening. Requires some (but minimal) training; 15 items rated on 4-point score (normal to very autistic). Scores >30 suggest autism. May overidentify in individuals with minimal language or more cognitive disability. Also used for diagnostic purposes.
Social Communication Questionnaire (SCQ) (Rutter, Bailey, & Lord, 2003)	Screen based on ADI; 40 yes/no items for parents (takes 10 minutes). Child must be older than 4 with mental age at least 2 years. Gives overall score and may suggest need for further evaluation.
Screening Tool for Assessment of Autism in 2-year-olds (STAT) (Stone, Coonrod, & Ousley, 2000)	Twelve items administered in a play-based setting. Requires some training. Early results encouraging.
Pervasive Developmental Disorder Screening Test–II (PDD ST-II) (Siegel, 2004)	Designed for use in various settings and age groups. Lack of data on large, unselected sample.
Social Responsiveness Scale (SRS) (Constantino, 2005)	Teacher/parent-completed rating (65 items) used in 4- to 18-year-olds. Provides total score, used in research, does not yield overall diagnosis.

who have major problems in conduct. If this term is inappropriately applied to a child with an ASD, this can result in a very bad situation because people will attribute problem behaviors to the child rather than focusing on developing the right program!

MEDICAL AND EDUCATIONAL LABELS

Medical Labels

- Autistic disorder, autism, childhood autism
- Rett's disorder
- Childhood disintegrative disorder
- Asperger's disorder
- PDD-NOS

Other Educational Labels (in addition to those above)

- Autism spectrum disorder
- Other health impaired
- Learning disabled
- Social–emotional maladjustment/behavior disturbed
- Neurologically impaired
- Multiply handicapped

The diagnosis can be important for other reasons. Federal and state laws and regulations may require some services for eligible children with autism or may specify kinds of treatment to which the child is entitled. In other instances, insurance reimbursement issues come into play (see Chapter 4).

COMPREHENSIVE ASSESSMENTS FOR AUTISM AND RELATED CONDITIONS

Various specialists and organizations around the country provide more comprehensive diagnostic assessments for children at risk or thought to have autism. Sometimes these more detailed assessments are provided by specialists working as individuals, who may then suggest other assessments by members of other disciplines. It is increasingly more common to find *groups* of specialists and interdisciplinary or transdisciplinary teams who work together to coordinate the child's assessment. (Interdisciplinary means individuals from different professions work together; transdisciplinary means that these individuals work very closely together, often watching each other work with the child.) There is tremendous variability in the country in terms of the level of expertise of such individuals and teams and the quality of the work they produce, although when the approach works well, it can work very well indeed.

Good places to look for resources for assessment can include university-based medical schools or clinics or children's hospitals. There are also now more states with state wide service programs as well as more private practitioners who offer assesment services. Parents and parent support groups and other organizations may be able to recommend people nearby. Working with an interdisciplinary team can be very helpful, since often you can coordinate with the team to do several things during the visit.

A comprehensive assessment will usually include a number of elements, varying a bit depending on the child's age and current levels of functioning:

1. *A history that you provide in response to the interviewers' questions:* This history is important for purposes of diagnosis and because it may suggest additional tests or evaluations that need to be done. It also provides information specific to the child and information relevant to the family and particular situation. This will include a history of the pregnancy, the child's early development and behaviors, medical history of the child, and history of other problems in family members.

2. *Psychological testing.* This includes testing of development and intelligence as well as other tests. This helps with the diagnosis as well as in planning treatment and intervention. This assessment will also look at **adaptive functioning**—that is, the child's ability to extend concepts to "real-world" situations and meet his basic day-to-day needs.

3. *A speech–language pathologist often will do an assessment of speech, language, and communication skills:* This may include tests of vocabulary, speech sound production, the ability to understand words and sentences, and the ability to combine words to form grammatical sentences. The speech pathologist will also want to look at actual language abilities. (Some children with autism may have a large vocabulary but don't always use their vocabulary on a regular basis or to interact with others.)

4. *Occupational and physical therapy assessments.* Evaluations of the child's **fine motor** skills (such as fastening zippers or buttons, handwriting, or using scissors) and of his gross motor skills (such as walking, running, using stairs) may be conducted as well, particularly if there are major difficulties in the motor area or many sensory issues/problems.

5. *Diagnostic instruments.* These may include either interviews with you about the child's history or direct assessment based on interaction with the child. These instruments are designed to help (but to not replace) informed clinical observation. We will talk about examples of all these tests later in this chapter.

6. *Medical evaluations.* This may be limited to a physical examination or be more complex, including specialists in areas like genetics or neurology.

You may see any of a number of different professionals while the child is being assessed. These often include a psychologist, a speech–language pathologist, and a physician, but may include other individuals as well. Often, a social worker or nurse may be involved in the assessment. The social worker may ask you for information on the family, with a goal of helping you find the best resources and help coordinating services; a nurse may be involved in taking the history and in working with the doctor in evaluating the child's physical health and developmental functioning. An audiologist may be involved in testing hearing, or an optometrist or ophthalmologist in testing vision. In the following discussion, we will refer to these various people as "the professionals," since they may come from different disciplines and backgrounds. Some of the features of these assessments are summarized below.

EVALUATION PROCEDURES: AUTISM AND PERVASIVE DEVELOPMENTAL DISORDERS

1. **Historical Information**
   a. Early development and characteristics of development
   b. Age and nature of onset at which concerns first appeared
   c. Medical and family history

2. **Psychological/Communicative Examination**
   a. Estimate(s) of intellectual level (particularly nonverbal IQ)
   b. Communicative assessment (receptive and expressive language, use of nonverbal communication, pragmatic [social] use of language)
   c. Adaptive behavior (how does the child cope with the real world)
   d. Evaluate social and communicative skills relative to nonverbal intellectual abilities

3. **Psychiatric Examination**
   a. Nature of social relatedness (eye contact, attachment behaviors)
   b. Behavioral features (stereotypy/self-stimulation, resistance to change, unusual sensitivities to the environment, etc.)
   c. Play skills (nonfunctional use of play materials, developmental level of play activities) and communication
   d. Various rating scales, checklists, and instruments specific to autism may be used

4. **Medical Evaluation**
   a. Search for any associated medical conditions (infectious, genetic, pre- and perinatal risk factors, etc.)
   b. Genetic screen (chromosome analysis and genetic consultation if indicated), fragile X testing
   c. Hearing test (usually indicated)
   d. Other tests and consultation as indicated by history and current examination (e.g., EEG, CT/MRI scan)

5. **Additional Consultations**
   a. Occupational or physical therapy as needed
   b. Respiratory therapy and/or orthopedic specialists (Rett's syndrome)

Adapted, with permission, from F. Volkmar, E. Cook, C. Lord (2002). Autism and pervasive developmental disorders. In M. Lewis (Ed.), *Child and adolescent psychiatry: A comprehensive textbook*. Baltimore: Williams & Wilkins.

The history will include a history of the child from birth to the present, including a history of the pregnancy, the child's development, and her medical and family history. Often, the person talking with you will try to get a sense of what the child was like as a young baby. For example, was she "easy" and happy to be left alone? Did she smile responsively at you? Was she very demanding and difficult? When did you first become worried about the child, and why were you worried? Don't be alarmed if people ask you about things you have never seen! Not all children with autism show every single feature, and, to complicate life, many children who don't have autism may show a few signs that suggest autism!

Sometimes it may be difficult for you to remember specific **developmental milestones** or events. Feel free to bring a baby book or other information that would help you refresh your memory, such as old videos of the child. The medical history will include a review of any medical problems the child has had, such as frequent ear infections. The person talking with you will also be listening carefully for anything you mention that might suggest the need for special medical tests. He or she will also want to know about the kinds of programs the child has been involved in. If you have reports from schools or service providers, you should bring them to show the assessment team. The family history is important because we are now much more aware of the possible genetic aspects of autism. It is clear that a number of conditions, including problems in language, learning, and social interaction, seem to be more common in families of children with autism.

Issues in Assessment of the Child, Adolescent, or Adult with ASD

Individuals with ASD typically exhibit some special challenges for assessment. Assessment of children with autism is both a science and an art. To do a good job, the people doing the assessment need to be able to do many things at the same time. They need to be able to see and interpret the results of their interactions with the child, keeping in mind both what is seen in typically developing children as well as in those with autism. Given the difficulties in social **engagement** and in learning, the examiners will have to use various methods to help ensure that the results are valid and reflect the person's "true" abilities at that specific point in time.

The science part of the assessment is that the examiner has to know exactly the limits within which he has to work (e.g., the specific ways a test must be done). The art part of the assessment is that the examiner also has to be flexible in understanding how, within the constraints of what is "legal" on the test, he or she can help the child be interested and invested in doing well. Usually, the goal for individually administered tests is that the examiner is trying to get the best possible performance out of the child while not violating the "rules" of the test. To this end, the examiner may use rewards or **reinforcements** (stickers, food, prizes, praise, and opportunities to play). A very good examiner will quickly have a sense of how he or she must adapt to the child and will often quickly get into a rhythm where the work with the child shifts easily from one task to another. For the experienced examiner often this information ends up being at least as valuable as the scores on the various tests and assessment instruments.

Parents often are concerned that their child's performance on a given day may not be typical or representative. We try to have parents observe the assessment either in the room with us, or, when possible, through a one-way mirror (you can see the child working but he can't see you). This gives parents a chance to observe what we do and tell us if they see things that are unusual. Occasionally, parents realize that if the examiner were to ask a question differently or if the child were tested with different materials, she might be able to do better—again, something we want to know (although we also want to know what the child will do when we show her something in a very standard way). Sometimes parents are surprised both at what the child can, and sometimes can't, do.

The importance of examiner experience cannot be overemphasized. For example, some tests of intelligence are very verbal, and, given the problems with language, children with autism don't always do so well with these tests. At the other extreme, there are some tests that are done totally without language, and, while the results of these tests may be helpful, they don't tell us much about what the child can do with language-based material. Sometimes we'll see the results of an assessment where an examiner has used a test that is inappropriate for the child; in this case, you'd get the same result (the child couldn't really do the test) each time you used it and would have great **reliability**, but the results wouldn't tell you much about what the child actually could do.

CHALLENGES FOR ASSESSMENT IN AUTISM

- Tremendous range of variability in levels of function (within and between children)
- Great variability in functioning across settings
- Behavioral problems may complicate assessment
- Lack of social interest makes it hard to get the child's cooperation

As part of his or her work with the child, the examiner will try to get a sense not only of what the child is capable of, but also areas of strengths, weaknesses, or special interests that may affect programming. Also, the person doing the assessment will be alert to specific problem behaviors that are important either because they help with the issue of diagnosis or because they are important areas for intervention. For example, aggression, self-injury, or stereotyped behaviors may be helped through behavioral (behavior modification) or pharmacological (drug) intervention.

Psychological Assessments

This part of the assessment is concerned with several things, often including establishing the child's overall levels of cognitive ability (intelligence quotient [IQ]), as well as describing her profiles of strengths and weaknesses. Any of a number of tests may be used (some of these are mentioned subsequently). Usually, this testing will include, at a minimum, a test of cognitive ability or intelligence and some assessment of adaptive skills (the ability to translate what you know into real-world settings), as well as observation of the child and discussion with you.

Observation of the child should be part of the assessment process—giving some psychological test is only one part of a broader assessment. This is important because individuals with autism are quite variable in their behavior. As we mentioned previously, there are many issues in assessing a child with autism. New situations can be a problem for the child. So can situations where the child is left to his own devices. Often the child's behavior is best in familiar settings and when his environment is very "structured," with clear expectations of what he is doing. The professionals evaluating the child should try to get a sense of the range of the child's behavior. You can also help them understand what is typical for the child.

Usually, for most of the assessment, the examiners will be working in a very structured way with the child in an effort to get her best possible performance within the limits of the test or assessment they are doing. We try to get the child's best performance by setting up a friendly but not overly stimulating environment and picking materials/tests that will be appropriate to the child's needs. As previously discussed, there is both a science and an art to doing assessment with children with autism. For some portions of the time with the child, the examiner must decide to "pull back" a bit to give the child more opportunities for less structured interaction. The examiner may also need to decide what the right pace of the assessment is—this again depends on the child; some children respond better to a rather rapid pace, while others like to take things slow and easy! Some of the different types of psychological tests and terms are described on the following page.

PSYCHOLOGICAL TESTS: CONCEPTS AND TERMS

Norm-referenced tests: Tests of this type compare an individual's score against a group of people (usually this is a large group selected to be representative of the general population). Scores derived from tests of this kind can be presented in various ways, including percentiles, standard scores, and age-equivalent scores (among others — see page 59). Typically, test results are distributed along what is called the bell-shaped curve (or what is technically called the normal distribution). The ability to compare scores across people of the same, and different, ages is a strength of this approach. A price, however, is paid in that considerable care has to go into exactly how the test is designed and administered; any deviation from the rules makes the scores difficult, if not impossible, to interpret.

Criterion referenced tests: Tests of this kind are *not* used to compare people to each other; rather, the comparison is to a specific criterion or standard. Taking a test to get a driver's license is a criterion-referenced test. For educational purposes, tests of this kind can be used to show that a student has demonstrated mastery of material (e.g., before moving on to a different grade or more advanced work).

Intelligence: This is a blanket term that usually refers to (and includes) a number of abilities, including the ability to reason, solve problems, plan, and use abstract/symbolic thinking and language. There are many different theories of intelligence and its components.

Intelligence tests: These norm-referenced tests are usually (for people with ASDs) administered individually by a psychologist who is very familiar with the test and the rules for giving and scoring it. Tests of intelligence sample various cognitive skills and are concerned with establishing how able the individual is to solve various kinds of problems. Typically, intelligence tests include various tasks that sample abilities that require more or less language and may look at issues such as how quickly an individual solves problems or what their general level of knowledge is.

Intelligence quotient (IQ): A score derived from tests of intelligence that gives an overall number summarizing a person's intellectual skills. Usually, the average is 100, with what is called a standard deviation of 15. About 97% of the population will score between IQ 70 and 130; about 50% at or above IQ 100, about 1.5% above 130, and about 1.5% below 70 (IQ 70 or below is often used as one of the essential aspects of defining intellectual deficiency or intellectual disability). Particularly for individuals on the autism spectrum, the overall IQ score can be very misleading because it represents an average of very different scores; in such cases, the psychologist may decide not to report an overall IQ score.

Developmental tests: Similar to tests of intelligence, but designed for younger children (birth to ages 3, 4, or 5 years or so). Although they have some (modest) relationship to intelligence in school-age children, the main function of these tests is helping us understand levels of ability in different areas (e.g., problem solving, language, motor areas). They are usually norm referenced.

Achievement tests: Unlike IQ tests, achievement tests are less concerned with how able the person is and more with how they have used their ability to learn (e.g., as applied in math or reading). In addition to standard scores, percentiles, and age equivalent, these tests also often give grade equivalent scores. These tests are often given in schools—they may be given to groups of children. Under the No Child Left Behind laws, tests of this kind have received more attention.

Projective and personality tests: These tests may be paper and pencil (self or parent report) or, in the case of some tests, are individually administered by a psychologist. Tests of personality may include scores related to levels of depression, anxiety, or problem behavior. Projective tests, like the Rorschach inkblot test, allow the individual to give a response to a very unstructured stimulus; tests of this kind may be used to look for unusual patterns of thinking or experience.

Neuropsychological tests: Tests of this kind are usually focused on a particular process such as memory, attention, or particular kinds of problem solving.

Standard scores: Refers to a score (from a normed test) that takes the average of the test and its distribution into account, often the standard score is 100, indicating the middle score for the population tested.

Age-equivalent scores: Compare the individual's ability to what would be typical for a person of a specific age. For example, an age-equivalent score of 5 years, 2 months might be computed based on a child's ability. The meaning of age-equivalent scores clearly varies depending on the child's age (the same 5 year, 2 month score would mean very different things if the child were 5 or 10 years of age).

Percentile scores: Presents a score based on what percent of scores are lower, for example, an 85th percentile score means the person scored higher than 85% of the people who take the test.

Grade-equivalent scores: Presents a score from a norm-referenced test that allows parents and teachers to compare a child's performance to what the typical grade (based on 9-month school year) would be for the score; for example, a score of 4.5 would be a score typical of a child in the fourth grade during the fifth month of school. These scores should be interpreted with care.

Validity: This term has various meanings in terms of testing, but the usual one people think about is whether the test is actually measuring what it is supposed to.

Reliability: This term also has several different meanings, but usually what people focus on is the ability of the test to give consistent results over time (test–retest reliability) or the degree to which items on the test hang together (internal consistency).

In our own assessment clinic for children with autism, we usually ask parents to observe all or portions of the assessment so they can tell us what is or is not typical for their child. This isn't always appropriate, for example for a higher functioning teenager and often this isn't even an option. But this has a number of advantages, including helping parents see what we and the child are doing. We do, however, have to remind parents of a couple of things. One is that, depending on the test or assessment we are using, we may have to ask a question in a very particular way. Sometimes parents will tell us afterward that the child could have answered the question if we'd asked it differently or used different materials. It is helpful for us to know this; at the same time, we are interested in how the child responds to a very standardized question or item and so must work within the constraints of the specific test or assessment procedure we are using. At other times, parents can be overly eager to help their child— sometimes up to the point of answering the question for her! When this happens if the parent is in the room we usually will see if the parent can watch the examination through a one-way mirror in the next room or by video. That way, they can tell us what is typical and what is not without influencing the child's responses.

Tests of Cognitive Ability

For younger children, tests of cognitive ability are usually referred to as developmental tests; these tests provide information on the child's functioning in different areas relative to other children of the same age. For somewhat older children (those nearing 5 or 6 years of age and sometimes younger), more traditional **intelligence tests** may be used. The distinction between developmental and intelligence tests is a somewhat arbitrary one and reflects, in part, the fact that results of tests of cognitive development and intelligence become more stable around the time most children traditionally enter schools. By stable we mean that the results will generally remain rather similar as the child gets older. Typically, psychologists will administer more traditional tests of intelligence, while a range of professionals can administer developmental tests. Tests of intelligence usually provide an overall or "full-scale" IQ score, as well as scores for verbal and nonverbal skills. Verbal skills often include such areas as the ability to define vocabulary words or explain similarities, whereas the nonverbal or performance skills can include areas such as the ability to recognize and reproduce patterns or assemble puzzles. For most IQ tests the average score is 100 with a standard deviation of 15. Scores fall on the famous, or infamous, bell shaped curve. Scores below 70 are usually thought of as falling in the delayed range.

In classical autism, particularly in younger children, nonverbal skills are usually much advanced over more verbal abilities. That is, it is common for a child to have a much higher nonverbal IQ. A child's nonverbal abilities might be, say, at a level corresponding to IQ 75 or 80 (**standard score**), while his verbal abilities might be at the IQ 40 level. For higher functioning children with autism, this gap is usually not as great but may still be there to some extent. There is some indication that this situation is reversed in Asperger's syndrome, where verbal skills are better than nonverbal skills.

There are many different intelligence tests available. The specific test or tests chosen will depend on several factors. For example, how much language is required (either to understand or respond), how much the test requires **transitions** and shifting, the social demands of the test, and how important speed of performance is. Generally, children with autism do best on tests that require less language and social engagement and fewer shifts and transitions. Since IQ tests can vary widely in how much they emphasize these factors, it is possible that the same child could get very different results on different tests. Thus, it is important that the psychologist choose the tests carefully, keeping in mind the specific circumstances and needs of the child. The choice of test (or tests) is up to the psychologist, who may try to start with something he or she thinks will be easier or more interesting to the child. Sometimes what seem to be minor differences in tests (more or less verbal tests) can actually result in major changes for a child with autism; thus, it is important that the psychologist have some experience in working with children with autism and be aware of the range of IQ tests available. Some of the more frequently used tests are listed in Table 3.3. We will give some specific examples of test results and how these inform the assessment team's results in subsequent chapters.

Adaptive Skills Assessment

In addition to tests of development and intelligence, often there will be some attempt to understand how the child does in more typical settings. This concern with *adaptive skills* is important because often children with autism can do something in a very structured way, but have more trouble generalizing the skills to real-world settings. Tests of adaptive skills are usually done by interviewing parents. The results often add an important "real-world" perspective and help identify areas the family and school can work on together.

Adaptive functioning (adaptive skills) is a concept *distinct* from IQ. For example, we have an adolescent patient with Asperger's syndrome who has a verbal IQ of 140 (genius level), one of whose major preoccupations is solving very complex mathematical equations. But this same patient cannot walk into McDonald's and get a cheeseburger and change! The latter skill—translating his mathematical ability into the real world—is what adaptive skills are all about. Given the major challenges individuals on the autism spectrum have with generalization, it is very

| TABLE 3.3 | SELECTED TESTS OF INTELLIGENCE/DEVELOPMENT |

Name	Comment
Wechsler Intelligence Scales: Wechsler Preschool and Primary Scale of Intelligence, 3rd edition (WPPSI-III, 2002); Wechsler Intelligence Scale for Children, 4th edition (WISC-IV, 2003), Wechsler Adult Intelligence Scale, 3rd edition, (WAIS-III, 1997)	Excellent series of tests covering preschool (around age 4) to adulthood; provide separate verbal and performance IQ scores. Some tasks (both on the verbal and nonverbal sections) are timed—a challenge for many children with autism and related conditions (this actually may help document need for untimed tests). Typical profiles of ability are seen in autism and Asperger's disorder.
Stanford Binet Intelligence Scale, 5th edition (SBS-V) (Roid, 2003)	Excellent test; can be used with somewhat younger children. Wide age range, nonverbal scale may underestimate abilities in ASDs.
Kaufmann Assessment Battery for Children, 2nd edition (KABC-II) (Kaufman and Kaufman, 2004)	Excellent test, can be used from 3 to 18 years of age. Some language is needed (but not much). Somewhat more flexible for children with autism. Many of the materials interest children with ASD. Language demands minimized and good sensitivity to possible cultural bias.
Leiter International Performance Scale–Revised (Leiter-R) (Roid & Miller, 1997)	A test originally developed for deaf children, recently redone. Provides assessment of nonverbal cognitive ability. (Can be used for children with no expressive speech.) Some teaching is allowed. Limitations: No verbal IQ, and the new materials are less interesting for children with autism.
Mullen Scales of Early Learning (Mullen, 1995)	Can be used with very young children. Provides scores in nonverbal problem solving, receptive and expressive language, and gross and fine motor skills. Scores from developmental tests like the Mullen are usually less predictive of later abilities.
Differential Ability Scales, 2nd edition (DAS-II) (Elliott, 2007)	Well-done test, covers wide range of ages and taps a number of different skills (not just overall IQ).

Note: Many other tests are available and tests are constantly being revised and reissued.

typical for there to be a big gap between what they know and what they can actually do in the real world. Accordingly, assessment of adaptive skills is important both at the time of first diagnosis and also over time.

The *Vineland Adaptive Behavior Scales* assesses capacities for self-sufficiency in several different domains of functioning:

Communication (receptive, expressive, and written language)

Daily Living Skills (personal, domestic, and community skills),

Socialization (interpersonal relationships, play–leisure time, and coping skills)

Motor Skills (gross and fine motor skills)

There is an optional maladaptive behavior section that focuses on problem behaviors.

There are three forms of the test, which itself was recently redone (what psychologists call *restandardized*). There is a teacher rating form (which is of much less interest to us only because it is meant more as a screening-type test) and what are called the survey and expanded form. The latter two are done as interviews with parents or caregivers or even the person involved. These interviews are called semistructured because the interviewer knows the specific questions but scores based on parents talking more generally about the person; that is, they don't come right out and ask you the question. Rather, they may say something like, "Tell me how Jimmy does getting dressed," and then may ask more detailed follow-up questions based on what the parent says. The expanded form is of most help for programming purposes and takes a bit longer than the survey form which usually takes an hour or less to do and gives information about overall levels of functioning, but not with the same detail as the expanded form. The Vineland produces the usual kinds of scores, that is, standard scores, age equivalents, and so on. Because items are arranged developmentally and with the addition of some other data on the person, it is possible, with the expanded form, to produce a very detailed list of reasonable next steps to work on in the individual's program. The survey and expanded form can be used for people from birth to 90 years of age. We will give some examples of use of the Vineland in developing programs in subsequent chapters.

A number of different research papers (some of which are included in the reading list) have used the Vineland to document social and communication problems for diagnostic as well as treatment purposes. For children with autism there is a fairly common profile on the Vineland with some areas such as motor and daily living skills being much stronger than socialization and communication skills. Interpersonal functioning is usually very low. In contrast, individuals with Asperger's still have lower socialization scores, but receptive and expressive skills may be better, while motor skills, particularly fine motor skills, are weaker. We'll give some examples of results from the Vineland when we talk about cases in later chapters. One of the important things to understand about tests of adaptive skills is that the issue is not whether the person can engage in a particular behavior or activity but whether they *usually* do so (this is especially important in autism, where often the child *can* do things in isolation but have horrible trouble translating behavioral gains into real-world settings).

Neuropsychological Assessment

Occasionally, specialized testing is needed, particularly if there is any question of a very specific difficulty. Neuropsychological testing focuses on specific abilities such as visual perception and visual–motor integration, learning and memory, **attention**, and executive functions. These tests are more often done when there is some indication of a specific learning problem or difficulties. For example, testing of visual–motor skills can help evaluate problems with handwriting and hand–eye coordination (sometimes a problem in children with Asperger's), and the results may then have some implications for intervention (for example, use of a computer or keyboard rather than cursive handwriting drills).

Other Psychological Assessments

A host of other assessment instruments are available, including personality tests, projective tests, vocationally related tests, and achievement tests. With the exception of achievement tests, these tend to be relatively less frequently used in children with ASDs. Achievement tests are frequently used, often in schools, to document academic progress. It is also helpful to have achievement testing in situations where the child appears to have an isolated ability; for example, some children with autism read to "decode" (sound out the words) and may have impressive reading abilities, but a test of reading understanding may show that the child's actual ability to use the information is at a much lower level. Achievement test results can also be viewed in relation to IQ scores and patterns of strengths and weaknesses may have important implications for classroom placement/activities. As children move into adolescence testing may be done to help with vocational placement or vocational interests.

Personality tests and projective tests are sometimes used, particularly in older individuals (adolescents and adults) with autism and particularly Asperger's disorder. These tests can be used to document problems in thinking and reality testing. They are not routinely done.

In classical autism, particularly in younger children, nonverbal skills are usually much advanced over more verbal abilities; that is, it is common for a child to have a much higher nonverbal IQ. We will give some examples of psychological testing in Chapters 7, 8 and 9.

Speech–Language–Communication Assessments

Difficulties in communication are one of the central features of autism and a main focus of intervention. This is true even for higher functioning individuals with autism and Asperger's disorder, who have significant problems in the social use of language even when they have good vocabularies. Typically developing children are quite communicative well before they begin to say words. In children with autism spectrum difficulties, these skills do not develop in the same way, so, for example, early (preverbal) methods of communicating such as reaching and pointing to show something to someone else may be quite deficient.

When children with autism do speak, their speech is remarkable in a number of ways. The prosody (musical aspects) of speech may be markedly off so that the child speaks in a somewhat robotic (what speech–language pathologists call *monotonic*) way. Use of pronouns (which are constantly shifting relative to who is speaking and being referred to) is an area of difficulty for many children with autism; often, children with autism reverse pronouns, saying, for example, you instead of I. Another very common characteristic is echolalia—repeating the same word/phrase over and over—such as saying "wanna cookie, wanna cookie, wanna cookie," having been asked, "Do you want a cookie?" Echolalia tends to persist over time, unlike in typically developing children where it gradually diminishes as the child becomes a more effective and sophisticated communicator. For the more able person with autism, difficulties in keeping up a conversation, in responding to more sophisticated language (e.g., humor, irony, sarcasm) may present significant obstacles. These are what speech–language pathologists refer to as *pragmatic* aspects (social aspects) of language.

It is important to realize that problems in communication do not exist in isolation. Rather, these difficulties have a major impact on the child's social, organziational, and problem-solving skills. For example, children who do communicate verbally may rely on very idiosyncratic communication, which further contributes to social difficulties. For example, the child may say "the mailman is coming" anytime something unexpected happens because she remembers once when the mailman came unexpectedly early. Her parents may understand what this phrase means, but most people would not.

Speech–communication assessments are important for all children with autism and related conditions, regardless of their level of functioning. For example, for children who are mute, an assessment of *comprehension* skills can be very appropriate. **Speech–language pathologists (SLPs)** are concerned with broader aspects of communication and not just speech, so they might, for example, consider ways in which a child who is not yet speaking could be helped to communicate through some other means.

The communication assessment should include several components. As was true for **psychological assessment**, the choice of tests and assessment procedures must reflect an awareness of the child's unique circumstances. For example, the SLP may be interested in assessing the child's ability to produce sounds and words if it seems like this is an area of specific difficulty. Various **standardized tests** of vocabulary (both of **receptive vocabulary**—what the child understands, and **expressive vocabulary**—what she can say) are available, as are more sophisticated tests that look at exactly how language is used. For very young children, fewer assessment instruments are available. Instead, observation of social functioning (such as during play) may augment the results obtained with more standardized tests. Scores are much like those derived from psychological assessments, and again test types, ages tested, format of test, and so forth vary. We'll give specific examples of speech–communication testing results in later chapters.

Depending on the child's age and ability to communicate, the SLP will assess different, usually multiple, areas. These include measures of preverbal communication, single-word vocabulary (receptive and expressive), as well as actual language use. There often is a significant gap between single-word vocabulary and the ability to use words regularly in conversation. As we mentioned before,

TABLE 3.4   **COMMONLY USED TESTS OF SPEECH–LANGUAGE–COMMUNICATION**

Name	Comment
Peabody Picture Vocabulary Test, 4th edition (PPVT-4) (Dunn & Dunn, 2007)	Measures receptive vocabulary (what the child understands). *Note:* This score may overestimate child's actual language ability. Age range 2½–90 years.
Expressive One Word Picture Vocabulary Test (EOWPVT) (Brownell, 2000)	Measures naming ability (what the child can label). Again, may overestimate child's actual language ability. Age range 2–18 years.
Reynell Developmental Language Scales, U.S. edition (Reynell) (Reynell & Gruber, 1990).	Useful from 12 months through age 6; provides measures of actual language use. Scores often lower than when single-word vocabulary is assessed. Provides scores for verbal comprehension and expressive language. Materials attractive to children.
Preschool Language Scale–4 (PLS-4) (Zimmerman, Steiner, & Pond, 2002)	Used to assess receptive and expressive language; frequently used in schools. This is a direct assessment. Good instrument for younger children. Age range 2 weeks–<7 years).
Comprehensive Assessment of Spoken Language (CASL) (Carrow-Woolfolk, 1999)	Used from ages 3 to 21, only a verbal or nonverbal (pointing) response required (no reading or writing ability expected) with test of various language abilities, including pragmatic ability (social language use) and figurative language.
Clinical Evaluation of Language Fundamentals, 4th edition (CELF-4) (Semel, Wiig, & Secord, 2003)	Used for children from 3 to 21 (two versions). Assesses various language skills related to school requirements. Useful for older and higher functioning children.
Test of Language Competence (TLC) (Wiig & Secord, 1989)	Focuses on more complex aspects of language (e.g., ambiguity, figurative language, abstract language), ages 5–18.

Note: Many other tests are available.

sometimes the assessment will include evaluation of specific problems in language speech production (such as articulation) depending on the special needs of the child. Evaluation of the child's ability to use language socially should always be included (see Table 3.4).

The kinds of tests used are quite varied. Some of them rely on parental report of the child's skills, while others are based on assessment of the child by the SLP. Some assessment measures have been developed specifically for children with autism and related disorders or communication delays; often these employ a more play-based format, as is appropriate to younger children and those with more restricted communication skills. For example, the Communication and Symbolic Behavior Scales (CSBS) looks at both language and the development of symbolic abilities in a play-based setting. It is used for children whose communication skills are between 6 and 24 months (the child can actually be up to 6 years of age). And also includes a caregiver questionnaire. It provides a range of scores in different areas.

For children who are not yet using words, the SLP is interested in the building blocks of language, including social interaction, play, and other behaviors with a strong communicative aspect. The goals include understanding what the child understands about communication with others (use of gestures and words), whether he understands communicative intent (the reasons for communicating), and the means for communicating (behaviors, words, vocalization, gestures). The SLP will also be interested in learning how effective and persistent the child is as a communicator. For instance, does he persist in trying to communiucate when the other person does not understand, or does he use more or less conventional ways to communicate? In addition, the reasons why the child communicates will be noted. That is, does he communicate only to get things, to protest, or to engage other people? The social quality, as well as the rate of communications, is also important. For example, does the child pair his communication with eye contact or gestures? The SLP will listen to whatever sounds the child does make.

When children are able to combine words, a different range of assessment tools becomes available. It becomes somewhat easier to assess the child's ability to understand receptive and expressive language and relationships between words. Specific tests are chosen based on both the child's age and her level of language. For this group of children, sometimes one needs to make compromises or accommodations to get information that is helpful for purposes of diagnosis and treatment planning. For example, if the child is older but has limited language, the SLP may choose to use a test originally developed for younger children. Or, if the child has specific issues that complicate giving the test the usual way, some **accommodation** may be made. These changes might include repeating instructions, using reinforcement, or giving additional cues to the child. When these strategies are used, it does complicate scoring and interpretation of the test but may give valuable information for treatment.

In addition to doing formal testing, the SLP will also usually include a period of play so that he or she can record a language sample. The latter, usually audio- or videotaped, can be used after the assessment to analyze the level and sophistication of the child's spontaneous language.

For older children and those with better language (including children with Asperger's disorder) the usual tests of vocabulary levels and language abilities may tend to be much higher than the child's actual communication ability and thus may mislead school staff. For such children, the assessment should focus on more complicated aspects of language, including social uses of language, such as understanding humor and non-literal language (for example, "His eyes were bigger than his stomach"). For these children, often the results of the Vineland (see above) are more informative than many of the more usual language measures. For individuals who do speak, the SLP will often pay special attention to the child's ability to modulate or moderate their tone of voice and volume as relevant to the specific topic or place.

Autism/ASD-Specific Tests and Rating Scales

A number of different rating scales, checklists, and other assessment instruments have been developed to help clinicians diagnose autism. Some of these are primarily checklists for *screening* for autism and have been discussed previously in this chapter (see Table 3.2, page 51). These **screening tests** were developed for health care providers or others to use to determine which children who show some signs of autism should have a comprehensive evaluation. Other tests and rating scales are more specifically concerned with *diagnosing* autism (and a few can be used for both purposes). These tests may take the form of either parent-completed rating scales or interviews, or they may be based on actual work with the child. That is, there are some checklists that are completed by professionals based on observation of and/or work with the child, while others are based purely (or largely) on parent or teacher report.

Many different issues are involved in the use of these instruments (again, a little knowledge can be a dangerous thing) and sometimes people will use them in ways that were not intended. For example, we encountered a well-meaning school administrator who got access to a rating scale, and, with no training in how to use it and very little experience with autism, decided a child "couldn't have autism" based on her (incorrect) completion of the rating scale (to make matters worse, her score, which was done with no training at all, came out half a point below the usual cutoff for autism). Some of the scales require very specific, and sometimes extensive, training to complete. None of these scales are a substitute for a careful, thoughtful assessment by an experienced clinician. Many (but not all) of these instruments are listed in Table 3.2 on page 69.

TABLE 3.5	DIAGNOSTIC TESTS/INSTRUMENTS FOR AUTISM

Name	Format and Comments
Autism Diagnostic Interview–Revised (ADI-R) (Rutter, LeCouteur, & Lord, 2003)	Interview with parents to verify diagnosis of autism based on history of child (requires substantial training). Very well-done test used for research as well. Items keyed to categorical (DSM/ICD) criteria. Typically takes 90 minutes or more. Used for children with chronological and mental ages above 2 years. Issues with borderline cases.
Autism Diagnostic Observation Schedule (ADOS) (Lord, Rutter, DiLavore, & Risi, 1999)	Assessment of the child, covering wide span in ability levels; assesses behaviors and features relevant to diagnosis of autism. Companion instrument to ADI-R, also very well done. Requires significant training. Items designed to elicit behaviors of type seen in autism. Four modules based on levels of individual's language. Less useful for nonverbal adults/adolescents.
Childhood Autism Rating Scale (CARS) (Schopler, Reicher, & Rennner, 1988)	Assessment of the child. Looks at severity of autistic behaviors; useful for screening. Requires some (but minimal) training. Fifteen items rated on 4-point score (normal to very autistic). Scores >30 suggest autism. May overidentify in individuals with minimal language or more cognitive disability.
Gilliam Autism Rating Scales, 2nd edition (GARS-2) (Gilliam, 2006)	Norm-referenced; focus is on ages 3–22. Takes 5–10 minutes. Forty-two items grouped in three categories. Structured interview format. Recently revised, can inform IEP development. Older version may have underidentified possible autism.
Psychoeducational Profile–Revised (PEP-R) (Schopler, Reicher, Lansin, & Marcus, 1990)	Assessment for preschool and some school-age children to identify areas for intervention. Flexible administration of items in several different domains; items rate as pass/fail/emerging with scores and age equivalents for domains. Some normative data available. Adult–adolescent version also available.

The two instruments that are probably most commonly used at present are the *Autism Diagnostic Interview–Revised* (ADI-R) and the *Autism Diagnostic Observation Schedule* (ADOS). The ADI is an interview done with parents that focuses on the child's social and communication skills, as well as other behaviors. This test, which can take a while to complete, was originally designed for research (to be sure that researchers in different parts of the world were diagnosing autism in the same way). It has the considerable advantage of being explicitly "keyed" or linked to the diagnostic criteria for autism in DSM-IV. The ADOS is a companion instrument to the ADI; it focuses on assessment of the child using various activities.

Other instruments commonly used at present include the *Childhood Autism Rating Scale* (CARS), along with several others. These scales measure severity of autism either on the basis of parent or teacher report or observation of the child.

Several other instruments are available for assessment of individuals with Asperger's disorder. Given that, at least as an official diagnosis, Asperger's has been around for comparatively much less time than autism, it is probably not surprising that there is less agreement about which of these scales is best to use. Table 3.6 summarizes some of these scales. Here, even more than for autism, use of a scale is *not* a substitute for a careful and thoughtful diagnostic/clinical assessment.

Medical Assessments

Depending on the specific situation, the child may be seen for a medical assessment as part of the comprehensive assessment, or may be referred for specific medical tests on the basis of the history and assessment of the child. Doctors may find correctable or treatable medical conditions (e.g., hearing loss or seizures) or other medical conditions (e.g., intellectual disability, language disorders) that may produce symptoms suggestive of autism or ASDs. Depending on the findings of the assessment, there should be a search for genetic conditions such as fragile X syndrome or tuberous sclerosis. Testing hearing or vision is important. More specialized testing for seizures may include a brain wave test (electroencephalogram [EEG]) or sometimes neuroimaging (magnetic resonance imaging [MRI] or computed tomographic [CT] scan). These tests are not routinely needed, however. Clearly, symptoms that suggest a possible seizure do require that more extensive assessment is needed.

There is no specific laboratory test for autism at the time we are writing this book. However, genetic testing, for fragile X or other conditions, is almost always done. There is also much interest at present in finding genes involved in autism, and so a blood test in the future is a real possibility, although probably, particularly at first, such tests will miss some children with autism. For children who have had a period of developmental regression, more extensive medical investigations are usually undertaken (see Chapter 13).

TABLE 3.6	DIAGNOSTIC TESTS/INSTRUMENTS FOR ASPERGER'S

Name/Reference	Format and Comments
Asperger Syndrome Diagnostic Scale (ASDA) (Myles, Bock, & Simpson, 2001)	Ratings done by someone familiar with student, 50 items (present/absent) on 5 subscales. Used ages 5–18. Provides an overall Asperger syndrome quotient (ASQ). Some issues relative to how instrument was standardized, used more to document change (not diagnose).
Childhood Asperger Syndrome Test (CAST) (Scott, Baron-Cohen, Bolton, & Brayner, 2002)	Parent-completed screen, 37 present/absent items; subset of items summed with score >15 is indicates need for additional evaluation. Used 4–11 years. No information on reliability.
Gilliam Asperger's Disorder Scale (GADS) (Gilliam, 2001)	Thirty-two-item norm-referenced scale for individuals familiar with student; ages 3–22 years. Large standardization group, but information on standardization sample lacking.
Krug Asperger Disorder Index (KADI) (Krug & Arick, 2003)	Rating scale (norm referenced); rater should be familiar with child. Two versions (ages 6–11, 12–21). Apparently good reliability, but diagnoses not verified independently.
A Scale to Assist the Diagnosis of Autism and Asperger's Disorder in Adults (RAADS) (Ritvo, Ritvo, Guthrie, Yuwiler, Ritvo, & Weisbender, 2008)	Seventy-eight-item self-rating based in DSM/ICD criteria. Small standardization sample; does not distinguish autism and Asperger's. Intended to identify adults at risk for disorder(s).
Autism Spectrum Screening Questionnaire (ASSQ) Ehlers, Gilberg & Wing (1999)	Screening instrument with 27 descriptions, each rated on 3-point scale; items grouped in five areas. Used for 6–17 years of age (teacher/parent versions). Scores >13 indicate more evaluation needed. Good sensitivity, but poor specificity (over pickup cases).

Occupational and Physical Therapy Assessments

Occupational and physical therapists may be involved either as members of the assessment team or in the school-based intervention program. Physical therapists are concerned with the child's ability to engage in gross motor (large muscle) movements, and occupational therapists are often more concerned with fine motor (hand) movements. They also may be needed to help assess the child if she has major sensory challenges. These specialists can provide input to classroom teachers as well as to parents on ways to help cope with and understand challenging behaviors, as well as motor difficulties, such as with writing and unusual sensitivities. Some selected tests of motor development or sensory–motor

TABLE 3.7   **MOTOR AND SENSORY MOTOR TESTS**

Name	Format and Comments
Sensory Experiences Questionnaire (SEQ) (Baraneck, 1999)	Thirty-five items; targets children with autism (6 months to 6 years); focuses on frequency of unusual sensory experiences.
Evaluation of Sensory Processing (ESP) (Parham & Ecker, 2002)	Used in children 2–12 years; 76 items on 5-point scale.
Sensory Profile (Dunn, 1999)	Normed on large sample of children (ages 3–10), 125 items (5-point scale) for caregivers. Focuses on unusual sensory responses.
Toddler Infant Motor Evaluation (TIME) (Miller & Roid, 1994)	Covers birth to 47 months, focuses on several domains based on rating of observed motor behaviors. Requires considerable training.
Test of Visual Motor Integration (VMI) (Beery & Buktenica, 1997)	Widely used and well-standardized individually administered instrument (includes adults). Used for ages 2 through adulthood. Assesses visual perception and motor coordination. Easily done by a trained evaluator. Useful in documenting fine motor and visual–motor delays.
Peabody Developmental Motor Scales (PDMS) (Folio & Fewell, 1983)	Norm-referenced scores for fine and gross motor abilities. Birth to 83 months.

abilities are summarized in Table 3.7. Issues of sensory difference are addressed in Chapter 16 (sensory chapter).

Understanding The Results

When the child's evaluation is complete, a variety of numbers will be available to describe his performance. This is especially true if the tests used were based or standardized on the "normal population." The professional(s) who work with the child will be able to interpret these for you. You should always feel free to ask questions, and the people doing the testing can reasonably be expected to explain the results in ways you understand. One of us once had the experience of being part of an assessment where a much less experienced member of the assessment team solemnly turned to the father and said something like, "Your child has a score of 7"—to which the father very correctly replied, "What in the world does that *mean*?"

Keep in mind that, for scores to be valid, the person doing the assessment has a number of rules he or she must follow in the assessment. If you give the child the answer in advance, of course she'd do well. But the results would not be *valid*. Sometimes deviations from these rules are needed and can be sensibly made, but when this is done, it will tend to make it more difficult to compare the child's performance to that of children in the normal sample. If the examiner really violates the rules, he or she cannot really use the norms provided for the test. Again, we cannot overemphasize that parents and teachers should always feel free to ask for an explanation of what scores mean and how the person who gave the test understands them. Having some number or numbers itself is just an academic exercise—the science, and art, of assessment is translating both the numbers/scores *and* observations into something meaningful about the child.

As we have discussed previously in this chapter different kinds of scores are available. In general, standard scores are the ones to be most interested in since they give a much better sense of how the scores compare to other children (regardless of age). Thus it is easy to understand an IQ score of 70 or 80 or 130 or 140. However, for most children, adolescents, and adults *not* on the autism spectrum the overall score, for example the overall IQ or intelligence quotient, is highly meaningful and informative, but that is because usually there is not much variability in subscores. In contrast, in individuals with ASD, it is not at all uncommon to have a great deal of scatter and it is just this scatter that starts to help with program development. Indeed, if the person has a dramatic range of scores, a discussion of strengths and weaknesses is much more informative than a single number—and often a single overall score won't be reported.

Although age-equivalent scores are easy to understand, they are often less useful than the standard scores. For example hearing that a 6 year old child has an age equivalent score of 5 years 2 months is harder to compare to a $5\frac{1}{2}$ year old child who has an age equivalent score of 5 years 3 months. In addition age-equivalent scores are usually much more likely to fluctuate than standard scores (performance on one or two items may increase or decrease the age-equivalent score more dramatically than it does the standard score).

Originally, standard scores such as IQ were computed by taking the child's **age-equivalent score (mental age)** and dividing it by the child's actual chronological age and then multiplying the result by 100. Thus, a child with a mental age of 3 years and an actual age of 5 years would have been said to have an IQ of 60 ($^3/_5 \times 100$). Nowadays, tests are developed and "standardized" in more sophisticated ways, but the general idea is the same. The distribution of standard scores falls on the famous (or infamous) bell-shaped curve. The average score will be in the middle, with other scores around it. For many IQ tests, the average or mean score in the general population is 100. That is, about 50% of people would score above 100, and 50% would score below it. These tests usually have what is called a **standard deviation** (measure of how the scores scatter around the average) of about 15. This means that most people (about two-thirds) taking the test will score within 15 points above to 15 points below the mean, or between 85 and 115. Only about 3% of people will score more than 30 points (two standard deviations) above or below the mean. That is, only about 3% of people would have scores of 70 or below. Some tests will have different means and standard deviations. Age-equivalent scores are easier to understand but standard scores are, in many ways, more useful since they take age into account. We will give examples of testing results in subsequent chapters to illustrate some of these points.

PUTTING IT ALL TOGETHER

Due to health insurance issues, geographical location, and other factors, parents unfortunately do not always have that much choice when selecting a team to assess their child. If you can, try to connect with people who have worked together previously and who have considerable experience in diagnosing autism and related conditions. Other parents and often school staff will be able to give you good information about qualified professionals. Often, the primary health care provider is the person who provides an initial referral to a team and then helps you obtain local services and resources. He or she then can help parents obtain local services and resources; this person may be able to direct parents to experienced people. Sometimes the school will have a well-functioning and experienced assessment team, since it is increasingly the case that school-based professionals (psychologists, speech pathologists, occupational and physical therapists) are more familiar with autism.

The best of the interdisciplinary teams work well together. Unfortunately, others don't. Sometimes parents and schools end up getting a plethora of individual reports with little integration and a report that lacks a single view of the child. Sometimes we've seen separate reports from six or seven different professionals working in the same group, but with little apparent awareness of each other's findings. This usually happens when the "team" members work as individuals rather than as a group. Ideally, what is desired is a single sensible and realistic view of the child.

At the risk of overstating what we hope is now obvious, parents and teachers should feel that reports, whether from a team or an individual care provider, should be understandable. Results should be translatable into programs for the person on the autism spectrum. For example, when we write reports, we tell parents that every one of the numbered "bullet points" in our recommendations is something that might well be included in the child's individualized education plan (IEP). As a consumer and parent, you should feel as if you can understand the reports and that the results have implications for how you or the child's teacher and others can work with her. Sometimes one can't help but see many different specialists; in this case, the lack of integration is often a major problem. In this situation, you can ask one of the specialists if he or she can assume a major role in coordination and integration of all the various reports. Sometimes the primary care provider can serve this function; at other times, a school-based professional may be able to do so.

DIAGNOSTIC CERTAINTY AND UNCERTAINTY

To make life complicated, many conditions that are apparent in the first years of life may be confused with autism. For example, significant intellectual disability (mental retardation) may result in language delay and lead parents and health care providers to suspect autism. Usually, however, these children have social abilities and communication skills that are pretty much on target for their overall intelligence or cognitive ability. At times, however, distinguishing between autism and intellectual disability can be difficult. One reason is that we know that many children with strictly diagnosed autism also go on to exhibit intellectual disability. Another reason is that sometimes children with intellectual disability exhibit some of the same kinds of unusual self-stimulating behaviors (e.g., hand flapping) seen in children with autism. Yet another reason is that we know that although they have their uses, the results of developmental and other tests become stable only as the child gets older.

Somewhat less commonly, there is confusion about autism for children with language difficulties. We often see children with very serious language problems who had, as a result, gotten a diagnosis of autism, but were in fact very socially related and sometimes very "communicative" even when they did not have any words. Occasionally, such children may seem to develop their own sign language system. They usually are very much interested in communication, even when their actual language is limited.

Although we continue to see that many children with autism have isolated areas of ability, professionals have become aware that when one looks at the *entire* intelligence test, often many—indeed, probably most—children with strictly defined autism do have some degree of associated intellectual disability overall. This is important for several reasons. First, it disproves the notion that arose in the 1950s and 1960s that, rather than having some degree of developmental delay, children with autism were "choosing" not to respond (negativism). It also contradicts the related idea that they could not be tested. While there can indeed be many difficulties in assessing children with autism, these days when we hear that a child is "untestable," this often says more about the examiner than the child. It is now clear that assessment can be done if the person doing the testing is flexible and is prepared to test developmental skills using techniques adapted for children with autism.

Consistent with Kanner's original report, we often see children with autism who have some good skills, particularly in problem solving, that do not make use of language. The observation of areas of "splinter skills" has been made repeatedly. The term *splinter* means just that—skills that are striking because they are so much better than other areas of the child's development. For some children with autism, these unusual abilities (e.g., in drawing, music, or calendar calculation) rise to the level of savant skills. Such skills tend to be very narrow and often involve memory for concrete events or trivial information (e.g., numbers, calendars) or visual–spatial skills (e.g., jigsaw puzzles). Many younger children with autism may have an unusual interest in letters and numbers, with some children teaching themselves to "decode" words, although they are usually much less advanced at understanding what they read. Unfortunately, splinter skills often don't contribute much to the child's ability to meet the demands of daily life.

For many parents, a diagnosis of intellectual disability seems, if anything, even worse than a diagnosis of autism. Given the difficulties in assessment and the limitations of testing for young (preschool) children, often the term *developmentally delayed* may be used at first. The question of whether intellectual disability is present is often settled only when the child is at or near traditional school age. Keep in mind that children with autism who also have some degree of associated intellectual disability will continue to grow and develop. Although not common, some children will also make major gains over time—particularly in the preschool years and, to a lesser extent, in adolescence. Also keep in mind that it is possible to drop a diagnosis of intellectual disability or autism if this is appropriate as a child grows older. Sometimes it may be important to keep labels; for example, in some states these may have implications for adult service programs.

CONDITIONS THAT MAY BE CONFUSED WITH AUTISM

Condition	Features That Help Differentiate It from Autism
Intellectual disability	Generally even pattern of cognitive and language delay. Social skills not much different from cognitive level. (*Note*: Intellectual disability may coexist with autism and related disorders; this is rare in Asperger's disorder.) Problems arise in distinguishing autism when stereotyped behaviors are present.
Language disorders	Nonverbal and social skills often preserved; the child can be very communicative even when a severe language disorder is present. Differentiation from autism can be complicated for very young children.
Deafness	In contrast to the more typical situation in autism, hearing difficulties are not very selective. (Hearing is affected in all/most situations, not just in certain situations, as in autism.) Hearing testing is critical; occasionally children with autism do exhibit deafness or other sensory impairment (see Chapter 16). Some deaf children will exhibit self-stimulatory movements.
Schizophrenia	In children, schizophrenia is very uncommon. Hallucinations (hearing voices) and delusions (bizarre beliefs) are present. Major deterioration in function may suggest childhood disintegrative disorder, but typical signs of marked social problems and other unusual behaviors more typical of autism are not seen. Schizophrenia is rare in children.

Obsessive compulsive disorder (OCD)	Usually the child voices active dislike of the symptoms, in contrast to autism and Asperger's disorder where repetitive behaviors or circumscribed interests seem to be preferred activities. Social skills usually preserved in OCD.
Reactive attachment disorder (RAD)	Lack of social interest is common in children reared in very neglectful settings (e.g., some orphanages) and the child may exhibit some unusual behaviors, but usually development significantly improves when a more appropriate environment is provided.
Selective mutism	Child talks only in some situations. While some social difficulties are present, these are not as severe as in autism, and child can communicate in some settings.

Special problems for diagnosis arise in several different situations. As we discuss in Chapter 7, infants and young children sometimes pose problems for diagnosis, since it is not uncommon for a child under age 3 to exhibit *some* but not all the features of autism. Usually, this takes the form of a child who exhibits the required social and communication problems but does not yet have the unusual motor **mannerisms** and interests typical of autism. Often, these children go on to develop more typical autism after age 3, but sometimes they do not. More rarely, we see a child at 2 or even near 3 who appears to have autism, but as time goes on, the child seems to have some other problem or, more rarely, appears perfectly normal. Some of the difficulties in early diagnosis partly reflect our real difficulties in assessment of younger children and partly reflect the fact that different kinds of problems can mimic autism early in life. As a result, however, the assessment team may discuss with you a provisional or working diagnosis and make it clear that the issue of final diagnosis will be made with certainty only over time.

Asperger's Disorder

Diagnostic issues also arise with children who are more cognitively able, particularly if they are very verbal. As we discussed in Chapter 1, some controversy has surrounded Asperger's disorder. Children with Asperger's disorder usually do not have delayed language—instead, their language skills are often a source of strength. Probably, in part, as a result of their much better language, parents don't seem to be worried as early as parents of children with autism. However, often their ability to communicate (not just talk) and their social skills, particularly with peers, are poor. There may be a fascination with letters and numbers early in life and, as time goes on, the child develops one or more highly specialized interests, such as in clocks, time, rocks, dinosaurs, snakes, or sometimes in much more esoteric areas, such as deep fat fryers or telegraph line pole insulators. The family will discover that their life revolves around the child's special interests, and these special interests dominate the child's life and interfere with learning. Often, unusual profiles of ability develop with much better verbal skills and poor nonverbal and motor abilities. There can, however, be complications in understanding the diagnosis in the first years of life, and sometimes the diagnosis is clarified as the child gets a bit older. Unfortunately, the precise boundary line between high-functioning autism and Asperger's disorder continues to be debated and, of course, children haven't always "read the book" and don't conform to more typical **syndrome** pictures. Diagnostic evaluations of children with Asperger's disorder are very similar to those of children with autism with the exception that since the children are more verbal, a wider choice of tests and other assessments often is available.

Pervasive Developmental Disorder Not Otherwise Specified (PDD- NOS)

PDD–NOS (also sometimes called atypical PDD, or atypical autism) is both an easy and a rather complicated diagnosis to make. It is easy in the sense that this category is reserved for children whose problems don't exactly correspond to the guidelines for autism or one of the other explicitly defined PDDs, but who have *some* problems in social interaction and either communication problems or stereotyped behavior patterns and interests. As a result, this is a category that really is very much based on the judgment and experience of the clinician.

One complication in making this diagnosis is that even though it is the most common of all the PDDs, it is also the least studied (mostly because it has been hard to define). The relationship of this category to more strictly defined autism and other disorders is now an area of much interest. Hopefully, research on it will increase in the near future. Another complication is that for those of us who deal with children with PDD–NOS, it is clear that there probably are many subtypes. For example, one possible subtype is a group of children with PDD–NOS who also have major problems with attention.

As a result of these issues, the child might get a diagnosis of PDD–NOS under several conditions:

- If she is younger
- If she is evaluated by someone with less experience in diagnosing children with ASDs
- If some aspects of the picture don't quite "fit" with the more usual presentation of autism or another autism spectrum condition

The various rating scales and tests used for other disorders can still be used and may provide important information for program planning.

Children who lose skills present very special problems for diagnosis. These include the rare children with childhood disintegrative disorder and Rett's disorder, as well as some children with autism who regress before 3 years of age. These children typically need more extensive medical evaluations. These issues are discussed in great detail in Chapter 13.

WHAT HAPPENS AFTER THE ASSESSMENT?

Parents, and whenever possible, teachers should be involved in assessments. The professional or team of professionals working with the individual with an ASD should be prepared to meet with parents and teachers and provide an understandable summary of the results obtained and the implications these results have for diagnosis and intervention. It is important that there is adequate time to talk about the results. The findings should translate into an easily understood, detailed, concrete, and realistic set of recommendations. As we discuss in the next chapter, these results and recommendations should be considered in developing the student's IEP.

SUMMARY

In this chapter, we have discussed both the uses and limitations of diagnosis and have reviewed some aspects of what a good assessment should include. Keep in mind that there will be considerable variability in diagnostic procedures and materials used, depending on the child and his specific needs, strengths, and weaknesses. It is important to realize that when we give examples, not every child will behave or develop in the same way. Also keep in mind that there are many good professionals to work with, but there are also many professionals with a lot to learn. You should pay attention to the experience of the assessor. If you feel that the child has not been accurately assessed or that your own views haven't been heard, think about going elsewhere. Unfortunately, the number of truly outstanding diagnostic centers around the country is relatively limited, but, as time goes on, more and more professionals are learning more about assessment of autism.

▪ READING LIST

American Psychiatric Association. (2000). *Diagnostic and Statistical Manual of Mental Disorders*, (4th ed., text revision). Washington, DC: American Psychiatric Press.

Baranek, G. T. (2002). Efficacy of sensory and motor interventions in children with autism. *Journal of Autism and Developmental Disorders*, *32*(5), 397–422.

Baranek, G. T., David, F. J., Poe, M., Stone, W., & Watson, L. R. (2006). Sensory Experiences Questionnaire: Discriminating response patterns in young children with autism, developmental delays, and typical development. *Journal of Child Psychology and Psychiatry*, *47*(6), 591–601.

Baranek, G. T., Parham, L. D., & Bodfish, J. W. (2005). Sensory and motor features in autism: Assessment and intervention. In F. Volkmar, A. Klin, & R. Paul (Eds.), *Handbook of autism and pervasive developmental disorders: Vol. 2. Assessment, interventions and policy* (3rd ed., pp. 831–857). Hoboken, NJ: Wiley.

Baron-Cohen, S., Allen, J., & Gillberg, C. (1992). Can autism be detected at 18 months? The needle, the haystack, and the CHAT. *British Journal of Psychiatry*, *161*(1), 839–843.

Baron-Cohen, S., Cox, A., Baird, G., Swettenham, J., Nightingale, N., Morgan, K., et al. (1996). Psychological markers in the detection of autism in infancy in a large population. *British Journal of Psychiatry*, *168*(2), 158–163.

Beery, K. E., & Buktenica, N. A. (1997). *Developmental test of visual-motor integration (VMI)*. Parsippany, NJ: Modern Curriculum Press.

Braaten, E., & Felopulos, G. (2004). *Straight talk about psychological testing for kids*. New York: Guilford Press.

Brownell, R. (2000). *Expressive one word picture vocabulary test (EOWPVT)*. Los Angeles: Western Psychological Services.

Campbell, J. M. (2005). Diagnostic assessment of Asperger's disorder: A review of five third-party rating scales. *Journal of Autism and Developmental Disorders*, *35*(1), 25–35.

Carrow-Wollfolk, E. (1999). *Comprehensive assessment of spoken language (CASL)*. Circle Pines, MN: American Guidance Service.

Carter, A., Volkmar, F. R., Sparrow, S. S., Wang, J-J., Lord, C., Dawson, G., et al. (1998). The Vineland Adaptive Behavior Scales: Supplementary norms for individuals with autism. *Journal of Autism and Developmental Disorders*, *28*(4), 287–302.

Charman, T., Baird, G., Simonoff, E., Loucas, T., Chandler, S., Meldrum, D., et al. (2007). Efficacy of three screening instruments in the identification of autistic-spectrum disorders. *British Journal of Psychiatry*, *191*, 554–559.

Constantino, J. N., & Gruber, C. P (2005). *Social responsiveness scale*. Los Angeles: Western Psychological Services.

Coonrod, E. E., & Stone, W. L. (2005). Screening for autism in young children. In F. R. Volkmar, R. Paul, A. Klin, & D. Cohen (Eds.), *Handbook of autism and pervasive developmental disorders: Vol. 2. Assessment, interventions and policy* (3rd ed., pp. 707–729). Hoboken, NJ: Wiley.

Corbett, B. A., Carmean, & Fein, D. (2009). Assessment of neuropsychological functioning in autism spectrum disorders. In S. Goldstein, J. A. Naglieri, & S. Ozonoff (Eds.), *Assessment of autism spectrum disorder* (pp. 253–289). New York: Guilford Press.

Dumont-Mathieu, T., & Fein, D. (2005). Screening for autism in young children. The modified checklist for autism in toddlers (M-CHAT) and other measures. *Intellectual Disability and Developmental Disabilities Research Reviews*, *11*(3), 253–262.

Dunn, L. M. & Dunn, L. M. (2007). *The Peabody picture vocabulary test* (3rd ed.) Circle Pines, MN: American Guidance Service.

Dunn, W. (1999). *Sensory profile*. San Antonio, TX: Psychological Corporation.

Ehlers, S., Gillberg, C., & Wing, L. (1999). A screening questionnaire for Asperger syndrome and other high-functioning autism spectrum disorders in school age children. *Journal of Autism & Developmental Disorders*, *29*(2), 129–141.

Elliot, S. D. (2007). *Differential ability scales* (2nd ed.). San Antonio, TX: Harcourt Assessment.

Faherty, C. (2000). *Asperger's . . . what does it mean to me?* Arlington, TX: Future Horizons.

Faherty, C. (2000). *Autism . . . . . what does it mean to me?* Arlington, TX: Future Horizons.

Filipek, P. A., Accardo, P. J., Ashwal, S., Baranek, G. T., Cook, E. H., Jr., Dawson, G., et al. (2000). Practice parameter: Screening and diagnosis of autism: Report of the Quality Standards Subcommittee of the American Academy of Neurology and the Child Neurology Society. *Neurology, 55*(4), 468–479.

Folio, M. R., & Fewell, R. R. (1983). *Peabody developmental motor scales and activity cards (PDMS).* Itasca, IL: Riverside.

Gamliel, I., & Yirmiya, N. (2009). Assessment of social behavior in autism spectrum disorders. In S. Goldstein, J. A. Naglieri, & S. Ozonoff (Eds.), *Assessment of autism spectrum disorder* (pp. 138–171). New York: Guilford Press.

Gilliam, J. E. (2001). *Gilliam Asperger's disorder scale.* Austin, TX: Pro-Ed.

Gilliam, J. E. (2006). *Gilliam autism rating scale, 2nd edition* (GARS-2). Austin, TX: Pro-Ed.

Goldstein, S, Naglieri, J. A., & Ozonoff, S. (Eds.), (2009). *Assessment of autism spectrum disorders.* New York: Guilford Press.

Hogan, K., & Marcus, L. (2009). From assessment to intervention. In S. Goldstein, J. A. Naglieri, & S. Ozonoff (Eds.), *Assessment of autism spectrum disorder* (pp. 318–338). New York: Guilford Press.

Hogan, T. P. (2003). *Psychological testing: A practical introduction.* Hoboken, NJ: Wiley.

Howlin, P. (2000). Assessment instruments for Asperger syndrome. *Child Psychology and Psychiatry Review, 5,* 120–129.

Kaufman, A. S., & Kaufman, N. L. (2004). *Kaufman assessment battery for children, 2nd edition: Manual.* Circle Pines, MN: American Guidance Service.

Klin, A. (2009). Subtyping autism spectrum disorders: Theoretical, research, and clinical considerations. In S. Goldstein, J. A. Naglieri, & S. Ozonoff (eds.), *Assessment of autism spectrum disorder* (pp. 91–116). New York: Guilford Press.

Klin, A., J. McPartland, & Volkmar, F. R. (2005). Asperger syndrome. In F. R. Volkmar, R. Paul, A. Klin, & D. Cohen (Eds.), *Handbook of autism and pervasive developmental disorders* (3rd ed., pp. 88–125). Hoboken, NJ: Wiley.

Klin, A., Saulnier, C., Tsatsanis, K., & Volkmar, F. R. (2005). Clinical evaluation in autism spectrum disorders: Psychological assessment within a transdisciplinary framework. In F. R. Volkmar, R. Paul, A. Klin, & D. Cohen (Eds.), *Handbook of autism and ervasive developmental disorders* (3rd ed., pp. 772–798). Hoboken, NJ: Wiley.

Klinger, L. G., O'Kelley, S. E. & Mussey, J. L. (2009). Assessment of intellectual functioning in autism spectrum disorders. In S. Goldstein, J. A. Naglieri, & S. Ozonoff (Eds.), *Assessment of autism spectrum disorder* (pp. 209–252). New York: Guilford Press.

Krug, D. A., Arick, J. R., & Almond, P. J. (1980a). Behavior checklist for identifying severely handicapped individuals with high levels of autistic behavior. *Journal of Child Psychology and Psychiatry and Allied Disciplines, 21,* 221–229.

Krug, D. A., Arick, J. R., & Almond, P. J. (1980b). *Autism screening instrument for educational planning.* Austin, TX: Pro-Ed.

Krug, D. A., & Arick, J. R. (2003). *Krug Asperger's disorder index.* Austin, TX: Pro-Ed.

Le Couteur, A., Lord, C., & Rutter, M. (2003). *The autism diagnostic interview-revised (ADI-R).* Los Angeles: Western Psychological Services.

Le Couteur, A., Rutter, M., Lord, C., Rios, P., Robertson, S., Holdgrafer, M., et al. (1989). Autism diagnostic interview: A standardized investigator-based instrument. *Journal of Autism and Developmental Disorders, 19*(3), 363–387.

Lord, C. (1997). Diagnostic instruments in autism spectrum disorders. In D. J. Cohen & F. R. Volkmar (Eds.) *Handbook of autism and pervasive developmental disorders* (2nd ed., pp. 460–483). New York: Wiley.

Lord, C., Risi, S., Lambrecht, L., Cook, E. H., Jr., Leventhal, B. L., DiLavore, P. C., et al. (2000). The Autism Diagnostic Observation Schedule-Generic: A standard measure of social and communication deficits associated with the spectrum of autism. *Journal of Autism & Developmental Disorders, 30*(3), 205–223.

Lord, C., & Rutter, M. (1994). Autism and pervasive development disorders. In M. Rutter, L. Hersov, & E. Taylor (Eds.), *Child and adolescent psychiatry: Modern approaches* (vol. 3, pp. 569–593). Oxford: Blackwell.

Lord, C., Rutter, M., & DiLavore, P. (1999). *Autism Diagnostic Observation Schedule-Generic (ADOS-G)* (WPS ed.). Los Angeles: Western Psychological Services.

Matson, J. (Ed.). (2008). *Clinical assessment and intervention for Autism Spectrum Disorders.* Oxford, UK: Academic Press.

Miller, L. J., & Roid, G. H. (1994). *The T.I.M.E.: Toddler and infant motor evaluation.* San Antonio, TX: Therapy Skill Builder.

Mullen, E. M. (1995). *The Mullen scales of early learning.* Circle Pines, MN: American Guidance Service.

Myles, B. S., S. J. Bock, et al. (2001). *Asperger syndrome diagnostic scale.* Los Angeles: Western Psychological Services.

Nadel, S., & Poss, J. (2007). Early detection of autism spectrum disorders: Screening between 12 and 24 months of age. *Journal of the American Academy of Nurse Practitioners, 19*, 408–417.

Nalieri, J. A., & Chambers, K. M. (2009). Psychometric issues and current scales for assessing autism spectrum disorders. In S. Goldstein, J. A. Naglieri, & S. Ozonoff (Eds.), *Assessment of autism spectrum disorder* (pp. 59–91). New York: Guilford Press.

Parham, L. D., & Ecker, C. L. (2002) Evaluation of sensory processing. In A. Bundy, S. Lane, & E. Murray (Eds.), *Sensory integration: Theory and practice* (2nd ed, pp. 194–196), Philadelphia: Davis.

Paul, R. (2005). Assessing communication in autism spectrum disorders. In F. R. Volkmar, R. Paul, A. Klin, & D. Cohen (Eds.), *Handbook of autism and pervasive developmental disorders* (3rd ed., pp. 799–816). Hoboken, NJ: Wiley.

Paul, R., & Wilson, K. P. (2009). Assessing speech, language, and communication in autism spectrum disorders. In S. Goldstein, J. A. Naglieri, & S. Ozonoff (Eds.), *Assessment of autism spectrum disorder* (pp. 171–208). New York: Guilford Press.

Reynell, J., & Gruber, C. (1990). *Reynell Developmental Language Scales-U.S. Edition.* Los Angeles: Western Psychological Services.

Ritvo, R. A., Ritvo, E. R., Guthrie, D., Yuwiler, A., Ritvo, M. J., & Weisbender, L. (2008). A scale to assist the diagnosis of autism and Asperger's disorder in adults (RAADS): A pilot study. *Journal of Autism and Developmental Disorders, 38*(2), 213–223.

Robins, D., Fein, D., Barton, M., Green, J., Kleinman, J., & Dixon, P. (2002, July). *The M-CHAT: An American modification of the CHAT detects autism at age 2.* Paper presented at the World Association of Infant Mental Health, Amsterdam, Netherlands.

Robins, D. L., Fein, D., Barton, M. L., & Green, J. A. (2001a). The Modified Checklist for Autism in Toddlers: An initial study investigating the early detection of autism and pervasive developmental disorders. *Journal of Autism and Developmental Disorders, 31*, 131–144.

Roid, G. H. (2003). *Stanford Binet Intelligence Scales* (5th ed). Itasca, IL: Riverside.

Roid, G. H. & Miller, L. J. (1997). *Leiter International Performance Scale-Revised.* Wood Dale, IL: Stoelting.

Rutter, M., Bailey, A., & Lord, C. (2003). *Social Communication Questionnaire (SCQ)*. Los Angeles: Western Psychological Services.

Schopler, E., Reichler, R. J., & Renner, B. R. (1986). *The Childhood Autism Rating Scale (CARS) for diagnostic screening and classification of autism*. Irvington, NY: Irvington.

Schopler, E., Reichler, R. J., Bashford, A., Lansing, M. D., & Marcus, L. M. (1990). *Psycho-educational profile revised*. Austin, TX: Pro-Ed.

Scott, F. J., Baron-Cohen, S., Bolton, P., Brayne, C. (2002). The CAST (Childhood Asperger Syndrome Test): Preliminary development of a UK screen for mainstream primary-school-age children. *Autism, 6*(1), 9–31.

Semel, E., Wiig, E. H., & Secord, W. (2004). *Clinical evaluation of language fundamentals* (4th ed.). San Antonio, TX: Pearson.

Shea, B., & Mesibov, G. (2009). Age-related issues in the assessment of autism spectrum disorders. In S. Goldstein, J. A. Naglieri, & S. Ozonoff (eds.), *Assessment of autism spectrum disorder* (pp. 117–137). New York: Guilford Press.

Siegel, B. (2004). *Pervasive Developmental Disorders Screening Test II (PDDST-II)*. San Antonio, TX: Harcourt Assessment.

Sparrow, S. S., Cicchetti, D. V., & Bella, D. A., (2005). Vineland Adaptive Behavior Scales: Second Edition (Vineland II), Survey interview form/caregiver rating form. Livonia, MN: Pearson Assessments.

Sparrow, S. S, Cicchetti, D. V., & Bella, D. A., (2008). *Vineland Adaptive Behavior Scales: Second Edition (Vineland II), The expanded interview form*. Livonia, MN: Pearson Assessments.

Stone, W. L., Coonrod, E. E., & Ousley, O. Y. (2000). Screening Tool for Autism Two-Year-Olds (STAT): Development and preliminary data. *Journal of Autism and Developmental Disorders, 30*, 607–612.

Ventola, P., Kleinman, J., Pandey, J., Barton, M., Allen, S., Green, J., et al. (2006). Agreement among four diagnostic instruments for autism spectrum disorders in toddlers. *Journal of Autism and Developmental Disorders, 36*, 839–847.

Ventola, P., Kleinman, J., Pandey, J., Wilson, L., Esser, E., Boorstein, H., et al. (2007). Differentiating between autism spectrum disorders and other developmental disabilities in children who failed a screening instrument for ASD. *Journal of Autism and Developmental Disorders, 37*(3), 425.

Volkmar, F. R., Carter, A., Sparrow, S. S., & Cicchetti, D. V. (1993). Quantifying social development of autism. *Journal of the American Academy of Child and Adolescent Psychiatry, 32*, 627–632.

Volkmar, F., Cook, E. H., Jr., Pomeroy, J., Realmuto, G., Tanguay, P., et al. (1999). Practice parameters for the assessment and treatment of children, adolescents, and adults with autism and other pervasive developmental disorders. *Journal of the American Academy of Child and Adolescent Psychiatry, 38*(12), 32S–54S.

Volkmar, F. R., Klin, A., Siegel, B., Szatmari, P., Lord, C., Campbell, M., et al. (1994). Field trial for autistic disorder in DSM-IV. *American Journal of Psychiatry, 151*(9), 1361–1367.

Volkmar, F. R., Klin, A. et al. (1994). Field trial for autistic disorder in DSM-IV. *American Journal of Psychiatry, 151*(9), 1361–1367.

Volkmar, F., & Klin, A. (2005). Diagnosis and classification of autism and related conditions. In F. R. Volkmar, R. Paul, A. Klin, & D. Cohen (Eds.), *Handbook of autism and pervasive developmental disorders* (3rd ed., pp. 5–41). Hoboken, NJ: Wiley.

Wechsler, D. (1997). *Wechsler Adult Intelligence Scale* (3rd ed.) San Antonio, TX: Psychological Corporation.

Wechsler, D. (2002). *Wechsler Preschool and Primary Scale of Intelligence* (3rd ed.). San Antonio, TX: Psychological Corporation.

Wechsler, D. (2003). *Wechsler Intelligence Scale for Children* (4th ed.). San Antonio, TX: Psychological Corporation.

Wiig, E. H., & Secord, W. (1989). *Test of language competence.* New York: Psychological Corporation.

Wiseman, N. D. (2006). *Could it be autism? A parent's guide to the first signs and next steps.* New York: Broadway Books.

Wodrich, D. L. (1997). *Children's psychological testing.* Baltimore: Brookes.

Zimmerman, I. L., Steiner, V. G., & Pond, R. E. (2002). *Preschool Language Scale-4.* San Antonio, TX: Psychological Corporation.

Zwaigenbaum, L., & Stone, W. (2006). Early screening for autism spectrum disorders in clinical practice settings. In T. Charman & W. Stone (Eds.), *Social & communication development in autism spectrum disorders: Early identification, diagnosis, & intervention* (pp. 88–113). New York: Guilford Press.

QUESTIONS AND ANSWERS

1. **Does the diagnosis really matter?**

    This is a good question. The answer is yes and a qualified no. The complication is that diagnosis is used for many different things—for research, for teaching people about commonalities in illnesses and disorders, for communicating rapidly, and for getting educational services. All of these are legitimate goals, and the needs for diagnosis will vary somewhat depending on what the goal is. Essentially, the diagnosis grounds us in the general territory we are dealing with, but, of course, to come up with a program or treatment, we need to take the needs of the individual child into account. Some people advocate against giving a diagnosis to avoid giving premature or stigmatizing labels. However, it is just these labels that sometimes help a child get services. For purposes of research, again, depending on what is being studied, often rather strict diagnostic labels are needed, that is, to avoid what would be confounding or complicating issues in interpreting the results of a research study.

2. **Can autism be diagnosed from an EEG or brain scan or a blood test?**

    No, autism is diagnosed based on history and clinical examination. The EEG is useful in the diagnosis of seizure disorders, which are sometimes associated with autism. Brain scans such as MRI or CT scans may be indicated depending on the history and examination of the child but don't diagnose the presence/absence of autism. In terms of blood tests, when genes for autism are clearly found, there may be some such tests in the not so distant future. At the moment, the only lab test that makes sense is the test for fragile X (a blood test) and a genetic assessment.

3. **What is the difference between DSM and ICD?**

The DSM system is the American system of diagnosis (published by the American Psychiatric Association). DSM stands for *Diagnostic and Statistical Manual of Mental Disorders*. The DSM is now in its fourth edition. This book is used for both clinical work and research; it includes guidelines (or criteria) for diagnosis. The ICD, published by the World Health Organization (based in Geneva Switzerland), is the *International Classification of Diseases*, now in its tenth edition. Unlike DSM, there are two versions: one for clinical work and another for research. For autism and related disorders, there are no major differences between the two systems. Hopefully, this will continue in the future (both systems are being revised at the time this book is written).

4. **On the intelligence test the school psychologist gave my 8 year old child, his verbal skills fell into the MR range, but his non-verbal skills were above the MR range. Does this mean he is mentally retarded? If he is will, he stay that way?**

You ask a great question. The diagnosis of mental retardation or, as it is now termed, intellectual disability is based on *two* things: full-scale IQ (this is, more or less, the average of verbal and nonverbal scores) and adaptive skills. Scores on both the full-scale IQ and measure of adaptive skills must be less than 70 for a diagnosis of intellectual disability. Often, children with autism have the pattern you describe; children with Asperger's may have the reverse pattern (higher verbal than nonverbal skills). In addition to the variability within the IQ test (often with areas of much greater ability and other areas with much worse skill), there can also be considerable variation in scores between IQ tests. Often, the overall abilities (full-scale IQ) of children with autism go down over time; that is, the IQ decreases because, although the child makes gains, the *rate* of gain is not as great as expected.

Although the diagnosis of autism (or Asperger's) is not based on test profile, it is something to look at because it may have important implications for intervention. In some states, it is important to establish a diagnosis of mental retardation (MR) since that label is more likely to help your (adult) child get services. Probably because of changes in diagnosis as well as early diagnosis and intervention, the number of students with autism is increasing.

Finally, we would need to look at the report of the assessment; this would tell us things like the test or tests used (results can sometimes vary dramatically based on choice of test; this is probably more true for children on the autism spectrum than others). Finally, we would want to see the observations the psychologist made during the testing. The fact that the nonverbal IQ is in the average range is generally a good sign.

5. **The school wants to treat my child as if his primary disability is MR and not autism. Is that okay?**

In the best of all possible worlds (of which this is *not* one), we should be programming to children and not to labels. That being said, the problem in the real world is that a label of MR (and not of autism) tends to imply the need for a general kind of intervention (e.g., with many opportunities for learning, stimulating environments, etc.). For a child with autism who also has intellectual disability, it is generally better to go with the autism label since this label implies the need for special services. One of the problems with general "stimulation" programs and classrooms designed for children with MR is that they may be overstimulating for the child with autism and also often lack the intensive focus on behavior and communication that is needed.

6. **My child wouldn't cooperate enough during intelligence testing for the school to obtain a score, but they decided he has MR anyway. Is this okay?**

The short answer is no. It is sometimes the case that children with ASDs are difficult to test. Psychologists who have had a great deal of experience are often able to test the child while less experienced psychologists may not be able to. Sometimes it helps to spend some time getting to know the child and then think about what kind(s) of tests may be helpful. Some tests are designed to be done without any language, for example. Even for children who are difficult to test, it is important to get some sense of their levels of cognitive ability; for example, if the child does or doesn't have the ability to remember something out of sight (what psychologists call *object permanence*), it may be a push to try more symbolically based interventions if the child does not have object permanence. Even when you can't test the child, parents can be interviewed in terms of the child's language and self-care abilities, and this can give important information, as can observation of the child in school or at home.

Getting Services

I n this chapter, we provide information on getting services for a child with an autism spectrum diagnosis. This chapter includes a discussion of legal rights and some of the key concepts relative to rights to educational services. It is important that parents and teachers have some basic understanding of these rights and concepts. We also discuss some of the issues involved in seeking insurance reimbursement for services. In the next series of chapters, we'll talk about overall approaches to programming and then more age-specific issues for infants and young children, school-aged children, and adolescents and adults. Keep in mind that, as in other areas, parents and parent support groups may be good sources of information. Also keep in mind that things can change—either through changes in the laws (by Congress) or new judicial decisions (by the courts)—so it is important that everyone involved be aware of current requirements.

THE INDIVIDUALS WITH DISABILITIES EDUCATION ACT (IDEA)

In thinking about getting services for any child, it is important to know a little bit about the history of educational services for children with autism (and, for that matter, other disabilities). Before 1975 only a small number, maybe around 20%, of children with disabilities received an education within public schools. In many schools, parents would be turned away and were often told to put their children in institutional settings where there was little proactive programming or education. As a result, many individuals with autism were placed in these institutions; probably not surprisingly, the major function of such placements was that it helped them learn to live in (i.e., remain in) institutions, and outcome was often poor. There were, of course, exceptions but these usually were situations where parents wouldn't accept a lack of services and advocated for, or sometimes started, their own private schools or programs. Many of the earliest schools for children with autism in the United States were started this way, and some remain active to the present. All this changed dramatically in 1975.

In 1975, Congress passed the Education for All Handicapped Children Act, also known as Public Law 94-142, which mandated school services. This law has been revised and amended many times. The current version is called the **Individuals with Disabilities Education Act (IDEA)**. (The IDEA is an alphabet soup of lovely acronyms that we will introduce to you in this chapter). This law applies to several areas, including early education as well as school-based and transition services and mandates meeting the educational needs of children with disabilities from the time they are born until they reach 21 years of age. Although the IDEA is thought of as a civil rights law, it technically does not require states to participate; rather, it gives them incentives to do so by funding programs when states meet certain requirements. All the states now participate. The IDEA was most recently amended in 2004.

KEY CONCEPTS AND TERMS	
IDEA	The Individuals with Disabilities Education Act—an act of Congress giving specific rights to children with disabilities for educational services.
PL-94-142	Public Law 94-142—the original (1975) law passed by Congress mandating school services to children with disabilities.
FAPE	Free and appropriate public education
IEP	Individualized education plan
LRE	Least restrictive environment
ADA	Americans with Disabilities Act
504 Plan	A plan developed to accommodate the special needs of a child with a handicap.
IFSP	Individualized family service plan—a plan similar to the IEP but for younger children (under age 3).

It is important for parents and teachers to understand what the law does and doesn't require. There are some key concepts that we'll review shortly. Also, it is important to realize that the age of the child has some relevance here. For example, after age 21 the IDEA does not apply, but other laws, such as the **Americans with Disabilities Act (ADA)**, may apply. The requirements for early intervention (before age 3) programs are different from those of public schools, and some of the terms and concepts will vary depending on the age of the child; some aspects of procedures may vary a bit from state to state. Also keep in mind that a vast number of children, over 6 million in 2006, were educated under the provisions of this law. This number includes children with a range of disabilities, not just autism. Autism is, however, mentioned specifically in the law as one of the conditions that meet the requirement for disability. As we discussed in the previous chapter, this can be one area where diagnostic labels are very important. Regardless of labels, parents and teachers should keep in mind that the intent of the law is to identify children whose disabilities interfere with their learning. Thus, even if a child with autism has normal cognitive ability (intelligence quotient [IQ]), he can still qualify under IDEA for services. The reading list at the end of this chapter provides information on a number of resources that can be helpful in understanding this law and how it works. Be aware, however, that in the legal arena, changes can happen at any time—these changes can come from changes in the statute (the underlying law), from court decisions (which interpret the law), from regulations enacted by the state and federal education agencies to implement the law, and by the passage of other federal laws, for example, the No Child Left Behind Act. Changes can occur even because of local issues that impact on school services/programs. For example, a gifted director of special educational services in a district can retire or be replaced, and sometimes, literally overnight, there can be a dramatic shift in the quality and nature of programs. This chapter is as accurate about the state of the law as we could make it at the time of publication; however, it is not a substitute for the advice of a lawyer. Do not take action relying on the descriptions of the law in this book. Consult a lawyer with expertise in this area of law.[1] Some states may have additional provisions about regulation of special education services. In general, federal statutes usually supersede state laws and regulations (called *preemption*). However, a state or local education agency may choose to require or provide more services or more protections than are guaranteed by the federal statute.

HISTORY OF THE IDEA

Legislative History

1975: The Education for All Handicapped Children Act (PL 94-142) mandates the right to education for all children with disabilities.

1990: The law is renamed the Individuals with Disabilities Education Act (IDEA).

1997: IDEA was amended in several ways including to provide coverage of delayed children between ages 3 and 9 years, and the use of mediation to resolve disputes was encouraged.

2004: The Individuals with Disabilities Education Improvement Act of 2004 (IDEIA) modified the law to conform with No Child Left Behind and also dealt with disciplinary issues for students in special education.

Supreme Court Decisions

Hendrick Hudson Central School District v. Rowley: Decision in 1982 (discussed in the chapter) that established the "Chevy, not a Cadillac" standard of an adequate, not optimal, special education program.

---

[1]For example, the state of the law on reimbursement for unilateral placements by parents in private programs has changed repeatedly in the past 5 years. That is an area where it is very important to obtain legal advice prior to taking action.

> ***Schaffer v. Weast***: This 2005 decision held that the "moving" party (usually the parent) in a placement challenge had the burden of persuasion.
>
> ***Winkelman v. Parma City School District***: In 2007 the Court found that, under IDEA, parents have independent enforceable rights, which are not limited to procedural and reimbursement-related matters but encompass the entitlement to a free appropriate public education for their child. This means that parents can sue "pro se" (without a lawyer or representing themselves) to enforce their own rights, which are the same as their child's rights.

Supreme Court's Restriction of Right to Attorneys' Fees for Prevailing Parents

> ***Smith v. Robinson, 1984***: Attorneys fees are not available under the Education for All Handicapped Students Act (EHA). In response to *Smith v. Robinson*, Congress amended the EHA to explicitly allow for attorneys fees retroactive to the day before the decision.
>
> ***Buckhannon v. West Virginia Department of Health and Human Resources, 2001***: Defined "prevailing parties" entitled to attorneys' fees in certain cases, including IDEA cases, to those awarded some relief *by a court*. This eliminated the entitlement of fees in settlements and fees awarded under the "catalyst theory" (that the filing of the court action was the catalyst which caused the district to change its behavior.)
>
> ***Arlington Central School District v. Murphy 2006***: IDEA does not authorize prevailing parents to recover expert fees. The Court held that IDEA provides that a court "may award reasonable attorneys' fees as part of the costs" to parents who prevail in an action brought under the act. It does not authorize prevailing parents to recover fees for expert witnesses in such actions.

KEY CONCEPTS AND PROVISIONS OF IDEA

Evaluation and Identification

The states are required to locate and evaluate children with disabilities who may need special services. This is known as the "child find" obligation. Children can be identified and referred for evaluation by parents or by health care providers, as well as by school personnel. Given the key importance of health care providers, it is especially important that they be aware of these rights, be familiar with programs and services, and be available to advise parents. The "child find" requirement—to **identify** and evaluate—applies to all children, including children attending private schools and children who are homeless or migrant. Special provisions are made for children under age 3. Once a child has been identified, the local school district (called the Local Educational Authority, or

LEA in legal speak) must determine whether the child is eligible for services under IDEA. Parents of children under the age of 18 are asked to give their consent for an evaluation. The evaluation should be sufficiently detailed as to provide a determination of whether the child does or does not meet the eligibility requirement of having a disability such that the child requires **special education** and/or **related services** in order to benefit from his/her education. Given the many different manifestations of autism and related conditions, multiple disciplines and evaluations are frequently involved to be able to provide a comprehensive assessment. For example, many children on the autism spectrum require speech and language evaluations as well as psychoeducational evaluations and occupational therapy assessments. The purpose of the assessment is both to establish whether or not the child is entitled to services and to assist the team in planning the educational program (**individualized education plan [IEP]**) that will provide and direct the services.

Parents can, of course, submit their own evaluations. The school district must take the evaluation into consideration, but is not required to accept such evaluations or to follow their recommendations. If the parents disagree with the evaluation provided by the school, they can also request an independent evaluation. If parents are careful to document that they disagree with the school's assessment, the school has to either pay for the independent evaluation or request a hearing (often called *due process*) to defend their evaluation and to show that an independent evaluation is not needed. When would a parent want to ask for an independent evaluation? There are several situations when this would make sense. If a school district does not identify a child as having a disability and the parent disagrees, an independent evaluation can be helpful. In other cases, sometimes the district identifies the child as disabled, but does not offer services because their evaluation does not show that the disability interferes with the child's ability to benefit from education. A review (usually repeat testing) at least every 3 years (triennial review) is required, with additional testing as needed to show continued need for services.

Free and Appropriate Public Education

One of the core key concepts of IDEA is that students must be provided with a free and appropriate public education (FAPE). Note the words *free and appropriate*. The meaning of *free* is clear: that parents do not have to pay. However, the question of what is appropriate for a particular child is often one that turns into a sticking point. Parents, understandably, want the best for their child. The law, however, uses the word *appropriate*, not *best*. Put another way, as set out by the United States Supreme Court in the case of *Board of Education of the Hendrick Hudson Central School District v. Rowley*, a school district satisfies its duty by providing an "adequate" education. In that case, Amy Rowley, a hearing-impaired child, was able to advance from grade to grade without the benefit of the requested sign language interpreter. The Supreme Court stated that law required "personalized instruction and related services calculated . . . to meet [a child's] educational need." The Court added that, because in this case they were presented with a handicapped child who was receiving substantial specialized instruction and related services, and who was performing above average in the regular classrooms of a public school system, they confined their analysis to that situation. Unfortunately, later court decisions and hearing officer decisions have frequently ignored the Court's limitation of *Rowley* (that is a situation where the child was performing above the average) and the *Rowley* case has limited the services required by the IDEA to minimally adequate to pass from grade to grade. This issue remains an important one and a source of frequent dispute between parents and schools.

Of course, if states or school districts choose to, they can do more than the minimum required. As a practical matter, there also is considerable regional variation in how services are provided and what services are available. This can be very dramatic across states and sometimes even within states. In our particular state, for example, variations from town to town can be quite dramatic and sometimes moving across the street can result in a major change for the better (or worse) in terms of the quality of the program.

Eligibility for Services

The IDEA includes a very specific list of covered disabilities, including autism as well as mental retardation, speech–language impairment, visual impairment, and hearing impairment. In addition, the law requires that the child must, as a result of his condition, require special education services. In other words, simply having a disability or a diagnosis alone does not make a child eligible for special education and related services. So if a hearing-impaired child, for example, could be helped with a hearing aid so that his disability was not interfering with his ability to learn, he would not necessarily qualify for services under IDEA unless some other condition that interfered with educational progress was present.

We want to stress two additional points: It is very important to keep in mind that educational progress is not limited to academic progress. The term *special education* is much broader than *book learning*. It is, under the law, "specially designed instruction, at no cost to parents, to meet the unique needs of a child with a disability." This includes:

- Instruction in the classroom and also in other settings
- Instruction in physical education

- Transition services designed to help the child move from school to employment, vocational school or other postsecondary education, adult services, independent living, or community participation

- Services based on the individual child's needs that take the child's strengths, preferences, and interests into account

- Instruction, related services, community experiences, the development of employment and other postschool adult living objectives, and, when appropriate, acquisition of daily living skills and functional vocational evaluation

This is a broad definition of education, well beyond academic subjects, and covers areas of critical importance for children with autism spectrum disorders (ASDs). Transition services also are available, and usually are delivered, after a child has completed and graduated from high school.

The second point is that even if a student doesn't technically qualify under IDEA, there are other federal laws, notably the ADA and section 504 of the Rehabilitation Act of 1973, which may apply, and the child may qualify for some accommodations or services under these laws. Both of these laws prohibit discrimination based on a person's disability, and require equal access to services. The ADA applies to public accommodations and governmental services, and the Rehabilitation Act to recipients of federal funds. Thus, it is likely that almost every public school system would fall under both acts. Both laws require that entities make reasonable accommodations, which are modifications to their policies and procedures that are required to permit a person with a disability to access the services or benefits provided. This applies in schools and means that even if it is determined that a child with a disability does not need special education in order to make progress in school, if she needs another modification to receive equal access it must be provided. Such modifications can be modified curriculum or transportation, preferential seating, or even being permitted to enter and leave classes early to avoid the difficulties of the crowds and disorder of the halls between classes. One important difference about accommodations under these acts from special education mandated under IDEA is that reasonable accommodations must be requested by the student or her parents—there is no requirement to seek out eligible students and offer such accommodations.

Autism is specifically mentioned as one of the eligible categories under IDEA. For young children, the possibility of a "developmental delay" category is given for children between 3 and 9 years of age so that children with developmental delays do not have to have a specific disability label. As a result of the emphasis on autism, there is often pressure to have children on the autism spectrum (more broadly defined) included within the autism category. Practices vary considerably from state to state and sometimes within states. It is also possible for children with ASDs to qualify under different categories, for example, speech and language impairment, intellectual delay, even "other health impaired." In theory the emphasis should be on the child's needs and not the child's label.

Individualized Education Plan (IEP)

The IDEA requires schools to create an individualized education plan for any child who is eligible for special education. This is required for any student who qualifies and is the most important element of the student's intervention program. This document is developed by parents and teachers and others (an "interdisciplinary team") using the information gathered by all of them and discovered in the evaluation. The document will be the guide for the school program and should set out exactly what kinds of services are to be provided, including the number of hours of each service, how much of that service will be provided in a setting with nonhandicapped peers, and what special arrangements or accommodations are made for the student. It should also include measurable goals and objectives (the term *goals* now includes the concept of objectives). We will discuss the IEP in much greater detail shortly.

It is important to understand that the purpose of the IEP is to be an individualized plan—a blueprint. The child should not be pigeonholed into whatever autism classroom the school or district has. Rather, the IEP should reflect the unique needs of the child. In theory, the IEP will include long-term goals, and short-term objectives should be developed without regard to what is available in the district's existing programs.

Parents should understand that the IEP is developed by an interdisciplinary team (called by different names in different states, i.e., planning and placement team [PPT], committee on special education [CSE or CSPE], or in many states simply IEP team), which includes mainstream and special education teachers, specialists (i.e., school psychologist, **social worker**, speech–language pathologist) and parents in a process that aims to achieve a consensus. The IEP is not something you vote on like a committee meeting. While the school can and should have regular meetings and deliberations among all the staff involved in working with the child, the law requires that parents (and older children) be invited to all formal meetings and be able to participate in a meaningful way. It is also important to realize that the IEP can include provisions for extending the school day or school year if that is necessary to the child's education. This is available particularly (but not only) if there is risk of regression for the child. The IEP also can include transition services even beyond high school graduation until the age of 21 (in many states, until the end of the school year in which a child turns 21.)

Special Education and Related Services

IDEA encompasses both special education and "related services." The latter includes the range of other interventions designed to meet the child's needs and enable him or her to participate in and benefit from special education, for example, speech and language therapy, occupational and physical therapy, or the services of a psychologist or an aide or paraprofessional. Assistive technology is also included. Transportation also falls into this category, for example, a special bus to and from school. However, most medical services are specifically excluded. We'll talk about insurance coverage of medical issues at the end of this chapter.

Least Restrictive Environment (LRE)

The law mandates that children be educated in the least restrictive environment appropriate to the child's learning. The intent of the law is for children to be educated in settings that are normative, that is, where they are with typically developing, nondisabled peers. This issue has been the focus of much litigation, and in many states the standard is now twofold: (1) can the child be adequately educated in the general classroom setting if additional services are provided, and (2) if the child is in a more restricted setting, how can he be integrated into mainstream settings to the maximum extent appropriate? This right not to be segregated is considered a civil rights issue, although some parents believe that their children will receive better or more appropriate services in separate specialized settings.

Several different and sometimes competing considerations can apply here. These include the benefits to the student of being in a regular classroom with support versus a self-contained special education classroom or other more segregated classroom, the benefits to the students/peers who don't have disabilities of being in an integrated classroom, and the disruption to the education of other students, if any, caused by the student's behavior. A child cannot be placed in an inappropriate setting because it is less costly.

Participation in Decision Making and Legal Protections

Families are specifically included in the decision-making process under IDEA. Parents and, to the extent possible, students should participate in meaningful ways in decision making. Parents have an important role in the entire process, and a series of safeguards are in place to protect their rights and those of the child. In reality, of course, many different things can impact on parents' abilities to be strong advocates, for example, their levels of sophistication, language barriers, and other competing concerns. Protections written into the law include the right of parents to review and receive copies of records, to attend IEP meetings, to participate in decision making, and to consent (or not) to the proposed program (IEP). There are specific requirements about notification of meetings, rights to request independent evaluations, and the provision to parents of notice and explanation of their rights. There is also a procedure to resolve disputes between parents and schools that is designed both to promote agreement among the parties and to protect the rights of the student. These dispute resolution mechanisms are mediation or what are called *due process* hearings. Due process is what the United States Constitution requires before depriving anyone of life, liberty, or property. By calling the special education appeal hearing *due process*, Congress was emphasizing the importance of the right to an education and of the process used to develop the plan. The courts consider adherence to these rights to due process as important as the content of the IEP and the nature of the educational program. In fact, ironically, the courts and hearing officers are more likely to reverse a decision of a school district because of a failure to provide due process safeguards than because of an educational decision. The hope and expectation is that a fair and open process should produce an appropriate educational program. The box below summarizes some of the key concepts in this area.

RIGHTS AND SAFEGUARDS UNDER IDEA

Notice requirements: The school must give written notice to parents of proposed changes (e.g., in placement or program) and of the parents' rights (e.g., to voice complaints or contest a planned change).

Consent of parents: Parents must give consent for an evaluation to be done or if reevaluation is done; schools have the right to seek such an evaluation if parents don't consent but must go through due process procedures or mediation to do so.

Mediation: Rather than go through due process parents and schools can use the more informal mediation process to resolve disputes.

Due process: Parents or the school can initiate a due process hearing to resolve disputes at any stage in the process (from evaluation, planning and placement, and review). Parents must be informed of their rights and the possibilities for free or low-cost legal representation. The due process hearing is similar to a regular court hearing (but less formal) and parents and/or the school may be represented by attorneys. An entire appeals process is also available.

Stay put: The stay put provision means that if a child is in a program and there is a dispute about moving the child to another program this cannot be done until a placement decision is reached, that is the school cannot unilaterally remove a child from a program (parents, of course, can). Practically, this usually means that when a dispute is under way, the child stays where he or she is until the dispute is resolved.

Young Children: Special Considerations

IDEA requires that special education services begin at age 3 years and also provides a program to support early intervention services in children from birth to 3. These programs (sometimes called "birth to three" as well as "early intervention" services) provide a range of services. The focus of this part of the law is on enhancing development of children with disabilities and enhancing the ability of families to meet their needs. This was intended to be a very comprehensive program of services. In reality, the degree of sophistication and intensity of these services again varies considerably from state to state and even town to town. Some young children with autism may require and may be entitled to more intense services than are typically offered in these programs.

Young children also present special issues for "mainstreaming." It is *not* usual for children younger than age three to be in group (school) settings. Sometimes parents have arranged for a home-based instruction program that is more typical for young children and a number of intervention programs have a strong home-based component (see Educating Children with Autism, 2001). Early intervention services are, accordingly, often provided in the home and a 1997 modification of the law included the term *natural environment* to be consistent with this idea.

In contrast to the IEP a different kind of plan is developed for young children. This plan is called the individualized family service plan (IFSP) and, in contrast to the IEP, it is meant to be oriented around the family. There is explicit recognition of the importance of the family in the development of very young children and that the family also needs support. So, for the IFSP, there may be specific attention focused on helping siblings or in helping parents learn ways to promote the development of their child.

Finding eligible children is a major concern of this program. The law mandates that an assessment be completed promptly and a meeting with the family to develop the IFSP be developed within 45 days of referral. The IFSP should include a discussion of the child's development, parental concerns, and a discussion of how service will be delivered and progress monitored. Unlike the IEP, the IFSP is reviewed every 6 months. As the child nears his third birthday, a written transition to school-based (preschool) services is required, and the IEP process may begin. The IDEA requires states to ensure that the process is completed by the time the child reaches his or her third birthday. For that reason, many states begin the process when the child is $2\frac{1}{2}$. The variability of programs from state to state and often within states makes it important for parents and health care providers to know what is available locally.

DISCIPLINARY ISSUES

Special issues arise if students with disabilities are disciplined by the school. Under IDEA, it is important that the child's disability be taken into account in disciplinary matters, and even under section 504 and the ADA, reasonable accommodations may be requested (and such requests should normally be granted); for example, a child with autism who is sensitive to loud noises should not be suspended from school if he has a panic attack and runs out of school during a fire drill. Schools should have appropriate behavioral intervention programs in place; if they don't, they can't suspend the child. If a student has a behavioral plan and problems still occur, the team needs to review the behavior plan. There are very specific issues, including consideration of whether the behavior is a manifestation of the disability, that must be considered before a student can be suspended, and lengthy suspensions particularly require careful review under IDEA. Even if a student is suspended, the school is usually obligated to continue to provide educational services. Suspension is not an excuse for excluding children with disabilities from school.

For very serious situations (e.g., involving guns or danger to other students), the child can be placed in an alternative setting for up to 45 days, during which time the IEP team will review the IEP and placement. There are special aspects of the "stay put" provision of the law and specific consideration for situations where the child's behavior is a danger to self or others. If a student's educational placement is being changed as a result of code-of-conduct violations, there must be a "manifestation determination" in order to determine whether the behavior was a result of the child's disability or of the district's failure to provide an appropriate educational program or an appropriate behavioral intervention.

THE IEP—PROCESS AND CONTENT

As noted earlier, the IEP is, as its name implies, designed to meet the individualized needs of the child for a free and appropriate public education in the least restrictive environment. Once a child has been deemed to qualify for special services, the IEP team is assembled to work on the plan. Usually, a report with a diagnosis of autism will be sufficient, but frequently the school will state that its staff is required to conduct its own assessment. Sometimes, no previous assessments will have been conducted. In these cases, with permission of the parents, the school can (and must) conduct its own assessment or refer the child for an outside assessment at the school's expense. For younger children (e.g., those moving into school from birth-to-three programs), a formal diagnosis may not be needed initially by the school. In any case, the results of this assessment should be shared with the parents and the IEP team. Similarly, for older children, the IEP should address needs relating to transition from school to work, vocational training programs, college, or other post–high school activities. (We discuss issues relevant to adolescents and young adults in Chapter 9).

The team to develop the IEP should include the following:

- The parents and the child as he or she gets older
- At least one regular education teacher—preferably the child's teacher
- At least one special education teacher
- A school psychologist or another professional who can help interpret evaluation results
- An administrator who is familiar with the range of available services
- Others, including, for example, the speech–language pathologist, behavior therapist, occupational or physical therapist, or the school nurse

Parents are also free to bring advocates to the meeting. This could be a friend, another parent, an attorney, or professionals (physicians/psychologists). It is always a good idea to bring along another set of ears to these meetings, where a large amount of information is being discussed.

The IEP covers the range of services the child needs. This includes whatever it takes to help the child benefit from special education including, but not limited to speech–language services, occupational therapy, physical therapy, psychological services, counseling, and assistive technology. School health services as well as social work services in school are also covered, as are transportation services. Any accommodations or modifications the child needs to benefit from the program should be spelled out; this includes any accommodations for standardized district or state tests. Extended-day or extended-school-year services, if needed, should be addressed in the IEP as well. The IEP is a written document, and parents should always have a copy.

Children on the autism spectrum have, of course, many of the same needs as other children. They also have some special issues, and it is important to keep these in mind. Academic goals should be reasonable relative to levels of cognitive ability. It is important that parents and teachers not be misled by the sometimes isolated special abilities seen in children with the autism spectrum disorders: some children may be able to read to "decode," but it is a mistake to program to this level of ability in general and even for reading in particular if the ability is an isolated one (that is where reading comprehension—understanding what is being read—is at a much lower level). In contrast to typically developing children, isolated areas of ability are fairly common in children with autism spectrum disorders. Occasionally, people assume that the isolated ability represents a general ability level and then program as if the child were functioning at that level in all areas. This can cause considerable frustration to the child. **Social skills** should be explicitly targeted. This can be done in a variety of ways, both in the classroom and through use of special supports like individual or small group work, for example, with a speech pathologist or psychologist, or in a social skills group, or both. If properly supported, opportunities for mainstreaming are very helpful. A common mistake is to mainstream older school-aged children into settings where they are most vulnerable, such as cafeteria, recess, or gym; these can be some of the *worst* settings for children on the spectrum because of the lower level of structure and lack of adult support and monitoring. Often, more academic settings or music or art can be better choices for social skills development. **Communication** needs to be encouraged, starting at whatever level the child is functioning at. Some individuals with Asperger's syndrome and higher functioning autism have better vocabulary abilities that may mislead school staff into thinking the child does not need to work with the speech pathologist. In fact, it is *communication* and not just vocabulary work that these children need. **Daily living skills** become increasingly important determinants of self-sufficiency and independence as the child gets older. An explicit focus on making skills functional, on having the family involved, and in working on generalization of skills is important. Sometimes an extended-day program is necessary to generalize daily living skills in the home. **Motor** and **sensory** issues can be addressed with the help of occupational and physical therapists. Consideration can be given to providing additional supports, for example, assistive technology such as computers, for children with fine motor coordination issues. Behavior issues/challenges need to be viewed in the context of the overall goals of the program and the safety of the child and classmates. This is an area where the efforts of behavioral psychologists can be extremely helpful and where objective data can really be helpful in informing the intervention plan.

Medical problems/issues are, strictly speaking, not part of the IEP plan, but obviously if there are major issues or problems, it is important that the school know about them. For example, if the child has seizures, is allergic to a food, or is receiving medications that impact on behavior, it is important that school staff be adequately informed. Appropriate accommodations can be made for medical problems. Vocational planning should start as children move through high school. We'll discuss this further in the chapter on adolescents and adults (Chapter 9).

Given that often many different people and specialties are involved in the child's life at school, it is good to specifically address issues of coordination of services and communication between service providers. How (and how often) will the team pass information back and forth to each other? How will they communicate with parents? Who will be the point person in talking with the parents? Who should parents primarily communicate with? When parents are appropriately involved and knowledgeable, the system can work well to help the child learn to generalize their knowledge from school to home and other settings.

The IEP fulfills several functions. First and foremost, it should be a plan for action with a reasonable presentation of the child's various abilities. Based on these strengths and needs, there should be an explicit statement of goals for his educational program—along with short-term goals and benchmarks for reaching those goals. The IEP should be explicit about what services will be provided including how frequent these are and their form and duration (e.g., 30 minutes of individual speech–language work with the school speech pathologist and one 30-minute group three to four students and speech pathologist—session each week). The goals should be operationalized in some way, that is, so you will know when the goals have been met. The law requires measurable goals, and therefore the IEP should set out how progress will be measured. This can be done in a number of different ways, but it is important that the IEP be explicit about how this is to be done. The degree to which mainstream activities are planned should also be made clear and what plans are in place (if needed) to help the student to be successful in mainstream settings. The IEP usually states the amount of time spent with typically developing peers.

The parents should be active participants in the process of developing the IEP. There are a number of excellent books/resources available to guide parents and educators in this process; many of these are listed in the reading list at the end of this chapter.

Regardless of whether the evaluations are done as part of the IEP process (i.e., by the school) or parents have independent evaluations, it is important that the evaluator understand the question(s) being asked. For example, is this an assessment primarily focused on diagnosis and eligibility or is the main goal to establish patterns of strength and weakness and to make program recommendations or primarily to monitor progress? Independent evaluations are most often needed in situations where parents and schools see a child and her needs so differently that they cannot agree on an appropriate program. School staff may have less experience with some of the intricacies of assessment of children on the autism spectrum. You want the evaluation (whether from within or outside the school district) to translate into goals that will move the child along the developmental line toward as independent an adulthood as possible and objectives that can be measured in order to monitor the child's progress toward the goals. Goals should cover academic and nonacademic areas: that is, in addition to progress in core academic areas such as math or writing, goals can include skills in the area of socialization, communication, self-help, and physical skills. As children become older, vocational and independent living skills may become important and should be addressed in the IEP goals.

The IEP should provide a summary of current skill levels in relation to the goals. The goals in the IEP should be written in a way that all involved can understand. Parents should always ask questions if something is not clear or does not sound like an accurate description of their child. (You know the saying that the only stupid question is the one you do not ask!) It should be clear how the goal is to be achieved and who will be monitoring progress. In general, being specific and precise is better than being diffuse and general. A goal that can be measured is better than one that can't. It is perfectly fine to have some big overarching goals ("Jimmy will improve his communication skills") as long as there are then very specific targets for assessing how this will be measured. Sometimes goals will be broken down into a specific time frame. While an appropriate goal is to improve reading comprehension, it is better if it is to improve reading comprehension by a particular amount, for example, one grade level. The objectives might be broken down to learning a certain amount of vocabulary or decoding accuracy as necessary components to improving overall comprehension. The long-term goals and short-term objectives must be measurable and should set out the methods of assessment: test scores, work product, teacher observation. This is particularly helpful when you are trying to build up ability (e.g., reading vocabulary or math) where it is possible to document progress in a very clear way. As students turn 16, the IEP should specifically address transition issues.

There are some things parents can do to be effective participants in the IEP process. First, they can bring (or, even better, supply ahead of time) any reports or documents relevant to the meeting, for example, reports from a private speech pathologist or documentation that the child has a need for occupational or physical therapy. Sometimes a pre-IEP meeting is helpful to review results of assessments or discuss preliminary plans. This can give parents an opportunity to digest the reports and discuss them with each other and any outside professionals before the planning meeting takes place. Parents can always bring someone to the meeting; this can be the other parent, an advocate, a professional, or an attorney. If appropriate, the child can also be part of the meeting. Parents can keep their own notes of the meeting and should remember to always have everything put down on paper—a verbal promise without written documentation won't work so well as a written promise. After the IEP meeting, the parents should receive a copy of the IEP and any documentation from the meeting. When it arrives, parents should read it carefully and submit additions or corrections, if there are any, in writing. Parents should try to participate actively in the meeting—they are the people who know the child best and who are in the best position to speak for him or her.

It is important for parents to keep a couple of things in mind. As we have emphasized, the legal standard is *appropriate* education, not the *best*. Also keep in mind that the school is *not* required to provide the specific method of instruction that you chose; for example, they do not have to provide only applied behavior analysis (ABA)-based instruction. It is the school's responsibility to be sure that parents understand the range of programs and services potentially available to their child. This may include private schools or even residential programs. The fact, by itself, that the school has, for example, an "autism classroom" does not mean that this will always be the right placement for a child with autism. Consistent with the law, the goal should be the least restrictive placement possible, and restrictiveness is measured by time spent with typically developing peers. Therefore, private schools and, particularly, residential programs are often tried only after other placements have not worked out. Remember as well that you don't have to have only a single meeting; if need be, multiple meetings can be held throughout the year to fine-tune the program.

Buddha supposedly once said that if we lived long enough and stayed in one place, we'd see everything; there is undoubtedly much to this. One of us has attended many meetings over the years and has reviewed thousands of IEPs. While things often go well, sometimes they don't. A few examples can illustrate this. The child can have a wonderful IEP, but if the school doesn't follow it, this won't be much help. On rare occasions, we've been surprised that the IEP was pretty poorly done but the school program was very good. We've also seen occasions where, in the attempt to capture every possible issue, the IEP was over 100 single-spaced pages long; in this case, the attempt to get everything right resulted in a document that was too complicated to be useful.

Private Services

Parents can withdraw their child from a school program they do not believe is appropriate. They can provide home-based instruction along with services such as occupational or speech therapy on a private basis. Schools may be liable for reimbursement of parents' costs if the IEP is found not to be appropriate and if the program provided by the parents was beneficial educationally. Parents should understand that there is no guarantee that they will be reimbursed—only that they can ask for reimbursement. A decision by the U.S. Supreme Court in 1993 said that parents could be reimbursed for a child's placement in a private program that was not state certified; this was in an instance where the local school's program was judged to be inappropriate.

DEALING WITH INSURANCE

The current crisis in the American health insurance system has an unfortunate impact on the quality and, for that matter, the quantity of care provided to individuals with all kinds of disabilities. Unfortunately, despite the considerable hype in advertisements about various insurance and health maintenance organization (HMO) programs, all of which seem to emphasize the word *care*, caring is often minimally available; unless parents and others are willing to act as strong advocates for obtaining quality care, such care often is neither available nor provided; in considering insurance plans, you should look at what the plan will provide in terms of continued care for developmental disorders, as well as for so-called "preexisting" conditions. Sometimes parents discover that insurance companies stop providing care when they switch insurance plans because the new insurance company claims the child was born with autism and had a "preexisting" condition. Another unfortunate tactic that insurance companies use is to try to avoid paying for ancillary but important services such as occupational or physical therapy or speech/language services; they may say these should be provided by the schools and not paid for by the insurance company, which may attempt to effectively limit access to more specialized care providers. This is unfortunate because even when primary care providers are very interested, often they need to have the option of asking very experienced specialists for help when problems arise.

As with anything else, if you do more homework in selecting an insurance plan, you are much more likely to be satisfied with it. It used to be the case that there were relatively few options available, and most provided about the same kinds and levels of insurance coverage. This is no longer the case. There are now many plans from which to choose—in some ways, too many. People are often not happy with their coverage but don't always know what to do about it. While the United States has, in many ways, the most advanced health care system in the world, we still do not have universal health coverage. Complexities with insurance arise because of understandable efforts on the part of both the government and the insurance industry to save money by making insurance plans efficient and cost-effective. On the other side, these efforts can also complicate your task in getting the best coverage for your child. The effort to save money also means that insurance companies may not be as interested in having individuals with chronic problems. Probably the first things to know about are the various kinds of insurance, which ones are available to you, and what their advantages and disadvantages are.

In selecting insurance you can easily feel overwhelmed by the range of choices. It is indeed the case that selecting the best program for your child and family can be a challenge. Given that in most situations you are selecting a program that everyone in the family must use, you have to consider everyone's needs. Therefore, you will have to keep in mind many factors. Relative to your child with special needs, it is very important to realize that often life is lived "in the fine print"; that is, you should be very careful to read all the details of descriptions of the programs. You have to be educated as a responsible consumer for your child. Do not be afraid to ask questions. You have to remember the level of needs that your child has in terms of medical care, as well as the potential for additional needs in the future. Sometimes what seems like a great option in terms of low-cost medical care does not, in fact, seem so great in reality when you spend hours on the phone arguing with the insurance company over obtaining basic services.

Kinds of Insurance

Several different kinds of health insurance plans are now available. These include HMOs, fee-for-service insurance plans, preferred provider plans, government-sponsored programs, and self-insurance.

Health Maintenance Organizations The basic idea of an HMO is that you (and/or your employer) pay a certain amount (the premium) each month for a specified range of services. Essentially, you are paying in advance for the services regardless of whether you use them; the idea of these prepaid programs is that the costs of all the various participants will average out over the month. One great advantage of these programs is that, in theory, you should not see another bill for medical services, having paid your monthly fee. Some plans, however, charge an out-of-pocket copay for certain services and/or for prescription medications. An HMO offers several advantages: it is—at least in theory—comprehensive, with a panel of possible caregivers, and it centralizes care and the finances. Having a centralized medical record, which occurs in some HMOs, can be a great help, as is having a primary health care provider who knows you and your child well. Another great advantage of the HMO is that preventive care such as regular checkups and so forth are well covered; this offers many advantages for parents of autistic children, as it gives you and your child time to know the doctors and staff in situations where your child is not acutely ill. This will help your child be more comfortable in seeing the doctor at times when she is not feeling well. HMOs are often somewhat less expensive than other plans. The HMOs do, however, have some limitations.

Problems with HMOs arise due to the basic structure of this form of health insurance. Given that health care is centralized within a specific system, you usually can see only doctors and other health care providers who are part of the HMO. Sometimes this is not a problem, as there may be many doctors on the staff from which to choose, including some who have experience in caring for children with autism and related conditions. However, in some plans, there may not be people who know much about the problems of autistic children or, for that matter, children with developmental difficulties. This can be a complication when you need additional services. For example, you may be perfectly satisfied with your pediatrician but then not like the choices available to you for a neurologist, ear doctor, or **psychiatrist**. In such cases, you may be able to ask if you can use "outside" care providers (i.e., providers who are not part of the HMO), but you may not be entitled to this and might have to pay out of your own pocket if you decide to use such a physician. This may also be a problem if you want the HMO to cover related services, such as speech therapy or occupational therapy. The HMO may tell you that these services should be offered by your child's school or that such services are not covered by your plan since this is not what it regards as part of routine, regular medical care. Because the HMO can be a relatively "closed" system, it may be hard for care providers to have access to the most advanced specialists who know about autism and similar conditions. Many HMOs have a point-of-service (POS) option. This costs a higher premium and, perhaps, higher co-pay per visit but allows you to see experts not on the HMO panel—a great advantage.

If you choose to use an HMO, it will be important for you to do some research in advance. You should find out exactly what services are covered, whether they have any doctors with special expertise in children with autism, whether you can use specialists who are not part of the HMO, how referrals to other doctors are made, and whether the program has any special exclusions that are relevant to your child. It is important that you look not only at the up-front cost (i.e., your monthly premium), but also the hidden costs, that is, the money you may have to pay for services that are not covered by the HMO, for example, costs to you for outside specialists or prescription drugs or for a psychiatrist or child psychiatrist to talk with you about medications for behavioral problems. It is also the case that the HMO may decide not to let you enroll if it is aware that your child has a chronic disability. One of the most important things to find out is whether any of the primary care staff (pediatricians and family care providers) know much about autism or are willing to learn and what specialized services the plan will cover. Sometimes, particularly in rural areas, the HMO may not give many choices for your primary care provider. You should also know that some programs, called combination programs, have features both of the HMO-type plan and more traditional insurance programs; in some cases, these may be particularly good choices for your child.

Fee-for-Service Insurance Plans   Fee-for-service plans are the "traditional" kinds of health insurance. For many years, only such plans were available.

Typically, these plans, which are now rare, are available either through your employer or are ones you can purchase yourself. These plans usually, but not always, give you greater flexibility for deciding what doctors (or hospital) you wish to use. This, in turn, may give you the greatest flexibility in finding a physician who has the greatest compatibility with you and your child. With these plans, you pay for the service and then you are reimbursed by the insurance company, or sometimes the insurance company gets the bill directly from the doctor. In either case, the doctor gets paid for the services provided. In contrast to the HMO, you may more often have to pay some costs out of pocket over and above the cost of the premium; this can include things like copays, deductibles, and some bills for services the plan doesn't necessarily cover. It is important to realize that "out of pocket" may not mean small change and that the costs can sometimes add up quickly. The definition of what is medically necessary can vary; sometimes it may refer only to acute care, and important aspects of routine care such as checkups or hearing aids may not be covered. For children with developmental difficulties, the lack of coverage of such basic services can be a problem.

As with the HMO, it is important in selecting a traditional fee-for-service plan that you know exactly what your policy will actually cover. Look especially under the section of the policy called Limitations or Exclusions. You should never just assume that all the services your child will need will automatically be covered.

Traditional fee-for-service programs are often provided by group plans to members or employees. The thought is that, as with the HMO, there is strength in numbers and group plans have some advantages in terms of lower costs given the larger number of persons covered. Copayments may also be lower with such plans. One of the problems with group plans is the enrollment period. Sometimes you can sign up for the plans only at a certain period in time. At those times, you may not have to fill out a health history, so the insurer may not necessarily know that your child has a disability.

Traditional fee-for-service plans can also be purchased on an individual basis, that is, for a person or family. This approach is often much more expensive than coverage provided by group plans.

Preferred Provider Organizations (PPOs)   The PPO is a variation on the HMO and is the fastest growing type of coverage. In this program, your employer or insurance company essentially makes a contract with a group of doctors or hospitals to provide care for you and your child; typically, the hospital or doctor agrees to take a reduced fee in return for the PPO sending more patients. PPOs have many of the same advantages/disadvantages as HMOs. Again, you have to be very careful to read the fine print to be sure that the particular plan is going to meet your needs.

Public Insurance Programs   Various public programs provide health care coverage for families who cannot afford other insurance. Such programs are funded by the federal government; the government of the individual state; a pool of funds; or some combination of state, federal, and private insurers. These include **Medicaid** or what sometimes is called medical assistance or Title 19. Medicaid is a program funded both by the state and the federal government. It provides medical care for individuals with low incomes, as well as individuals who are eligible for **Supplemental Security Income (SSI)** or people who receive what is now called Temporary Assistance to Needy Families (TANF). If you are enrolled in a Medicaid program, you receive a card that you must show every time you visit your doctor or receive medications or other medical supplies. Since the mid-1990s, most states administer Medicaid through managed care organizations.

A range of services are provided under Medicaid, including both in- and outpatient hospitalization services, laboratory services, services from physicians and laboratories, and x-rays. Although states generally must make some services available to individuals within certain groups, there is some variation from state to state. Usually, the primary care provider must ask for authorization for more specialized services; the range of choices of such services may be more limited than for other kinds of insurance.

In some cases, even if your income is a bit higher than would typically be allowed, you can still qualify for support through this program, particularly if you have a child with a disability. This can also happen, for example, if large medical bills reduce your family's income. Eligibility for such programs varies from state to state, and it is important that you check the requirements in your state.

Medicare is a federal government program that covers a range of services. It applies to individuals who are senior citizens (over age 65) and to some people with certain disabilities. Although Medicare and Medicaid have similar names, they are in fact very different programs.

Health Savings Accounts   Health savings accounts were created by public law 108-173 in 2003. Any adult who is covered by a high-deductible plan can establish one of these accounts. The person or family can make contributions to this account (and these are deductible), and so can the employer.

Self-Insurance Plans   Sometimes an employer may be large enough to set up its own insurance plan. These so-called self-insured programs may seem in many cases very similar to either HMOs or private traditional insurance plans. However, the kinds of services provided may not be as extensive as those provided by other kinds of programs. Sometimes states mandate certain benefits. It is sometimes the case that individuals in self-insured plans are not given all the mandates available. Another problem with self-insured plans has to do with denial of benefits. With the traditional programs or with HMOs, you often can file a complaint. The complaint is dealt with at the state level by the agencies that regulate these programs. Because self-insured plans are private, filing a complaint is more complicated, and you have to be very careful to understand what is entailed in filing a complaint or using the so-called appeals process before you make a decision.

State Children's Health Insurance Program (SCHIP or CHIP)   This is a federally sponsored, state administered program, created in 1997 to provide health care subsidies to children whose families earn too much for Medicaid, but who cannot afford other health insurance. The majority of states accept families who earn 200% over the federal poverty level. Information can be obtained from your state department of social services. The rules for this vary from state to state, and you must check with your state to see whether you qualify. Usually, the family pays premiums as in traditional programs and, as with the traditional programs, there may also be deductibles, other kinds of copayments, and various health care options.

Preventing and Dealing with Insurance Problems

Be an Informed Consumer   As the saying goes, an ounce of prevention is worth a pound of cure. Do as much work as you can before selecting an insurance policy. If you use benefits provided by your employer, see exactly what plans are available. If both parents are employed, you may have even greater access to a range of choices in insurance. Unfortunately, reading the description of an insurance plan, much less the policy itself, can be very confusing. Feel free to ask for help. For example, your employer may have an insurance office that can help answer your questions. If you are using a private insurance agent, this person can also answer many questions. Your current health care provider may be able to give you good information; parents of other special needs children, particularly if they also are employed by your company, can be good sources of information as well. It is very important to educate yourself about what is covered—you want to be sure that you do not have an unexpected surprise in discovering that the plan won't cover services your child needs. Be sure to understand exactly what is covered, your deductibles and copays, and what the exclusions are. Be careful not to be misled by what appear to be lower deductibles. Sometimes it will cost you more to have a plan that has a lower deductible than a higher one.

Particularly if you are using a group insurance plan provided by your employer, you may not always have easy access to the actual insurance policy or agreement between your employer and the insurance company. In this situation, what you often see is a fancy-looking brochure; although this may be beautifully done and seem very reassuring, please remember that this brochure is *not* the policy and is not what is legally binding. Always ask to see the actual insurance policy or contract to look at and feel free to ask your employer's benefits office for help in understanding it.

In looking at the insurance policy, be careful to look at what is *not* covered (excluded services). Looking at this section of the policy will give you a lot of information about what is not covered. These exclusions often include medications or certain therapies and specific services, such as mental health services or occupational or speech therapy. Check to see whether "preexisting conditions" are excluded, since autism and related disorders are always going to be preexisting because you already know your child has a problem. Sometimes there is a waiting period for so-called preexisting conditions. You might have to wait six months or sometimes even as much as a couple of years before you can receive reimbursement for some services.

Remember that insurance companies also must abide by the laws, which vary from state to state in terms of kinds of benefits that must be made available. Some states mandate certain services that must be available for children with autism. Look into other questions such as whether there is a cancellation provision to the policy, that is, whether the insurance company can decide to cancel your plan either for you as a group or for your individual child. Look to see whether there are rights of so-called conversion, that is, whether you can take a group policy and change it to an individual policy. This is important to know when your employer decides to change the group policy. It may be very difficult for your child to be enrolled in a new program, but it would then be important that you could continue the old policy as an individual policy.

There are some other things to check as well. Look to see what the maximum liability of the policy is. Sometimes insurance policies have a clause that states the total amount of money the insurer will pay over the life of the child. This may also include a certain maximum amount for a year's coverage. Check to see whether there is so-called coordination of benefits. This applies when both a mother and a father receive different insurance programs through their employer. It provides rules as to whose insurance is used to cover certain services.

It's important not to let yourself be caught by surprise, for example, when you discover that the doctor you have used for years does not participate in the plan you have just joined. Sometimes, even when you have done all your homework, problems will arise. You might, for example, discover that a private insurance program has changed its policy so that a previously approved service is no longer covered or that the care provider you really wanted is no longer participating with the insurance plan. Sometimes you may want services that the insurance plan says are not covered but that you feel should be either because you have read the policy or because you know that in your state such services are mandated, by law, to be covered.

Dealing with Disputes

Even when you have done your homework well, problems may arise. Keep in mind that a basic motivation of the insurance company is to make money and avoid spending it. Also keep in mind that a large insurance company may have a large staff with a fair amount of turnover (always try to talk to the same person if you can, and in any case, always keep a record of whom you talked to). Some insurance plans will have specific ways for dealing with disputes. There may be a person with the insurance company or HMO that you can use. This person may be called a patient representative or counselor or benefits coordinator; often, particularly if you are dealing with a large company or HMO, this will be the one person you can expect to be able to call on over time and who can help you deal with problems from within the system.

In dealing with disputes with the insurance company, you'll already be in a stronger position if you have done your homework—both on the specific insurance policy and what is legally mandated in your state. You should be careful to know the name of the office in your state that regulates insurance programs; this office can also help you know your rights and sometimes may be helpful in resolving problems with the insurance company. The kinds of problems you'll face will vary somewhat depending on your insurance coverage. For an HMO or PPO, for example, the problem may be in getting the plan to approve a service so that your child receives it; with the more traditional plans, the problem may be getting yourself (or your child's doctor) reimbursed once your child has received a service. It will be very helpful to you to know, in advance, how your plan is set up to deal with problems. Each plan should have a method for dealing with problems and complaints.

The following are some of the principles that can guide you in resolving problems:

- *Be an effective advocate for your child.* Always remember that you are your child's best advocate. You will know what your child needs and should not be shy in asking for it. While you should be assertive, try not to be angry or confrontational. Being assertive means you should be knowledgeable but also willing to listen. You should not be content to have a problem or complaint swallowed up in red tape.

- *Keep a record.* Always keep a record of whom you talked to and when and what you were told. Keep in mind, however, that while you are keeping a record, the HMO or insurance company may as well—including a computer record of each time you talk with someone at the company. Keep copies of any letters or other materials that support your request. Also keep copies of any information or correspondence from the insurance company. After you have a phone conversation, make a note to yourself or write a short letter that summarizes your discussion and send it to the insurance company or HMO (but keep a copy for yourself). It may be easiest if you keep a notebook and then put things in chronological order so you can easily find them.

- *Be prepared.* You should know, in advance of talking with the company, exactly what you want and what the problem is. Be prepared ahead of this call with all the basic information such as policy number, claim number, and so on. If you have any additional information that supports your request, be prepared to share it, for example, additional supporting letters from doctors or copies of articles that support the use of the treatment you request.

- *Make good use of others.* Particularly if you are using a group insurance plan, the insurance office in your company may be helpful in dealing with the insurance company. Your health care provider may also be very helpful. Sometimes the support of other parents or other individuals who have had experience within your organization with the same insurance program can also be helpful. Use parent advocacy groups at the local, state, and national levels as sources of information as well.

- *Know the system and try to work with it.* You should know what your rights are within your state and within the insurance company. You should try to move your dispute through the system as quickly as you can. Sometimes you will discover that the person you are talking to at the insurance company is not the person who will actually make the decision about your request—if this is so, ask to speak with the person really in charge. Also think about asking your child's doctor to write a letter or offer to speak with the person in charge. If things seem to have stopped dead in their tracks, call or write again; sometimes the insurance company may hope that your complaint will go away if it takes its time responding to you.

- *What to do when the system doesn't work.* Usually, you will not want to file a complaint with the state insurance agency until you have used all your options in dealing with the insurance company or HMO. However, too many parents do not realize that they do have the right to file a complaint with the state. Similarly, you usually should not immediately think about a lawsuit; this is very expensive and there is no guarantee that you'll win in the end. However, for some parents, there may be legal advocacy groups who could help you on a reduced fee basis.

Parents should carefully consider insurance plans and the special needs of their child when they consider relocating or changing jobs. Until the time that we have universal health care coverage in this country, such concerns should, unfortunately, be central in the minds of parents.

Coordination Between School and Private Providers

Occasionally, parents will be able to obtain insurance coverage for some ancillary services. At other times, parents pay out of pocket. It is important to realize that if multiple care providers are involved, there is the potential for either duplication (which is not always bad) or therapies that are in competition. For example, a child might be getting one approach to stimulating vocabulary development in school and a very, very different approach in private speech therapy. Keep in mind that sometimes this can be a good thing, but what is really critical here is to have the two professionals (school and private) have some discussion with each other. This is also very important if they are doing their own assessments. There is some potential for scores to be inflated if the child is unwittingly given the same assessment instrument more than once within a short period of time; this can mislead clinicians about what is actually going on.

SUMMARY

In this chapter, we have reviewed some of the issues involved in getting services for children on the autism spectrum. In the United States, the passage of Public Law 94-142 and its various successors marked a turning point in our approach, as a society, to children with disabilities and resulted in a much greater effort to include children with autism in the lives of schools and communities. One important result of this effort has been the general trend toward improved outcome. Despite its many advantages, IDEA is not perfect. Schools understandably complain about paperwork and lack of funding from the federal government, which has never lived up to its original commitment. Parents complain that the law is not fully implemented and that procedures aren't followed. They also complain that they want the best for the child, not just what is appropriate. Although the schools aren't required to pay for medical treatments, there are some treatment modalities (e.g., speech therapy, physical therapy, occupational therapy) that clearly fall into a gray zone of being quasi medical and that the schools are required to provide as related services. However, as we've discussed, medical insurance coverage is often minimal, so if parents pursue additional ancillary services outside the school setting, there may be little if any reimbursement.

At the time this chapter was written, Congress had just passed a new law requiring parity for mental health benefits to take effect in 2010; this law would require that limitations for mental health coverage be no more restrictive than those for other medical problems. This may increase access to some services for children whose families have private insurance.

▪ READING LIST

Addison, A. (2005). *Unfolding the tent: Advocating for your one-of-a-kind child.* Shawnee Mission, KS: Autism Asperger.

Anderson, W., Chitwood, S., & Hayden, D. (2008). *Negotiating the special education maze: A guide for parents and teachers* (4th Ed.). Bethesda, MD: Woodbine House.

Bateman, B., Herr, C. (2006). *Writing measurable IEP goals and objectives.* Verona, WI: Attainment/IEP Resources.

Cohen, J. (2006). *Guns a' blazing: How parents of children on the autism spectrum and schools can work together without a shot being fired.* Shawnee Mission, KS: Autism Asperger.

Cohen, M. (2009). *A guide to special education advocacy: What parents, clinicians and advocates need to know.* London: Jessica Kingsley.

Eason, A., Whitbread, K. (2006). *IEP and inclusion tips for parents and teachers—handout version.* Verona, WI: Attainment/IEP Resources.

Fouse, B. (1999). *Creating a win-win IEP for students with autism: A how-to manual for parents and educators.* Arlington, TX: Future Horizons.

Graham, J. (2008). *Autism, discrimination and the law: A quick guide for parents, educators and employers.* London: Jessica Kingsley.

Hyatt-Foley, D., & Foley, M. G. (2002). *Getting services for your child on the autism spectrum.* London: Jessica Kingsley.

Lentz, K. (2004). *Hope and dreams: An IEP guide for parents of children with autism spectrum disorders.* Shawnee Mission, KS: Autism Asperger.

Mandlawitz, M. R. (2005). *Educating children with autism: Current legal issues.* In F. R. Volkmar, R. Paul, A. Klin, & D. Cohen (Eds.), *Handbook of autism and pervasive developmental disorders* (3rd ed. , pp. 1161–1173). New York: Wiley.

National Research Council. (2001). *Educating children with autism.* Washington, DC: National Academies Press.

Pierangelo, R., & Giuliani, G. (2007). *Understanding, developing, and writing effective IEPs: A step-by-step guide for educators.* Thousand Oaks, CA: Corwin Press.

Shore, S. (2004). *Ask and Tell: Self-Advocacy and Disclosure for People on the Autism Spectrum.* Shawnee Mission, KS: Autism Asperger.

Siegel, L. (2005). *The complete IEP guide.* Berkeley, CA: Nolo.

Siegel, L. (2007). *The complete IEP guide: How to advocate for your special ed child* (5th ed.). Berkeley, CA: Nolo.

Siegel, L. (2007). *Nolo's IEP guide: Learning disabilities.* Berkeley, CA: Nolo.

Silver Lake Publishing. (2004). *Kids and Health Care: Using insurance, cash, and government programs to make sure your children get the best doctors, hospitals and treatments possible.* Los Angeles, CA: Silver Lake.

Winkelstern, J. A., and Jongsma, A. E. (2001). *The special education treatment planner.* Hoboken, NJ: Wiley.

Wright, P., & Wright, P. (2006). *Wrightslaw: From emotions to advocacy: The special education survival guide* (2nd ed.). Hartfield, VA: Harbor House Law Press.

Wright, P., & Wright, P. (2007). *Wrightslaw: Special education law* (2nd ed.). Hartfield, VA: Harbor House Law Press.

■ **WEB SITES**

www.autism-society.org/site/PageServer?pagename=life_edu_IEP
www.ed.gov/policy/speced/guid/idea/idea2004.html
http://idea.ed.gov
www.504idea.org/idearesources.html
www.ldanatl.org

■ **QUESTIONS AND ANSWERS**

1. **My child has been diagnosed with PDD-NOS, but the school has given him the label of autism. Is this okay?**

    Labels used by schools often differ somewhat from those used by medical professionals. These labels also vary considerably from state to state and sometimes within states! Often, for purposes of getting appropriate services, the label of autism is used very broadly, so in this case, it may be perfectly fine for your child. Keep in mind that you need to evaluate labeling issues in the context of your child's particular needs and that you can always ask to discuss the label and change or drop it.

2. **My daughter had a diagnosis of PDD-NOS when she was younger. Now she is 10 years old and has been included in a regular class for 2 years. She has not needed special services. Can we now drop the label that used to get her special services that she no longer needs?**

    Yes, you can indeed drop the label. If it turns out, for whatever reason, that she needs some special services in the future, you can revisit this issue with the school.

3. **My husband and I are having a disagreement with the school district. We think the goals are too broad and want something where there is something more objective, like actual data on something, but the school seems to want things very general ("Jimmy will improve his math skills"). Who is right on this, and do we have to wait until next year to fix this?**

    We'd want to know a bit more about the particulars of the situation, but we agree with you that the goals objectives need to be stated in such a way that they can be monitored. Some goals can be fairly broad (to indicate areas that need to have work), but having some specifics is helpful. This can also help to connect them to specific services/service providers; for example, communication goals might be monitored by the speech pathologist. You should ask for a meeting to review this issue. You do not have to wait for an annual meeting.

4. **We have already had some trouble with our school district not following the IEP. When should we get a lawyer?**

In general (with exceptions), we would encourage parents to try to work with the school in as cooperative a way as possible. It is possible to have another parent or an advocate come with you to meetings with the school and this may well help the process. It also is the case that you can talk with other parents ahead of time in an effort to discover if there is anything special you need to know about the school or program and to learn from their experience. Getting a lawyer will typically make the process much more of an adversarial one and, in the early stages, this may actually slow things down. However, if you have what you think are serious problems and if your concerns are not being heard or you feel your child's rights are being violated, it may be very appropriate to consult an attorney. Indeed, once you are at the point of starting "due process" proceedings, having a lawyer may help move things along. Keep in mind that you need to do some homework yourself to be sure the attorney is experienced with special education cases (you can often ask other parents and you can talk to the attorney about this as well). Also keep in mind that lawyers are expensive, and you can discuss costs with him or her, but it may be that just visiting the lawyer to go over your case and seek advice may itself be very helpful. There are some provisions in the 2004 amendments to IDEA that discourage claims that are not well founded. The school district should give you a list of low-cost legal services. Parent groups, including local autism groups and the Learning Disabilities Association of America, often have lists of advocates you can work with.

5. **We have just moved to a different state. When we went to enroll our 12-year-old in school, the school social worker said he was "too high functioning" to have an IEP and that he could have a 504 plan instead, but he has never had one of these and I'm not sure what it means.**

Your question brings up several different issues. First (and probably most important), having an IEP does *not* have to do with being low (or high) functioning; rather, it has to do with meeting the requirements of IDEA and needing special interventions. A 504 plan refers to section 504 of the Rehabilitation Act and the Americans with Disabilities Act and has to do with not excluding children (or adults) from participating in programs that are federally funded based on a disability (this includes schools). A 504 plan might be written, for example, if a child had an illness like diabetes and needed some special accommodations (such as monitoring his blood sugar during the day). Similarly, if a student had significant grapho-motor (writing) difficulties, it would support providing a keyboard or laptop for taking notes. In contrast, the IEP is an educational plan that outlines what the child needs over and above the regular program provided by the school. A 504 plan does not primarily have to do with special educational services. Sometimes students will start with a 504 plan, but if it becomes clear that special services are really needed, parents and school will move to develop an IEP. Basically, if the child needs special instruction and services, an IEP is the way to go—it is more involved than a 504 plan, but that may well be appropriate in this instance. If the school is telling you that your child has sufficiently improved and that an IEP is no longer necessary, we'd say to be careful that this is discussed thoroughly with you, and remember that even if you agree to this, you would have the option, if this doesn't work well, to ask for a meeting and talk about reimplementing an IEP.

Your question also raises the issue of what to do when you move. This happens frequently in today's world. If possible be in touch with the school or district well ahead of time—that way, they have a chance to meet you (and maybe your child) and see past records. Be sure they have copies of all the relevant materials, including the IEP. While the school can just adopt the old IEP, they may want to do their own assessment and may want to meet with you to develop a new one.

6. **The speech pathologist in school seems to be doing things very differently from everyone else. This is causing my son to be confused. When I asked for a meeting to discuss this, I was told I had to wait for another year for a review. What can I do in the meantime?**

It isn't quite clear from the question whether the problem has to do with differences between the speech pathologist and other school providers or outside providers. Regardless of which is the case, you can ask for a meeting *anytime*. If an outside provider is involved, then invite them to the meeting. You do *not* have to wait for another year to go by.

7. **I just found out that the school changed my child's program dramatically (they eliminated speech–language services) but we didn't know about it. What can I do?**

First, be sure that your information is correct. If so, then you should contact a parent advocate or an attorney. Your input is required, and the school can't arbitrarily change the IEP.

An Overview of Educational Programs

The goals for education of children with autism and related disorders are the same as for all other children: helping develop their potential for personal self-sufficiency and independence. For children with autism spectrum disorders (ASDs), there are additional challenges. These include social–communication challenges, behavioral and sensory issues, and problems with organization and transitions. Starting in the 1950s, parents and teachers began to try to deal with these problems and educate children with autism. Some of these early attempts, particularly the ones begun by parents, resulted in schools or programs that still are very active today. These programs were started because at that time public schools were not mandated to serve all children. Another strategy had been the attempt by some well meaning but misguided professionals to "correct" what they saw as poor parenting by providing intensive psychotherapeutic interventions to children with autism; this idea rested on the "refrigerator mother" idea of what caused autism (see Chapter 2), and as this idea was shown to clearly be wrong, many of these programs either closed or turned their attention to other kinds of problems.

Other factors did, however, increase interest in providing educational services to children with autism. These factors came both from research and public policy. On the research side, an awareness that behavioral interventions could improve the development of children with autism stimulated a tremendous interest in developing better methods for intervention. On the social policy side, passage of Public Law 94-142 in 1975 mandated schools to begin providing appropriate educational services to children with autism. Before this law was passed only a minority of children with autism received school based service. Since the passage of Public Law 94-142, more and more children on the autism spectrum have been enrolled in school programs and been able to make substantial progress. As a result of this and subsequent laws, the schools and educational intervention have assumed a central role in helping children make gains in social, communicative, and more traditional academic areas. They have adopted and adapted many of the methods first used in research work to help children profit from school settings. For purposes of our discussion, we'll talk about several different kinds of programs. These basically fall into three general categories, although some programs include aspects of more than one.

- *Center-based programs* provide services in a special setting. This might be in a special school or clinic (possibly affiliated with a college or university program in some way). These programs may be segregated (only children with ASDs or special needs) or inclusive (include some typically developing children).

- *Home-based programs* provide services mostly within the home (although sometimes there is additional time in outside support programs or actual classroom/intervention time as well outside the home).

- *School-based programs* provide services within the schools. This might be in an integrated, inclusive classroom (a mix of typically developing children and some children with ASDs or other problems) or a specialized (segregated) autism or special ed classroom (and many variations in between).

As we discuss shortly, these programs sometimes have different theoretical backgrounds. Sometimes they make use of identical or very similar intervention techniques; occasionally, programs will have some special techniques or terms that they use. Some of the more common procedures used include the following:

- *Applied behavior analysis (ABA)* is a rather broadly used term but basically refers to the application of principles from behavioral psychology in the study and change of behavior.

- *Discrete trial teaching* is one of the more frequently used ABA techniques. Typically, what is going to be taught is broken down into smaller steps, each of which is then taught (often many times) using prompts/rewards, which are then gradually faded over time.

- *Pivotal response training (PRT)* interventions are also based on ABA procedures but focus on behaviors seen as being key to learning and other skills, An important goal of this intervention is generalization of skills (use of same skills across settings with different people or materials). PRT procedures have been used to facilitate language, play, and social skills.

There are some excellent resources (listed in the reading list for this chapter and some additional ones in the next chapter), including books written specifically for parents and teachers on ABA and behavioral methods.

Although the vast majority of children with autism are educated within school-based programs, much of the research on intervention techniques has come from other settings. Accordingly, an awareness of all the various models of service provision is important for parents and teachers alike. In this chapter, we review some of the issues involved in providing appropriate educational programs to children on the autism spectrum. In subsequent chapters, we will discuss specific interventions. In this chapter, we begin with a discussion of model programs of service delivery and then move on to talk about how aspects of these programs can be successfully implemented in public school settings. In addition to programs designed for more "typical" children with autism, we also discuss special issues presented by students with Asperger's and higher functioning autism. In this chapter, we talk about services from several different perspectives and will give examples, in later chapters, of how some of these perspectives can be integrated in planning for students of different ages. Keep in mind, as we discussed in the previous two chapters, that assessment and planning the individualized education plan (IEP) are very much interwoven with the school program. In the ideal world, the assessment result and IEP process inform the school program.

For parents and teachers who are interested, there is an excellent and very detailed report from the National Research Council (NRC) called *Educating Children With Autism* (particulars of this book are included in the reading list[1]). This report summarizes much of what we know about what does and doesn't work in providing education to children on the autism spectrum. This report, stimulated by a request from the U.S. Department of Education, focused on those programs that have published peer-reviewed data to support their effectiveness. Although concerned primarily with the needs of younger children, much of what this report has to say applies to older children as well. It is very useful to begin with some of the findings that have emerged from this report about what we know works and what doesn't. As always, of course, when we are talking in a more general way, it is important to recall that one of the challenges in autism (and for the team doing the IEP) is to come up with a program tailored to the specific child. The reading list for this chapter provides a selection of the many excellent resources available to teachers (and parents) about educational interventions for children with ASD. We will mention some of these in the text, but others are listed in the reading list as well.

MODEL PROGRAMS

Educating Children With Autism summarized a number of the model programs around the country and focused on programs that had published data showing that they worked for at least some children with autism. This focus on programs

---

[1]One of us (FRV) was one of the members of the panel that put this report together.

with a research basis is important, and, not surprisingly, given the emphasis on research, all these programs had some connection to colleges/universities. It is important for parents to realize that it is in these programs where much of the research on intervention is conducted—and this is one of the reasons these programs, which actually serve only a very small fraction of students with autism, are so well known. They also have tended to focus, and now increasingly focus, on young children. Table 5.1 (reprinted from *Educating Children With Autism*) summarizes some aspects of these programs.

These programs employ somewhat different, and occasionally mixed, models of service delivery. Some programs are primarily home based; that is, most of the child's treatment, at least initially, is done in the home by one or more service providers. At some point, these children usually will transition to a school setting. This model is the one employed originally by Lovaas and his colleagues at the University of California at Los Angeles (UCLA) but has been used by others as well. Note that many programs include a home component, but the truly home-based programs are fundamentally and primarily based in the home. In

TABLE 5.1   FEATURES OF COMPREHENSIVE PROGRAMS

Program	Mean Age at Entry (range), in Months	Hours per Week	Usual Setting[*]	Primary Teaching Procedure
Children's Unit	40 (13–57)	27.5	School (S)	Discrete trial
Denver Community- Based Approach	46 (24–60)	20	School (I), home, community	Playschool curriculum
Developmental Intervention Model	36 (22–48)	10–25	Home, clinic	Floortime therapy
Douglass	47 (32–74)	30–40	School (S and I), home	Discrete trial; naturalistic
Individualized Support Program	34 (29–44)	12	School (I), home, community	Positive behavior support
LEAP	43 (30–64)	25	School (I), home	Peer-mediated intervention; naturalistic
Pivotal Response Training	36 (24–47)	Varies	School (I), home, community, clinic	Pivotal response training
TEACCH	36 (24 and up)	25	School (S), clinic	Structured teaching
UCLA Young Autism Project	32 (30–46)	20–40	Home	Discrete trial
Walden	30 (18–36)	36	School (I), home	Incidental teaching

[*]S, segregated classroom; I, inclusive classroom
SOURCE: Reprinted from *Educating Children With Autism*, by permission of the National Academies Press.

contrast, center-based programs provide the majority of their services within a specialized (nonpublic school) setting. These programs include the Douglass Program at Rutgers and the Children's Unit at Binghamton Universities. Training for parents and family members is provided and is often focused on generalization of skills to the home setting. The goal is eventual integration of children on the autism spectrum into classes in the public school or within the center.

The majority of children with autism are given services within school-based settings. Again, there are many variations, ranging from self-contained classes within a public school to partial or full inclusion in mainstream educational settings. The Treatment and Education of Autistic and Related Communication Handicapped Children (TEACCH) program is a good model of such a program where services are provided to regular schools throughout the state of North Carolina. There are many variations on these basic themes. The following provides a brief summary of a number of these programs; a web address for additional information is included at the end of each summary.

The UCLA Young Autism Project

This program was begun by Lovaas based on some of his earlier research on autism in the 1970s, which was followed by his work on early intensive intervention services provided to young children with autism in their homes (Lovaas, 1987). This program has, in many ways, been the inspiration for a number of other programs, particularly those providing services in the home but extending to center- and school-based programs as well. In his original (1987) report, Lovaas provided intensive (40 hours a week) instruction for a prolonged period using trained undergraduates. Parents were also given training so that there was an intensive teaching/intervention environment throughout the child's day. This model relied on ABA interventions with an emphasis, during the first year, on dealing with problem behaviors, and then, during the second, a focus on verbal language and play skills helped children relate to peers and community settings with the introduction of preschool exposure. By the third year, the focus was on learning through observational and preacademic tasks. There was a strong emphasis on moving children into mainstream school settings. Children who participated were compared to two other groups, including one where a much smaller amount of ABA was provided each week. The original results of the study were very positive, with almost 50% of the intensively treated children reported to be in regular educational settings and to have normal cognitive ability, as compared to 2% of control children. The findings persisted on follow-up. Two of the more controversial aspects of this program had to do with the substantial time commitment from parents and the use of aversives (negative consequences or punishment). A replication, in part, of this work was undertaken by

Smith and colleagues (2000). The study was less intensive (25 hours/week), and parents were required to spend only about 5 hours a week engaged in the treatment. Aversives were also less frequently used. A comparison group included parents who had participated in some ABA training. Again, progress was greater in the children who went through the more intensive treatment, but the degree of progress was not as great as in the original study, with only 27% of children able to attend regular education classes. Several factors may have affected the results, including a somewhat greater degree of cognitive impairment in the treated cases and the reduced intensity of treatment. Visit www.lovaas.com for more information.

Princeton Child Development Institute (PCDI)

Begun in 1970 by McClannahan & Krantz (2001), this program now includes service programs for preschool, school-age, and adult individuals with autism. The program is based on an ABA approach. Strengths of the program include high levels of staff training and supervision. The program has been well known for the use of activity schedules to structure teaching around relevant, meaningful activities (see Chapter 6). The web site for PCDI is www.pcdi.org.

Pivotal Response Training
University of California at Santa Barbara

This program began in 1979 and was developed by Lynn and Robert Koegel (see Koegel and Koegel 2006) at UCSB. Originally somewhat more broadly focused, the program now primarily works with younger children. The early stage of this program uses a behavior analytic approach with discrete trial training but with a shift to more naturalistic approaches. Some areas are particularly targeted, including communication, self-help, social, academic, leisure time, and so forth. The focus on certain critical areas (e.g., motivation, self-management, initiation) is a central theme, with the goal of enabling the child to participate in, and learn from, more normative settings. The program includes work both at home and at the center, along with participation in the public school intervention program. For additional information on the UCSB Koegel Autism Center, visit http://education.ucsb.edu/autism/.

Children's Unit for Treatment and Evaluation (Children's Unit)

This program, based at the State University of New York at Binghamton, was established in 1975 (Romanczyk et al., 2000). It serves a range of children with serious difficulties (not just those on the autism spectrum). There are preschool and school-age programs that run year-round. The emphasis of the program is on identifying factors that interfere with learning. The program uses both more traditional ABA and more naturalistic methods as children move through the program. The program is highly individualized, with close monitoring of data obtained on the child's progress. For additional information, visit the program's web site: http://icd.binghamton.edu.

Douglass Developmental Disabilities Center (DDDC)

Established in 1982 at Rutgers University by Dr. Sandra Harris (2001), the DDDC has expanded from the original school to include preschool and adult services. Services include home-based intervention as well as center-based learning in small classes. Both integrated and segregated classes are available. The approach is guided by ABA methods, using a discrete trial format and then moving to more naturalistic procedures. The curriculum is developmentally sequenced. Basic skills are initially targeted, for instance, aspects of socialization, communication, compliance, self-care, and behaviors that interfere with learning. For additional information, visit the program's web site: http://dddc.rutgers.edu.

Treatment and Education of Autistic and Related Communication Handicapped Children (TEACCH) at the University of North Carolina

This statewide program was begun in 1972 under the leadership of Eric Schopler (1997) and now Gary Mesibov. This program provides a range of services to individuals with autism and their families. In addition to its main office at the University of North Carolina, TEACCH has a number or regional centers across the state that implement special classrooms within the public schools. TEACCH is a program that is both developmentally and behaviorally based with an emphasis on several areas, including an awareness of areas of strength and vulnerability for individuals with autism with a focus on structured teaching with careful attention to the learning environment. There is a strong parent and family component and commitment to skill development and individualized planning. There is also explicit respect for supporting people and their differences rather than only on eliminating behavioral differences. The program has a long history of careful attention to teaching methods and ways the environment can be used to support learning and to acquire communication skills (Mesibov, 1997). The web site for this program (www.teacch .com) has valuable information on autism in general as well as on the specifics of the TEACCH approach.

Walden Early Childhood Programs (Walden)

Originally established at the University of Massachusetts–Amherst in 1985, the program moved to Emory University in Atlanta in 1991 (McGee et al. 2001). Walden provides a range of services to young children with autism as well as to typical peers. There is a strong emphasis on incidental learning as well as on social and language development. Parents are actively involved. Visit www.psychiatry .emory.edu/PROGRAMS/autism/Walden.html for more information.

Learning Experiences, an Alternative Program for Preschoolers and Their Parents (LEAP)

Originally based in 1982 at the University of Pittsburgh (Strain & Cordisco, 1994), this program now is based at the University of Colorado School of Education and operates within the Denver Public School system. This program emphasizes the importance of supported integration and the potential for peer teaching. It includes both classroom-based work and parent training. Although ABA methods are used, the program is strongly developmentally based. For additional information, visit http://depts.washington.edu/pdacent/ sites/ucd.html.

Denver Model at the University of Colorado

This program began in 1981 with a grant to Sally Rogers based on her developmental model of autism (see Rogers and Lewis, 1988 and other papers by Rogers in the reading list). In this approach, interventions are designed to address core problems in social skills such as imitation, perception of other people, and understanding their feelings and intentions. The intervention uses play, other learning activities, and relationships to increase communication and build capacities for symbolic thinking. The program aims to minimize the negative effects of social difficulties and provides consultation to school districts with children with autism treated in inclusive settings. Although strongly based in a developmental approach, the model uses behavioral methods and structured teaching as well. For additional information, visit www.jfkpartners.org.

Individualized Support Program—University of South Florida

This parent training program originated in West Virginia before it was moved to Florida in 1987 (see papers by Dunlap & Fox in the reading list). This program is provided in home and community settings with a period of intense involvement and then ongoing follow-up. The program is meant to be added to ongoing daily special education intervention. Goals include helping the family become more knowledgeable about their children's needs and fostering communication and social skills. The emphasis on family support is an important aspect of this program.

Developmental Intervention Model (Floortime)

In this model, developed by Stanley Greenspan, the emphasis is on relationships and is strongly developmentally oriented. Individual sessions are used, in which the adult follows the child's lead in play and social interaction. Children also receive other therapies. The program focuses on several areas in particular: shared attention and regulation, reciprocity of affects, social engagement, communication, and development of symbolic thinking and use of ideas (Greenspan & Wieder, 2009) (www.icdl.com/dirFloortime/overview).

What Do These Models Tell Us About Intervention for Autism?

Each of the models we've just reviewed has its stronger and weaker points. But one of the most important things about these programs is their commitment to research, in terms of changes made over short and long time frames. Work of this kind has advanced and will continue to advance the field. As the NRC report *Educating Children With Autism* makes clear, a number of things can be said about the importance of intervention in the lives of children with autism and related conditions. All this being said, what are the limitations of what we know?

Clearly, the research base for each of these treatments is highly variable. In some cases, there has been elegant and rigorous research, although often with a small number of subjects. Most of the work has, probably understandably, focused on very young children. One of the problems is that we don't have much research that compares different approaches; to put the issue another way, how do we know what approach works best for what child?

Weighing the Pros and Cons of the Various Treatment Models

There are pros and cons to the various treatment models. Home-based treatments have some advantages for preschool children. The child is already in the environment where learning will take place, and it is more "normative" for services to be provided where children live at this age. But the commitment to a home-based treatment model can be daunting for parents, particularly when, as is now frequent, both work. The expectation that a parent quit his or her job to be able to provide a home-based program is unrealistic except for highly affluent families or those where the family can survive on one parent's income. The intensity of this work also entails some special burdens on those delivering the services and may have important implications for family life and the marital relationship. However, this approach quickly enables parents to become versed in intervention techniques that can then be applied consistently throughout the child's day.

Center-based approaches have other pros and cons. One great advantage is bringing together in one place an entire group of people knowledgeable about autism and in regular communication with each other. The family does not need to transport the child to various sites for service. Backup is readily available; for example, if one staff member is sick, another trained staff member can take over. This can be a greater challenge in the public school setting, e.g., when there may be only one school psychologist or speech pathologist. Although parents are very much involved in center-based programs, the intensity of their, involvement is considerably lessened as compared to home based programs. The absence (often, but not always) of typically developing peers is a major drawback. More and more center-based programs now include a mainstream component (e.g., with an integrated classroom). It is also possible to combine approaches, for example, with special classes within schools with opportunities for mainstreaming or, for younger children, an option for a gradual transition into more normative preschool settings with some time at the center-based program and other time in the typical preschool.

School-based programs have the substantial advantage of the potential for considerable exposure to peers and mainstream, normative experiences. All the many resources available in school settings are available, including the possibility of additional services from professionals like the school psychologist or speech pathologist or occupational therapist. That being said, successful integration of students on the autism spectrum into public school settings does require thoughtful planning. Many of the techniques developed in center- and home-based programs for children with autism can be implemented readily in school settings, although maintaining the intensity of some of these interventions and their supervision can be a challenge. Preparation of teaching staff, particularly teaching assistants and paraprofessionals, is critical. A frequent challenge is that it may be easier for the aide to do something for the child rather than facilitating the child's engagement in the behavior/activity. The routine of a typical classroom day can be used to great advantage, for example, in terms of structuring mainstream exposure time, insuring predictability, and so forth. These routines also have great potential for use in teaching adaptive skills. Challenges for staffing have to do with training levels for teachers and other classroom personnel. Given the complexity of supports required, it is imperative that teachers be particularly well organized. Teachers must be familiar with a range of potential intervention techniques and have a detailed lesson plan that can be readily implemented. Opportunities for more intensive interaction with parents are also often much more limited.

SPECIAL EDUCATIONAL NEEDS OF THE CHILD WITH AN ASD

There are some excellent resources (many listed at the end of this chapter) describing school- and center-based programs developed to address the special needs of children on the autism spectrum. *Educating Children With Autism* summarizes areas of both agreement and divergence across the 10 comprehensive programs it surveyed. Probably most important is that there was consensus from all the programs that early intervention can make a major difference for many children, although not all children improve to the same degree. There was also agreement on the importance of several things about intervention programs:

- Intervention needs to be planned and intensive.
- Specific curricula should be used.
- Intervention programs must be interdisciplinary with good integration of services.
- Teachers and other service providers need experience, training, and ongoing support.
- Family involvement is critical to help the child generalize skills.
- Child engagement is essential—the child has to be actively involved.
- Functional behavior management procedures should be used to foster behaviors that facilitate learning.
- Attention must be paid to transition planning.

In the report, programs that appeared to work for younger children were year-round and "averaged" about 25 hours/week. (Note the quotation marks around "average" since, in fact, there were tremendous variations in how programs were organized and it was difficult to come up with a single number that captures this variation.)

There was also much consensus on the kinds of things that need to be worked on. These include social skills, communication skills, play (for younger children and leisure time for older children), behavioral issues and obstacles to learning, organizational and "learning-to-learn" skills (the ability to sit, pay attention to a task, and engage with the teacher or activity in learning), and to generalization and the translation of knowledge into real-world settings (adaptive skills).

Physical Space

The setting of the intervention was also felt to be important, given the difficulties children on the autism spectrum have in regulating their attention—particularly in more complex environments. This would usually imply a need for a balanced approach with "pull-outs" and opportunities for more intensive work mixed with classroom and small group work. It also implies that attention needs to be paid to the classroom environment, which can help or hinder the child's ability to attend. Having continuity and a consistent approach is also important. Having the team work together in a flexible and collaborative way is helpful in implementing the program and monitoring the IEP goals.

> ### THE CLASSROOM ENVIRONMENT FOR THE CHILD WITH AN ASD
>
> **Goals:** The physical environment should *enhance* and *not distract* engagement and attention for children with ASDs.
>
> *Organization of the Room*
>
> - Place materials/furniture to help organize the child (natural boundaries).
> - Look out for obvious distractions; place desks so the child looks at the teacher (not outside).
> - Don't have computer displays running where the child can see them.
> - Have an area in the room with few distractions where the child can "retreat" if he or she needs to.
>
> *Respect Visual Learning Style and Difficulties with Generalization/Organization*
>
> - Masking tape can be used to mark out specific areas, e.g, where the child sits in the classroom.
> - Visual schedules/supports should be used; these can transition into other organizational supports for older children (preteaching, organizational software).
>
> *Attend to the Social Environment*
>
> - Think about entrance/exit issues; for example, children's cubbies should be away from the door.
> - Consider proximity issues, for example, desk spacing, activity areas.

Applied Behavior Analysis(ABA)/Behavioral Treatments

Programs differ in the ways they manage behavioral issues and problems and in their approaches to teaching skills. A range of approaches can be used, but many methods derive from the ABA literature. This literature has been remarkably productive over the past decades in helping us understand effective ways to teach children with autism, particularly children who lack learning-to-learn skills and need real help in being able to profit from the school environment. These methods also apply to older and more cognitively able children. They can include a combination of several different strategies, including discrete trial training, pivotal response training, and use of functional routines. Discrete trial methods can be used for very basic skills. This procedure results in having a clear sequence where concepts are broken down into tasks that can be targeted. In the discrete trial, a cue is given to the child, who then responds and receives a reward or consequence of some kind before the procedure is repeated. Careful data are kept, and there is a larger vision of what is to be accomplished; that is, basic things like sitting in the chair are targeted first, and then as activities become more complex they are pulled together to help the child achieve higher skill levels. Pivotal response training focuses very much on the environment, broadly defined, and ways in which the reinforcement can be a natural consequence; this has the great advantage of making it easier to carry the procedure throughout the day and simplifies the task of generalization. It also meshes nicely with an approach that looks at functional routines. The functional routines approach focuses on a sequence of predictable events such as snack or circle time or going to lunch. These routines can then be used as the basis for various teaching activities, e.g., use of words, social skills, concepts, and so forth. Because typical children also are engaged in such activities, this method can seem to be very natural. Methods that use these behavioral techniques must, of course, develop a clear vision of expectations for the child. A few models have been developed that try to use child preference more actively; we discuss these in greater detail later in this chapter.

Social Skills Teaching

Social skills are usually taught using a balance of methods. These vary somewhat with the age of the child. For younger children, peer-mediated approaches are frequently used, while for adults, direct instruction is most frequent, and for school-aged children, what might be called "hybrid" methods are often used, for example, a social skills group where there is an adult leader (or leaders) with a peer group; this group might include other children with ASD as well as typically developing peers. Various combinations of these approaches are also possible, of course; for example, a speech pathologist might work with a child in a small group, like a "lunch bunch" and individually. Play skills should typically be explicit targets of intervention in younger children. There are many ways to teach play skills, including specific ABA-type instruction with development of scripts and functional play routines. Modeling by peers can also be helpful. Social skills intervention is always an important aspect of the plan for children on the autism spectrum. Chapter 6 reviews social skills interventions in greater detail.

Language/Communication Interventions

Language and communication skills are also an essential aspect of intervention, given that we know that the language levels and the capacity to speak are better signs for long-term outcome. We believe that with early intervention, the number of children with more prototypical autism who manage to be able to speak by age 5 is around 75%; this is a marked increase from a decade or two ago when the number was more like 50%. As we discuss in Chapter 6 and subsequent chapters, there are many different approaches to intervention in this area. It is important to keep in mind that even for children who don't speak, a focus on communication is essential, and for such children augmentative approaches can be used.

More verbal students on the autism spectrum present some interesting challenges for the system. Occasionally, the communication needs of more able children with Asperger's are minimized or ignored. We have heard statements like "He has such a great vocabulary, he doesn't need to see the speech pathologist," but this is said of a child who can't carry on a conversation except about his topic of interest. This is, of course, just the reason he needs to see the speech pathologist. Language and communication skills should be targeted at multiple levels, depending on the child's needs, for example, both expressive and receptive language as well as social language should be targeted.

AUGMENTATIVE COMMUNICATION STRATEGIES

- Provide "workarounds" for communication for students with limited or no spoken words.
- These workarounds can take various forms:
  - Picture exchange
  - Manual sign language
  - Computerized communication systems
- Typically, emphasize the stronger visual learning style of children with autism.
- Use of these augmentative strategies does *not* prevent children from learning to talk—it should increase their ability to talk if they are capable of it.

Organizational Issues, Learning to Learn, and Adaptive Skills

One of the obstacles for learning arises from the tendency of children with autism to be overly focused on details and not see the "big picture." This likely is very much related to the social difficulties and difficulties with dealing with change. These difficulties result in problems in developing joint attention and other early emerging social skills, which "set the stage" for the child in terms of learning what to and what not to focus on. This leads to problems in what psychologists call executive functions (the ability to get the big picture and multitask) and requires specific intervention for children at all ages and cognitive levels. For younger children, this can take the form of visual aids, for example, the classroom schedule on a bulletin board in picture format. As children become more cognitively able, these can be supplemented by other supports, for example, written lists/schedules, organizers, computer software, and so forth. Another problem that arises from difficulties with organization and a tendency to hyperfocus is a failure to appreciate that the skills learned in one context can be applied in another. This activity is called **generalization**. It becomes truly critical if children are to achieve independent living skills. Accordingly, it is important that schools and families work together to be sure that there is carryover of activities into home and other settings. Organizational aids can also help, as children need to do homework or help with simple household activities like shopping. Providing a structure, in advance, can prevent many problems from happening. It is important for parents and teachers not to teach skills in isolation. Generalization should be encouraged at every opportunity, as this will facilitate the acquisition of skills necessary for ultimate adult independence and self-sufficiency. We talk about daily living and other skills in the next chapter.

Sensory–Motor Issues

Sensory and motor issues can sometimes be a source of great difficulty for children on the autism spectrum. It is important that, as part of the IEP, the occupational and/or physical therapist be involved to develop procedures specific to the individual child. For some children, help with gross and particularly fine motor activities may be needed. The child with Asperger's may, for example, have particular problems with cursive handwriting, and it may be possible to justify alternatives (e.g., a laptop) if these difficulties can be documented. Both the speech pathologist and occupational therapist can be helpful around eating/feeding issues.

Use of the child's natural motivations and of more developmental approaches has been somewhat less common than ABA-based approaches, but these approaches have been effectively used. With these approaches, as indeed with typically developing children, the idea is that learning is easiest when it follows the natural inclinations/leads of the child. This approach also often assumes that, in general, normal developmental progressions are followed—that is, that you can make reasonable predictions of what a sequence of skills learning will be.

As with other approaches, and perhaps even more with this one, it is important to (1) pay attention to the child's learning environment and (2) be sure that the child is producing enough leads to follow. We have seen children enrolled in such programs fail to progress if they are not producing enough in the way of cues/leads for the teacher to follow.

AREAS OF VULNERABILITY AND POTENTIAL RESPONSES

Area of Vulnerability	Potential Responses
Organizational problems	Stepwise approach Consistency and predictability Use functional routines Give plenty of time Support organization with visual aids, organizers, computers, etc.
Attentional problems	Isolate the most relevant information Pay attention to the learning environment Structure environment/minimize distractions Support attention whenever possible
Problems in sequencing	Use routines, predictability, and sequencing Use visual schedules, stepwise approaches
Difficulties with rigidity	Use planned changes (choice times, predictable surprises)
Problems with time management	Use timers (including visual timers and cues) Give extra time Give concrete instructions (do X for 5 minutes) Establish clear expectations/feedback
Visual learning style	Provide visual supports (pictures → written words) Limit verbal language Keep language short and simple
Gestalt learning style (learns in "chunks")	Present material across settings Encourage generalization (family involved) Breakdown tasks into component parts
Trouble understanding social cues	Exaggerate social cues Pair gestures and words Teach in context Keep language simple Be explicit, explicit, explicit

Behavioral Management Issues

Programs vary in the ways they manage behavioral issues and problems and in their approaches to teaching skills. As mentioned earlier, ABA methods have been very helpful in giving us more effective ways to teach children with autism. These methods work both in encouraging the kinds of behaviors and skills that parents and teachers want to develop and in dealing with problem behaviors that can arise. These methods also work for older and more able children. They can include one or several different strategies, including discrete trial training, pivotal response training, and use of functional routines. Methods that use these behavioral techniques must, of course, develop a clear vision of expectations for the child, i.e., what behaviors are to be developed and encouraged and what behaviors are to be decreased and/or discouraged. A few models have been developed that try to use child preference more actively; we discuss these in greater detail in Chapter 14.

MAINSTREAMING

Under the law, it is presumed that children with autism and related conditions should be mainstreamed as much as possible. With the growing sophistication of support methods for both affected children and typically developing peers, it is increasingly possible to support children with ASDs in more typical, mainstream settings. If the process of identification and intervention starts early, it is frequently possible to have children fully included by the time they reach first grade, and even those not fully included are more able to relate to their typical peers and to achieve at least partial inclusion.

Various terms are used for mainstream settings, these include *full inclusion* and *integration*. Various possible models are available; for example, a special education integrated class might include some children who were typically developing. Usually, mainstream classes are structured around a traditional classroom model, while an integrated class also includes work individualized for specific students. A wide range of models are available including ones where both a regular classroom teacher and special ed teacher work together in the same inclusive class.

When considering inclusion of the child with an ASD in mainstream settings, parents and the school must take into account the needs of the child, the context of inclusion, the need for adult supervision, the expectations of peers, and so forth. Attention to activities used in the class, the structure and routine of the interaction, and the physical environment all contribute to successful social interaction. The teacher often needs support to learn techniques for inclusion and managing problem behaviors. Support staff such as teacher assistants and paraprofessionals may also benefit from training, with one of the goals being to help support the child in the environment through an emphasis on peer-mediated, rather than adult, intervention.

One of the great advantages of mainstream/integrated classes is the potential for fostering social skills. Most of the work that has taken place to date has centered on preschool children, although some work on older children has appeared as well. That being said, it is clear that simply putting the child with an ASD in the classroom is not, by itself, sufficient. Rather, the teacher and peers must be appropriately prepared if peers are to be helpful and effective models. An entire body of work has now emerged on strategies and procedures for teaching social skills in these contexts using typical peers and free play and other situations. Adult supervision is typically used to help initiate interaction and monitor ongoing activities. Peers can be very effective agents of change—if given the special license to do so. For older children, more complex and sophisticated strategies are needed. Even here, benefits can be shown from peer interaction and self-monitoring. The experience can be a valuable one for peers as well as for the child with ASD. As might be expected, younger peers need more support and monitoring than older ones.

Strategies for increasing interaction in a mainstream setting are varied. These include social scripts, for example, in teaching fantasy play (an area of great difficulty for many children on the autism spectrum). Teaching both response to social overtures and initiation is important. It is critical that the child with an ASD be able to both initiate and respond appropriately; the latter is much easier, of course. Videotapes can be used as effective adjuncts to the teacher; for example, the child can review the tape, observe when things go wrong, discuss alternative responses, and so forth. Video feedback can be highly effective, given the visual learning style in autism.

Researchers have developed various models of inclusion. For less cognitively able children, the emphasis may be on skills relevant to community involvement. This may be reflected in initial classes with an emphasis on one-on-one teaching with an eventual move to small group and more inclusive classes, eventually with typically developing peers. Transitions to mainstream settings should be carefully planned and supervised. Unfortunately, school districts often attempt to mainstream children into what are, seemingly, the easiest settings to manage: gym, recess, and cafeteria. Unfortunately given the lack of structure and reduced levels of adult supervision for children on the autism spectrum, these are usually the absolute worst situations to begin mainstreaming.

The goal is to have a successful mainstream experience. To this end, a well-worked-out transition plan with a gradual increase in exposure of the child to the mainstream setting is valuable, with careful, thoughtful adjustment based on response of the child. For preschool children, situations readily used for mainstream activities include story time and free play as well as snack or lunchtime. With appropriate support, recess can also be used. For older children, music and art and similar activities can be positive times. For the more cognitively able child, some mainstream academic classes may be appropriate (and easier than less structured activities). The greater complexity of middle schools and high schools presents significant challenges, although even here mainstreaming can be successful. Issues do arise for lower functioning students, where the balance of benefit (of exposure to normal peers) versus trade-off (need for more vocationally focused, transitional activities) can be an issue. For example, in one case with which we are familiar, a very cognitively disabled teenager who was not yet showering independently enrolled in a traditional American history class; in this case, whatever benefit came from being exposed to a discussion of the U.S. Constitution was probably greatly outweighed by a lack of attention to basic self-care skills.

INTERVENTIONS TO SUPPORT INCLUSION

Peer-based interventions (e.g., peer modeling, buddy systems)

Teach play skills

Participation in social skills groups

Provide visual activity schedule for classroom

Teaching social scripts (and then fade scripts over time)

Teaching self-management skills (initiation, staying on task, social routines)

Support inclusion (encouraging peer response, teacher responds to child through peer, environment supports peer interaction)

Management of problem behaviors

Adapted, with permission, from Handleman, J. S., Harris, S. L., & Martins, M. P. (2005). Helping children with autism enter the mainstream. In F. R. Volkmar, R. Paul, A. Klin, & D. Cohen (Eds.), *Handbook of autism and pervasive developmental disorders* (3rd ed., pp. 1038, Table 40.1). Hoboken, NJ: Wiley.

STUDENTS WITH ASPERGER'S

There are somewhat different challenges for more cognitively able students, particularly those with Asperger's. Often, the problem here is a lack of awareness, or minimization, of the child's level of social disability. Put another way, the very good language (but not communication) skills of the child overshadow an awareness of the child's vulnerability. Typically, this is reflected in comments like "He is too bright to be in special ed" or "She is too verbal to be on the spectrum." This is a bit like saying, "He's too bright to have pneumonia" or "She is too verbal to have polio."

The communication goals for the child with Asperger's may have a somewhat different focus than those of the child with autism. For Asperger's, these usually will include work on social communication (**pragmatics**). Issues such as carrying on a conversation with a beginning, middle, and end are important, as are issues of topic sharing, reciprocity, humor and irony, expectations for turn taking, and building on what the other person just said. Teaching self-monitoring and self-correction is important; even very rigid phrases like "Am I talking too much?" or "Would you like to talk now?" can elicit helpful feedback. Video and audio feedback can be valuable ways to learn self-monitoring and gauge progress. Work on **prosody** and voice volume can be helpful in this way as well. Most of us have hundreds, if not thousands, of different voices we use for different people and/or different settings. For individuals with ASDs who are verbal and who tend to be monotonic and loud, having three voices is very helpful (soft, medium, and loud) as long as the individual knows which one goes where (soft for church, medium for class, loud for playground).

Many of the same challenges and strategies for inclusion we have discussed previously (see the text box on page 137) apply to the student with Asperger's. There are a couple of potentially important differences. Two of these things make life a bit easier for teachers: (1) Often, there is a strong motivation on the part of the student to "fit in," and (2) better verbal abilities make it easier to teach explicit (verbal) strategies and rules for self-regulation and mastery of classroom routine. However, the one-sided social approaches may be off-putting to the typically developing students, so careful support and work with peers is important. Bullying (which we discuss in greater detail in Chapter 8) can start to be a problem, particularly as children become a bit older.

For students with Asperger's, another contributing factor to lack of recognition of the child's difficulties is the relatively frequent variability of the child's behavior across settings; for example, the child may seem engaged and enthusiastic in class, but the same child may literally be lost on the playground or the lunchroom. Often, behavior problems develop when the social difficulties are not attended to. These behavior problems can then lead to highly inappropriate labels; these vary from state to state, but terms like *BD (behavior disturbed)*, *ED (emotionally disturbed)*, or *SEM* (social–emotionally maladjusted) are used, and then the child is placed in a classroom with truly conduct-disordered children—usually boys—and all hell usually breaks loose very quickly. We're aware of one case where a very bright but quite socially limited first grader was put in a BD class for having talked back to his teacher (reminding her repeatedly that circle time was running late). He was in this BD class for no more than 5 minutes when a truly behavior-disturbed boy (who was very socially sophisticated) told him to "go pull the handle of that bright red box on the wall—a lot of stuff will happen," and indeed it did. This kind of placement leads to the worst possible mismatch. The support of the communication specialist is often very helpful in dealing with communication issues that contribute to behavior problems. Behavior management procedures can be effective but should be informed by the child's patterns of strengths and weaknesses and attempt, as much as possible, to help the child engage in self-monitoring/self-management.

> ## ADDRESSING AREAS OF VULNERABILITY FOR CHILDREN WITH ASPERGER'S
>
> - Be explicit, explicit, explicit:
>   - Put things/rules into words.
>   - Teach social rules.
>   - Assume nothing.
> - Make things verbal:
>   - Use video examples to explain ongoing stories and personal reactions.
>   - Teach narrative and observation skills (child as "detective" or "reporter"—a person who asks all the Wh questions: who?, what?, where?, when?, and why?).
> - Teach emotions and the language of emotions:
>   - Self-awareness of feelings, problem situations.
>   - Teach about the experience of anxiety, depression, reactions to novelty.
> - Teach explicit coping strategies:
>   - Include verbal self-talk and verbal coping.
>   - Increase self-monitoring capacities and invitations for feedback ("Am I talking too much?").
>   - Teach alternative solutions when child is aware of starting to have problems—for example, a pass to visit an adult at school (his or her "safe address") and then rapid return to the class.

Behavioral strategies for management of problem behaviors in more able individuals should be informed by an understanding of the child's disability. What can seem like very inappropriate behaviors may be much better understood from the child's point of view. An excessive tendency to follow the rules can lead to trouble; for example, the child may be quite insistent on a routine partly because she or he has learned to use it as a lifeline. The special interests often seen in students with Asperger's and sometimes with other students on the autism spectrum can present some challenges for the student and teacher alike. Whenever possible and when appropriate it may be helpful to use the students' natural interests/motivations in a positive way. Sometimes the task is helping the student learn to contain an interest, for example, to have something to talk to other students about apart from rocks or dinosaurs; in these cases, giving the child the opportunity (for very discrete periods) to pursue his or her interest may be used as an incentive for other work. We talk more about behavioral strategies and other approaches in Chapters 8, 9, and 14.

Family Support

Support of the parents and siblings is essential for many reasons. First and foremost, the family remains with the child when school staff do not. Also, unlike school staff, they don't come and go over time. They have particular advantages when it comes to work on generalization of skills and helping the child on the spectrum make connections between academic and real-world knowledge. As we discuss later on in this book (Chapter 19), support for siblings and parents is important.

TRANSLATING WHAT WE KNOW TO SCHOOL PROGRAMS

Fortunately, many of the interventions derived from model programs discussed earlier are readily used in school settings. These can be used to systematically analyze tasks, build new skills, and generalize skills to nonschool settings. A number of resources that illustrate application of these techniques have appeared and are listed in the reading list at the conclusion of this chapter. Arick, Krug, Loos, and Falco (2005) have developed a comprehensive curriculum for preschool and elementary school, the STAR program, which serves as one helpful model combining effective instructional strategies in the service of a well-conceptualized curriculum (www.starautismprogram.com). Table 5.2 summarizes some of the different instructional strategies used in the STAR program, which combines these approaches very effectively.

Given the sometimes intense needs for immediate support, it is critical for parents and teachers to not lose sight of the big picture. While all the behavioral techniques of ABA represent powerful tools, it is essential that schools and families have a longer term vision for the child and that the teacher, in particular, be prepared to implement an appropriate curriculum with realistic, objective, and measurable goals. Methods derived from pivotal response training and functional routines also offer powerful approaches to address fundamental problems in learning and facilitate generalization.

As we describe in greater detail in subsequent chapters, specific areas for instruction will, understandably, differ depending on the child's age and levels of functioning. For preschool children, appropriate tasks involve receptive and expressive language, social engagement (particularly joint attention, which becomes critical for profiting from a classroom environment), basic learning-to-learn skills (staying in the chair, attending to materials at hand), play skills, and preacademic abilities. The latter include use of areas of strengths, for instance, in nonverbal problem solving or visual spatial skills, to help the child learn to read words that can serve as prompts for specific behaviors. For the school-aged child, more traditional academic skills become more important. In addition to the continued need for supporting social and communicative development, there may be a growing awareness of the child's areas of vulnerability, and problems with anxiety may loom larger. Sensory processing problems may also

TABLE 5.2	INTERACTION OF INSTRUCTIONAL STRATEGIES AND CURRICULUM AREAS

Curriculum Area Used in STAR Program	Instructional Strategies Used in STAR Program		
	Pivotal Response Training	Discrete Trial Training	Teaching Functional Routines
Expressive language	All expressive language	Specific imitative sounds/words Specific labels Most midlevel and advanced programs	Develop generalization of expressive language
Receptive language	Taught incidentally within context of other Pivotal Response Training programs	All receptive language programs	Generalize use of receptive language within routines
Spontaneous language	All spontaneous language instruction program	Reinforce spontaneous language when it occurs	Set up situations in which the student needs to use spontaneous language
Functional routines	Expand expressive language using PRT strategies within routines	Expand receptive language use during discrete trial within routine	All activities comprised of a predictable chain of behaviors
Preacademic skills	Expand and generalize use of preacademic skills	All preacademic programs	Generalize use of preacademic skills within routines
Play skills and social interaction skills	Play skills are taught with PRT play programs and incidentally during PRT language	Social interaction and play are taught incidentally during one-on-one discrete trial sessions	Develop appropriate play and social interaction during all appropriate routines (e.g., play a game with peer, recess routine with peer buddy)

Adapted, with permission, from Arick, J., Krug, D., Fullerton, A., Loos, A., & Falco, R. (2005). *Handbook of autism and pervasive developmental disorders* (Chapter 39, p. 1013, Table 39.2). Hoboken, NJ: Wiley.

become more prominent (see Chapter 16). Problem behaviors (see Chapter 14) may also loom larger in importance. New strategies for teaching social skills may be needed, for example, social skills groups and direct instruction. The seemingly simple task of negotiating a more complex middle school may represent its own problems, with endless potential for the student to be sidetracked by others or the tremendous social demands of moving about in hallways filled with children (one of many possible solutions is to have the child move just before the bell rings and to give practice when the school is empty, along with visual supports, if needed). Organizational issues also loom larger (see Chapter 6) as academic demands increase. Using areas of strength to address areas of weakness and respecting different potential approaches to problem solving is important. For individuals with more "classical" autism, the visual learning style should be used in a positive way to facilitate coping and organization; for the student with Asperger's, an emphasis on verbal scripts and strategies may be equally as important.

High school (see Chapter 9) presents its own special challenges. For students who are unable to participate in part or fully in regular educational settings in high school, there is tremendous potential for social isolation. Fortunately, often by this age, behavior problems start to diminish and, whenever possible, the child's motivation for success can be a valuable ally. As in middle school, having an advocate within the school is highly valuable. This person can help the diverse range of teachers and staff the child has to deal with to understand the nature of autism and advocate for appropriate accommodations. At this time, thinking about next steps and transitions to work or college or other activities should begin (see Chapter 9).

Summary

In this chapter, we have surveyed current best practices in educating children with autism as exemplified by a range of model programs, each of which has at least some empirical research support. The issue, for the individual child, of exactly what approach is most suitable remains a challenging one. As we have noted, significant gaps in research exist, and although we can rightly point to many accomplishments, much remains to be done. In particular, the issue of helping develop a program designed for the child rather than trying to force a child into a program remains a common source of difficulty. Unfortunately, there is a lack of good studies that replicate findings in other locations and in which different interventions or models of intervention could readily be compared. As noted, even with very intensive service, many children continue to have significant learning challenges. For the present, the choice of program should be based, as much as is possible, on the individual needs of the child and family, while keeping in mind that things needed at one point in the child's life may not be needed later on.

◼ READING LIST

Arick, J. R., Krug, D. A., Loos, L., & Falco, R. (2005). School-based programs. In F. R. Volkmar, R. Paul, A. Klin, & D. Cohen (Eds.), *Handbook of autism and pervasive developmental disorders* (3rd ed., pp. 1003–1028). Hoboken, NJ: Wiley.

Dunlap, G., & Fox, L. (1996). Early intervention and serious problem behaviors: A comprehensive approach. In L. K. Koegel, R. L. Koegel, and G. Dunlap (Eds.), *Positive behavioral support: Including people with difficult behavior in the community* (pp. 31–50). Baltimore: Brookes.

Dunlap, G., & Fox, L. (1999). A demonstration of behavioral support for young children with autism. *Journal of Positive Behavioral Interventions, 2,* 77–87.

Dunlap, G., & Fox, L. (1999). Supporting families of young children with autism. *Infants and Young Children, 12,* 48–54.

Greenspan, S. I. (2006). *Engaging autism: Helping children relate, communicate and think with the DIR floortime approach.* New York: Da Capo Lifelong Books.

Greenspan, S. I., & Wieder, S. (2009). *Engaging autism: Using the floortime approach to help children relate, communicate, and think.* Cambridge, MA: Da Capo Lifelong Books.

Handleman, J. S Frogber, & Harris, S. L. (1994). *Preschool education programs for children with autism.* Austin, TX: Pro-Ed.

Handleman, J. S., Harris, S. L., & Martins, M. P. (2005). Helping children with autism enter the mainstream. In F. R. Volkmar, R. Paul, A. Klin, & D. Cohen (Eds.), *Handbook of autism and pervasive developmental disorders* (3rd ed., pp. 1029–1042). Hoboken, NJ: Wiley.

Harris, S. L., Handleman, J. S., & Jennett, H. (2005). Models of educational intervention for students with autism: Home, center and school-based programming. In F. R. Volkmar, R. Paul, A. Klin, & D. Cohen (Eds.), *Handbook of autism and pervasive developmental disorders* (3rd ed., pp. 1043–1054). Hoboken, NJ: Wiley.

Ivannone, R., Dunlap, G., Huber, H., & Kincaid, D. (2003). Effective educational practices for students with autism spectrum disorders. *Focus on Autism and Other Developmental Disabilities, 18,* 150–165.

Koegel, L. K., & LaZebnik, C. (2004). *Overcoming autism.* New York: Penguin Books.

Koegel, R. L., & Koegel, L. K. (1995). *Strategies for initiating positive interactions and improving learning opportunities.* Baltimore: Brookes.

Koegel, R. L. & L. K. Koegel, Eds. (2006). *Pivotal response treatments for autism: Communication, social, and academic development.* Baltimore: Brookes.

Lovaas, O. I. (1981). *Teaching developmentally disabled children: The me book.* Austin, TX: Pro-Ed.

Lovaas, O. I. (1987). Behavioral treatment and normal educational and intellectual functioning in young autistic children. *Journal of Consulting and Clinical Psychology, 55,* 3–9.

Lovaas, O. I. (2003). *Teaching individuals with developmental delays: Basic intervention techniques.* Austin, TX: Pro-Ed.

Matson, J. L., Benavidez, D. A., Compton, L. S., Paclawskyj, T., & Baglio, C. (1996). Behavioral treatment of autistic persons: A review of research from 1980 to the present. *Research in Developmental Disabilities, 17,* 433–465.

Maurice, C. R., Foxx, R. M., & Greene, G. (2001). *Making a difference: Behavioral intervention for children with autism.* Austin, TX: Pro-Ed.

Maurice, C., Green, G., & Luce, S. C. (1996). *Behavioral intervention for young children with autism: A manual for parents and professionals.* Austin, TX: Pro-Ed.

McClannahan, L. E., & Krantz, P. J. (2001). Behavior analysis and intervention for preschoolers at the Princeton Child Development Institute. In J. S. Handleman and S. L. Harris (Eds.), *Preschool education programs for children with autism* (Rev. ed.), pp. 191–213. Austin, TX: Pro-ed.

McGee, G. G., & Morrier, M. J. (2005). Preparation of autism specialists. In F. R. Volkmar, R. Paul, A. Klin, & D. Cohen (Eds.), *Handbook of autism and pervasive developmental disorders* (3rd ed., pp. 1123–1160). Hoboken, NJ: Wiley.

McGee, G. G., Morrier, M. J., & Daly, T. (2001). The Walden Early Childhood Programs. In J. S. Handleman & S. L. Harris (Eds.), *Preschool education programs for children with autism* (2nd ed., pp. 157–190). Austin, TX: Pro-Ed.

Mesibov, G. B., Shea, V., & Schopler, E. (2004). *The TEACCH approach to autism spectrum disorders*. New York: Springer.

National Research Council. (2001). *Educating children with autism*. Washington, DC: National Academies Press.

Olley, J. G. (2005). Curriculum and classroom structure. In F. R. Volkmar, R. Paul, A. Klin, & D. Cohen (Eds.), *Handbook of autism and pervasive developmental disorders* (3rd ed., pp. 863–881). Hoboken, NJ: Wiley.

Rogers, S. J. (1998). Empirically supported comprehensive treatments for young children with autism. *Journal of Clinical Child Psychology*, 27: 168–179.

Rogers, S. J., Hall, T., Osaki, D., Reaven, J., & Herbison, J. (2000). The Denver Model: A comprehensive, integrated educational approach to young children with autism and their families. In J. S. Handleman and S. L. Harris (Eds.), *Preschool Education Programs for Children with Autism* (2nd ed., pp 95–133.) Austin, TX: Pro-Ed.

Rogers, S. J., Herbison, J. M., Lewis, H. C., Pantone, J., & Reis, K. (1986). An approach for enhancing the symbolic, communicative, and interpersonal functioning of young children with autism or severe emotional handicaps. *Journal of the Division for Early Childhood*, 10: 135–148.

Rogers, S. J., & Lewis, H. (1988). An effective day treatment model for young children with pervasive developmental disorders. *Journal of the American Academy of Child and Adolescent Psychiatry*, 28: 207–214.

Schetter, P., & Lighthall, K. (2009) *Homeschooling the child with autism*. San Francisco: Jossey-Bass.

Schopler, E. (1997). Implementation of the TEACCH philosophy. In F. R. Volkmar, R. Paul, A. Klin, & D. Cohen (Eds.), *Handbook of autism and pervasive developmental disorders* (3rd ed., pp. 767–795). Hoboken, NJ: Wiley.

Schreibman, L. (2005). *The science and fiction of autism*. Cambridge, MA: Harvard University Press.

Smith, T. (1996). Are other treatments effective? In C. Maurice, G. Green, & S. Luce (Eds.), *Behavioral intervention for young children with autism: A manual for parents and professionals* (pp. 45–59). Austin, TX: Pro-Ed.

Smith, T., & Buch, G. A. et al. (2000). Parent-directed, intensive early intervention for children with pervasive developmental disorder. *Research in Developmental Disabilities*, *21*(4): 297–309.

Strain, P. S., & Cordisco, L. (1994). LEAP preschool. In J. S. Handleman and S. L. Harris (Eds.), *Preschool education programs for children with autism* (2nd ed., pp 225-244.) Austin, TX: Pro-Ed.

■ **WEB SITES**

Behavior Analyst Certification Board: www.BACB.com

Children's Unit for Treatment and Evaluation (Children's Unit) at the State University of New York at Binghamton: http://icd.binghamton.edu

Developmental Interventions Model (Floortime): www.icdl.com/dirFloortime/overview

Douglass Developmental Center at Rutgers University: http://dddc.rutgers.edu

Homeschooling: http://homeschooling.gomilpitas.com/weblinks/autism.html

Lovass Method: www.lovaas.com

Princeton Child Development Institute (PCDI): www.pcdi.org

Treatment and Education of Autistic and Related Communication-Handicapped Children (TEACCH) at the University of North Carolina: www.teacch.com

University of California at Santa Barbara Koegel Autism Center: http://education.ucsb.edu/autism

Walden Early Childhood Programs at Emory University: www.psychiatry.emory.edu/PROGRAMS/autism/Walden.html

■ QUESTIONS AND ANSWERS

1. **We are thinking about home schooling our 10-year-old with autism. Are there any resources available to help with this?**

   You don't tell us much about your 10-year-old, so it is hard for us give very specific advice. We would advise you to think carefully about not availing yourself of the services and opportunities provided for peer interaction in schools. That being said, there are some resources on this topic (see reading list), including a helpful web site and at least one book. We do know some parents who have been able to do this successfully, sometimes using local services to help with special things. Pay attention to opportunities for peer interaction.

2. **My wife and I have a young child with autism. He has just started ABA but only at 4 hours a week, and we're not sure this is enough. Also, the person providing the services (who is very expensive) doesn't seem to be as good or as well organized as the person working with the child of a friend of ours (who is getting much more service). Is there any kind of standard for ABA?**

   Your question raises several different issues, including how much time is enough, how to evaluate the quality of an ABA therapist, and the issue of standards for therapists. The question of time is hard to answer without knowing the particular child and without knowing the circumstances (e.g., is the plan to increase services after a short period of getting to know your son?). The original Lovaas model was very intensive, with 40 hours of service a week. In the National Research Council Report, it seemed that about 25 hours a week was a rough kind of average (of very different types of programs). The professionals who helped you with the diagnosis ought to be able to talk with you about services available. The issue of quality of the ABA therapist is complicated for several reasons. First, keep in mind that there are some ABA specialists who may have different levels of experience or who have worked more with some age groups than others. As with all therapists, there can be variability. Other parents can be excellent sources of information as well. There have been some attempts to establish minimum qualifications and certification procedures. Visit Behavior

Analyst Certification Board (www.BACB.com or www.abainternational.org) for more information.

3. **Our 4-year-old grandchild has been enrolled in a special pre-school program for children with autism over the last year. He doesn't seem to have made much progress at all as far as we can tell. He has horrible behavior problems and limited communication. He has some special interests (including some computer games) but says words only now and then. His parents tell us that they were told we'd have to wait for several years to see progress; they also told us that the school didn't want to try anything like the computer for teaching language, as they think that will hold his language back.**

Unfortunately, even with good programs, not every child gets better or as much better as we would like. Lack of progress should prompt a re-assessment and serious look at the program. As we've pointed out in this chapter, there are many different models of teaching, and some children may do better with one over others. Part of the assessment should include a careful look at your grandchild's communication skills and updated recommendations for intervention. The fact that he has interest in the computer is something to mention to the person or people seeing him—it might be something that could well be used in programming for him. Some of the new augmentative communication devices may be helpful given the interest in the computer; you might suggest an evaluation with this specifically in mind.

4. **What states have the best programs for autism?**

Actually, there are a number of different models in the various states. In a few states, like North Carolina, Delaware, and some others, there are statewide programs. In other states, the model is very different, with almost all services provided within the public school settings. In some states (such as Connecticut), services vary substantially from town to town. In other cases, there is a mix of both private school and public school programs. A few states have a model where regional schools are funded. In other words, there is tremendous variability. If you have the luxury of being able to move to a state of your choice, do your homework and try to find a state (or town) with good services.

5. **What do you see as the current needs for research on interventions in schools?**

An excellent question with a multipart answer. In the first place, as a society, we've done an increasingly good job in doing research on autism and its psychological and neuropsychological basis. We've not done such a good job in translating research into schools. Many different intervention methods and programs are now out "on the market," and some of these appear very promising, but we need careful, well-designed studies to understand better whether they work and how they work (and who they work for). On the school side of the equation, we should be doing a better job of understanding what works for what children; all too often, the child is expected to "fit in" with whatever model the school has going. However, we should be doing a better job of tailoring interventions for the individual child.

6. **What is the role of the parents and family in helping teachers and school professionals?**

    Parents and family members have several important roles to play. First and foremost, parents can and should act as advocates for the child. They should participate actively in the process of developing the IEP and monitoring the child's progress. They should be actively involved in the school program so that they can help with the generalization of skills across settings, from school to home and community. There are also some resources which offer parents and schools possible programs visable to all parties (see www.rethinkautism.com).

Educational Interventions

Individuals with autism spectrum disorders (ASDs) need developmental help in a variety of ways. As a result of the changes in public law we described in Chapter 4, services are now—for the most part—delivered in public schools. In Chapter 5, we reviewed the range of approaches to helping children with autism. They share many commonalities and a few areas of difference. In this chapter, we review interventions commonly used in school-based programs. In the next series of chapters, we focus on programs for particular age groups and give some examples to make the differences among them clearer.

Intervention strategies need to be carefully planned to fit each child's current needs and abilities, and they must be consistent with the long-term plan or vision for the child. Areas of intervention typically address the core diagnostic features of autism—deficits with social interaction and communication—but also include other issues including learning. Strategies need to include problems of weak organizational skills that can be an obstacle to efficient learning as well as the acquisition of real-life skills. Behavioral and sensory–motor issues also must be addressed (see Chapters 14–16). And, of course, schools must focus on academic skills and a curriculum designed to meet the child's needs. The report from the National Research Council on Educating Children with Autism underscores several of the important priorities for intervention. Although this report was focused primarily on younger children, these priorities apply, with some adaptation, to individuals of all ages. They include:

- Development of functional, spontaneous communication
- Social instruction in various settings
- Enhancing play skills and peer play abilities (for older individuals, this can be expanded to include a range of leisure-time activities)
- Enhanced academic and cognitive growth including a range of abilities and problem-solving skills

- Positive behavioral interventions for problem behaviors
- Functional academic skills and integration in mainstream setting as appropriate

The overarching goal is to help the individual acquire as many skills as possible to enable him or her to be as productive and self-sufficient as possible as an adult. As we and others have repeatedly emphasized, family involvement is essential to this effort. To the extent possible, the individual person also needs to be a part of the planning process, particularly as he or she matures.

Work in the area of educational interventions has increased dramatically over the past decade. As a result, we'll be presenting summaries of what we see as some of the important areas for intervention. A fairly long list of resources is provided at the end of this chapter. In addition to the many excellent resources we list, others are available as well. Keep in mind that any distinctions we draw are necessarily somewhat arbitrary. For example, when is an intervention more for social skills and when it is more focused on communication? Or should we think about use of pictures in teaching self-care skills as an organizational strategy or one for fostering adaptive skills. Clearly, there are many different ways to organize this information, and none is perfect. The happy news here is that what might seem like a problem for us as authors is good news for parents and teachers, for whom interventions are often good for addressing a number of different issues. As always, keep in mind the needs of the specific child, adolescent, or adult—what works for one person may not be as good a choice for another, and similar strategies often will work with individuals of different ages.

Autism-Focused Curricula

As with other areas of work in autism, the past decade has seen more and more attention focused on school-based services and the development of curricula specific to children on the autism spectrum. Also, as with other areas, research has sometimes not kept pace with the materials being produced. Similarly, the literature showing the effectiveness of treatments is somewhat less advanced than the production of teaching materials. As a result, any review of materials will necessarily be selective. In this section, we review some of the materials available. It is important for parents and teachers to keep in mind that more of these materials are appearing all the time. Whenever possible, we'll highlight evidence on effectiveness of the various treatments. Unfortunately, often, even when studies are available, they may be limited in important ways. For example, frequently researchers have tracked only a small number of children and have not addressed how their techniques might be applied by others and for whom they do and do not work. There is an increasing movement toward evidence-based treatments in education—as there now has been for a while in medicine—and we hope that, over the next decade, a more substantial research base for these treatments will emerge. Table 6.1 lists some of the available materials and curricula for students with autism.

An effective curriculum will be individualized and include observable goals and objectives (and realistic consent) within the context of a longer-term vision for the student. It cannot be overemphasized that the curriculum should

| TABLE 6.1 | SOURCES OF INFORMATION AND CURRICULA FOR STUDENTS WITH AUTISM |

Source—Publisher/Address/Web Site	Materials Produced
Academic Communication Associates, Inc. P.O. Box 4279 Oceanside, CA 92052-4279 www.acadcom.com	A range of speech, language, and special education products: books and software in several languages; information on augmentative communication
Autism Society of North Carolina Bookstore (source for many autism publications) 505 Oberlin Road, Suite 230, Raleigh, NC 27605-1345 www.autismsociety-nc.org	Wide range of materials available include information on Treatment and Education of Autistic and Related Communication-Handicapped Children (TEACCH) program
Brookes Publishing P.O. Box 10624 Baltimore, MD 21285-0624 www.brookespublishing.com	Excellent set of books on autism for teachers, psychologists, speech pathologists, physicians, and parents; books on pivotal response, SCERTS model
Future Horizons, Inc. 21 West Abram Street Arlington, TX 76013 www.fhautism.com	Books and materials and links for conferences; resources for parents and teachers and children's books
Jessica Kingsley Publishers 116 Pentonville Road London, N1 9JB. UK www.jkp.com	Wide range of books and other materials relevant to autism and ASD; books on social skills, eating problems; materials for parents and teachers
LinguiSystems 3100 Fourth Avenue East Moline, IL 61244 www.linguisystems.com	Range of materials particularly helpful to educators for teaching social and communication skills
ProEd 8700 Shoal Creek Boulevard Austin, TX 78757-6897 www.proedinc.com	Tests, teaching activities, and materials on a wide range of problems, including many products focused on autism, ASD
Sopris West 4093 Specialty Place Longmont, CO 80504-5400 www.sopriswest.com	Materials on behavioral assessment, social skills, and other materials

(Continued)

TABLE 6.1 CONTINUED	

Source—Publisher/Address/ Web Site	Materials Produced
Special Needs Project 324 State Street, Suite H Santa Barbara, CA 93101 www.specialneeds.com	Bookstore devoted to materials (books, videos, DVDs, and other materials) for educators, parents, and others; very large collection of books on autism spectrum disorders
Woodbine House 6510 Bells Mill Road Bethesda, MD 20817 www.woodbinehouse.com	Books and some materials with a focus on children with special needs for parents and teachers; excellent set of books on autism

SOURCE: Adapted, with permission, from Olley, J. G. (2005). Curriculum and classroom structure, In F. R. Volkmar, R. Paul, A. Klin, & D. Cohen (Eds.), *Handbook of autism and pervasive developmental disorders* (3rd ed., vol. 2, Table 33.1, p. 864). Hoboken, NJ: Wiley.

fit the child and not vice versa. As discussed earlier, the curriculum also is just one part of the academic content of the program. Careful attention must be paid to the learning environment and other factors that affect the child's ability to learn within his or her program. For example, the use of simple organization aides, such as visual schedules or use of functional routines and activity schedules, can enhance learning by helping with transitions, providing a structure for learning, and decreasing problem behaviors. We talk more about curriculum in Chapter 8.

The curriculum for students who are fully included requires special planning. This typically entails a well-done individualized educational plan (IEP) with critical support from teachers and aides. Interestingly, sometimes the commitment to full inclusion can present significant obstacles for the child with autism or ASD; for example, it may require the child to learn some activities in the community, but this will remove the child from the traditional classroom settings and time learning with peers.

Many children on the autism spectrum exhibit an area of strength in reading, which is sometimes isolated. They often seem to have an interest in visual images, which frequently starts with an interest in things like signs or hood ornaments on cars, but often extends into letters and numbers. It is not uncommon for very young children with autism to be fascinated by the letters or numbers on building blocks but ignore their use as building materials. As discussed later in the chapter, it is sometimes possible to use the child's relative interest in visual materials in other ways, for example, to help with organization. However, this early interest often leads to an interest in written words and frequently to early reading abilities. The term *hyperlexia* has sometimes been used to describe this phenomenon. Hyperlexia is the isolated ability to read single words with greater proficiency than one would otherwise expect given the child's age or other areas of difficulties.[1] Some children with autism or other ASD (e.g., those with Asperger's) can become effective early readers. Sometimes, however, reading to "decode" (to say the word out loud) may greatly exceed the child's ability to understand. For example, the child might be able to read a phrase of instruction on a card but *not* be able to then carry out the instruction. Some children are able to read better than they can actually talk, making their reading ability even more isolated. For students who have some understanding of what they read, use of written materials can be very helpful as part of the intervention program. Good tests of reading ability are available and it is important to make sure that good reading includes understanding as well as decoding before making this a major part of the child's program.

We are not totally sure why reading so frequently emerges as a skill area in children with ASDs. It may very much relate to the nature of visual images (static, invariant) as opposed to the much faster pace and higher memory requirements related to spoken language. It may be a manifestation of some of the ways the brain is organized differently in individuals with ASD. Occasionally, students with Asperger's, who often have greater strengths in the auditory areas, will show a similar phenomenon. For instance, one preschooler we know was home for a week with chickenpox and watched a Spanish-language channel the entire time and became reasonably fluent in Spanish.

SOCIAL SKILLS INTERVENTIONS

Kanner's original description of autism highlighted social difficulties as one of the essential elements of the autistic syndrome. As we mentioned in Chapters 1 and 2, these difficulties continue to be of central importance for a diagnosis of ASD, and research has clarified some aspects of why social difficulties are so central to autism. Along with increased research on the basis of social problems, there has been a noteworthy interest in therapeutic interventions for social difficulties. In some sense, of course, social skills intervention has always been a target for intervention. Some of the earliest behavioral intervention studies in autism emphasized the importance of child engagement and "learning-to-learn" skills, which included important aspects of engaging with teachers and other adults. Similarly, the many programs designed to stimulate language and communication skills are intrinsically also concerned with social engagement. Or, put another way, the whole point of being able to communicate is to communicate with someone. Over the past 10 years or so, there have been more and more

---

[1]Note that hyperlexia is seen in conditions other than autism as well.

reports of programs/curricula specifically designed to enhance social skills in autism.

It is important to realize that although we, and others, often talk about social and communication skills separately they are actually fundamentally inter-related and are important for other areas of development as well. Indeed, for typical children past about age 3, language becomes the primary (but not the only) means for social interchange. Having better social (and social-communicative) skills is essential for students on the autism spectrum to achieve higher levels of peer acceptance and integration into the community. As we discuss in Chapter 9, one of the unfortunate problems for more cognitively able individuals in adolescence can be an awareness of social differences from peers. This awareness and the social isolation sometimes seen can be associated with depression and mood problems. In this section, we review some of the current approaches to teaching social skills.

Essentially, three different approaches are used: adult-led approaches (teacher or clinician instruction/therapy), peer-based approaches, and combination approaches (e.g., social skills groups with peers and an adult or adults present). The peer-based approaches have, by far, the strongest base in the research literature and tend to revolve around integration of preschoolers and young school-aged children in mainstream educational settings. Often, approaches are combined.

Preschool Social Skills Interventions

We know from studies of typically developing children that there is a tremendous growth in social–communication abilities between ages 3 and 5. For the typical child of 3, language is used for play, for engaging in pretend, and in resolving conflicts with other children. Even for children on the autism spectrum (e.g., those with Asperger's) who develop early language and have good vocabulary, the *social* use of language often presents a problem that is usually seen in the child's play. For example, the child with an ASD may not be able to engage in cooperative or dramatic play without considerable support—the fast pace, the movement of roles back and forth, the use of imagination, and the heavy emphasis on social communication make for difficulties. This social deficit is often a problem for the preschool child with ASD, as most preschool programs have a strong basis in play. This may lead children with ASDs enrolled in such programs to be isolated or to approach peers in one-sided and very eccentric ways. In contrast to the usual programs for children with autism, which are highly structured and adult organized with considerable use of routine and predictability, those for typical preschoolers are usually just the opposite.

Accordingly, some modifications must be made for the child with an ASD to effectively participate in mainstream programs. This can be done in several ways. One approach is to focus on adult coaching/instruction of the child with ASD, and another is to engage peers in helping the child with an ASD. Of all the various social skills interventions, probably the most extensive and well-conducted research has focused on peer-based interventions in the preschool age group. A large body of work, from a number of different centers, has shown that when appropriate supports are provided, preschoolers with autism can be significantly helped. We discussed some of this in Chapter 5 when we talked about mainstreaming issues.

Much of the early work in this area focused on adult-mediated interventions, for example, through use of applied behavior analysis (ABA)/reinforcement procedures to develop and encourage play skills. This could take the form of encouraging attention to peers, minimizing reinforcement of initiations to adults, and by using prompts and coaching from a teacher. Focusing just on the child with ASD does carry a risk, however, in that it ignores the other half of the play relationship. Indeed, some work suggests that at baseline perhaps only 50% of the bids for interaction from the child with autism get a response from the typical peer. Accordingly, adding a peer-training component may substantially increase such behaviors. As one can imagine, the training of the typical peer has to be kept simple to be effective. Various methods have been used, including development of teacher scripts and roles for play with initial teacher involvement, which is gradually reduced. Other approaches focus on specific play skills and issues, for example, responding to peers, expanding play themes, building on play themes, and so forth. Sometimes scripts are used but then "faded" over time. Several good guides to these approaches are available (and listed in the reading list). These programs are most effective if the teacher is able to plan the materials, activities, and settings with the needs of the child in mind. Activities that have a natural ending may be good, and initially the focus may be on activities that minimize the need to wait or share to give the child on the autism spectrum a chance to learn through observation without becoming involved in a fight over materials!

Approaches where adults are heavily involved may not work out because the child may become very dependent on the adult's presence. Teachers may feel reluctant to be so involved, and even if they are willing to do so, they need training to be effective. More recently, the focus of work in preschoolers has shifted to approaches in which peers are the primary agents of change. Originally, the hope was that simply exposing the child with autism to typical peers would be sufficient. It quickly became apparent that gains made, if any, by mere exposure tended to be small. Strain and colleagues have produced an impressive body of research on peer-mediated social skills teaching. In this approach, the typical peers become "play organizers" and are taught what to do by adults before they work with other children. This approach has been particularly interesting since the results seem to generalize both across setting and to classmates with ASDs. The children who serve as organizers work by sharing, helping, giving affection, and praising. Peers are taught these skills in role-playing activities with adults and then are cued and are more readily maintained without adult involvement. These approaches have, however, been more difficult to implement in regular school settings. Accordingly, a different approach to peer-mediated teaching has attempted to streamline and simplify procedures, for example, the Goldstein "stay, play, talk" with your buddy approach in which typical peers are trained for relatively short periods of the school day to do just what is implied—staying, playing, and talking with their assigned partner. Research using this and similar techniques suggests considerable promise.

It is sometimes hard for parents, and occasionally even teachers, to understand the importance of play in early child development. For the typically developing infant and toddler, play skills develop with no formal instruction and have a usual sequence going from object manipulation (banging a rattle to make a noise), to functional use of objects (rolling a small car), to pretend and imagination (taking the car on a pretend trip to the zoo). Play skills have their roots in social development as well as in communication and also help develop cognitive and symbolic skills. For children on the autism spectrum, these skills must be taught.

Some of the models of intervention we discussed in Chapter 5 strongly emphasize teaching play skills, and the availability of typical peers offers many opportunities for developing play. Methods for teaching include peer modeling, teaching basic aspects of play through reinforcement and discrete trial, developing play through pivotal response, and so forth. Some uses of the pivotal response approach are summarized in Table 6.2. Some approaches have used preteaching or "priming" as a way for the child to practice with materials or with an adult before moving the venue to child–peer interaction. Many of the individual treatments provided (e.g., speech or occupational therapy) will adopt a play-based approach, with the added advantage of teaching specific skills relevant to play. Symbolic–imaginative play is, as one might expect, the most challenging for children with autism—it is fast paced, requires sophisticated language and symbolic skills, is highly social, and requires multitasking and a tolerance for novelty. Various approaches can be used to help develop these more sophisticated play skills. These approaches include explicit teaching, video modeling, visual supports, and scripting. These approaches can also be used in school-aged children.

TABLE 6.2	USES OF PIVOTAL RESPONSE TRAINING

Pivotal Behavior	Rationale	Methods	Examples
Responding to multiple cues	To reduce stimulus over selectivity	*Within stimulus prompting:* Exaggerating the relevant components of a stimulus, then gradually fading these exaggerations *Conditional discriminations:* Requires the child to discriminate on the basis of more than one feature	When teaching the sign for "more," the sign is first demonstrated with large, sweeping arm motions and exaggerated closing of the hands, which are gradually faded. When teaching colors, the child is asked to get a blue sock and is presented with a blue sock, a white sock, and a blue shirt, so that s/he must consider both the color and the item name in making a choice.
Increasing motivation	To increase responsiveness to social environment and enhance spontaneity and generalization	*Child choice:* Allow child to select preferred materials, topics, toys, and activities within teaching situations *Natural reinforcers:* Rewards that are directly and functionally related to the task, so emitting target response naturally leads to obtaining reward *Interspersing maintenance trials:* Provides practice of previously learned activities often to give a child a sense of success and positive affect *Reinforcing attempts:* Uses shaping to reward any goal-directed behavior, even if it is not the direct target	When teaching colors, child is allowed to choose colored candies. When teaching "cup," the child is given a cup with juice in it after s/he names the object. Teaching a new skill is preceded by several trials of a well-learned skill that has a high probability of being performed correctly. When teaching a pointing gesture as a request, a fist point is rewarded if it clearly indicates communication, then is shaped by gradually increasing requirement for index finger isolation.

(Continued)

TABLE 6.2   CONTINUED

Pivotal Behavior	Rationale	Methods	Examples
Increasing self-regulation	Allows more active involvement in the intervention process; improves independence; provides more opportunities for social interaction without direct supervision	*Target behaviors are operationally defined:* Child has clear idea of what to monitor. *Reinforcers are identified:* Rewarding consequences are identified. *Self-monitoring device is selected and trained:* A simple method of tracking child's own behavior is provided. *Use of self-monitoring is validated.*	Through repeated modeling, child is taught to touch a teacher's arm whenever peer moves too close to him for comfort. Child is rewarded for alerting teacher, rather than pushing a peer, by being allowed to play a favorite music box. Child gets a star and puts it on his hand each time he alerts teacher rather than pushing peer. Teacher checks child's hand after free-play period and provides praise for the number of stars he earned.
Increasing initiation of communication	Increase opportunities for spontaneous social learning and increased social competence	*Motivation to communicate is provided.* *Prompt/fade and shaping techniques are used to increase initiations.*	Preferred objects are placed in an opaque bag. Child is prompted to ask, "What's that?" Child is allowed to play with toy after asking question. Prompts are gradually faded.

SOURCE: Reprinted with permission from Paul, R., & Sutherland, D. (2005). Enhancing early language in children with autism spectrum disorders. In F. R. Volkmar, R. Paul, A. Klin, & D. Cohen (Eds.), *Handbook of autism and pervasive developmental disorders: Assessment interventions and policy,* (3rd ed., vol. 2, pp. 954). Hoboken, NJ: Wiley. This was adapted from Koegel, L. K., Koegel, R. L., Harrower, J., & Cater, C. A. (1999). Pivotal Response Intervention. *Journal of the Association for Persons with Severe Handicaps, 24,* (3) 174–186.

School-Aged Child Social Skills Interventions

For the typically developing child, the shift from preschool to elementary school entails a shift in peer interaction away from play to interaction focused on specific interests or activities (e.g., games with rules). More intense friendships also typically develop at this time, and the child with ASD may become aware of feeling isolated. As a result of these differences, social skills interventions in this age group tend to more frequently involve adults (i.e., with one-on-one instruction) or hybrid methods (social skills group in which an adult and other children are present).

Adult-based approaches range from more focused ABA activities for more cognitively or socially impaired students to more naturalistic ones. For example, several studies have used a time-delay approach (waiting for a specified period of time), rather than immediately responding to increased verbal responses from the child during play. A somewhat different approach has focused on child-centered interventions, such as imitating the child. Teaching of social skills may go on in individual sessions with the speech pathologist, work then done with the teacher and parents to help generalize skills. Behavioral techniques can be used to increase both the quantity and quality of social interactions.

Visual supports can be used to facilitate other aspects of social interaction in school-aged as well as younger children. These visual supports range from picture sequences to written rules to development of stories and narratives; as always, these supports should be appropriate to the individual's levels of communicative and cognitive ability. These supports can be used to facilitate generalization of skills to anticipate problem situations such as transitions and novel situations and anticipating change. Monitoring and observation can also be encouraged. These various strategies can be used to increase social skills and enhance social awareness and perspective taking. They can be combined with behavioral techniques and can also be used to help children become better observers of social interaction and its rules.

Often, children with ASDs are interested in another form of visual material: videos. Video modeling methods can be used to teach specific skills. Materials used might include specially produced films/film clips, videos made of the child interacting with a typical peer, or even more traditional movies and cartoons. The child can be helped to spot inappropriate as well as appropriate social behaviors. With the appropriate permissions from parents, the speech pathologist or psychologist might videotape a peer group discussion or social skills session and then use parts of it in individual work with the child, discussing what went wrong or what went well. The interest that many children on the autism spectrum have in watching videos is an advantage for these approaches.

There are two other frequently used strategies for teaching social skills. One approach focuses on the creation of joint narratives or stories. This is the format of Social Stories, which teaches new strategies for solving problems and producing more socially acceptable solutions. This approach, originated by Carol Gray and her colleagues (2004), aims to increase social awareness through use of an explicit, visual teaching approach that can enhance both social and communication skills. An explicit focus on the perspective of the person is adopted; this focus is important and central to maintaining productive social interaction.

Simple visual materials and strategies such as pictures, text, and cartoons are used, along with color-coding cues. There is an emphasis on the social context and thus on what is appropriate, with a focus on what issues in the situation are most important. Appropriate responses are explicitly discussed, as well as possible responses of the social partner and his or her perspective. Explicit teaching is provided on why certain responses/behaviors yield positive outcomes. This approach has the advantage of making complex social interactions more explicit and teachable. So, for example, if a student is about to do something new, like attending a first dance, development of a story could be used in advance as a chance to both teach and rehearse socially appropriate responses and initiations. A great advantage of this approach, particularly for more able students, is the explicit focus on positive rather than negative behaviors, that is, a focus on helping the individual acquire tools that will help him or her adapt to potentially very problematic situations. Furthermore, these interventions can be designed specifically for the situations at hand.

A related method, also from Carol Gray (1994), is called Comic Strip Conversations. This approach has the great advantage of teaching some important social distinctions (e.g., what is literally said versus what is thought). By producing a simple comic strip narrative, the child is helped to use a series of standard "thought" and "word" bubbles in producing a visual depiction, frame by frame, of a social interaction. Figure 6.1 shows these conversation symbols, which can be used to great advantage with little required other than rudimentary drawing ability. Variations of this technique can include things like use of color to indicate emotions. These methods can be used successfully in school and generalized to home and other environments. There is some research on these methods, although not as much as on the peer interventions we described for preschoolers.

Relationship Development Intervention (RDI) is a somewhat different approach to social skills teaching developed by Steven Gutstein and his colleague Rachelle K. Sheely (2001, 2002). This approach can be used for students of all ages. It uses a developmental approach to increase motivation for social interaction and the ability to be more effective in interacting with others. This method is family based (rather than school based), with parents receiving training along with individualized assessment and intervention. This method is available only through consultants trained in the method. There is some supporting research, although it is minimal at present.

Social skills groups are one of the most frequent methods for teaching social skills particularly in the elementary and middle school years. These groups can be limited to children with difficulties or can include typical peers—the latter becoming valuable role models. Groups can be time limited or ongoing. These can be conducted within school settings, by the speech pathologist and psychologist, for example, or can be done independently from school. In these "hybrid"

Conversation Symbols Dictionary

FIGURE 6.1   **Conversation Symbols**

Courtesy of Carol Gray – Comic Strip Conversations, 1994, Arlington, TX: Future Horizons. Reprinted with permission.

methods, one or more adult leaders work with the group, which can take advantage both of peer-based and adult-based learning approaches. The group will often have its own set of rules and a relatively standard format for sessions. Depending on the ages of the individuals in the group, the length may be longer or shorter and the group may include some time for a game or snack. One of the other advantages of the group format is that some activities or issues for discussion can be planned by the adult leader(s), but usually some of the topics for discussion will arise from the group itself. The adult(s) monitor the ongoing group activity, intervening as appropriate, but with the goal, as much as possible, of having group members provide helpful feedback. Sometimes a parallel group is held for parents, and depending on how the group is set up, teachers might be included as well. Topics in the group can include social problem solving (with problem description and discussion, role playing, and group discussion of similar experiences) as well as teaching about conversations and providing encouragement from group members to try new skills or approaches outside the group. Depending on the needs of the group, other areas may be targeted, for example, dealing with anger and difficult emotions or coping with novelty, encouraging independent living abilities, and so forth. A number of excellent resources for social skills groups and social skills training are available including books by Baker (2003) and McAfee (2002). Issues specific to children with Asperger's disorder have also been discussed (e.g., Myles and Southwick, 2005). In this population, explicit verbal teaching of social rules, role playing, and explicit teaching of play skills can be helpful. Much more research is needed on these groups, and modification can and should be made depending on age and ability levels of those involved.

Parents looking for social skills groups outside the school setting should talk with other parents to learn about their experiences and to obtain names of experienced group leaders. It is important to realize that social skills groups are conducted by individuals with a range of training (there is no formal certification program). Groups are frequently conducted by psychologists, social workers, speech pathologists, and others. Parents can also use many of the excellent books developed for social skills teaching.

The Circle of Friends program is focused on helping children who have trouble making friends (see Perske, 1988). In this approach, the child helps develop a social "map" showing social contacts, and these are then arranged in a series of concentric circles, with those individuals closest to the child—usually siblings and parents—closest to the center of the circle, while a middle circle will usually include some important adults, and the outer circle peers who are friends, with another ring drawn for a best friend. The system is then discussed in the classroom, starting with some volunteers who explain how it works. Children who are more isolated have a chance to do their maps. Other children are asked to volunteer to be on the child's circle. These classmates then can act as special mentors and receive some additional support. Teachers/adults need some training, but the whole classroom can benefit from this activity (see also Schlieder, 2007; and Keating-Velasco, 2007).

Dunn's Social Skills in Our Schools (the SOS. program) (2005) uses both peer- and adult-based teaching approaches for verbal children on the autism spectrum. This program includes a staff-training component and ongoing consultation, along with a combination of small group sessions, peer mentoring, and parent training.

Adult-based teaching clearly has an important role in the classroom. Use of regular routines; careful attention to the structure of the class and the physical environment; and coordination with the school psychologist, speech patholo-gist, and family members can all provide a highly supportive environment for students on the autism spectrum. Within this environment, they can be helped to generalize skills learned into the classroom settings and obtain sensible feed-back from a supportive adult. It is essential that teachers recognize that social functioning is an area in which students with ASD specifically need support. One of the functions that diagnostic assessment and testing can sometimes per-form is to concretize for teachers how significant social problems are for specific students (we give some examples of this in the next several chapters). Explicit teaching can also be conducted to improve social skills, such as using the concept mastery approach (Heflin & Alaimo, 2007). There are a number of resources that can help teachers thinking about teaching social skills (Baker, 2001; McAfee, 2002).

Adolescent and Adult Social Interventions

Unfortunately, there is little research on adolescent and adult social skills inter-ventions, although more resources are appearing. Many of the methods previ-ously described can be used, particularly for individuals who are less verbal. Sadly, by this age, typical peers have dramatically moved ahead in their social experience, and peer-based methods are not as simple to use given this disparity. However, adult-based approaches can be quite effective particularly for helping the individual learn specific skills/tasks. Because language becomes the primary means for social interaction in these age groups, careful attention also must be paid to this part of social interaction, that is, attending to the social "rules" of language (what can and can't be discussed). Humor, jokes, irony, and sarcasm may be difficult for the adolescent with ASD to understand. Even tone of voice or voice volume can be problematic. Fortunately, there are some saving graces in that, for many adolescents, interaction can now revolve around texting or the Internet—media that are intrinsically less challenging given that social demands are (to some extent) minimized.

Interventions for adolescents and adults have typically included a major focus on developing conversational skills; for example, in taking a turn, the person has to reflect on and build upon something the conversational partner just said. Some methods have used explicit scripts that can then be faded. Other approaches have focused on relevant conversational skills, such as periodically making eye contact. Given their problems in generating comprehensive narratives, helping students with ASDs build a focus on all relevant aspects of the situation is helpful. This can be done by using the metaphor of a reporter or detective who asks all the relevant "wh" questions (*who, what, where, when,* and *why*).

Another important area for intervention has to do with organization and self-management. For the more verbal individual with an ASD, particularly those with Asperger's, "self-talk" may be used to help the person develop and implement specific protocols or rules for problem situations. Using self-talk, the student might, for example, recite to himself a set of rehearsed strategies. Such verbally mediated strategies can then be generalized to other settings.

Social skills groups and peers can be used with adolescents and adults. Peers can be helped to foster social skills in regular meetings as well as, sometimes, outside the group session; outside contact is most likely in groups going on within schools. Again, some degree of preparation is important. Even for more able individuals, use of explicit (written) rules or visual prompts may be helpful. Attention should be paid to generalization and maintenance of skills learned, through reinforcement techniques such as "homework." Role playing can be effectively used to help teach social perception and the ability to "read" the social cues of peers. Training in the rules of social interaction and conversation as well as attention to the (many) topics off limits from usual discussions can be helpful. As with most other skills in life, practice, practice, practice is essential. Role playing can be used to practice interactions in a relatively safe situation, either in individual work with a student or even in groups. Role playing can also be particularly effective in groups by providing consensus feedback ("Dude, you really got to look at the guy interviewing you—at least once!") and may validate and reinforce observations made in individual work.

In their book *The Hidden Curriculum*, Brenda Smith Myles and her colleagues Melissa Trautman and Ronda Schelvan give an overview and discussion of some common social situations and ways that more able individuals on the autism spectrum can be helped to deal with them. They emphasize the importance of observation and listening (as opposed to just talking—a significant problem for people with Asperger's) as well as asking questions and learning. This explicit approach also involves awareness of options, choices, and potential consequences. They also emphasize construction of social narratives, with an emphasis on relating social issues more broadly to include generalization. They also talk about use of visual strategies like the Power Card (Gagnon, 2001).

Adreon and Myles (2001) also described the social autopsy approach. In this approach originally used by Richard Lavoie, a specialist in learning disabilities, social mistakes are analyzed, with an emphasis on finding positive solutions for the future. For more able individuals, explicit instruction can be used. This can take the form of a very focused psychotherapy or counseling approach, emphasizing specific problem solving and development of explicit strategies for dealing with problem situations. Approaches from the body of work on cognitive behavioral therapy can also readily be adapted for older individuals on the autism spectrum, such as practicing relaxation in stressful situations or understanding the origins of anxiety when exposed to novelty or situations where there is conflict. For more able, older individuals, the emphasis has to be on "explicit, explicit, explicit" problem solving with discussion, in advance, of problem situations and with opportunities for homework, role playing, and positive practice. Books by McAfee (2002), Patrick, (2008), and Baker (2001) provide helpful strategies which can work for older individuals. We talk more about social skills in subsequent chapters.

LANGUAGE AND COMMUNICATION PROGRAMS

For the typically developing child, the onset of language proceeds seamlessly during the first months of life. At birth, typically developing babies will orient to the faces and sounds of their parents. By 6 months, they vocalize with good intonation (the musical aspect of speech), are beginning to respond to voices even without a visual cue, are starting to detect feelings conveyed by the voice, and are beginning to respond to their own name. By a year of age, a truly tremendous amount of development has occurred in terms of language development, even before the child says his or her first word. Between the first and second year of life, an explosion of language ability typically occurs, with infants able to begin to think more symbolically. This also is the time when children develop what is called *object permanence*, so that things that go out of sight don't go out of mind. By the second birthday, the child will often have several hundred words. The situation in autism and related disorders is, in general, a very different one. We have come to recognize that difficulties in language and communication are a core challenge for individuals on the autism spectrum and that these are important target areas for **early intervention**, given their importance for long-term outcome.

As discussed earlier in this book, early warning signs of difficulty in autism include a lack of interest in speech and failure to attend to one's own name or engage in joint attention, with limited vocalization and requesting. These problems also highlight how much early social development is intertwined with early communication and language development. For example, in contrast to children whose main problem is language (but who have reasonably good social skills), young children on the autism spectrum are less likely to use nonverbal means to communicate. In this section, we consider the language/communication needs of younger children on the spectrum and the use of augmentative communication strategies before moving to consideration of the needs of older and more able individuals. There are a number of challenges for enhancing social communication that must be addressed depending on the age and level of ability of the individual. These are summarized in Table 6.3.

In developing the communication program, it is important to keep several things in mind. In the first place, the child's particular characteristics should be considered: age, levels of ability, particular learning style. It is also important to recognize that, as much as possible, learning should not be limited to just one setting or person. A range of activities and situations should be used, including individual to small and large group. Using typically developing peers should be

---

TABLE 6.3   CHALLENGES FOR ENHANCING SOCIAL COMMUNICATION ABILITIES AT VARIOUS DEVELOPMENTAL LEVELS

A.   Prelinguistic level
1.   Establishing communicative intentionality
2.   Uneven developmental profiles (developmental discontinuities)
3.   Problem behavior and communication limitations
4.   Establishing nonspeech communication alternatives (gestures, picture communication, sign language)
5.   Establishing joint attention and reciprocal action

B.   Emerging and early language levels
1.   The shift from presymbolic communication to language may be slow
2.   Unconventional verbal behavior may be produced for communicative as well as noncommunicative purposes
3.   Generalization of early creative language and gestalt forms may be slow
4.   Early language forms are typically used for a limited range of communicative functions or purposes. Although language may be used in a symbolic or quasi-symbolic manner, there is limited flexibility in the use of language forms
6.   Early language use is greatly influenced by socioemotional factors, such as emotional regulation, and situational variables such as familiarity with activities
7.   There may be considerable difficulties comprehending communicative partners' language and nonverbal signals

C.   Challenges and issues at more advanced language levels
1.   Language comprehension and social–cognitive limitations experienced by persons with ASD adversely affect conversational ability (e.g., perspective taking abilities)
2.   Verbal and nonverbal conventions of discourse, such as conventions for initiating, maintaining, and terminating conversations may be violated affecting the success of communicative exchanges
3.   Learned verbal "scripts" may be applied too rigidly, with few, if any adjustments for different communicative or situational contexts
4.   Ability to recognize and repair communication breakdowns may be limited
5.   Unconventional verbal forms and idiosyncratic language used with clear intent may be difficult to "read," especially for unfamiliar partners
6.   Language use in more socially complex and less familiar social situations may be especially challenging.

SOURCE: Adapted and reprinted, with permission, from Prizant, B., & Wetherby, A. (2005). Critical issues in enhancing communication abilities for persons with autism spectrum disorders. In F. Volkmar, A. Klin, R. Paul, and D. Cohen (Eds.), *Handbook of autism and pervasive developmental disorders* (3rd ed., p. 927). Hoboken, NJ: Wiley.

considered. In setting goals and developing a program, it is important to be explicit about several things:

- What methods are used?
- How will progress be measured?
- How are family members to be involved?
- What materials and strategies can be used?
- Will visual strategies be incorporated? How will natural teaching contexts be used? What are the short-, medium-, and long-term goals for the child?

See Prizant and Wetherby (2005) and Paul and Sutherland (2005) for more detailed discussion of these issues.

Approaches to Intervention

There are several different approaches to language interventions. Some are more didactic, teacher-directed methods that are based in learning theory. Other approaches are more naturalistic, using similar principles but in more natural settings, often trying to incorporate the child's natural motivations. Another set of approaches is sometimes called developmental or pragmatic; here, the emphasis is on using a range of materials, an awareness of normal progressions of skills, and a systematic evaluation of what works. Some methods are more heavily teacher directed; others try to maximize naturalistic approaches with attention to child interest/motivation.

It is important to realize that the ability to communicate also is very closely related to behavior. Imagine what would happen if you suddenly had no way of communicating—it would be very frustrating. Similar problems arise when children on the autism spectrum have either limited or very unusual (and sometimes very idiosyncratic) ways of communicating. Accordingly, it is important to recognize that what appear to be behavioral challenges or issues may serve, at least to some degree, important communicative functions. That is, what might seem to be, and is, a very problematic behavior may be one of the few ways the child has for expressing frustration. Communication issues also can arise, somewhat paradoxically, in older and more able children and adults. The person with Asperger's may talk on and on but have real trouble having a genuine conversation with a back-and-forth information exchange. Accordingly, a focus on communication should always be a major part of the program for any individual with an autism spectrum diagnosis. In the following sections, we first consider the communication needs of younger children and then move to consider intervention needs for somewhat older students. Keep in mind that this is a somewhat artificial distinction and that, as always, it is the individual child who needs a program appropriate to his or her needs.

Communication Needs of Young Children with ASD

Behavioral Approaches   An entire body of work has centered on the use of Discrete Trial Instruction (DTI) to help younger children be more attentive to language and start to use language on their own. These techniques include prompts and shaping as well as reinforcement to encourage desired behaviors. This work was pioneered by Lovaas in his work on intensive behavioral treatments (see Chapter 5). In addition to discrete trial instruction, other ABA-based methods can be used. These typically will include a study to reveal what happened before the child exhibited an undesired behavior and a planned series of desired behaviors. These goals are broken down into small steps and then systematically taught, with "chaining" used to gradually build the entire desired response. For example, the goal might be to say a word, and the beginning of the process would be to focus on having the child imitate the beginning of the word. This process is also occasionally reversed (e.g., you might teach the last step in a sequence and then move backward, as it were, to produce the desired response). An important aspect of the ABA approach is the careful attention to what motivates the child; this knowledge is then used in providing rewards for the child during teaching. There is ample evidence that approaches based on these methods can be used in teaching the early forms of communication, including increased responses to language and simple word use with gradually increasing complexity. One of the criticisms of this approach is that the child has a somewhat passive role rather than the much more active role in typical learning. Generalization is another complexity; that is, you have to teach with a view toward helping the child "get" the concept at hand. Put another way, getting the child to say *dog* to his or her own dog is wonderful, but the next step is teaching "dogness," so that pictures of a range of dogs, stuffed animal dogs, and/or plastic toy dogs all are seen as dogs in the overall conceptual sense.

Functional communication training has been used, with good results, to teach communication responses. This training gives the child some alternatives to resorting to maladaptive behaviors. This approach has the great advantage of not only helping deal with the problem behavior but also giving the child an idea of the potential communication has for making her more effective in getting what she wants. In this approach, the first step is a functional analysis to try to understand the function of the behavior, whether it be escape, attention seeking, protest, or something else. Then effective communication alternatives are introduced. In one study, Durand and Carr (1987) were able to teach the phrase "help me" to a boy who engaged in many escape behaviors. This approach can be combined with other behavioral methods to teach a range of other communication and social skills (e.g., pointing to request things). For children in whom oral speech is a major issue, teaching a few effective manual signs can be an alternative and can be very helpful.

The Verbal Behavior Approach was developed by Sundberg and Partington (1995) and promoted by Vincent Carbone (www.drcarbone.net) and others (see Barbera & Rasmussen, 2007). This method takes a very behavioral approach to fostering language learning, with a carefully arranged sequence of goals and skills designed to enhance language in children who can use symbols and help them develop more sophisticated language. This approach combines a range of effective behavioral methods and discrete trial teaching both in more natural settings as well as more intensive teaching sessions. Goals include imitation of verbal behavior, production of verbal behaviors that have an immediate effect (called *mands*), use of labels, responding to frequently used words, and increasing language responses to others. This approach also can be adapted to children's alternative communication forms, such as nonverbal responses or augmentative communication approaches.

Some of the concerns about the somewhat artificial nature of language learning in some of the early behavioral programs led to approaches thought to be more in keeping with natural language learning. These naturalistic approaches focus on materials and objects that are of interest to the child and then use learning principles to increase language production around these. These methods can be used to target both beginning expressive language and more complex social–pragmatic language skills. Some of these approaches blend behavioral techniques and more natural settings. Examples of these approaches appearing in the reading list include the work of Koegel, O'Dell, and Koegel (1987); Laski, Charlop, and Schreibman (1988); Charlop and Trasowech (1991); and McGee, Krantz, Mason, and McClannahan (1983).

The milieu approach to teaching embeds language teaching very firmly within natural environments so that, for example, the teaching may go on throughout the day in the classroom as opposed to a daily 30-minutes "pull-out" session with the speech pathologist. Prompts and cues are used to follow up when the child initiates an activity, and care is given to the arrangement of the environment so that there are materials and activities that will likely get the child's interest. A variation of this approach (called the *minimal speech approach*, developed by Potter and Whittaker, 2001) has the adults reduce the complexity of their language to one or two words, and pause to allow the child time to respond. One important feature of this variation is the focus on making the child less adult responsive and more independent. The Natural Language Paradigm (NLP) approach (Koegel, Koegel, & Carter, 1998) uses a range of interesting materials and language models with reinforcement for communication and the chance to be engaged with the interesting and motivating play materials. In this approach, there is constant reinforcement throughout the day for verbal communication and communicative attempts. Pivotal response methods (Koegel, Carter, & Koegel, 2003) have also been used to develop specific, highly relevant behaviors, such as increasing motivation and the initiation of communication. Table 6.4 gives examples of some of the milieu teaching approaches.

A somewhat different approach was originally developed in adults and then extended to children. This system, called Prompts for Restructuring Oral Muscular Phonetic Targets (PROMT) is based on the idea that motor difficulties in producing sounds are a major problem. The program focuses on using stimulation of the mouth and sound structures to produce better speech.

TABLE 6.4   EXAMPLES OF MILIEU TEACHING METHODS

Method	Source	Example Activity
Prompt-free	Mirenda & Santogrossi (1985)	Several pictures of toys or snacks are placed within a child's reach. When the child touches one of the pictures (whether clearly intentionally or not), the child is given the object pictured. This continues until the child uses the pictures intentionally and spontaneously to request desired objects.
Mand-Model approach	Rogers-Warren & Warren (1980)	Objects the child likes are placed in sight but out of reach around the classroom. The teacher observes the child and when interest in some object, even fleeting interest is noted, the teacher "mands" (requests) an utterance from the child with a stimulus such as "What's that?" If the child responds with the target word or gesture, he receives the toy to play with for a short time. It is later replaced so it can tempt him again.
Incidental Teaching	Hart & Risley (1975)	Objects the child likes are placed in sight but out of reach around the classroom. The teacher waits for the child to indicate interest in an object by looking at it or pulling her toward it. When he does, she looks at him and uses expectant waiting, to allow him to initiate a request. If the child does not produce a conventional request, the teacher prompts with "What do you want?" If the child produces the target response (pointing to or naming the object), he receives the desired object to play with for a time. It is later replaced so it can tempt him again. If the child does not produce the target, the teacher provides a fuller prompt, such as request for direct imitation of the target ("You want the bear? Say *bear*.") and receives the toy.

SOURCE: Reprinted, with permission, from Paul, R., and Sutherland, D. (2005). Enhancing early language in children with autism spectrum disorders. In F. Volkmar, A. Klin, R. Paul, & D. Cohen (Eds.), *Handbook of Autism and Pervasive Developmental Disorders* (3rd ed., vol. 2, chap. 37, p. 951). Hoboken NJ: Wiley.

Augmentative Approaches   Another line of approach, also originally developed to help individuals with significant motor–speech problems is termed *augmentative and alternative communication* (AAC). In this approach, the individual is helped to communicate in various ways. This may include teaching about use of gestures or manual signs (like that used for deaf children). Signs can also be used with speech (what is termed the *total communication approach*). Although signing has been used extensively to help children with autism, it seems most helpful in teaching first words. Kathleen Quill's book *Teaching Children With Autism* (1995) has some wonderful examples and discussion of these and other approaches to increasing social and communication abilities.

A somewhat different approach uses pictures as a medium of communicative exchange and development. The Picture Exchange Communication Systems (PECS) (Bondy & Frost, 1998) teaches words by using a picture to substitute for the desired object. Once the child has the idea, the pictures can then be used as the basis for building more sophisticated language, including full sentences. As you can imagine, there is importance in using different people, environments, pictures, and reinforcement to build up to the broader goal of stimulating overall communication development. There is some data suggesting the usefulness of this approach, particularly when it is used to support the transition from photographs to more symbolic representations of things and actions. For children who are able to make this transition, programs like Boardmaker (www.mayer-johnson.com) can be used to build language even further with more sophisticated language based on sentence strips. Visual aids can also be used to stimulate language development—we talk about these in the next section of this chapter.

Yet another approach uses devices that essentially talk for the child. For example, the child may push a button and the machine says "hello" or "cookie." These devices are very sophisticated, but, unfortunately, their ability to produce a broad range of language initiations or responses is rather limited. For some children, all these approaches are still too advanced. In these cases, use of actual objects may be helpful.

It is important for parents and teachers to realize that alternative communication approaches can be combined with other approaches and that there is no good evidence that adopting, for example, picture exchange, will slow down the child's ability to speak. However, as our colleagues Rhea Paul and Dean Sutherland (2005) have pointed out, much more research is needed and particularly on the issue of whether use of such approaches helps children learn to talk faster than they otherwise would have. On balance, however, the available data suggest that these approaches can help children learn to communicate more effectively and do not (as parents sometimes worry) slow down communication development. Some aspects of augmentative communication approaches are summarized in Table 6.5.

TABLE 6.5   AUGMENTATIVE ALTERNATIVE COMMUNICATION STRATEGIES: AN OVERVIEW

Method/Concept	Comments
Unaided Systems	
Manual sign	May be combined with speech (total communication approach) may help with beginning to learn words; fine motor skill deficits can be a problem
Teaching gestures/body language	Such as pointing, showing, nodding, waving; may be first step in teaching communication skills
Aided Systems	
Picture boards	Used to indicate choice (e.g., of activity or food)
Picture Exchange Communication Systems (PECS)	Moves from teaching exchange (picture for object) to more complex language forms, addresses generalization in different environments; some supportive evidence
High-tech devices	Various devices can be used, for example, child touches a picture and the device says a word; these devices don't provide more complex language

Developmental Approaches   Another line of intervention for early language development in autism has focused on more naturalistic and developmental approaches. One approach of this type was developed at the Hanen Centre to help parents stimulate language development in children with various disabilities; the book *More Than Words* by Fern Sussman (1999) uses this approach to outline a series of developmentally based interventions, including imitating the child's sounds and words, modeling and engaging in games, using visual support and music, and following any leads produced by the child. In this model, any behavior is treated as a form of communication. Another approach, Floortime, similarly encourages following the child's lead and following up on attempts at communication. Some of the more social skills intervention programs such as RDI (discussed previously) also have a strong focus on social interaction, which may stimulate language.

The Denver model developed by Dr. Sally Rogers (Chapter 5) similarly has emphasized developmental methods and approaches in fostering language development. Another population program, the Social Communication Emotional Regulation Transactional Support (SCERTS) model (Prizant and colleagues, 2004, 2005; and www.scerts.com) uses a multidisciplinary approach focused on communication and social–emotional development of young children with autism and related disorders. Areas of emphasis include social communication, helping the child regulate his or her emotions, and supporting transactions with others. Family are actively involved in this process. More information on the SCERTS approach is provided by Prizant and Wetherby (2005) and at the SCERTS web site (www.scerts.com).

Quill (2000) similarly has developed a curriculum focused on enhancing social and communication skills. Her approach draws on a range of methods including both highly structured and more natural settings. Typical peers are given coaching and then used to help the child with ASD learn to be more effective as a communicator and play partner.

The more naturalistic and developmentally based methods are very popular with schools and parents. However, rigorous research comparing all the various approaches is pretty limited. In contrast to the much more structured, behaviorally oriented approaches, naturalistic ones require considerable training of all concerned and, to some extent, can be much more dependent on the presence of a sensitive member of the treatment team who "gets" the importance of the particular approach. It is important to realize that use of one of these more naturalistic teaching methods still requires considerable planning and work if it is to be implemented successfully.

Expanding Language Abilities and Unusual Language Features   Once children start using some words, and maybe start putting words together, a wide range of methods can be used to enhance communication skills. These can include ABA-based discrete trial or pivotal response approaches as well as more naturalistic approaches, for instance, setting up situations where children will be tempted to use their language. *Teach Me Language* (Freeman & Dake, 1997) has a well-developed approach to help children move from single words to more sophisticated language.

Often, as language increases, unusual aspects of language also become more apparent. These can include echolalia (repeating things over and over); problems with the musical aspects of language (prosody), which take the form of mono-tonic or robot-like speech; problems with pronouns; and problems with the social use of language. Some children use idiosyncratic language, that is, where the child uses some word or phrases whose meaning is unique to them. Some children learn to say many words, but their language understanding lags behind what they can say (the reverse of what happens in normal development). Echoing can be immediate (the child repeats a statement back to you) or delayed (he echoes a phrase from a game show in greeting someone new). Many of these language features were first described by Kanner in his original (1943) paper on autism. Our understanding of them has, however, changed over time. Tager-Flusberg and colleagues (2005) give an excellent overview of many of these features.

Early on, people speculated that maybe echolalia was somehow bad, perhaps an attempt by the child to distance him- or herself from other people. Accordingly, the goal often was to treat it as a problem behavior and eliminate it. However, as time went on, it became clear that, as with many of us learning a new language, echoing can have important functions. It can, for example, be something to say when you don't know what else to say or a way to try to keep something in mind. Prizant and Duchan (1981) have talked about some of these possible functions. It also may be the case that the tendency to echo is part of a general processing style in autism—a tendency to take in things as a whole "clump" rather than to break them up; this is what is called a **gestalt processing** style. Echoing is often greatest as children are learning language and lessens over time as they become more capable communicators. In any event, both immediate and delayed echoing clearly can have important functions in communication, and we now try to understand these functions rather than simply trying to eliminate the echoing. Often, as children are learning to be more flexible with their language, they start to "mitigate" their echoed language—that is, to change a little bit of it. This speaks to the tendency they have to learn things as entire chunks.

Similarly, pronoun problems initially were thought to be fundamentally related to social difficulties in autism. As time has gone on, our understanding of this has also changed. Pronouns are very complicated, since the choice of pronoun reflects several different things (who is being talked about and the context). Kanner himself pointed out that part of the problem with pronouns may also come from echoing (i.e., in tending to repeat the last pronoun heard). As language improves and expands, the pronoun problems tend to diminish. At present, most people see pronoun problems as one aspect of the whole host of difficulties that have to do with fast-paced, socially dominated conversational exchange. Similarly, idiosyncratic language, in which a child uses some word or phrase which has a unique meaning only to them, may reflect the child's unique history and association of some experience with a word. Kanner gave several examples of this kind of language. For instance, one boy had once dangled his stuffed animal over a railing; thereafter, whenever the going got tough, he would repeat the phrase, "Don't throw the dog out the window," which he'd heard his mother tell him at the time!

Some areas of language development usually don't need so much work, such as articulation or the way words are actually said; occasionally, children will have trouble with this and may need special help, but usually not. Other areas are much more likely to be targets for intervention. For example, social language skills are typically important targets for intervention at whatever level of language the child has. As children start to develop some language and use it to express their experience, social interchange becomes more important. As previously discussed, peers can become very effective teachers for younger children and have the great advantage of fostering skills in natural contexts. It is important to foster language independence, particularly with peers. Some children with ASD end up directing more of their communications to teachers and other adults. Goals for pragmatic or social language development relate to use of non-verbal cues in interaction (e.g., gaze, tone of voice), initiating and maintaining conversations, giving appropriate amounts of information and having reasonable expectations for conversational "back and forth," and so on.

Goals for Students with Asperger's and Higher Functioning Autism

For individuals with Asperger's and higher functioning autism, both similar and somewhat different issues arise. For these students, communication issues often have less to do with saying words and vocabulary building and much more to do with social language use. Communication goals are often very much linked with social goals, and the speech pathologist may be working on social functions and communication at the same time. Problems can arise in many different ways. For some children, prosody and talking in a very loud voice can be a major problem. Work on prosody (the musical aspect of speech) can be done in various ways, but it is important to know that research in this area is relatively sparse. Procedures can include use of audio- or videotape recorders or other devices (for practice and feedback). Some computer programs have been developed for prosody problems in other conditions that may be useful in autism. For children with a very loud voice (what speech pathologists call *register*), it probably doesn't make much sense to try to develop the many different levels of voice that most of us have. Rather, it may make more sense to focus on three voice loudness levels—soft, medium, and loud—and then teach which one goes where: loud voice at recess, medium voice in class, soft voice at church.

Work on conversational and social skills can dovetail nicely with social skills groups or social skills teaching programs. This can include work on listening and turn taking, inviting feedback, and the use of language to express feelings and to help with self-monitoring and self-regulation. For highly verbal individuals, words can be used as an area of strength for teaching social skills, for instance, by teaching scripts that can be faded over time. For more able individuals with autism, visual supports (written cues and other static visual cues) may still be helpful. The speech pathologist will want to consider a program to help the individual be more broadly effective in one-on-one situations, in group and classroom situations, and in even large community or family settings.

Explicit teaching of social conventions can be helpful. The tendency for individuals on the autism spectrum to be highly literal can lead to all kinds of miscommunications. Accordingly, aspects of figurative language, idioms, and slang can be explicitly taught (see Myles et al., 2004, for some helpful examples). There are several excellent resources in the reading list for help in this area. The chapters by Paul and Sutherland (2005) and Marans, Rubin, and Laurent (2005) in the *Handbook of Autism and Pervasive Developmental Disorders* have much helpful information.

ORGANIZATIONAL ISSUES/SUPPORTIVE TECHNOLOGY

Individuals with ASD have a number of challenges for learning. As discussed in earlier chapters, some of these are probably a direct result of the social disability itself, while others come about basically as "fallout" of the social problems. Put in a simple (but probably pretty accurate) way, if one is not drawn into the world of people early in life, he doesn't learn to focus on the importance of what other people think, and, as a result, he can have very different and sometimes very idiosyncratic ways of viewing the world. There may be early problems in such basic things as learning-to-learn skills (a major focus of ABA and other interventions in preschool children), and one may have trouble as he gets older in being an efficient learner who can multitask and organize well. This area of vulnerability has a fancy name in psychology: *executive functioning*. Developing executive functioning means one can be oriented to long-term goals and includes things like flexibility, planning, organization, self-monitoring, and multitasking. These issues are important throughout life. In early childhood they can interfere with learning, and in later childhood they can interfere with academic progress and also with translation of knowledge to real-world settings. These problems are not unique to autism but can have serious consequences for learning.

EXECUTIVE FUNCTIONING DEFICITS—IMPLICATIONS FOR ASD	
Problem Area	**Resulting Difficulty**
Planning and evaluation	Difficulties in forward planning and monitoring lead to focus on short-term goals, failure to see "big picture"
Flexibility	Rigid thinking patterns see only one solution to a problem, results in child getting stuck on one step/stage of a project, can't do "work-arounds"; novelty can create behavioral issues
Inhibition	Tendency to perseverate, stick with previous responses/strategies, can't shift to changed problem

We discussed in Chapter 5 some of the important foundations to learning that are typically targeted in behavioral intervention programs for very young children—learning-to-learn skills such as sitting in your chair, waiting a turn, sharing a focus of interest, and engaging in imitation. We discussed in this chapter the importance of augmentative communication aids. These same types of strategies can be used very effectively to deal with problems of organization and executive functioning deficits. These can take many forms. One of the simplest to use in the classroom (and at home) is visual supports. Say, for example, that a 4-year-old child with autism has significant difficulties with transitions. One approach within the classroom (and at home) would be to put up a visual schedule with pictures of the daily activities. Depending on the child's language and cognitive levels, variations on this theme can be adopted; for instance, there can be a written label "circle time" if that is appropriate. Similarly, at home, the child's day can be put up on the fridge with magnets, with each photograph turned over when an activity is done. At the end of the day, you can review what the child did. You can also start to build in other things like choices (to bring in an element of unpredictability—but be sure to start with choices the child will like!). An entire literature on visual supports now exists and has proven very helpful to teachers and parents alike. A series of excellent books by Linda Hodgdon (2003) on the use of visual strategies is very practical and gives helpful guidance to teachers and parents on how to use these approaches in the classroom and at home, and in dealing with behavior problems. Other books are available as well. Cohen and Sloan (2007) give examples of the use of visual support to improve social skills, attention, motivation, memory, and so forth. The Power Cards approach developed by Gagnon (2001) is particularly helpful for more cognitively advanced students with autism and Asperger's.

As children become older and more cognitively able, other approaches are available as well, and more are coming out all the time. These fall, more or less, into two different camps that we might call low tech and high tech, and both have their uses. For children with problems in organization, many of the same things that adults use to organize themselves can be useful, such as written (or visual and written) schedules and use of lists, organizers, and day planners. For children engaged in doing longer term projects, the use of a team approach, with another child as a mentor, can be helpful. Helping the child with autism develop a specific plan or series of steps to a specific goal in written form can be helpful. Similarly, in the classroom, some preteaching around critical concepts may help the child remember what it is important to attend to (this can be as simple as having the child have a short list of critical concepts or topics that he or she should listen for). We've also had students who had trouble remembering and/or writing quickly use aids like a special homework sheet from the teacher or one of the small, handheld audio recorders that can be quickly pulled out and used when the teacher is going over complicated material or giving homework assignments. Within the classroom, some focus on the environment such as placement of the child's desk and helping him or her keep a distraction-free (i.e., uncluttered) desk and work space can improve his or her ability to focus.

Keep in mind that, on the low-tech end, some of the same activities that can help with adaptive or daily living skills can be used to help teach organizational abilities. Having a regular schedule with chores, for example, provides structure for the child and practice in using a visual or other schedule. Similarly, in the classroom, various things can be done to help the child get and stay organized. These can include giving extra time, doing some preteaching and attending to "big-picture" issues with the child (e.g., developing a schedule or sequential checklist for a project, giving extra time before/after class). The teacher can reinforce successful self-management or attempts at self-management.

These issues often surface, particularly, with reference to homework. Homework can present many challenges; there is the potential for not planning time well so that students get "stuck" on one task. They may have particular trouble with homework that involves either organization or more abstract skills. There are many potential interventions that can be helpful. For some students, doing the homework at school (e.g., in an after-school study group with a peer or other tutor) can be helpful. Similarly, helping students learn to plan time can be helpful. A visual timer that gives students a clear visual sense of what time is left (these timers are a bit like the old hourglass in that there is highly visible, maybe red, circle or semicircle that gradually diminishes in size). Particularly when students have trouble "getting stuck" (this often happens in things like spelling, where the English language rules do not always reflect the operation of logic), think about having the student assignment be to work on the spelling list for 30 minutes as opposed to mastering the list. This time can then be appropriately expanded (or contracted), depending on the child's other homework—the idea is to help the child get some sense of the need for the entire set of homework assignments and not just be totally stuck on one of them.

At the higher tech end, electronic organizers, tape recorders, and computers have their many uses. Even within the high-tech end, some approaches are fairly simple to implement. For example, a fourth-grade boy who was very high functioning (but quite disorganized) had the task of writing a two- to three-page paper on the history of Egypt. The boy was excited to be able to use the computer and quickly amassed literally hundreds of facts/pictures from the Internet and other sources. His problem was in how to translate this into a paper. In talking with his father, a salesman, we suggested that the father get out his computer and boot up his slide-maker program and set up a series of several slides, each with a title only. The first slide was "Egypt: A History" and had the child's name, the next slide was "Egypt at the time of the pharaohs," the next "Egypt at the time of Jesus," the next "Egypt at the time of Mohammed," and finally "Egypt today". The boy then went back and filled in the bottom half of the slide with five or six relevant points/facts. The father and boy then turned this visual presentation into an outline and each of the slides became a paragraph of the paper, with each of the five or six bullet points becoming a sentence. Keep in mind that in our increasingly computer- and internet-focused society, knowing computer skills can be a very handy thing as children get older and think about job choices.

For children with Asperger's in particular, the use of a laptop computer from very early on in school has considerable advantages. Often, cursive writing is a real struggle, and the laptop offers a highly functional work-around. Laptop and keyboard skills also can provide access to other important technologies, for example, spell checking and so forth (if the parents and teachers wish it to). It is important for parents and teachers to understand that this can indeed be a reasonable accommodation. Depending on the circumstance, computers can be equipped with all kinds of supports, including spell check, text-to-speech voice synthesizers, and so forth. One of us once had the experience of a teacher at a planning meeting saying very loudly that offering a laptop was a "crutch" to the child; we replied that this was true and that if she were missing a leg and we gave her a crutch, that would be a good thing!

A range of other supports on the computer is available, including organizational software programs like Inspiration and Kidspiration (www.inspiration .com). For more able students, it is very much worth having parents and teachers visit web sites focused on the needs of children with other problems like learning disabilities (www.ldpride.net) or **attention deficit disorder (ADD)** (e.g., www.addwarehouse.com) to look for new materials, software, and so forth. Keep in mind that, depending on the context, some of the lower tech approaches can be very helpful. For instance, a tag on the backpack that says on one side "What I Take to School" and on the other "What I Bring From School" may be very helpful in reminding the student about homework, lunch, and so forth. Keep in mind that the goal, as much as possible, is to have the student participate in the organization and planning so that, for example, developing a checklist for homework completion can be a homework task. There are some excellent books that discuss executive function and organizational issues. The book *Smart but Scattered* (Dawson & Guare, 2009) is very teacher/parent friendly and has many valuable suggestions. The book *Executive Function in Education: From Theory to Practice* (Meltzer, 2007) covers a range of issues and disorders. In that book, the chapter by Ozonoff and Schetter (2007) is focused on autism and ASD in particular, and other chapters include some focused on specific academic/curricular areas.

ADAPTIVE SKILLS AND GENERALIZATION

Adaptive skills involve self-sufficiency in real-life situations, that is, the skills to translate knowledge across settings, from school to home and community in meeting the demands of daily life. The concept of adaptive skills applies to all ages and levels of functioning. These abilities are one of the major factors that determine ultimately how independent and self-sufficient a person is. Our goal is to help people be as independent as they can possibly be. For individuals with ASD, there are some real challenges to acquiring this self-sufficiency. In the first place, the real world is unpredictable—a problem if you have a preference for sameness. Second, the real world is highly social—a problem if you have social vulnerabilities. Third, the real world is fast paced, with many demands and bits of information coming to you at a time. And, finally, if you tend to learn things in a very narrow kind of way, you will have significant problems generalizing skills. If, for example, you can use the toilet at home but not at school, that is a problem. Similarly, if you can solve complex math equations in your head but not order a cheeseburger in a fast-food restaurant, you're in trouble. It is almost always the case that individuals with ASD exhibit lower—and often very much lower—levels of ability in real-world contexts than they exhibit in familiar and highly structured settings. Accordingly, it is critical that schools and parents specifically consider the issues of generalization and adaptive skills as part of the child's program.

TEACHING SELF-CARE SKILLS

- As with other skills, an explicit and focused approach is helpful.
- Try to use the child's natural motivations as much as possible.
- Be explicit in teaching.
- Use routines/scripts, which can then be faded.
- Teach generalization (different materials/situations/contexts for same behavior).
- Use the same methods used in schools:
  - Visual schedules
  - Written materials
  - Photographs
- Be consistent (gradually introduce variations).
- Use natural environments (rewards and consequences) as much as possible.

We discussed assessment of adaptive skills in Chapter 3. The Vineland Adaptive Behavior Scales are probably the most widely used instrument to assess adaptive behavior. We'll give some examples of results from the Vineland in later chapters. Other instruments are available as well, but are not as frequently used. It is important to realize that Vineland test results are based on what the person usually does—not what they *can* do. This is why the test is particularly helpful for individuals with ASD. As you'll see in the next chapters, when combined with other testing, the Vineland can also yield some very specific recommendations for areas of work in the domains of social, communication, and daily living skills (and motor skills as well for younger children).

A range of intervention methods can be used in teaching adaptive skills of various kinds. Of course, much of the work on social skills and communication we've already discussed is concerned with translating abilities learned in the classroom into real-world settings. There are a number of approaches to teaching daily living, coping, and self-help skills as well. Some of the earliest work in this area focused on using behavioral techniques to teach specific skills in children with autism, including self-care (McClannahan et al., 1990) and toilet training (Ando, 1977). Peer modeling/tutoring has also been used successfully. McClannahan and Krantz's book *Activity Schedules for Children with Autism* (1999) provides an excellent introduction to a behavioral approach aimed at teaching independent behaviors. As noted in the previous chapter, the use of routines and pivotal response training can be highly productive in encouraging such behaviors. Any of a number of approaches can be used, including various kinds of reinforcers (ranging from things like food to more complex systems like stickers and tokens). In thinking about these approaches, it is important to keep things as simple but also as natural as possible and to have a longer term vision. You'll want to gradually fade the rewards system and move on to something else.

Several excellent resources are available for parents and teachers. The book *Taking Care of Myself* (Wrobel, 2003) provides an explicit curriculum for teaching hygiene, modesty, self-care, and so forth, and is targeted at adolescents. A series of books by Beverly Plass (see reading list) provides well-done stories and teaching material (aimed at students of different levels) focused on community, work, and leisure/recreational activities. These books focus on expanding knowledge using picture supports and increased communication skills to enhance independence. *Self-Help Skills for People with Autism* (Anderson, Jablonski, Thomeer, & Knapp, 2007) has some excellent examples and is very practical and easy for both parents and teachers to use. This book is particularly good at illustrating how complicated tasks can be broken down into smaller, teachable steps and includes chapters on dressing, eating, toileting, and generalization of skills. We talk about some of these issues in the next several chapters, including working on toilet training, personal hygiene, and sexuality.

Summary

In this chapter, we surveyed some of the various approaches to teaching particular skills and have discussed several interventions in different areas: curriculum issues, social skills, communication skills, daily life (adaptive) skills, and organizational issues. As always, it is important for parents and teachers to remain focused on a particular child and his or her needs. It is important for parents and educators to work together in developing individualized education plans that address the strengths and weaknesses of the particular child. Parents and families have a very important role in helping generalize skills across settings, that is, in helping the child learn to use what he learns in school in other contexts.

While we wish there was more research on these various intervention methods, there is at least some, and fortunately there are more and more tools for parents and teachers to work with. It is particularly important to include a focus on real-world skills and generalization given the learning style of individuals with autism and related disorders. Parents (and teachers) should not be misled by isolated areas of strength—when these are present, they can be important considerations in program development, but keep in mind that other areas need intensive work.

Many different approaches to teaching have been developed. These use a range of methods and require thoughtful consideration of the ways that different areas interact, for example, the interaction of social vulnerabilities in learning play skills and motor imitation. Keep in mind that a range of approaches is available, and the challenge, as always, is selecting a method appropriate for the particular individual with ASD. Don't lose sight of the big picture, that is, the overall goals and vision for how parents and teachers want the child to develop. As is true in other areas, an awareness of general developmental principles and sequences of development is helpful, but parents and teachers should also be aware that the sequences are commonly violated in children with ASD. Frequent sources of confusion in Asperger's include isolated special abilities combined with what initially appear to be good language skills. It is important for parents and teachers to have a balanced approach with a clear vision of what may be possible and a clear awareness of where the child is at any particular point in time.

■ READING LIST

Adreon, D., & Myles, B. S. (2001). *Asperger syndrome and adolescence: Practical solutions for school success.* Shawnee Mission, KS: Autism Asperger.

Al-Ghani, K. I. (2009). *The red beast: Controlling anger in children with Asperger's syndrome.* Philadelphia: Jessica Kingsley.

Anderson, S. R., Jablonski, A. L., Thomeer, M. L., & Knapp, V. M. (2007). *Self-help skills for people with autism: A systematic teaching Approach.* Bethesda, MD: Woodbine House.

Ando, H. (1977). Training autistic children to urinate in the toilet through operant conditioning techniques. *Journal of Autism and Childhood Schizophrenia, 7*(2), 151.

Baker, J. (2001). *Social skills picture book: Teaching play, emotion, and communication to children with autism.* Arlington, TX: Future Horizons.

Barbera, M. L., & Rasmussen, T. (2007). *The verbal behavior approach: How to teach children with autism and related disorders.* Philadelphia: Jessica Kingsley.

Beukelman, D. R., & Mirenda, P. (2005). *Augmentative and alternative communication: Supporting children and adults with complex communication needs* (3rd ed.). Baltimore: Brookes.

Bondy, A., & Frost, L. (1998). The picture exchange communication system. Seminars in *Speech and Language, 19*, 373–389.

Buron, K. D., & Myles, B. S. (2004). *When my autism gets too big! A relaxation book for children with autism spectrum disorders.* Shawnee Mission, KS: Autism Asperger.

Carter, M. A., & Santomauro, J. (2007). *Pirates: An early-years group program for developing social understanding and social competence for children with autism spectrum disorders and related challenges.* Shawnee Mission, KS: Autism Asperger.

Charlop, M., & Trasowech, J. (1991). Increasing children's daily spontaneous speech. *Journal of Applied Behavior Analysis, 24*, 747–761.

Cohen, M. J., & Sloan, D. L. (2007). *Visual supports for people with autism: A guide for parents and professionals.* Bethesda, MD: Woodbine House.

Coulter, D. (2005). Manners for the real world: Basic social skills (DVD). Coulter Video.

Dawson, P., & Guare, R. (2003). *Executive skills in children and adolescents: A practical guide to assessment and intervention* (The Guilford Practical Intervention in Schools Series). New York: Guilford Press.

Dawson, P., & Guare, R. (2009). *Smart but scattered: The revolutionary "executive skills" approach to helping kids reach their potential.* New York: Guilford Press.

Delmolino, L., & Harris, S. L. (2004). *Incentives for change: Motivating people with autism spectrum disorders to learn and gain independence.* Bethesda, MD: Woodbine House.

Dunn, M. A. (2005). *SOS. Social skills in our schools: A social skills program for children with pervasive developmental disorders, including high-functioning autism and Asperger syndrome, and their typical peers.* Shawnee Mission, KS: Autism Asperger.

Durand, V. M., & Carr, E. G. (1987). Social influences on "self-stimulatory" behavior: Analysis and treatment application. *Journal of Applied Behavioral Analyses, 20*(2), 119–132.

Fein, D., & Dunn, M. (2007). *Autism in your classroom.* Bethesda, MD: Woodbine House.

Fovel, J. T. (2002). *The ABA program companion: Organizing quality programs for children with autism and PDD.* New York: DRL Books.

Freeman, S., & Dake, L. (1997). *Teach me language: A language manual for children with autism, Asperger's syndrome, and related developmental disorders.* Langley, BC, Canada: SKF Books.

Gagnon, E. (2001). *Power cards: Using special interests to motivate children and youth with Asperger syndrome and autism.* Shawnee Mission, KS: Autism Asperger.

Goldstein, A. P., Sprafkin, R. P., Gershaw, N. J., & Klein, P. (1980). *Skill-streaming the adolescent: A structured learning approach to teaching prosocial skills.* Champaign, IL: Research Press.

Goldstein, H. (2002). *Promoting social communication: Children with developmental disabilities from birth to adolescence.* Baltimore: Brookes.

Goldstein, H., English, K., & Shafer, K. (1997). Interaction among preschoolers with and without disabilities: Effects of across-the-day peer intervention. *Journal of Speech, Language, and Hearing Research, 40*, 33–48.

Gray, C. (1994). *Comic strip conversations.* Arlington, TX: Future Horizons.

Gray, C. (2000). *The new social story book: Illustrated edition* (2nd ed). Arlington, TX: Future Horizons.

Grigorenko E. L., Klin, A., & Volkmar, F. (2003). Annotation: Hyperlexia: disability or superability? *Journal of Child Psychology and Psychiatry, 44*(8), 1079–1091.

Gutstein, S. E., & Sheely, R. K. (2002). *Relationship Development Intervention with children, adolescents and adults*. Philadelphia: Jessica Kingsley.

Gutstein, S. E., & Sheely, R. K. (2002). *Relationship Development Intervention with young children: Social and emotional development activities for Asperger syndrome, autism, PDD and NLD*. Philadelphia: Jessica Kingsley.

Hart & Risley (1975). Incidental teaching of language in the pre-school. *Journal of Applied Behavior Analysis, 8*, 411–420.

Heflin, L. J., & Alaimo, D. F. (2007). *Students with autism spectrum disorders: Effective instructional practices*. Upper Saddle River, NJ: Prentice Hall.

Hodgdon, L. (2001). *Visual strategies for improving communication: Practical supports for school and home*. Troy, MI: QuirkRoberts.

Hodgdon, L. (2003). *Solving behavior problems in autism: Improving communication with visual strategies*. Troy, MI: QuirkRoberts.

Kanner, L. (1943). Autistic disturbances of affective contact. *Nervous Child, 2*, 217–250.

Keating-Velasco, J. L. (2007). *A is for autism, F is for friend: A kid's book for making friends with a child who has autism*. Shawnee Mission, KS: Autism Asperger.

Koegel, L., Carter, C., & Koegel, R. (2003). Teaching children with autism self-initiations as a pivotal response. *Topics in Language Disorders, 23*, 134–145.

Koegel, L. K., Koegel, R. L., & Carter, C. A. (1998). Pivotal responses and the natural language teaching paradigm. *Seminars in Speech and Language, 19*, 355–371.

Koegel, R., O'Dell, M., & Koegel, L. (1987). A natural language teaching paradigm for non-verbal autistic children. *Journal of Autism and Developmental Disorders, 17*, 187–200.

Kranowitz, C. S. (1995). *101 activities for kids in tight spaces*. New York: St. Martin's.

Krantz, P., & McClannahan, L. (1999). *Activity schedules for children with autism: Teaching independent behavior*. Bethesda, MD: Woodbine House.

Laski, K., Charlop, M., & Schreibman, L. (1988). Training parents to use the natural language paradigm to increase their autistic children's speech. *Journal of Applied Behavior Analysis, 21*, 391–400.

Marans, W. D., Rubin, E., & Laurent, A. (2005). Addressing social communication skills in individuals with high-functioning autism and Asperger syndrome: Critical priorities in educational programming. In F. R. Volkmar, R. Paul, A. Klin, & D. Cohen (Eds.). *Handbook of autism and pervasive developmental disorders* (3rd ed., vol. *2*, pp. 977–1002). Hoboken, NJ: Wiley.

McAfee, J. (2002) *Navigating the social world*. Arlington, TX: Future Horizons.

McClannahan, L. E., & Krantz, P. J. (1999). *Activity schedules for children with autism: Teaching independent behavior*. Bethesda, MD: Woodbine House.

McClannahan, L. E., & Krantz, P. J. (2005). *Teaching conversation to children with Autism: Scripts and script fading. Topics in autism*. Sandra L. Harris, Series Editor. Bethesda, MD: Woodbine House.

McGee, G., Krantz, P., Mason, D., & McClannahan, L. (1983). A modified incidental teaching procedure for autistic youth: Acquisition and generalization of receptive object labels. *Journal of Applied Behavior Analysis, 16*, 329–338.

Meltzer, L. (Ed.) (2007). *Executive function in education: From theory to practice*. New York: Guilford Press.

Mirenda, P., & Iacono, T. (2009). *Autism spectrum disorders and AAC*. Baltimore: Brookes.

Mirenda, P., & Santogrossi (1985). A prompt-free strategy to teach pictorial communication system use. *Augmentative and alternative communication, 1*, 143–150.

Myles, B., & Southwick, J. (2005). *Asperger syndrome and difficult moments: Practical solutions for tantrums, rage and meltdowns*. Shawnee Mission, KS: Autism Asperger.

Myles, B. S., Trautman, M. L., & Schelvan, R. L. (2004). *The hidden curriculum: Practical solutions for understanding unstated rules in social situations*. Shawnee Mission, KS: Autism Asperger.

Patrick, N. J. (2008). *Social skills for teenagers and adults with Asperger syndrome: A practical guide to day-to-day life*. London: Jessica Kingsley.

Paul, R., & Sutherland, D. (2005). Enhancing early language in children with autism spectrum disorders. In F. R. Volkmar, R. Paul, A. Klin, & D. Cohen (Eds.), *Handbook of autism and pervasive developmental disorders* (3rd ed., vol. 2, pp. 946–976). Hoboken, NJ: Wiley.

Pepper, J., & Weitzman, E. (2004). *It takes two to talk: A practical guide for parents of* children with language delay. Toronto, Ontario: The Hanen Centre.

Perske, R. (1988). *Circles of friends: People with disabilities and their friends enrich the lives of one another*. Nashville, TN: Abingdon Press.

Plass, B. (2008). *Functional routines for adolescents & adults—community*. East Moline, IL: LinguiSystems.

Plass, B. (2008). *Functional routines for adolescents & adults—home*. East Moline, IL: LinguiSystems.

Plass, B. (2008). *Functional routines for adolescents & adults—leisure & recreation*. East Moline, IL: LinguiSystems.

Plass, B. (2008). *Functional routines for adolescents & adults—work*. East Moline, IL: LinguiSystems.

Potter, C., & Whittaker, C. (2001). *Enabling communication in children with autism*. London: Jessica Kingsley.

Prizant, B. M., & Duchan, J. F. (1981). The functions of immediate echolalia in autistic children. *Journal of Speech and Hearing Disorders*, 46(3), 241–249.

Prizant, B. M., & Wetherby, A. M. (2005). Critical issues in enhancing communication abilities for persons with autism spectrum disorders. In F. R. Volkmar, R. Paul, A. Klin, & D. Cohen (Eds.), *Handbook of autism and pervasive developmental disorders* (3rd ed., vol. 2, pp. 925–945). Hoboken, NJ: Wiley.

Prizant, B. M., Wetherby, A. M., Rubin, E. M., Laurent, A. C., & Rydell, P. J. (2005). *The SCERTS model: A comprehensive educational approach for children with autism spectrum disorders* (2 volumes). Baltimore: Brooks.

Quill, K. (1995). *Teaching children with autism: Strategies to enhance communication and socialization*. New York: Delmar.

Quill, K. (2000). *Do watch listen say: Social and communication intervention for children with autism*. Baltimore: Brookes.

Rogers-Warren & Warren. (1980). Pragmatics and generalization. In R. L. Schiefelbusch (Ed.), *Communicative competence: Assessment and intervention* (pp. 157–201). Baltimore: University Park Press.

Rosaler, M. (2004). *Asperger syndrome*. New York: Rosen.

Sabin, E. (2006). *The autism acceptance book: Being a friend to someone with autism*. New York: Watering Can Press.

Sanders, R. S. (2002). *Overcoming Asperger's: Personal experience & insight*. Murfreesboro, TN: Armstrong Valley.

Savner, J. L., & Myles, B. S. (2000). *Making visual supports: Work in the home and community: Strategies for individuals with autism and Asperger syndrome*. Shawnee Mission, KS: Autism Asperger.

Schlieder, M. (2007). *With open arms: Creating school communities of support for kids with social challenges using circle of friends, extracurricular activities, and learning teams.* Shawnee Mission, KS: Autism Asperger.

Stewart, K. (2002). *Helping a child with nonverbal learning disorder or Asperger's syndrome: A parent's guide.* Oakland, CA: New Harbinger.

Sundberg, M., Michael, J., Partington, J., & Sundberg, C. (1995). The role of automatic reinforcement in early language acquisition. *Analysis of Verbal Behavior, 13,* 21–37.

Sussman, F. (1999). *More than words: Helping parents promote communication and social skills in children with autism spectrum disorder.* Toronto, Ontario: The Hanen Centre.

Tager-Flusber (2005). Language and communication in autism. In F. R. Volkmar, R. Paul, A. Klin, & D. Cohen (Eds.), *Handbook of autism and pervasive developmental disorders* (3rd ed., vol. 1, pp. 335–364). Hoboken, NJ: Wiley.

Wheeler, M. (2007). *Toilet training for individuals with autism or other developmental issues* (2nd ed.). Arlington, TX: Future Horizons.

White, S. W., Koenig, K., & Scahill, L. (2006). Social skills development in children with autism spectrum disorders: A review of the intervention research. *Journal of Autism and Developmental Disorders, 37,* 1858–1868.

Wrobel, M. (2003). *Taking care of myself: A hygiene, puberty and personal curriculum for young people with autism.* Arlington, TX: Future Horizons.

Zeedyk, M. S. (2008). *Promoting social interaction for individuals with communication impairments: Making contact.* London: Jessica Kingsley.

◼ WEB SITES

Vincent Carbone: www.drcarbone.net
Hyperlexia association: www.hyperlexia.org
Mayer-Johnson, LLC: www.mayer-johnson.com
Carol Gray: http://www.thegraycenter.org
Scerts: www.scerts.com
Organizational software: www.inspiration.com
Learning Disabilties: www.ldpride.net
Attention deficit disorder (ADD) supports: www.addwarehouse.com

◼ QUESTIONS AND ANSWERS

1. **My 6-year-old has a tremendous ability to read. He can read at about a fifth-grade level. The school has totally oriented his program around written material, but this doesn't seem to have helped him much—in some ways his behavior has gotten worse. Why is this?**

   You mentioned his ability to read (what is technically called decoding) at a fifth-grade level, but you didn't mention his level of understanding. If, for example, you give him a written instruction, can he follow it? It is often, but not always, the case that children on the autism spectrum read to decode at a much higher level than they understand. This can be a source of great confusion to parents and teachers and a source of great frustration to the child, that is, if people are treating him like he should be understanding something that he isn't. Our first suggestion would be to have someone assess his actual understanding of what he reads.

2. **My 4-year-old is not yet talking. She seems to jabber a lot, and every now and then we think we hear her say something, but she doesn't repeat it. It is hard for us to get her attention and have her focus. There are times, though, when we can get her involved in games—if we make a "raspberry" sound, she may try to do this back at us. The school has been pushing visual supports and picture exchange but we worry that these may hold back her speech development. Is it impossible that she'll speak? What are the best methods for teaching her to talk?**

Life is lived in the details, and so it would be important to really know your child before giving advice that was specific to her. That being said, your question points out a couple of important things. Probably most importantly, you mention that she engages in sound imitation and that she makes a range of sounds. These are good signs. Your question also suggests that she has some difficulty with "learning-to-learn" skills (sitting and focusing), and this is something that ought to be a major focus of intervention since it is hard to teach her if she doesn't have this. As we mention in this chapter, there are many different approaches to teaching, and you can think about any of them. For a child with significant learning-to-learn skills, we might suggest starting with a more focused behavioral approach, but other approaches can be used as well—particularly if she has some motivation to communicate at times. The important thing is to adopt a strategy and approach and stick with it. There are some children who certainly learn to speak after age 4, although this gets harder as time goes on. If the use of visual supports helps her get the idea of communication, they are a good idea.

3. **My 8-year-old son with Asperger's has dreadful self-care skills. He doesn't like to shower or change clothes. For the life of me, I can't get him to clean up, and it embarrasses his older sister when we go out (among other things because he has a lot of body odor). We fight about this all the time. The only thing he seems to enjoy is his special interest in sports facts (particularly the local college basketball team).**

You are correct that having good personal hygiene skills is increasingly important as kids get older. If your child is in a social skills group or situation where he can get feedback from other children, that might be helpful. Taking a very explicit approach (written schedule or sequence of what he has to do when he showers) might be helpful—maybe even including an audible timer to let him know how long he needs to spend in the shower. We have seen some children do well when they worked with somewhat older peers/mentors; for example, if you can find a trustworthy older (high school or college) boy who can go with him to the swimming pool (where the rules require him to take a shower) and then out for pizza (or some other enjoyable activity) and *then* to a basketball game, it might "detox" the situation with you and give him a situation where he is motivated to shower. The various books on self-care activities in the reading list have some helpful suggestions as well.

4. **I am having trouble toilet training my 3-year-old with autism. I think he is refusing to toilet train to frustrate me! What should I do?**

There are some good resources in this area (the book by Wheeler in the reading list is an excellent place to start). Keep in mind that toilet training can be a challenge (and a challenge for children of this age) for typically developing preschoolers. We usually think that for toilet training to work you need several different things to be true: the child has to have the motor abilities (often, this is not true until around 2 to 3 years of age), the child has to have an awareness of what is wanted (again often not true until around 3 years even for typically developing children), *and* the child has to have the motivation to do what you want (a real challenge for children with ASD). For some typically developing children (and maybe even for your child), toilet training is a chance to "play out" some issues with parents—around control, for example. Given all these issues, it is not at all uncommon for children with autism to be late in toilet training. For children with Asperger's, the motivation and understanding may be there, but the motor abilities may be a problem. For children with autism, the motor abilities may be there, but the motivation and understanding of what is wanted may be lacking. There are some questions to ask yourself. Can you tell when the child is going to go to the bathroom? Does he seem to notice when he has soiled his diaper? Are there any medical problems that complicate toilet training (sometimes restricted diets and/or unusual food preferences lead to constipation). Do you have a regular and consistent toileting routine? Use of an explicit schedule and behavioral reinforcement techniques can be helpful once the child is ready. There are many different approaches that can then be used. In addition to the Wheeler book, there is a good discussion of toilet training in the book by Anderson and colleagues on teaching self-help skills to people with autism.

5. **My daughter gives me horrible fits when we go shopping. She gets overwhelmed by the store and wants to buy everything in sight. She gets angry very quickly when I say no. How can I help her be more functional?**

    You may want to talk with the school psychologist or behavioral consultant or, for that matter, the speech pathologist who knows your daughter. Depending on the specifics of the situation any of several different strategies might be useful. For children who are less verbal, develop a very specific behavior plan—you might want her to spend literally 1 minute in the store and then go outside, and then gradually build up the time she can tolerate being in the store (which may be very overstimulating to her). Come up with a visual shopping list (or, if she reads, a written list), and then plan this almost like a military mission with a quick entrance and exit; then try to build on success by gradually expanding the time involved. Think about turning this into a teaching activity—giving her something to do while you are doing your shopping or giving her a very focused activity to engage in (rather than having a meltdown about being overwhelmed). If the activity level in the store is a problem, go at less busy times. Or go only when she has earned enough money to buy a desired item.

    For more able children with Asperger's, there are some good resources on anger control, for example, the book by Al-Ghani in the reading list.

6. **My son has Asperger's and has a horrible time with cursive handwriting and with timed tests. Can special accommodations be made for him?**

    The short answer is yes. Special accommodations can include untimed tests or tests given in more solitary environments (to minimize distractions). It is not at all uncommon for individuals with Asperger's to have such accommodations (reasonable accommodations for individuals with disabilities are a right in the United States). For individuals with fine-motor and grapho-motor (handwriting) problems, use of a computer can easily be justified.

7. **My daughter with autism is high functioning and in the fifth grade. She seems to have horrible troubles in some classes (social studies and English) but not others (science and math). How can we help her be successful?**

    In thinking about teaching for specific academic areas, it is helpful to step back and think about "big picture" issues. Social studies and English are, for example, classes where several things may conspire to make life more complicated for the student with autism. In contrast to science and math, they are less fact focused and more concerned with understanding abstract issues, including social motivations, cause-and-effect relationships, and abstract concepts. It may be possible to help the child using preteaching (the teacher explains exactly what is going to be taught, what the most important concepts are, etc.). Having a schedule/visual outline may also help. The outline or schedule can be color coded; for example, key concepts can be in one color, important facts another. The book *Autism in Your Classroom* (Fein & Dunn, 2007) gives a number of helpful suggestions for teachers working with students on the autism spectrum.

8. **I am a father of 10-year-old boy with Asperger's. He knows a lot about some things but is really clueless about others. He would like to have more friendships, and I was thinking sports would be a good way to go. Do you have any suggestions for specific sports?**

    As always, the place to start is with whatever the special interests/motivations are for the particular child. If he has any, this would be the place to begin the discussion. That being said, there are some generalizations to make; however, as with all generalizations, there can be very reasonable exceptions. Team sports (basketball, soccer, baseball) can be some of the most problematic because they are fast paced and very social and involve high levels of motor ability. Often, going in the other direction can be helpful. So finding sports where you go at your own pace, where you are more socially supported (one-on-one or small group), and where motor abilities are more developmentally progressive can be good. This would mean things like judo or martial arts (where the child proceeds at his or her own pace and where the program is developmentally progressive, that is starts simple and gets more complicated over time) can be good. Swimming or skiing can also be good. If you want more socially interactive sports, then activities that are more dyadic (two people) can be good, for example, tennis.

9. **My 15-year-old with autism is high functioning but often seems frustrated by his inability to understand jokes. It seems either like other kids are laughing at him when he isn't meaning to be funny or he is seeing something as funny that other kids don't. How can I help him?**

    Your observation is a good one. Often, children on the autism spectrum run into trouble because they have problems understanding and interpreting the (tremendously) sophisticated social communications of typically developing peers. The child may feel like others are making fun of him (when they are not) or may not understand when others are seeing something as humorous. Explicit teaching here is very helpful. You can use real-life experiences or situations. You can also use any of the various social skills teaching techniques. Keep in mind that figurative language can be a source of great confusion, and it is possible to explicitly teach many concepts. See *The Hidden Curriculum* (Myles, Trautman, & Schelvan, 2004) for specific examples.

10. **We have a 6-year-old son with autism. My wife and I think he has a good school program and he's made progress, but we'd like more input on what they are doing at school so we can work on it at home as well. Any suggestions?**

Your question in an important one—working on generalization of skills across settings is important and you have important opportunities to help your son make connections between school and the larger world. You can do any of several things. You can ask the teacher to be in occasional touch (by phone or e-mail) about what is going on at school. You can also ask to have some of your son's work sent home to get an idea of what he is working on. As part of the IEP process you can ask for some attention to the issue of communication and generalization of skills. Think about family and recreational activities than can be a source of pleasures as well as learning. Finally there are a number of resources—including some web based ones—that are good sources of information and suggestions. One of the new ones of these, www.rethinkautism.com, has an ABA based curriculum with videos, lessons, and so forth that parents and teachers can use.[2]

---

[2]One of us (FV) is on their professional advisory board.

CHAPTER 7

Working With Young Children

It may seem a little paradoxical but our understanding about how autism first presents itself has, until relatively recently, been pretty limited. One of the big problems was that almost all the data came from parent reports of their children at age 3, or 5 (or later) when the children first were diagnosed. Essentially, parents were asked to look back and recall information accurately, which is not so easy to do. Another approach was to look at videotapes of children at first birthday parties, at Chanukah, or Christmas, and observe their behavior looking backward in time. Both of these approaches gave us some information, but it was frustrating for researchers not to be able to see and work directly with very young infants with autism. This situation is now changing dramatically. This has implications for services since it seems for many children that early diagnosis and treatment can make the biggest difference. It also has important implications for research because we can try to sort out important aspects of *how* development happens in autism. Perhaps that knowledge will let us develop better treatments. Being able to know the first warning signs of autism, perhaps even very subtle ones, would also help us do a better job of screening.

In this chapter, we review what is known about autism as it appears in infants and young children and some of the intervention methods used. Keep in mind that, in contrast to some other areas in autism research, this is an area where knowledge is evolving very rapidly. Also keep in mind that what we do know is mostly about autism. Children with Asperger's come to diagnosis much later while those with "autistic-like" features (pervasive developmental disorder not otherwise specified [PDD-NOS]) are variable in terms of when they come to professional attention. At least some of what we know about autism probably applies, however. We talk about early development in these conditions later in this chapter.

In his original report, Leo Kanner suggested that autism was congenital, something the child was born with. Studies that ask parents about when they were first concerned about their child's development tell us that for children

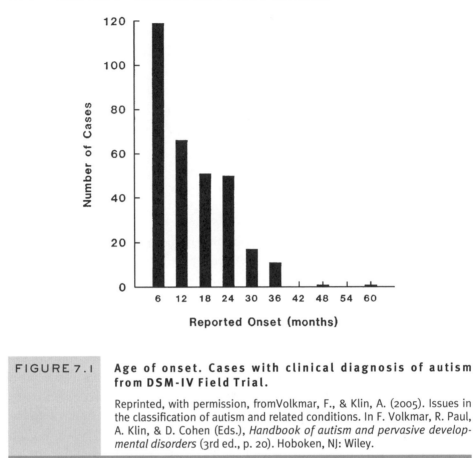

FIGURE 7.1   **Age of onset. Cases with clinical diagnosis of autism from DSM-IV Field Trial.**

Reprinted, with permission, fromVolkmar, F., & Klin, A. (2005). Issues in the classification of autism and related conditions. In F. Volkmar, R. Paul, A. Klin, & D. Cohen (Eds.), *Handbook of autism and pervasive developmental disorders* (3rd ed., p. 20). Hoboken, NJ: Wiley.

with autism, most parents are concerned in the first year of life, about 90% are worried by 24 months, and essentially all parents are by the time the child is 36 months of age. Figure 7.1 shows data on reported age of onset from the work done as part of the *Diagnostic and Statistical Manual of Mental Disorders*, 4th edition (DSM-IV) definition of autism. Keep in mind that this is when parents were worried, *not* when very subtle signs of difficulty might have been seen by specialists. Those difficulties probably might be detectable even sooner. Given the data we do have, what are the kinds of things that worry parents (and professionals) early in life?

Observing babies is complicated because they change so quickly and also because, even within a single day, behavior can vary tremendously. Furthermore, they usually sleep a lot and, accordingly, being able to catch the baby at just the right moment is critical for people who want to observe them. Also, some behaviors that are perfectly fine at one age may be a warning sign at a later age. For example, some of the simple play that babies do in exploring things with their mouth becomes worrisome if it isn't replaced by more advanced play skills as the child gets older. In infants, there can normally be what appear to be major "disconnects," for example, between what the baby seems to want and how good he or she is at getting it, such as being able to reach for something *and* signal the parent with eye contact that he or she is interested in it. Such abilities develop in the first year of life. Given variability in the child's state (awake/asleep) and behavior and motivation, it may be hard for parents to get the child to demonstrate things that show either normal development or worrisome behavior. This creates some problems for assessment (people who work with babies learn to be patient!). There are also many reasons babies can be slow to do things. Some develop alternative methods for doing something.

Another issue, which we discuss in much greater detail in Chapter 13, is the problem of regression. That is, some babies seem to develop normally and then lose skills. Often, this can be seen with word use. Twenty percent or more of parents of children with autism report the rapid or gradual loss of words. The child then seems less interested in social interaction. Research on this group of cases is complicated for a number of reasons. Given that, until recently, we almost always are looking backward, as it were, our sources of information are limited. Research using video tapes suggests that in some cases the children do indeed look good at around the first birthday but then regress. That being said, other work suggests that sometimes what parents see as a regression is actually more of a failure to progress; that is, the child has developed reasonably normally but development then slows down. In other cases, even though parents report a regression, careful discussion with them reveals that there was reason to be worried even earlier! Given these complications, as you can imagine, it is hard to know how best to think about regression in these cases. It is clear (see Chapter 13) that a very late onset with perfectly normal development to age 3 or 4 and then a profound regression is not a good sign—those children tend not to do well. Research is under way to try to understand the meaning of regression in autism.

SIGNS OF AUTISM BEFORE 1 YEAR OF AGE

In most cases children don't seem to regress, but parents become concerned as the child fails to develop words or to respond to sounds or seems socially "disconnected." In his first report on autism, Leo Kanner emphasized this social disconnectedness in his use of the word *autism*. He was careful to say that, unlike typically developing children, the infant with autism didn't engage in early social routines and seemed to lack social interest. Other behaviors that he also described in older children, for example, echolalia or motor mannerisms/stereotypies, require more developmental skills than young babies can muster.

There is good reason to stick with what Kanner said about focusing on social abilities because we realize those are things present in the typical child from birth. Interestingly, Kanner also thought that infants with autism had trouble in adjusting their bodies when they were picked up or in assuming what are called "anticipatory postures" when the parent is getting set to pick them up (adjusting themselves to be held). A general lack of social engagement and limited interest in eye contact is often reported, as are problems in imitation. Problems in imitation can include copying motor things (pat-a-cake) or vocal ones (babbling to imitate). Sometimes babies who go on to have clear autism are described as easily startled or "on a high wire act" all the time. When picking up the baby, by 6 months or so he or she may seem to be floppy (what is called low tone) or too stiff (high tone).

Parents, of course, notice many different things. But most of the studies that try to group these find that early parental concerns often cluster around the social difficulties and some of the problems in what we call arousal and regulation. In a study from our Center, we talked to parents of preschoolers with autism about behaviors that emerge very early in life in typically developing children.[1] We found five of these behaviors that children with autism didn't do; this was true even when we compared the children to another group of children without autism but who were developmentally delayed. These five behaviors were:

- Showing anticipation of being picked up
- Showing affection toward familiar people
- Showing interest in children or peers other than siblings
- Reaching for a familiar person
- Playing simple interaction games with others

Other studies have also found early differences in what is termed *temperament* (a shorthand term for baby personality style). These studies have found that parents of children with autism who noted troubles early often reported the child to be either very difficult or very passive. Typically developing babies are interested in faces from very early in life, and by 8 or 9 months old they have become so good at looking at faces that the readily recognize familiar people and usually become afraid of strangers. Children with autism may not show this.

Using home movies and videos has also shown some differences in the first year of life in children with autism. It is often found that children who go on to

---

[1]Klin & Volkmar (1992). The development of individuals with autism: Implications for the theory of mind hypothesis. *Journal of Child Psychology and Psychiatry, 15,* 317-331.

TABLE 7.1	SYMPTOMS OF AUTISM IN THE FIRST YEAR OF LIFE

Social Symptoms
  Limited ability to anticipate being picked up
  Low frequency of looking at people
  Limited interest in interactional games
  Limited affection toward familiar people
  Content to be left alone
Communication Symptoms
  Poor response to name (doesn't respond when called)
  Does not frequently look at objects held by others
  Restricted interests and stereotyped behaviors
  Mouths objects excessively
  Does not like to be touched

SOURCE: Reprinted, with permission, from Chawarska, K., & Volkmar, F. (2005). Autism in infancy and early childhood. In F. Volkmar, R. Paul, A. Klin, & D. Cohen (Eds.), *Handbook of autism and pervasive developmental disorders* (3rd ed., p. 230). Hoboken, NJ: Wiley.

have a diagnosis of autism seem less likely to look at other people or to smile or vocalize to others. They may be less likely to seek out others. As babies get a little older, they start to respond to their own name, but children with autism, by about 8 to 10 months, often don't seem to do this. Infants with autism may put things in their mouths more than other infants—even ones with delays. They may seem not to like to be touched. Some of the unusual sensory behaviors seem to develop a bit later than others and sometimes don't become really striking for another year or more.

Overall, it seems that many infants with autism do display differences in the first months of life. Sometimes parents will notice differences from very early on. More frequently, parents start to notice problems at 6 to 8 months of age, as the child seems not very interested in interaction with them. The infant with autism may still have an interest in the nonsocial world. Failure to respond to name is one of the striking manifestations by the end of the first year of life (and an item frequently included in screening instruments for autism). Symptoms suggestive of autism in the first year of life are summarized in Table 7.1.

SIGNS OF AUTISM BETWEEN 12 AND 36 MONTHS

By about a year of age even more sophisticated social skills start to emerge, for example what are called *joint attention skills* are usually starting to develop and these skills help the infant engage with their parents and learn to focus on what is important. Although we know a lot about this issue based on parent reports and looking back at home videos, only now are we starting to get good information collected *at the time*. This is coming from a series of what are called *prospective* (forward-looking) studies following large numbers of children at risk for autism, starting at birth to see how the first symptoms of autism develop.

Even when they are worried early on, it is presently most typical for parents to start to seek help after the child turns one. Many parents are told to "wait and see" or that "he'll grow out of it" or that "Einstein didn't talk until he was 5." In a study some time ago, it was typical for several years to elapse between the time parents were first worried and the child's diagnosis. Fortunately, awareness of autism has grown both on the part of parents and on the part of health care providers. All that being said, it still can be hard to diagnose autism in very young infants, and parents often start pursuing assessments after the first birthday. What kinds of things trigger this? Common reasons for parents to seek assessment include:

- Speech delay
- Lack of response to speech (worries the child may be deaf)
- Regression or loss of skills or failure to make usual gains in skills
- Unusual behaviors (preoccupations, early repetitive movements)
- Limited interest in playing and interacting with others

The unusual interests and behaviors usually appear sometime after 12 months and before age 3 years. These can include staring at fans or spinning things or developing repetitive movements (often of the hands or fingers). After 1 year of age, the kinds of things parents start to notice correspond with the kinds of things we look at in older children in making a diagnosis of autism: problems in social interaction and communication and play, and unusual responses to the environment. Of the behaviors required for a diagnosis, this last category seems to be the one that comes later, sometimes raising problems in diagnosis if a baby has trouble in the other two areas but not yet the third one.

After 12 months, problems in communication often become more notable. These include delays in both development of language and nonverbal means of communication, that is, gestures and eye contact. Young children with autism typically do not use pointing gestures, do not show things to other people, and rarely give objects to others to share or to get help. Young children often engage in what experts call **joint attention**, which refers to the two way back-and-forth between people around a third thing, often an object. So if, say, something interesting (or scary) happens, or maybe just something a little new, the typically developing baby will more or less immediately "check in" with the parents, looking at them to get their take on the situation. Or the child will look at the parent and then look at the thing they are concerned about and then back to parent, drawing the parent's attention to it. Toddlers with autism may use their finger to point to something they want but not usually with eye contact with their parent. The child may not follow if the parent points to something and may have little interest in imitating parents or siblings. The child's preference for being left alone may also be dramatic. The child's emotional response to things may be unusual—not happy with things other children would be happy about, but panicked around other things. The child may seem less sensitive to pain or may start having marked taste sensitivities and unusual food preferences (often refusing to eat new foods).

By this age, research studies often are able to compare toddlers with autism to toddlers with other kinds of problems, such as toddlers whose language is delayed. Compared to such children, those with autism have trouble with pointing to show and in using gestures. Children with other language problems are able to do these things. As children get a little older those with autism may not be using imagination in play. Signs of autism between 12 and 36 months are summarized in Table 7.2.

In one of the first follow-up studies of 2-year-olds referred for possible autism, Cathy Lord (1995) followed a group of 30 children and found several items at age 2 that predicted which ones were likely to have autism. These included a lack of a number of social behaviors (shared enjoyment, interest in other children, social reciprocity, greeting behavior) and use of the other

---

TABLE 7.2   SYMPTOMS OF AUTISM: AGES 1 TO 3 YEARS

Social Symptoms
Abnormal eye contact
   Limited social referencing
   Limited interest in other children
   Limited social smile
   Low frequency of looking at people
   Limited range of facial expression
   Limited sharing of affect/enjoyment
   Little interest in interactive games
   Limited functional play
   No pretend play
   Limited motor imitation
Communication Symptoms
   Low frequency of verbal or nonverbal communication
   Failure to share interest (e.g., through pointing, sharing, giving, showing)
   Poor response to name
   Failure to respond to communicative gestures (pointing, giving, showing)
   Use of other's body as a tool (pulls hand to desired object without making eye contact, as if *hand* rather than person obtains object)
   Restricted interests and stereotyped behaviors
   Hand or finger mannerisms
   Inappropriate use of objects
   Repetitive interest/play
   Unusual sensory behaviors
   Hyper/hyposensitivity to sounds, texture, tastes, visual stimuli

person's body as a tool. When you see toddlers with autism try to get something, such as something out of reach, or if they want something to happen (like ringing a bell), they may take your hand to the object but without looking at you—it is as if the *hand* rather than the person is supposed to get the object. Other problems included attending to voice, pointing, and understanding of gestures. Some of the repetitive and restricted behaviors also were noted, including unusual hand and finger movement and odd sensory behaviors. Abnormality in two of the behaviors (showing and attending to voice) could be used to correctly classify over 80% of cases. One of the things that was very helpful about this study was the clarification that some children, at age 2, did not show the unusual finger/hand movements or sensitivities characteristic of autism, but did start to do so by age 3. In other words, it seemed that some children only gradually developed all the symptoms needed technically for a diagnosis of autism, but did so by 3 years of age. Much less commonly, a child who looked like he had autism *before* age 3 did not look like he did by age 3.

Some children who go on to have PDD-NOS (or what it sometimes called autism spectrum disorder [ASD]) may look like they have autism early on, but then develop more skills and lose some of the unusual behaviors. For children who continue to have strictly defined autism, the social and communication behaviors remain very consistent. By around age 3, the child may seem more easily distracted and may have unusual reactions to sounds.

Given their problems in social interaction, it is important to know that young children with autism do form attachments to their parents. At first, this might seem counterintuitive, given what parents often report as their experience of the child. But experimental work does demonstrate that children with autism do form such attachments. Interestingly, the process of attachment formation can sometimes also be a bit indiscriminate. For example, the child may develop attachments to unusual objects. Attachments to objects are frequently seen in typically developing children (the technical term for this is a *transitional* object, since it helps the child deal with transitions like being left in day care or going to sleep at night). When these are seen in typically developing children, the objects are usually soft (teddy bear, blanket) and the actual object is very important (one of us once pawed through a dumpster at a McDonald's on interstate 95 looking for our older daughter's puffy, which she was very attached to and had, as is typical, inadvertently thrown out in the trash!) In autism, these objects differ in two respects: They are unusual in that they are typically *hard* and not soft and may be unusual in other respects (e.g., *Reader's Digest* magazine, Wheaties boxes, bundles of sticks, rocks, metal airplanes, firetrucks), *and* the specific object is not so important as the class of object (any magazine of the same type will do). It may be that the attachments we see in autism are "strategic" rather than "affiliative," that is, that they have to do less with purely social connections.

To briefly summarize, in the first year of life, the earliest signs of autism are decreased interest in looking at people and in responding to being called by their name. Problems in the sensory area may be noted, but this is much less consistent; similarly, it is less likely that infants under 1 year of age have some of the kinds of mannerisms and repetitive behaviors and interests that seem to develop a bit later with autism. After the first birthday, though, the features of autism usually become more apparent. Many different aspects of the child's development are affected. Occasionally, infants seem to develop normally and then either have development slow down or they actually lose skills. For the typically developing child, by 2 years of age, there usually will be tremendous social interest and many words, along with the beginnings of more imaginative play, while toddlers with autism seem to have little interest in others—including other children—and may prefer to be left on their own. The child's emotional range, as reflected in their smiling and taking pleasure in things, may seem restricted. After the first birthday, problems in communication start to become more noteworthy. Words are often delayed, and some of the usual gestures and nonverbal behaviors may not develop. Pointing without prompting to show things and difficulties understanding the gestures of others may be seen, and the problem with ignoring their own name usually continues. With toddlers who have some words, echolalia (repeating) may start. The unusual motor behaviors seem to emerge for many children between ages 2 and 3. These often include hand and finger mannerisms. They may also include unusual sensory preoccupations or fears, such as staring at the blades of a fan for long periods or developing panic about the sound of a vacuum cleaner.

Asperger's and PDD-NOS

Much less is known about the early development of children with Asperger's and PDD-NOS, although some infants with early delays of the type seen in autism clearly develop into the latter category. In Asperger's, most of what we know comes from reports of parents and, in general, is fairly consistent with what Asperger said in the first place. If, like Asperger, you think of the condition as one where social difficulties occur in the face of what seem to be good language (but not necessarily communication) skills, you might suspect that these are children whose parents would be worried much later—and this indeed usually is the case. The typical time for parents of a child with Asperger's to become concerned is at entry to preschool when social difficulties become much more noticeable. Asperger reported things like the child's talking before walking, and it is not uncommon for parents to report this or to say (as Asperger did) that "words are his lifeline." Motor delays are usual, but parents are typically not very concerned because they see the child as very bright and verbal. In contrast to autism, the unusual motor manifestations are less likely to develop early on, and the child is more likely to start exhibiting unusual interests and preoccupations that start to interfere in other ways with the life of the child and family. These may include things like train or bus schedules, the weather or the Weather Channel, dinosaurs, or astronomy. Sometimes the child is interested in something that originally frightened him. For instance, he may develop an interest in snakes because he is afraid of them. Usually, however, parents are not so worried until the child goes into preschool and they receive a call from a concerned teacher that the child isn't fitting in. Often, the child is interested in being social, but his attempts to make friends put off other children—hugging children he barely knows or engaging them in long discussions about his topic of interest. Sometimes the child will have trouble tolerating changes in the schedule—if circle time is supposed to happen at 10:15, it had better not happen at 10:16. We talk more about Asperger's in the next two chapters.

Are parents always the ones who are first concerned? The answer is no. Often, parents particularly first-time parents aren't the experts in child development they will become after they have had a child. Parents may not be worried if the child has developed some language. While parents are often the first ones to be worried, sometimes it is grandparents (who have had a lot of experience) or other family members. Sometimes it is the pediatrician or health care provider (and, as we talk about in the next section, screening for autism is increasingly common). We have now had the experience of having day care providers worried about autism in a child who seems not to be developing normally. All this reflects the greater awareness of autism and the greater access to information about it.

SCREENING FOR AUTISM—FIRST STEPS IN GETTING A DIAGNOSIS AND SERVICE

As we discussed in Chapter 3, a number of different screeners for autism have been developed. Some of these are specific to autism. Others assess development more generally. Some are based on parent report, some on observation by a professional, and others use both sources of information. Essentially all of these try to tap into some of the characteristics in autism. At this point, what are critically needed are more objective, physiologically based, screenings, based, for example, on how the child takes in social information. Efforts are under way to develop such techniques. An example of one potential method is shown in Figure 7.2 (baby eye tracking).

Usually, the first person parent's talk to when they have concerns about their child's development is the child's pediatrician or other health care provider. If the pediatrician has not followed the child since birth, he or she needs to meet with

FIGURE 7.2   **Eye gaze pattern in a 2-year-old with autism. This image, generated using infrared eye tracking shows the unusual gaze of a toddler with autism. Rather than looking at any of the characters in the scene, the child focuses on what, to most toddlers (and adults), would be irrelevant details.**

Reprinted, with permission from Klin, A., Jones, W., Schultz, R., & Volkmar, F. (2003). The enactive mind—from actions to cognition: Lessons from autism. *Philosophical Transactions of the Royal Society*, p. 350.

the parents and take a thorough history, starting with a family history, the details of any problems during the pregnancy and delivery, and careful developmental history of the child up to the current time. The pediatrician will want to focus on speech and language development, fine and gross motor skills, social skills, and whether any restrictive interests, stereotypies, or repetitive behaviors exist.

After taking a careful history, a thorough physical exam (including looking at the child's growth charts) needs to be done to see if there are any signs of underlying disorders that can be found with developmental delays. An underlying disorder is rare, but the ones to consider with autism are fragile X, and tuberous sclerosis (see Chapter 10). The child also needs to have a good hearing test done, since children with hearing loss can have speech delays or some autistic features. That may be done in the pediatrician's office, or you may be referred to a specialist for this testing. If there is any suggestion that the child has a seizure disorder, he or she will need an electroencephalogram (EEG) or appointment with a neurologist. Depending on what is found during the history or physical exam, the pediatrician may order some blood work or other diagnostic testing.

Once your health care provider is concerned about a developmental delay, he or she will probably have you fill out one of several screening questionnaires that we referred to earlier. The age of your child will help direct your health care provider to a specific screening test. The American Academy of Pediatrics (www.aap.org/healthtopics/autism.cfm) has recently come out with a Resource Toolkit for Clinicians to help pediatricians evaluate children for ASDs.[2] For children under 18 months old, they recommend a screener called Communication and Symbolic Behavior Scale Developmental Profile (CSBS-DP). For children 18 to 24 months old, they have recommended a screener known as the Modified Checklist for Autism in Toddlers (M-CHAT). Parents answer a series of questions, and the pediatrician then scores the test. If, after putting all of the information together, you and your doctor are concerned about an ASD, your child will probably be referred to a state-run early intervention program that provides evaluation and treatment of children from birth to 3 years old. These have been funded through money provided by the Individuals with Disabilities Education Act (IDEA). You and your doctor may also want an evaluation by a team of specialists in ASDs, but that may take longer to arrange.

Keep in mind that the idea of screening is to quickly see if there is reason for concern. Children can "fail" screens for many reasons other than having autism. For example, language problems or cognitive delays may be picked up on a screening test. For somewhat older children, problems with attention may also turn up in the screening.

Some aspects of development are more affected by autism than others. As a result, sometimes you see areas where the child with autism is relatively (or sometimes absolutely) advanced. This can result in what are called *splinter skills* or "savant" abilities. In autism, these usually are skills that are nonverbal (puzzles), whereas in Asperger's, verbal abilities often are an area of strength. In any case, the sometimes very divergent abilities within a single child can make for real challenges in intervention. It is important that teachers and parents are realistic about where the child is functioning and aim neither too high nor too low.

Diagnostic Assessments

For younger children, assessment issues can be complicated. Many of the behavioral problems associated with autism, along with lack of social interest and communication problems, can interfere with assessment (see Chapter 3; also see the reading list for additional reading—particularly chapters by Bishop, Lustyer,

---

[2]Other good web sites with information on early diagnosis of autism include First Signs (www.firstsigns.org) and the CDC's autism website (www.cdc.gov).

Richler, and Lord; Chawarska and Bearss; Paul; and Baranek and colleagues, 2008—all in a recent book on autism in infants edited by one of us and our colleagues Chawarska, Klin, and Volkmar, 2008). Young children with autism may have trouble with new materials and transitions and become frustrated easily. Accordingly, patience and often multiple sessions may be needed to get a good sense of the child's profile of strengths and weaknesses. For older children, it is common for a psychologist to give various tests, including tests of intelligence. For preschool children, developmental tests are often used. These are like traditional IQ tests in many ways, but by avoiding the use of the term *IQ*, there is more emphasis on emerging skills and less stress on long-term prediction. Several different tests can be used. We summarize a few of them here:

- *Bayley Scales.* These scales are based on one of the oldest of the developmental tests, which have been revised and updated recently as the Bayley-III (Bayley, 2006). The Bayley Scales have traditionally been the most generally used tests in infants and toddlers for both research and clinical work. This test is used for infants from 1-to 42-months and includes several different scales focused on cognitive, language, motor, social–emotional, and adaptive behavior development (only the first three of these are given to the child; the other two are done with parents).Testing time varies, depending on age of the child.

- *Battelle Developmental Inventory.* This is a test developed for children from birth to 7 years of age. It assesses development in several areas, including personal-social, motor, communication, adaptive, and cognitive. Compared to other tests, it takes a long time to administer—up to 2 hours. There are some potential drawbacks to this test based on the way it was developed (normed), and there can be some issues in understanding the scores.

- *Mullen Scales.* The Mullen Scales of Early Learning can be used in children up to 58 months of age. This test yields what are called T scores (the average is 50, and the standard deviation is 10) as well as age-equivalent and percentile scores. One great advantage of this test is its use of multiple scales assessed separately: gross and fine motor skills, visual reception (somewhat like nonverbal learning), and **receptive and expressive language.** The ability to disentangle language skills from nonverbal learning is a plus, since it appears that nonverbal abilities may be a better predictor of an ultimate ability to develop language. The test takes from 15 minutes to an hour to administer, depending on the age of the child. This test is now fairly frequently used in developmental assessment of children with autism.

All the tests we've just mentioned assess an infant's or toddler's skills against some standard. Another approach focuses on expected competencies. This approach, called criterion-referenced testing (as opposed to norm referenced testing) is more focused on sampling skills, which can be important for intervention. Tests of this type include the Brigance Diagnostic Inventory of Early Development Revised and the Hawaii Early Learning Profile (HELP). A similar test, the Rossetti Infant Toddler Language Scale, focuses only on communication and parent–child interaction. While these tests can help clarify some of the things the child can and can't do, they typically do not replace norm-referenced tests in a diagnostic evaluation.

Delays in development of speech and communication are common in children with autism, and, as compared to typically developing children, they tend to develop language later than other children and their language is unusual in many ways. For example, the range of babble the baby with autism produces may be more limited (few sounds and unusual sounds) and problems in nonverbal communication are common. Similarly, at around 9 months of age, typically developing infants start to coordinate eye contact and gestures when they request things (looking at the parent while reaching for an object) and a shared focus of interest becomes important. As compared to infants with other problems, those with autism are not as likely to use conventional gestures like pointing and showing. They may use the hand of the parent as a tool to get objects (without making eye contact). In this situation, it is almost as though only the hand, but not the person attached to it, exists. For children with autism, behaviors that signal a *joint* attentional activity tend to be reduced in frequency, as are other communicative behaviors, like responding to their own name.

The communication portion of the diagnostic assessment usually is done by a speech pathologist, although some of the assessments can be done by a psychologist or other trained professional. It focuses on several different aspects of communication development, including vocabulary word knowledge, both receptively and expressively as well as more general communication skills. Usually one, or often several, of the standard speech-language tests are used to establish levels of functioning. If delays are found, areas known to be specifically at risk in autism are targeted. Following are some of the tests that are used:

- *Peabody Picture Vocabulary Test.* This tests looks at understanding of words (single word vocabulary) in children from age 2 years 6 months through adulthood. This is a well-established, frequently used test. The child is given a word and asked to select it from a panel of pictures.

- *Expressive One-Word Picture Vocabulary Test.* This test is used with children age 2 to 18 years. As you might expect, it assesses the ability to name (as opposed to understand) objects, actions, and concepts. The child is shown a picture and asked to provide a name. The test is well done and is also frequently used.

- *Rossetti Infant-Toddler Language Scale.* This test assesses communication (not just vocabulary) in children from birth to age 3. It is a criterion-referenced test that looks at both verbal and preverbal communication skills. Information comes from both direct observation and parental report.

- *Reynell Developmental Language Scale.* This test assesses both receptive and expressive language, but more broadly than only vocabulary; that is, it looks more at communication. It takes about 30 minutes to be administered and uses materials that interest most children. It is well standardized, and information can be readily translated to an intervention plan.

- *Communication and Symbolic Behavior Scales.* This norm-referenced, standardized instrument uses a play-based format to look at children's language as well as symbolic development. It can be used in infants and toddlers whose language abilities are between the 6- and 24-month levels of the typical population (up to age 6 years for children with delays). It takes an hour or so to complete.

In addition to formal testing, the speech pathologist will be looking at the entire range of behaviors involved in communication, including the range and types of sounds produced, unusual language features (such as echoed language, pronoun reversal), unusual or idiosyncratic language (word/phrase use that is unique to the individual), and other language abnormalities frequently seen in autism. For children who have some spoken language, a focus on their social use of language (what speech pathologists call **pragmatics**) will also be included.

As part of the assessment, the speech pathologist may engage in a number of behaviors that parents might see as odd or even a bit disrespectful. For example, she might seem to tempt the child with a toy, but then keep it to herself or offer the child something that is hard to reach or in a container. She may pretend not to understand something the child says or seems to want. All of these are ploys to see what the child will do to ask for help, to protest, request, and so forth. Often, the speech pathologist will try to get a language sample (if the child is verbal). Even if the child isn't yet using words the speech pathologist will be interested in the range of sounds the child makes and the kinds of communications he uses and their function (e.g., does the child only communicate to get something?). It is very typical for assessment of younger children to include both informal, naturalistic observation (often play based) as well as more formal assessment instruments.

Sensory and motor assessments are available as well. These are described in greater detail in Chapter 3. These can include parent report measures (e.g., the Vineland Adaptive Behavior Scales for motor skills or the Sensory Experiences Question for sensory responses) or be direct assessment (the Mullen Scales for gross and fine motor skills).

In addition to the results of formal testing, the observations of the occupational therapist, psychologist, or speech pathologist can also add to intervention planning. For example, while the professional may have to give certain items in certain ways to correspond to the way the test has to be done, there are many opportunities to see how the child approaches tasks, what kinds of things the examiner can do to get the child interested, and ways you can get the child engaged. These kinds of observations can often readily then be used to help develop the intervention program.

Depending on the child's age and levels of function some of the more traditional diagnostic assessment instruments can be used such as the Autism Diagnostic Interview-Revised (ADI-R). Particularly for young children, there is considerable potential for developmental change. Evaluators have to make judgments about how representative results are and be aware that tests may have specific requirements; for instance, the child's mental age or developmental level may have to be at a certain level to use the test appropriately.

Access to Services for Very Young Children

As we discussed in Chapter 4, the law in the United States mandates school responsibility for providing a free and appropriate public education (FAPE) for every child, starting when the child is 3. Before that time a different federal law, sometimes called Part C, applies and is designed to "enhance the development of infants and toddlers with disability and minimize their potential for developmental delay."[3] This eligibility applies to all infants and toddlers with disabilities and delays in physical, cognitive, social, emotional, communicative, or adaptive development and, at the discretion of the state, to give services to children at risk who might experience delay if they were not given early intervention services. Unlike the law for children of school age, states have a choice to participate in offering early childhood services. Parents can be asked for part of the cost, but families who can't pay still should be able to get services.

As part of this program, early intervention services, known as EI (early intervention) or as Birth-to-Three or other such names, are supposed to develop a program of coordination across responsible state agencies. As a practical matter, the lead state agency is often either the department of education or the department of developmental disabilities (these have different names in the different states). Once a child is referred to the agency, it should provide an evaluation and develop what is termed an individualized family service plan (IFSP) that is similar to the individualized educational plan (IEP) developed for school-aged

---

[3]The actual law is found in 20 USC §§1431 and subsequent sections.

children. It differs in that the plan is focused on early intervention and must emphasize services for the family. Parents have to be involved in the process and have to consent to delivering services. Given the focus of the IFSP on the family, there usually will be discussion about helping parents foster the child's development and helping other family members (e.g., the siblings) cope. Typically, there is a regular review of the IFSP at 6-month intervals. Many of the same considerations that apply in being involved in an IEP (see Chapter 4) apply here. There are some special issues for families of younger children, and supporting the family and child is particularly important (see Bailey, 2008).

As a practical matter, early intervention services are quite variable around the country and sometimes even within the same county or town. As we described in Chapter 5, there are a number of different programs that may be applicable to your child. Sometimes these are center-based (the child goes for some hours each day or some days during the week to an early intervention center). Sometimes the service providers come into the home. In some cases, the child works with trained professionals; in others, parents are trained in simple procedures aimed at helping the child develop new skills, and often different approaches to early intervention are combined. Often, an early intervention program will include educational therapy, speech-communication, and occupational or physical therapy. There may be work on family issues and training. Even when the forms of early intervention differ, the goals are generally the same minimizing any disruption that autism or another condition has on the child's development and enhancing the child's cognitive, communicative, and adaptive skills.

Early intervention programs commonly draw on the range of special education services and interventions provided to slightly older children. The law specifically encourages providing services in the "natural environment"—the home. Providers of care may come into the home on a regular basis. A special education teacher might visit and work with the child but also give suggestions to parent(s). The speech pathologist or occupational therapist might come into the home and work with the child and family, or they might work in a center-based program. Toddlers with autism are very good candidates for early intervention. They can be taught using various methods, and it is while they are young that they are most likely to learn new skills. As children turn 3, the school district is obligated to provide services, and in many cases this works well because a more intensive program can be provided and it is easier to coordinate all the services in one setting. Occasionally, parents will continue home-based programs until the child is a bit older. This is particularly true if the child seems to be making good progress and the parents can support (and sometimes afford) the level of services provided. One of the problems with home-based programs is the lack of access to typical peers, who can be powerful teachers of social skills. A number of excellent books on teaching social and play skills appear in the reading list.

Usually, parents will have let the school district know that they have a child who is 3 or nearly 3 and in need of special preschool services. Almost intrinsically, there will be some logistical problems, since schools are less focused on the family and more likely to use a center-based approach. The early intervention providers should work to coordinate a smooth transfer. Parents must be part of this process and give consent. As we describe in Chapter 4, the school may wish to do its own assessment and will involve the parents in developing the IEP, which then takes the place of the early IFSP.

Program Content

As we discuss in Chapter 5, a large body of work has now shown the importance of early diagnosis and intervention for improving long-term outcome. The report from the National Research Council that we discussed in detail in Chapter 5 emphasizes that the evidence for many programs' effectiveness is strong. These programs have similarities and differences, as we've discussed. In some programs, the teacher very much sets the agenda; in others, the child is allowed some role in this process. Some programs emphasize more traditional developmental principles, trying to build on the child's behavior in a systematic way consistent with what happens in typical development. As we mentioned in Chapters 5 and 6, regardless of their differences, these programs also have a number of things in common. This includes providing a reasonably intensive treatment, a focus on data-based instruction and record keeping, and an explicit focus on intensive teaching and helping the child become more independent.

The applied behavior analysis (ABA) model is probably the most well-known and most common treatment approach and has a solid research basis (Harris and Weiss, 2007). Other programs may focus more on natural settings and target what are thought of as highly critical and important behaviors (that is, pivotal response training programs; Koegel et al., 2008). Other programs are more developmentally based, giving the child a role in helping set the agenda for what is learned; the Greenspan approach (Greenspan, 2009) and SCERTS models (Prizant et al., 2004; Wetherby and Woods, 2008) are examples of these approaches. In other cases, programs are what might be called eclectic picking and choosing based on a range of techniques; the book *Educating Children With Autism* (National Research Council, 2001) has good summaries of all these programs. Increasingly, states are adopting explicit guidelines for early intervention in autism. In a handful of states (e.g., North Carolina and Delaware), statewide service programs have been established. Given how diverse children with autism are, it may not be surprising that there are so many choices!

Unfortunately, as we talked about in Chapter 5, there can be some issues. It is typical for the school to want the child to be in their autism program, sometimes this is like trying to fit a square peg into a round hole! Put another way we don't always do as good a job as we might in terms of matching children up to the programs that are best suited for them. Fortunately, many—probably most—programs work well for most children. But when there is an exception, parents and teachers need to be more creative in thinking about solutions. Sadly, there also is a lot of variability—in some states, this variability is marked from one town to another or one county to another, or sometimes even from one school to a different school in the same town.

To a great extent, what is worked on in early intervention and preschool school–based programs will have to depend on the child and his or her special needs and issues. There are, however, some general things that often run through good programs. These include a very explicit focus on teaching communication and social interaction skills. There also will be a focus on dealing with problems in behavior, particularly if these interfere with learning. Given difficulties in social interaction and play, there is also often a very explicit focus on teaching play skills (one of the areas where typical peers can be very helpful). Given the tendency children with autism have to be very rigid in what they learn, there usually is a strong focus on adaptive skills (taking skills into the real world) and on generalization.

Early intervention programs typically will focus on a number of areas that cause trouble for young children with autism. Given difficulties with social engagement, it is probably not surprising that problems arise with organization and attention. Organizational difficulties (technically referred to as executive functions) have to do with what you might think about when planning your work agenda. Usually, these start to emerge as the child reaches school age, but some organizational difficulties can be seen early on. These can be addressed in various ways, including pictures, schedules, and other supports (see Chapters 5 and 6). Being able to focus one's attention is also important. One of the difficulties in young children is not that they don't attend but what they attend to. Accordingly, programs will work on helping the child learn to use joint attention (social cues). Attention may be fostered in a number of ways, including keeping the environment simple so that the child is forced to focus on what is relevant. Given the importance of communication for subsequent development, a focus on fostering communication is almost always part of the early intervention program. There should be a focus on all relevant aspects of communication, including both understanding (receptive language) and speaking (expressive language). Because communication is also intrinsically social, there is usually a focus on social aspects of language and communication. The kinds of activities that are worked on include imitation of other people's movements or sounds they make, building up vocabulary, using words for objects/actions or both, developing sentences, and then adding the "bells and whistles" of language, starting with things like yes and no and moving to more sophisticated concepts. For children who have trouble with verbal communication, a variety of alternative methods are available, including picture exchange, computerized systems, or sign language. As we discussed in Chapter 5, parents sometimes assume that if the therapist wants to use these methods, it means they've given up on the child's talking. In fact, anything that can be done to help the child learn to communicate can help the child eventually learn to speak.

Self-help skills (see Chapter 6) are usually an area of real trouble for children with autism. Any variations from the usual or routine can cause trouble. This likely reflects the fact that they may have a rigid and context-dependent learning style and, lacking the social "glue" that most of us have for pulling the world together, children with autism are constantly relearning solutions to old and recurrent problems. As a practical matter, personal independence and self-sufficiency in adulthood starts with teaching adaptive skills in preschool. These include dressing and undressing, personal care, how to behave in the community, using the toilet, and so forth.

TOILET TRAINING

Requirements for Toilet Training

- Understanding what is wanted
- Motivation to do what is wanted
- Motor coordination

Obstacles to Toilet Training in ASDs

- Cognitive problems (may not understand what is wanted)
- Social problems (problems with imitation, problems with body awareness)
- Motor and sensory issues (may interfere)

Approaches to Toilet Training

- Develop a routine—be aware of optimal times
- Develop system for communicating need (words/pictures/object swap)
- Plan clothing ahead of time (to expedite the attempts)
- Use visual schedules/supports
- Identify problem areas (sound of the toilet)
- Think about motor issues (step stool may help child)

- Praise/reinforcement for success
- Keep language simple (also use visuals)
- Practice in less familiar environments (encourage generalization)

For a detailed discussion of issues and procedures, see Wheeler, M. (2007). *Toilet training for individuals with autism and other developmental issues.* Arlington TX: Future Horizons.

Some young children with autism have fairly good motor skills early on; others have delays. As time goes on, motor skills often become much more social (think about how socially related you have to be to play football or baseball or soccer). To foster development of these skills, early intervention often focuses on activities that involve big muscle movements (gross motor skills) like riding a trike or kicking a ball, as well as more fine motor abilities (fine motor skills) like building with blocks, tracing a diamond, or cutting paper with scissors. Both kinds of skills are important. Often, in relation to work on motor problems, there is work on sensory skills. This might focus on helping the child tolerate a greater range of sensations or materials (see Chapter 16 and also Baraneck, et al., 2008). Often, the physical—and particularly the occupational—therapist will be involved in sensory and motor interventions.

Teaching Play Skills

You might think that play is something you wouldn't need to teach, but for children with autism, you'd be wrong. For the typical child, early play involves a lot of exploration of the feeling, color, and smell of objects or the sounds they make.For the child with normal social abilities, this changes dramatically in the second year of life, when play focuses more on the function of things (cars are to roll, cups to drink from). This is then followed by much more complicated imaginative play. Play sets the stages for a number of different developments critical for the growing child. It helps the child learn flexibility: The cup can be a cup, or a bathtub, or a rocket—whatever you want it to be. Play also becomes very social, with children learning to move very quickly in play with roles of people and materials changing rapidly. Among its many other functions, play also helps children develop more sophisticated ways of thinking; it is the beginning of being able to imagine how things could be and to be able to take the world apart and put it right back together, sometimes in very creative ways. Because play it also very symbolic, it is intimately related to language development. For the typically developing child then, play opens up whole new worlds and the child learns to seek new experiences from which he or she can learn. In children with autism, there are many challenges for play. They don't much like social interaction. They also don't particularly like new things and the challenges that new things bring.

Accordingly, children with autism start to exhibit problems in play, often around a year or so of age. In contrast to the developing imaginative play of the typical child, the child with autism may fixate on one aspect of the material— sometimes one that isn't very productive, such as its taste or smell. By age 2 the unusual patterns of play are often very striking, and by age 3 they tend to be very dramatic. Imaginative play does not "kick in" as usual. Instead, children tend to be fixated on a narrow range of materials, often wanting to play with simple cause-and-effect toys (push a button and something happens)—the sort of play behavior more typical of much younger children. Fortunately, it is possible to explicitly teach skills needed for play. The use of typical peers can be very helpful in this regard (see Chapters 5 and 6).

Harris and Handleman (2000) have created a particularly helpful summary of 10 early intervention programs. We reviewed many of these in Chapter 5. Research on early intervention and early diagnosis is now proceeding at a much more rapid pace. Work on specific problems (e.g., joint attention) is now highly focused, with rigorous control groups and good scientific methods. Although some differences in emphasis exist, the preschool intervention programs share many similarities. These include a focus on social skills (particularly imitation, joint attention, affective engagement), expressive and receptive language, motor and self-help skills, and play, as well as the more usual pre-academic and pre-school skills (Weiss, 2001; Baker, 2003). An explicit focus on learning readiness skills is also typical. Also, as we noted in Chapter 5, there are some variations between programs. Some programs may emphasize use of routines, schedules, and visual support, while others may emphasize peer interaction or incidental teaching. Still others focus on more naturalistic methods while others focus on discrete trial learning, particularly at the beginning of treatment (see Wetherby and Woods, 2008 and Koegel et al., 2008).

Unfortunately, we still don't know why some children respond better to intervention than others. Sometimes it seems (with the wisdom of hindsight) predictable, for example, the child who was very, very uninterested in other people versus the child who was interested but very odd. It does appear that children who have greater cognitive delay when treatment starts may be less likely to improve, although, of course, they are also starting from a position where even more catch-up is required. Parents understandably want an opinion about the child's long-term prognosis, but this is inevitably impossible to give. The good news is that there is much potential for change. The bad news is that we don't always know who will change and in what direction. Another major problem for prediction is that in the preschool years, the tests we use to look at cognitive development and language tell us about the child relative to other children the same age but not about the future. The reason for this is that only as the children (of all types) become older do traditional tests of intelligence or cognitive ability start to tap the kinds of skills closely related to school success.

CASE REPORTS

The following reports are based on actual cases, although names and other identifying materials have been changed. These three cases illustrate the range of needs exhibited by young children on the autism spectrum and some of the challenges in programming for them. They share some similarities but also, of course, some differences.

Case 1: Bob

Robert, called Bob by his parents, was a 24-month-old boy brought to us by his parents for an opinion on diagnosis and treatment. He was the second of two children born to an immigrant family in which both parents had college degrees. The pregnancy with Bob was uncomplicated; he was delivered by cesarean section because he was breech but was in good condition at birth. Early developmental milestones were within normal limits. He was walking by 12 months and said first words around that time as well. However, his language did not seem to "take off" as expected. His parents assumed that this was because they spoke their native language in the home, while Bob was exposed to English only at day care. At his 18-month check-up, his pediatrician noticed that in addition to expressive language delays Bob also seemed less related to his parents than expected. He had a placid and easy disposition and was undemanding. The pediatrician expressed some concern and asked to see Bob again at 20 months; at that time, he did a screening test for autism given the delayed language and what seemed to him lack of engagement. At 20 months on the Modified Checklist for Autism in Toddlers (M-CHAT; see Chapter 3) Bob failed three of five critical items and was referred to the local state Birth-to-Three agency. That agency did a screen of his development at 21 months. At this screen there was considerable concern. Bob was exhibiting significant delays in expressive and receptive language (on the screening instrument, expressive skills were at the less than 1year level, and receptive skills at about the 15-month level). Fortunately, his personal social and gross and fine motor and problem–solving skills appeared (on this parent report screen) to be within age-expected limits. Bob was enrolled in two sessions of speech-communication therapy a week. His parents sought an evaluation with us.

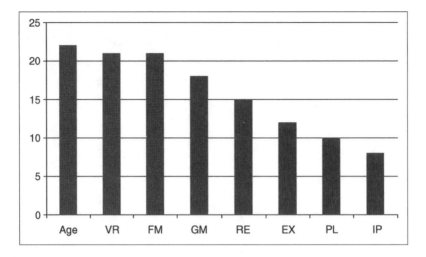

FIGURE 7.3   Assessment results for Bob at age 22-months (results expressed in age equivalents). Results from the Mullen Scales of Early Learning. VR = visual reception (nonverbal problem-solving), FM = fine motor, GM = gross motor, RE = receptive language, EX = expressive language; results from the Vineland Adaptive Behavior Scales for PL = play, and IP = interpersonal.

As part of his assessment with us, Bob was seen for developmental testing, speech-communication assessment, and psychiatric assessment. He was also referred for some additional medical testing. A behavioral hearing test had been done, but the results were equivocal, so a more definitive test was requested and completed and showed that Bob had normal hearing. The results of Bob's developmental assessment using the Mullen Scales of Early Learning are presented in Figure 7.3.

Bob showed average skills in the areas of visual reception (nonverbal problem solving) and fine motor skills, both at the 21-month level. His score in the gross motor area was below average (18-months age equivalent). Both receptive and expressive language were significantly delayed, at 15- and 12-month age levels, respectively. During the testing, the psychologist noted that it was often difficult to get Bob's cooperation—he was often out of his seat, exploring various parts of the room, and was easily frustrated. He had few "learning to learn" skills. His eye contact was poor, and he responded to his name less than half the time. He would respond to requests for joint attention-that is, if something interesting happened, he could be prompted to notice but never initiated such interactions, nor was he interested in showing things to his parents or the examiner. He did make more overtures to his mother than to the examiner, but sometimes used her hand (without making eye contact) to obtain desired objects. Although not yet very dramatic, we did note that Bob was starting to engage in some repetitive activities. There was one occasion when we saw what might have been the beginning of hand flapping. His parents told us that for some time he had been interested in watching spinning things, and that certain sounds, like the garbage disposal or vacuum cleaner, were very upsetting.

On the Vineland Adaptive Behavior Scales, based on his mother's responses to the semi-structured interview, Bob's gross and fine motor skills were areas of relative strength for him, being closest to age level. Daily living skills were somewhat delayed, but play and socialization skills were quite delayed at the 10- and 7-month level, respectively. The levels of receptive and expressive language ability were slightly higher than observed by us on the Mullen, probably reflecting his slightly greater difficulty in a new situation in showing us all that he was capable of in a more familiar context.

During the speech-language communication assessment, various materials were used to elicit intentional communications. Bob was heard to possibly use the word *hi* on one occasion, and several times said "no," but otherwise no words were heard. His mother indicated that she had not heard the word "hi" before, although the family had been working with him on greeting and leave taking, and he was now occasionally saying "bye." The Reynell Developmental Language Scales were used to assess his speech, language, and communication skills, along with a play session during which he was presented with a series of situations to tempt him to communicate. Bob was interested in some games but wouldn't engage in play with a familiar toy in the new setting; as reflected in this and other examples, it appeared that he had some difficulty in generalizing skills learned at home to new contexts. Bob did enjoy playing one simple game with a cause-effect toy. In addition to his occasionally using the word *no*, Bob more frequently would attempt to avoid tasks, for example, by leaving the table, lying on the floor, failing to look, or pushing with his hand to move something away from him. His parents reported that this was typical in his work with the speech pathologist. His parents reported that he had used some words in the past but that these had seemed to drop out of his vocabulary; for example, he used to say *car* and *open*, but could not demonstrate these for us during the assessment. He did have some interest in pictures and was able to produce a few words. He also produced runs of syllables during play including "ahsee," "hoola," "to-to-to," but these seemed devoid of meaning, intent, or awareness. His **prosody** (the melodic aspect of speech and language) was unusual. On the Reynell, his expressive and receptive language skills were severely delayed.

During the assessment, Bob generally related to his parents and the examiner when he needed something. He generally could not be engaged in tasks that involved either motor or vocal imitation. Occasionally, he would lean against the person who was working with him but had little apparent awareness that he was in physical contact. He was probably most engaged when his mother sang a familiar song to him; he notably brightened and seemed to sway with the music but did not ask for more when the song was over.

In reviewing the history with the family, it became clear to us that although the parents had reported his language to have developed on time, this actually was rather questionable. Both parents were concerned about his language delay and probably had over-interpreted the sounds he did make.

Medically, apart from these developmental problems, his physical examination did not reveal any likely medical cause for his difficulties. Fragile X testing and chromosome analysis were normal, as were some screening laboratory and genetic studies.

Recommendations and Follow-up   We shared with the family that our impression was that Bob very likely had autism, although we emphasized that this would be clarified over time. At this point, our major concern was helping him be enrolled in a much more intensive program. We pointed out that he had some important strengths. Notably, his nonverbal problem-solving skills were close to age-expected levels, he had a few words, and he enjoyed a few social activities that might be used to motivate him. At the same time, we expressed significant concern about his delayed social skills, his problems tolerating adult intrusions, and some of the problematic behaviors, all of which interfered with his learning. We also were concerned about fostering his language and the broader notion of communication. We had a number of recommendations to discuss with them. These very specific recommendations were grouped into a number of areas.

Bob needed considerable work on his behavior and on his learning to learn skills—that is, he needed to be able to sit and work without quickly going off task. He had some behaviors that also interfered with learning, and these needed to be targeted as one part of his overall intervention program. We strongly suggested an ABA program, given what seemed to be his major behavioral needs.

Goals for communication included developing consistency in responding to people (e.g., around greetings). We emphasized that adults' bids for communication should be highly contextualized and relevant to his ongoing routine. Second, we recommended that his program attempt to increase the frequency and the consistency with which he communicated, through use of either words or picture exchange to request a range of things: objects, food, actions, refusal, cessation of activity, recurrence, protest, greeting, and leave taking. We also recommended that an important goal would be to increase the frequency with which he initiated his own requests for things he enjoyed, such as music and games. We also helped his parents develop a vocabulary checklist so they could consistently use words relevant to his daily experience. We also talked with the parents about potential uses of visual schedules and visual materials to help Bob be (and feel) more organized.

Goals for occupational and physical therapy had to do with use of materials to foster his problem-solving abilities, turn taking, body awareness, and tolerance of physical touch. We also flagged for the staff his potential to get lost in off-task exploration of toys (e.g., absorption in their contours, texture) or visual stimulation.

In going over the results of the Vineland with the parents, we outlined a set of goals that would be reasonable next steps to work on in terms of self-care and other skills. Following our assessment, Bob was enrolled in a new center–based program with a strong ABA emphasis. The amount of time Bob spent in a program was dramatically increased to 4 hours a day, 5 days a week, and his parents were able to attend school on occasion to work on generalization of skills and ask questions. His new program included some individual therapies (speech-language and occupational therapy), and a staff member visited the home once a week. This included discrete trial training to work on basic learning to learn and other skills. As part of his beginning work at the center-based program, a list of reinforcers was produced and his team worked with us to develop a set of immediate, medium, and long-term goals for Bob. These included developing a consistent work routine to enable him to spend increasing time in one-on-one work with an adult. There was also an emphasis on functional use of behaviors and generalization of skills. Objectives were broken down into explicit steps, with a plan for building basic social and communication skills. His intervention plan included a focus on developing more social skills, such as tolerating work with adults and following the adults' lead, expanding joint attention, and so forth.

Although progress was initially slow, within 6-months Bob had started to show major gains in his organization, learning, and language. He is now, as an 8-year-old, enrolled in a regular public school class (second grade) with pull-out support for speech-communication work.

Case 2: Adam

Adam, age 4 years, was seen at the request of his parents for a consultation. He had started preschool (shortly after his third birthday) and had experienced significant problems with peers. Adam, a first child, was born after an un-complicated pregnancy, labor, and delivery. His early development had not caused his parents' concern. He had spoken words before a year (at 10 months) and had walked at around 14 months. From early in life, words had seemed his "lifeline," according to his parents. He seemed to use language for many different purposes and at a very sophisticated level. His parents thought that, if anything, his development was advanced over his peers (and in many respects it was).

Adam had an early interest in letters and numbers. His first interest had been in car hood ornaments. He learned to sound out words early. When he entered preschool at about age 3½ years, he had major difficulties with peers. He was very interested in interacting with other children, but approached them in very one sided (and off-putting) ways, for example, coming up behind and hugging peers in his class. He was distressed when they did not respond positively. His medical history did not reveal any unusual problems. His paternal grandfather was noted to have been somewhat isolated and a bit of an eccentric; he had worked as a map-maker for many years but had a wife and several children.

At the time of our assessment, Adam was given the Wechsler Preschool and Primary Scale of Intelligence, 3rd edition (WPPSI-III). On the WPPSI-III (see Chapter 3), his areas of greatest ability were in the verbal areas with scores in the superior and above-average range, as compared to his performance (nonverbal) abilities (in the average range). For example, his scaled score in the information subtest was 16, while his block design subtest score was 12. His full scale IQ was 120, with a verbal IQ of 127 and a performance score of 108 (98th vs. 70th percentile, respectively). His reading (both understanding and comprehension) was at about the first grade level. During the communication assessment, he had very good expressive and receptive vocabulary (at, or even somewhat above, his verbal IQ), but his social language use was quite impaired, and he had major difficulties carrying on a conversation and producing coherent narratives.

On the Vineland, his written communication skills were high but his "real world" receptive and expressive skills were lower than would be expected given his scores on the individually administered language communication assessments. His daily living skills were moderately low, and his socialization skills significantly impaired. His age-equivalent score in the interpersonal relationship area of the Vineland was at the 2-year level. He had some problems with **visual–motor** coordination, as shown by a test (the Beery Developmental Test of Visual–Motor Integration) of his ability to copy designs. His parents reported problems with attention, as well as significant social difficulties with peers. The school program was working hard to foster Adam's academic abilities, seeing his reading, in particular, as an area of strength. At the same time, there was much less of a focus on teaching social skills.

At the time of our assessment, Adam had a number of important strengths, including some in the area of social motivation. He was very interested in interpersonal interaction and genuinely puzzled by why his peers seemed oblivious to him. In interacting with adults, his social motivation was very apparent, as were his many areas of social vulnerability. Indeed, in many respects, and consistent with his scores on the Vineland, Adam acted like a child half his age. He had difficulties delaying gratification, had problems in using eye contact to help regulate social interaction, and was basically lost at sea when it came to fast-paced play activities. Although his preoccupation with letters and numbers seemed to represent an area of strength, this served, in many respects, to further isolate him from other children. In play, for example, he would assign each participant a letter or number, and then refer to them as such—a rather unusual procedure for dealing with typical peers. He had some unusual sensory interests and sensitivities, although these were not particularly striking and didn't seem to interfere at school.

Recommendations and Follow-up   In discussing the results of our assessment with Adam's parents, we emphasized his young age and the need to follow him over time. We did, however, flag for them the possibility that he was exhibiting Asperger's disorder, with good verbal abilities and more impaired nonverbal and visual-motor and severely impaired social skills. Although Adam's parents and school had been understandably impressed by his areas of strength, we indicated that his areas of vulnerability were not being adequately addressed. Accordingly, we recommended a program that emphasized acquisition of social skills (with exposure to typical peers in a structured, supported context), explicit teaching of social and other skills, and an emphasis on areas of weakness, as well as areas of strength. We made a number of recommendations for both school and home. These included supported exposure to typically developing peers and individualized interventions, with a specific focus on social goals in natural contexts using discrete trial and pivotal response training. An explicit parent component to his program was recommended to encourage generalization of skills over various settings. Explicit social skills teaching was recommended, along with a focus on teaching play skills. Speech-communication therapy focusing on social use of language (pragmatics) was also recommended. Occupational and physical therapy interventions were recommended for dealing with gross and fine motor skill areas. We underscored with his parents the need to help Adam manage his strong interest in letters and numbers and place it within a broader context. We also suggested to them that, over time, his areas of interest may change and that it would always be important to help him get the "big picture" even while trying to use his natural motivations and interests.

At the time of follow-up, at age 6½, Adam continued to exhibit a somewhat eccentric and one-sided social style. He had, however, made major gains with peers and was fully mainstreamed. He did receive some special services to support gross and fine motor as well as social communication skills, but he had made a good adjustment to school. At the time of our last visit, he had a relatively strong interest in one fairly circumscribed area (dinosaurs) but was able to use this in connecting with typical peers.

Case 3: Helen

This case differs from the two previous ones in several ways. Probably most importantly, Helen was seen at the ages of 15, 34, and 50 months, and we have presented her case as an example of a very young child with autism (this is published in more detail in Klin et al., 2004; and summarized in Klin et al., 2008).

We have known Helen since she was 2 weeks of age (when her older brother was just diagnosed as having an ASD). This is a reminder of the potential for families to have multiple affected children (see Chapter 2) given the strong genetic base of autism. Helen's case also serves as a reminder that, for some children, noteworthy developmental regression can occur and that sometimes improvement is very slow even when good services are provided.

Early History   Helen was born after a pregnancy complicated by her mother's thyroid disease, which was treated during the pregnancy. She was observed for a short period of time after delivery in the newborn special care unit because of low blood sugar, but then did well. She was smiling by 3 weeks of age, sitting at 4 months, crawling at 6 months, and walking by 12 months. At that point in time, her parents (and her pediatrician [LW]) noted that she was saying a number of words, including *hi, baby, mommy*, and *daddy*. Unfortunately, at around 14 months, she seemed to become less socially engaged and stopped not only talking but making many sounds at all. Within a few weeks, when she was seen for a comprehensive assessment, she had developed a dislike of loud noises and bright lights.

Family and Medical History   Helen's brother had exhibited features of autism shortly after birth. Apart from his history of difficulty, there was no history of developmental or psychiatric problems in members of the family. Except for several (four) ear infections, Helen had been in good general health, and her development had been closely followed by her pediatrician, given her brother's history. Originally, her parents wondered if her loss of words had to do with an ear infection.

On genetic and medical evaluation at 15 months, Helen had a large head size (>95% of the population of children her age). At 6 months, her head circumference was at the 50th percentile (her brother and parents also had large heads). Otherwise, genetic screening and neurological consultation (including neuroimaging studies) did not reveal any abnormalities (see Chapter 2).

Assessment at 15 Months   At this age, Helen was scoring at age-expected levels in terms of her nonverbal problem-solving abilities (her ability to use objects,

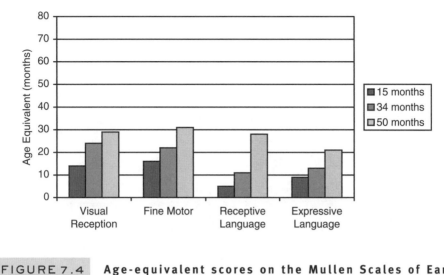

FIGURE 7.4   **Age-equivalent scores on the Mullen Scales of Early Learning achieved by Helen.**

Reprinted, with permission, from Klin, A., Caulnier, C., Chawarska, K., & Volkmar, F. (2008). Case studies of infants first evaluated in the second year of life. In K. Chawarska, A. Klin, & F. Volkmar (Eds.), *Autism spectrum disorders in infants and toddlers* (p. 145). New York: Guilford Press.

discriminate shapes) as well as in both her gross and fine motor development (running, scribbling, throwing a ball). Unfortunately, her language at the time of the assessment was very delayed, with receptive skills 6-months delayed and expressive skills 8-months delayed (her scores on developmental testing over time are presented in Figure 7.4).

During the speech-communication assessment, Helen would pull a person's hand to get desired objects without making eye contact. She exhibited no gestures to communicate and was happy to be left on her own. She inconsistently would seek out her parents if she was upset and did respond to some verbal directions if these were kept simple and exaggerated visual cues were also provided. She was not heard to use any words at that time and made a limited range of sounds that were not directed at other people.

On the Vineland Adaptive Behavior Scales, she had severe delays in socialization and expressive language skills. Her motor skills were somewhat stronger, as were her receptive language skills (i.e., within familiar contexts at home she was scoring somewhat higher than she did during her session with the speech pathologist). Her scores on the Vineland over time are provided in Figure 7.5.

Observations of her behavior at 15-months revealed a child who presented as very isolated and self contained. She tended to fixate on some kinds of toys and had troubles with transitions. She also had some unusual interests, for example, in

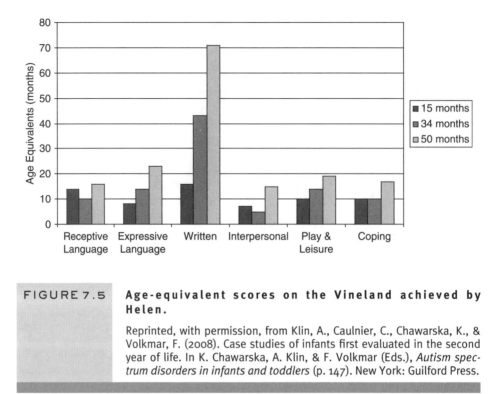

FIGURE 7.5 **Age-equivalent scores on the Vineland achieved by Helen.**

Reprinted, with permission, from Klin, A., Caulnier, C., Chawarska, K., & Volkmar, F. (2008). Case studies of infants first evaluated in the second year of life. In K. Chawarska, A. Klin, & F. Volkmar (Eds.), *Autism spectrum disorders in infants and toddlers* (p. 147). New York: Guilford Press.

certain textures. At the same time, her social engagement was very concerning. She had only occasional eye contact with others and often seemed to ignore other people. When she did smile or seem happy, this seemed to be in response to her own experience and not some shared enjoyment with another person. She often ignored adults, and it was impossible to engage her in simple games like peek-a-boo. Her interest in more representational toys was quite limited. Frustration led Helen to make a number of high-pitched, unpleasant sounds. Unlike many young children with autism, she exhibited stereotyped mannerisms (hand flapping and finger posturing) even at 15-months of age. She had some trouble with change and novelty. We shared with her parents our concern that even despite her young age, she was exhibiting a profile very, very suggestive of autism.

Within a month, she began to receive 3 hours of speech-language therapy and 1 hour of occupational therapy each week through the state early intervention program. In addition, 8 hours a week of applied behavior analysis (ABA) were provided, along with a 1 hour play group each week. Over the next months, these services were all increased in intensity until she transitioned into the school system at age 3.

Assessment at 34 Months We saw Helen again at 34 months. During the interval between these two visits, she had made slow but steady progress. Her fine motor and problem-solving skills were at the 20- and 22-month levels. Language continued to be her area of greatest vulnerability (along with social skills). At 34 months, her language skills were about 2 years delayed (i.e., at around a 10 month level). During the speech-communication assessment at 34 months, she had not made many gains. She was mostly interested in observing herself in a mirror and had little evidence of differential responses to adults (e.g., parents vs. stranger), although she would, at times, turn to her parents for help or support. All communication functions (verbal and nonverbal) were significantly delayed. She did some singing (including one nursery rhyme) but made little eye contact and was very unengaged with the adults. Interestingly, by this time Helen had become fascinated with letters and numbers.

Diagnostically, Helen was very much the same child at 34 months. She had few consistent words, and her language was unusual for its self-stimulatory quality and limited range of intonation. She did seem to like to label things (a frequent activity in her intervention program) but did not use words to communicate in a consistent way. She did enjoy rough and tumble play with her parents, but even then often seemed more engaged with herself than her parents. She was exhibiting higher levels of motor stereotyped behaviors and unusual sensory behaviors at this age.

Helen was enrolled in a public school program at age 3. By the time she was just past her fourth birthday (at 50 months), she was receiving ABA services 4 hours a day 5 days a week in the morning, with an afternoon preschool program that included typically developing peers and opportunities for pull out work with the occupational therapist and speech langauge pathologist, as well as about 10 hours a week of individual special-ed work.

Evaluation at 50 Months   When she was seen at 50-months of age for her third assessment, she had made progress in her communication skills, although her growth in terms of problem-solving/nonverbal reasoning and fine motor development had slowed. Her levels of delay ranged from 19 to 29 months. During the speech-communication assessment at 50 months, Helen knew a number of words but primarily only labeled things (i.e., she didn't use the words to communicate in other ways). She could follow very simple, two step directions but more complex language was beyond her. It was easiest for her to respond when language was kept very simple, with short phrases rather than long sentences. Sometimes her use of language was very idiosyncratic (she would use a word in a very odd way that most people wouldn't understand). Although she had made progress in her vocabulary, her overall language/communication skills remained severely impaired.

Helen continued to exhibit delays in adaptive skills, although her profile of delay was scattered with social and receptive/expressive skills most severely delayed and motor skills closer to age level. By this time, however, her reading abilities were quite strong. She was reading to "decode" at about the 6-year level, but her understanding of what she read was minimal; for example, one could give her a written instruction like "sit down," and she could sound it out but not follow the direction.

By 50 months, Helen had made some important gains in terms of her ability to focus, tolerate adult intrusion, and engage with adults (if only for short periods of time). She was also less likely to engage in stereotyped mannerisms or even self injurious behavior when she was frustrated or tired. Importantly, she was beginning to use some words, on occasion, to communicate her needs and was starting to use words with a point to request objects. Her language was mostly single words and continued to have an unusual "robot-like" quality.

Discussion   Helen seems to have developed well until shortly after a year of age. Even at the time of her first comprehensive assessment, her presentation was fairly classic for autism. Even though she appeared to have had major losses of skills in some areas, motor and nonverbal problem-solving remained close to age level at the time of our first assessment. She gradually made gains in the areas of socialization and communication, but significant vulnerabilities persisted despite provision of a reasonably intensive program. Her ability to read to decode had emerged as an isolated area of strength but was not matched by her ability to understand what she read. Although provided with reasonably intensive intervention, she had not, unfortunately, made as much progress as we would have hoped.

Helen now, at around 6 years of age, has not made as much progress as her older brother. She is enrolled in a special school for children with autism. She has a few words, but generally her communication skills remain an area of great vulnerability. She has had a number of behavioral challenges and been treated with several medications for behavior problems.

Summary

In this chapter we reviewed some of what we know about autism and related conditions as they appear in infants and young children. As we mentioned, until recently most of the information on this topic came from either parent memories or the retrospective study of children through videotapes. Most parents of children with autism become concerned about the child's development in the first year or two of life. The earliest features of autism tend to fall into two groups—one involves social engagement and the other relates to early communication abilities. Although unusual sensory interests and motor behaviors develop, they often develop somewhat later—usually by age 3 but can be preceded by unusual sensory sensitivies that, as Kanner suggested, stand in stark contrast to the child's lack of interest in the social world.

When parents are concerned the health care provider is usually the initial professional to see the child, conduct an initial assessment, and suggest more extended testing. Depending on the results of this assessment, services can be provided even before the child is eligible for school-based programming (at age 3). The unusual profiles of strengths and weaknesses in children on the autism spectrum can present some challenges for intervention. It does appear that, on balance, early and more intensive intervention is the most effective. Parents must negotiate the challenges of dealing with two systems—the early intervention system and then the public schools. A range of well-documented programs are available for slightly older children; as interest in early diagnosis of autism increases, there will undoubtedly be more interest in evaluating programs for children under 3 as well. Overall, it does appear that early intervention makes an important difference for the better; that being said, there are still individual differences, and predicting what will happen to a specific child is often difficult. A major challenge for current research is the development of better tools for screening/assessing children with possible autism or related disorders. Several studies are under way at present in different places around the country, often studying children who are siblings of those with known autism. We hope that this research will lead to earlier and more effective interventions.

■ READING LIST

Bailey, K. (2008). Supporting families. In K. Chawarska, A. Klin & F. R. Volkmar (Eds.), *Autism spectrum disorders in infants and toddlers: Diagnosis, assessment, and treatment* (pp. 300–326). New York: Guilford Press.

Baker, J. (2003). *The social skills picture book teaching play, emotion, and communication to children with autism.* Arlington, TX: Future Horizons.

Baranek, G. T., Wakeford, L. & David, F. J. (2008). Understanding, Assessing, and Treating Sensory-Motor Issues. In K. Chawarska, A. Klin & F. R. Volkmar (Eds.), *Autism spectrum disorders in infants and toddlers: Diagnosis, assessment, and treatment* (pp. 104–140). New York: Guilford Press.

Barbera, M. L., Rasmussen, T. (2007). *The verbal behavior approach: How to teach children with autism and related disorders.* London: Jessica Kingsley.

Baron-Cohen, S., Allen, J., & Gillberg, C. (1992). Can autism be detected at 18-months? The needle, the haystack, and the CHAT. *British Journal of Psychiatry, 161*(1), 839–843.

Bayley, N. (2006). *Bayley scales of infant and toddler development, Third Edition.* San Antonio, TX: Harcourt Assessment.

Begun, R. W. (Ed.). (1995). *Ready-to-use social skills lessons and activities for grades prek–k.* San Francisco: Jossey-Bass.

Brinton, B., Robinson, L. A., & Fujiki, M. (2004). Description of a program for social language intervention: "If you can have a conversation, you can have a relationship." *Language, Speech, and Hearing Services in Schools, 35*, 283–290.

Bishop, S. L., Luyster, R., Richler, J. & Lord, C. (2008). Diagnostic Assessment. In K. Chawarska, A. Klin & F. R. Volkmar (Eds.), *Autism spectrum disorders in infants and toddlers: Diagnosis, assessment, and treatment* (pp. 23–49). New York: Guilford Press.

Bondy, A. & Frost, L. (2001). *A picture's worth: PECS and other visual communication strategies in autism*. Bethesda, MD: Woodbine House.

Bretherton, A. V. & Tonger, B. L. (2005). *Pre-schoolers with autism – An education and skills training programme for parents (Manual for parents)*. London: Jessica Kingsley.

Cafiero, J. M. (2005). *Meaningful exchange for people with autism: An introduction to augmenting and alternative communication*. Topics in Autism. Sandra L. Harris, Series Editor. Bethesda, MD: Woodbine House.

Chawarska, K. & Bearss, K. (2008). Assessment of Cognitive and Adaptive Skills. In K. Chawarska, A. Klin & F. R. Volkmar (Eds.), *Autism spectrum disorders in infants and toddlers: Diagnosis, assessment, and treatment* (pp. 50–75). New York: Guilford Press.

Chawarska, K., Klin, A., Paul, R., & Volkmar, F. (2007). Autism spectrum disorder in the second year: Stability and change in syndrome expression. *Journal of Child Psychology & Psychiatry & Allied Disciplines, 48*(2), 128–138.

Chawarska, K., Klin, A. et al., (Eds.). (2008). *Autism spectrum disorders in infants and toddlers: Diagnosis, assessment, and treatment*. New York: Guilford Press.

Chawarska, K., & Volkmar, F. R. (2005). Autism in infancy and early childhood. In F. R. Volkmar, R. Paul, A. Klin, & D. Cohen (Eds.), *Handbook of autism and pervasive developmental disorders* (3rd ed. , pp. 70–78). Hoboken, NJ: Wiley.

Dawson, G., Meltzoff, A. N., Osterling, J. & Rinaldi, J. (1998). Neuropsychological correlates of early symptoms of autism. *Child Development, 69*(5), 1276–1285.

DiLavore, P. C., Lord, C., & Rutter, M. (1995). Prelinguistic autism diagnostic observation schedule. *Journal of Autism and Developmental Disorders, 25*(4), 355–379.

Eikeseth, S., Smith, T., Jahr, E., & Eldevik, S. (2002). Intensive behavioral treatment at school for 4- to 7-year-old children with autism: A 1-year comparison controlled study. *Behavior Modification, 26*(1), 49–68.

Goldstein, H. (2002). *Promoting social communication: Children with developmental disabilities from birth to adolescence*. Baltimore: Brookes.

Greenspan, S. I. (2006). *Engaging autism: Helping children relate, communicate and think with the DIR floortime approach*. Cambridge, MA: De Capo Lifelong Books.

Handleman, J. S., & Harris, S. L. (1994, 2001, 2008). *Preschool education programs for children with autism*. Austin, TX: Pro-Ed.

Harris, S. L., & Weiss, M. J. (2007). *Right from the start: Behavioral intervention for young children with autism* (2nd ed.). Bethesda, MD: Woodbine House.

Hodgdon, L. (2001). *Visual Strategies for Improving Communication: Practical Supports for School and Home*. Troy, MI: QuirkRoberts.

Hoskins, B. (1996). *Conversations: A framework for language intervention*. Eau Claire, WI: Thinking Publications.

Jahr, D., Eldevid, S., & Eileseth, S. (2000). Teaching children with autism to initiate and sustain cooperative play. *Research in Developmental Disabilities, 21*, 151–169.

Kasari, C. (2002). Assessing change in early intervention programs for children with autism. *Journal of Autism and Developmental Disorders, 32*(5), 447–461.

Klein, M., Cook, R. E. (2001). *Richardson-Gibbs, A. M. Strategies for Including Children with special Needs in Early Childhood Settings*. Albany, NY: Delmar.

Klin, A., Chawarska, K., Paul, R., Rubin, E., Morgan, T., Wiesner, L., et al. (2004). Autism in a 15-month-old child. *American Journal of Psychiatry, 161*(11), 1981–1988.

Klin, A., Saulnier, C., Chawarska, K. & Volkmar, F. R. (2008). Case Studies of Infants First Evaluated in the Second Year of Life. In K. Chawarska, A. Klin & F. R. Volkmar (Eds.), *Autism spectrum disorders in infants and toddlers: Diagnosis, assessment, and treatment* (pp. 141–169). New York: Guilford Press.

Koegel, L. K., Koegel, R. L., Fredeen, R. M. & Gengoux, G. W. (2008). Naturalistic Behavior Approaches to Treatment. In K. Chawarska, A. Klin & F. R. Volkmar (Eds.), *Autism spectrum disorders in infants and toddlers: Diagnosis, assessment, and treatment* (pp. 207–242). New York: Guilford Press.

Lord, C. (1995). Follow-up of two-year-olds referred for possible autism. *Journal of Child Psychology and Psychiatry and Allied Disciplines, 36*(8), 1365–1382.

Lord, C., Shulman, C., & DiLavore, P. (2004). Regression and word loss in autistic spectrum disorders. *Journal of Child Psychology and Psychiatry, 45*(5), 936–955.

Lytel, J. (2008). *Act Early Against Autism: Give Your Child a Fighting Chance from the Start.* New York: Perigree Trade.

Maestro, S., Muratori, F., Barbieri, F., Casella, C., Cattaneo, V., Cavallaro, M., et al. (2001). Attentional skills during the first 6-months of age in autism spectrum disorder. *Journal of the American Academy of Child and Adolescent Psychiatry, 34*(3), 147–152.

Matson, J. L., & Minshawi, N. F. (2006). *Early intervention for autism spectrum disorders: A critical analysis.* Elsevier.

Maurice, C., Green, G. & Luce, S. C. (Eds.). (1996). *Behavioral intervention for young children with autism: A manual for parents and professionals.* Austin, TX: Pro-Ed.

McClannahan, L. E. & Krantz, P. J. (2005). *Teaching conversation to children with autism: Scripts and script fading.* Bethesda, MD: Woodbine House.

McGinnis, E., & Goldstein, A. P. (1990). *Skillstreaming in early childhood: Teaching prosocial skills to the preschool and kindergarten child.* Champaign, IL: Research Press.

Mullen, E. (1995). *Mullen scales of early learning-AGS Edition.* Circle Pines, MN: American Guidance Service.

National Research Council (Ed.). (2001). *Educating children with autism.* Washington, DC: National Academy Press.

Osterling, J. A., & Dawson, G. (1994). Early recognition of children with autism: A study of first birthday home videotapes. *Journal of Autism and Developmental Disorders, 24*(3), 247–257.

Paul, R. (2008). Communication Development and Assessment. In K. Chawarska, A. Klin & F. R. Volkmar (Eds.), *Autism spectrum disorders in infants and toddlers: Diagnosis, assessment, and treatment* (pp. 76–103). New York: Guilford Press.

Pepper, J. & Weitzman, E. (2004). It Take Two to Talk: A Practical Guide for Parents of Children with Language Delay. Toronto, Ontario: The Hanen Centre. www.hanen.org.

Prizant, B. M., Wetherby A. M., Rubin, E. M. S., Laurent, A. C., Rydell, P. J. (2004). *The SCERTS model: Enhancing communication and socioemotional abilities of children with autism apectrum disorder.* Baltimore, MD: Brookes.

Prizant, B. M., Wetherby, A. M., Rubin, E., Laurent, A., & Rydell, P. (2006). *The SCERTS model: A comprehensive educational approach for children with autism spectrum disorders.* Baltimore, MD: Paul H. Brookes.

Quill, K. (1995). *Teaching children with autism: Strategies to enhance communication and socialization.* Albany, NY: Delmar.

Quill, K. (2000). *Do watch listen say: Social and communication intervention for children with autism.* Baltimore, MD: Brookes.

Robins, D. L., Fein, D., Barton, M. L., & Green, J. A. (2001). The Modified Checklist for Autism in Toddlers: An initial study investigating the early detection of autism and pervasive developmental disorders. *Journal of Autism and Developmental Disorders, 31*, 131–144.

Siperstein, G., & Richards, E., (2004). *Promoting social success.* Baltimore: Brookes.

Stone, W. L., Ousley, O. Y., Hepburn, S. L., Hogan, K. L., & Brown, C. S. (1999). Patterns of adaptive behavior in very young children with autism. *American Journal on Mental Retardation, 104*(2), 187–199.

Strain, P. S., Kerr, M. M., & Ragand, E. U. (1979). Effects of peer-mediated social initiations and prompting/reinforcement procedures of the social behavior of autistic children. *Journal of Autism and Developmental Disorders, 9*, 41–54.

Weiss, M. J. & Harris, S. L. (2001). *Reaching out, joining in: Teaching social skills to young children with autism.* Bethesda, MD: Woodbine House.

Wetherby, A. M. & Woods, J. (2008). Developmental Approaches to Treatment. In K. Chawarska, A. Klin & F. R. Volkmar (Eds.), *Autism spectrum disorders in infants and toddlers: Diagnosis, assessment, and treatment* (pp. 170–206). New York: Guilford Press.

Wetherby, A. M., Yonclas, D. G., & Bryan, A. A. (1989). Communicative profiles of preschool children with handicaps: Implications for early identification. *Journal of Speech and Hearing Disorders, 54*(2), 148–158.

Whalen, C., & Schreibman, L. (2003). Joint attention training for children with autism using behavior modification procedures. *Journal of Child Psychology and Psychiatry and Allied Disciplines, 44*(3), 456–468.

Wheeler, M. (2004). *Toilet training for individuals with autism and related disorders: A comprehensive guide for parents and teachers.* Arlington, TX: Future Horizons.

Wiseman, N. D. (2006). *Could it be autism? A parent's guide to the first signs and next steps.* New York: Broadway Books.

Wolfberg, P. J. (2003). *Peer play and the autism spectrum: The art of guiding children's socialization and imagination. Integrated Play Groups Field Manual.* Shawnee Mission, KS: Autism Asperger.

■ WEB SITES

http://www.aap.org
http://www.cdc.gov/ncbddd/autism/index.htm
http://www.firstsigns.org

■ QUESTIONS AND ANSWERS

1. **My son and his wife have an 8-month-old son, their first. I know I may be an overly concerned grandmother, but I worry that Billy doesn't seem to respond like other children. He doesn't seem as interested in things as my other grandkids. He does not turn when his name is called, and he doesn't seem to smile when we talk to him. He seems to like to stare at things that move. Is this too young to be worried about autism?**

    It is not too young. You are absolutely right about the kinds of things to worry about at this age—lack of response to people and a greater interest in things. While being sure of a diagnosis at this age is not always possible, it is possible to start intervention if there are good reasons to do so. You should express your concern to your son and his wife and ask them to talk to their health care provider, who may want to do some developmental screening and/or refer them to the local early intervention program for an assessment.

2. **Our 4-year-old was diagnosed with autism at age 2. She has made very good progress with an ABA program. This has been fairly intensive and structured with some time each week (and more this past year) in a typical preschool setting. My wife and I are just starting to think about a transition to a typical kindergarten next year (with some supports). When can you tell if a child is "cured"?**

   First and foremost, it is very good indeed that your daughter has responded well to treatment. You explicitly ask one question but also raise another important issue: transitions. Changes in program go best when a lot of planning has gone on and the child and program are well prepared. The people who have been helping her already will undoubtedly have a number of suggestions. Having her enrolled in some experience with typically developing children also will make the transition easier. There are a number of things you can do well ahead of time to smooth things along— pictures and visits to the new classroom and teacher. In developing the IEP, look at both where she has come from and where the team would like her to go. It may be easier to have more supports at first, and then if things go well, you can phase them out or cut back. Your explicit question asks about cure. This is always difficult to answer since the answer depends on how you define *cure*. Many children on the autism spectrum are going on to have productive experiences in mainstream settings and sometimes continue to do so even without much in the way of formal support. Often, even the most able people on the spectrum have some residual personality quirks or eccentricities as adults, as do many typically developing people. You should take pride in her accomplishments to date and see how the transition to a typical kindergarten goes. Good luck!

3. **I am a retired pediatrician. My first grandchild is now 15- months old and still not talking. I worry because he doesn't respond to his name and doesn't seem to "click" with people (he won't look at me if I make a funny sound). My grandchild has had a number of ear infections, although once these clear up, his hearing is fine (it has been tested several times now). My daughter-in-law gets very anxious whenever we talk about this and won't agree to pursue an**

evaluation by the local early intervention team. Do you have any suggestions?

You are right to be concerned. The process of coming to grips with a child's developmental vulnerabilities can be a difficult one for parents, particularly if this is a first child and they don't have a good comparison. Obviously, you have a long history of experience but also the complicating role of being the father-in-law. In situations like this it may be worth having a private discussion with your son to share your concerns. It may also be worth suggesting that the parents take the child to a play group or other setting where they will be able to see typical peers and make some observations of what typical behavior at this age is like.

CHAPTER 8

Working with School-Aged Children

Children with autism spectrum disorders (ASDs) face new challenges in primary and middle schools. Expectations change based on increased psychological and physical maturity. Additional challenges come because there are new expectations for independent, self-directed learning and new transitions within, and often between, schools with increasing changes in teachers and programs. Fortunately, more and more children with ASDs are doing well in school, and gains in social learning often occur. A range of options is available to students, going from fully included, mainstream academic settings, to programs that provide both mainstream experiences and special education services, to fully segregated learning environments. Many of the same issues and program considerations relevant to younger children (Chapter 7) continue to apply, although there usually will be more emphasis on academics. The paths children follow in their learning and development will, of course, differ. There are some generalizations that can, however, be made.

In the preschool years, earlier diagnosis and intervention are associated with progressively better outcomes if we look at the entire group of children with ASDs. That being said, by first grade there will start to be major divergences, with some children having made substantial progress and others continuing to have significant challenges. We still do not know why some children seem to do better than others, even in what appear to be rather similar and appropriate programs. By around age 6, we can have a much better sense of the child's ability to communicate and his verbal abilities. Around this time, tests of intelligence begin, for both the general population and those students with ASDs, to become more predictive of later performance. Starting around this time, the psychologist can use intelligence (IQ) tests that tap more and different kinds of skills to more precisely identify areas of strength and weakness. In contrast to the preschool years, social isolation and oddity can contribute to isolation and more obvious differences from typically developing students in school. Factors contributing to this include problems in play and making friends, unusual patterns of interest and behavior, and unusual language and communication patterns. Repetitive behaviors and interests may become more striking and also serve to make the child with an ASD stand out, particularly in less structured situations. Paradoxically, some of the places where typically developing children have the greatest enjoyment of "down time" (e.g., recess, physical education, cafeteria) can be some of the most stressful for the child with an ASD.

In this chapter, we focus on some of the challenges, opportunities, and issues that children and their parents and teachers face in the primary school years (roughly ages 6 to 12). In the next chapter, we'll move to another set of challenges as children enter adolescence.

DEVELOPMENT AND BEHAVIOR

Social Skills and Social Style

As discussed in Chapters 1 and 2, we know more about various factors that contribute to social problems, including unusual processing of social stimuli in the brain and unusual patterns of looking and gaze in viewing social scenes. Data from our research using eye-tracking methods (see page 202) suggests that a considerable amount of information is lost simply as a result of where the child looks. Other investigators have noted that the multiple cues, as are usually present in social interaction, also are a source of difficulty (Pierce, & Schreibman, 1998).

Social difficulties do, however, persist, and often the child's style of social interaction becomes more apparent. Wing and colleagues (Wing & Gould, 1979) have described three general styles of social interaction in children with ASDs. These styles have some implications for intervention. They can also change over time.

Children with the *aloof* social style tend to be those usually thought of as having the most "classic" form of autism. Typically, they are largely oblivious to social interaction. They don't seek out others and may actively avoid social contact. The child may become distressed when intruded upon. Individuals with this style tend, on balance, to have greater degrees of cognitive/learning difficulty. Levels of communication ability tend to be low. Often, there is little interest in peer or peer-play activities. It may be difficult to get their attention—often physical prompts and cues are needed given their lack of interest in the social world. Behavioral problems can be striking, but it may also be difficult to relate the behavioral problems to obvious precipitants. These children present more behavioral challenges and often require the most intensive behavioral and educational support.

Children with what Wing has termed the *passive* social style tend to be just that. They passively accept social interaction but don't seek it and aren't particularly upset if it isn't there for them. In contrast to the aloof group, those with the passive style will accept it but don't have the typical child's marked interest in seeking social contact. They may have trouble in responding to social cues, often relying on rigid and one-sided or idiosyncratic responses. Play patterns are often more sophisticated than those in the aloof group but still tend to be somewhat rigid and perseverative.

These children tend to have fewer problem behaviors and lower levels of motor sterotypies. They can be approached by other children, but their difficulty in responding appropriately and in initiating often lead to isolation from peers unless special provisions for inclusion are made. Often, children with this style started with a more aloof one but became more tolerant of social interaction over time and with intervention.

The final group that Wing and colleagues described is what they termed the active but odd group. Often, these tend to be the most cognitively able children—with autism, Asperger's, or pervasive developmental disorder not otherwise specified (PDD-NOS)—who actively seek other children but do so in rather eccentric, one-sided ways. Language levels tend to be highest in this group. Even when good verbal abilities are present, language/communication may be one-sided and rather eccentric, for example, coming up to other children and beginning a discussion of the child's topic of special interest. These children may be well known to teachers because of their repetitive questioning, literal adherence to rules, narrow interests, and social eccentricities. Although strongly motivated to relate to others, the lack of empathy and ability to put themselves in the other person's place can lead to major difficulties with peers. The child may say something literally true but very inappropriate. There may be, particularly as time goes on, an awareness of being different and feelings of depression and distress as a result. Behavioral difficulties tend to be associated with predictable stressful events (e.g., novelty), although the general level of behavior problems in this group is somewhat less. The unusual social style can lead to peer rejection and sometimes bullying (discussed subsequently in this chapter).

Emotional Development

From very early in life, typically developing children learn to understand and express feelings. The strong social and communicative context for this experience is undoubtedly an essential part of learning to recognize one's own emotions as well as those of others. This process of self–other observation parallels other changes in the child's understanding. By the time typically developing children enter first grade, they are highly experienced in reflecting on their own feelings and those of others. Children are easily aware of what makes them, or other people, happy, anxious, or sad and use these feelings and observations to help regulate their behavior.

Children on the autism spectrum seem to have rather different experiences of emotional and affective development (Hobson, 2005). These problems are not necessarily unique to autism; for example, children with learning problems or Down syndrome may also have difficulties in this area. As a practical matter, parents and teachers frequently observe unusual emotional responses. This may take the form of highly idiosyncratic responses of pleasure or displeasure in response to what otherwise seem trivial events. However, the child might have minimal reaction to what most of us would see as a major life event. When more cognitively able people with autism write about their experience of emotions, they often report feelings of anxiety, fear, and frustration (see the box below). Children may say things (often things that are quite true) that are very hurtful of other people's feelings with little appreciation of this.

ANXIETY AND AUTISM

I was living in a world of daydreaming and fear revolving about myself. I had no care about human feelings or other people. I was afraid of everything! I was terrified to go in the water swimming (and of) loud noises; in the dark I had severe, repetitive nightmares and occasionally hearing electronic noises with nightmares. I would wake up so terrified and disoriented I wasn't able to find my way out of the room for a few minutes. It felt like I was being dragged to Hell. I was afraid of simple things such as going into the shower, getting my nails clipped, soap in my eyes, rides in the carnival. . . .

Reprinted, with permission, from Volkmar, F., & Cohen, D. (1985). The experience of infantile autism: A first person account by Tony W. *Journal of Autism and Developmental Disorders, 15,* 47–54.

A number of studies have now shown that children with ASDs have trouble in recognizing the feelings of other people (Hobson, 2005). There are also differences in the ways they show feelings; for example, expressions may be very idiosyncratic. It is likely that the constellation of social difficulties and communication problems, often coupled with some degree of cognitive processing problem, account for these difficulties. As we mentioned in Chapter 2, differences in basic things like how the brain processes social information may also have an impact; for example, differences in face processing may speak to a reduction in the importance of the face as a source of information. The fast pace and multimodal nature of usual social interaction pose further challenges. Some programs have been developed to train emotional recognition and improve responding, although it is not always clear how readily the results translate into real-world settings.

Play

As with other skills, an expected sequence of play usually emerges in the typically developing child, going from simple object manipulation to increasingly complex imaginative play, so that by the time children enter school they are capable of very sophisticated and elaborate pretend play and engaging in games with others. Play activities help children learn and foster a range of skills such as self-regulation, language, and memory. Given their multiple areas of challenge, it is not surprising that children with ASDs come into primary school settings without these skills. As younger children, they are less interested in play, particularly social play, and their play may consist of repetitive action rather than more dramatic imagination. By school age, many children with ASDs will have acquired at least some play skills. These can be supported and expanded upon in school programs.

Various techniques have been used to enhance play skills. These include both teacher-directed and peer-focused efforts (we'll talk more about the use of peers shortly). Behavioral reinforcement techniques can be used to increase interactive play, for example, by reinforcing interaction and a wider range and use of play materials. For some children, more basic skills, such as joint attention or basic language skills, need to be taught. Modeling play can be effective. For some students, providing scripts is helpful. Using the child's specific motivations (e.g., toys that are of greatest interest to the child) may help. Peers can be highly effective as play teachers, particularly if peers are given some structure and guidance (Carter, Cushing, & Kennedy, 2009).

Language and Communication

Problems in communication are universal for children with ASDs. In the past, as many as 50% of children with strictly diagnosed autism were largely nonverbal at the time they entered school; with earlier detection and intervention, that number has now apparently been significantly reduced—maybe to 30%. As with other areas, the range of levels of function is broad. Some students may come into first grade with minimal language. Others—those with Asperger's—may have amazing vocabularies but still have problems with communication. Minimally verbal students may have problems with some of the basic social aspects of communication, for example, joint attention or understanding simple gestures. It is clear that having at least some language by the time of school entry is a significant indicator of better prognosis. That being said, even in students with minimal language, further gains are possible and desirable. In general, improved language levels will strongly relate to better social skills, fewer behavior problems, and ultimately more personal independence and self-sufficiency.

Verbal children may have language that is unusual in various ways. These include a number of different problems, including echolalia, pronoun reversals, unusual speech intonation and volume (what speech pathologists call *register*), and problems in social language use. **Echolalia**, the repetition of speech, is seen in typically developing very young children. It is common for verbal individuals with ASDs but is not always seen. It can be immediate (repeating something just heard/said) or remote (something said days, weeks, or months ago—including on TV or radio). Early on in the history of autism, echolalia was viewed as something bad and something to be eliminated. Several different lines of work have changed this view. As noted, normally developing infants echo, and many different, adaptive functions of echoing have been identified, for example, in trying to keep a conversation going or to remember something. Echolalia is also viewed now as one manifestation of a more general problem in learning, with a tendency for many children with ASDs to learn language in whole chunks rather than in terms of single words. As children with ASDs learn more complex language, echolalia tends to decrease. An intermediate step in this process occurs when the child starts to transform some part of the echoed speech (termed *mitigated echolalia*).

Problems with pronoun use were first noted by Kanner in his original description of autism. Errors in use of personal pronouns (particularly I/you **pronoun reversal**) have long been described as characteristic of verbal children with ASDs. Among typically developing children, pronoun use becomes reasonably well established by age 2 to 3. Pronouns are complicated because the nature of the pronoun changes depending on context (e.g., if I have a red pen, it is *my* red pen, but if I give it to Mary, it is *her* red pen). The tendency to echo also may contribute to pronoun problems; for example, if the child repeats the last pronoun heard, it will often be incorrect. Pronoun problems may be more frequent in autism than in Asperger's. When pronoun problems occur, they can be a source of confusion—sometimes because the child's language otherwise seems well organized.

Problems with **prosody** and **register** (speech volume) are also frequent in more able, verbal children with ASDs. Prosody, the musical aspect of speech, may be quite impaired, so the child talks in a robot-like or monotonic voice. Prosody helps in conversation by indicating, among other things, areas of special importance and emphasis. In ASDs, there may be some inflection of speech, but the inflection pattern may not correspond to ordinary use (e.g., atypical words are inflected). Problems in register mean that in contrast to most of us, who use hundreds of different voice volumes, the child with an ASD has only one—often loud. Prosody has been the focus of relatively little study, but there is limited research available, for example, the work of our colleague Rhea Paul (2005).

Difficulties in the social use of language, termed **pragmatics**, are areas of great difficulty to more able students with ASDs. These problems include difficulties with carrying on a conversation, for example, only wanting to talk about one thing and not allowing the conversational partner a turn. Some of the difficulties may reflect the social problem of putting oneself in the other person's place (e.g., in starting a conversation in the middle as opposed to the beginning). A particular area of difficulty results from the subtle combinations of language features, such as discrepancies between word use and tone, as in sarcasm. Humor, irony, ambiguous language, and figurative language may pose great obstacles to communication. Myles, Trautman, and Schelvan (2004) provide a very helpful list of figurative speech phrases and idioms that can be explicitly taught. Seemingly simple tasks that involve politeness may be a problem. For example, a man with autism who once worked for one of us doing copying was left a paper with a yellow note on top asking him if he could make three copies; the paper was returned with the word *yes* written on the note—but no copies.

A final area of challenge can be in the ability of the child to develop the ability to tell stories and narratives. Typically, a story will have a beginning, middle, and end. There are some basic—culturally determined—rules (e.g., about characters, plot, feeling, etc.). Generative narratives can be an area of challenge for the child with ASD. If you find a book with pictures (but no words) and ask the child with an ASD to tell the story, he or she may focus on only one element and not get the "big picture." The significance of difficulties in this area relates, among other things, to the importance of people being able to generate their own internal narratives, for example, to recall the events of the day and plan and organize their lives. These difficulties can be seen in older and more able children as they struggle in English class with novels or short stories that focus on feelings and nuances of communication and interaction with less emphasis on generation of facts. Various approaches can be used to help children, including explicit focus on identification of relevant plot/narrative aspects, for instance, *who* is involved, *where* are they, *what* are they doing, *when* are they doing it, and *why* are they doing it. Some computer resources (e.g., the Storybook Weaver program) can be used for children to work on developing their own narrative abilities.

As discussed in Chapter 6, a number of different strategies can be used to facilitate communication in children with ASDs. For children with limited verbal language, an emphasis on communication, broadly defined, is indicated. Behavioral techniques can be used to increase word use. As discussed previously, for children with limited or no words, picture or object exchange or other augmentative communication aids may be helpful. For the verbal child with an ASD, a host of intervention techniques are available and must be tailored to the specific needs of the child. Often, there is an early emphasis on vocabulary building, but it is important not to neglect issues of generalization and developing more complex language. For the most cognitively able students, particularly those with Asperger's, the child may have a tremendous vocabulary but rather poor communication skills. The child's speech may be oddly inflected and pedantic with a rather "professorial" aspect (a major problem for peers). For this group, there should be a strong emphasis on explicit teaching of conversational rules, with many opportunities for practice and critique coupled with a strong social skills acquisition program. Language and social skills are intimately related. Often, but not always, gains in both areas proceed in tandem. For some children, even major gains in language abilities may not be associated with similar social gains, such as the ability to put oneself in the other person's place (theory of mind). Poor social judgment coupled with rigidity and an emphasis on telling the truth can lead to some complicated situations. Fortunately, when given appropriate supports, children with ASDs can become more communicative, and often teachers and parents discover that the child has a lot to say.

Sensory and Behavioral Issues

Stereotyped and repetitive behaviors are frequent in school-aged children. These tend to be somewhat more common in students with lower levels of cognitive ability. For more able children, the unusual behaviors may take the form of intense, often unusual, interests/preoccupations; for instance, the child may be fixated on the weather channel or train/bus/TV schedules. These unusual behaviors may also be observed along with unusual sensory responses.

Observations of children over time often reveal some change. For example, early repetitive behavior may start in a rather simple fashion but come to be much more complicated. Unusual rigidity and difficulties dealing with new situations are common. Some studies have suggested that these unusual behaviors, particularly the more common stereotyped movements, become less common as children move into adolescence, although some individuals will retain these into adulthood. Occasionally, the rigidity and repetitive nature of some of the behaviors exhibited is taken to suggest the presence of obsessive–compulsive disorder. However, the more traditional stereotyped movements seen in children with autism are usually less complex than those of obsessive–compulsive disorder. For more able children, another differentiation is that children with obsessive–compulsive disorder do not usually *like* their preoccupation—that is, they would like *not* to be so preoccupied; this is not the same in more able children with Asperger's, who usually like their special interest.

It is important to note that unusual sensory responses and stereotyped behaviors are seen in a range of developmental disorders, including mental retardation/intellectual disability (see Chapter 3). When they are present, however, they can present significant obstacles for intervention. Both behavioral methods (Chapter 14) and drug treatments (Chapter 15) can be used very effectively. As with other areas, there is always a need to balance potential benefits and risks. Unusual behaviors and sensory responses that interfere with the child's learning are ones that appropriately might be targeted either for medication or behavioral intervention. There is some evidence that, when carefully done, these interventions can significantly enhance the child's learning.

Gender Differences

With the notable exception of **Rett's disorder** (see Chapter 13), more boys than girls are usually thought to have autism and ASDs—with rates three to four times higher in boys. Among individuals with Asperger's disorder, the rate may be much higher—with boys outnumbering girls 20 or more to one. This has, unfortunately, meant that information on girls with ASDs is generally rather limited. Researchers have, for example, sometimes excluded girls from participation in research studies. There are some suggestions of differences in presentation. For girls with autism, as a group, there are often more severe cognitive problems. When girls with autism or ASDs are higher functioning, there are some suggestions of differences in how they present; for example, girls may be more concerned about the impression they make on peers. Girls with autism and Asperger's may have even more trouble "fitting in" socially than boys. However, they may have fewer behavior problems and the degree of the social difficulties may be somewhat less. By middle school, girls with ASDs may be more anxious than boys and stressed by social demands. However, girls may also have stronger play and communication skills and may be less prone to attentional problems than boys (Nichols, Moravick, & Tetenbaum, 2009). They also may face special challenges in terms of personal safety (Chapter 11) and sexuality (Chapter 9). It is important that parents and teachers think about the special problems that girls with ASDs face.

Various theories have tried to account for differences between boys and girls. A British researcher, Simon Baron-Cohen (2003), has suggested that perhaps these differences relate to sex differences in the brain. However, some of the differences in clinical presentation of autism and Asperger's in girls may relate to more general sex differences. Regardless of its cause, the fact that girls less commonly have ASD makes for some challenges in school programs; for example, girls in special ed class settings are likely to be significantly outnumbered by boys, and opportunities for interaction with other, typically developing girls may be limited.

SCHOOL-RELATED ISSUES

School presents many challenges for the child with an ASD. These include the complicated learning environment as well as the social–communication, emotional, and academic challenges intrinsic to the school experience. Differences in response to situations/contexts become much more important, and the child has, for the first time, to become much more differentiated in his behavior and responses. There are many more expectations for self-directed learning, and organization usually comes from within the child as opposed to external structure. Problems with social interaction and communication can have a negative impact on peer interaction. For the more cognitively able student, this may be combined with a growing awareness of being isolated and feeling different.

Some students with ASDs will do well academically, particularly in more "fact-based" areas and most particularly those where they have a special interest or ability. Other children will have variable kinds and degrees of learning difficulties. Some children reach school age but are nonverbal or largely nonverbal, and, accordingly, traditional academic subjects hold little interest for them. In such cases, increasing communication skills and participating in structured learning situations are relevant goals.

Teachers and others often take the child's language skill to give an estimate of overall ability; for children who are typically developing, this is often reasonable. However, for children with ASDs, there are some pitfalls. Children with more classical autism presentations may have much less well developed verbal than nonverbal abilities, and there is a danger that schools will program *only* to the lower verbal skills. Conversely, students with Asperger's may have much better verbal skills but areas of great difficulty with other kinds of tasks; therefore, teachers may over estimate many abilities in this group. It must be emphasized that appropriate supports be provided given the individual's specific needs. The book by Mackenzie (2008) in the reading list discusses these issues in some detail.

Academics and Curriculum

Several considerations arise in thinking about objectives for the academic program. Students with ASDs present teachers with some unusual challenges. In addition to all these considerations, it is important that the objectives are spelled out for students in their individualized education plan (IEP) and that their classroom settings be developmentally appropriate. These objectives also have to be realistically placed within the broader context of the curriculum. What is appropriate will vary considerably from child to child. Sometimes the regular program, often with some modification, may meet the child's needs. At other times, a smaller teaching setting will be more helpful. As we have noted, the profiles of strengths and weaknesses can and will vary considerably from one child to another; accordingly, there is not a simple one-size-fits-all approach (Tsatsanis, 2004). While cognitive profiles are of some help in thinking about the most appropriate teaching strategies and goals, other issues—for example, behavior problems, social difficulties, sensory issues, and difficulties with transitions and change—may also need to be considered. Difficulties with attention and organization, combined with a lack of social attention, pose other problems. When medications are given to help with associated problems, side effects can complicate teaching. The age of the student may also be relevant; for instance, activities or materials that are appropriate for much younger children might attract the interest of the child with an ASD, but there is a risk of typical peers reacting negatively.

Goals targeted will usually include social interaction skills and expanding communication, as well as more traditional academic goals (see Kluth, 2003, for a discussion of teaching procedures and strategies). Fostering other skills, such as leisure time and adaptive skills, is also important. Some of the general areas that are addressed in the IEP for a school-aged child are listed in the text box below. Keep in mind that this is a general list and the IEP must be tailored to the individual student; also keep in mind, as we've discussed, that the IEP needs to strike a sensible balance—having some short-, medium-, and longer term (vision) goals along with objective data to monitor progress. Continued communication with parents is important.

AREAS TO CONSIDER ADDRESSING IN THE IEP FOR THE CHILD OF SCHOOL AGE

Social Skills/Social Difficulties

- Social skills teaching methods
- Understanding social cues/emotions
- Appropriate social responding, initiation
- Teaching social routines
- Explicit teaching regarding social problem solving

Emotional and Self-Organizational Skills

- Increasing awareness of feelings/emotions
- Using appropriate strategies to deal with anxiety and problem situations

Communication and Language Skills

- Using augmentative communication if appropriate

(Continued)

- Increasing complexity of spoken/written communication
- Increasing self-expression (and self-advocacy)
- Understanding social language (nonverbal cues, prosody, voice volume)
- Conversational and pragmatic skills (starting and stopping a conversation, responding to cues, learning figurative/nonliteral language)

Organizational Skills

- Visual, written organizers (schedules/lists/color codes)
- Working independently for longer periods
- Management of materials and tasks (including self-correction)
- Learning when to ask for help
- Keyboarding (as appropriate) and computer resources

Behavioral and Sensory Issues

- Address specific behavior problems or sensory issues
- Increase flexibility and ability to deal with transitions

As discussed in Chapters 5 and 6, there are a number of ways to support learning. These must be tailored to the needs of the individual student. They can range from simple organizational aids (written or visual schedules) to much more technologically sophisticated procedures (computers, personal digital assistants, text-to-speech programs, etc.). For some students, there is a genuine pull toward computer-based technology—it is predictable and rule governed, the information load can be tailored to the student, and it can combine auditory and visual information in very interesting ways. Moore (2002) makes a number of suggestions for assisting with organizational issues; for example, color-coding can help all students in the classroom. Technological supports have become increasingly sophisticated; the speech pathologist and occupational therapist can often be helpful in thinking about use of assistive technologies (see Chapter 6). Computer-assisted instruction can be helpful in a host of ways. Students who have difficulty in writing may profit from use of organization software (e.g., kidspiration, www.inspiration.com), and if the child can use a laptop, the potential for other aids (spelling and grammar checking) is also present. For some students, speech recognition software may be useful; this turns the student's spoken words into text and may be particularly helpful for students with fine motor problems. In thinking about such systems, any difficulties the student has with the flow of speech should be considered; for example, some systems can accommodate students whose speech is slower due to articulation problems. The occupational therapist may be helpful in thinking about approaches to writing problems and a range of alternatives from more sophisticated computer programs to much simpler interventions, like using a slant board to assist in handwriting (Myles 2005) may be helpful. In this regard, it is important to note that the value of some of the simplest things—visual schedules, preteaching, use of lists/checklists, charts, and so forth—should not be underestimated. Technology is certainly not a replacement for effective instruction.

Whenever possible the special interests/motivations of the student with an ASD should be used; Kluth and Schwarz (2008) give some good examples of this. Often, considerable "incidental" teaching can occur around the topic of special interest or fascination. This isn't always easy to do, but even when it isn't giving the student the opportunity to spend some time on an area of special interest, it can be used as a reward and motivator. Challenges for children with ASDs—particularly those whose verbal skills are less advanced than nonverbal and other abilities—include difficulties in auditory processing. Spoken language is fast paced and ephemeral (in contrast to pictures and the written word). Teachers should plan, in such situations, to give extra time for processing, provide relevant visual supports (outlines, checklists), and keep their language simple and direct (Myles & Adreon, 2001). For more cognitively able students who have trouble with the pace of the class, the use of written notes (e.g., from another student) or even tape recordings of class lecture/discussion may be very helpful. Moore (2002) has some very helpful suggestions, including various possibilities for assisting students with note-taking strategies. Scott, Clark, and Brady (2000) give an excellent review of a range of educational supports.

Teachers should also be aware that while small groups can be good learning environments for students with ASDs, group work needs to be carefully monitored. The student with an ASD will often need support ahead of time, such as reviewing key concepts, terms, and goals, with written or visual supports available if needed as well. First and foremost, the teacher and then other students (hopefully modeling the teacher's behavior) should show consideration and respect for the student with an ASD; for example, if the student makes an off-topic comment, the teacher can help redirect the conversation to the topic at hand. We'll talk more about ways to help peers shortly.

Some children on the autism spectrum have an early—and sometimes very precocious—interest in iconic symbols, including letters and numbers. Some of these children become early readers, occasionally even what has been termed **hyperlexic** readers (very advanced reading skills for the child's chronological age). In contrast to spoken language, written language is static and, for many children, much easier to master. As previously noted (page 64), it is important for teachers and parents to understand that reading "decoding" (literally sounding out words) may be much higher—misleadingly higher—than the child's actual understanding.

Several steps can be taken to encourage literacy. These include availability of books and word processing programs, giving children time for reading, and encouraging reading and related literacy skills. Some of the available computer programs (e.g., Living Books) can be highly motivating to students. The reading program should be sure to include an emphasis on strengthening comprehension skills. It is important that teachers keep in mind the possibility that students with ASDs will do well with comprehension of basic facts but may miss other key aspects of stories relating to emotions, intentions, and the like. For testing purposes, teachers may wish to consider ways to minimize the burden of additional language processing; for example, as opposed to open-ended questions, multiple choice, yes/no, and fill-in-the-blank questions may more accurately reflect the student's ability to understand the information conveyed.

Spelling can be quite challenging for students with ASDs. This is particularly true for the English language, which borrows heavily from other languages and has a complex set of rules. Students can use a range of different strategies, and it is important to understand the sources of errors in an attempt to provide remediation (Attwood, 1998). Computers can be used to help teach and, when appropriate, to help students spell-check their work. Peer tutoring can also be used. Sometimes spelling, or some other area, may be such a difficult homework task that it becomes all consuming and the student with ASD is spending all his homework time stuck on it, e.g., working on spelling to the exclusion of everything else. When this happens, modification to the rules can be helpful, for example, using a visual timer to give the student a set amount of time to focus on spelling—at the end of the time, he is done regardless of where he is on the spelling list (Myles & Adreon, 2001, provide an excellent discussion of homework-related issues).

Mathematical abilities are highly variable. Basic math concepts may present tremendous challenges for some students, while other students may, literally, be years ahead of their classmates. Some individuals can engage in prodigious savant skills (e.g., calendar calculation) (Thioux and others 2006). Others are interested in certain types of equations or areas of mathematics. Visual cues and multisensory approaches (e.g., TouchMath) may be helpful. Some children are very good at understanding the basic math facts due to their strengths in rote memorization; the same students may not have nearly as good an understanding of the underlying principles. Peer tutoring and use of concrete materials (e.g., money) can be helpful. As with other skills, generalization is important.

Teaching Procedures and Programs

We discussed specific teaching procedures extensively in Chapter 6 and listed some of the many potential resources and programs teachers can appropriately use in work with children on the autism spectrum (see page 151). As discussed in Chapter 5, these programs have many areas of similarities and some areas of difference. Most are strongly behaviorally based using procedures like discrete trial and pivotal response training and work with teaching functional routines. Others have a stronger developmental component where following the child's motivation becomes more important. It is important that the curriculum be appropriate to the child's level of ability and also consider the child's chronological age and, to the extent possible, specific interests and motivations. Curricular materials and teaching strategies need to be carefully considered. Pivotal response procedures can, for example, be used for various purposes (see page 157). There are advantages to using various strategies and teaching materials approaches, for example, for enhancing generalization of skills (see Arick Krug, Fullerton, Loos, & Falco, 2005, for a discussion). For school-aged children, sensory issues may need to be addressed to enhance learning. Teaching approaches (e.g., use of visual materials, provision of organization aids and supports) need to be adapted for the individual student. As children progress through school, academic demands become more challenging, with greater expectations for abstract thinking and self-organization. This can lead to attentional and/or behavioral difficulties, and teachers should be careful to monitor students to be sure that what appears to be a lack of attention does not, in fact, reflect greater cognitive challenge; accordingly, periodic assessment should be accomplished.

As noted in Chapter 6, various models of instruction and curricula have been developed. For example, the Support and Treatment for Autism and Related Disorders (STAR) program provides a range of training and teaching materials useful in developing individualized behavioral treatment programs for children and their families. It makes use of a number of different methods (e.g., discrete trial, pivotal response training, picture exchange, verbal behavior, and other behavioral procedures). The Web site (www.starautismprogram.com) provides additional information and links to training and other materials, including DVDs. This program has the great advantage of providing detailed lesson plans along with teaching materials and data systems, including curriculum-based assessments in a number of relevant areas such as functional routines, receptive and expressive language, and so forth. The data system helps monitor progress and can be used to help document progress as specified in the IEP. Other programs may use the Treatment and Education of Autistic and Related Communication Handicapped Children (TEACCH) method. This approach, based at the University of North Carolina at Chapel Hill, was begun by Eric Schopler and continues under the direction of the Gary Mesibov. This approach draws on a number of different methodologies in development of individualized programs for students and their families. It includes careful attention to teaching methods, the structure of the learning environment, and use of visual and other supports in teaching. Materials and information on training are provided on the TEACCH Web site (www.teacch.com). Some excellent summaries of the range of behavioral and curriculum approaches useful to teachers are available (e.g., Hall, 2008).

Programs like TEACCH emphasize the importance of careful consideration of the classroom and classroom structure for learning. For example, placement of the child with an ASD at the front of the class (to be near the teacher) may be appropriate. Classroom rules, schedules, and so forth can be prominently displayed at the front of the room. Moore (2002) makes a number of suggestions for helping the child with Asperger's syndrome, and many of these would apply to other students on the autism spectrum as well. Attention to physical aspects of the classroom environment may reveal specific factors/distracters that need to be addressed, for example, moving the child to an area where he has an opportunity for reduced exposure to extraneous stimuli. For children who must move from one classroom to another, the possibility of the child's moving just before the bell rings may be helpful. Use of visual supports and clear directions is also helpful. Instructions should be considered relative to the child's language level. For students—particularly those with Asperger's—who have handwriting problems, or for students whose anxiety interferes, modified test taking may be appropriate; for example, taking a test in the library or a quiet area or using a different format (oral versus written examination) or doing the test in several shorter periods, can be considered. Depending on the material changes in format of the test (e.g., true–false or multiple choice), there may be better choices for assessing knowledge than open-ended tests (see Moore, 2002). Grades can sometimes be a source of anxiety, and the teacher and student can often work together to develop a straightforward way of giving feedback with explicit guidelines about how grades are calculated.

MAINSTREAMING AND PEER PREPARATION

Students with ASDs are increasingly included in mainstream settings. Early diagnosis and more intensive intervention have resulted in many children with ASDs who are ready to be fully included by the time they reach first grade. For other children, the opportunity to spend at least part of the day in a mainstream setting can provide important opportunities for positive peer interaction and academic success (see Handleman, Harris, & Martins, 2005, for a detailed discussion; and Myles, 2005, for strategies specific to students with Asperger's syndrome).

Various terms are used, more or less interchangeably, to describe mainstream educational opportunities (e.g., *inclusive classrooms, inclusion,* or *integration*). Various models of **mainstreaming** have been developed. For example, at times children, particularly younger children, may be in a special ed classroom where there are some typically developing peers. In general, the inclusion refers to any time the child with an ASD is with typically developing peers within school. Many variations in inclusion are possible. The child with an ASD may be included in some classes and not others. Specific strategies can used in particular situations; for example, the peer-assisted learning strategies (PALS) method has been used in work on math and reading (see Utley & Mortweek, 1997). The most cognitively able students with ASDs (e.g., those with Asperger's) may be most readily included in academic classes, while special services can be provided at less structured times when the child is more likely to have difficulty (e.g., lunch, recess, physical education [PE]). In some instances, peer buddy systems and other supports may appropriately be used at such times to support inclusion of the child with an ASD. Networks of support can be created in several ways, such as using the Circle of Friends approach (Schlieder, 2007). A range of peer support procedures is available (see Carter et al., 2009).

For children with ASDs who have greater cognitive and behavioral challenges, inclusion may occur only in very specific contexts where high levels of adult support can be provided. While much of the work on mainstream procedures has been based on work with younger children, there has been an increasing focus on school-aged children, and it is clear that the typically developing peer can be a wonderful model for the school-aged child with an ASD. Indeed, peers can be highly effective teachers and supporters, although some degree of training and/or support is needed if peers are to be effective; that is, just having the child with an ASD in the classroom is not of itself sufficient (Carter et al., 2009). Several programs have used typical peers of elementary or junior high school age to increase social contacts and peer relationships (e.g., Haring & Breen, 1992; and Morrison, Kamps, Garcia, & Parker, 2001). In one study, Pierce and Schreibman (1997) were able to train elementary school–aged peers in a modified version of pivotal response training (PRT) with notable success.

Various considerations go into selecting peers to work with the child with an ASD, such as the level of disability that the child with an ASD exhibits, the motivation and interest of the typical peer, the degree of supervision/support that the typical peer needs, and so forth. Carter and colleagues (2009) have summarized some of the pros and cons of different approaches for recruiting peers into programs, such as student identification, teacher recommendations, classroom announcements, and so forth. Peers may need training in areas such as language level and methods of demonstration as well as in dealing with or ignoring inappropriate behaviors. Typical peers may benefit from this work. Peers can be assigned as peer buddies or can participate in social skills groups. For younger and less socially advanced students with ASDs, preteaching, social scripts, and other supports may be of help. Another approach has used videotape review of social interaction with typical peers for teaching social skills (Thiemann & Goldstein, 2001). There are many different activities that can incorporate peer support, from walking with the student from one class to another to helping with homework, reviewing lessons/course content, sharing materials, and helping with communication, to name just a few (see Carter et al., 2009).

Peer supports can be particularly helpful at what are some of the most challenging times of the day for students with ASDs—notably, lunch, recess, transitions from one classroom to another, and PE. PE can be particularly challenging for students with ASDs; for example, changing clothes can take longer than for other students; the social back-and-forth in the locker room (particularly for boys) may be very confusing; and team sports can be very challenging, given the combination of organizational, motor, and social skill requirements. Adaptive PE can be used when appropriate with specially trained teachers who work with students in smaller settings.

Teachers and school staff should also keep in mind the more general importance of providing information to the entire student body about disabilities. This can take a more general and generic approach in the beginning, for example, encouraging discussion of ways people cope with difficulties and disabilities, having students participate in activities that help them understand the challenges disabilities present, and using videotapes and a class/school discussion section to present information and encourage an atmosphere of mutual tolerance and respect. Various specific resources relevant to autism, Asperger's, and related disorders are now available, including some excellent videos and children's books (see reading list below). All students will know someone with a disability (even if it is as "minor" a disability as wearing glasses). We have fond memories of attending one of our daughter's second-grade classes and doing an inservice on disability in general, which included having children practice what it is like to be sightless (with a blindfold on and a cane to try to get around), or in a wheelchair or being on crutches.

PEER INFORMATION/RESOURCES

Amenta, C. A. (1992). *Russell is extra special: A book about autism for children*. New York: Magination Press.

Cook, J., & Hartman, C. (2008). *My mouth is a volcano!*. Chattanooga: National Center for Youth Issues.

Donlon, L. (2007). *The other kid: A draw it out guidebook for kids dealing with a special needs sibling*. Coral Springs, FL: Llumina Press.

Gosselin, K. (2002). *Taking seizure disorders to school: A story about epilepsy*. Hawthorne, NY: JayJo Books.

Hoopmann, K. (2001). *Blue bottle mystery: An Asperger adventure*. Philadelphia: Jessica Kingsley.

Hoopmann, K. (2001). *Of mice and aliens: An Asperger adventure*. Philadelphia: Jessica Kingsley.

Hoopmann, K. (2002). *Lisa and the lacemaker: An Asperger adventure*. Philadelphia: Jessica Kingsley.

Hoopmann, K. (2003). *Haze*. Philadelphia: Jessica Kingsley.

Keating-Velasco, J. L. (2007). *A is for autism, F is for friend: A kid's book for making friends with a child who has autism*. Shawnee Mission, KS: Autism Asperger.

Welton, J. (2003). *Can I tell you about Asperger syndrome? A guide for friends and family*. Philadelphia: Jessica Kingsley.

In addition to peer preparation, the classroom teacher will benefit from training in methods to support inclusion. The teacher needs to consider the role of the peers, the nature of the activities, support for the peers, and the needs of the child with an ASD. Picking activities that are fun and motivating will increase the interests of typical peers and the student with an ASD. The teacher should also consider the physical arrangements of the room and have plans in place, in advance, for dealing with behavioral issues. In general, the goal should be for the teacher to be a background presence and facilitator once activities are under way with, as much as possible, interaction and feedback coming from the students interacting with each other. It must be emphasized that peers need preparation and support, particularly in the early phases of the process.

Discussion of peer and teacher support strategies also raises an important issue, providing enough but not too much support. Readily available supports, like peers, are much less intrusive and often more effective than other supports (e.g., paraprofessionals). Aides and other paraprofessionals have an important role but, as with students and teachers, need preparation for their role. They are present in the classroom to facilitate the accommodation of the student(s) with special needs but must maintain a careful balance, e.g., in encouraging peer interaction and increasing levels of autonomy and independence for the student with ASD. Having a paraprofessional who sticks like glue to the student with an ASD can be off-putting to peers. They should always keep in mind the overall goal of fostering classroom inclusiveness and participation and think about how their intervention can help the student become more independent. There are some good books written specifically for the child with an ASD that may be helpful as well (see the text box below).

INFORMATION FOR CHILDREN WITH ASDs

Cook, J. & Hartman, C. (2008). *My mouth is a volcano!* Chattanooga: National Center for Youth Issues.

Larson, E. M. (2006). *I am utterly unique: Celebrating the strengths of children with Asperger syndrome and high-functioning autism.* Shawnee Mission, KS: Autism Asperger.

Lears, L. (2002). *Becky the brave: A story about epilepsy.* Morton Grove, IL: Albert Whitman & Company.

Ludwig, T., & Manning, M. J. (2006). *Sorry!* Berkeley, CA: Tricycle Press.

Naylor, P. R. (1994). *King of the playground.* New York: Aladdin Paperbacks.

Strachan, J., & Schnurr, R. G. (1999). *Asperger's huh? A child's perspective.* Gloucester, Ontario: Anisor Publishing.

Bullying and Teasing

Unfortunately, one of the issues that comes about with exposing children on the autism spectrum to typically developing peers is the potential for teasing or bullying to occur. Although the data on this topic are in some ways limited, it is fairly clear that children with ASDs—probably particularly those with Asperger's and high-functioning autism—are more likely to be bullied than their typically developing peers. The higher functioning individuals with ASDs are also, unfortunately, the ones who have greater potential for subsequent problems with self-esteem and other problems given their higher cognitive abilities. Given that these are the individuals most likely to be mainstreamed, there clearly is potential for significant trouble.

Some of the factors that predispose children with ASDs to teasing and bullying include their difficulties in reading social cues and in dealing with the fast pace of social interaction. Unusual interests may make them stand out from peers and be perceived as profoundly uncool. Language issues may be a problem—difficulties with more sophisticated language and figures of speech may lead to confusion. The child with an ASD may say something not intended to be funny and feels badly when laughed at.

Bullying can be verbal or physical. It can also be either very overt or much more subtle, for example, involving exclusion or isolation from a group. It can take the form of malicious gossip. There can sometimes be a fine line in deciding what bullying is or isn't (e.g., the teacher who uses sarcasm or ridicule). Bullying can be an isolated instance but can also be ongoing and frequent. As Heinrichs (2003) notes, bullying types vary with the developmental level of the child so that younger children are more likely to exhibit physical or verbal aggression toward same-sex peers, while in early adolescence social and other kinds of bullying become more common and impact both same-sex and opposite-sex peers. In later adolescence, sexual aspects of bullying may be more prominent.

Factors that seem to increase the potential for being bullied include social isolation and social awkwardness. Difficulties with language use in general and social language use (pragmatics) in particular, are also risk factors. Individuals with ASDs have trouble understanding more sophisticated forms of humor and this, along with idiosyncratic communication styles also contribute to risk for being bullied. Social eccentricity, social isolation, and what appears to be self-centeredness likely also contribute to this problem. One study (Little, 2002) found that children with Asperger's or the nonverbal learning disability (NLD) profile had a fourfold increase in bullying. Bullying leads to stress and symptoms of stress. Bullying may also precipitate aggression as well as depression and symptoms of anxiety. In his original description of the condition that now bears his name, Hans Asperger commented on the potential for these problems.

Although definitions of bullying vary somewhat, they almost all involve some sense of one student's having power over another one. As Attwood (2008) notes, bullying is more likely to occur in situations where adults are not closely monitoring things (e.g., hallways, recess, sports/gym). Bullying can also happen outside of school, for example, on the neighborhood playground or even with siblings. As noted, teachers and other adults in authority can sometimes use sarcasm to the point that this becomes bullying. Attwood (2008) also comments on a problem that we've seen fairly frequently—rather, overly trusting children on the autism spectrum can be "set up" by other students who use the child's desire for friendship and acceptance as a path to getting them to engage in inappropriate behaviors, for example, the boy who pulls the fire alarm on a dare at the suggestion of a peer who says he's "chicken" otherwise.

Unfortunately, some of the same problems that contribute to bullying in the first place also make it less likely that the more able child with an ASD will report the bullying. The child may be afraid of retaliation/"payback," he may not understand the motivation of the bullying, and he doesn't often think about asking adults for help. As a result, sometimes the awareness of teachers and parents of bullying emerges only when the child comes into treatment for symptoms of anxiety or depression (Attwood, 2008). Sometimes children will start having major meltdowns over seemingly trivial things, and it may emerge that the child has been under considerable stress due to bullying. It is important for parents and teachers to be alert for signs of possible bullying. It is also important that the school environment be one that discourages bullying.

The nature of bullying and difficulties in reporting are obstacles to prevention; for example, bullying will tend to occur in settings where adult supervision is minimal or nonexistent and the children involved often don't report it. Preventing bullying requires a broad-based approach with staff and teacher training, explicit discussion and class rules against bullying, monitoring and intervention when bullying occurs, and promotion of social competence for all involved (including the bully). Zero tolerance of bullying might, at first blush, seem to be a good solution, but carries its own problems (e.g., relative to children who have been repeatedly bullied but then act out); zero tolerance also may potentially discourage reporting (Heinrichs, 2003). Having an explicit discussion with all students and an established school code of conduct can be helpful. An effective bullying prevention program will also include sensible strategies for helping students being bullied and those who bully (sometimes there is overlap of the two groups). Finally, as Heinrichs points out, it is important to help the student with an ASD understand the differences between normal peer conflicts and bullying. These clarifications can be particularly helpful to more able students with ASDs who have trouble disentangling the normal ups and downs of social relationships from bullying. This is helpful as well in educating the student with an ASD about what bullying actually is and what they can do to get help. Various resources to prevent and deal with bullying are provided by Heinrichs (2003) and Dubin and Carley (2007).

TEN BULLYING STRATEGIES FOR KIDS WITH ASPERGER SYNDROME

1. Keep telling adults when you are bullied or teased. Find out who will listen to you and take action.

2. If you are being bothered at recess, stay closer to an adult and play with or around other kids when you can.

3. If someone is bothering you and won't stop, say "Stop that" loudly, turn around quickly, and walk away.

4. As you walk away, try to remember who you see standing around; they may be a witness to what happened.

5. Say something assertive like "Back off," instead of attacking back by saying something mean like "You're an idiot, too."

6. If someone asks you to do something or say something to someone else that you don't feel right about, stop, think, and say, "Why don't you do it yourself"; then don't do it!

7. Stay away from kids who are mean to you, and don't keep trying to make them like you no matter how popular they are.

8. Talk to and hang around with kids who are nicer to you but may not be as popular as others; they may need a friend.

9. If someone tells you to stop doing something, they probably mean it. So stop.

10. Watch kids who usually get along with most everyone, including the teachers, and see how they act in different situations. You might get some good ideas for how to behave.

Reprinted, with permission, from Heinrichs, R. (2003). *Perfect targets—Asperger syndrome and bullying* (p. 177). Shawnee Mission, KS: Autism Asperger.

CASE STUDIES

Case 1: Jack

Jack was a 12-year-old adolescent who was enrolled in the seventh grade in middle school who had been seen by us four times since he was 3. At age 3 we had made a diagnosis of autism, and his family and school had provided extensive supports for him. He had made slow but steady progress, and at the time of the current evaluation, he was participating in many mainstream activities with some special ed classroom time. He was no longer receiving individual speech–language or occupational therapy (OT) services (those had stopped when he transitioned to junior high school last year). A social skills group was provided on a weekly basis (and led by his former speech pathologist). His parents sought the current assessment because starting in grade 10 he would have to transition to high school and they wanted an update on his progress. They also were concerned that he was increasingly making negative comments about himself and was more anxious in school. Some weeks before our assessment, he had been started on a selective serotonin reuptake inhibitor (SSRI) medication (see Chapter 15) to help deal with anxiety and behavioral rigidity.

Over the years, Jack's cognitive functioning had consistently fallen in the low average to borderline impaired range but with notable strengths in skills in tasks that involved rote memory and weaknesses in tasks that involved verbal skills or where fast processing was required. During the current testing, Jack was cooperative and compliant. He was careful and thoughtful in his approach and would ask for clarification if he didn't understand. He responded well to praise, and the psychologist also noted that after completing a difficult item, he would comment on his performance, saying "I got it!" He was occasionally anxious when tasks were more difficult, even though he'd been told that some things would be more difficult for him. He had some occasional off-task behaviors that involved some hand mannerisms, but these generally didn't cause him trouble. The psychologist felt that the scores obtained were reasonably valid indicators of current levels of ability.

Jack was given the Wechsler Intelligence Scale for Children, 4th edition (WISC-IV) (see Chapter 3) to evaluate his level of cognitive functioning. He had been given other versions of this test previously, and it was chosen because of its appropriateness for Jack and its ability to assess various areas of cognitive functioning.

On the WISC-IV Jack exhibited significant scatter in his scores. The WISC-IV provided several index scores as well as a full-scale IQ all with a mean of 100 and a standard deviation of 15. Jack's index scores were 71 for verbal comprehension, 102 for working memory, 82 for perceptual reasoning, and 73 for processing speed. His overall IQ score was 79, although in the report we emphasized the importance of looking at the pattern and range of his scores and not the overall IQ. The discrepancy between his lowest and highest scores was statistically significant.

An analysis of the specific subtests that go into the various index scores was of interest in further understanding his profile of strengths and weaknesses. For example, in looking at the tasks that went into his verbal index score, Jack had the most trouble with a task called comprehension (which involves some understanding of social rules and judgment) but did much better with understanding word meaning (vocabulary) and similarities (e.g., how are a cat and dog alike). Both tasks that went into the working memory score were solidly average. Within the perceptual reasoning subtest, his area of greatest weakness was block design (usually an area of strength for people with autism but not one for Jack), while other subtests in this area were in or near the average range. One of the reasons he did poorly with block design was his tendency to not carefully check his work, thus losing points because he missed a small detail. In fact, his actual score on the task was unchanged from the previous time we had seen him. On a different task in this area, he was asked to identify pictures from a group of conceptually similar pictures. The psychologist noted that Jack talked himself through this task and did better as a result.

Tasks that involved speech in processing were difficult for Jack. He had trouble working at a rapid pace and also had some problems with the tasks that also involved his crossing out pictures; that is, the combination of a handwriting aspect and a need to move quickly were particularly challenging for him. In comparison to his previous testing, Jack's overall cognitive abilities have remained consistent, indicating that he has made age-related gains. Additionally, his pattern of personal strengths and weaknesses has also remained consistent; he continued to demonstrate personal strengths in rote memory and mental control and personal weaknesses in verbal reasoning and speed of processing.

The psychologist administered some items from other assessment instruments. He noted that when Jack was able to use language to help solve a problem (particularly one with a visual component) he did better than if the problem were more abstract. She also noted that he had a tendency to "get stuck" and didn't always change his strategy in response to a new situation. A similar pattern was reported by his parents on an instrument looking at executive functioning—his parents noted that Jack had problems in the areas of flexibility and being able to inhibit his responses. They also noted that he could become overly emotional in response to changes in plans, transition, and so forth, and that sometimes seemingly little things could cause an angry or tearful outburst.

Jack's parents also reported that he has difficulty with inhibition. They reported that he acts impulsively and without thinking, blurts out statements, and has trouble staying seated.

The speech pathologist reviewed Jack's IEP and noted that he was getting some small group social skills work but otherwise no individual speech–language services. His IEP had a number of good goals for social development as well as some curriculum-based speech–communication goals. Social goals had to do with carrying on a conversation, dealing with transitions and turn taking, and decreasing perseverative speech. During the speech–communication assessment, Jack was polite and cooperative. He was given a brief schedule of the assessment activities, including breaks, which were checked off during the session. With the support of the checklist, Jack complied with all assessment tasks, made frequent comments, and remained engaged with each of the testing activities. Although he was cooperative, Jack exhibited a high level of anxiety and needed constant reassurance, asking, "Is that right?" As during the psychological assessment, he would become worried if he made an incorrect response. Also consistent with the psychologist's observation, Jack often got stuck when he made a wrong response. The speech pathologist noted that when he was more anxious, that is when tasks were more difficult, his language tended to become more scripted. Unfortunately, this often seemed to worsen his performance since, instead of taking in the new situation, he would be preoccupied with the previous question/task. Jack had made some nice gains in his ability to carry on a conversation. He responded well to simple and direct questions. He had more difficulty if the pace of the language increased or if the level of the language was more complex. Although he exhibited relatively little variability in his tone of voice, he did have good eye contact and had easy-to-read nonverbal cues.

The speech pathologist used several different tests to evaluate Jack's communication skills. She also collected a sample of his communication by tape recorder for subsequent analysis. On the Comprehensive Assessment of Spoken Language (CASL) his standard scores ranged from 56 to 86 (with a mean of 100 and standard deviation of 15). He had the greatest difficulties with nonliteral and pragmatic language. His abilities to understand synonyms and make grammar judgments were in the average range. As with the IQ test results, an analysis of the subtest scores helped to clarify areas of strength and weakness. His ability to understand ambiguous language and idioms was weak. Overall, while he had made gains from his previous assessment, his language use remained very concrete. Jack had substantial difficulty with implied or indirect meanings.

Jack's ability to tell a story was at the low end of the average range. For a child of his age, he was not yet able to construct more complicated plots. He had trouble putting aspects of his story together with time markers and, as he became tired, he often left out important aspects of the story. While Jack could understand major elements of a story, he was producing less mature stories. This was seen as likely impacting his written language and his participation in mainstream classrooms as materials became more complex.

The sample of Jack's spontaneous language showed that most of his sentences were well formed but generally simple and not very elaborate. He did resort to scripted language at times and occasionally had word-finding problems. As noted previously, his prosody was unusual. He had numerous pauses in his speech and unusual patterns of intonation, but these didn't affect his ability to be understood.

Jack appeared to enjoy engaging in reciprocal communication. At times he would initiate conversation and wait for a response. He had a clear ability to engage in reciprocal conversation and comment on joint activities with positive affect, which confirmed significant progress since his last evaluation. However socially, Jack did not yet show an appreciation for the perspective of others or recognize and repair communication breakdowns.

The Vineland Adaptive Behavior Scales, expanded form, were used to assess Jack's adaptive skills. Results could be compared to his previous assessment, and his relatively stable standard scores showed that he was making age-appropriate progress in the areas of communication and socialization (standard scores between 65 and 70). His daily living standard score was lower (45) reflecting less progress than expected given the passage in time. Compared to his cognitive ability, his adaptive skills were significantly lower than expected, particularly for the area of daily living.

During Jack's time with the psychiatrist, there was an opportunity to see Jack in a less structured situation and to talk with him and his parents about his feelings of frustration, anxiety, and loneliness. Jack was quite responsive and clearly enjoyed talking. He had obvious social vulnerabilities. When asked to describe his friends, he said he had only one friend, David, but then couldn't really talk about why David was a friend other than to say that David has some interest in video games. He talked about some of the difficulties he had with a peer at school who seemed to be making fun of him. Jack had not really talked to his parents or teachers about this and didn't have any strategies to help in dealing with it. Similarly, Jack was able to provide clear descriptions about situations that led him to experience negative emotions, such as anxiety, sadness, and anger; again, he was not able to describe any coping strategies for managing these negative feelings.

Jack was also able to engage in brief reciprocal conversations, particularly when the evaluator asked direct questions or when he was able to talk about his experiences and interests. When describing his interests, he could become overly wordy and then had trouble letting the psychiatrist have a chance to talk. Sometimes, in describing situations or his own emotions or feelings, he seemed to resort to scripted language. When listening to more complicated speech, he would sometimes echo portions of it, apparently in an effort to remember it while working on his response. Jack made appropriate and consistent eye contact, used various gestures, and responded to nonverbal gestures.

At the time of this contact, Jack was just beginning to show physical signs of puberty. He did talk with the psychiatrist (the only male among those seeing him) about his interest in girls and his wondering about the changes in his own body. He had an interest in understanding more about girls and sex but had a fairly rudimentary understanding of all that was involved in having a meaningful relationship.

Jack demonstrated a few unusual behaviors. He occasionally squinted his eyes, rubbed his hand across his head, and one time he slapped his arm. Jack also seemed to have strong interests, including movies and Pokemon.

In our feedback with Jack and his parents and in our subsequent report, we emphasized several things. Most importantly, we talked about the gains he had made since the time of our last visit. He had made major gains in his ability to get along with others, to engage in conversation, and had greater social awareness and engagement. We also pointed out that in some respects these also made him more aware of areas of difference, which continued to exist for him, with vulnerabilities in some important areas of his life.

The psychological testing revealed that Jack's difficulties increase when he needs to independently abstract and/or meaningfully organize information that is implicit in a learning situation or experience but that he did better with some supports to guide him (these could be rules, a sequence of steps, or visual templates). Given his capacity for reasoning within a structure, it seemed important not only to give him specific information but also to define the problem, his options, and the general rules that would guide his problem solving. Given his age and the onset, in the near future, of adolescence we also suggested the importance of prioritizing functional academic and adaptive skills with a view toward enhancing his independence.

Our report included a number of different recommendations, particularly in light of the transition to high school in a year's time. These included a range of academic and social supports, with an emphasis on beginning transitional planning and thinking about fostering adaptive skills and functional abilities. We recommended a number of potential changes for his school program, including some individual work with the psychologist and speech pathologist as well as continued group social skills training. Work with peer mentors and explicit targeting of problem situations with peers (bullying) was noted to be a critical area. We also discussed with his family the option for him to attend a summer camp for children with special needs. We recommend a move toward highly functional academic goals and a focus on Jack's areas of potential vocational interest.

As part of social skills development, we recommended several things, including explicit teaching in his small group setting followed by individual work and use of the Social Stories approach to help him have a better awareness of social situations and to prime (i.e., cue) appropriate responses. We recommended after-school and extracurricular involvement with typical peers with support of a "peer buddy." Given the transition to high school in a year or so, we suggested some beginning activity in the new school with the potential of a peer buddy to help Jack build up an awareness of the new school and to increase his confidence in being able to negotiate it.

It appeared that, given the onset of adolescence and his interest in understanding more about girls and sexuality, Jack should receive concrete and specific information about social norms and relationships, as well as risks of danger and abuse. We recommended that a same-sex adult work with Jack in understanding some of the basics about sexuality, public and private behavior, personal boundaries, and appropriate and inappropriate touching and sexuality.

We agreed with Jack's parents that it was not too soon to begin thinking about transitional planning. We made some connections for them with local services in their state disabilities service and vocational programs.

For Jack's teachers we made a number of recommendations about teaching strategies, for example, in making tasks explicit, to use preteaching and practice in natural settings, in use of a task-analytic approach for more complex tasks, and to use functional routines along with repetition to encourage generalization. In dealing with more abstract/complex materials, we suggested first presenting things at a more concrete level and then moving to more abstract examples. We also noted the continued need for using visual and other supports to help Jack in learning.

In terms of some of Jack's behavioral problems, we suggested a number of strategies to help him deal with new situations. These included using routine and consistency to decrease anxiety with explicit teaching about novel and anxiety-provoking situations with explicit strategies for Jack to use in dealing with such situations. He could be provided with decision trees to represent possible scenarios. For instance, the identified problem could be "bothersome peer," and Jack, with help from an adult, can identify various ways to manage the situation. We provided his parents and school with a flowchart that could be readily adapted to create visual supports for this and similar situations.

In our discussions with him, Jack was not able to identify a single coping strategy for dealing with negative feelings. We also made some suggestions about helping Jack deal with feelings of anxiety and issues of self-esteem. These included an explicit focus on helping him recognize and label his feelings, developing some new coping strategies, and learning specific relaxation and other techniques. Given Jack's clear desire for feedback, we also suggested that his teachers and parents provide positive feedback but keep in mind that the overall goal was for Jack to monitor his own performance accurately; for example, he should be encouraged to self-monitor and be praised for doing so. Jack's frequent requests for help seemed to be a potential useful starting point for developing enhanced self-monitoring skills. We also noted that in conversation Jack often used questions as a way of maintaining the conversation but without necessarily building on what he had just heard his conversational partner say, so we recommended that Jack be taught additional appropriate ways to maintain conversation.

As part of his social skills program, we recommended the continued use of a peer with the addition of a peer-mentoring component and use of a range of strategies, including small groups, social activities, continued teaching of social skills, role playing, and instruction on the social rules/norms of his peers.

A number of goals for individual work with the speech pathologist were identified, including building up Jack's ability to use and comprehend narrative language and building on the important gains he had made in receptive and expressive language.

Our report discussed the pros and cons of medication and the importance of careful monitoring and a thoughtful implementation of other supports to help Jack feel less anxious. We also suggested careful monitoring of his self-esteem issues and noted the potential for some adolescents with ASDs to become more overtly depressed.

Finally, we outlined for Jack and his parents a number of goals in the area of adaptive skills, with a particular emphasis on the importance of independent daily living skills. We recommended a number of books and talked about the options for using written/visual schedule in activities of daily living.

Discussion Jack's case illustrates several things. First, with early intervention Jack has done rather well. When first seen at age 3, he was not yet talking but by the time of this assessment he had made a number of gains and was largely main-streamed. However, it appeared to us that some supports—notably, some of the individual work with the speech pathologist—had been pulled a bit too quickly. Jack's growing ability to self-monitor and his motivation to do well were impor-tant strengths but also carried the potential for feelings of anxiety and depression. His experience of being bullied by another student is, unfortunately, not un-common. Neither was the fact that his parents and teachers were unaware of it. Although Jack had made a number of gains, his overall abilities remained signifi-cantly scattered.

With support, Jack was able to make a number of gains in the year following this assessment and was able to transition relatively easily to high school. He had made a relationship with two peer buddies in the high school program before his arrival and felt comfortable there by the time he arrived for actual classes. Jack and his family were also delighted to discover that he could do well on his own at a special needs summer camp.

In high school there was a strong emphasis on functional skills, and Jack enjoyed his work in a convenience store as well as a major discount store. Jack and his family made greater use of a psychologist in the community who has become a major resource for him around behavioral issues which gave him a chance to actually apply skills in community settings. As a teenager Jack has con-tinued to receive a relatively low dose of an SSRI medication, which he feels helps him with anxiety.

Jack is now almost done with high school and planning on going to a techni-cal school after high school. He has become much more independent and self-sufficient but still relies on his parents for some support and plans to continue to live with them during technical school. He has now had several friends and one relationship with a girl.

Case 2: Tammy Jo

Tammy Jo ("TJ") was a $6\frac{1}{2}$-year-old girl who was seen for follow-up evalua-tion. TJ had previously been seen by us at 2 years of age, when autism was diagnosed. TJ's parents were concerned about her progress and current school placement. In addition to our multidisciplinary evaluation, we did conduct a school visit.

TJ's parents were first worried about her when she was a year of age. At that time, she was not talking. Although they had expressed concern to their pediatrician, they had been reassured by him, given TJ's apparently good motor skills and her ability to solve puzzles. By 18 months, language still had not developed; at that time, the pediatrician performed a hearing test, which was normal, and then referred her to us for an assessment. At that time, she was producing a very limited range of sounds, had no actual words, was socially very isolated, and had shown some troubles with change and in responding to the environment. She wasn't responding to her name, nor was she engaging in social routines. She seemed very isolated and "in her own world." At that time, we told the parents of our concern and discussed the difficulties of early diagnosis but recommended intensive intervention services. These had included a (parent-funded) home-based applied behavior analysis (ABA) program and, starting at 3, school-based services.

TJ's parents reported that her interest in people had increased over the last several years and her communication skills had improved. They had been generally pleased with her progress. The school had provided a reasonably intensive support program and had suggested that she repeat kindergarten. At the time of our assessment, she had just entered the first-grade program, where she was having some noteworthy behavior problems, which we'll talk about momentarily.

As part of our assessment, TJ was seen by several different professionals. During the speech-communication assessment, TJ was generally cooperative but seemed to do best when given visual cues and a visual schedule. She also worked well when given stickers as rewards and frequent breaks. Her expressive single-word vocabulary was an area of strength and higher than her understanding of single words (standard scores of 88 and 50, respectively, where 100 is the average and 15 is the standard deviation). Her actual use of language was much lower, at an age equivalent of 4 years for language comprehension and $3\frac{1}{2}$ years for language expression. Her speech was mostly understandable (she still used some jargon) but had an unusual sing-song quality. During the psychological assessment, we chose to use a test of nonverbal intelligence—the Revised Leiter International Performance Scale. This test was chosen because we wanted a good measure of nonverbal problem solving (see Chapter 3). On this instrument, TJ's score of 82 was in the low-average range. The psychologist attempted to administer a more traditional test of intelligence, but TJ's behavior quickly became problematic. She was noted to have developed an ability to sound out (decode) single words and was starting to read, although her understanding of what she read was at a much lower level.

On the Vineland Adaptive Behavior Scales, her scores ranged from close to age-expected levels for written language and motor skills to significantly delayed—with areas of greatest delay in receptive and expressive communication (age equivalents of nearly 4 years for receptive language and 3 years for expressive language) and in socialization skills (interpersonal age equivalent of 2 years 6 months).

TJ's parents met with the psychiatrist to talk about their concerns with her behavior. Since her enrollment in first grade, her parents had felt that her behavior significantly worsened, with higher levels of stereotyped behavior (particularly body rocking and hand mannerisms) and the onset of a self-injurious behavior (face slapping). They were concerned because the stereotyped behaviors had seemed much worse since her new placement and the face slapping was hard for them to interrupt. The child psychiatrist observed TJ during parts of her assessment and also spent time with her. He noted that she was more related to her parents than other people and made more eye contact with them. She was able to engage in some simple social routines and could take pleasure in this. Attention varied with task difficulty and seemed most impaired if supports weren't provided. TJ used play materials for simple functional play and early pretend play. Stereotyped mannerisms were most common when she was frustrated or overwhelmed with tasks. She was developing some early abilities for self-monitoring but engaged in task avoidance when activities were more challenging for her.

Review of the IEP and then a follow-up discussion with her school program revealed some areas of concern. The combination of her much higher expressive vocabulary and ability to sound out words had been taken to suggest a much higher level of understanding of language/written words than actually was the case. As a result, much of her academic program was more advanced than she was able to understand and, consequently, she appeared to be frustrated during much of her time in the first-grade classroom. During the school visit, the absence of some of the problematic behaviors during her "special" times (when working in a more structured situation on skills more appropriate to her level) also seemed to reflect the combination of inappropriately high academic goals and difficulties responding in more complex environments. In talking with the school and with her parents, we suggested some modifications in her program to take into account the significant scatter in her skills. We suggested increasing a number of the more structured out-of-class times with service providers like the speech pathologist. We also suggested implementing a number of supports for TJ in the classroom and emphasized the importance of responding to the range of her abilities.

TJ's problematic behavior rapidly diminished when she was given a modified program more appropriate to her levels of ability. She continued to be in the mainstream setting for some classes but had more opportunities for learning in a structured setting at school. Her face slapping decreased quickly.

Now, some months later, her school is beginning to again increase mainstream class time, but they are careful to do this slowly and to monitor for any signs of frustration. TJ has continued to make progress, and her parents have been pleased that the problem behaviors have diminished dramatically.

Case 3: Danny

Danny was a boy of almost 9 years of age who had a long history of problems in social interaction, but who seemed to have good language skills. His school raised the question of whether he might have autism because he seemed "too verbal." Danny's early history was remarkable for early development of words (he was saying single words by 8 months and talking in sentences by 18 months) but slow motor development (he didn't walk until 16 months and was always described as somewhat clumsy and poorly coordinated). His parents noted that he had early, long-standing special interests in things like trains, geography, and astronomy. His parents reported that he was a sensitive child who seemed to notice changes and disliked certain foods. But they had not been worried about him until he was 4 and started preschool, where his teachers reported concerns about his peer relationships and difficulties dealing with change. At the time of this assessment, he was completing second grade in a public school (having repeated kindergarten because of poor social skills). His school had suggested an evaluation for possible attention deficit hyperactivity disorder (ADHD), given his tendency to be impulsive and very verbal.

He had been evaluated at $5\frac{1}{2}$ by a developmental pediatrician, who suggested he might have PDD-NOS. In school, he was given OT and speech therapy but mainstreamed for much of the time. At the time of the current assessment, he was in regular classes with 1 hour a week for occupational therapy.

On psychological testing, Danny was a talkative 8-year 8-month-old boy. On meeting the examiner, he launched into a discussion of outer space events. His attention was somewhat variable, but, in general, he seemed to cooperate with assessment procedures. When given any opportunity, he would become very "professorial," assuming a "lecture-like" stance with the examiner and explaining his views on topics having to do with astronomy. His social style was very one-sided. Although he could follow a story, he often returned to a discussion of stars, planets, and so forth. A visual schedule with routines and reinforcement for staying on task (and off space topics) was helpful. The psychologist noted that Danny had poor hand–eye coordination and particular trouble with tasks that involved manipulative or graphomotor skills. On psychological testing, his verbal IQ was 104 and his nonverbal IQ 78 (mean of 100, standard deviation of 15). He exhibited much scatter on the test of intelligence with strengths in the areas of auditory memory, fund of knowledge, and to a lesser extent, verbal reasoning. Areas of specific deficits included visual–spatial orientation, facial recognition, and computational skills.

The psychologist noted that Danny tried to use verbal strategies to cope with nonverbal tasks and that when tasks became nonverbal he often had difficulties attending. He talked throughout the assessment. On a test of visual–motor integration, his standard score was 72. He had difficulties with visual perception and motor planning. During speech–communication assessment, Danny's expressive single-word naming emerged as a strength (standard score of 119). Receptive vocabulary was solidly average (standard score of 99). When tasks were more complicated, he had moderate to severe delays in formulating language. He made a few articulation errors. His prosody was somewhat unusual. He tended to talk at a very fast rate but could slow down if asked to do so. Whenever possible, he would try to turn the discussion to one of his topics of special interest. His language tended to be slightly pedantic, with a tendency to use more sophisticated words but in a somewhat unusual way. He had significant difficulties carrying on a conversation. He did not respond to nonverbal cues.

During the psychiatric assessment, Danny was noted to be an overtly sociable little boy but one whose sociability was rather superficial and one-sided. While clearly related to his parents, he was inconsistent in use of eye contact. He had trouble in responding to nonverbal cues and with pragmatic language. He had trouble with figurative and ambiguous language and significant troubles understanding sarcasm. Danny did have trouble with distraction, but when provided with support, he could focus for long periods of time. He had some difficulties with transitions/changes in activities. He talked excessively about his areas of special interact. He had trouble responding to cues from his conversational partner. He tended to rely excessively on verbal skills to mediate the ongoing social interaction. His affective range was rather limited. He was generally happiest when engaged in discussion of some topic of particular interest to him. He did sometimes take pleasure in interaction in successful task performance and was, at such times, able to share the focus of happiness with the examiners. When excited, some toe walking was observed. His use of play materials tended to be rather rigid and stereotyped. Some degree of motor difficulty was noted, as Danny had problems with poor coordination, clumsiness, and unstable gait. Neither his gross nor fine motor skills appeared to be at age level. During this time with the psychiatrist, Danny drew a rather poor sketch of the solar system, but his verbalization about the various planets and the controversy over whether Pluto should be considered a planet was at a much higher level.

On the Vineland Adaptive Behavior Scales, Danny's standard scores ranged from 32 to 52, i.e., very delayed relative to his cognitive ability. He had isolated strengths in written and expressive language but major areas of weakness in social and expressive communication, and daily living skills. Interviews with his family revealed a paternal grandfather with problems similar to Danny's.

Although his school has raised the question of attention deficit disorder, our impression was of a youngster with Asperger's disorder. On cognitive testing, there was significant discrepancy between his verbal and nonverbal intelligence. He had gross and fine motor difficulties. He relied heavily on verbal strength to solve problems. Problems with inattention and impulsive behavior were noted but usually in response to more challenging (nonverbal) tasks. He similarly had marked scatter in his language skills, with strengths in single-word vocabulary but weaknesses when asked to cope with more complicated language tasks— particularly if these involved social language use. His social difficulties, reliance on verbal mediation strategies, circumscribed interests, motor problems, and other features were consistent with Asperger's disorder and his psychological testing consistent with the NLD profile.

In our report, we emphasized that his unusual developmental profile put him at a real disadvantage in dealing with peers and certain academic subjects. We made a number of recommendations for developing social and communication skills and an appreciation of nonverbal social cues. Individual speech therapy along with OT and physical therapy (PT) were recommended, as was a social skills intervention program.

Comment   In this case, as was particularly true in the past, Danny's better vocabulary skills combined with behavior difficulties initially suggested attentional difficulties. The severity of his social (and other) problems was masked by his good verbal abilities. Provision of a more appropriate intervention program proved very helpful to Danny. He was able to learn to use verbal mediation strategies to help with social situations and in dealing with novelty. He currently is enrolled in the ninth grade, where he receives some special supports and accommodation (including use of a laptop and untimed tests). His interest in space and astronomy has continued.

SUMMARY

In this chapter we've talked about some of the issues that impact school age children and their families. In some ways this age group is the one we know the most about, at least in terms of research. There are many opportunities for positive growth and behavior change in this age group. On the other hand behavioral management issues can also become much more important. Parents and teachers should pay attention to both academic and non-academic skills. There is the potential for children to learn skills in isolation and the family has a critically important role in helping children learn to generalize skills. Parents and teachers should also be alert to the potential for problems with bullying in this age group.

■ **READING LIST**

Aarons, M., & Gittens, T. (1998). *Autism: A social skills approach for children and adolescents.* Bradwell Abbey, Milton Keynes, UK: Speechmark.

Adreon, D., & Stella, J. (2001) Transition to middle and high school: Increasing the success of students with Asperger's syndrome. *Intervention in School and Clinic, 36,* 266–271.

Arick, J. R., Krug, D. A., Fullerton, A., Loos, L., & Falco, R. (2005). School-based programs. In F. Volkmar, R. Paul, A. Klin, and D. Cohen (Eds.), *Handbook of autism and pervasive developmental disorders* (3rd ed., pp. 1003–1028). Hoboken, NJ: Wiley.

Aspy, R., Grossman, B., & Mesibov, G. B. (2007). *The Ziggurat Model: A framework for designing comprehensive interventions for individuals with high-functioning autism and Asperger syndrome.* Shawnee Mission, KS: Autism Asperger.

Attwood, T. (2008). *The complete guide to Asperger's syndrome.* London: Jessica Kingsley.

Attwood, T. (1998). *Asperger's syndrome: A guide for parents and professionals.* London: Jessica Kingsley.

Baker, J. (2001). *Social skills picture book: Teaching play, emotion, and communication to children with autism.* Arlington, TX: Future Horizons.

Baron-Cohen, S. (2003). *The essential difference: Male and female brains and the truth about autism.* New York: Basic Books.

Baron-Cohen, S. (2008). *Autism and Asperger syndrome (the facts).* New York: Oxford University Press.

Bishop, B. (2003). *My friend with autism: A coloring book for peers and siblings.* Arlington, TX: Future Horizons.

Brock, S. E., Jimerson, S. R., & Hansen, R. L. (2006). *Identifying, assessing, and treating autism at school.* New York: Springer.

Buron, K. D. (2007) *A 5 is against the law! Social boundaries straight up.* Shawnee Mission, KS: Autism Asperger.

Buron, K. D., & Curtis, M. (2004). *Incredible 5-point scale: Assisting students with autism spectrum disorders in understanding social interactions and controlling their emotional responses.* Shawnee Mission, KS: Autism Asperger.

Burrows, E. L., & Wagner, S. J. (2004). *Understanding Asperger's syndrome: Fast facts—a guide for teachers and educators to address the needs of the student.* Arlington, TX: Future Horizons.

Carter, E. W. (2008). *Peer support strategies for improving all students' social lives and learning.* Baltimore: Brookes.

Carter, E. W., Cushing, L. S., & Kennedy, C. H. (2009). *Peer support strategies for improving all student's social lives and learning.* Baltimore: Brookes.

Carter, M., & Santomoura, J. (2004). *Space travelers: An interactive program for developing social understanding, social competence and social skills for students with AS, autism and other social cognitive challenges.* Shawnee Mission, KS: Autism Asperger.

Cook, J., & Hartman, C. (2008). *My mouth is a volcano!.* Chattanooga: National Center for Youth Issues.

Coulter, D. (Producer/Director). (2000). *Asperger syndrome: Success in the mainstream classroom* [DVD]. Winston Salem, NC: Coulter Video.

Coulter, D. (Producer/Director). (2006). *Intricate minds: Understanding classmates with Asperger syndrome* [DVD]. Winston Salem, NC: Coulter Video.

Coulter, D. (Producer/Director). (2006). *Intricate minds II: Understanding elementary school classmates with Asperger syndrome* [DVD]. Winston Salem, NC: Coulter Video.

Coulter, D. (Producer/Director). (2006). *Intricate minds III: Understanding elementary school classmates who think differently* [DVD]. Winston Salem, NC: Coulter Video.

Crary, E., & Casebolt, P. (1990). *Pick up your socks . . . and other skills growing children need.* Seattle, WA: Parenting Press.

Dubin, N., & Carley, M. J. (2007). *Asperger syndrome and bullying: Strategies and solutions.* London: Jessica Kingsley.

Dunn, M. A. (2005). *S. O. S. social skills in our schools: A social skills program for children with pervasive developmental disorders, including high-functioning autism and Asperger syndrome, and their typical peers.* Shawnee Mission, KS: Autism Asperger.

Edwards, A. (2001). *Taking autism to school.* Hawthorne, NY: JayJo Books.

Ernsperger, L. (2002). *Keys to success for teaching students with autism.* Arlington, TX: Future Horizons.

Faherty, C., & Mesibov, G. B. (2000). *Asperger's: What does it mean to me?* Arlington, TX: Future Horizons.

Fein, D., & Dunn, M. (2007). *Autism in your classroom: A general educator's guide to students with autism spectrum disorders.* Bethesda, MD: Woodbine House.

Flowers, T. (1996). *Reaching the child with autism through art: Practical, "fun" activities to enhance motor skills and improve tactile and concept awareness.* Arlington, TX: Future Horizons.

Grandin, T. & Barron, S. (2006). *The unwritten rules of social relationships: Decoding social mysteries through the unique perspectives of autism.* Arlington, TX: Future Horizons.

Gray, C. (2000). *The new social story book.* Arlington, TX: Future Horizons.

Gutstein, S. E. (2001). *Autism Asperger's: Solving the relationship puzzle—a new developmental program that opens the door to lifelong social and emotional growth.* Arlington, TX: Future Horizons.

Hall, Laura J. (2008) *Autism spectrum disorders: From theory to practice.* Upper Saddle River, NJ: Prentice Hall.

Handleman, J. S., Harris, S. L., & Martins, M. (2005). Helping children with autism enter the mainstream. In F. Volkmar, R. Paul, A. Klin, & D. Cohen (Eds.), *Handbook of autism and pervasive developmental disorders* (3rd ed., pp. 1029–1042). Hoboken, NJ: Wiley.

Haring, T. G., & Breen, C. G. (1992). A peer-mediated social network intervention to enhance the social integration of persons with moderate and severe disabilities. *Journal of Applied Behavior Analysis, 25,* 319–333.

Heflin, L. J., & Alaimo, D. F. (2007). *Students with autism spectrum disorders: Effective instructional practices.* Upper Saddle River, NJ: Pearson.

Heinrichs, R. (2003). *Perfect targets: Asperger syndrome and bullying—practical solutions for surviving the social world.* Shawnee Mission, KS: Autism Asperger.

Hobson, P. (2005). Autism and emotion. In F. Volkmar, R. Paul, A. Klin, & D. Cohen (Eds.), *Handook of autism and pervasive developmental disorders* (3rd ed., pp. 406–424). Hoboken, NJ: Wiley.

Howlin, P. (1998). *Children with autism and Asperger syndrome: A guide for practitioners and careers.* Hoboken, NJ: John Wiley & Sons.

Jaffe, A., & Gardner, L. (2006) *My book of feelings: How to control and react to the size of your emotions*. Shawnee Mission, KS: Autism Asperger.

Kluth, P. (2003). *You're going to love this kid: Teaching students with autism in the inclusive classroom*. Baltimore: Brookes.

Kluth, P., & Chandler-Olcott, K. (2008). *A land we can share: Teaching literacy to students with autism*. Baltimore: Brookes.

Kluth, P., & Schwarz, P. (2008). *Just give him the whale: 20 ways to use fascinations, areas of expertise and strengths to support students with autism*. Baltimore: Brookes.

Koegel, R. L., & Koegel, L. K. (1995). *Teaching children with autism: Strategies for initiating positive interactions and improving learning opportunities*. Baltimore: Brookes.

Koegel, R. L., Koegel, L. K., & Brookman, L. I. (2003). Empirically supported pivotal response interventions for children with autism. In A. E. Kazdin & J. R. Weisz (Eds.), *Evidence-based psychotherapies for children and adolescents* (pp. 341–357). New York: Guilford Press.

Koegel, L. K., & LaZebnik, C. (2009). *Growing up on the spectrum*. New York: Penguin Books.

Larson, E. M. (2006). *I am utterly unique: Celebrating the strengths of children with Asperger syndrome and high-functioning autism*. Shawnee Mission, KS: Autism Asperger.

Little, L. (2002). Middle-class mothers' perceptions of peer and sibling victimization among children with Asperger's syndrome and nonverbal learning disorders. *Issues in Comprehensive Pediatric Nursing, 25,* 43–57.

Ludwig, T. (2006). *Just kidding*. Berkeley, CA: Tricycle Press.

Mackenzie, H. (2008). *Reaching and teaching the child with autism spectrum disorder: Using learning cpreferences and strengths*. London: Jessica Kingsley.

McClannahan, L. E., & Krantz, P. J. (2005). *Teaching conversation to children with autism: Scripts and script fading*. Bethesda, MD: Woodbine House.

McKinnon, K., & Kremps, J. L. (2005). *Social skills solutions: A hands-on manual for teaching social skills to children with autism*. New York: DRL Books.

Moore, S. T. (2002). *Asperger syndrome and the elementary school experience: Practical solutions for academic and social difficulties*. Shawnee Mission, KS: Autism Asperger.

Morrison, L., Kamps, D., Garcia, J., & Parker, D. (2001). Peer mediation and monitoring strategies to improve initiations and social skills for students with autism. *Journal of Positive Behavior Interventions, 3,* 237–250.

Myles, B. S. (2001). *Asperger syndrome and sensory issues: Practical solutions for making sense of the world*. Shawnee Mission, KS: Autism Asperger.

Myles, B. S. (2005). *Children and youth with Asperger syndrome: Strategies for success in inclusive settings*. Thousand Oaks, CA: Corwin Press.

Myles, B. S., & Adreon, D. (2001). *Asperger syndrome and adolescence: Practical solutions for school success*. Shawnee Mission, KS: Autism Asperger.

Myles, B. S., & Southwick, J. (1999). *Asperger syndrome and difficult moments: Practical solutions for tantrums, rage, and meltdowns*. Shawnee Mission, KS: Autism Asperger.

Myles, B. S., Trautman, M. L., & Schelvan, R. L. (2004). *The hidden curriculum: Practical solutions for understanding unstated rules in social situations*. Shawnee Mission, KS: Autism Asperger.

Naylor, P. R. (1994). *King of the playground*. New York: Aladdin Paperbacks.

Nichols, S., Moravick, G., and Tetenbaum, S. P. (2009). *Girls growing up on the autism spectrum*. London: Jessica Kingsley.

Ozonoff, S., Dawson, G., & McPartland, J. (2002). *A parent's guide to Asperger syndrome and high-functioning autism: How to meet the challenges and help your child thrive*. New York: Guilford Press.

Paul, R., Augustyn, A, Klin, A., Volkmar, F. R. (2005). Perception and production of prosody by speakers with autism spectrum disorders. *Journal of Autism and Developmental
Disorders, 35*(2): 205–220.

Pierce, K., & Schreibman, L. (1997). Multiple peer use of pivotal response training to
increase social behaviors of classmates with autism: Results from trained and untrained
peers. *Journal of Applied Behavioral Analysis, 30*(1), 157–160.

Pierce, K., & Schreibman, L. (1998). Using peer trainers to promote social behavior in
autism: Are they effective at enhancing multiple social modalities? *Focus on Autism &
Other Developmental Disabilities, 12,* 207–218.

Quill, K. (1995). *Teaching children with autism: Strategies to enhance communication and socialization.* New York: Delmar.

Schlieder, M. (2007). *With open arms: Creating school communities of support for kids with social
challenges using circle of friends, extracurricular activities, and learning teams.* Shawnee Mission,
KS: Autism Asperger.

Scott, J., Clark, C., & Brady, M. (2000). *Students with autism: Characteristics and instruction
programming.* San Diego, CA: Singular.

Silverman, S., & Weinfeld, R. (2007). *School success for kids with Asperger's syndrome: A practical
guide for parents and teachers.* Waco, TX: Prufrock Press.

Small, M., & Kontente, L. (2003). *Everyday solutions: A practical guide for families of children with
autism spectrum disorder.* Shawnee Mission, KS: Autism Asperger.

Strachan, J., & Schnurr, R. G. (1999). *Asperger's huh? A child's perspective.* Gloucester, Ontario: Anisor.

Strong, C. J., & North, K. H. (1996). *The magic of stories.* Eau Claire, WI: Thinking
Publications.

Thiemann, K. S., & Goldstein, H. (2001). Social stories, written text cues, and video feedback: Effects on social communication of children with autism. *Journal of Applied Behavior Analysis, 34,* 425–446.

Thioux, M., Stark, D. E., Klaiman, C., Schultz, R.T. (2006) The day of the week when you
were born in 700 ms: Calendar computation in an autistic savant. *Journal of Experimental
Psychology: Human Perception and Performance, 32*(5), 1155–1168.

Tsatsanis, K. D. (2004). Heterogeneity in learning type in Asperger syndrome and high-
functioning autism. *Topics in Language Disorders, 24*(4), 260–270.

Tsatsanis, K. D., Foley, C., & Donehower, C. (2004). Contemporary outcome research and
programming guidelines for Asperger's syndrome and high functioning autism. *Topics in
Language Disorders, 24*(4), 249–259.

Utley, C. A., & Mortweek, S. L. (1997). Peer mediated instruction and intervention. *Focus
on Exceptional Children, 29*(5), 1–24.

Vicker, B. (2007). *Sharing information about your child with autism spectrum disorder:
What do respite or alternative caregivers need to know?* Shawnee Mission, KS: Autism
Asperger.

Volkmar, F., & Cohen, D. (1985). The experience of infantile autism: A first person account
by Tony W. *Journal of Autism and Developmental Disorders, 15,* 47–54.

Weber, J. D. (2000). *Children with fragile X syndrome: A parents' guide.* Bethesda, MD: Woodbine House.

Wing, L., Gould, J. (1979). Severe impairments of scoail interaction and associated abnormalities. *Journal of Autism and Developmental Disorders, 9*(1), 11–29.

Winter, M. (2003). *Asperger syndrome: What teachers need to know.* London: Jessica
Kingsley.

■ QUESTIONS AND ANSWERS

1. **I am a relatively new speech pathologist who works in a public school. I happened to see one of my students last week in the mainstream class he attends for reading (he is in the second grade). Usually, I see him individually for pull-out from his resource room program. He was with his aide, and I realized that he was sitting at the back of the room—mostly staring out the window while the teacher was reading. The aide, who is a very nice, grandmotherly type person, seemed to always run interference for him with the other students. He was humming to himself and doing some self-stim while looking outside and watching the trees and bird feeder. He wasn't making any trouble, but I wasn't sure how much, if anything, he was learning. He has made good progress in his individual work, but I wonder if we should take a look at his mainstream time—I wasn't sure this was doing a lot of good.**

   You have made a number of important observations and also are in a position to be helpful since you are already part of the team. Your question raises several different issues: the value of his mainstream experience, the issue of the pros and cons of having his own aide in the setting, and your own individual work with him. There are several steps you and the teacher can think about to make the mainstream time more valuable. If he is seated nearer to the teacher, she'll be better able to keep an eye on him. Second, the teacher could work with the aide and special ed teacher to do some preteaching; for example, maybe he should see the book ahead of time or have a visual support (pictures of important things to attend to). The aide could be involved in working on this with him before the class. As you point out, having an aide raises some potential risks for his being isolated from his peers. It would be worth working with her a bit to give him a bit more space and have more possibilities for peer interaction. You and the teacher could work with her about effective ways to help him be more interactive and to encourage peers when they want to interact with him. Finally, depending on how things with you are going, you might consider some work with a small group of peers from his mainstream class, for example, so that he could have some practice in interaction in a small-group setting with some peers who might help him generalize his skills in the larger setting.

2. **My fourth-grade daughter has a profound interest in insects. She has had other interests over the years, but this one has been the most enduring. She occasionally drives her mother and me crazy**

with wanting to go get books on insects or look for TV programs or movies that feature insects. She has a whole insect collection of stuffed animals. Is there any way to get rid of this? If we can't, is there any way to get some control over it?

You've asked two very good questions. In his original paper, Asperger pointed out that the special interests he saw in children tended to be all-encompassing, interfered with the child's learning other things, and often came to dominate family life. Interests often do change somewhat over time. Occasionally, students are able to use their interests in an adult occupation. Getting rid of the interest is probably not so easily done. Rather, try to see how you can work with it—there are some good books on the topic in the reading list, for example, the book by Kluth on using special interests. Often, a lot of incidental learning can occur when the child is given projects that build on her interest in some way; for example, math can focus on multiplying insects. Books or movies with insect characters can be used to teach about narrative and plot and feelings. It might help to put children who are overly preoccupied on a schedule where they get time to pursue their interest as a reward for other work, for example, setting up a homework schedule where your daughter gets time to pursue her insect interest as a reward for getting her homework done.

3. **My 9-year-old son with autism can be a bit of a handful in terms of his behavior. My husband and I would like to take some time off to go to the movies or out to a restaurant occasionally. Our parents and siblings live several towns away, so we can't use them except occasionally. Do you have any suggestions about finding a good babysitter?**

    You are wise to think about getting some time for yourselves and for your child to have the opportunity to be with other caretakers. Often, other parents or sometimes teachers and school staff can suggest possible babysitters. Sometimes parents of other children with special needs are willing to do babysitting swap arrangements. If you live near a college or university, sometimes putting up an ad in the psychology department or school of education can be a good source for finding college students with an interest in children with special needs who may be willing to babysit. Sometimes state departments of developmental disabilities (called different things in difference states) maintain programs to provide parents with respite care. There is a book by Vicker (2007) in the reading list with information that babysitters and other caregivers need to know.

4. **Our 7-year-old son with Asperger's has trouble with explosive outbursts. We've identified some of the triggers for these**

(unexpected transitions and changes in schedule) but not for others. Both we and his teacher notice that we can sometimes tell when he is "about to blow"—he starts to look angry or upset, but he doesn't seem aware of this. Are there any things we can do to help?

You are right that often there are triggers, and you have identified some of them already—new situations and transitions are frequent sources of difficulty, and changes in schedule can be a real problem. There are several different things to do. First, continue to pay attention to when these situations happen—location, setting, who the child is with, and so forth. Second, you, and eventually your son, should start to work on helping him have an increased awareness of when he is "going to blow." He may be having trouble knowing when he is getting angry and upset. There may be physical signs he could pay attention to and then use as a cue to do something about it. Finally, there are some good resources to help children learn about their emotions—look at the reading list for some of the books by Buron and by Jaffe and Gardner. For children with Asperger's, learning to put things into words is a good first step. We talk about some of these issues in Chapter 14.

5. **Our 8-year-old with an ASD has a problem with showing affection. He has gotten more interested in people but sometimes will come inappropriately close to them or he will go up and hug other kids. We are not sure what to do about this. It is getting him into trouble.**

There are several things you can do. As we discussed in this chapter, some children with autism and autism spectrum disorders develop the "active but odd" social style. Their social interest is a plus, but their ability to translate this interest into appropriate behavior can be a problem. There are some resources for teaching about boundaries and personal space. We talk more about this in the next chapter as well. The book by Buron in the reading list on social boundaries is a good place to start. These issues become even more important as children become adolescents (and we talk more about it in the next chapter) so this is a good time to start working on the problem.

6. **Our 7-year-old with an ASD is starting to ask questions about why he is different from other kids. How should we deal with this?**

Children often start to develop an awareness of being different in the early school years sometimes earlier and sometimes later. Parents should try not to be defensive but answer questions honestly with an appropriate amount of information. Discussion about strengths and weaknesses is appropriate. So is pointing out the range of people with disabilities of varying degrees. Simply giving a label to a child isn't horribly helpful; don't say "you have Asperger's disorder" and leave the topic. There are some books written specifically for children with ASDs about having an ASD (see the book by Strachan and Schnurr in the reading list). Usually, this is a topic children will keep coming back to. For some children, being able to talk to a knowledgeable professional (physician, psychologist, teacher) can be helpful. Keep in mind that it is important to emphasize areas of strength as well as vulnerability (see the book in the reading list by Larson, written for children on just this issue).

7. **I am a fourth-grade teacher. We are about to have a student with Asperger's included in the class for most of the day. What would be the best way to do this? We are a relatively new middle school, and many of the children won't know each other or the student coming into the class.**

There are several things you can do. There are some excellent video resources (see the reading list for Coulter videos) that may be helpful with somewhat older elementary school children. There are also a number of children's books written for peers or siblings (see the text box on pages 250–251). You need to walk a fine line here—you want to give the classmates good information but you don't want to "set up" the child with a difficulty to be in trouble from the start! A lot of this will also rest on your attitudes and responses; for example, if the child with Asperger's has a problem with blurting out an answer, a supportive but corrective response from you will set the tone for classmates dealing with interruptions.

Adolescence, Adulthood, and the Future

A dolescence brings many changes for child and parent alike. Sexual maturation takes place as well as physical growth and many emotional and developmental changes. This can be a difficult time for both children and parents—even for children who are developing typically. It can be even more difficult for children who have sexual feelings but whose social and communication problems make it hard for them to talk about these feelings. For the highest functioning adolescents with autism or Asperger's disorder, the interest in others may be complicated by their difficulty in making connections with peers or feeling rebuffed when they attempt to do so. Adulthood brings another set of challenges. For an increasing number of individuals on the autism spectrum, this means going to college or vocational school—with all the changes entailed in being independent. For other individuals, the goal may be living apart from parents, in a setting where some minimal or moderate level of supervision is provided. For some individuals, it may mean living at home but having a job, perhaps with support, in the daytime. For others, there may be an option for a group home with supported employment.

In this chapter, we discuss some of the issues that impact adolescents and adults with autism and what parents and teachers may do to make things go more smoothly. We start with a discussion of the facts about adolescence and puberty and then move on to talking about sexuality and coping with some problem behaviors in adolescence. We then move on to discussing adulthood and future planning issues. Although we have separate sections in this chapter focused more on adolescents or on adults, keep in mind that, of course, many of the issues discussed apply to both age groups. It is the case that many of the same issues and concerns relevant to children can still apply to adolescents and adults. Fortunately, there are more and more resources available, and some of these are included in the reading list at the end of this chapter.

ADOLESCENCE: BASIC FACTS

Although most of us tend to think of adolescence as a time of turmoil, research has shown that this is not always so for typically developing children—indeed, it probably isn't even usually so. It is true that some children with autism spectrum disorders (ASDs) go through adolescence fairly smoothly. Still, **puberty** (which also means the beginning of adolescence) involves a set of dramatic changes in a child's body, which can pose problems for any child. An increasingly adult body is also associated with a new set of societal expectations—which can be especially difficult for individuals with autism to grasp. What is acceptable and cute in a 4-year-old may not be so easily accepted in a 14-year-old.

Children enter puberty when they begin the process of sexual (reproductive) maturation. The overt physical changes of puberty are the result of complicated processes that really start before birth. Hormone systems, which previously had been relatively inactive, become much more active, resulting in dramatic changes in growth and in the body. In fact, the bodily changes of puberty are really only surpassed by those of infancy! It may not be surprising, then, that for some children on the autism spectrum, puberty can be a difficult time.

The bodily changes of puberty usually emerge over a period of about 4 years or so. Girls, on average, mature about 2 years earlier than boys. As levels of hormones start to increase, changes in both body size and what are called the "secondary sex characteristics" (increases in body and facial hair, changes in the voice, and in the breast and genital organs) become marked. In fact, the hormonal changes that trigger puberty start some years before the observable body changes. Various stages of puberty have been defined (see Table 9.1) in both boys and girls and serve as a rough guide to where in puberty an individual child is.

TABLE 9.1   STAGES OF PUBERTY (TANNER)

	Boys	Girls
Stage 1	Preadolescent	Preadolescent
Stage 2	Slight amount of pubic hair, slight enlargement of penis and scrotum	Sparse pubic hair, breasts begin to develop
Stage 3	Increased pubic hair, penis longer, testes bigger	Increased pubic hair, breasts enlarged
Stage 4	Pubic hair pattern resembles adult pattern, but still sparser than in adult	Abundant pubic hair (less than in adult), nipple becomes more prominent
Stage 5	Adult male distribution of pubic hair, adult-size testes and penis	Adult female pattern of pubic hair, breasts of mature adult

SOURCE: Adapted, with permission, from Tanner, J. M. (1962). *Growth at adolescence* (2nd ed.). Oxford, UK: Blackwell; and Daniel, W. A. (1977). *Adolescents in health and disease.* St. Louis: Mosby.

Sex Differences in Puberty

There are differences between boys and girls in how puberty develops. As mentioned, girls tend to mature before boys. For girls, signs of the beginning of puberty include breast development, with the onset of menses (**menarche**) happening fairly late in the process. For boys, growth of the penis and testicles and development of pubic hair will often be the first signs of puberty. Changes in hair (first in the underarms and then in the face) and voice happen a bit later. There are wide variations for both girls and boys related to when puberty starts, and how long it takes to unfold. It does seem that with better nutrition and health care, puberty now occurs earlier than it used to. Both boys and girls typically go through a "growth spurt," during which they may grow three or more inches a year. The growth spurt in boys is usually longer than it is in girls.

Perhaps the area of greatest concern during adolescence is that of growth and sexual development. Parents often worry when their children develop either very early or late. The pediatrician can provide helpful information to parents on changes to expect.

Adolescence in Children with ASDs

Puberty is driven by biology and not developmental status. It is not typically delayed in children with autism and related disorders. However, the transitions and changes of puberty can be much more difficult for children with ASDs for many reasons. First and foremost, it is not always possible to totally prepare the child for the changes that she is about to experience. She may lack good communication skills or be unable to fully understand what parents are trying to explain. In addition, the rapid mood changes that the parents of all adolescents try to cope with, and often find frustrating, can be magnified in children with disabilities. Aggressive behavior toward others and self-injurious behaviors can escalate. These behaviors can be harder to physically manage as the adolescent or young adult with an ASD becomes larger and stronger (we discuss this shortly).

It is hard to know when behavior changes merely signify "normal adolescence" and when they are clues to new underlying problems such as the pain of an ear infection or a toothache. Sometimes parents may need to go to the doctor in order to rule out medical problems. In general, the start of adolescence is a good time for the child to have a scheduled physical—that is, at a time when the child is not sick and parents (and the child) can spend more time with the doctor talking about changes in adolescence. Adolescents with autism or pervasive developmental disorder (PDD) may develop any of the medical problems that other adolescents develop during this time of life. In addition, adolescents with autism have an increased risk of developing seizure disorders (see Chapter 12).

Adolescents need to eat more during growth spurts, so if the child is a very picky eater, it may require new efforts to get him to eat all that is needed. For some adolescents, obesity may be a concern, especially if the adolescent or young adult with an ASD doesn't have as many outside activities or sources of exercise as a typical teenager.

Leo Kanner, the man who first described autism, also was one of the first people to do follow-up studies, made an interesting observation. He noted that some children with autism improved with adolescence while others lost skills. Subsequent work has tended to support his observation. Often, even children with more severe behavior problems seem to have a general improvement. In some cases a child seems, in the early teens, to become very motivated to become part of a peer group. The number of children who improve varies from study to study, and also depends on how improvement is defined, but seems to be between 40 and maybe 80% of cases. These gains include gains in communication, social skills, and behavior. In some cases, the improvement is very significant, and sometimes the person, as a young adult, may even seem to "lose" the diagnosis of autism.

However, some children seem to take a downturn in adolescence. This, fortunately, is relatively less common and may be seen in perhaps 10 to 20% of cases. Sometimes this is associated with the onset of seizures, and then it is difficult to know how much of the change is from the seizures, the medicines used to treat the seizures, or both. Even when deterioration doesn't happen, some children continue to have behavior problems, and larger physical size and new preoccupations (e.g., sexual behaviors) may pose new challenges.

BEHAVIOR PROBLEMS IN ADOLESCENCE

For some children with ASDs, the hormonal changes that precede the onset of puberty may exacerbate preexisting behavioral difficulties such as aggressiveness and self-injurious behaviors. In other children, the start of adolescence will bring on these types of behaviors for the first time. To complicate things further, the many changes in the body and an emerging sexuality may only add to life's confusions. Unfortunately, this is also a time when children are moving into more complex social and physical environments such as high school.

Behavior problems in adolescence often seem to start a year or so before the bodily changes that signal puberty. These may take the form of greater irritability, decreased attention, higher levels of activity, and stereotyped behaviors. Often, these behaviors get better as the child enters puberty, but the increase in the child's physical size and the potential seriousness of the behaviors may be very problematic. As the adolescent or young adult with an ASD becomes older, parents may consider medications to help manage behavior problems, or, if she is already on medications, parents may need to increase the dose or change to new medications. The strategies we discuss in Chapters 13 and 14 can be used effectively. Talk to the young person's school staff as well about strategies that may help the adolescent or young adult with an ASD cope at school. An increase in physical activity may, for example, be helpful to some children. We talk about other potential approaches to behavior problems in Chapters 15 and 16. As we emphasize in those chapters, an important first step is to try to "get the big picture" and put the behavior problem in a broader context.

Individuals who make major improvements in adolescence often have an emerging sense of being different and of wanting to "fit in." For these adolescents, it is important to support their desire and motivation to work toward more typical peer relationships. These individuals are the ones who often will receive the least amount of services in school (because they indeed are doing well) but who also would profit the most from explicit teaching about social relationships and real-world skills. These more able individuals are also often the ones who can become, at times, depressed or anxious about feeling "different." They also can respond very well to structured psychotherapy/counseling approaches (see Chapter 14) and to medications (Chapter 15).

SEXUALITY

Developing sexuality poses a complicated set of issues for typically developing children, much less those with some developmental vulnerability. Some adolescents with autism will have strong sexual feelings; others won't. Some children, particularly higher functioning children, may be very motivated to have a girl-friend or boyfriend, and sometimes this extra motivation helps the child make important gains. It is important to realize that sexual feelings are very much tied up with feelings about relationships—which means they are even more problematic for children with autism and related difficulties.

For typically developing children, sexual awareness comes early. Toddlers are aware of the differences between boys and girls by around age 3 and know their own gender. They also have a growing sense of their own bodies, and, through toilet training, an awareness of the distinction between public and private behaviors. As children become older, they want to understand more about their bodies and where babies come from. For the typically developing child, parents, teachers, and peers are all important sources of information. By adolescence, there will be an interest in bodily changes such as menstruation and wet dreams and a strong awareness of appropriate and inappropriate sexual behaviors. Older adolescents cope with issues such as the distinction between love and sex, the importance of contraception and preventing sexually transmitted disease, and more adult-like notions of what long-term relationships mean.

For a child with an ASD, education about sexual issues is complicated by both language and communication difficulties and social problems. Sexual feelings can sometimes be quite intense—for lower and higher functioning children alike. Unfortunately, one of the prime sources of information available to typically developing children (i.e., their peers) is not so readily available to the child with an ASD. The child's learning difficulties and adults' anxiety may both pose further challenges to learning!

People used to believe that the social problems of autism prevented sexual interest or relationships, but we now know that this isn't true. With earlier intervention and an emphasis on programs in communities, more people with ASDs are having meaningful relationships—sometimes including sexual relationships. Parents of adolescents with ASDs, like many parents, may have trouble viewing the adolescent as a sexual being, and parents may be concerned that the adolescent may be taken advantage of. However, it is important for the individual's emotional health for parents to allow her or him to explore their sexuality at the same time the child is learning other positive ways to relate to others.

In helping the person learn to develop relationships, keep in mind that parents want to:

- Make the learning process as positive an experience as possible.
- Help the child learn about what *not* to do as well as what *to* do (there are some absolute no-nos like talking about a desire to have sex!).
- Remember that the overall goal is to help the adolescent develop a more positive view of herself or himself.

As with other activities, experience is helpful. This experience may need to be carefully planned and monitored. For example, mixed (male–female) group activities present excellent opportunities for socializing. Explicit teaching can be helpful here, particularly for more verbal young people, and can emphasize important (but complicated) distinctions, such as the difference between what we think and what we say (Myles, Trautman, & Schelvan, 2004; Myles and Adreon, 2001). Understanding the distinction between public and private behavior is also important. Again, teaching the adolescent or young adult with an ASD when to say no, who can touch what and where, and when touching might be appropriate is also essential. For children who have not yet mastered them, there will be many chances to learn some of the appropriate social rules. Guided rehearsal and practice may also help—for example, in teaching the adolescent or young adult with an ASD how to act during a date. Many of the resources we mention in discussing social skills interventions (see Chapter 6) are very appropriate here (see also Baker 2003, 2006a,b). If the adolescent or young adult with an ASD has the chance to attend a social skills group with other teenagers, that may also be a big help.

Sometimes adolescents with Asperger's disorder or autism can be quite pre-occupied with sex or with the issue of wanting a girlfriend or boyfriend. To some extent, these concerns are age appropriate and expected. They can, however, re-sult in some very awkward moments if the adolescent or young adult with an ASD takes a rather literal, one-sided approach to trying to obtain what she wants. For example, one teenager we know with Asperger's disorder would pick a girl and stare at her during lunch in the high school cafeteria. The girl would eventu-ally come over to ask him what he wanted and he would then make a very explicit sexual request! This young man had to learn that while the girl had indeed asked him what he wanted, there is a rule against answering as frankly as he did.

In general, parents should help the adolescent or young adult with an ASD deal with emerging sexuality by having open discussions with them, with re-sponses pitched to a level she or he can understand. These discussions should also make clear what the rules are for socially acceptable behaviors. It is impor-tant to keep in mind that sex is only part of what needs to be discussed. The adolescent or young adult with an ASD also needs to understand the role that relationships play in sexuality and to understand the differences between having a friendship and a sexual relationship.

Occasionally, particularly for individuals with greater cognitive impairment, parents may need the help of a specialist in dealing with sex education issues. For example, parents may want to consult a specialist if the adolescent or young adult with ASD has real difficulty understanding basic issues such as masturba-tion and the need for privacy. Potential resources include the adolescent's or young adult's school and physician or agencies such as the state department of developmental disability. Other parents can also be sources of good information.

Teaching About Sexuality

It is important to realize that helping prepare the child for adolescence and emerging sexuality really begins much earlier in life. Parents and teachers should try, whenever possible, to affirm the things that the child can do, and encourage an awareness of the importance of others and the many different kinds of rela-tionships we can have. Early relationships with brothers and sisters and with par-ents will usually provide opportunities for learning about the differences between the sexes as well as about the child's own body. Because sexual issues are also very much relationship issues, it is important, early on, to encourage social skills, as discussed in Chapter 6. Encouraging relationships both within and outside the home is important since these relationships will provide oppor-tunities for learning and generalizing skills.

When teaching about sexuality, the first consideration is, of course, determining where the child is in understanding these issues. If the child is younger or more cognitively challenged, teaching must start at a lower level, for example, helping facilitate an understanding of privacy issues, of basic differences between the sexes, and so forth. As understanding increases, parents can begin to discuss issues that will be more relevant in adolescence, such as menarche and masturbation. It is also important to teach children about appropriate and inappropriate touching—that is, who can and can't touch the more private parts of their bodies (an issue that often will have come up already with their doctor). There are some excellent guidelines and curricula developed (see the reading list at the end of the chapter).

Privacy and Modesty   Often, the first difficulty parents face is teaching some ideas about privacy and modesty. This issue often arises early because parents may need to spend a longer time teaching the adolescent or young adult with an ASD skills such as toileting and dressing. Modesty is a difficult concept because it requires a *judgment* and an *appreciation of context*. It is important to understand, that it is all right to be naked in the shower or while changing clothes in a locker room but not "in public." The child with an ASD often has difficulty in appreciating context, and this, combined with a tendency to be rigid, can make for some problems in teaching. Teachers and school staff can be a tremendous help in this regard by reinforcing appropriate behavior and setting guidelines for children to apply in and outside school.

Problems in appreciating privacy and modesty rules cause endless troubles—sometimes starting at a fairly young age. A friend of ours, who once worked in a group home, tells a wonderful story of taking one of the clients in the home to a classical music concert. This rather large, nonverbal young man with autism loved classical music and seemed to enjoy the performance very much. The only problem arose when he went into the bathroom by himself. Shortly, a torrent of men were pouring out the door. It turned out that the young man with autism had learned early in life that when you go to the bathroom, you take off all your clothes first, and his doing this in the concert hall bathroom probably did not seem at all out of the ordinary to him!

In thinking about teaching modesty, there are several important considerations to keep in mind. First, what are the situations where privacy/modesty is needed? And second, whom do parents know who can help do some teaching? For example, grandparents and siblings may be good resources, but casual acquaintances are not. Teachers and school staff can help but should be sure that parents are actively involved in the discussion process. Third, as with other tasks, parents have to think about what they want to teach and the challenges for teaching. So, for example, given the difficulties children with autism have in generalization, parents might want to teach the child to get dressed in his or her bedroom or bathroom and nowhere else (at least at first). Similarly, bathrooms are a good place to teach personal self-care and grooming (see Chapter 6). Parents can make a point of shutting the door to "have some privacy." Beginning early in life, parents can also gradually teach the names of body parts and can point out differences between boys and girls and men and women. Some parents find it helpful to teach their child that the private parts of the body are the ones that are covered by a swimming suit. For additional guidance, parents may want to refer to Schwier and Hingsburger (2000).

Masturbation   Most children with autism and related conditions will learn to masturbate. This can be a source of discomfort for parents and teachers. It is important to realize, however, that masturbation is very common in all children and adolescents and that the task for children with autism is to learn that if they do this, they need to do it in the privacy of their bedroom. Often, masturbation will start in the preschool or early school years and parents and teachers have the opportunity to explain (in as simple language as is needed) that we don't engage in that behavior in public—obviously, that means the child needs to understand what private spaces are. A matter-of-fact attitude is much better, since parents may otherwise teach the adolescent or young adult with an ASD a very effective and problematic way of always getting attention!

Some parents tell their child that bad things will happen to their bodies when they masturbate—this only adds to the child's confusion since it is untrue! Often, much patience and work is needed. Visual supports and other learning aids can be helpful—for instance, learning to put out a sign that says "Do not disturb" (as in a hotel).

Sometimes masturbation during school can be a problem. Giving the student opportunities for frequent movement or objects to manipulate with the hands as an alternative activity may be helpful. (An occupational therapist [OT] can often recommend materials.) Exercise, too, can help. The OT and special education teachers may help come up with some strategies for helping the adolescent or young adult with an ASD learn that masturbation in school is not appropriate.

Teaching About Boundaries   The possibility of sexual or physical abuse is always a concern for parents. Parents of lower functioning children are often worried that they might not know about abuse if it occurs, and parents of higher functioning children worry that their child may easily be misled into inappropriate sexual activity. Fortunately, most children with ASDs are closely supervised in their day-to-day activities and the opportunity for abuse does not occur. Planning for activities and work should include consideration of whom the adolescent or young adult with an ASD will be with and the safety of the situation. This may be a greater concern for more high functioning children because they may be allowed more independence and less supervision. They may not fully understand other people's intentions, however, and at times other people may not understand their behaviors.

> ### SIGNS OF POSSIBLE ABUSE
>
> Sexual or physical abuse can sometimes be easy to detect and sometimes more difficult. Among the many clues to possible abuse in typically developing children (which may also be seen in children with ASDs) are:
>
> - Unusual changes in behavior
> - Increased anxiety or depression
> - Avoidance of certain people or situations
> - Increased agitation or aggression
> - Withdrawal
>
> Sometimes a marked increase in sexual activity (such as masturbation) may be the only sign. Physical symptoms or signs of sexual activity are obvious warning signs.
>
> Discuss any suspicion of sexual abuse with your health care provider. And remember that, by law, the provider must contact child protective services if he or she thinks there is a possibility that the adolescent or young adult with ASD has been abused.

Part of growing up is learning about boundaries and appropriate behavior on the part of others. Various programs and curriculums are available (see reading list). These programs can help to teach about levels of intimacy in a very concrete way and help convey the idea that different adults have different relationships with the child. For example, handshakes are appropriate for adult strangers; for closer friends and family members, other kinds of contact such as hugs may be appropriate. Clearly, teaching about strangers and being appropriately wary of strangers is important. For children who are verbal, the "No, Go, Tell" strategy may be useful. This method, described by Schwier and Hingsburger (2000) involves being able to say no to an activity, getting away from the situation, and telling others what has happened. There are some other excellent resources in the reading list at the end of this chapter.

Unfortunately, there will inevitably be some exceptions to the various rules parents teach, and sometimes these will come back to haunt parents. For example, if parents teach the adolescent or young adult with an ASD not to let strangers touch her, sooner or later she will see a new doctor who is a stranger to her, but who has a legitimate need to touch her.

Girls in Adolescence: Physical Changes and Medical Issues

As their breasts enlarge, girls with ASDs need to understand that breasts are a private part of the body. They should know that other people should not be attempting to touch their breasts and that they should not show them to others. Higher functioning girls will want to know more about the functions of the breasts. As the breasts develop, the doctor will want to talk about breast exams (see the reading list for some helpful books).

Like all girls, girls with ASDs should be prepared in advance for the onset of their period. The reading list gives some resources that may be helpful in educating girls about their bodies and the changes to expect. For children who are verbal, the chance to talk with their mothers or older sisters can be a big help. Do not overwhelm the girl with information that she may not be interested in, but be prepared to answer her questions in a matter-of-fact way. For example, she may or may not want to know why women menstruate, but if she asks, provide truthful, factual information.

Some girls will be able to manage on their own with the help of their caregivers, but others may require more direct supervision or help during their periods. When your daughter is having her period, it may be helpful to teach her to change her pad at specific times, such as after math class and after lunch (particularly if she has trouble making this judgment herself). As with other self-help skills, teaching the steps involved may be useful for less cognitively able students.

At least initially, someone may need to keep track of how often the girl has a period and how long it lasts, and at times be sure that the pads are changed when necessary. Personal hygiene may require more intervention than before for some girls. Additional discussions about privacy may also be needed. For instance, more verbal and talkative girls will need to learn that one's periods are not a topic for general conversation. Parents and teachers should also, of course, be mindful of the need to respect privacy and be sensitive to the situation and context in discussions of these issues.

Some girls have cramps with their periods. These can start a day or so before the period or at the beginning of the period. Usually, they last only a few days. For girls with poor communication skills, cramps may be a cause of behavior change at this time of the month. Menstrual cramps are often treated with nonsteroidal anti-inflammatory drugs (NSAIDs) such as ibuprofen. If the pain is severe and interfering with normal functioning, birth control pills may be used to prevent the cramps.

Birth control pills or other types of hormonal contraception can be very useful in helping teenage girls and young women with autism manage their periods. First, they can help reduce heavy menstrual flow. Second, they make it easier to predict when a girl's period will start. That may be very helpful when a girl has major behavioral changes with her period or needs quite a bit of supervision when changing her pads and with general hygiene when she has her period. If birth control pills are used, someone needs to be sure that they are taken every day as prescribed. Hormone injections, given every 3 months or implants that last longer, have also been used for birth control or to control the periods and symptoms caused by them. For girls who have trouble remembering to take a pill every day, or for those who might take a patch off, the injections or implants can be very helpful. This may be particularly helpful in girls and young women with ASDs who have a very hard time coping with their periods and any associated symptoms.

There are many potential side effects to hormonal birth control, but in general it is very safe in teenage girls. The hormones can interact with some drugs, especially some antiseizure medications, so be sure that the doctor prescribing the birth control pills knows whether your daughter is on any other medications. Most teenagers placed on birth control pills are put on what are called "low-dose" pills. That means that the amount of hormone in them is lower than in the past and there are many fewer side effects. As we discuss concerning other medications, it is always important that parents discuss the potential benefits and risks of any birth control medication for their daughter with her physician before deciding to use these.

Premenstrual Syndrome (PMS)   It is important to realize that girls with autism may have PMS, but that it may be harder to diagnose in girls with severe communication problems. In such circumstances, it is important that parents are aware of the timing of what appear to be unusual, monthly "behavioral difficulties," which may actually represent a response to discomfort. PMS symptoms can vary greatly among girls. Some will have few or no symptoms, while others, unfortunately, can have many different symptoms. Both physical and emotional symptoms can be a part of PMS. Some of the most common physical symptoms include headaches, breast swelling and tenderness, change in appetite, weight gain, tiredness, and achy muscles and joints. Common emotional symptoms include irritability, depression, anxiety, poor concentration, and social withdrawal (which may be hard to separate from some girls' underlying behavior and social difficulties that are part of the ASD). Changes in sleep, with either trouble sleeping or sleeping more than usual, have also been described as a part of PMS.

The symptoms of PMS, as the name implies, usually appear in the second half of the menstrual cycle before the period starts. No one treatment has been found to work for all of the symptoms of PMS or for everyone. For some girls, being aware that these symptoms can be expected at a certain time of the month can be helpful in dealing with them. Others have found that exercise is helpful in preventing or lessening the symptoms. Sometimes taking 1,200 mg of calcium per day is recommended as a way to prevent PMS. This is the amount of calcium that is recommended anyway for children and adolescents during their years of rapid growth so that they will develop strong bones. NSAIDs such as ibuprofen and naproxen sodium, which are over-the-counter drugs, or prescription medicines of this type can be helpful for some of the physical symptoms of PMS. For girls with severe symptoms of PMS, birth control pills have been used with very good results. Remember, parents want to carefully weigh the potential risks with the hoped-for benefits before starting these. Antidepressants have also been used at times for severe PMS symptoms and have been very helpful for some people.

Pelvic Exams   At some point, all girls need to start having an annual pelvic exam. If a girl is not having any problems with her periods or other aspects of her gynecological health and she is not sexually active, she can wait until sometime between age 18 and the early 20s before starting the annual exams. If there are problems sooner, she will need to be examined at that time. Some young women will find it hard to have a pelvic examination and sedation or even anesthesia is sometimes needed.

Boys: Physical Changes and Medical Issues

Many changes also occur in the bodies of boys during puberty. As mentioned earlier, these include increased hair, growth of the body, change in voice, and development of the genitals. They also include wet dreams (emission of semen during sleep) and erections as sexual maturation moves along. These occurrences can be confusing. Boys who are higher functioning may be relieved to hear that this is a normal part of growing up. As with girls, advance preparation is helpful; often, the father or a brother would be a good person to do this!

By this time in adolescence, it will be important that the doctor include examination of the genitals as part of the regular physical examination. This is also an opportunity for the doctor to teach the young man about self-examination of the testicles for lumps, if this is appropriate—that is, if the boy can understand the reason for doing it.

Contraception and Protection from STDs

There are a variety of reasons that it might be appropriate to think about safe sex for a son or daughter with autism. Some adolescents and young adults with ASDs may be able to enter into a longer term relationship that involves a sexual relationship. For other young people, contraception might be an important safeguard to consider when they move into a community living situation. Occasionally, birth control pills may be used to treat painful periods (dysmenorrheal) and sometimes for other medical reasons as well (see the earlier section on birth control pills).

Usually, the issue of birth control looms larger in the minds of parents of girls, but even parents of boys with ASDs should realize that sexual activity brings potential risks of sexually transmitted diseases (STDs) as well as of pregnancy. That is, if a young man is going to be sexually active, he must understand the risks of unprotected sex. Some higher functioning young men may need help to understand the use of condoms.

The issue of birth control and an awareness of the risks of unprotected sex (including pregnancy) should be discussed with the sexually active teenager and young adult. The health care provider of the adolescent or young adult with an ASD may be helpful to parents in the process. As far as we know, individuals with ASDs are just as fertile as anyone else. In addition, if someone with autism conceives a child, there is some potential that she will pass along the risk for autism, if not the actual disorder, given that there seem to be strong genetic aspects to autism.

In the past, it was common for individuals (particularly women) with intellectual disabilities to be made infertile (sterilized) without their consent. Currently, laws about sterilization—as well as marriage and guardianship—vary significantly from state to state. In considering what is best for your own child, it is important to realize that sexuality does not have to lead to childbearing and sterilization won't of itself make her less vulnerable to abuse. Parents should also remember that anyone who has the cognitive ability to make decisions about her own health care is entitled to do so, and decisions about the reproductive status of an adolescent or young adult with an ASD very well may not be the parent's to make.

HIGH SCHOOL: CHALLENGES AND OPPORTUNITIES

High school presents some challenges for typically developing children, and in some ways even more so for children on the autism spectrum. There are many different sources of challenge:

- Typically developing adolescents in high school function at a *very* high social level. Students with ASDs often are several, and sometimes many, years behind in terms of their social sophistication and ability to tolerate the fast pace and nuanced social interaction of high school.

- Academic/cognitive demands are greater; this may present a very significant challenge for the less cognitively able student.

- Demands for self-directed learning, self-monitoring, and organization skills are high; students are expected, often, to work largely independently, and issues such as time pressure and organization may pose significant obstacles for students with ASDs.

- The physical environment of high schools can be challenging—often these are large schools where students move frequently from class to class, and hallways are noisy places where a lot of socializing goes on.

- Demands for self-care and personal hygiene are high; adolescents are often meticulous (even when they sport a studied nonmeticulous look) about appearance, cleanliness, and so forth.

- This is often a time when typically developing adolescents start to orient to peers (over parents and siblings) and so peer group issues and peer acceptance can loom large.

As noted in Chapter 4, the whole process of getting services should extend well into adolescence for those students who continue to need individualized education plans (IEPs). Work on adaptive, social, and communication skills should continue (see Chapter 6). There are some excellent resources for teaching social, organization, and other skills specifically written for high school students and young adults (e.g., Baker, 2006a; Wehman, Smith, & Schall, 2009). Transition planning should also be an important part of the IEP process, with the longer term goal/vision of enabling the student to be as independent and self-sufficient as possible in adulthood. This should include careful consideration of the student's interests, abilities, and areas of challenge. It should be highly individualized. Depending on the level of the child, services in high school can be provided up to age 21 (or even longer in some states) or until goals and objectives are met. It is important for parents to realize that graduation from high school at age 17 or 18 does *not* have to occur and that many adolescents can remain in the high school system for several years more. Also, it is important to realize that as part of the IEP process vocational and other assessments can be requested. This should also include consideration of whether the student may be able to learn to drive independently. If not, other skills (e.g., using the bus) should be explicitly taught. Other considerations include any special needs, for example, relevant to the work environment.

Experiences of teasing/bullying or, more frequently, social isolation can be problems, particularly for more cognitively able students at this age, and it is important that some adult or adults are on the lookout for such situations (see Chapter 8). Bullying is probably most common in lower and middle school-aged children but sometimes continues into high school and beyond. Occasionally, students on the autism spectrum run into problems in college where their ten-dency to be more isolated and/or their special interests make them more vulnerable to hazing and harassment. It is important to realize that such behavior is not only inappropriate but also can quickly become illegal. The flip side, inappropriate pursuit of other students—either as friends or romantic partners—is sometimes seen. This can also be the source of great difficulty, and many schools/colleges are relatively rigid about setting limits for such behavior and continued pursuit/harassment (a fine line between them may or may not exist) can result in expulsion. Many of the steps previously discussed on teaching appropriate social behaviors and distance will help.

Transition to College or Vocational Program/School

For the more cognitively able student with an ASD, college or vocational school may be a good possibility. An increasing number of special programs around the country are designed to help with explicit teaching about the skills needed for attending college and living independently (see reading list). A number of different considerations apply in these cases. It is important for parents and students to realize that unlike elementary and high school, college attendance is *not* a right. Rather, the applicable law (see Chapter 4) refers to nondiscrimination for students with disabilities. As a practical matter, this has several important implications for students with ASDs in college:

- Students must self-identify as having some disability to the college disability office. Parents *cannot* do this for the student. Once the student does self-identify, a number of different, reasonable accommodations can be made, including tutors, help with organization, untimed tests, and so forth.

- Students must learn to be appropriate in their interactions with other students; this issue frequently surfaces when a student who has an ASD is perceived by other students as threatening or harassing.

- Students must be able to function reasonably autonomously, or special provision for support must be made; this can take the form of peer mentorship, roommates who have identified as having special interests in common with the student with an ASD, and so forth.

- Use of peer mentors and continued individual/group therapies may be helpful; for example, an individual therapist may work on problem issues such as depression or anxiety or explicit social teaching.

- Vocational training programs may be appropriate for many students. These can include an opportunity either to sample a range of potential vocational options or, for a student with a strong interest, to enroll in a program of study designed to teach specific skills (e.g., computer programming).

Keep in mind that the issue of job choice requires (1) a realistic awareness of strengths and weaknesses and (2) usually a situation where social–interpersonal demands are kept minimal.

- Independent living skills should be explicitly targeted. This includes everything from self-care to study habits, dealing with the cafeteria and student union, doing laundry, and so forth. For students who can make the transition, there are many advantages to colleges and vocational schools, especially those with residential campuses. For example, only a few places will serve food, libraries are relatively self-contained, and so forth. Even for students who live at home (e.g., attending a 2-year college program or nearby vocational programs), it is important to foster independent living skills.

There are now a number of excellent resources available, including several mentioned in the reading list at the end of this chapter including books by Harpur, Lawlor & Fitzgerald (2004) and Wolf, Brown, and Bork (2009).

HYGIENE AND SELF-CARE SKILLS

Bathing and grooming and similar skills become increasingly important for adolescents. Idiosyncratic habits, routines, or rituals may sometimes unintentionally provide an additional life complication for adolescents on the autism spectrum. For example, one higher functioning adolescent boy we know desperately wanted a girlfriend. Among many challenges he faced was the fact that he wore only one set of clothes, almost never bathed or showered, and made no attempt to make himself look more attractive. He spent a considerable amount of time in a social skills group complaining until eventually another group participant pointed out to him that girls were hard to please and that what people had to do to "get to first base" was be clean and presentable!

Modeling self-care skills at home when children are younger is one of the most useful (and least time-consuming) means parents can use to help the individual with an ASD learn what she needs to do. For girls, the chance to watch Mom and sisters put on makeup and fix their hair can be important; for boys, watching a father or older brother shave similarly can be helpful in the long run. Parents should also talk with the adolescent or young adult with an ASD and praise the child for his interest in being more "grown up." Some adolescents with ASDs may overdo the interest in perfumes, aftershaves, or antiperspirants at first, but they can always learn to scale back a bit, and this skill will be helpful for them in the long run.

Teachers and school staff may be a big help in teaching self-care activities and independence (see Chapter 6). Various resources are available, including the use of visual schedules, pictures, picture books, social stories, and so forth.

Moving to Adulthood

Outcome in Autism and Related Conditions

Predicting the future is hard for most things, and this is true for how any child will do. One of the things parents are, understandably, most concerned about is having some estimate/guesstimate of how well their child will do over time. As previously discussed, there are many, many difficult factors that make prediction difficult for the individual child—we start to get better when we predict about *groups* of children. Another problem is that there have been changes in how the diagnosis of autism is made, and other conditions, such as Asperger's, are now included in the group of autism spectrum conditions. Yet another and very important factor is that as a society we are doing better at providing early diagnosis and services to children on the autism spectrum. Given all these issues, what can we say about adult outcome in autism?

If parents look at the first studies—by Kanner and his student Leon Eisenberg in the 1950s—we see a range of outcomes. Some individuals remained very dependent, but others, about one-third, had a "moderate social adjustment." This is particularly impressive given that, at that time, there was not nearly as much known about treatment and what treatments were effective in autism. While some students achieved independence, Eisenberg also noted that social problems tended to remain (e.g., one young man was asked to speak at a sports rally and announced, quite truthfully, that the school's team was about to lose). One of the problems in understanding many of the early reports was a lack of clarity about diagnosis. Despite this problem, people like Kanner kept very good records and noted some of the factors we still look at in guesstimating outcome—communication skills and levels of intelligence were, for example, strong predictors. It was while doing these follow-ups that Kanner and Eisenberg noticed that some children seemed to do particularly well in adolescence as they tried to gain better social skills. In some cases, individuals grew up to have their own homes, and one was married and had a child; in other cases, individuals (particularly those with more communication and cognitive impairments) remained with their families. Several studies suggest that the severity of autistic symptoms decreases with age, and this improvement can be observed in various areas of functioning. Usually, even in the cases with the best possible outcome, some degree of social oddity will persist.

For Asperger's disorder, the outcome may be even better than that in autism. Although this issue is the focus of some debate, it is interesting that Asperger himself suggested that the outcome was probably better and this might not be so surprising given that communication and cognitive abilities often were areas of strength. It is also the case that Asperger tended to think of the condition he described more as a personality style rather than a developmental disorder,

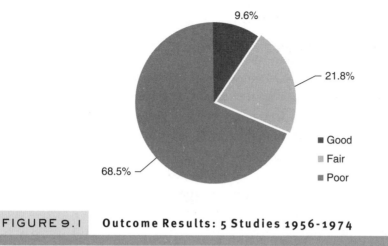

9.6%

21.8%

68.5%

- Good
- Fair
- Poor

FIGURE 9.1   Outcome Results: 5 Studies 1956-1974

suggesting a potential "shading off" of the condition. Similarly, his observation that other members of the family, often fathers, have similar problems would seem to suggest good potential for long-term relationships. We'll talk more about marital and couples issues for higher functioning adults on the autism spectrum shortly.

There have been a number of studies of outcome of autism and related conditions (see Patricia Howlin's excellent chapter in the *Handbook of Autism* (2005) for a summary). As Howlin emphasizes, there are a number of problems in comparing studies, given changes in diagnostic terminology and different approaches used in defining outcome. In her recent review, Howlin tried to summarize these data by sorting cases into good, fair, and poor outcome (good outcome cases were largely independent, while those with poor outcome remained very dependent). Over time, it appears that the number of good outcome cases has almost doubled (before and after 1980), with fewer individuals having poorer outcomes over time. Figures 9.1 and 9.2 summarize these changes over time in selected studies.

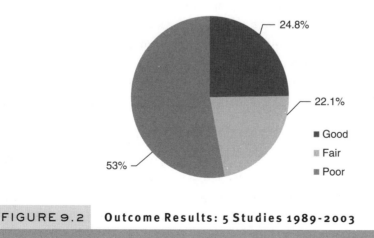

24.8%

22.1%

53%

- Good
- Fair
- Poor

FIGURE 9.2   Outcome Results: 5 Studies 1989-2003

Several factors appear to be important in predicting ultimate outcome. One is the presence of truly communicative speech (by around age 5), another is non-verbal cognitive ability in the normal range, and yet another is the person's capacity for self-sufficiency and independence. Some work has tried to refine early predictive factors; for example, vocabulary size has been thought to be a good predictor of outcome, although this is controversial.

Usually, adaptive skills (capacities for personal self-sufficiency and independence) are much lower than cognitive ability. This is one of the reasons that family involvement (from very early on) is so important in treatment (see Chapter 19). For example, in one study of adolescents, even though the mean intelligence quotient (IQ) was in the average range, only about half of the students were truly independent in self-care activities. This is reflected in a myriad of ways, including personal hygiene, ability to live and travel independently, and so forth.

Mental Health and Medical Issues

In general, the trend during adolescence is for decreased difficulties, although sometimes new problems emerge. These may have to do with trouble with change, compulsive behaviors, sexual behaviors, aggression, or other problems. For the more able individuals, including those who improve in other ways, problems with depression and anxiety can become much more striking. This is, sadly, something of a "double-edged sword" phenomenon; that is, sometimes the awareness of being or feeling "different" can motivate change on the one hand but lead to greater anxiety and depression on the other (Ghaziuddin, 2005). Studies of family history and genetics also suggest a potential genetic vulnerability for anxiety and depression (Rutter, 2005). When individuals are less able cognitively and have behavior problems, the literal increase in body size can, of itself, represent a new, and important, challenge.

As adolescents become young adults, they may need to find new health care providers. Some pediatricians may be willing to continue to care for the adolescent or young adult with an ASD into her 20s. As she reaches her 30s, or earlier with some doctors, parents will need to find an internist or family physician to take care of her. The main reason parents will eventually need to switch to an internist or family practice physician is that as the adolescent or young adult with an ASD grows older, the individual will develop the same kinds of medical problems that other older people get. That is, adults with autism are subject to all adult-related medical conditions, such as high blood pressure, high cholesterol, heart disease, and so on. The pediatrician may not feel comfortable treating these problems if they are not seen in children, and at times the pediatrician may not even recognize or think of problems that are seen only in adults.

Although autism has been recognized since the 1940s, relatively little has been written about adults with autism and their medical care. A particular challenge for parents of adults with autism and other PDDs is that many health care providers who typically work with adults are not knowledgeable about these disorders. Internists and general practitioners may have little or no training at all in the area of developmental diagnosis or developmental disability and may be hesitant to assume care for young adults with autism. Sometimes they are surprised or even shocked by the lack of cooperation on the part of an adult with autism. Other parents with older children with autism or PDD may be able to recommend doctors they have found who are willing to take on these young adults. The pediatrician may be able to help in the transition by speaking directly with the new doctor about the adolescent or young adult with an ASD and her special needs. For individuals who have seen a family doctor this may not be an issue at all.

VOCATIONAL ISSUES

The abilities to live and work independently as an adult should be the goal for persons with ASDs. Even when learning and behavior problems make this less likely the overall goal should be to help the individual attain as much self-sufficiency and independence as possible. For more and more individuals, adult independence is possible and, while challenges remain, more resources are available to help the individual, his family, and his school work for this goal. Unfortunately, there is considerable variability from state to state in what is actually available. There are some federal supports for vocational training for students who have substantial handicaps to employment and who can benefit from vocational services. Typically, state departments of vocational services (sometimes called voc rehab or DVR) often are the agencies mandated to provide these services. If adults qualify, a plan for employment—similar to the IEP—can be developed. Various other federal, and sometimes state, laws can apply. These have to do with discrimination against individuals with disabilities. At the federal level, the Americans with Disabilities Act of 1990 is often most relevant. It prohibits discrimination based on disability. This act applies in a range of settings, including most private employers, public accommodations, and so forth.

Community resources often lag behind what we need to help adolescents and adults enter the workforce. It is important for everyone concerned to realize that there are no mandates or rights relative to adult employment, unlike the right to a free and appropriate education in the United States. Rather, relevant laws have to do with rehabilitation and protection of persons with disabilities from discrimination. Transition planning is mandated for children with disabilities as part of a student's IEP beginning no later than their 16th birthday. This acknowledges the need for a coordinated transition process with involvement of all relevant parties and ongoing collaboration. Other laws mandate equal access to jobs but not to necessary support services.

There are a number of challenges in transitional planning. These include costs involved in supporting students and community-based supports. Even the best planning is, of course, of little benefit if few opportunities and supports are available to adults who need them. For many persons, the family—particularly the parents, but also siblings and other family members—can be an important part of the planning process. At a minimum, they can serve as advocates for the person with autism. They can also have an important role in helping various agencies/service providers work together.

The marked individual presentations of individuals on the autism spectrum itself poses some obstacles for vocational planning. Some characteristics do have overarching importance; for example, in general, social vulnerability is a core shared feature and, accordingly, jobs that deemphasize social skills (to the extent possible) often work best. The Americans With Disabilities Act (ADA) prohibits discrimination based on disability. Employers must make reasonable accommodation for the disability. It is important to realize that the law doesn't require that companies hire people with disabilities; instead, it says that employers can't refuse to hire based on a person's having a disability. It also should be noted that there are other important qualifications to the law. There are also specific procedures and legal safeguards for individuals who feel that they have been discriminated against because of disability. The earlier law (Rehabilitation Act of 1973) also has specific provisions that apply in federally funded programs. Lawyers with experience in this area are the most helpful in answering questions about disability discrimination. It is important to realize that these laws may apply in many different areas; for example, federal fair housing laws make it illegal to discriminate against individuals with disabilities (including autism) in housing. These laws also set forth standards for "reasonable accommodations" of persons with disabilities.

The marked variability in social, communicative, and cognitive abilities pose significant problems for vocational programs. Individuals do vary. They range from the man who talks too much about his favorite topic to the individual who rarely says anything and gets upset with change. Accordingly, it is important that individual interests and their strengths and vulnerabilities always be taken into account. A range of options is usually available and includes the following:

- *Sheltered workshops.* For many years, this was the most frequent placement for adults with autism who also had significant cognitive challenges. These workshops provide, as the name implies, a protected work environment.

Often, this meant minimal challenges for the person with repetitive work and many periods of downtime and, of course, fewer opportunities for community engagement and further learning.

- *Secured employment.* In this mode, there is an attempt to support individuals with autism in less restrictive settings (e.g., in the community). This emphasis on a more typical life experience has been a great attraction. These programs, as parents can imagine, are more intensive in terms of initial assessments and continued support. There is typically a lifelong commitment by the agency to support of the individual. In this setting, a focus on behavioral and adaptive skills is also typical.

- *Supported employment.* In this approach, employment is combined with ongoing support (e.g., a job coach). This has been an increasingly common approach, and strategies to help individuals with ASDs have become much more sophisticated. Supported employment can take various forms. Intensive training and support is provided and the job coach and other supports are needed in the beginning, but their services may be gradually reduced over time. If an entire group of individuals can be supported at the same time, there may be some savings in terms of staff (job coach) time. However, continued support is often needed, even at a low level, and the move to decrease supports should not be too fast. Factors such as employer engagement, attitudes of coworkers, demands for social interaction, and productivity all are important, as is the ability to match, as much as possible, the preferences/strengths of the individuals with the job. Many factors/issues (*not* just economic ones) should be considered.

- *Independent (competitive) employment.* For more individuals on the autism spectrum, independent employment opportunities are increasingly available. Kanner himself observed that some of his patients were able, as adults, to enter into independent employment. Typically, these positions "played to strengths" of individuals with ASDs; for example, social requirements tended to be minimal and might include work in the computer industry, as a laboratory technician, in accounting, and so on. Higher functioning individuals, probably most particularly those with Asperger's, have been able to secure employment as academics (in areas like astronomy, cartography, mathematics, chemistry, and computer science). Sometimes individuals are able to adapt to positions that might not, at least theoretically, seem to be good "fits" for the person on the ASD spectrum (Keel, Mesibov, & Woods, 1997). Clear expectations and routines still often seem to be important, and other issues (e.g., transportation access and money management skills) may also be very important.

Living Arrangements for Adults

As with vocational programs, an increasing number of potential living arrangements are available. For typically developing children, late adolescence is usually a time to transition from living with parents to living semi-independently (in college or vocational programs or the military) before moving on to total independence as young adults. Even this pattern is changing, however, with many typically developing individuals moving back into their families of origin for periods of time. For individuals with ASDs, the challenges faced are significant ones with expectations for dealing with skills of daily living and coping with the challenges and frustrations of the work on a 24/7 basis. Fortunately, more and more options are available. That being said, many individuals, particularly those with autism, continue to live with their parents well into adult life. Individuals who experience the greatest challenge are those with the double handicap of an ASD and significant intellectual disability/cognitive delay.

Some of the traditional options have included group homes and supported apartments. In the former, a group of individuals with disabilities lives together with regular (usually 24/7) support from staff. In supported apartments, an individual or individuals may live with the periodic support of staff. In some instances, individuals may be able to live largely independently with occasional help from parents/family members. A number of transitional programs have grown up around the country that specialize in helping teach independent living skills to foster as much personal self-sufficiency as possible in adulthood. Other programs, sometimes referred to as skill development or host family homes, have the possibility for the individual to reside with a family who've been specially trained to teach self-care, community, and similar skills. Residential programs may be associated with specialized schools or autism treatment centers or may have more general associations with state departments of disability services. Increasingly, the trend has been for individuals living in group homes or other residential facilities to have significant community involvement. A myriad of options have been arranged by families, depending on the unique needs of the individual— for example, an apartment near the parents or a sibling. It is important that supports be flexible and consider the needs of the individual. One of the case examples given at the end of this chapter illustrates some of the problems that can come with inappropriate residential placement. In considering these programs, it is important for parents and the individual to be involved in the process of looking at the various options. There should be a feeling that staff and program are supportive and knowledgeable about the needs of a person on the autism spectrum.

In thinking about housing, it is also important to realize that, for adults, there may be special financial assistance available. It is important that parents and those working with young adults be aware of local, state, and federal supports. The reading list has a number of resources relevant to these issues and the specifics of skills needed for independent living.

PLANNING FOR THE FUTURE

Health Insurance

We discuss some of the issues involved in health insurance coverage in Chapter 10. As children become adults, they face several potential challenges in terms of health insurance support, that is, apart from their parents' coverage. Some states prohibit discrimination in insurance based on disabilities, although various loopholes also give "outs" to insurance companies. Increasingly, states are passing laws that force insurance companies to cover individuals with disabilities and what are called *preexisting conditions*. Sometimes special insurance programs are available if parents can show that a person can't obtain coverage elsewhere.

Government Benefits

There are two major federally supported programs that provide additional support for individuals with disabilities who can't support themselves. These programs are called Supplemental Security Income (SSI) and Social Security Disability Insurance (SSDI). The SSI program (www.ssa.gov/ssi) provides a basic payment to individuals or couples every month. The amount paid is reduced by the amount the person earns as income. The program is designed for people who cannot bring in substantial income or what is called *substantial gainful activity,* which means they can't engage in work. For children, the disability test has to do with "marked and severe functional limitations"; a specific set of guidelines for children and adolescents is provided. The web site listed earlier in this paragraph gives more information. In addition to being disabled, there is also a test based on financial need. Income past a very low threshold reduces the benefit on a dollar-for-dollar basis. There are some work incentive aspects to the program, for example, if additional income will help the person be able to work. For children and adolescents under 18 years of age, it is the parent's income that determines eligibility. Accordingly, many individuals with autism and severe disability become eligible as they turn 18. For this to happen, however, the individual has to have assets below a certain threshold. Keep in mind that it may be particularly important to have SSI if only for purposes of obtaining health insurance, i.e., Medicaid, coverage.

The SSDI program is a bit different. The test of eligibility is the same as for SSI, but families don't have to have very low income to be eligible. As with SSI, the amount of income that can be earned is very small. There are several ways to qualify, including being single and having a disability that began before age 18 or if the person is a child of someone covered by Social Security who has retired or passed away. There is more potential for earning at least a small amount of money each month with the SSDI program. Many individuals with autism and severe disability qualify for this program as their parents retire or die. More information is available online (www.ssa.gov/disability).

Keep in mind that other benefits are potentially available; for example, there are special benefits associated with federal employees. One of the most important things about SSI and SSDI is that they also give access to Medicare and Medicaid insurance programs (see Chapter 10). Parents should think about these possibilities in their long-term planning; in particular, they should take care not to jeopardize eligibility for programs with a "means test" (i.e., where parents have to demonstrate income below a certain level). So, for example, Medicaid and SSI have a "means test," but SSDI and Medicare do not. Other programs (e.g., housing assistance) may also have a specific means test. An important bottom line is to get some help in thinking long term relative to estate planning. Parents might, for example, think about a discretionary special-needs trust, which may avoid the problem of jeopardizing eligibility.

Guardianship and Legal Issues

As children become adults, they automatically assume legal and societal responsibility unless some special provision is made. Unless that happens, individuals become independent as they reach the legal age of adulthood—usually age 18 years. Parents of less cognitively able children (and sometimes those with more able children) just assume that they can continue to make decisions for the individual as he or she becomes an adult, but this is not, in fact, the case.

Depending on the situation, parents (or brothers and sisters or other family members) may wish to become **guardians** as the person with autism becomes a "legal" adult. Procedures and issues vary somewhat from state to state. There are different levels of guardianship—this may involve all kinds of decisions about the person, or it may be much more limited (e.g., to money-related issues). A person who is a guardian of property can make investments for the person. Depending on how the guardianship is done, this individual can make all decisions including living arrangements, medical treatments, and so forth. Typically, some—often very formal—legal proceeding is (rightfully) involved in this. Because laws vary from state to state, it is very important for parents to talk with a knowledgeable lawyer. Some of the issues involved are summarized on the next page.

GUARDIANSHIP

Definitions

A **guardian** has legal rights (fully or partially) to make decisions about housing, medical care, and so forth, for a person.

A **conservator** has special responsibilities for controlling finances for a person who is incapable, or only partially capable, of managing his or her own funds and property.

Terms and responsibilities can vary a bit from state to state. Often, the two positions are combined.

When Is a Guardian Needed?

If a person can't take care of his or her own needs, is in some degree of risk or danger, or has no one with responsibility for making decisions for them.

How Is a Guardian Appointed?

Procedures vary from state to state but usually involve someone (e.g., a parent) filing a petition with the probate court seeking guardianship. The petition will usually have some evidence (e.g., medical affidavits or other statements) that indicate the individual is incapable of independent decision making. The court may then appoint a temporary person (guardian ad litem) who makes an independent report to the court after meeting with all those involved. The court may also appoint a physician or psychologist to examine the person who is said to be in need of a guardian. A trial or court proceeding may be held with the person present being given the opportunity to have a lawyer. The judge makes a decision and, if a guardian is appointed, issues special legal documents indicating just what the guardian can and can't do.

Duties of the Guardian

These vary depending on need and the court's decision. They can range from minimal involvement to basically being involved in all decision making for the individual, for example, where he lives, who takes care of him, and so forth.

Court Review and Supervision

There is usually some provision made for periodic review, for example, to be sure the person still needs it.

Termination of Guardianship

Can be done by the court if it determines that the person no longer is in need. Various special provisions can be made, for example, for having co-guardians (who must then agree on decisions) or indicating how provision should be made if the original guardian dies.

Parents can list (nominate) guardians for children in their wills, so the process of guardianship (or at least its first consideration) can begin when the person is a child. There are advantages and disadvantages to guardianship arrangements. In some states, when a person has a legal guardian, he or she loses specific rights (e.g., to vote or marry). Laws vary from state to state, but in almost all cases the process of having a guardian for an adult is typically somewhat complicated. Unfortunately, sometimes the court proceedings involved are tedious or, in the worst case, even humiliating to the person who is getting a guardian. Accordingly, working with a knowledgeable lawyer is important.

Estate Planning

The range in outcome for children with ASDs poses challenges for parents (and lawyers). Parents are forced to grapple with difficult issues—some common to all parents doing estate planning and others very specific to individuals with ASDs. **Estate planning** should begin once anyone has a child—this should include provision for care and custody of any minor children and also guidance for disposition of life insurance, trusts, and so forth. The temptation to delay planning is enormous. Unfortunately, so are the risks of not planning. Several different sets of issues arise including provision for children, considerations for adolescents and adults, and complications involved in the potential need for the person to have help in adulthood (e.g., in administering money from life insurance). It is important for parents to realize that sometimes state agencies can collect funds designated to support individuals with disabilities as part of what is called *cost of care* liability. Accordingly, simply leaving money, property, or other assets to a child in a will may not be the best approach in estate planning. Even setting up a special trust account in the child's name may simply result in it going to the state if the child needs care as an adult.

Again, talking with a lawyer is critical. In some instances, it may be best to leave funds to siblings or other trusted family members or friends and specifically discuss with them parental desires for long-term support of the individual with an ASD. It is a bit confusing for parents, but, in fact, it is usually essential that this is voluntary on their part—that is, if parents superficially designate that the money is to go to support a child with an ASD, the state may be able to claim it. There is, of course, a major risk in that if the person to whom parents leave the money decides to spend it on something else, he or she can indeed do so.

Some states now have "special needs" trusts that allow the person (the trustee in charge of the trust) to use funds to benefit the designated person. As long as there is no specific legal requirement for the money to be spent for a special purpose on behalf of the individual, it may be relatively safe from being taken. However, other trusts that require funds to be used to support a person with a disability may indeed be subject to claims by the state. Talking with an attorney experienced in the laws of the particular state is clearly very, very important.

If the preceding information sounds a bit confusing, parents should, on the one hand, be reassured that it is and, on the other, realize that this means parents often need help from professionals in thinking about long-term planning for children with disabilities. Additional complications arise from the fact that laws can vary substantially across the various states and that while some programs are federal, it is often the state laws that will have to do with the intricacies of wills and other aspects of estate planning. The bottom line is that getting some professional help is important.

There is a natural tendency on the part of all of us to not think about long-term issues, particularly if they are unpleasant ones (like our not being around). It is important that parents fight against this natural tendency to put things off. Keep in mind that once parents have a will and or have begun the estate planning process, parents can always go back to change things, depending on the specifics of the situation. Also, parents should *not* assume things like "Jimmy will take care of Bobby when we no longer can"; instead, it is important to talk to siblings, family members, or other responsible parties. We've seen some tragic situations where a parent just assumed something would happen when they were no longer around but had not made appropriate arrangements. This can be particularly bad when parents haven't made a will. Part of estate planning means looking at retirement plans, life and disability insurance, and, at times, having discussions with the child's grandparents if they want to think about providing some resources in their will.

If parents don't make a will, it usually is the case that children receive equal shares of whatever the person owns when they die. This means that the child with autism could receive money or assets that could jeopardize eligibility for support from many important programs. It is a dreadful mistake for parents to die and not have a will.

Parents who have wills can take various steps to ensure the care of their children, including those with disabilities. Often, it is the case that parents will appear to "leave out" the child in the will just to avoid the problem of "cost-of-care liability." Even leaving money to a trust may pose some problems, as the trust may be factored into the cost-of-care liability. As a result, parents need to have a discussion with an experienced attorney who can work on this problem with them.

Similar issues arise with life insurance. If a sum of money goes to the person with autism on the parent's death, this may also jeopardize their eligibility for important programs. Accordingly, the disposition of life insurance or retirement plan benefits should be carefully thought out as part of the estate planning process. As we have emphasized, including other relevant people (e.g., family members such as siblings or grandparents) in the planning is important.

Even having a bank account in a child's name under the Uniform Transfers to Minors Act (UTMA) can cause trouble. Funds placed in the account become the child's as he or she reaches 21 years of age and at that point also become involved in cost-of-care calculations. This can be a special problem for a person who, at age 18, has qualified for SSI and Medicaid, but who 3 years later has access to assets that then disqualify him from these programs. The bottom line here is that it may not be a good idea to set up a bank account in the child's name.

LEGAL PROBLEMS FOR ADULTS

There is a small literature, mostly involving adults with Asperger's, who have trouble with the law. For lower functioning adults, "crimes" mostly relate to issues of behavioral meltdowns, for example, in response to sensory sensitivities, or unusual interests. In more able individuals, particularly those with Asperger's, the unusual interests can, at times, produce legal problems; for example, one young adult was so fascinated by animal life that he broke into a zoo. This literature mostly consists of case reports relating to a very small number of people. Sometimes the apparent legal problems represent a long-standing pattern of *over-*compliance, for example, the person who doesn't exercise good judgment and stops in the middle of a crosswalk when the light changes. Occasionally, the desire for friendship and social contact, combined with eccentric social overtures and overwordiness, lead to trouble, for example, the high school student who makes explicit sexual requests because he doesn't understand all the myriad steps involved in having an intimate relationship. Finally, in some cases, individuals can be "set up" by peers or others given the desire to please and lack of social sophistication and common sense. There are some case reports, mostly British, suggesting some potential for violence, although in our experience this is, in fact, rather rare. In general, our experience is that adults on the autism spectrum are more likely to be victims than to victimize others.

PSYCHIATRIC COMORBIDITIES IN ADULTS

As we have discussed, there does appear to be an increased risk for anxiety and mood problems (particularly depression) in late adolescence and early adulthood. It remains unclear how much this reflects a more basic (and potentially inherited) predisposition and how much comes from a lifelong pattern of social isolation and rejection. We talk about some of these issues and potential interventions in Chapters 14 and 15.

A small literature, consisting mostly of case reports, does suggest some increased vulnerability for either schizophrenia or bipolar disorder (what used to be called manic depression) in adulthood. However, one major problem is the tendency of many individuals to talk without self-censoring—a phenomenon that often appears to the outside observer to be suggestive of psychosis.

Marriage

Some individuals, particularly those who are high functioning, are able to marry and have families. This seems to be more common in Asperger's disorder than in autism, although even in autism this is observed (Szatmari, Bartolucci, Bremmer, Bond, & Rich, 1989). Family history studies also have sometimes revealed members of the family who had married but who also appeared to have problems on the autism spectrum. Several accounts of these experiences are now available and listed in the reading list; in addition, books outlining specific support and coping strategies for couples are now available.

CASE REPORTS

Case 1: Timothy

Timothy, or as he preferred to be called, Tim, was a 15-year-old boy who was seen for evaluation at the request of his parents, who were divorced. Tim was attending a private school and enrolled in advanced academic classes but had very few friends and poor social skills. He lived 50% of the time with each parent. One of his teachers had attended a workshop on Asperger's syndrome given by one of the authors and then talked to Tim's parents and suggested an evaluation. His parents significantly disagreed about the necessity of this; his father insisted that Tim was bright and gifted, and his mother insisted that he was far behind his peers socially— both were correct.

History   Tim was an only child born to two very successful parents. His father was an engineer and his mother a scientist at a major university. Tim was talking by about 9 months and walking by a year. He was speaking in full sentences by 14 months, and both parents regarded him as precocious. They did report that he had some problems with both gross and fine motor coordination but weren't at all concerned until he attended a prekindergarten program at age 4, where he was noted to have some problems with attention and getting along with peers. He also had a strong interest in astronomy and space travel that verged on being abnormal only because he was so fixated on the topic. His parents moved him to a very different and much more academic preschool program, where he did well although continuing to be somewhat isolated from his peers. His parents both mentioned, independently, that he was more interested in astronomy and space than in having friends. He had a very strong vocabulary. He subsequently was enrolled in a rigorous private academic program. Although he had occasional behavioral difficulties, he did very well academically. For the first time in primary school, he was able to make a few friends with other boys who were usually described by their peers as "geeks." These friendships usually were not close ones, however.

His difficulties with some aspects of organization and rigidity combined with his tendency to talk a lot and be clumsy led to a series of medical evaluations. A pediatric neurologist thought he might have attention deficit hyperactivity disorder (ADHD) and gave a trial of stimulant medications, which did not seem to particularly help Tim. Other medicines tried over the years had focused on anxiety, attentional difficulties, or thinking problems and included trials of several selective serotonin reuptake inhibitors (SSRIs) and one trial of a major tranquilizer (see Chapter 15). Although his parents disagreed somewhat over how well these worked, they did feel that one of the SSRIs, given for a presumptive diagnosis of obsessive-compulsive disorder, had been the most helpful. In the early school grades, Tim received some occupational therapy privately because of his handwriting and fine motor difficulties. Interestingly, despite his large vocabulary, he also had received some speech therapy because of problems in having conversations. Both treatments had stopped before third grade.

At the time of our assessment, his parents had been divorced for about a year. As noted, Tim spent half time with each parent, who lived reasonably close to each other. There was some, but minimal, friction between them. Tim had seemed to tolerate the divorce reasonably well, being primarily concerned with the new custody arrangement.

Over the years, Tim had experienced some behavior difficulties in school. In the fourth grade he hit a teacher and was put on probation. The details of this incident were somewhat murky but apparently involved a dispute over one of Tim's routines. Psychological testing in the fourth grade showed a 30-point discrepancy between his verbal and nonverbal IQ, favoring the verbal. Academic achievement was consistently well above age level.

Starting in the sixth grade, he switched to a new private school that he could remain in throughout high school. He developed some other special interests and achieved some prominence for his science abilities. He almost never was able to participate fully in sports or gym programs, and his schools had allowed him to skip gym to focus on his special interests. He had been enrolled in a martial arts program, where his father was proud to report he had advanced to a high level.

At the time of our assessment, Tim had returned from a summer spent at a special science camp at a major American university. He was now in the high school program (ninth grade) at his school and was doing well in many areas but struggled with English in particular. Even in his favorite classes (advanced chemistry and math), he had some troubles with organization and particularly with tests—most particularly if these were "pop" quizzes. He had some friends at school, but these were not children he spent any time with outside school. His social life mostly revolved around his special interests and his interest in chess and some computer games. He had met a number of people online, but his mother, in particular, was concerned because he didn't seem to have great judgment and was easily swayed by these acquaintances.

As noted, there had been some ongoing tension between the parents about Tim's problems. His mother reported that an older half-sibling by the father's previous marriage had similar problems. She also suggested that the father himself was socially isolated. It was clear that both parents wanted the best for Tim and were very supportive, although they differed dramatically in how they viewed Tim and his problems.

Assessment Results   During our assessment, Tim was a very likable boy who was hardworking and eager to please. He had more trouble with some activities than others and, when he had trouble, tended to become first anxious and then defensive about his difficulties. He was very talkative and adopted a somewhat professorial style, sometimes seeming to lecture the various staff members. He was verbose; for example, in response to the question "Who was Christopher Columbus?," he set off on a long disquisition about who had actually discovered America, veered off onto a discussion of the role of the Spanish Inquisition, and came back to the exploits of other famous explorers. He often tried to talk himself through problems. Although very verbose, he sometimes caused himself trouble by not listening to all of the directions for a task and jumping ahead.

On the Wechsler Intelligence Scale for Children, 3rd edition (see Chapter 3), his verbal IQ was 127, while his nonverbal IQ was 89—a significant discrepancy. This particular test provided several index scores to examine specific cognitive function. On the verbal comprehension index, his score was 127, perceptual organization was 94, freedom from distractibility was 131, and processing speed was 72. If one were to assign percentile scores to these results, they ranged from the 3rd to the 98th percentile. He had trouble with tasks that involved some measure of social judgment and visual–motor coordination. On an additional test of visual motor integration, his standard score was 89.

During the speech–communication assessment, Tim was noted to have a highly superior receptive and expressive vocabulary (both about the 95th percentile). On a test that tapped more into his communicative competence, his scores were more varied. Tim had major difficulties using language to make inferences (25th percentile), reflecting significant problems in putting together information to interpret the intent of others in basic social situations. His speech was somewhat monotonic and tended to be at a high volume most of the time. He had trouble with the social aspects of a conversation, for example, in allowing his conversational partner to shift the topic. He had particular difficulties in use of eye contact and responding to gestures and tone of voice. His own use of gaze was unusual—he tended either to stare fixedly or to avoid eye contact.

During his time with the psychiatrist, Tim was noted to have a rather eccentric and one-sided social style. He enjoyed interaction but frequently commented on how he did much better with adults than other children his age. He tended to talk for long periods without giving his conversational partner a chance to talk. He did not seem to notice when, at one point, the psychiatrist got out a newspaper and held it up and started reading while Tim was engaged in a monologue about problems in the Mars Lander space program. Tim did not exhibit unusual mannerisms but was noted to be rather slow and deliberate in his movements. He had some feeling of being "left out" by other students in terms of school life, but then proceeded to minimize this. He denied feelings of depression but did indicate that he could get very anxious if unexpected things happened, particularly if there was a time pressure aspect.

Both parents were interviewed, separately, to complete the Vineland Adaptive Behavior Scales. Interestingly, although they both had their own perspectives on Tim, they gave rather similar reports of what he was capable of doing independently on the Vineland. Tim's age-equivalent scores on the Vineland are summarized in Figure 9.3. As can be seen, his expressive and written language skills are areas of strength for him. Receptive language and interpersonal skills were

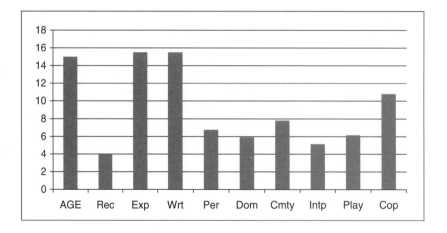

FIGURE 9.3 **Vineland Adaptive Behavior Scores**

Age—chronological age (15 years), then Vineland Adaptive Behavior Age Equivalent Scores for Receptive, Expressive, and Written (communication areas); Personal, Domestic, and Community (daily living skills areas); and interpersonal, play–leisure time, and coping (socialization areas).

very significantly delayed (around the 5-year level), while daily living skills were, on average, around the 8-year level. Fine motor skills were also delayed (below the 4-year level).

In talking to his parents and to Tim about the results, we first emphasized how impressed we were by his work with us and his clearly strong motivation to do well. We also emphasized that no single number did justice to his overall ability, which clearly ranged dramatically from quite impaired to quite advanced. When we talked with his parents, his father voiced the notion that both parents were correct—that is, that the mother's perception of his significant social delay was correct, and so was the father's impression of high verbal abilities. In talking about the diagnosis, first with the parents, and then with Tim, we agreed that the Asperger's label most effectively described his history and current difficulties. We also talked about the nonverbal learning disabilities profile (see page 12) as a way of thinking about his unusual pattern of strengths and weaknesses.

We made a number of recommendations for intervention within and outside of school. Tim's significant issues with processing speed, anxiety with time pressure, and visual–motor problems justified giving him extra time for tests and making special provisions to deal with the problem of pop quizzes. We also discussed how some of his problems with social awareness and judgment were translating not only into his interactions with peers but also into some of his academic problems (e.g., with his English class). We suggested specific work with a speech–language pathologist to focus on both communication and explicit teaching of social skills. Services of an experienced mental health individual were suggested for dealing with anxiety and monitoring medication. Recommended teaching strategies included use of a systematic, step-by-step verbal approach in dealing with new materials, with concrete verbal and visual cues and clear expectations and a focus on generalization. Explicit work on organization and effective communication was also suggested, and several computer resources were provided. A major portion of our report focused on approaches to teaching social skills, cultivating social awareness, understanding social cues, and teaching specific verbal problem-solving strategies.

Interestingly, Tim was, if anything, relieved to have a clear picture of his own strengths and weaknesses. He researched the issue of Asperger's syndrome quite diligently and found it helpful to have a single term that helped account for some of his problems. Although he has continued to have some significant social and learning issues, he has gone on to be successful in a major college, where he is completing his junior year. He intends to go to graduate school and is living apart from his parents. He has developed some real friendships and, for the first time, has a girlfriend.

Case 2: Jane

This 28-year-old woman had recently been deinstituionalized from a residential setting where she had been placed as a school-aged child. She had a long history of autism and significant intellectual disability. Her parents had placed her in this large state program and had some, but only sporadic, contact with her over the years. As the state institution was closing, staff began to look for possible placements for Jane.

Jane was somewhat verbal and often echoed language. She was an attractive woman whose disability was not immediately obvious. In addition, she had one isolated skill—she was very good at reading. She did not, unfortunately, understand much of what she read but she did read compulsively.

In her previous residential placement, Jane spent much time in her room reading or engaged in body rocking. She did go out every day to work at the cafeteria for two hours and had a well-established routine. She was well known at the institution and had very few behavior problems.

A relatively new group home became interested in having Jane join their facility. Jane's parents (who had been opposed to moving her in the first place but now had no choice since the state institution was closing) visited and liked it. Jane had a single visit and seemed to do well. The group home staff were impressed by her ability to read. They also were impressed by her long record of regular work and were eager to find her a job in the community. They had not previously had much experience with individuals with autism but were eager to have her join them.

Within 1 week of Jane's move, she was having severe behavior problems. She had been taken to look for a job as a bagger in a grocery store but had had a melt-down there. At the group home, attempts to interrupt her reading or to take her on community outings were met with resistance. Staff provided her with written materials, including a schedule and plans for the day, but this seemed minimally helpful. Jane's behavior difficulties led her to break several items in the home, and she began to slap herself compulsively. Her parents and the group home staff were worried and contacted her (new) doctor, an internist, who was surprised she wouldn't let him examine her. The group home rightfully felt that the situation was going downhill rapidly and sought a consultation from one of us.

In looking at Jane and her history and recent events, it was possible to make a number of recommendations. In the first place, we suggested that either the staff needed urgent training about dealing with behavior problems in a person with autism or they seek a group home with more experience in the area. Second, we pointed out that although Jane seemed to read, her understanding of what she was reading was pretty minimal and hence couldn't really be used to organize her. Instead, we suggested a number of visual aids and other strategies, including a large bulletin board in her room that displayed the week in pictures. This made it possible for staff to review with Jane what would be coming next, what she had done before, and so forth. Rather than engage in so many new things at once, we suggested that an initial step might be for Jane to have jobs around the house and then be given periods of time where she could be allowed to be on her own (with some supervision and observation, of course). Given that she had a number of bruises from self-injury, we also suggested a trial of medication once she had been seen by a local pediatrician who was experienced in examining individuals with autism (and indeed her physical exam was fine). The medication produced a fairly rapid and dramatic decrease in the problem behavior, although it was coupled with a number of other recommended changes (ideally, one would like to change only one thing at a time, but this was an emergency). Rather than force Jane into community outings in a range of settings, we suggested work with a consultant who could think about vocational and community issues. This individual realized that Jane had considerable sensitivity to noises and that outdoor activities worked well for her. Eventually, things stabilized for Jane in her new placement. She now works outdoors in a supported employment situation in a local park. She is variably involved in community activities with other residents of the group home but has done better as she has adjusted to the new situation. Medications could be tapered and then stopped after some months. Although Jane remains relatively impaired, she has had a much better quality of life with minimal behavioral difficulties. She continues to read avidly, although her understanding of what she reads remains relatively limited. However, she has taken to the use of visual prompts and schedules, and levels of daily living skills have improved significantly.

Jane's history points out the pitfalls of rapid and poorly considered moves and the importance of supports appropriate to individuals with autism. Although her original placement (in a state-run residential facility) was unfortunate in many respects, it had been something she was familiar with and had mastered. Her new group home's enthusiasm should have been a bit tempered by the lack of experience in dealing with individuals with autism. In some respects, the crisis created by her transition has, in the end, been a productive one.

Case 3: Ned

Ned is a 30-year-old who has achieved a large degree of independence without being totally independent of his family. He is a man who had a fairly classic history of autism. His parents noted troubles early on but were told to "wait and see." They started getting services only after he was nearly 5. Ned did start to talk just before his fifth birthday. Although his parents were initially given very pessimistic projections for the future, they refused to give up on him. He was enrolled in school and received many special services. In addition to the benefit of having concerned parents (and a large extended family with several brothers and sisters), Ned benefited from a great deal of community involvement. This came from his family's church and their prominence in the community, as they had, for two generations, operated a local restaurant.

Ned made important, if somewhat slow, progress in elementary school. IQ testing revealed nonverbal abilities in the average range, but verbal skills were close to the intellectually deficient range. Fortunately, with many siblings and an involved family, Ned was included in a myriad of activities and was comfortable with new situations and people as well as being out in the community. His daily living and adaptive skills were particularly a source of strength for him.

In adolescence, Ned developed an awareness and concern about being "different" from other children. Fortunately for him, rather than becoming depressed, Ned used this motivation to work very, very hard to be like other children. He was able to be more or less totally included in high school with some special supports.

In the middle of high school, he and his parents started the process of transition planning. Unlike his siblings (all of whom went to college), Ned strongly indicated his preference to enter the family business. He loved the routines of the restaurant and particularly liked to cook. Accordingly, he was switched to a vocational school where the emphasis was on real-life skills and, for Ned, on learning to cook (he also enjoyed being one of the few boys in the cooking classes). On completing high school, his parents tried to enroll him in a local community college, but it quickly became clear that Ned very much wanted to work in the restaurant, so this was arranged.

Ned started at a fairly low level, doing dishes and food preparation. As time went on, he began to be a more independent employee and developed some special areas of expertise. As a cook, he was meticulous and very consistent (both real pluses when it comes to restaurant work). Although he had some trouble with math, once he had learned a recipe, he was readily able to repeat it without change. He also enjoyed the camaraderie of the kitchen staff, and the fact that his father was around much of the time was also a plus.

Once he was settled into his job at the restaurant, Ned decided he should live apart from his parents. He found a garage apartment about five blocks from his family home. Although he had some challenges initially in terms of organization, he quickly became a good tenant and enjoyed being somewhat independent from his parents. In his mid-20s, he became aware of feeling more dependent on his father, who usually drove him to work. Ned saved money for a car and, more importantly, his parents found a driving instructor able to work with a special needs student. Ned was rightly proud of obtaining his driver's license and having his own car (at age 25). He was careful not to drive on freeways or in places where there was a lot of traffic.

In addition to his nearby parents, Ned has several siblings in relatively close proximity. He can walk to his church and attends mass on a regular basis and is active in a children's program. He is well known and accepted in his community. He has occasional difficulties in response to change but generally has made a very good accommodation to adulthood.

At the time of this writing, Ned has just purchased a condominium closer to the family business. His parents have been pleased to have him as an employee. He is the only child in the family to have gone into the restaurant business. They have made arrangements that his siblings and he will inherit the family business and have discussed, in detail, their wishes for his siblings to remain involved in Ned's life in the future.

The delay in diagnosis in Ned's case was unfortunate. However, he had the good fortune to have a committed and involved family and community. He also developed, as sometimes happens in adolescence, a strong motivation for learning new skills and "fitting in." For most purposes, Ned is now an independent adult. He has occasional times of relying on his parents for help or support. He has become an active member of his community and can take pleasure in his success.

Summary

Children with autism and related conditions grow up to become adolescents and adults. We want them to live as full and independent lives as they possibly can. As with other children, adolescence can bring changes and be a time of growth for some and challenge for others. Helping adolescents and young adults with ASDs cope with sexual feelings is important. Teaching about privacy, intimacy, social norms, and different kinds of relationships should start in childhood.

Fortunately, the overall outcome in autism appears to be significantly improving. This probably represents the combination of several factors: better (and earlier) diagnosis, early and more appropriate intervention, and (possibly) expanded definitions of autism. A number of adult vocational options, ranging from college to supported employment, are available, and more and more are living independently. Even when adults aren't fully independent, they can live rewarding and fulfilling lives.

It is important for parents to be aware of the changes in entitlements that come with age, particularly in the transition from school age (basically under 21), where education is a right, to older ages, where entitlements to services can vary dramatically from state to state and where, for many problems, the applicable set of laws relates to the mandate not to discriminate based on disability. In college, technical, vocational, and other programs, it is essential that the program be informed—usually by the student—of any special needs related to disability.

For more and more adults, independent living is now possible, and many individuals, particularly the most cognitively able, are involved in family life—sometimes having long-term relationships and families of their own. Even when this is not possible, the goal should be as much independence and self-sufficiency as possible. Planning for adulthood starts *many* years in advance. In addition to cognitive and language abilities, self-care skills (see Chapter 6) are critical. For many adults, there is a significant gap between overall cognitive ability and capacities for adult independence and self-sufficiency.

READING LIST

Aston, M. C. (2003). *Aspergers in love: Couple relationships and family affairs.* London: Jessica Kingsley.

Aston, M. C. (2009). *The Asperger couple's workbook: Practical advice and activities for couples and counsellors.* London: Jessica Kingsley.

Attwood, S. (2008). *Making sense of sex: A forthright guide to puberty, sex and relationships for people with Asperger's syndrome.* London: Jessica Kingsley.

Attwood, T. (2004). *Exploring feelings: Cognitive behavior therapy to manage anxiety.* Arlington, TX: Future Horizons.

Baker, J. (2006a). *Preparing for life: The complete guide for transitioning to adulthood for those with autism and Asperger's syndrome.* Arlington, TX: Future Horizons.

Baker, J. (2006b). *Social skills picture book for high school and beyond.* Arlington, TX: Future Horizons.

Baker, J. (2003). *Social skills training for children and adolescents with Asperger syndrome and social–communications problems.* Shawnee Mission, KS: Autism Asperger.

Bashe, P. R., Kirby, B. L., Baron-Cohen, S., & Attwood, T. (2005). *The OASIS guide to Asperger syndrome: Completely revised and updated: Advice, support, insight, and inspiration.* New York: Crown.

Bellini, S. (2006). *Building social relationships: A systematic approach to teaching social interaction skills to children and adolescents with autism spectrum disorders and other social difficulties.* Shawnee Mission, KS: Autism Asperger.

Bentley, K., & Attwood, T. (2007). *Alone together: Making an Asperger marriage work.* London: Jessica Kingsley.

Bolick, T. (2001). *Asperger syndrome and adolescence: Helping preteens and teens get ready for the real world.* Gloucester, MA: Fair Winds Press.

Boushey, A. (2007). *Talking teenagers: Information and inspiration for parents of teenagers with autism or Asperger's syndrome.* London: Jessica Kingsley.

Buron, K. D. (2007). *A 5 is against the law! Social boundaries: Straight up! An honest guide for teens and young adults.* Shawnee Mission, KS: Autism Asperger.

Coulter, D. (Producer/Director). (2001). *Asperger syndrome: Transition to college and work* [DVD]. Winston-Salem, NC: Coulter Video.

Coulter, D. (Producer/Director). (2006). *Intricate minds: Understanding classmates with Asperger syndrome* [DVD]. Winston-Salem, NC: Coulter Video.

Coyne, P., Nyberg, C. & Vandenburg, M. L. (1999). *Developing leisure time skills for persons with autism: A practical approach for home, school and community.* Arlington, TX: Future Horizons.

Debbaudt, D. (2002). *Autism, advocates, and law enforcement professionals: Recognizing and reducing risk situations for people with autism spectrum disorders.* London: Jessica Kingsley.

Duncan, M., & Myles, B. S. (2008). *The hidden curriculum 2009 one-a-day calendar: Items for understanding unstated rules in social situations.* Shawnee Mission, KS: Autism Asperger.

Edmonds, G., & Beardon, L. (2008). *Asperger syndrome and social relationships: Adults speak out about Asperger syndrome.* London: Jessica Kingsley.

Edwards, D. (2008). *Providing practical support for people with autism spectrum disorders: Supported living in the community.* London: Jessica Kingsley.

Fegan, L., Rauch, A., & McCarthy, W. (1993). *Sexuality and people with intellectual disability* (2nd ed.). Baltimore: Brookes.

Fein, D., & Dunn, M. (2007). *Autism in your classroom: A general educator's guide to students with autism spectrum disorders.* Bethesda, MD: Woodbine House.

Fullerton, A., Stratton, J., Coyne, P., & Gray, C. (1996). *Higher functioning adolescents and young adults with autism: A teacher's guide.* Austin, TX: Pro-Ed.

Gaus, V.O. (2007). *Cognitive–behavioral therapy for adult Asperger syndrome.* New York: Guilford Press.

Getzel, E. E., & Wehman, P. (Eds.). (2005). *Going to college.* Baltimore: Brookes.

Ghaziuddin, M. (2005). *Mental health aspects of autism and Asperger's syndrome.* London: Jessica Kingsley.

Goldstein, A. P., McGinnis, E. (1997). *Skillstreaming the adolescent: Student manual.* Champaign, IL: Research Press.

Graham, J. (2008). *Autism, discrimination and the law: A quick guide for parents, educators and employers.* London: Jessica Kingsley.

Grandin, T. (2008). *The way I see it: A personal look at autism and Asperger's.* Arlington, TX: Future Horizons.

Grandin, T., & Duffy, J. (2004) *Developing talents: Careers for individuals with Asperger syndrome and high functioning autism.* Shawnee Mission, KS: Autism Asperger.

Gutstein, S. E. (2001). *Autism Asperger's: Solving the relationship puzzle: A new developmental program that opens the door to lifelong social and emotional growth.* Arlington, TX: Future Horizons.

Harpur, J., Lawlor, M., & Fitzgerald, M. (2004). *Succeeding in college with Asperger syndrome.* London: Jessica Kingsley.

Harpur, J. Lawlor, M. & Fitzgerald, M. (2006). *Succeeding with interventions for Asperger syndrome adolescents: A guide to communication and socialization in interaction therapy.* London: Jessica Kingsley.

Henault, I., & Attwood, T. (2005). *Asperger's syndrome and sexuality: From adolescence through adulthood.* London: Jessica Kingsley.

Hingsburger, D. (1995). *Just say know! Understanding and reducing the risk of sexual victimization of people with developmental disabilities.* Quebec: Diverse City Press.

Hollins, S., & Downer, J. (2000). *Keeping healthy down below.* London: Gaskell and St. George's Hospital Medical School.

Hollins, S., & Perez, W. (2000). *Looking after my breasts.* London: Gaskell and St. George's Hospital Medical School.

Hollins, S., & Roth, T. (1994). *Hug me, touch me.* London: St. George's Mental Health Library.

Howlin, P. (2004). *Autism and Asperger syndrome: Preparing for adulthood* (2nd ed.). London: Routledge.

Howlin, P. (2005). Outcome in autism spectrum disorders. In F. Volkmar, R. Paul, A. Klin, & D. Cohen (Eds.), *Handbook of Autism and Pervasive Developmental Disorders* (pp. 201–222). Hoboken, NJ: John Wiley.

Hoyt, P. R., & Pollock, C. M. (2003). *Special people, special planning.* Orlando, FL: Legacy Planning Partners.

Hudson, J., & Myles, B. S. (2007). *Starting points: The basics of understanding and supporting children and youth with Asperger syndrome.* Shawnee Mission, KS: Autism Asperger.

Jackson, L., & Attwood, T. (2002). *Freaks, geeks and Asperger syndrome: A user guide to adolescence.* London: Jessica Kingsley.

Jackson, L., & Willey, L. H. (2003). *Asperger syndrome in adolescence: Living with the ups, the downs and things in between.* London: Jessica Kingsley.

Keel, G. H., Mesibov, G. M., & Woods, A. B. (1997). TEACCH supported employment program. *Journal of Autism and Developmental Disorders, 27*(1), 3–9.

Koegel, L. K., & LaZebnik, C. (2009). *Growing up on the spectrum.* New York: Penguin Books.

Korin, E. S. H. (2007). *Asperger syndrome: An owner's manual 2 for older adolescents and adults: What your parents and friends, and your employer need to know.* Shawnee Mission, KS: Autism Asperger.

Korpi, M. (2007). *Guiding your teenager with special needs through transition from school to adult life: Tools for parents.* London: Jessica Kingsley.

Lovett, J. P. (2005) *Solutions for adults with Asperger syndrome.* Beverly, MA: Fair Winds Press.

McAfee, J., & Attwood, T. (2001). *Navigating the social world: A curriculum for individuals with Asperger's syndrome, high functioning autism and related disorders.* Arlington, TX: Future Horizons.

Meyer, R. N., & Attwood, T. (2001). *Asperger syndrome employment workbook: An employment workbook for adults with Asperger syndrome.* London: Jessica Kingsley.

Morgan, H. (1996). *Adults with autism: A guide to theory and practice.* New York: Cambridge University Press.

Murray, D. (2005). *Coming out Asperger: Diagnosis, disclosure and self-confidence.* London: Jessica Kingsley.

Myles, B. S., & Adreon, D. (2001). *Asperger syndrome and adolescence: Practical solutions for school success.* Shawnee Mission, KS: Autism Asperger.

Myles, B. S., Trautman, M. L. & Schelvan, R. L. (2004). *The hidden curriculum: Practical solutions for understanding unstated rules in social situations.* Shawnee Mission, KS: Autism Asperger.

Nadeau, K. G. (1994). *Survival guide for college students with ADD or LD.* Washington, DC: Magination Press.

Nadworny, J. J., & Haddad, C. R. (2007). *The special needs planning guide.* Baltimore: Brookes.

Newport, J., & Newport, M. (2002). *Autism-Asperger's and sexuality: Puberty and beyond.* Arlington, TX: Future Horizons.

Palmer, A. (2005). *Realizing the college dream with autism or Asperger syndrome: A parent's guide to student success.* London: Jessica Kingsley.

Patrick, N. J. (2008). *Social skills for teenagers and adults with Asperger syndrome: A practical guide to day-to-day life.* London: Jessica Kingsley.

Perry, N. (2009). *Adults on the autism spectrum leave the nest: Achieving supported independence.* London: Jessica Kingsley.

Plass, B. (2008). *Functional routines for adolescents & adults—community.* East Moline, IL: LinguiSystems.

Plass, B. (2008). *Functional routines for adolescents & adults—home.* East Moline, IL: LinguiSystems.

Plass, B. (2008). *Functional routines for adolescents & adults—leisure & recreation.* East Moline, IL: LinguiSystems.

Plass, B. (2008). *Functional routines for adolescents & adults—work.* East Moline, IL: LinguiSystems.

Robison, J. E. (2007). *Look me in the eye: My life with Asperger's.* New York: Three Rivers Press.

Rodman, K. E., & Attwood, T. (2003). *Asperger's syndrome and adults . . . is anyone listening? Essays and poems by partners, parents and family members.* London: Jessica Kingsley.

Rutter, M. (2005). Genetic influences and autism. In F. Volkmar, R. Paul, A. Klin, & D. Cohen (Eds.), *Handbook of autism and pervasive developmental disorders* (3rd ed., pp. 425–452). Hoboken, NJ: Wiley.

Sabin, E. (2006). *The autism acceptance book: Being a friend to someone with autism* (spiral-bound). New York: Watering Can Press.

Santomauro, J., & Santomauro, D. (2007). *Asperger download: A guide to help teenage males with Asperger syndrome trouble-shoot life's challenges.* Shawnee Mission, KS: Autism Asperger.

Schopler, E., & Mesibov, G. (1983). *Autism in adolescents and adults.* New York: Plenum Press.

Schwier, K. M., & Hingsburger, D. (2000). *Sexuality: Parentsr sons and daughters with intellectual isabilities.* Baltimore: Brookes.

Shore, S. (2003). *Beyond the wall: Personal experience with autism and Asperger syndrome* (2nd ed.). Shawnee Mission, KS: Autism Asperger.

Sicile-Kira, C. (2006). *Adolescents on the autism spectrum: A parent's guide to the cognitive, social, physical, and transition needs of teenagers with autism spectrum disorders.* New York: Penguin.

Silverman, S., & Weinfeld, R. (2007). *School success for kids with Asperger's syndrome: A practical guide for parents and teachers.* Waco, TX: Prufrock Press.

Smith, M. D., Belcher, R. G., & Juhrs, P. D. (1995). *A guide to successful employment for individuals with autism.* Baltimore: Brookes.

Sohn, A., & Grayson, C. (2005). *Parenting your Asperger child: Individualized solutions for teaching parentsr child practical skills.* New York: Perigee Trade.

Stanford, A. (2002). *Asperger syndrome and long-term relationships.* London: Jessica Kingsley.

Stevens, B. (2002). *The ABC's of special needs planning made easy.* Phoenix, AZ: Stevens Group.

Szatmari, P., Bartolucci, G., Bremmer, R., Bond, S., & Rich, S. (1989). A follow-up study of high-functioning autistic children. *Journal of Autism and Developmental Disorders, 19*(2), 213–225.

Taymans, J. M., & West, L. L. (2000). *Unlocking potential: College and other choices for people with LD and AD/HD.* Bethesda, MD: Woodbine House.

Vermeulen, P. (2000). *I am special: Introducing young people to their autistic spectrum disorder.* London: Jessica Kingsley.

Wall, K. (2007). *Education and care for adolescents and adults with autism: A guide for professionals and carers.* Los Angeles: Sage.

Wehman, P., Smith, M. D., & Schall, C. (2008). *Autism & the transition to adulthood: Success beyond the classroom.* Baltimore: Brookes.

Willey, L. (1999). *Pretending to be normal: Living with Asperger's syndrome.* London: Jessica Kingsley.

Winter, M. (2003). *Asperger syndrome: What teachers need to know: Written for Cloud 9 Children's Foundation*. Philadelphia: Jessica Kingsley.

Wolf, L. E., Brown, J. T., & Bork, G. R. K. (2009). *Students with Aspeger Syndrome: A guide for college personnel*. Shawnee Mission, KS: Autism Asperger.

Wrobel, M. (2003). *Taking care of myself: A hygiene, puberty and personal curriculum for young people with autism*. Arlington, TX: Future Horizons.

■ WEB SITES

Videos and materials available from James Stanfield Company (P.O. Box 41058, Santa Barbara, CA 93140; 800-421-6534/www.stansfield.com):

Circles 1: Intimacy & relationships (social boundaries)
Circles 2: Stop abuse (recognize and avoid sexual abuse)
Circles 3: Safer ways (avoiding sexually transmitted diseases)
    No-Go-Tell The Gyn Exam

■ QUESTIONS AND ANSWERS

1. **My daughter is supposed to have her first gynecological exam soon. Do we need to schedule this for the hospital where she can have anesthesia?**

    As for other developing young women, at some point the pediatrician or family doctor of an adolescent or young adult with an ASD may recommend that parents consult with a gynecologist. This may be routine—as the teenager approaches adulthood and needs regular care—or it may be because there is some problem. Parents should not assume that the adolescent or young adult with an ASD will absolutely have to have anesthesia. Probably, it would be best to make an appointment for an initial visit with the gynecologist to let the adolescent or young adult with an ASD meet the doctor and have a discussion about what approach makes the most sense. When parents schedule the visit, parents should be clear about the adolescent's or young adult's having special needs so that a longer time can be given if it is needed. Often, mothers may decide to have their daughter use their own gynecologist, in which case parents can discuss this issue with the doctor at their own checkup. See the reading list for some resources (including picture books) that may help in preparation for the visit to the gynecologist.

2. **Our 14-year-old has made some nice gains in his cognitive and communication skills, but has a lot of trouble with self-care. His father still needs to get him into the shower. Is there some way we can work on his self-care skills?**

    Absolutely. Parents might want to talk with the school psychologist to get an assessment of current levels of self-care (adaptive) skills.

There are several very good tests that can be used to do this, and, in conjunction with any cognitive or IQ testing already done, the psychologist may be able to generate for parents a list of reasonable goals. The issue here is to pitch things at the right level for the adolescent or young adult with an ASD, keeping in mind that it is better to start a little slower and with things that are easier, and then build on success as parents move along. An experienced teacher or person who works with developmentally disabled children may also be helpful. Sometimes it works well to have someone other than the parents involved. For example, one young man we know had pretty bad self-care skills but was really interested in fitting in at school. He took up swimming with the supervision of a college student who was able, fairly quickly, to get him up to speed! This activity helped him learn about getting dressed and undressed, as well as showering before and after swimming—one of the "rules of the pool."

3. **Our 15-year-old has autism but is very high functioning. He is now mainstreamed for all classes and doesn't get special help in school. We are planning on moving to a new district. Can we just assume that this district will automatically have to give him services?**

    An excellent question. Even though autism is included in the legislation that mandates services, having a diagnosis does not, necessarily, confer eligibility for services. This needs to be established, and sometimes the school can oppose it.

4. **My 18-year-old with Asperger's has a girlfriend for the first time. Are there any good resources I can steer him toward?**

    There are several good books in the reading list, including the book by Aston and the book by Edmonds and Beardon on relationships of adults with Asperger's. The book by Duncan and Myles (2008) is also excellent for teaching rules about social situations. There are also some good resources on Asperger's and sexuality; for example, see Henault and Atwood (2005).

5. **My adult son with autism is interested in getting a job. He is a good worker and very high functioning, although I think he misses a lot of social cues. Are there any good books about employment?**

    There are several excellent books about employment of adults on the autism spectrum listed in the reading list. Meyer and Atwood (2001) have a book on employment of adults with Asperger's. Also see the book by Howlin (2004).

6. **Our daughter with autism is more than a little bit a "couch potato." Are there any ways to get her more active?**

   Yes, there are some good resources. See the book by Coyne and colleagues (1999) on leisure time and recreational activities.

7. **Our son with Asperger's really wants a job. Are there any good resources?**

   You didn't state your son's age. If he is still in school, you should try to use some of the school-based resources. If he is out of school, state agencies and state services may be helpful. There are several good books on helping more able individuals obtain employment; for example, the book by Meyer (2001) and the book by Smith and colleagues (1995) are good resources.

8. **Our 13-year-old has autism, and things were going pretty well until adolescence hit. He has had a lot more difficulty with attention and impulsive behavior. Our pediatrician tried stimulant medicines, but these seemed to make things worse. What else can we try?**

   There are a number of different medications—depending on the specifics of the situation of the adolescent or young adult with an ASD — that could be tried. Alternatives to stimulants include some new medications that work differently for attentional problems; sometimes medicines like the SSRIs are used. You should talk with your doctor about all these options. (See Chapter 15 for more information about medications.)

9. **Our daughter wants to go away to college. She has been able to make it through high school and does well academically; it is the social and independent living issues we are concerned about. What steps can we take in selecting a college or post–high school program?**

   College is a major decision for everyone, and parents of all children need to be involved in the process. More and more children on the autism spectrum are going to college; this is great but presents some challenges for the person, family, and college. First, do your homework, and then go and visit some colleges that seem to be good fits for your daughter and her interests and needs. Keep in mind a couple of things: A smaller program may be better, although some larger state schools have good support programs. Your daughter needs to identify herself as having special needs if she wants any special provision made for her in college (e.g., relative to tests, help with notes, etc.). As we talked about in this chapter, it is important to remember that the laws relating to colleges are different than those mandating public school education. Also see the reading list for some good books on college programs. Finally, keep in mind that there are now a number of transitional programs around the country (there is a list at the Yale Child Study Center web site, http://childstudycenter.yale.edu). These vary in terms of what they provide. For some students, junior college and living at home can also be a good option.

10. **Our son turns 18 in a few months. He is already a client of the state department of developmental disabilities. Does this mean we automatically are his legal guardians?**

    Not at all is the short answer. It is very important to realize that becoming an adult, under the law, is generally an automatic thing. There are no automatic exceptions for disabilities. You should speak with a lawyer now about the steps you need to take to become a legal guardian.

CHAPTER 10

Managing Medical Issues and Problems

Fortunately, having an autism spectrum disorder (ASD) and being healthy are not mutually exclusive. Although there are some medical problems that are more common in ASD, most children with autism are born with the same potential to live healthy lives as anyone else. However, the communication and behavior challenges that go along with autism can make it harder to detect, treat, and manage problems that might affect health. In this chapter, we discuss some of the issues involved in providing quality health care to individuals on the autism spectrum.

CHALLENGES IN PROVIDING HEALTH CARE FOR CHILDREN WITH AUTISM

Not surprisingly, two of the major problems in autism—difficulties with communication and social skills—can pose major challenges for health care. For the child (or adult) with limited verbal abilities, an acute disease may actually present itself in very different ways. These may include changes in behavior such as irritability, decreased appetite or refusal to eat, acute weight loss, or behavioral changes such as head banging or self-injury. Sometimes it seems like the opposite occurs because the child seems to be doing better! In addition to the problems in communication and relating, other problems may come because the child does not like to be touched or won't cooperate when being examined. Even going to the doctor's office can be a major chore! While most parents occasionally have trouble getting their younger children to cooperate with routine medical procedures such as examination of the ears or mouth, even the most minor procedures pose potentially major problems for the parents of a child with autism or other pervasive developmental disorder (PDD). Just sitting in the waiting room for a long period of time can be stressful for both child and parents. Because children with autism often need extra time getting used to the doctor and the setting, the usual rapid pace of medical care—which only seems to increase over time—may make examination more difficult.

Dealing with medical professionals can be complicated for any parent and is even more complicated for parents of a child with significant developmental problems. It is important that parents find health care professionals who understand the child's special needs. A good relationship with a **pediatrician** or other primary care provider is important; the long-term goal is to help individuals on the autism spectrum participate as much as possible in the process of getting good health care and learning to be as informed and as active in the process as possible. Therefore, probably the most important thing to look for in any health care provider is his or her interest in making the relationship a success over the long haul.

Although autism and related disorders are still not as well understood as they should be by many physicians, more and more health care providers know at least something about these conditions. By the time a child is first diagnosed with an ASD, the family will probably already have a primary care provider who, hopefully, has been helpful to them in getting a diagnosis and obtaining services (see Chapters 3 and 4). If the family is satisfied with the care they have been receiving, there is no reason to switch doctors, especially if the doctor is willing to accommodate the child's special needs and to learn about autism. However, sometimes other considerations may lead parents to switch providers. If a new doctor is needed, other families and school staff can often provide helpful information about finding someone new.

Preventive care is particularly important for children with autism, both because it tries to prevent problems that may be even more difficult to deal with in a child with an ASD and because it helps give the child and health care provider an opportunity to know each other apart from times when the child is ill. Routine screening by physical exam and laboratory testing are important to detect problems early—when treatments can be helpful and prevent more severe or permanent conditions. Poor growth, dental problems, sensory impairments, curved spine (scoliosis), and high blood pressure are a few of the disorders that might be found at a routine preventive care exam. Follow-up care is especially important if a child is on regular medications. Immunizing children against many previously common infectious diseases is an important part of preventive care.

Helping Medical Visits Be Successful

Both parents and the doctor and his or her staff can take steps to make visits to the office successful. As we emphasize routine visits are important in helping the doctor have a baseline sense of the individual's functioning when she is not ill. Having the child become familiar with the doctor's office and procedures when she is well also makes cooperation during an illness much more likely. Although it can seem easier to skip well-child visits, this usually leads to other problems over the longer haul. Fortunately, there are several steps that the doctor and his or her staff and the parents can take to make things go well.

Parents can take several steps to help prepare the child for a visit to the doctor. If the child is going to a new office, try to get some pictures of the staff ahead of time and even drive by the office to show it to the child. Look in the library (or bookstores) for books about going to the doctor that you can use with the child. For some children, particularly those with significant communication problems, using a visual storyboard or pictures of the doctor and the office may be helpful each time you visit. For more able children, Social Stories may be helpful. The idea is to try to make things as familiar as possible, given that people with autism have trouble with change. If you can get them cheaply, equipment or pretend equipment, like a stethoscope, blood pressure cuff, or even an **otoscope** (the instrument doctors use to look in the ear) can help the child feel less anxious. If possible, visits should be scheduled for a time when waiting time is likely to be minimal, such as the first appointment of the day or of the afternoon. Or if there is more than one waiting area, ask for the smaller and quieter one. Parents can plan ahead and bring an activity (or activities) that the child enjoys. Usually, a period of talking precedes the exam. This can help the child relax. When it comes time for the exam, it may help if the doctor goes slowly and explains what will happen. When possible, it's important that a parent or other caregiver who knows the child be present and available to help calm him and make him feel comfortable.

In his or her approach to the child, the doctor will usually want to give ample time for "warm-up" and familiarity (as we discuss later, this is not always possible—particularly in emergency situations). Taking a careful and thoughtful approach and telling the child in advance what is going to happen will help. Doing less stressful parts of the examination first also makes sense—so that looking in the mouth and ears may be saved until the end. Sometimes the doctor must modify the usual examination procedure; for example, much of the examination of the young child can be done while the child is sitting on a parent's lap. If lab studies are needed, you can ask about applying an anesthetic cream ahead of time to make the blood drawing less painful. This may help if the child has to have regular bloodwork, such as checks of anticonvulsant blood levels if the child has seizures.

Sometimes the pediatrician may suggest laboratory tests or consultations with medical or nonmedical professionals (hearing tests, psychological tests, or tests of communication skills or of nutrition). Parents should always feel free to ask why a doctor recommends a specific test or procedure. For example, the child's pediatrician might wish to have the opinion of a psychiatrist or a child psychiatrist if behavior-modifying prescription medication is being considered. If the child has seizures, the pediatrician might suggest a consultation with a neurologist, who would then work with the pediatrician in the management of the seizures. Generally, the pediatrician or primary care provider will supply names of specialists, but parents can also get names from friends or other parents. Parents should feel free to ask the specialist questions, particularly if medication is prescribed. The pediatrician or primary care provider should be given the report of the specialist's recommendations and informed about any new medications prescribed.

Other Members of the Health Care Team

In addition to physicians, there are several other health care specialists who have a valuable role in helping individuals with autism and related conditions. For those children who need medication, an understanding and helpful pharmacist can make a big difference for parents and families. The pharmacist may be able to compound (make up) medications for children who don't like the taste/flavor of the usual kind of medicine. Using the same pharmacist for all medications also ensures that the pharmacist can be on the alert for medication allergies or problems that come about when combinations of medicine have the potential to cause trouble. These complicated medication situations are particularly likely when children are seeing many different specialists who may all be prescribing medications.

Within the school setting, the school nurse will often be the person who is most knowledgeable about the child's medical problems. She or he may be involved daily if the child needs to take medication while at school. The school nurse should know about changes in medication (including doses) to be on the lookout for **side effects.** The nurse and teachers should have a plan in place in advance to deal with any emergencies—anticipated (e.g., allergies) or unanticipated (accidents and falls). If the child has seizures, the nurse should know what to expect (see Chapter 12).

Medical Conditions More Common in Autism and Related Disorders

Fragile X Syndrome

As we discussed in Chapter 2 fragile X syndrome is a syndrome associated with intellectual disability, and, sometimes, with autism. The condition is X-linked and, occurs more frequently in boys.

GETTING HIGH-QUALITY MEDICAL CARE

There are several steps parents (and teachers) can take to be sure the individual with autism receives high-quality care.

1. *Always be a careful observer.* Particularly if the child has limited expressive language skills, often the doctor, nurses, and other professionals have to rely on you for information. Not uncommonly, a change in behavior may be the clue that an illness is beginning.
2. *Discuss and try to anticipate the child's special needs.* Try to anticipate what you and the doctor and his or her staff can do to make the child as comfortable as possible.
3. *Don't pass up the routine checkups.* It is particularly important for the child to see the doctor for routine checkups under circumstances that are less stressful. Regular well-child visits give the doctor a chance to observe the child when she is not ill.
4. *Ask questions and get information.* The doctor can provide you with valuable information, as much as you can provide the doctor. If you don't understand something, you should always ask.
5. *Keep a record.* Parents may want to keep a notebook with reports of previous evaluations and past specialists. A short (one-page max) summary may be very helpful; this can be with the child at school as well as in case of emergencies. It should list any chronic medical problems such as allergies or unusual responses to medications, neurological problems, seizures, past illnesses, hospitalizations, or surgeries.
6. *Teach health care.* Teach the individual about going to the doctor through books, pictures, play, videos, and other sources. Work to teach some basic aspects of personal self-care, including personal hygiene.

SUMMARY OF MEDICAL HISTORY INFORMATION

Child's name: _____

Parents' names: _____

Date of birth: _____

Address: _____

Home phone: _____

Work phone: _____

Health care provider name: _____ Phone: _____

Other person to contact in emergency: _____

School: _____

PDD diagnosis: _____

Level of communication and behavioral issues: _____

Medical problems (e.g., seizures, asthma): _____

Medications patient is taking (name and dose): _____

Allergies to medications: _____

Other allergies: _____

Unusual reactions to medications: _____

Hospitalizations: _____

Surgeries: _____

Associated problems in fragile X syndrome include mild intellectual disability (although sometimes the intelligence quotient [IQ] is in the normal range). Boys with the disorder may have some unusual body features such as large ears and genitals; the face may be long and narrow; and the palate (the roof of the mouth) may be unusually high and arched. Some individuals with this condition have seizures.

In addition to intellectual disability, behavioral problems can include hyperactivity, difficulties with attention, anxiety, repetitive motor mannerisms **(stereotypies),** aggression, impaired speech and language skills, difficulty making eye contact, and extreme shyness. Children with fragile X syndrome seem particularly likely to have greater degrees of attentional difficulty than other children with intellectual disability. Medical treatments for many of these behavioral difficulties are discussed in Chapter 15. Some excellent resources on this condition are provided in the reading list.

Tuberous Sclerosis

Tuberous sclerosis is a disease that is rare but has been noted to be significantly associated with autism. Symptoms of tuberous sclerosis include the growth of unusual tissue (tubers) or benign tumors in the skin, eye, brain, and other organs, as well as white patches on the skin at birth. The tumors associated with this disorder are often seen in the preschool years and may increase in frequency during puberty. These growths are "benign" in the sense that, unlike cancer, they do not spread but the effect on growth and development can be very serious. For this reason, the child may need to have computed tomography (CT) or magnetic resonance imaging (MRI) scans to monitor the growth of tubers in his brain.

Although the effects of the disorder can be severe, the degree of severity in individual children is quite variable. Sometimes the first symptoms are seen in infancy or early childhood—often with the onset of seizures. Between 50% and 60% of affected individuals show intellectual disability, and about 80% have seizures. See Chapter 12 for information about medical treatment of seizures.

Studies of individuals with autism show that a small number—probably fewer than 1%—may also have tuberous sclerosis. This figure is higher if only individuals with autism and seizures are included. About 8–12% of these people may have tuberous sclerosis. If you look at the problem the other way around, roughly one-third of children with tuberous sclerosis have autism. The ratio of boys to girls with autism associated with tuberous sclerosis is about the same (it is equally likely in boys and girls); this is in contrast to autism in general, where the rate of autism is several times higher in boys than girls.

Children with tuberous sclerosis may have speech delays and learning problems, even if they do not have intellectual disability. They often have motor problems as well. All children with developmental delays and seizures should be carefully examined for the physical signs of tuberous sclerosis.

Seizure Disorders

Epilepsy (recurrent seizures) is the medical condition most commonly seen in autism and related disorders. Because as many as 25% of children with strictly diagnosed autism may develop epilepsy, we devote an entire chapter to seizure disorders and their treatment later in this book (Chapter 12).

COPING WITH COMMON MEDICAL PROBLEMS

Dealing With a Sick Child

Generally speaking, children with autism are no more or less susceptible to the usual range of childhood illnesses. However, when children with autism *are* ill, the child's difficulties communicating what is wrong and often an unwillingness to be examined complicate matters. It goes without saying—even though we are now saying it—that the information provided here is *general* information and the child's health care professional is the best source of information *specific* to the child. Also, it is important to keep in mind that parents are an important part of the medical treatment team—they can provide information on history and the child's past responses to illness and treatments—an invaluable part of the health care process.

How to Know When Your Child Is Sick

There are many different ways that parents can tell when their children are sick. The child can have a fever, a rash, a cough or runny nose, upset stomach with vomiting and diarrhea, or one of many other symptoms. Sometimes a change in behavior is the only sign of an illness. It can, at times, be a real detective project to find the cause of the changes that you notice. Many children with autism or other PDDs are on medications to help with behavior or to treat a seizure disorder. At times, these medications can cause adverse reactions, and sometimes this can complicate the task of figuring out what is really going on when the child is ill.

Children who are not yet talking present special problems for medical professionals. Of course, in some ways, these problems are similar to those faced by pediatricians every day as they deal with infants. When the person can't communicate very well, the doctor has to rely a lot on the history or information others provide about the illness. The doctor also can rely on what he or she sees while watching the child as well as on physical examination findings and, sometimes, on laboratory tests, x-rays, or other special procedures. There are some major differences, however, between dealing with a nonverbal 8-month-old and a nonverbal 8-year-old. Some of these are discussed below. One of the important considerations is helping the child communicate about pain and discomfort.

HOW TO KNOW WHEN YOUR CHILD IS IN PAIN

There are several reasons that it can be difficult to recognize that a child with ASD is in pain. First, children with autism may not experience pain in the same way that other children do. And, second, they can have a great deal of difficulty communicating about their pain.

Some children with autism don't seem to mind pain very much. We've known children with appendicitis who didn't complain at all. Sometimes the doctor may be surprised the child was not "acting sicker." Other children may be bothered quite a bit even by a small amount of discomfort. For these children, difficulties with change and inability to deal with even minor annoyances can create major behavior problems. As the child gets older, you'll have an increasingly better sense of how he deals with pain.

Children who are not yet using words to communicate present the greatest challenges when they are ill. As the individual who knows the child best, be alert for any changes in the child's behavior or appearance. Behaviors that suggest pain in children with ASD include:

- *Moaning, whimpering, or unusual crying.* These vocalizations may or may not be associated with changes in facial expression suggesting pain.

- *Changes in eating or sleeping habits.* For example, the child may refuse favorite foods or seem to be sleeping more.

- *Changes in activity or behavior.* This can include either unusual lack of activity or overactivity. Some children may start to become self-abusive if they are in pain, for example, hitting their head on the floor or with their hand if they have an earache, dental pain, or sinus infection. Pain in an arm or leg might result in changes in the child's movement. Occasionally, parents tell us that their child's behavior actually *improves* when the child is sick. For example, the child may be more talkative (this is probably related to the stress of being ill).

Sometimes, particularly when pain or discomfort is chronic, you and the doctor have to turn into real detectives to try to track down the source of the behavior change. It can be helpful to think about things by taking a broad view of the child. For example, for an adolescent girl who has behavior difficulties on a monthly basis, you might wonder about whether she is having discomfort in relation to ovulation. Similarly, changes in behavior in association with the seasons might suggest seasonal allergies. As we mentioned, the sudden onset of self-injurious behavior can also be the first sign of illness due to pain from an ear infection or new teeth (this can include the eruption of the "wisdom teeth" [the third molars] in adolescence).

- *Changes in appearance.* Although it can sometimes be hard for you to put into words in a very exact way, you'll sometimes notice that the child just looks ill. As the person who knows the child the best, you may be the first person to realize this.

For children who don't yet use verbal language, it is important to be aware of possible warning signs that the child may be in pain (see the box above). The child who can communicate with words may be able to talk about pain or discomfort. However, he may use very personal or "idiosyncratic" language. For example, saying, "My stomach hurts," may, for some children, mean many different things. Other children may have an unconventional way of saying they are in pain. Sometimes they may say a phrase that they first heard when they were sick; for example, "I got a booboo" may be used to refer to any discomfort anywhere in the body and, clearly, language of this type would be very difficult for a doctor to understand correctly without the help of a familiar adult. Other children may have some language, but not enough to communicate in detail, or be able to use conventional gestures that otherwise might help localize pain. Use of visual aids and other communication supports may be helpful. For instance, you can show a child a picture of a child or a doll and ask the child to indicate where on the doll it hurts. Or you can show her pictures of children's expressions and ask her to point to the one that shows how she feels.

Some excellent resources are provided in the reading list at the end of this chapter. Picture books have been specifically developed to review in advance what happens when a child goes to the doctor or a hospital to help him communicate about what happens there. Other books were designed for typically developing children but also can be quite appropriate. Parents can also make their own picture books (preferably using photos of the child) and work with the speech pathologist about being sure that the child has some words he can use to communicate about pain and feelings of discomfort. If the child doesn't seem to understand the meaning of the word *pain* or *hurt,* you need to try and teach that concept by saying, "Ouch, that hurts," every time you sustain a minor injury or pointing out when the child must be hurting.

Common Medical Problems

Children with autism or other PDDs can develop any of the medical problems that typical children can develop. Because of their communication and developmental difficulties, it can be harder for a parent or a medical professional to recognize that a child with autism is sick. It can also be harder to diagnose the problem. In this section, we discuss only a few of the medical problems seen in children on the autism spectrum. Others, such as celiac disease, are discussed in other parts of the book (Chapter 18).

Infections, unfortunately, are part of growing up. Fortunately, many steps can be taken to reduce the frequency and severity of infections in children with ASD. These include teaching good hygiene (hand washing, use of tissues), reducing exposure to situations likely to cause infections, and **immunizations** (which we discuss later in this chapter). Infections occur when viruses or bacteria invade the body; the body's natural defenses (the immune system) then become active in fighting off the infection in various ways. In some cases, particularly with bacterial infections, the doctor can supply medicine (antibiotics) that help the body do its job of fighting off infections. These medicines may help shorten the length of an infectious illness or its severity. For viral infections, fewer medicines are available, although immunizations can be given to prevent some viral illnesses in the first place. While infections can involve any part of the body, the most commonly seen involve the ears, eyes, nose, throat, sinuses, and skin, and the respiratory, gastrointestinal, and urinary tracts.

Infections can be harder to diagnosis in children with ASD because the child is less likely to complain of pain or discomfort. The infection may present itself only as a dramatic change in your child's behavior or as a fever. Observing your child and keeping track of the events leading up to the time your child goes to the doctor help the doctor understand the way the illness developed and may help determine the cause of the illness.

FEVERS

Children frequently get fevers when they are sick. It is often a parent's first clue that their child has some kind of infection. Fever by itself is not necessarily bad. Some children tend to have higher or more frequent fevers than other children. The height of the fever does not indicate how serious the infection is. Discuss this issue with your doctor and ask if there is a specific temperature at which you should call.

We treat fevers for several different reasons. An important reason is that a child will often feel better and act more like herself when the temperature comes down. In addition, fevers can lower the seizure threshold. That is, if your child has seizures, she may be more likely to have one when she has a fever. Most pediatricians recommend acetaminophen (Tylenol) or ibuprofen (Motrin or Advil) to bring down a temperature. Many children respond better to the use of one of the newer thermometers that measure the temperature in the ear or on the forehead from the temporal artery than they do to the use of a thermometer that requires insertion into their mouth or rectum. Temperatures taken this way are generally pretty accurate and make for less trouble for children who may not want anything like a thermometer in their mouth!

Gastrointestinal Infection (GI "Bugs")   A gastrointestinal (GI) infection is any infection in the stomach or intestinal tract. Often, this leads to stomachache, vomiting, diarrhea (or all three). It can be referred to by several different names—gastroenteritis, GI bugs, or intestinal flu. GI bugs are easy to pass around, and sometimes poor toileting skills, especially if there are large numbers of people in a school or a group setting, may result in GI disease occurring in an entire grade or school group at the same time. Usually, the diagnosis of GI illness is not difficult because the vomiting and/or diarrhea is quite obvious.

Finding the cause of a GI infection may take some time. Most of them are caused by viruses and are self-limited and will be over in a week or less. If they last longer or there is diarrhea with blood, or signs of **dehydration** such as decreased urination or lack of tears when crying, more of an evaluation is needed. Treatment for most GI infections usually consists of dietary changes and encouragement of fluids to avoid dehydration. Usually, doctors recommend clear liquids and avoidance of dairy products. A BRAT diet (bananas, rice, applesauce, and toast) is recommended by some doctors for younger children or a generally bland diet for older children. Avoidance of fatty, fried, or spicy foods is recommended. A few GI infections are treated with antibiotics. The most important aspect of caring for a child with vomiting and/or diarrhea is the prevention of dehydration. If your child shows signs of dehydration, you should contact your doctor immediately.

The best way to prevent GI infections is to foster good hand-washing routines in children after they use the bathroom and for caretakers involved in diapering or toileting to be extra careful about washing their own hands. Having sick children stay out of day care or school until their vomiting or diarrhea has completely stopped is another important way to prevent the spread of GI infections.

A parasitic infection with pinworms (enterobiasis) can also contribute to behavior change because it can cause intense rectal itching. Pinworms can be hard to detect unless the doctor knows of the severe itching it is causing and instructs you to look for the pinworms in the anal area late at night or first thing in the morning; they are small but visible and will move. Sometimes people just put a piece of adhesive tape over the area with the pinworms; they will stick to the tape and can be taken to the doctor for inspection. Or you can obtain a pinworm kit from your health care provider that includes a plastic paddle to help collect the pinworms. When found, the pinworms can be treated with medication.

Urinary Tract Infections (UTIs)   UTIs occur when bacteria infect the urinary tract. These infections are much more common in girls than in boys. Poor hygiene and cleaning after going to the bathroom can make this kind of infection more likely. Children need to be reminded to wipe first in the front and then in the back. Irritation of the perineum from soaps or bubble bath may make UTIs more likely for some children, as can **constipation**.

The most common symptoms of a UTI are pain on urination, increased frequency of urination, and urgency (which means feeling like you have to go immediately). Fever, general irritability, abdominal discomfort, and low back pain may also develop. At times, vomiting and diarrhea are the only clues. If your child develops new onset of daytime or nighttime wetting after she has been routinely dry, you should look for a UTI.

A child with autism or PDD with a UTI may not complain of pain on urination as other children might. A fever or new onset of bedwetting or daytime accidents may be the only clues. Your child may suddenly be going to the bathroom more often than usual. Sometimes a change in behavior—such as increased irritability—can be a clue.

Respiratory Infections and Sinus Infections   Colds are infections that affect the upper respiratory system. Infections of the lower respiratory system are called bronchitis and pneumonia. Sometimes the sinuses (air spaces in the head) can become infected (sinusitis). A simple cough or runny nose often won't need to be seen by the doctor. However, if there are symptoms and signs of strep throat, including sore throat; possibly swollen, red **tonsils;** and sometimes white patches on the tonsils, there are now quick tests available, and antibiotic treatment can be started. Prolonged cough and congestion, with the child looking sicker, should be checked out by a doctor. Sinus infection may be suspected if there is prolonged nasal congestion (a week to 10 days or more) with thick and discolored mucus.

Middle Ear Infections   Infections of the middle ear **(otitis media)** are one of the most common problems for which children are taken to the doctor. Ear infections are also common in children with ASDs; given the potential of ear infections to interfere with hearing, prompt treatment and control is important.

With these infections, fluid in the middle ear (on the other side of the eardrum from the ear canal) becomes infected. Most children have at least one ear infection by the age of 2, and many have more. As your child gets older, you can expect the frequency of these infections to decrease.

Anything that makes your child more congested, such as an upper respiratory infection or **allergy,** will make an ear infection more likely to occur. They can also occur in someone who is otherwise perfectly healthy.

The signs and symptoms of an ear infection will vary with your child's age and with his ability to communicate. Ear infections can cause fever and pain as well as impaired hearing and disturbed balance. As a result, some of the common symptoms of an ear infection are irritability, especially when your child is lying down; poor feeding; trouble sleeping; inattention; and increased oppositional behavior. The signs can include pulling at the ears or hair or banging the head against the floor, crib, or bed. Poor balance and falling can also indicate a middle ear problem. Fever can at times be the only clue that your child has an ear infection, although not every child will have a fever with every ear infection. Occasionally, the only symptom of an ear infection is a cough. Some children never have any symptoms from an ear infection and it is discovered at a routine health check.

Your pediatrician will make the diagnosis of a middle ear infection by looking into your child's ear and looking at the eardrum with a special instrument called an otoscope that lights up and magnifies the area. The doctor will probably need your help in holding your child still to look in the ear. Giving your child the chance to get acquainted with the doctor (and his or her instruments) while not ill makes it easier to examine her when she is not feeling well.

Ear infections can be caused by either viral or bacterial infections. The doctor cannot tell which is causing it just by examining the ear. Bacterial infections can be cured by antibiotics.

We treat ear infections with antibiotics for several reasons: first, to make the child more comfortable and to correct whatever other problems the infection has caused, such as decreased hearing or poor balance; and second, to prevent any more serious infections from developing, such as mastoiditis (an infection of the mastoid bone behind the ear) or meningitis (an infection of the covering of the brain). These complications are, fortunately, very rare. In fact, recently there has been more of a problem with the overuse of antibiotics and the development of bacteria that are now resistant to the commonly used antibiotics. Because of this, your pediatrician may recommend giving your child something such as acetaminophen (Tylenol) or ibuprofen (Motrin or Advil) for pain relief and then waiting and watching for a day or two to see if the ear infection will clear up without antibiotics. If it doesn't improve on its own, or if your child is very uncomfortable when the ear infection is diagnosed or appears quite ill to your doctor, he or she will probably prescribe antibiotics right away.

Sometimes parents note improvement fairly quickly after starting antibiotics and take this as a sign that the infection is cleared; this may not be the case. It is important to take antibiotics for the full length of time prescribed, even though your child should feel better in 1–2 days. Most of the antibiotics are taken for 10 days, but a few are taken for only 3–5 days. Rarely, a single shot of antibiotics is used. If the ear infection does not clear up on the first antibiotic, your doctor will need to prescribe another. Unfortunately, as mentioned, with more widespread use of antibiotics these days, there are now bacteria that are resistant to many of the antibiotics.

If your child has frequent ear infections, your pediatrician may recommend that he take a low dose of an antibiotic on a daily basis for a few months to try to prevent, or at least decrease the frequency of, the ear infections. If this does not work, or if fluid remains in the middle ear after an infection for 3 months or longer, your child may need to have **pressure-equalizing** (PE) **tubes** placed in the eardrum to restore hearing or prevent infections. Surgery is required to place these in the ears.

There are times when enlarged adenoids contribute to the problem of recurrent ear infections by blocking the **eustachian tubes** and making it hard for the middle ear fluid to drain out. In such cases, their removal will be recommended along with the placement of pressure-equalizing tubes. The tonsils are not usually removed unless they have also been infected repeatedly or are causing other problems such as sleep apnea.

The decision to have surgery to put in pressure-equalizing tubes will be made only after weighing the risks and benefits involved. Your child will require general anesthesia and usually a short stay in an outpatient surgery center. You will want to have an anesthesiologist and an ear, nose, and throat **(ENT)** surgeon **(otolaryngologist)** who are experienced with children. For children with language and communication problems, often the risk is worth the greater potential benefit of improved hearing and fewer infections. However, decisions are always made jointly by you and your doctor.

Swimmer's Ear (Infection of the Ear Canal)   Children with autism should be taught to swim for many reasons. It is great exercise and (more importantly) helps prevent drowning (see Chapter 11). Children who spend a great deal of time swimming can develop swimmer's ear (**otitis externa**). This is an infection and inflammation of the ear canal (the part of the ear from the outside of the ear leading up to the eardrum). It can also be caused by local trauma, such as having a cotton tip applicator pushed too far or too forcefully into the ear canal. Usually, this is done in an attempt to remove wax, but more often it pushes the wax further in and can injure the sides of the ear canal. If your child has swimmer's ear, she will usually complain of pain (or look as if she is in pain) when you move the ear or push in front of it. It may also be painful for her to lie on that ear or to open her mouth wide, which may move the affected area.

Swimmer's ear is diagnosed in the same way as a middle ear infection, that is, by looking into the ear with an otoscope. It is usually treated with eardrops—either antibiotics alone or a combination of antibiotics and steroids to help reduce the inflammation. Occasionally, oral antibiotics are also needed. Sometimes if the infection is very bad, a wick is placed in the ear canal to make it easier for the drops to get into the ear.

If your child gets recurrent swimmer's ear, it is worth trying to prevent it by using special eardrops to try to dry out the ear canal after swimming. There are many nonprescription brands of drops intended for this use. You can check with your pharmacist about which brands he carries. Do not use them if your child has pressure-equalizing tubes in his ears, however. Most ENT doctors recommend that children with pressure-equalizing tubes wear specially molded ear plugs while swimming.

Conjunctivitis   Conjunctivitis, or pink eye, is an inflammation of the outer covering of the eye. It can be caused by either allergies or infection. The infections can be either viral or bacterial; only bacterial infections improve with antibiotics. You will know that your child has this problem if you see that her eye looks red, and at times you will also see drainage. With bacterial infections, the drainage is usually thick and either yellow or green. If you wipe it away, more will appear. In the morning, there may be crusting along the edges of the eyes and the lids may at first seem stuck shut. With viral infections, the drainage may be thinner and is less likely to be discolored. There may be no drainage at all with allergic conjunctivitis. There are other causes of red eyes, so you should check with your health care provider if you notice this in your child.

The treatment varies, depending on the cause. Bacterial infections are treated with antibiotic eye drops. Occasionally, oral antibiotics are used if there is also an ear infection or if it is impossible to get drops into the eyes. When conjunctivitis is due to allergies, it is treated with antihistamines, taken either orally or as eyedrops.

Skin Disorders   Skin conditions can be especially problematic in children with autism spectrum disorders. The itching, pain, or appearance of skin conditions can be very irritating or distracting, and children with autism may react by scratching and picking. Some of the most common are **eczema** (itchy, dry skin), **impetigo** (infected skin), and acne.

Your pediatrician can make suggestions to help you deal with these problems. Sometimes topical medication will be required, and at other times your child may need to take something orally. Medications that help with itching may be all that is necessary at times, while in other situations an antibiotic may be required.

If your child picks at his skin, monitor him carefully. Quickly treat any minor scratches or infections that develop, in order to prevent more serious problems.

Noninfectious Gastrointestinal Problems   In the past several years there has been much interest in GI problems in ASDs. This interest came about for several reasons: the flurry of interest in the gut hormone secretin (see Chapter 18) and an awareness of the frequency of GI problems in children on the spectrum. Clearly, any GI problem can occur in children with autism/PDD. There are also good reasons problems like constipation or loose stools could be more frequent; for example, many people on the autism spectrum tend to be sedentary and don't get enough exercise or they have unusual eating habits. One of the problems with GI difficulties is that these cause discomfort but aren't readily observable. Common problems that are painful include gastroesophageal reflux disease, constipation, diarrhea, and lactose intolerance.

Gastroesophageal reflux involves the passage of stomach contents back up into the esophagus, throat, or mouth, where it is either silently swallowed or actually spit all the way out of the mouth. It occurs in many people without causing any symptoms, but when it does cause symptoms, it is considered a problem known as gastroesophageal reflux disease **(GERD).** It can start right after birth or it can develop later in childhood. In children, symptoms of GERD include:

- Vomiting, which at times may be severe enough to limit growth
- Esophagitis (irritation of the esophagus), which can cause pain and irritability
- Respiratory symptoms such as cough, hoarseness, stridor (noisy breathing), and wheezing; less commonly, apnea and recurrent pneumonias.

Your child may stop eating because of the pain or have behavioral changes such as irritability or loss of interest in food. These types of changes require investigation to understand their origin. A careful history of the relationship between eating and the pain may allow a doctor to diagnose GERD. Sometimes testing is required. Your pediatrician may refer you to a pediatric gastroenterologist for this testing. Because testing for GERD usually involves something unpleasant, such as placing a tube into the stomach, many doctors will treat GERD on the basis of the history to start with. There are now several different kinds of medication that can be used to treat gastroesophageal reflux very effectively.

Constipation   One of the most common GI problems in all children is constipation. This can mean either having infrequent bowel movements or having hard or difficult-to-pass bowel movements. Some children can have such severe pain from constipation that they are admitted to the hospital to be watched for appendicitis. Often, constipation makes children lose their appetite.

There are many different causes of constipation. Some of the most common include dietary problems, lack of activity, and behavioral issues such as reluctance to use the toilet. Some medications can also cause constipation, so if your child develops constipation after starting a new medication, talk to your doctor. There are also many medical problems that can cause constipation, so if the problem persists, again, consult with your doctor.

As a parent, you may be able see the problem starting to develop by paying close attention to your child's bowel patterns. Watching how frequently she has a bowel movement and how large or hard it is may allow you to correct a problem before it becomes too severe. If your child is too old or independent for you to be directly monitoring her bowel habits, try to be alert to changes such as your child spending increasing amounts of time in the bathroom or complaining of stomach pain.

Dietary changes can help prevent or correct constipation if your child will allow the changes. Some changes that may help include:

- *Increasing the child's intake of fluids.* If it's hard to get your child to drink much, you can try to sneak fluid into his diet with gelatin, popsicles, and other foods with high water content that your child does like.

- *Increasing the amount of fiber in your child's diet.* Adding many fruits and vegetables, especially the leafy green ones, can be helpful, although frequently children have constipation because they don't like these foods. Adding bran cereals or whole-grain breads, rice, and pasta will also increase the fiber in the child's diet. Bear in mind that bananas, apples, or dairy products can constipate some children. Even if your child doesn't like fruits or vegetables, you may be able to get her to eat some by adding ground-up vegetables such as carrots or zucchini to sauces or cookies or making fruit smoothies. It is possible to buy juice boxes with added fiber that will help some children. You may have to ask your doctor where you can order them.

- Occasionally, your child may require a stool softener such as mineral oil or docusate (Colace) or polyethylene glycol (Miralax).

Trying to successfully adjust the diet of a child with autism to correct constipation may require the input of many specialists. Your doctor may refer you to a dietitian or a gastroenterologist.

Diarrhea   Acute diarrhea, lasting less than 7 days, is a common problem in all children. It is most commonly caused by infection. Sometimes foods will cause diarrhea, especially large quantities of juice, or intolerance to milk, wheat, or many other foods. If your child has severe or persistent diarrhea or if you see blood in the bowel movement, you should see your pediatrician.

Lactose Intolerance   Some children develop lactose intolerance as they get older. They lack either some or all of the enzyme lactase, which is needed to digest the sugar lactose that is found in dairy products. As a result, if they consume too much dairy, they can develop gas, abdominal pain, or diarrhea. Any of these can cause a child to be uncomfortable and fussy.

Cutting down on or eliminating dairy products helps. The Lactaid products available at the grocery store are a good substitute for many people. These are dairy products without the lactose sugar. You can also buy Lastase pills, which provide some of the missing enzyme and allow some people to comfortably eat small amounts of dairy products. There are tests for lactose intolerance, but often diagnosis can be made without testing by eliminating dairy products for a trial period. If symptoms recur when dairy products are reintroduced, your child is presumed to have lactose intolerance.

Eating Problems

Children with autism and related disorders can have a number of problems with eating and food. These often include:

- Unusual food preferences and sensitivities, which can lead to a restricted diet
- Obesity
- Pica (eating nonnutritive substances such as dirt or string)
- Rumination (regurgitation of food that has already been eaten)

In this section we'll consider some of these problems and potential solutions. Again, keep in mind that this is a general discussion with general suggestions and that when you need specific advice, various professionals (as well as many parents and well-intentioned friends and relatives) will be there to make suggestions!

Unusual Food Preferences and Sensitivities

Children with autism or other pervasive developmental disorders may have unusual eating habits. Some have pronounced likes and dislikes when it comes to food. Sometimes these habits keep the child from having a good diet. Some children are extremely sensitive to certain food textures or tastes or smells.

Some children may eat only certain kinds of food (e.g., foods that are soft and mushy). Other children may resist new foods or may not tolerate foods of certain temperatures. Sometimes children eat the same foods over and over again. We've seen children who would only eat white food, who would only eat cold food, who would only eat French fries and certain fast foods.

The attempt to introduce new foods at mealtimes can lead to temper tantrums and other difficulties. Occasionally, these escalate to the point that the child becomes malnourished, although this is unusual. Avoidance of certain foods (such as dairy products) may have important implications for other aspects of health such as developing strong bones and teeth. These unusual food preferences are not always easy to understand. When problems start early, they often seem to get worse as the child becomes a bit older, so it is worth trying to help the child when these problems first develop.

To some extent the unusual food preferences of some children with ASD resemble the problems seen in typically developing toddlers, who often engage in struggles over food. The endless reminders from your mother to eat your peas or broccoli may come to mind! These problems are, however, often much more marked and severe in children with autism. Several things help the typically developing child cope, for example, being motivated to imitate the models provided by family members eating a range of foods or enjoying praise from parents for trying new foods.

Unfortunately, children with ASDs often feel less social motivation and desire for praise. In addition, heightened sensitivities to foods, rigidity and difficulties with change further complicate attempts to introduce new foods into their diets. These problems can be even more complicated when parents are also pursuing dietary interventions (see Chapter 18) that further restrict what the child can eat. For example, some parents restrict the diet so much that the young child may not be able to participate effectively in educational programming because the only foods available to him as reinforcers are unappetizing to him.

Helping Your Child Tolerate More Foods

Dealing with unusual food preferences is not easy. Strategies for coping with this problem are quite varied. One approach is to attempt very *gradual* change—very, very gradually introducing new foods. This might work well, for example, for a child who eats only white foods. For this child, you could gradually begin to introduce color into the food. Blenders and food processors can be a real help in this regard. Sometimes unpopular foods can be hidden in other blenderized foods; this may make the texture more tolerable as well. Depending on the child's preferences, it may be possible to add to foods she does like. For example, if she will drink milkshakes, you can try adding different kinds of foods to the shake.

For some children, varying the way in which the food is presented may be the trick. Sometimes freezing pureed vegetables into popsicles may make them more interesting! Or a child who would never eat cooked peas might respond if they were present in frozen form. Other children might be willing to try dried peas, available in some Asian food stores! The usual rule of thumb is to try gradually introducing new foods. Even though it is a hassle, keep at it since, otherwise, the tendency is often for the child to become even more rigid.

Sometimes children are delighted to try foods that they have been involved in preparing. This approach can also have payoffs if you need to plan school lunches or snacks. You can try a visual approach to help involve the child in cooking. For example, make up a set of index cards illustrating how to prepare spaghetti and put them in order, in a notebook or on a ring. (Photos might show the child getting the spaghetti box out of the cupboard, getting the pot out, and putting water in it, etc.) For children who can read, the printed words may be sufficient.

You might also try involving the child in grocery shopping to try to spark his interest in new foods. You can consult with the child's school staff about ways to make this a positive learning experience. For example, you can make a visual shopping list ahead of time. Use a digital or instant camera and make photographs of the actual items the child will need in the store. You can put these onto a shopping list using Velcro tabs. This special list can help the child shop with you in the store while you are doing your shopping. Start with very simple foods and gradually increase the complexity as time goes on. This is a wonderful way to make grocery shopping a positive learning experience for the child and help him take pride in his abilities. You also help encourage adaptive behaviors and important community and daily living skills.

If poor weight gain is an issue, more calories may be added. Adding whole milk to the diet can provide added calories. You may want to try adding a commercial instant breakfast or a product such as Ensure or Pediasure that provides both calories and many needed nutrients for the day.

Getting Professional Help

A range of behavioral approaches can also be used to help the child learn to tolerate a greater range of foods. It is important to have the help of an experienced professional in setting these up. Often, a gradual, step-by-step approach is used with carefully selected rewards for more appropriate eating. The specific plan is individualized, depending on the child's needs and problems. Praise, time-limited meals, ignoring food refusals, and more frequent "mini-meals" (with limited snacks in between) can all be used in various combinations. As with everything else, it is important to weigh the pros and cons of the various approaches. Children whose limited diets put their growth and development at risk are the ones who will need the most intensive intervention programs.

Various professionals can be helpful to you in dealing with the food preference problem. Behavioral psychologists may help you design a plan for gradually introducing new foods and expanding the child's range of foods. Especially if the child eats a very narrow range of food, it may be worth meeting with a dietitian to review your child's diet and think about ways to supplement it. Often, it is the texture, rather than the taste, of food that seems to be a problem. Speech–language pathologists or occupational therapists may be able to work with you in developing ways to help the child be able to tolerate a greater range of textures or help with other aspects of the "presentation" of foods.

Overeating and Weight Gain

Excessive body weight is now a very common problem in our society. We tend to eat foods that are high in calories and don't engage in the degree of physical work that our forefathers did. This is of concern because **obesity** is a risk factor for many **chronic** diseases, such as heart disease and type 2 **diabetes.** The overweight child with autism often becomes even less likely to exercise, and a vicious cycle sets in, which only adds to the weight problem and makes it even harder to manage the child physically.

Children with autism and related disorders can be at risk for obesity for several different reasons. Often, a lack of interest in team sports and in physical activity means that children with autism may not burn enough calories. For other children, food functions very effectively as a reinforcer to the point that the child lives for snacks and treats. Other children seem never to reach the point of feeling full and eat and eat until interrupted. Occasionally, some medications used for emotional or behavioral difficulties (such as risperidone) may actually stimulate the appetite and lead to weight gain.

Sometimes the overweight problem results from children having unrestricted access to food. This may happen in school or adult programs. It may be more difficult to control food intake in a private home when other members of the family want to have their own access to food. Occasionally a husky adolescent or young adult may become aggressive if food or snacks are denied. It's important to balance carefully the degree of weight control desired and the effort it will take to achieve this goal. If the amount of overweight is relatively minimal, it may not be worth the effort.

Undernourishment

Inadequate weight gain or even weight loss in children with autism is usually caused by eating too little of the right kinds of food due to unusual food preferences, as described above. Rarely, this occurs because of very restricted diets that children are put on. In addition, some medications such as **methylphenidate** (Ritalin) and other stimulants may make children feel less hungry and contribute to difficulties gaining weight. If weight loss occurs, your pediatrician will need to do some testing to rule out medical explanations as the cause.

Unusual Eating Behaviors

Eating Nonfood Substances (Pica)   Some children with ASDs have trouble with eating nonfood substances. This is known as **pica.** Some will eat dirt, paint chips, string, or anything they find on the floor. Other children will chew on materials or keep them in their mouths without swallowing them (or sometimes swallowing them by mistake). Still other children may be tempted to eat the leaves of plants (some of which are poisonous). Some may even eat their own feces. It is unclear why pica is more common in children with ASDs, although it probably reflects more general problems with cognitive development. Pica also occurs in children with intellectual disability who do not have autism.

Eating nonfood items can lead to various medical problems, such as obstruction of the bowel, and increase the child's risk for lead poisoning, depending on what is eaten. There is a strong association between pica and iron deficiency **anemia.** This can be tested for at the same time that a lead level in the blood is checked.

Various strategies can be used for dealing with inappropriate eating and mouthing behaviors. The choice of strategy depends on the age and developmental level of the child, your ability to restructure the environment to prevent the problem, and the nature of the trouble. Sometimes children really like the experience of moving their mouth and/or chewing. If this is the case, you can try several different things. For very young children, a pacifier may be helpful. For somewhat older children, increased access to foods that are crunchy or chewy may help decrease the desire to chew on other things. (You can try chewing gum, but avoid excess sugar!) An occupational therapist might also be able to suggest appropriate nonfood items for your child to chew on, such as rubbery "chew tubes." Occasionally, children engage in these behaviors when the environment is too complicated for them—that is, they use chewing as a stress reducer. You can see if reducing the level of environmental stimulation helps with the problem. Occasionally, using an electric toothbrush (sometimes several times a day) can help deal with the child's apparent need for oral simulation (this also has advantages for dental care).

Various professionals may be helpful in reducing pica. The speech–language pathologist or occupational therapist may help you think about new ways to cope with the problem and give the child alternative behaviors. A psychologist or physician with experience in developmental disabilities may also be helpful in suggesting behavioral interventions to try. Sometimes you can find a substitute or alternative behavior such as eating ice chips (with or without flavor). Sometimes your reactions to the behavior may be an important part of what keeps it going. You may need to learn to ignore the behavior if it is not endangering the child's health, and instead give her plenty of praise and attention when she is not chewing on nonfood items.

Lead Exposure   If the child eats or mouths nonfood items, it is essential to take precautions against lead poisoning. The most frequent source of unexpected lead in the United States is from indoor house paint that was used before it was banned for health reasons in the 1970s. It can also come from lead solder used to connect water pipes in older homes. If you live in an older home, you should have both the paint and the water checked for lead. Painting over lead paint will prevent a child from eating loose paint chips. If the original windows are still part of the house, there is the possibility that a fine dust with lead paint in it will fall on toys and other objects in the room when the windows are opened and shut. If the child puts one of these toys into his mouth, he will ingest lead. The solution is to scrape the wooden window frames down to bare wood and repaint them with lead-free paint or replace them with new windows.

Elevated lead levels cause different symptoms, depending on how much lead is ingested and the age of the child who has ingested it. Usually, when children have elevated lead levels, their parents do not notice any symptoms, but they may actually suffer from some subtle neurodevelopmental problems. The Centers for Disease Control and Prevention considers any lead level of 10 micrograms per deciliter or above to be abnormal, and it should prompt a search for the source of the lead. Higher levels, usually of 40 micrograms per deciliter or above, may cause more side effects such as anemia. Extremely high levels of 60 micrograms per deciliter or above may cause worse problems such as behavioral changes, regression of newly acquired skills, and most seriously, acute brain toxicity with seizures and coma. Obviously, higher levels must be treated promptly. It is possible to die from the effects of extremely high lead levels.

The pediatrician will probably screen the child for lead routinely when she is young. You may want to request a lead level at an older age if you think there has been any possible exposure. If the child tends to mouth everything or to eat nonfood substances, it is worth having the doctor check a lead level with a blood test. If a high lead level is found, various treatments are available. In addition, efforts must be made to discover the source of the lead and remove it.

Rumination   This unusual behavior—which, fortunately, is not very common—refers to the habit of regurgitating food and chewing it again. This behavior is occasionally seen in typically developing infants but is most common among people with intellectual disability (with or without autism). For the latter group, it may start at more or less any point in time. Problems related to **rumination** can include dental complications, food **aspiration** (food passes into the lungs rather than the stomach), and growth problems. To complicate life, gastroesophageal reflux may contribute to the problem at least some of the time. Various interventions can be used to deal with rumination, particularly if serious medical complications are present. The assistance of an experienced behavior management professional is really needed to deal with the behavioral aspects of this problem. He can, for instance, figure out what the child "gets" out of the behavior and come up with substitute behaviors to teach instead.

Celiac Disease (Gluten Intolerance)

Celiac disease is a disorder of the small intestine. People who have it cannot eat foods with gluten in them because it damages the lining of the small intestine. This can lead to malabsorption of nutrients and poor weight gain or weight loss, fatigue, diarrhea, and discomfort. Other symptoms can at times also be experienced. The disorder can develop in infants and children, but many times it is not diagnosed (and possibly may not develop) until adolescence or adulthood.

In recent years, it has become easier to screen for celiac disease. As a result, it is now known that celiac disease is much more common in the general population than previously thought. Some studies report as many as 1 in 133 people in the United States have celiac disease. Children with autism are no more likely to have celiac disease than typical children, but because more people in general are being diagnosed, there will also be more people diagnosed who also have autism.

Gluten is a protein that is found in wheat, rye, and barley, and sometimes oats (if they have been contaminated with wheat). These substances are found in a wide range of foods. Treatment for this disorder requires avoidance of all gluten in the diet. This usually requires the help of a dietitian or nutritionist, at least initially. Some people with gluten intolerance also have lactose intolerance because of the damage that the gluten has done to the small intestine. This will improve as the intestine heals.

If there is a suspicion that the child may have celiac disease, the pediatrician can do a blood test to assess the likelihood that the child has the disorder. To definitively diagnose celiac disease, however, a biopsy (sample of tissue) needs to be taken from the child's small intestine while she is either sedated or under anesthesia. Testing needs to be done *before* the child starts on a gluten-free diet, or her intestine may heal before the biopsy can confirm that it has the damage typical in celiac disease.

COPING WITH THE EMERGENCY DEPARTMENT AND THE HOSPITAL

Dealing With the Emergency Department (ED)

In dealing with an emergency, remember that all the doctors, nurses, and other health care professionals want to provide quality care to your child and indeed to all patients. Unfortunately, they often have little experience with children with autism and related disorders and often are working in a very fast-paced and busy setting. Not surprisingly, the combination of inexperienced staff and an overly stimulating environment can increase the child's anxiety, complicating visits to the ED.

As with other areas of medical care, parents or adults with the child have an important role in this process. Parents have to be persistent and effective advocates for their child when dealing with the ED, and can be assertive and helpful without being hostile and overbearing. Obviously, in an acute emergency, the health care professionals will do whatever is necessary to manage the situation. That is, if the child is not breathing or her heart is not beating, resuscitation may have to be carried on. This requires the full attention, effort, and energy of all the ED, and parents or other adults will probably have relatively little role in the process.

More typically, however, the problem is one of an acute illness or injury that is not really life threatening. Many of the same considerations come into play in the ED as in other settings. For example, as with school programs, children with autism often do better in situations where there are fewer distractions—a quieter and less distracting room is better than a busy and overstimulating one. Similarly, although there will be many people around the ED, it will be better if you and the child interact with as few of them as possible. Hopefully, the ED staff will pay close attention to the information that you can give them. Keep in mind that it's easy to overwhelm them with information. The important things to be able to tell them are that the child has autism or a similar disability and that you are the parent and know the child's medical history. Use of a MedicAlert bracelet can be helpful (in case parents are not around). The school should have basic information that needs to be conveyed in the event of an emergency, and the school nurse can be helpful in being sure this is collected and available if needed.

If there are important issues such as allergies to medications, information relevant to the current emergency, or chronic health care problems, this should be communicated very quickly and briefly to the ED. The doctors and staff will also want to know the name of the local primary care physician. This doctor may be very helpful to you as well. For example, he or she could call ahead to let the ED staff know you're coming or talk with the ED staff to alert them to what works best for the child.

As in the doctor's office, the doctors and health care providers should be thoughtful and considerate in dealing with you. Except in a life-threatening situation, they should introduce themselves to you as well as to the child. If someone comes into the room without doing this, you should introduce yourself to them. It's important to realize that the staff of the ED may be misled by the child's appearance. Indeed, Leo Kanner, in his original report on autism, noted the ED staff to overestimate levels of functioning. If you notice that this seems to be happening, let them know. Obviously, if it's possible, the individual should be able to answer questions about his injury or illness. More typically, however, parents or teachers will be the people to do this, particularly for younger individuals. Again, the primary care provider may be able to provide information by phone or in person that will help the ED staff.

In a non-life-threatening situation, parents or familiar adults can usually be present to assist the staff in working with the child. The presence of familiar people will generally help calm the child, and they can also tell the doctors if, for example, there are any "tricks of the trade" in working with the person. For instance, you may know that the child particularly hates having her ears looked at. If this is so, you may tell the doctor that he or she may want to save this part of the examination to the very end. If the child has a favorite activity, engaging in this may help the child feel more comfortable.

Like the child's regular physician, the ED doctor should be very aware of several issues that often cause behavioral difficulties and acute behavioral change, particularly in doing a physical examination. Problem areas often include examination of the mouth and ears; unfortunately, these are just the places that can cause pain and discomfort (from an ear infection or an impacted wisdom tooth). Indeed, particularly in nonverbal children, problems in the mouth and ears can often result in acute behavioral change. A child who previously has been in good control may suddenly begin hitting herself on one side of the head or the other. This is often a clue that the child is suffering pain in some area.

If the child has breathing problems or allergies, it's important that the doctor listen to the chest and consider the possibility of pneumonia or other chest infection. The doctor will listen to the heart to be sure the child does not have an unusual heart rate or murmurs. The doctor will want to examine the child's abdomen by gently feeling different parts of his belly. The doctor will be looking for signs that indicate an acute infection, such as the point tenderness of appendicitis, or other problems. The doctor also may wish to do a rectal examination to see if the child is losing any blood in the digestive system and to be sure that constipation or bowel impaction is not causing the trouble.

Particularly if the child has recently fallen or had another injury, the doctor will also be alert to the possibility that she might have a broken bone or been knocked out. The doctor will wish to look at the child's arms and legs to look for swelling of the joints and so on. The doctor will also be looking for any problems in the skin, such as rashes or skin infections or any signs of injury. If the child has seemed to lose abilities over a short period of time, the doctor will also want to do a careful neurological examination. That involves checking the function and strength of many parts of the body, as well as checking reflexes with a reflex hammer. It is hard to do a thorough neurological exam with an uncooperative child, but the doctor will have to do the best that he or she can.

For girls and women with autism, a gynecological examination may sometimes be needed. It will be very important that the doctor or nurse practitioner know whether your child has previously had a gynecological examination.

Sometimes, even after a thorough search, the physical examination does not show any particular disease or evidence of injury. Often, the doctor will then want to order laboratory tests. These may include things such as analysis of the urine, a complete blood count, blood chemistry, tests of liver function, an electrocardiogram, or x-rays. Depending on the circumstance, the doctor may also wish to look for blood levels of medications your child is currently on. If your child has apparently ingested something he should not have, the doctor may also order toxicology screens. These can be either urine or blood tests.

If blood tests are needed, you may want to ask if an anesthetic cream can be used to numb your child's skin before the blood is drawn. EMLA (lidocaine/prilocaine) cream is one brand that is frequently used. It can make blood drawing a much less painful and upsetting process for your child. Unfortunately, the cream is meant to be applied to the skin an hour before the blood drawing in order to be maximally effective. In the emergency setting, this is often not possible.

Occasionally, a new illness will be heralded by an acute change in behavior or a level of functioning, and again the doctor will be alert to this. If there is a marked change in the child's level of consciousness or awareness of the environment, the doctor may order a computed tomography (CT) scan or conduct a lumbar puncture (spinal tap) in order to check for bleeding or signs of infection around the brain.

Sometimes it may be preferable for more invasive tests and procedures such as the vaginal examination, lumbar puncture, or even treatment of broken bones to be done with some degree of sedation. By this we mean that your child can be given some medication to make her less anxious or somewhat sleepy without putting her completely to sleep, as happens with general anesthesia. Medications to sedate your child can be given by the doctors in the ED either by mouth or as a shot in the muscle or intravenously. If general anesthesia is required, an anesthesiologist (a specialist in anesthesia) will be needed and your child will probably need to be taken to the operating room. This can sometimes take a long time to arrange.

It is important that the doctor realize that sometimes people with autism have "paradoxical" reactions to some sedatives; that is, they become more agitated, rather than calm. Consultation with an anesthesiologist may be helpful if sedation is needed. If you know that a particular medicine has been used before with good results—for example, at the dentist's—be sure to let the ED doctors know this. Similarly, if you know that some medicine resulted in a worsening of behavior rather than sedation, be sure to mention this. Be sure the anesthesiologist is aware of any medications that your child is on.

It's important that the primary care doctor realize that you have been to the ED and that the staff there communicate results of their assessment and any lab or other studies directly to him or her.

IS A TRIP TO THE ED REALLY NEEDED?

Sometimes it will be obvious that you need to go to the ED: The child will have a dramatic change in behavior, a broken bone, or a laceration requiring stitches. Other times, you may be unsure how urgent the situation is. For example, the child may have changes in response to illness that can be difficult to understand and may be difficult to put into words. That is, you may notice more irritability, changes in sleep patterns, weight loss, or what may seem to you to be a change in level of functioning. **It is always a good idea to check with your primary care provider first unless there are life-threatening problems. He may be able to give you some advice over the phone and/or see your child in the office, allowing you to avoid a visit to the ED altogether.**

Coping with the Hospital

In contrast to visits to the ED, hospitalizations are usually planned in advance. This gives some opportunity to prepare the child, adolescent, or adult and the hospital staff for his stay. As a general rule, it is best to try to avoid hospitalizations if possible due to the stress of having uncomfortable or painful procedures done in an unfamiliar environment by unfamiliar health care providers. This means that whenever possible, tests such as brain wave tests (electroencephalograms), hearing tests, or minor medical or surgical procedures such as having wisdom teeth removed, are best handled on an outpatient basis. When this isn't possible, a one-day admission to the hospital sometimes can be arranged so the child does not have to stay overnight. These possibilities should always be explored with the child's health care provider.

Sometimes it is impossible to avoid a hospital stay. For example, if your child has to have her appendix removed or if she has an infection that has to be treated by intravenous (IV) antibiotics, hospitalization may be mandatory. If it is possible to anticipate a hospital stay, however, you can at least take some steps to prepare the child.

Sometimes there is only one option in terms of a nearby hospital, particularly for less serious problems. At other times, there may be several choices and the task becomes more complicated. Often, for simpler problems, a community hospital may be best. These hospitals tend to be smaller, with fewer staff members. Often, the environment is less threatening and noisy, and if the hospital is closer to home, it makes it easier for parents and family members and others to visit. When problems are more complicated or medical procedures are more extensive, however, the child will have to be in a larger hospital setting. The strengths here have to do with the number of doctors and specialists available and their expertise. The downside, unfortunately, is that often many different doctors and staff are involved in the child's care and the hospital will be much busier and the pace more rapid.

Especially in a larger or teaching hospital, it's important for you to identify which doctor is primarily responsible for the child and work with him or her to be sure that medical care is well coordinated. Often, the pediatrician or primary health care provider will be involved on a regular basis. As in working with the regular doctor, you should never hesitate to ask questions. There may, of course, be times when either the situation is so urgent or the doctor is so busy that he or she will not at that point have time to discuss something with you. However, the doctor should always be able to go over your concerns or questions with you later. You should be made to feel and should feel that you work with the hospital staff as part of the team of people who are helping to provide the child with high-quality health care.

Depending on the individual's level of understanding, she should be informed about the hospitalization in advance in a calm way. It usually is not necessary to go into great detail. It may be helpful for the child to understand a little about what is going to happen. This is a judgment call based on the parents' and the doctor's knowledge of the child. Sometimes parents manage their own anxiety by trying to tell the child more than she needs to know. Again, try to strike a reasonable balance. Particularly if the admission is an elective one, it would be good to have the child, adolescent, or adult visit the hospital ahead of time. They should meet the staff and the doctors, if possible, and even have a tour of the operating room and recovery room facilities. Use of picture books, photographs, and other visual aids may be helpful. School staff might also be able to help prepare the child for the visit. For adults who are more cognitively challenged, it may be particularly helpful to have an introductory visit—in this case, as much for the medical staff as for the patient!

Many hospitals have what are called **Child Life** programs in which a trained professional will try to help the child understand what is going to happen in the hospital before he gets there. This is particularly helpful when the child is going through elective surgery or other kinds of procedures. The Child Life staff member may be able to show the child the room where he will go to sleep, the room where he will wake up, the kinds of materials he will see, and the staff he will meet. Occasionally, these individuals can be called on if there are adolescents or adults with developmental disabilities.

Whenever possible, you should talk to staff about ways to add as much familiarity to the hospital stay as possible. You can bring in a few familiar activities, videos, toys, and so forth. Maybe you can bring favorite music on an MP3 player or the child's familiar blanket. If the individual likes to watch his favorite videos, as is often the case, find out if there is a video or DVD player in the room or if one can be brought in.

The child should be accompanied by a family member or another familiar person who is aware of the child's communicative abilities. This person can be a teacher, a staff member, or a family friend, as well as a family member. The availability of this person helps the hospital seem like less of a strange place. This person can also help negotiate with hospital staff and try to explain, in terms the child will understand, all that is going to happen. In most hospitals, a parent or family member can "room in" with the child. This should be utilized whenever possible. Sometimes hospitals will provide staff members called "sitters" to help the family. This is a person who can stay with the child if there is no familiar person available for a time. If this service is available, it's important that the staff member have some familiarity with children with autism. Ideally, it would be someone who can communicate easily with the child by whatever modality she uses. Sometime teachers, aides, or other school staff (or friends or family members) can take over this role. If the child is not yet verbal but can use visual aids, you can use them to help her have a sense of what to expect—that is, use photographs to make visual schedules, use pictures to explain what will happen, and so forth.

CONSENT TO MEDICAL TREATMENTS

If your child with autism is in his late teens (the exact age varies from state to state), you need to make sure you understand what your state law says about giving consent for medical treatment. Once your child reaches a specific age, the power to withhold or grant consent for medical treatment will ordinarily pass from you, the parents, to your child. This may not be a problem if your child has good communication skills and is likely to understand the need for routine and emergency medical care. However, if your child is likely to refuse needed medical care due to comprehension or communication difficulties or because he has an aversion to doctors, you may need to take steps to retain control of medical decision making for him. Usually, this involves you, the parents, becoming the legal guardians of your child. In some situations, it may work well for you to establish some kind of limited guardianship in which you are responsible only for medical and/or financial decisions for your child.

If you have questions about medical consent, talk to your family lawyer or other parents to see what is needed. If possible, discuss the issue with your son or daughter as well. It is important to do this *before* you actually need it.

Preparing the hospital staff is as important as preparing the child for his stay. Hospital staff readily learn to "tune out" all the noises, smells, lights, and myriad activities and stimulations that occur on the hospital floor. They may not understand that a blinking light can be very distracting for a child with autism. Or they may not understand why a loud noise coming from a heart monitor may send him into a frenzy of activity or aggression. If possible, talk to staff about any potential difficulties the child might have before they occur.

Whenever possible, the hospital staff should know and use the child's routines to help her feel more comfortable in this strange place. So, for example, tell them about the child's ability to engage in self-care activities, her sleeping routines, such as the use of music or a story or a favorite object for comfort, and her favorite recreational activities. If the child is not feeling too unwell, school-based activities will also be a good way to help her spend some time and engage in familiar activities. Try to plan these in advance with the child's teacher.

More and more frequently these days, hospitals are set up for patients to have single or private rooms. If this is not the case, your child will need to share a room with another patient. You and the staff should carefully consider who they put in the other bed in the room. It may be hard for your child to have a fussy child in the room or someone with many visitors.

Staff should also be educated about any safety measures your child needs. It is a bit surprising, but in fact the hospital can be a somewhat dangerous place. If your child is impulsive or tends to act out behaviorally, are there provisions for his safety? Questions to consider might include:

- Does she need a room where the windows are protected—for example, so that she cannot be tempted to throw things out or jump out?

- Does she need an adult in the room all the time?

- Does she need some of the room furniture to be removed?

- Can familiar objects be placed in the room to make her feel more comfortable—within reason?

- If the child is self-abusive, does she need to wear a helmet or mittens?

- What behavioral techniques help the child avoid difficult behaviors? What techniques are most effective? What techniques are less effective?

Parents can help hospital staff immensely by conveying this kind of information.

Hospital Procedures

At the time of admission, whether it is an emergency admission or an elective admission that has been scheduled, it will be important to review the child's history with members of the treatment team. Be sure also to let hospital staff know if the child is receiving medications on a regular basis. If he is coming for an elective admission to the hospital, it is easy for parents to bring along bottles of medicine. If this is an emergency admission, it's important that the parent or staff members have a list of medications readily at hand so that the hospital knows exactly what medicine the child receives and when. This is particularly important if the child takes seizure medications or medicines that help address behavior problems.

Once the child has been admitted, there are several things you can do to make the hospital experience less traumatizing:

- *Ensure that the child feels as safe as possible in her own room.* Some procedures, such as blood drawing, are uncomfortable and whenever possible should not be done in the child's hospital room. A treatment room is preferable so that the child feels as safe as possible in her own room. Everything should be ready in the treatment room by the time the child arrives, so that the procedure can be done as quickly and as safely as possible. You or another caregiver may need to assist with the procedure. If you choose to leave the room, extra hospital staff may be needed.

- *Make sure the child knows what is going to happen.* Before beginning, the hospital staff should explain to the child what is involved in as much detail as he needs. It's important in telling children about procedures to be honest. Well-meaning lies such as "It won't hurt" cause more trouble in the long run than the truth. If the child can and does ask whether something will hurt, tell the truth. You do not have to go overboard on this, but you should be honest and straightforward.

Preparing the child is especially important when she has elective surgery. Here, the opportunity for her to meet the staff and to see the recovery room and the operative suite of rooms can be very helpful. With the permission of those involved, you can take photographs, which can be put in a book that you can review with the child before (and after) the experience of surgery.

- *Create a diversion, when possible.* Procedures such as lumbar puncture and throat culture may present particular challenges. During uncomfortable procedures, you can sometimes help the child by taking his mind off the procedure by counting, listening to a favorite story, or talking about the child's favorite interests. Using rewards both during and after the procedure may also be helpful. It is very important for parents to try to stay calm. If the parent is calm, it is more likely the child will be calm.

  Some procedures, such as electroencephalograms (EEGs), CT scans, or MRIs require a much longer period of time. It may be impossible to get a child with autism to cooperate long enough for these without sedation or general anesthesia. In our research with MRIs, we use a mock scanner (i. e., a replica of a real one) for children to use to become familiar with what it feels like to be in an MRI machine.

- *Avoid restraining your child if possible.* Sometimes this can be done through careful preparation, but sometimes children cannot cooperate with procedures and have to be restrained. It is best to avoid this if possible, but when it is necessary, it is better if a number of trained people are available to help things go as smoothly as possible. Although it can be difficult to watch, your child is less likely to hurt herself or others if a number of people hold her still.

- *Reduce pain as much as possible.* Sometimes pain or anxiety can be avoided by premedication. We discussed the use of EMLA cream, sedation, and anesthesia earlier in the section on dealing with the ED. If you know ahead of time that a certain medication will be used for sedation, you may want to try it first at home to see how your child reacts to it. *Be sensitive to the child's needs.* As with other patients, it's important that hospital staff be sensitive to the needs of the child and the family. Sometimes children (or parents) may overhear aspects of conversations that are not necessarily about them but may be upsetting to them. Usually, it is not good to have "secrets" from the child—often, these end up not being secrets at all and they have the potential to backfire in unfortunate ways. Thus, conversations about the child's medical care, current medical status, and future procedures are probably best done outside the room with the parents and doctor first, and then, immediately afterward, in a briefer and more relevant form with the child. Of course, all information should be given to the child with tact and sensitivity. Older and more able individuals can and should be involved in discussions of their care whenever possible and realistic.

Surgery

If surgical intervention is being considered (unless on an emergency basis), there should be a careful discussion of the benefits and risks for the child. In considering the benefits and risks, it is important to realize that surgery has the potential for disrupting ongoing programs, causing the child some discomfort, and always has the possibility for complications and infections.

The child's regular doctor can be very helpful to you in balancing the pros and cons of surgery. Sometimes the pro is that the procedure is easier to do when the child is younger or that the problem may become worse as he gets older. Sometimes the procedure may significantly increase the child's ability to profit from educational or other programs. For example, the placement of pressure-equalizing tubes may allow the child to hear better. Other times, such as with appendicitis, surgery is not elective but absolutely necessary.

If the child is having elective (i.e., nonemergency) surgery, you fortunately will have time to explore the various options and prepare the child, as much as is possible and appropriate, for the experience. As mentioned earlier, the Child Life specialist will be able to assist you in helping prepare the child for the experience. Of course, since you know the child so well, you may also have important information about her to share with the Child Life specialist. Again, you might want to take some pictures ahead of time to introduce the child to the hospital and the staff. You don't want to be horribly intrusive, but you may be able to take a few pictures during the visit to use in talking to the child afterward. Alternatively, if the child can make use of more verbal modalities, Social Stories might be helpful.

Anesthesia   If the child will need **anesthesia,** try to schedule a time to speak with the **anesthesiologist** (a doctor who administers anesthesia) or nurse–anesthetist (nurse who administers anesthesia) to talk to them in advance about the child's special circumstances. These should include his ability to cooperate and understand, any special fears or anxieties you and the child may have, and the child's medical history. Particularly if the procedure or surgery is being done in a one-day surgery center or in anticipation of discharge to home immediately afterward, be sure to listen to the instructions that you are given. For example, usually the child should not eat for some hours prior to anesthesia.

The anesthesiologist will usually talk to you about the kind of anesthesia that she or he plans to use. Sometimes anesthesia is "local" (such as when the dentist numbs up a tooth before putting a filling in); sometimes it is "general" (when the person is basically put to sleep). Some children with autism may need general anesthesia for even minor procedures because they may become so agitated when people try to do anything to them that they cannot be controlled easily. Other children may do just fine with local anesthesia for procedures such as getting a cut stitched up.

Sometimes a small amount of sedation can help a child be able to use local anesthesia. Sedation will make the child less anxious, and the local aesthetic will prevent pain in the area of the procedure. Often, before general anesthesia, some sedative agent is given to help the child feel less anxious. The question of what type of anesthesia is something you can discuss with the doctor.

Recovery Room   After a procedure or surgery, the child may be moved back into a recovery room—a special place where nurses and doctors can keep a close eye on the child until they know that things are okay and that he is awake. Usually, the child should have seen the recovery room ahead of time (assuming that this was not an emergency procedure). It will help if you are around and can stay calm and collected. If possible, arrange for a favorite toy, game, or other familiar object to be nearby when the child awakens. You should ask to join the child as soon as is practical after the surgery. As with other things, an ounce of prevention is worth a pound of cure. Try to anticipate problems and discuss the child's needs in advance with the staff in the recovery room.

DENTAL CARE

As is true in other areas, an ounce of prevention is worth a pound of cure when it comes to dental care. Children who have inadequate prevention are at risk for major problems as they get older. For example, dental pain may cause self-injurious behavior, and untreated dental problems can lead to other medical problems—sometimes severe ones. Sadly, some children and some adults with autism we know are only able to have a dental examination and dental procedures under general anesthesia! The goal should be to try to prevent the development of such fears of dental care. Unfortunately, that is not always possible.

Occasionally, dental problems first present themselves as behavior changes in children and adolescents with ASD. This is particularly common in children who have more difficulties with communication skills and who have had limited ongoing dental care due to their lack of cooperation (sometimes despite the best efforts of parents!). This may happen, for example, when a cavity has progressed into a very painful dental **abscess.** In such a circumstance, the child's behavior may gradually, or more abruptly, deteriorate and self-injurious behavior may develop. The self-injurious behavior usually takes the form of face slapping or head banging and may be quite severe. Sometimes an abscess may be visible on the face as a swollen and puffy bulge in the cheek, but this doesn't always happen. Occasionally, an older adolescent with autism may develop these problems as the wisdom teeth come in. Younger children with autism sometimes also develop self-injurious behavior (although usually in a somewhat less severe form) as their teeth come in.

Children with autism and other PDDs are at increased risk for dental problems due to the same symptoms of autism that complicate other aspects of health care. These include many of the problems also faced in dealing with going to the doctor's office as we discussed earlier in this chapter. They may be particularly difficult due to the child's unusual sensitivities (e.g., to the smell or taste or grittiness of toothpaste), difficulties with oral "defensiveness" (an unwillingness to have things in the mouth), or difficulties with attention (making it difficult to sit for a long period in the dental chair).

Children with specific diagnoses along the autism spectrum may have additional dental problems. For example, children with Rett's disorder who have problems in eating and swallowing may retain bits of food in the mouth, making cavities more likely. Children with fragile X syndrome may have specific malformations such as crowding of the teeth.

Coping with the Dentist's Office

Most children with autism spectrum disorders should start seeing a dentist around age 3 unless problems have been noted earlier. A big part of these early visits to the dentist is to help the child become comfortable with the office and the dentist. It also gives the dentist a chance to get to know the parents, and to provide information on dental care and preventative measures such as fluoride. The dentist may also help think about ways to encourage good dental care (tooth brushing and flossing).

While all this is happening, the child can (within limits and with supervision) get more familiar with the office and its operation. A chance to see and maybe hold the instruments may be helpful. As time goes on, modeling the behaviors needed at the dentist and with dental procedures can be useful, with parents and siblings showing the child what to do.

You should be thoughtful and careful in selecting the child's dentist. Good sources of information on potential dentists include the primary physician or other health care provider, as well as other parents. Some dentists have special expertise in working with children or individuals with developmental problems. If the child has difficulty working with a regular dentist, it may be worth trying to find a pediatric dentist with special expertise in this area; sometimes these dentists will also work with older individuals who have developmental challenges.

Just as with visits to the doctor's office, visits to the dentist's office will go more smoothly if you try to anticipate potential problems. Sometimes the child may need to visit the dentist's office to see it before she is ready to actually begin having examinations or dental procedures. The use of picture books in advance of the visit and a visual schedule for procedures may be helpful. Some commercial books are available (see the reading list at the end of this chapter), and you can make your own as well.

Some dentists, particularly those especially trained in working with children, pride themselves on taking it "slow and easy" with a new patient with autism. They will realize that the new situation has many potentially overwhelming sights and sounds and may be a bit of a push for the child with an ASD. They may try to work out a program for the child in which they gradually do more and more actual dental work. For instance, the first goal may be for the child to just sit in the dental chair and go up and down or sit on your lap on the dental chair. Next, they may work on having the child tolerate the dentist/hygienist looking inside his mouth without touching it and so on. This can take time.

You can also talk to the dentist and the dental hygienist about "tricks of the trade" they may have heard about. For example, some children may not like the texture or taste of certain toothpastes or polishing compounds (sometimes the gritty texture makes for special trouble). A patient dentist will be willing to take the time needed to make the child feel more comfortable because he or she knows that the treatment will be more likely to be successful in the long run.

Occasionally, particularly for more challenging or painful procedures, the dentist may want to use sedative medications or other specific techniques (e.g., nitrous oxide [laughing gas]) to make them more tolerable for the child. Except in cases of emergency, you'll have the chance to discuss these ahead of time. Keep a couple of things in mind when discussing options for anesthesia or medication. In general, don't try something for the first time and expect it to work. As discussed earlier, some children with autism get more agitated with anesthesia or premedication. In our experience, when premedication is going to be used, it may be worthwhile to try a "test dose" at home (or in the dentist's office) and see how the child tolerates it.

Sometimes the dentist may want to treat the child in a hospital on a day admission or in an outpatient hospital facility where anesthesia is available. The dentist may recommend this for routine examination if he or she has not been able to do a good exam even after several attempts to help the child be more comfortable.

TIPS ON DENTAL HEALTH

- Start early. Tooth brushing should be started as soon as the teeth begin to come in. Try to make this an enjoyable game or have a special (favorite) activity after.

- Try different toothpastes. Different flavors are available. Brushing without toothpaste is better than not brushing at all!

- Talk to the dentist (also maybe to the pharmacist) about ways to give the toothbrush a taste that is interesting.

- For children who don't tolerate the toothbrush, work on a plan to help introduce it.

- Try brushing teeth in front of a mirror. Sometimes children are interested in watching themselves. You can also try tooth brushing as a family activity (occasionally children with autism will get into the swing of this).

- If the child won't brush her teeth, encourage water drinking immediately after meals (to try to clean out as much food as possible from the teeth and give the bacteria that cause cavities less food to grow on). You can do this with a bottle for very young children or through a straw or squeeze bottle for older children.

- Think about other approaches. Some children like mechanical things and might be willing to try an electric toothbrush or one of the water irrigators.

- Avoid foods that are known to cause cavities. This means limiting sweets, particularly sticky sweets. Some candies are particularly likely to stick to children's teeth, such as "fruit roll-ups" and dried fruits such as raisins. Keep in mind that many drinks have large amounts of sugar as well. Try to encourage use of other (nonsweet) foods as snacks. For children who receive foods as reinforcers, try to encourage a range of foods.

- If the child has motor difficulties talk with the occupational therapist or physical therapist about adapted toothbrushes that may give the child more stability and control.

- For more able children, "disclosing tablets" (which show areas where more brushing is needed) might be both helpful and instructive.

You don't want to turn tooth brushing into a daily battle, but try to turn it into a regular and routine habit. Flossing can also be started early on for children who will tolerate this (not all will, but it is worth trying). Fluoride is a chemical that makes tooth enamel harder and more resistant to decay and is now commonly added to the drinking water in the United States. If your water has no fluoride added or you have well water, you can talk to the dentist about ordering fluoride for daily use. For some children, sealants can make a big difference in reducing cavities.

IMMUNIZATIONS AND AUTISM

In the past, there were many childhood illnesses that almost all children had to suffer through in order to become immune to them. In the past, many children died from these illnesses and others suffered permanent brain damage. For example, Helen Keller became both blind and deaf as a result of a childhood infection that today could have been prevented. Now many infectious diseases can be prevented by vaccination. Some illnesses, such as smallpox, have been eliminated, which is why there is no longer a routine immunization requirement for smallpox. Other illnesses, such as polio, will hopefully be eliminated in the not-too-distant future. Sometimes the reason for immunization is to protect the child from a serious illness; at other times, it may be to prevent the illness in adults. If a pregnant woman develops rubella, there can be very serious consequences for the fetus. The use of immunizations to prevent childhood illness and reduce childhood disability and death is a triumph of medicine in the last century. There are now a number of illnesses that can be prevented through immunization; this list changes all the time as new immunizations become available. See the Advisory Committee on Immunization Practices (www.cdc.gov/vaccines), the American Academy of Pediatrics (www.aap.org), and the American Academy of Family Physicians (www.aafp.org).

Over the past several years, there has been much concern that autism might sometimes be caused by the measles immunization in the measles, mumps, and rubella **(MMR)** vaccination, or by the **mercury**-containing preservative **thimerosal** in some **vaccines.** The measles connection was suggested in a study in the prestigious British medical journal, *The Lancet,* in which it was stated that persistent measles virus could be found in the gastrointestinal (GI) tract of a very small number of children with autism. It was theorized that this finding in the gut was somehow connected with a change in the brain, causing the children to become autistic. The conclusions of this article were later retracted. The fear that measles immunization (particularly the MMR combination) could cause autism led many parents, starting in Great Britain, to refuse the shot for their children. As a result, there have now been increasing numbers of cases of measles in Great Britain but, unfortunately no decrease in the number of cases of autism. Similarly, even though there was no good data suggesting that the thimerosal was the cause of autism, it was taken out of all of the vaccines except for multiple-dose vials of influenza vaccine used for children over 3 years old. And once again, as with the decrease in the use of the measles vaccine, there continued to be more and more cases of autism diagnosed.

It is true that some children with autism seem to be doing fine until some specific event, after which they seem to regress (see Chapter 13). This is not the case in the majority of cases of autism; however, there are several things that make this whole business difficult to sort out. In the first place, it is likely that the apparent association between an immunization such as measles and the onset of regression is just that—only an *apparent* association. They may have occurred at the same time, but one may not have caused the other. This seems possible since the vaccine is usually given at a time when parents start to notice possible developmental problems anyway. A recent report from the National Academy of Sciences (see the reading list) did not find convincing evidence for the association of measles immunization with autism.

A number of well-done scientific studies have now been conducted and do not support the idea that immunizations cause autism. Studies done around the world have failed to find good evidence that either the measles vaccine itself or the preservative might cause autism. For example, in Denmark, the rates of autism increased *after* the preservative was eliminated from the vaccine. A study by Taylor and his coworkers (1999) found no change in the rates of autism with the use of MMR vaccine. Similarly, rates of autism don't seem to change in sensible ways in relation to changes in the MMR vaccination formulation. The reading list provides more information on this topic.

If your child has had an unusual reaction to immunizations or if you are concerned about the MMR immunization, you should discuss this with your child's doctor.

Summary

In this chapter, we reviewed some aspects of health care in autism. We emphasized that finding a good health care provider is really important and worth spending extra time on. We also discussed the importance of helping the child become familiar with the doctor's office and office staff and of paying attention to routine care and immunizations. We advocated for keeping a short medical summary with the child, particularly if he has any important medical conditions. Even if he doesn't, it will be good to have a summary that can be used in case of emergency. We finished with a discussion of some of the most common medical problems you may encounter, as well as other disorders that have been associated with autism.

We also discussed some aspects of illness in children with autism, as well as injuries, the ED, and hospitalization. Obstacles to effective diagnosis and treatment for children with ASDs include difficulties in communication and unusual behaviors. There are many steps that you can take to ensure that the child receives high-quality health care.

Obviously, you want the child to be as healthy as possible. Whenever possible and appropriate, medical conditions should be treated promptly and thoroughly. However, sometimes children with autism may have relatively minor problems for which treatment may not always be appropriate or a priority. You sometimes have to decide if the child would be better off suffering the symptoms of a minor condition, rather than suffering from the cure. To the extent possible and appropriate, the child should be involved in discussions about her treatment. Since the medical care of children with autism is not always cut and dried, it is vital that you are able to make informed decisions about the child's care. This is best done by building a strong working relationship with the doctor and the other health care providers who are part of the treatment team.

▮ READING LIST

Acs, G., & Ng, M. W. (2001). Dental care for your child with special needs. In M. L. Batshaw (Ed.), *When your child has a disability: The complete sourcebook for daily and medical care.* Baltimore: Brookes.

Ahearn, W. H., Castine, T., Nault, K., and Gina, G. (2001). An assessment of food acceptance in children with autism or pervasive developmenal disorder not otherwise specified. *Journal of Autism and Developmental Disorders, 31,* 505–511.

Attwood, S. (2008). *Making sense of sex: A forthright guide to puberty, sex and relationships for people with Asperger's syndrome.* Baltimore: Jessica Kingsley.

Batshaw, M. (2002). *Children with disabilities* (5th ed.). Baltimore: Brookes.

Civardi A., & Bates, M. (Eds.). (2001). *Going to the dentist (first experiences).* Tulsa, OK: EDC.

Civardi, A., & Bates, M. (Eds.). (2001). *Going to the hospital.* Tulsa, OK: EDC.

Cornish, E. (2002). Gluten and casein free diets in autism: A study of the effects on food choice and nutrition. *Journal of Human Nutrition and Dietetics, 15,* 261–269.

Duyfee, R. L. (2002). *American Dietetic Association complete food and nutrition guide* (2nd ed.). New York: Wiley.

Fombonne, E., & Cook, J. E. H. (2003). MMR and autistic enterocolitis: Consistent epidemiological failure to find an association. *Molecular Psychiatry, 8,* 133–134.

Hollins, S., Avis, A., and Cheverton, S. (1998). *Going into hospital.* London: Gaskell and St. George's Hospital Medical School.

Hollins, S., Bernal, J., & Gregory, M. (1996). *Going to the doctor.* London: St. George's Mental Health Library.

Kedesdy, J. H., & Budd, K. S. (1998). *Childhood feeding disorders: Biobehavioral assessment and intervention.* Baltimore: Brookes.

Legge, B. (2002). *Can't eat, won't eat: Dietary difficulties and autistic spectrum disorders.* London: Jessica Kingsley.

Mayer, M. (1990). *Just going to the dentist.* New York: Golden Books.

Murkoff, H. (2002). *What to expect when you go to the dentist.* New York: Harper Festival.

Offit, P. A. (2008). *Autism's false prophets: Bad science, risky medicine, and the search for a cure.* New York: Columbia University Press.

Pace, B. (2002). *Chris gets ear tubes.* Washington, DC: Gallaudet University Press.

Rogers, F. (2002). *Going to the hospital.* Tulsa: EDC.

Stratton, K., Gable, A., & McCormick, M. (Eds.), (2001). *Immunization safety review: Thimerosal containing vaccines and neurodevelopmental disorders.* Immunization Safety Review Committee–Institute of Medicine. Washington, DC: National Academies Press. (Can be ordered online at www.nap.edu.).

Stratton, K., Gable, A., Shetty, P., & McCormick, M. (Eds.). (2001). *Immunization safety review: Measles-mumps-rubella vaccine and autism.* Immunization Safety Review Committee–Institute of Medicine. Washington, DC: National Academies Press. (Can be ordered online at www.nap.edu.).

Taylor, B., Miller, E., Farrington, C. P., Petropoulos, M. C., Favot-Mayaud, I., Li, J., et al. (1999). Autism and measles, mumps, and rubella vaccine: No epidemiological evidence for a causal association [see comments]. *Lancet, 353*(9169), 2026–2029.

Taylor, B., Miller, E., Lingam, R., Andrews, N., Simmons, A., & Stowe, J. (2002). Measles, mumps, and rubella vaccination and bowel problems or developmental regression in children with autism: Population study. *British Medical Journal, 324*(7334), 393–396.

Weber, J. D. (2000). *Children with fragile X syndrome: A parents' guide.* Bethesda, MD: Woodbine House.

■ QUESTIONS AND ANSWERS

1. **My daughter is really phobic about going to the doctor. She freaks out when she sees the stethoscope, not to mention the thing the doctor looks in her ears with. We get so anxious taking her to doctors. What can we do to prevent all this?**

   There are a couple of things you can do. One is to attempt to gradually have your child become more familiar with medical "stuff." See if you can get her a doctor's kit to play with. Sometimes doctors' offices will have old stethoscopes children can see. One of the functions of "playing doctor" for typically developing children is to deal with their anxieties about going to the doctor. In that respect, your daughter's response may be pretty normal. She may, however, lack some of the abilities to put all this into words. See if looking at some books about going to the doctor helps. You could also try taking pictures and/or developing a story about going to the doctor. If the problem persists, talk with the school psychologist or someone with experience in managing behavior problems to see if you can come up with a way to make the experience more positive for her.

2. **My husband's employment recently changed and we have a new insurance company. It seems like we'll have to change our son's pediatrician since he doesn't participate. Is this a good idea?**

   If you have had a good experience so far with your current pediatrician, it is *not* a good idea. See if you can find out why your pediatrician doesn't participate or whether you might have a choice of insurance plans and still be able to have the same doctor. Although switching of pediatricians is more and more common (for the reasons you mention), it is not a good idea for someone with chronic medical problems or with difficulties adjusting to new people and places.

3. **My child hates going to the doctor's office, so I usually go only when I have to. Is this a mistake?**

Yes, it is a mistake. The more familiar you and your child are with the office, the less traumatic it will be to go--particularly when your child is not feeling well anyway. Talk to your child's doctor and maybe the office staff to see what they can do to help you (e.g., giving you the first appointment of the day or giving your child a room of his own to wait in). Try to go just to get acquainted and have a special treat for your child waiting at the office. If need be, get the help of a behavioral psychologist so that you can work out a plan to help your child feel more comfortable. It will pay off in the long run!

4. **Our daughter won't let anyone brush her teeth, but she doesn't do a good enough job on her own. She's already had two cavities and had to have general anesthesia to fill them. What can we do?**

Children on the autism spectrum can be very sensitive about having things done in or near their mouths, so this can be a problem. You seem to suggest that she is at least doing some brushing of her teeth. Try to encourage this. Talk to her speech pathologist and maybe to the occupational therapist, as well as the dentist, to think about ways to help her with doing a better job brushing. Some children like (while others hate) electric toothbrushes. Ask your dentist about having sealants and/or fluoride treatments to help prevent cavities.

5. **My son has a dreadful allergy to some antibiotics. My wife and I worry that if he is ever injured and we are not around, he might be taken to a hospital or doctor who doesn't know this. What can we do?**

You can do several things. If your child can be persuaded to wear it, a MedicAlert bracelet can go with him all the time. In any case, your program/school staff should all have a basic record of special medical needs. A copy of this record should travel with your child—to outings, to summer camp, on sleepovers. If your child keeps a wallet with him, you can also put a copy there.

6. **My child has to have some elective surgery. There is a large teaching hospital about 50 miles away and a community hospital in our town. Which one should we use?**

This really depends on the nature of the surgery. The advantages of staying in town are pretty obvious, so the question is, are there advantages to the larger teaching hospital that outweigh these known positives? If it is a complicated or specialized surgery, has the staff at the larger hospital had more experience with it? How much of a hassle will it be for you to go to the larger hospital? Can you stay with your child in the hospital? Your child's pediatrician should be a good person to advise you on this.

7. **My child seems to get a lot of colds and infections and runs a fever when she is sick. Is a fever dangerous?**

Your question is really a two-part one. A fever by itself is not necessarily dangerous. A fever is a sign of infection, and, obviously, that is something that needs to be looked into. But fevers per se are not necessarily dangerous—unless your child has seizures or the fever is very high and could trigger fever-related (febrile) seizures. You also mention that your child has many infections. Has she recently started to go to school or into day care? Sometimes children who have not previously had many infections will start to get them when they are exposed to other sick children (one of the reasons why you should try *not* to send your child to school or day care when she is sick!).

8. **My child hates taking medicines. Are there any tricks to getting him to do so?**

Here are several ideas to try:

- Give him something that he likes to taste first and then give him the medicine followed by another helping of whatever it is he likes.

- Similarly, you can mix many medications with foods or drinks that taste better, but be sure to talk to your doctor or pharmacist to check on this first.

- Ask your pharmacist if there is any way for him to mix the medicine in a liquid form that might taste better.

- Parents have told us many different things that worked for their children. One parent mentioned having the child suck on a cold Popsicle to numb the taste buds and then give him the medicine!

9. **Are there specific genetic tests for autism?**

There are tests for some disorders (like fragile X) often associated with autism. There are also now a number of genes being studied as potential causes of autism and it may be that tests for at least some of these genes will be available in the not so distant future. Knowledge in this area is changing rapidly. Genetic studies can now look for more subtle changes, for example, breaks and rearrangements in chromosomes. Talk with your doctor about current recommendations on genetic testing.

CHAPTER 11

Ensuring Safety

All children have accidents and injuries. The occasional hurt or "owie," broken bone, bump, fall, cut, or scrape is part of growing up. This is true for all children, but children with autism and related conditions are probably at increased risk for injuries and accidents. This happens for several reasons. An understanding of important safety concepts (such as that hot things are dangerous) can come later than for most children. In addition, children on the autism spectrum may be more impulsive. Younger children with autism, in particular, seem to have an unusual combination of poor judgment and good motor ability. Other children with autism spectrum disorders (such as Asperger's disorder) may have poor judgment and poor motor ability. Either situation can lead to trouble. The unusual sensory interests sometimes seen in autism and related conditions can also be a problem. For example, the autistic child may not mind the taste of something that most of us would find bitter or might be interested in something vibrating or twirling, like the wings of a bee or the twirling blades of a fan. Children with autism can also surprise you. The child who is otherwise fearful of new things or situations may seem driven to explore a new construction site, or the child who is otherwise afraid of the water may be preoccupied with a neighbor's swimming pool. Likewise, the child who is usually fearful of things and has been once stung by a bee may not seem to learn from that particular experience. For all these reasons, you should take extra care in trying to prevent problems before they happen. In this chapter, we consider some of the issues involved in being sure children on the autism spectrum are safe. This chapter includes some general information on safety and focuses on issues specifically related to children with pervasive developmental disorder (PDD). It is not meant to be an exhaustive discussion of all aspects of safety in children. There are many good books devoted entirely to that topic. Several are mentioned in the reading list at the end of this chapter. As you will see, we divide this chapter into several sections on safety at home, safety at school, and safety in the community. There may be points in each section that are relevant to the others. Keep in mind that the child's level of development, as well as her size, will greatly influence what she will find enticing and appealing and the kinds of problem situations that can arise.

ACCIDENTS AND INJURIES

- Injuries are the leading cause of death in children and adolescents in the United States.
- Fatal injuries are just the tip of the iceberg: For every fatal injury, another 18 children end up in the hospital and over 200 are treated in the emergency department.
- The good news (and sad news) is that most of these injuries are preventable.
- Available data suggest that children with autism are at increased risk for serious injury and even death due to accidents such as drowning and suffocation.

GENERAL HOUSEHOLD SAFETY

An ounce of prevention is worth a pound of cure. Take sensible precautions as you would for any child. This is especially true for younger children with autism, who have a knack for finding dangerous situations or places. Even for normally developing youngsters, you cannot always anticipate what they will get into. Many children with autism or PDD will require safety supervision longer than other children. Their judgment about which places are safe and what might be hot or sharp may not be as good as you would like. As children on the autism spectrum get older and consequently larger and stronger, you may need to re-think what will keep them safe. For example, an older child may be able to undo a standard plastic outlet cover but not yet realize the dangers of poking something into the outlet. Screw-on covers that are harder to remove may be helpful. LectraLock (http://lectralock.com/residential.htm) is a company that provides ideas and products for this kind of safety. Many children with autism, particularly young children, are not safe unless someone is watching them all the time. The ways to provide a safe environment vary with the child's age and surroundings. For younger children and for many older children with PDD, you will need to either: (1) have someone keep an eye on them constantly, (2) take them along when you need to leave the room briefly, or (3) have a safe area where they can be left alone briefly without any risk of harm. A crib or playpen may be a safe place for a younger child. The child's bedroom can be a safe and secure place to leave him briefly if he can't get out on his own. Keep in mind that you want to teach safety; this means modeling the behavior you want, reminding the child about safety through regular and routine discussion and reminders, and so forth.

Safety steps to take include covering electrical sockets; locking cabinets that contain poisonous cleaning supplies and paints; putting in door latches and stair gates; and storing knives, scissors, and other sharp objects out of reach. Check for the obvious hazards—things like open stairwells, areas where the child could easily fall, sharp objects protruding from walls or floors, and so on. Be sure windows are secured and that the child cannot fall out of them. Use window guards on windows, particularly for rooms on the second story and higher. And, of course, if there are any guns in the home, be sure they are unloaded and locked away out of all children's reach. The absolute safest way to avoid gun accidents is not to have guns in the house.

You also want to keep the home safe from fire or poisonous gases. Matches, flammable materials, candles, and electrical cords can all be dangerous in the hands of a child. You should have a smoke detector and a carbon monoxide detector, as well as a working fire extinguisher on each floor of the home. Be sure the child cannot turn on the stove herself. Also be sure that the furnace or any wood-burning stove or other heaters are working properly. Know what number to call in your area if you have a fire emergency. In many places, it is 911.

IMPORTANT NUMBERS TO POST ON THE PHONE

- 911 or local police and fire department numbers
- Pediatrician's name and phone number
- Local hospital's emergency departments number
- Poison Control Center number: 800-222-1222

In addition to the more general safety precautions, go room to room with an eye for potential safety hazards relative to the child with an ASD. For example, what looks colorful and interesting? What would be tempting to pull at? Are the fans or things that spin within the child's reach? Something that looks unappealing and unappetizing to you may look delicious to the child. This is even more of a problem when some medications may look and, indeed, even taste like desirable candies.

Overall, the kitchen and bathrooms are probably the most dangerous areas in the home. Take a particularly careful look at these rooms and remove dangerous objects that the child could get hurt with, and block access to places where he could get injured.

Like other children, those on the autism spectrum tend to spend most of their time in their bedroom, so be sure it is a safe place. Depending on the child, it may be best to keep the room sparsely furnished (this may help with sleep at night as well; see Chapter 17). Take a careful look for things that can be a source of danger, for example, a bookcase that can be pulled to a window or over on a child. You can use an intercom to alert you when she is leaving the room, especially at night. Another option that can work nicely is to use a Dutch door; you can then lock shut the bottom half of the door and keep the top half open so you can either see or hear the child. If the child with autism shares a room with an older sibling, be sure that none of the older child's belongings present a safety hazard. If the autistic child shares a room with a younger child, be sure that she doesn't allow the younger child to get into trouble such as by opening a gate or door and letting the younger child out of the room without a parent's knowing about it.

Falls, such as down the stairs or out a window, are mostly a problem for younger children, but some older kids with autism may misjudge a distance or a height and have an unexpected accident. If the child likes to move chairs around and climb, be sure that he can't climb onto a windowsill and then fall out of the window. Make sure all windows have screens that can't be easily dislodged. You may need to block the space in front of windows if the child is a good climber. Gates can be used to protect children from falling down stairs. You may need to fasten the gate to the wall if it is at the top of a staircase. Pressure gates may give way if a bigger child pushes into it.

Poisoning

Poisonings can occur at any age. Harmful household cleaners and detergents as well as medications, both prescription and nonprescription, and paints and solvents are common sources of poisonings. Cosmetic products and household plants can also be poisonous if eaten.

COMMON HOUSEHOLD POISONS

Kitchen

- Dishwasher detergents
- Drain cleaners
- Ammonia
- Oven cleaners
- Glass cleaners

Bathroom

- Medicines (over-the-counter and prescription)
- Toilet bowel cleaners
- Thermometers containing mercury
- Deodorizers

Laundry Area

- Detergents
- Bleach

Basement or Garage

- Automotive materials
- Antifreeze
- Windshield cleaner/deicer
- Insect killers
- Glues
- Paints
- Paint thinner/remover
- Kerosene
- Brake fluid
- Gasoline
- Rat/mouse poison
- Lighter fluids/charcoal starter

Other Areas

- Alcohol
- Cigarettes
- Furniture polish
- Moth balls/cakes

To guard against poisoning:

- Keep prescription (and nonprescription) medicines in safe and secure spots with child-resistant caps. (Be aware, however, that even child-resistant caps are not 100% effective.)
- Be aware that unfinished alcoholic drinks are potentially dangerous if they are consumed by younger children.

- Keep in mind that even a medication or vitamin that you regularly give to the child can be harmful if the child decides to feed herself too many of them.

- Keep poisons in places where the child can't reach them. This can be different places at different ages. Child-resistant latches on cabinets offer some protection, as do child-resistant bottles, but don't underestimate the child's ability to get into things! Substances that are quite poisonous should be kept under lock and key.

- Keep things in their original containers so you know what they are.

- For children who can understand its meaning, use bright colored stickers to indicate which substances may be harmful. Mr. Yuk stickers have been used successfully for this purpose by many parents. These stickers can be procured from the Pittsburgh Poison Center at the Children's Hospital of Pittsburgh (http://chp.edu/CHP/mryuk).

POISONOUS OR TOXIC FLOWERS AND PLANTS

Common House Plants and Flowers

- Philodendron
- Dumbcane
- Peace lily
- Amaryllis
- Foxglove
- Monkshood
- Lilly of the valley
- Aloe
- Caladium
- Elephant ear
- Narcissus
- Daffodil
- Oleander
- Larkspur
- Poinsettia
- Chrysanthemum

Wild Flowers and Plants

- Nightshade (various varieties)

- Henbane
- Hemlock
- Morning glory
- Mountain laurel
- Mistletoe
- Jimson weed
- Hellebore
- Buttercup
- Castor bean
- Rhododendron
- English holly

Note: This is just a partial list.

At home (and also at school) the Poison Control Center number should be posted near the phone or school nurse's office. (The national number—which can put you in touch with the local center—is 800-222-1222). When you call the Poison Control Center, you should have some basic information:

- Your name and phone number
- The child's name and age
- The child's weight
- The name of the product or plant or whatever the child ingested, the amount you think she ingested, and when it was ingested

It is also important to recognize the warning signs that the child may have gotten into something. These include finding open containers of medicines or cleaning supplies near the child or stains on the child's clothing, or the child's suddenly becoming sick (vomiting, seizures, abdominal pain, etc.). If the child is sick, call 911 first, then poison control. Be especially careful when you have visitors who bring medications or cigarettes with them, or when you go to other people's homes who do not have young children and therefore have not child-proofed their homes.

Mouthing can be a serious problem for young children and even older children with autism spectrum disorders (ASDs). If the child likes to explore objects with his mouth, you should be sure that lead-based paint was not used at home or in school on walls or toys or even cribs. Lead-based paint has not been used for indoor paint in this country since the end of the 1970s, but some people still live in houses with old paint, or it may persist in the soil outside the house. You may need to avoid toys with small pieces past the usual recommended age of 3 years if the child likes to mouth things.

Wandering

Wandering can be a problem at home as well as at school and in the community. Children who wander put themselves at risk. If this happens at home, there are several steps parents can take. Special locks for outside doors make it harder, hopefully impossible, for the child to open the outside door on her own. Some people use deadbolt locks; some use a regular lock or a hook-and-eye-type lock very high up on the door (well out of the child's reach). Another choice is to put alarms on the windows or doors that go off when they are opened, alerting parents to a child's trying to leave the house. One web site that provides such products is Radio Shack (www.radioshack.com).

If the child has a tendency to wander, help her learn to wear a MedicAlert bracelet. The bracelet can have the child's name, parents' names, and cell phone number and can even state that the child has autism or ASD. We have seen one instance where the child's tendency to bolt/wander was so severe that her parents obtained a special helper dog that went with the child everywhere. The child and dog were basically tied together and the dog was trained that when the child started to bolt, he (a massive dog) would just sit! Other options are increasingly available (e.g., global positioning systems). We talk more about wandering later on when discussing safety issues in the community.

Another area that deserves consideration is the yard outside the home. Swimming pools are an obvious hazard and need to be surrounded by secure gates and fences as well as alarms that go off if a child goes through them or gets into the water. Even without a pool, a yard can be the source of many dangers. Be sure the child can't get out of the yard on his own and that he can't find any poisonous plants to ingest. Walk around the yard periodically and see what might look inviting to a child of different ages.

SAFETY AT SCHOOL

Safety issues at school are somewhat different than at home. Some hazards are less frequent than at home, but other issues are more common and more complicated to deal with. Having other students around leads to potential difficulties, and areas where typically developing children are less supervised (recess, gym, even cafeteria) may be much more likely to surface as trouble spots for children on the autism spectrum. As we noted previously, teaching safety is important and an awareness of potential safety concerns is important in preventing problems. In this section we discuss some of the problems that can arise in the school itself. The following section (on safety in the community) discusses auto and bus safety concerns as well as water safety.

Staff Preparedness

As with other activities, planning is important to prevent accidents and injuries, but because some emergencies may happen, it is critical to have staff trained and ready to cope if necessary. Teachers should all be trained in basic safety issues and simple first aid. In situations where there are potential danger areas (e.g., if there is a pool at school or if there is access to potentially toxic materials), children should never be left unsupervised. For children on the autism spectrum, adequate supervision is always appropriate. In contrast to typical children, those on the autism spectrum may need more, not less supervision on playgrounds, recess, and similar activities; failure to be aware of this often leads to trouble.

Teachers and school staff should establish rules and routines to prevent accidents and have an important role in teaching basic safety concepts that can be generalized to home and community settings. They should also rehearse what to do in the event of an illness or emergency.

Teaching Safety Concepts

As the child gets older and acquires more language, parents and school staff should make a point of teaching safety concepts. You can use picture schedules and visual cues to help children who are just learning language. Topics to teach include what things are dangerous (hot objects, electrical outlets), how to cross the street, and, as children get older, the appropriate use of household items that have some potential for being dangerous (electrical appliances).

Keep in mind that there is some (relatively slight) potential for "overdoing" this teaching—that is, you could end up making the child frightened of certain situations if you make them sound too dangerous. Focus on concepts important for the child's safety in the real world. Use explicit teaching at whatever level is appropriate to the child. If a situation makes *you* very anxious or frightened, think about having someone else work on this with the child (or work with you first) so that your own anxiety is not part of what the child learns.

Teach *generalization* of safety concepts; don't, for example, let the child learn to cross the street only in one spot! Given the tendency of children with autism toward rigidity, you should work very specifically on generalization and "teaching the big picture." There are some important exceptions to the rule—one child we know with Asperger's would stop in midstreet if the "don't walk" sign came up, obviously putting him at more danger because of his literal response to being taught about safe crossing!

Outdoor Activities and the Playground

Going to the playground at recess or after school can be a great way for the child to get exercise and meet other children. Even when more interactive play is a challenge, the opportunity to be in a new environment and play alongside other children is important. In outside areas, look for worn play equipment that is unsteady or ready to break, sharp edges, or exposed nails/screws. Keep safety in mind, particularly when you look at play equipment. For example, if the child is a fearless climber, you might want to limit the height of playground structures so she won't be tempted to jump. Be sure there are no poisonous plants in the playground or backyard. Even when an area is fenced in, keep in mind the potential for the child's getting out. Never assume that the child can't get out of a fenced area! Be aware that items like swings, slides, and seesaws may be a particular source of danger, given problems in social awareness, organization, and judgment. There are guidelines for playgrounds relative to Americans With Disabilities Act (ADA) standards. As we noted in the chapter on medical conditions, having a one-page medical summary and/or permission for emergency treatment for the child is helpful. The school nurse can take an active role in this process; this helps him or her get to know the child and family and be more helpful in actual emergency situations.

Many children receiving special education services who are out of the mainstream classroom for parts of the day are included with the rest of the class for recess and gym. Unfortunately, these times (when typically developing children need the least supervision) are just the times when children on the autism spectrum may need the most attention! Difficulties in peer interaction, communication, and play may prevent the child from being included. For younger and more cognitively impaired children, this is even more likely to occur. For the more able children, there is significant potential for teasing and social ostracism. This means that, depending on the child's levels of ability, the teacher may want to be proactive in preventing problems. Fortunately, a number of good resources are available (see the reading list for this chapter as well as for Chapter 7). For younger children, use of an assigned peer buddy during recess can be helpful. A similar procedure can be used with older and more able children, for example, giving the child on the autism spectrum a task he can engage in with an assigned peer during recess. As we have discussed elsewhere in the book, teaching social and play skills is critical. Dealing with the typically developing students is also important; various resources, including videos and reading materials, can be used to help avoid bullying and teasing. Similarly, teaching the more able school-aged or adolescent student about responses to teasing, understanding humor, and similarly sophisticated social skills can be important.

Classroom Safety

As at home, it is good to take a look at school or day care facilities for obvious dangers in the building itself. Often, difficulties will arise around times of transition—always a stressful time for the child on the autism spectrum. Have plans in place for dealing with emergencies. The fire drill may be a source of great anxiety and lead to disorganization in the child with ASD. Have a plan in advance that can be rehearsed with the child; practice this often enough that it feels routine to the child. For more able children, you can teach routines of what to do and have the child practice; for less able children, take appropriate steps so that, for example, in case of an evacuation, the child is assigned to a responsible adult. In some parts of the country, storm drills such as for tornados may occur, and practicing for these situations may also be helpful.

Establishing classroom rules will lend a sense of structure to the child with ASD, and it can also help prevent accidents and injuries. As on the playground, the rules must be tailored to the situation, environment, and students. Once rules for the classroom are clear, they should be used and applied consistently. As part of lesson planning, teachers should consider risk and safety issues. The teacher should also look at the classroom for safety issues, including availability of scissors or other sharp materials, electrical appliances or shock hazards, cleaning supplies or other materials that may be poisonous, and so forth. Art materials should be nontoxic.

Field trips represent special opportunities for encouraging generalization of skills. They also present some risk, particularly for children on the autism spectrum who may become upset with new situations or changes in the environment. It is important that teachers plan appropriately for community activities and field trips by obtaining parental permission, having a plan in place for monitoring students, being prepared to deal with emergencies, and so forth.

In some cases, children will have known medical problems, for example, allergies or seizures. Teachers should be prepared to cope with these problems if they arise. For children with severe allergies, training in the use of the EpiPen is appropriate; this pen can be lifesaving if a child has a severe allergic reaction.

Aggression

Aggression in school can be a major problem and present many challenges for teachers and school staff. Aggression may be directed against other children, the staff, or against the self (self-injurious behaviors). Unfortunately, aggressive behavior of any type tends to "energize" similar responses in those observing it, including staff. It is important to train staff to be as calm and collected as possible, rather than inadvertently contributing to further escalation.

Verbal aggression can be an issue in more able children on the autism spectrum. This can include name calling, swearing, threats, and so forth. At times, this may have been provoked by teasing or bullying or similar behavior from other students; at other times, it may arise as the person on the autism spectrum misinterprets a comment or joke. Verbal aggression can go on to escalate into physical aggression and fighting. If possible, interrupting the verbal aggression is important by removing the parties from each other and redirecting them. When possible, try to understand what went on and help the child develop alternative responses—thus making this a learning experience for some or all concerned. Giving the child something new to focus on is helpful.

Physical aggression can be difficult to manage. This can range from hitting, biting, and kicking to self-injurious behaviors. For children who have problems with physical aggression, it is important to have a behavioral plan in place in advance. Alertness to signs of an impending blow-up can often prevent escalation. As with verbal aggression, remaining calm helps. Physical restraining should be done only when there are no other alternatives and/or in situations where risk of injury is extreme. If there are some children who will possibly need restraint, this should be planned for ahead of time. There should be explicit plans that everyone involved knows about in advance so that no one will be hurt or surprised by the actions that are taken.

Although self-injurious behavior is relatively uncommon, when it occurs, it may be so severe that it can cause significant physical injury or may interfere significantly with the child's educational program. Self-injury is most common among children with the most significant degree of developmental delays and seems to increase around adolescence as well as during times of stress. As with aggressive behavior, careful observation may help clarify what sets the behavior off and what warning signs to look for, for example, temper tantrums that escalate to more challenging behaviors.

Self-injurious behaviors can range from repeated scratching and gouging of the skin and eyes, to self-inflicted bites and occasionally to severe head banging—sometimes severe enough to break bones. Sometimes, self-injuries are connected to a medical problem. For example, among adolescents, self-injury may start only when the wisdom teeth cause difficulties, or sometimes nonverbal children may start to bang their ear because they have a painful ear infection. Various methods, including medicines, protective equipment, and behavioral interventions can be used to control self-injury. Often, multiple methods are used together. When these methods are used, parents, doctors, school personnel, and others need to be involved so that everyone works together in a coordinated way in the child's best interest.

COMMUNITY SAFETY

Wandering/Running/Bolting

As discussed in the section on general household safety, some children on the autism spectrum have trouble with running away/bolting from caregivers. Sometimes this takes the form of impulsive running/darting away, at other times it can seem more premeditated. These times are, as you might expect, times when the child is in the most danger, for example, darting into a street, jumping from a car onto a highway, or jumping in front of a train (sadly, all examples of cases we knew). As always, there is a balance between wanting to encourage appropriate adaptive skills and maintaining safety. For children for whom this is known to be a problem, it is important to maintain constant adult supervision, with the child always visible to the teacher, staff member, or parent and with continued observation of the area. A behavioral plan for dealing with the behavior should be developed. Sometimes a loud noise or loudly spoken instruction will interrupt the behavior and do the trick in terms of stopping the behavior. Use physical intervention if appropriate to ensure safety. In community situations, continuous visual contact is important and assistance should be obtained when needed. Running/bolting should not be ignored given the seriousness of such behavior; however, try not to make the "chase" into part of a game that inadvertently reinforces the behavior. We give some examples of dealing with running/bolting in Chapter 14.

Auto and Bus Safety

Many children are hurt each year in car accidents. You can minimize the chances of injury by following National Highway Traffic Safety Administration recommendations (www.nhtsa.dot.gov). They suggest using the child safety locks on the back doors of the car to keep kids from opening the doors from the inside. They also recommend that parents use a window lock to prevent children from being able to open the windows themselves. And, most important, they recommend that children under 12 sit in the back in age-appropriate safety restraints. That means infants from birth to at least 20 pounds and 1 year of age need to be rear facing in a car seat appropriate for their weight. Children from 1 to approximately 4 years old should be in a safety seat facing forward. Older and larger children (starting at 40 pounds) can be in a booster seat and there are now safety seats that can be used for children up to 60 to 80 pounds.

In deciding when to switch the older child to a seat belt, the National Highway Traffic Safety Administration web site advises, "Use vehicle lap and shoulder belt for children who have outgrown a booster seat and can sit with his or her back straight against the vehicle seat back cushion, with knees bent over the vehicle's seat edge, without slouching, and feet on the floor (approximately 4″9′)." Recently, there has been a move to keep children in booster seats longer and until they are bigger. This is thought to be safer than switching to a regular seatbelt at age 4 years. Some states now require a booster seat until the child is through the sixth year and 60 pounds. Many local fire and police departments provide a free inspection to be sure that you have the car seat or booster seat installed properly.

If the child does not like being restrained, you will need to be sure that he cannot undo the safety belts or restraints. You may want to have another person sit next to him in the back seat to keep him safely buckled up. There are also some products available that can make it harder for the child to un-buckle his seat belt. Several products that may be helpful are available from E-Z-ON (www.ezonpro.com). If the child gets out of his car seat or seat belt, be prepared (as soon as you can do so safely) to make a point of pulling over and stopping the car so you can get him back into the car seat or seat belt.

If the child has a hard time in the car in general, you may be able to make the trip more enjoyable with toys to play with or a DVD player or TV to watch.

If the child rides in a bus or van to school, be sure someone supervises her getting properly seated before the ride home. Some children with ASDs need an aide on the bus to be sure they don't undo the safety restraint and get out of their seat.

Water Safety

Some parents may find that their child enjoys being in the water, and that this has a calming effect on him. However, you need to be careful that the child is never left alone in or near the water, not even briefly. This is especially true of any child with seizures. Drowning can occur at home in the bath or outside in a pool, even a small child's pool. Drowning is one of the more frequent causes of accidental death in autism. So if the school uses an inflatable pool for younger children in the summer, it's safest to empty it each time the class is finished with it for the day. If you have a larger pool at home, you need adequate gates, locks, and covers to keep the child from trying to swim on his own. As we discussed earlier in the household section, a safety alarm that lets you know when some-thing, or someone, has hit the surface of the pool is a worthwhile investment. Teach good safety around the pool—no running, no diving into shallow parts of the pool. Also keep in mind that if you have a pool, you'll also have pool chemicals around, which are probably poisonous and need to be inaccessible to the child.

It is a *very* good idea to have the child learn to swim. She is less likely to drown if she knows how to swim. Furthermore, swimming is a great sport—it provides good exercise, offers opportunities to learn some self-care skills (such as changing clothes), and can be a good way to meet other children and adults in a more controlled and less threatening situation. Its repetitive and somewhat isolative aspects can be a source of pleasure to children on the autism spectrum, and unlike team sports (which are highly social), swimming can be a sport you can do in the presence of other people but one that is not very social.

SUMMARY

In this chapter, we talked about some of the steps you can take to help the child be safe at home, at school, and in the community. Prevention is nine-tenths of the battle here. Go through the home, classroom, and playground with an eye for potential danger spots for the child. If the child is small, get down to her level on the floor and take a look around (the world can look quite different). Keep in mind the child's special interests and abilities as you are childproofing the environment. Help others in the household and at school be aware of safety issues. Some new approaches are using computers and virtual reality simulations to teach safety skills. These approaches are just emerging but hold considerable potential for highly focused, repetitive teaching and their use of less complicated learning environments may make it easier for the child with ASD to learn.

Because you can't prevent all injuries or accidents, you should be prepared to deal with them effectively. Post poison control and other important numbers near the telephone. Read a book on first aid and take a first aid course that includes cardiopulmonary resuscitation (CPR) training. Putting together a first aid kit to have at home or to take along on family trips may be helpful. Finally, keep in mind that issues of safety can change for children over time as they become older. Periodically, take a look at the environment to be sure it is still as safe as possible for the child. There is a child autism safety web site (www .MyPreciousKid.com) that is very helpful. It includes suggestions for products that may help keep the child safe, including ID tags, locators, door alarms, and other products.

■ READING LIST

Boyd, B. (2003). *Parenting a child with Asperger syndrome: 200 tips and strategies*. Philadelphia: Jessica Kingsley.

Chavelle, R. M., Strauss, D. J., & Picket, J. (2001). Causes of death in autism. *Journal of Autism and Developmental Disorders, 31*, 569–576.

Cook, J., & Hartman, C. (2008). *My mouth is a volcano!* Chattanooga, TN: National Center for Youth Issues.

Dubin, N. (2007). *Asperger syndrome and bullying: Strategies and solutions.* London: Jessica Kingsley.

Fancher, V. K. (1991). *Safe kids: A complete child-safety handbook and resource guide for parents.* New York: Wiley.

Jagoda, A. (2004). *Good housekeeping family first aid book* (rev. ed.). New York, NY: Hearst.

Kim, Y. S., & Leventhal, B. (2008). Bullying and suicide: A review. *International Journal of Adolescent Medicine and Health, 20*(2), 133–154.

Ludwig, T. (2006). *Just kidding.* Berkeley, CA: Tricycle Press.

Ludwig, T., & Manning, M. J. (2006). *Sorry!* Berkeley, CA: Tricycle Press.

Marotz, L. R., Cross, M. Z., & Rush, J. M. (2005). *Health, safety, and nutrition for the young child* (6th ed.). Clifton Park, NY: Thompson Delmar.

Naylor, P. R. (1994). *King of the playground.* New York: Aladdin Paperbacks.

Reich, J. B. (2007). *Babyproofing bible: The exceedingly thorough guide to keeping your child safe from crib to kitchen to car to yard.* Beverly, MA: Fair Winds Press.

Rodgers, G. C., Jr., & Matyunas, N. J. (1994). *Handbook of common poisonings in children* (3rd ed.) Elk Grove Village, IL: American Academy of Pediatrics.

Shaw, E. (2001). *Keep kids safe: A parent's guide to child safety.* Appleton, WI: Quality Life Resources.

Shore, K. (2001). *Keeping kids safe.* New York: Prentice Hall.

Strickland, D. C., McAllister, D., Coles, C. D., & Osborne, S. (2007). An evolution of virtual reality training designs for children with autism and fetal alcohol spectrum disorders. *Topics in Language Disorders, 27*(3), 226–241.

Unintentional injuries in children. 2000. *The Future of Children* (a publication of the Packard Foundation), *10*, www.futureofchildren.org.

■ QUESTIONS AND ANSWERS

1. **When David was first diagnosed, the doctor did several lab studies. These all came back normal except for his lead level, which was slightly elevated. It was not high enough to treat, but the doctor has followed it since that time and we have been careful to keep an eye on what he puts in his mouth. Why does this happen?**

Lead poisoning is an important health problem in children. Several studies have suggested that children with autism may be more likely to have higher lead levels. This is usually because they may like to put non-food items in their mouths or may be more likely to lick things than children without developmental difficulties (normally developing toddlers also may be at greater risk for lead poisoning). The worry here is not that the lead level caused the autism but that higher lead levels may contribute, over time, to other developmental difficulties (e.g., inattention). Periodic screening is thus important in autism (this can be done with a simple blood test), particularly if the child likes to put things in his mouth. Treatment can be indicated if the lead level is high, although here, as in much of the rest of medicine, an ounce of prevention is worth a pound of cure; parents should be alert to the problem, and particularly if the child has a high lead level, look for the sources of lead in the environment and remove them. These are most likely to be found in paint in old houses and, sadly, in toys from abroad.

2. **My son has no sense of danger and will go with anyone—is there any way to help him get a sense of appropriateness with strangers?**

   The answer really depends on your child's age and level of cognitive ability as well as his ability to communicate. For children who are verbal and have better cognitive abilities, there are some good children's books that teach about safety. Some of the curricula developed for schools in teaching about use of personal space may also be appropriate. It will be important that your school know about, and work on, this issue.

3. **The company I work for is relocating and we have to move. Are there any precautions my wife and I should think about when looking for a new place to live? Our 4-year-old with ASD seems to be into everything!**

   Keep in mind that for older homes (built before the mid-1970s), you should be sure the house (and grounds) are free from lead-based paints. There are companies that can test for this. As you think about a house, keep safety in mind; for example, are you on a busy street or a quiet one? Are there danger areas (pools, cliffs, highways) nearby? Are there things that might particularly attract your child and be dangerous?

4. **I teach a second-grade class (along with another teacher and a paraprofessional), and we have a child with autism who is included for most of the day. Are there any special times of the day that accidents are more likely to happen? Are there any things we can do to make the classroom safe?**

   Transitions are characteristically stressful times for children on the autism spectrum, and the most likely times for children to have all kinds of difficulties, including injuries. So keep a special eye on the child at these times. Take a careful look at the classroom for obvious and less obvious safety hazards. Depending on the level of ability of the child, this may take a different form—are there poisons, sharp objects, dangerous materials?

5. **Our 6-year-old likes to eat everything. A friend told me we should keep a bottle of ipecac syrup in the house in case he eats something he shouldn't. When should we use this?**

   Basically, you shouldn't. Call poison control (or 911 if your child is in obvious distress). Doctors now feel that the dangers in using ipecac outweigh the risks.

6. **There is a student with Asperger's in my home room in junior high. He gets very preoccupied with the fire drills and will be anxious for weeks and weeks after they happen. Is there anything I can do to make him less anxious?**

   The anxiety likely stems from various sources; you can try to sort out some or all of these and do as much as you can to address them ahead of time. Practice even when there is no drill. Have a clear set of directions for the student so he knows exactly what do to. Giving him a very specific job may also help. If he is afraid of the noise, seat him as far away as you can from the source of the sound. Doing a project on firefighters or fire prevention may also help (although there is some potential that he will end up learning a *lot* about this!).

7. **My 8-year-old with autism has a tendency to wander. As it happens so does my elderly grandfather—for him my parents have found a GPS tracking device. Are there similar things that can be used for children with autism? Also, my husband wants to get a dog—are they any good for helping children with autism?**

   As you point out there are increasing uses for both low- and high-tech "devices" to deal with safely issues. GPS monitoring can be used—typically this involves the person wearing a device of some kind (see www.people trackusa.com, www.heartofsailing.org/Docs/AutismSafetyToolkit.pdf, or www.nationalautismassociation.org/safetytoolkit). Information on service dogs is also available (www.autismservicedogsofamerica.com).

CHAPTER 12

Dealing With Seizures

This chapter covers seizure disorders, which may occur in children with autism and related conditions. Seizure disorders are the most frequently encountered medical complications associated with autism. They may also be observed in other pervasive developmental disorders (PDDs). Only a minority of children will have seizures. If this chapter is not relevant, that is, if you don't have a child with seizures or don't teach any children with seizures, don't read it! However, if your child or student has seizures or you think he might have seizures, this chapter can provide helpful information. The next chapter focuses on a related problem: regression. For readers for whom seizures is an important topic, there are a number of excellent resources provided in the reading list at the end of this chapter. Because seizure disorders can have their onset at any time during the child's development and because these disorders can sometimes be difficult to recognize, it is important that parents and professionals alike be familiar with some aspects of these conditions.

WHAT IS A SEIZURE?

A **seizure** is a sudden change in behavior, consciousness, or sensation caused by a change in brain activity. Seizures (also called convulsions, fits, spells, or attacks) are caused by uncontrolled and sudden episodes of abnormal electrical activity in the brain. Some part of the brain begins to "fire" or activate in an uncontrolled fashion, and this activity spreads to other parts of the brain and is associated with changes in behavior, the motor system, or sensations. Sometimes the person falls down and loses consciousness, but at other times she may simply seem to "tune out" for a few seconds.

Often, clues about the origin or location of the starting point of a child's seizures are provided by the symptoms exhibited. A child may experience what is called an **aura**—a kind of warning sign at the start of certain kinds of seizures. It might take the form of an unusual experience or a change in behavior; for example, a person's lip might begin to twitch or he might experience an unusual smell. Depending on the nature of the seizure, more and more brain cells may be involved, and the seizure then becomes more widespread (this is called **generalization**). The seizure itself can take different forms, which we'll discuss shortly.

Following the seizure, there is often a period when the person is somewhat confused or disoriented as the brain recovers from the seizure. This is called the **postictal period** (meaning after the attack). After some seizures, the person may go to sleep for a time. The various phases of the seizure can be a bit confusing. That is, the seizure itself may last only a minute, but the person can be confused or sleep for a longer period.

Many different kinds of seizures have been identified, and you will get a quick education about these types here. You may ask yourself whether all this stuff makes a difference; in this case, the answer is yes! Different kinds of seizures are treated differently—that is the reason why neurologists make such a fuss about all of this and why it is important for you to understand something about it.

WHAT IS THE DIFFERENCE BETWEEN SEIZURES AND EPILEPSY?

If the child has a single seizure, it will be called just that—a seizure. However, if he goes on to have another seizure, doctors will probably diagnose him as having epilepsy. Epilepsy is a chronic disorder of the brain that involves recurrent seizures, and it can be associated with a range of learning, behavioral, and other problems.

A seizure can be observed as an isolated finding. Sometimes, for example, very young children with autism will have a seizure only in relation to a high fever. These so-called febrile convulsions are not technically classified as epilepsy. Similarly, other seizures can be caused by certain drugs or drug withdrawal, alcohol, or an imbalance of body chemicals. In these instances, epilepsy would not be diagnosed, since the seizures are caused not by a chronic brain disorder, but by something outside of the brain. It is important to realize that a single seizure does not necessarily mean the individual has epilepsy.

How Common Are Seizures?

In the general population, about 5% of all children experience a seizure by the time they are 15 years old, and half of these will be seizures associated with a high fever (febrile seizures). Febrile seizures tend not to come back after about the age of 6, and do not, of themselves, constitute epilepsy. Only a small number of children with febrile seizures go on to develop chronic seizures or **epilepsy**. Children who are more likely to go on to develop nonfebrile seizures, or epilepsy, are those who have (1) underlying brain disorders, (2) what are called focal (localized) or prolonged seizures, and (3) a family history of epilepsy.

Although most children with autism do *not* have seizures, the risk of having a seizure is still much higher than in typical children. One review of epidemiologically based samples suggested that the percentage of individuals with autism who had epilepsy was from 0 to 26% or so of the sample (the median percentage in all studies was 16.7). Several different things make it hard to get an exact number; for example, we have changed the ways we diagnose autism, and the chance of developing seizures may change with age (so the age of the sample is important). Risk also seems to be increased in children with autism who also have significant intellectual disabilities. It is clear that the rate of epilepsy in autism is much higher throughout childhood and adolescence than for typically developing children. This has been known for some time, and an appreciation of this was one of the lines of evidence that made people think autism was a brain-based disorder.

Children with seizures but without other developmental problems often do quite well and may outgrow them. However, children with autism tend to develop seizures that are not just due to fevers, and their seizure disorders tend to persist and can further complicate the task of intervention. Figure 12.1 shows

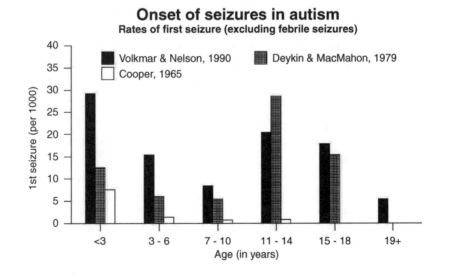

FIGURE 12.1   Rates of first seizure in two samples of individuals with autism (Volkmar & Nelson, 1990; Deykin & MacMahon, 1979) and a normal British sample (Cooper, 1975).

the rates of seizure in two different samples of children with autism and a nor-mative sample of British children. As you can see, the risk for developing epilepsy is increased in autism relative to the normal population throughout childhood with an increased risk early in life and again starting in early adolescence.

TYPES OF SEIZURES

There are many different kinds of seizures—well over 30. Most of the seizures that are seen in autism, however, fall into a few general categories. The main distinction made now is between generalized seizures (which involve the entire brain from the beginning of the seizure) and partial seizures (which originate in one part of the brain and may or may not spread to involve the entire brain). Sometimes children have both generalized and partial seizures.

In the past, people used other terms to talk about seizures, and you sometimes may hear people still use these old terms, particularly grand mal or petit mal. A **grand mal** (which means a "big and bad" seizure) tended to be used as a term for what people thought of as "big" seizures (e.g., where the child fell down and lost consciousness), while the term **petit mal** ("small and bad") was used for seizures that seemed less serious. However, these terms were not used very consistently and often confused things for people. Seizure types are listed in Table 12.1. There are generalized seizures, which include tonic–clonic, absence, atonic, and akinetic seizures; and partial seizures, which include three types of **simple partial seizures**—adversive, jacksonian, and focal—as well as two types of **complex partial seizures**—temporal lobe seizures and psychomotor seizures.

Even with this newer classification system, it can be quite confusing when people talk about the different types of seizures. If your child or student has a seizure disorder, be sure that the child's physician clarifies which type of seizure the child has.

Generalized Seizures

Generalized seizures affect both sides of the brain at the same time. These account for about 40% of seizure disorders in the general population and about 70 to 75% or so percent of those seen in autism.

Generalized Tonic–Clonic Seizures   Generalized tonic–clonic seizures are what most people think of when they think about a seizure. These seizures affect the whole body. Usually, there's no warning before the seizure starts. The child may fall and lose consciousness. The body then stiffens (the tonic part of the

TABLE 12.1   COMMON TYPES OF SEIZURES*

Name	Other names	Symptoms
Generalized Seizures (Nonfocal Seizures)		
Tonic–clonic	Grand mal	Loss of consciousness, alternating contraction and relaxation of muscle groups, child may fall, may lose bowel and bladder control. Often confused (postictal) after seizure.
Absence seizures	Petit mal	Loss of consciousness, with staring, eye fluttering, and maybe facial twitching.
Atonic	Drop attacks	Symptoms due to loss of muscle tone; child drops and loses consciousness but there are no generalized convulsions. Recovery is rapid.
(Akinetic) Myoclonic	Jerk attacks	Muscle jerks (usually arms or head), usually very brief, loss of consciousness.
Partial seizures		
Simple partial seizure	Adversive Focal motor Jacksonian	Isolated in one part of the body (movement or sensation). Person remains conscious.
Complex partial seizure	Temporal lobe Psychomotor seizure	Abnormal response to environment, variable across people. Seizures start in one part of the brain and then generalize and the person may lose consciousness.

*Selective list.

seizure) and muscles begin to alternately contract and relax (the clonic part of the seizure). This gives rise to the jerking movement that is typical of such seizures. Breathing may be affected and might even stop briefly as the muscles become stiff. If this happens, the child may turn blue. The seizure may go on for some minutes, with a gradual slowing of the jerking. Often, the child may lose bladder or bowel control. Sometimes people will sleep for hours after such a seizure. Usually, the seizure itself lasts only a few minutes unless someone is in what is called **status epilepticus**, which means the seizure is continuous. That constitutes a medical emergency but, fortunately, does not happen with most seizures.

Generalized, tonic–clonic seizures are the most common seizures observed in autism. In one study of children with autism, 70% of the children who had seizures had the generalized tonic–clonic type.

Absence Seizures   Previously known as petit mal seizures, this seizure type involves a very brief loss of consciousness. During this time, which may last only a few seconds, there is staring and there may be eye fluttering, mild face twitching, or eye blinking. There are no warning signs before the seizure begins. The child does not fall down, and, once the seizure passes, she is back to normal (but usually cannot remember the seizure).

Often, this kind of seizure is very subtle and may be missed. The child "tunes in" and "tunes out" very frequently. This is one of the most common kinds of seizure in children in general. Sometimes children with these seizures have several hundred seizures a day. As might be imagined, these seizures can interfere significantly with learning. Often, absence seizures stop before a child reaches adulthood.

These seizures can be confused with simple partial seizures since both kinds of seizure can involve staring; the treatment, however, can be quite different. It can also sometimes be difficult to distinguish this kind of seizure from complex partial seizures. Absence seizures are less common in autism than tonic–clonic seizures and represent maybe 15% of all seizures in autism. An electroencephalogram (EEG) will determine which type of seizure the child has. See "Evaluating a Seizure Disorder" later in the chapter.

If the child has absence seizures, it is especially important that teachers and other people in his life know what these look like so they don't think that it's just "autistic behavior" when the child is staring ahead and not listening to them.

Myoclonic Seizures Myoclonic seizures involve jerking of the muscles (the word *myoclonic* means muscle jerk). You might see the child kick out unexpectedly. She might fall down if, for example, muscles in the leg are jerking and other muscles are moving. These seizures can be difficult to diagnose in children with autism, given the high rates of stereotyped movements, and, to further complicate life, not all muscle jerks are due to seizures.

Atonic seizures are also sometimes seen. These are like **myoclonic seizures** except that instead of a muscle's stiffening, there is actually a loss of muscle tone; that is, suddenly the legs or arms may go limp and the child collapses to the ground. These are sometimes called akinetic seizures.

This seizure type accounts for less than 10% of seizures in autism.

Partial Seizures

Partial seizures probably account for around 10% or so of seizures in autism. The partial seizure may include what is called either a *simple partial* or a *complex partial* seizure.

In a simple partial seizure, consciousness is impaired (not totally lost), but in a complex partial seizure, consciousness is lost. The features of simple partial seizures vary depending on what part of the brain is involved. You may see jerking of one part of the body. This might be accompanied by a tingling sensation, but as we have emphasized, the child does not lose consciousness.

Complex partial seizures (sometimes known as temporal lobe seizures or psychomotor seizures) are characterized by unusual but purposeless activity. Consciousness or awareness is altered. There is tremendous variability from person to person, but individuals tend to experience similar symptoms each time they have a seizure. Often, there is a warning sign of the seizure. This so-called aura is very stereotyped. For example, the child may always be aware of an unusual sensation immediately before a seizure. During the seizure itself, the child may be somewhat confused or disoriented and may make lip-smacking movements, or may appear drunk or drugged. Abnormalities in sensory perception often occur, particularly at the beginning of the seizure. Although the individual is not violent, he may struggle or fight if restrained. Usually, after the seizure, the child is very confused but has no memory of the seizure. Typically, such seizures last for 1 to 3 minutes. These seizures are somewhat less common in autism compared to generalized seizures.

Partial seizures can involve other symptoms, such as change in heart rate and blood pressure or extreme emotions. The way that partial seizures develop may provide important clues as to where in the brain the seizure gets its start.

Febrile Seizures

As we have mentioned, **febrile seizures** are fever related, are most common in young children (under age 6), and often do not come back. Do not, however, fail to have the child evaluated following a febrile seizure, since you need to be sure that the seizure was not due to something else (like a brain infection). After examination and possibly some lab work, the doctor will likely not recommend more extensive assessment for an isolated febrile seizure.

There is some suggestion that the susceptibility to febrile seizures runs in families. If you have other children with febrile seizures or if there is a history of seizures in your family, be sure to mention this to your health care provider even if your child has not developed seizures. You should also know that if your child has had one febrile seizure, she is at somewhat greater risk for another. There is a small chance of developing nonfebrile seizures or epilepsy if the child has had a simple febrile seizure and there is no family history of seizures nor an associated neurological disorder.

In the past, febrile seizures were treated with antiseizure medicines. That is now uncommon, since it is clear that most children don't go on to have seizure disorders and there are potential adverse effects from medicines used to treat seizures.

The rates of different kinds of seizures in children with autism vary a bit from study to study. In a study one of the authors was involved in some years ago, of 41 children with seizures the most frequent type was tonic-clonic seizures

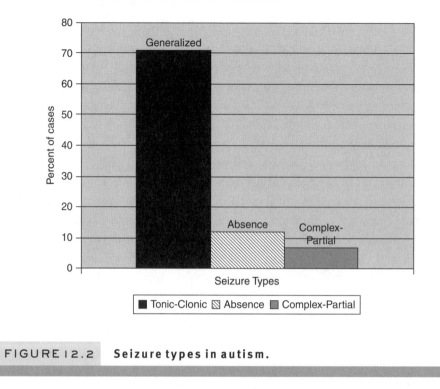

FIGURE 12.2   Seizure types in autism.

(71%), with absence (12%) and complex partial seizures (7%) less common (see Figure 12.2).

EVALUATING A SEIZURE DISORDER

If there is a possibility that the child is having seizures, you should consult the child's doctor. He or she may send you to a **neurologist** or **pediatric neurologist** (a specialist in diseases of the nervous system, including the brain). You should explain exactly what you are worried about, and the child's primary doctor can help you decide how urgent this is. Even before he or she sends you to a neurologist, he or she may want to do some tests or get an EEG (brain wave test). Depending on the results, the child's doctor may then want you to see a neurologist.

The neurological consultation will typically include a comprehensive medical evaluation and a review of your child's and family's history. The neurologist or pediatric neurologist will ask for a very detailed description of what appears to be the seizure. For example: How common are the episodes? Do they always happen in exactly the same way or at certain times? Can they be interrupted? How long do they last? Does the child seem to lose consciousness? Did the child have a fever before the seizure? The doctor will want to know how the episode progresses over time. All this information may provide important clues about whether the child had a seizure, and if so, what kind, and maybe even where it starts in the brain.

The neurologist will do a physical examination with a very detailed examination of the central nervous system. This neurological examination will include testing the child's reflexes, looking for specific signs of brain dysfunction. Typically, an EEG will also be obtained if it hasn't been already (or it may be repeated). The EEG is done by pasting small electrodes onto the child's scalp at certain points. A very sensitive machine then picks up very small changes in electrical activity and records these. There is nothing painful involved. Still, it is probably best to try to prepare the child in advance for the EEG. Some children with autism may not like the sensation of paste on their head, but others will have no problem. Some may have difficulty staying still and may need help (e.g., giving them a favorite video to watch). Discuss the logistics of all this in advance either with the neurologist or the person doing the EEG. In general, it is important to avoid sedating the child since drugs can, themselves, sometimes affect the EEG.

During the EEG, the child might be exposed to some of the conditions in which seizures are most likely to occur, such as going to sleep or watching a flashing light or even hyperventilating. Sometimes you might be asked to bring the child in after a period of sleep deprivation. Sometimes the doctor will suggest a 24-hour EEG. If so, the child may need to stay in the hospital while a computer records the EEG for a whole day to get a good sense of the various changes in the EEG over the day. Two advantages of 24-hour EEGs are: (1) any unusual behaviors can be noted by parents and the nursing staff and then related to the EEG, and (2) a longer EEG record is more likely to show abnormalities. The disadvantage is that it is even more of a nuisance to the child and you! Sometimes a special video EEG will be used to observe the child during the possible seizure itself.

The EEG is examined ("read") by a neurologist, who takes into account the age of the child as well as clinical symptoms. The doctor looks for the rhythm of the EEG; for differences between, for example, the right and left side of the brain; and whether there is unusual electrical activity suggestive of seizures. Depending on the history and examination, the doctor may want some other tests done as well, for example, an MRI (magnetic resonance imaging) or computed tomography (CT) scan to look at the actual structure of the brain. Some of these studies, such as CT scans, involve radiation, but others, such as an MRI, do not. The doctor may also ask for blood tests in order to look for chemical imbalances, infections, and other factors that might predispose to seizures. In preparing the child for these tests, many of the same considerations apply as for the EEG. For some of these tests, however, sedation may be an option. You can discuss this with the doctor.

Unfortunately (as with the diagnosis of autism itself), there is no simple blood test that absolutely tells you whether what you have seen really was a seizure. You have to rely on the experience of the doctor, who will consider the results of the EEG and other tests and rely on your history and description of the event. Perhaps at this point you are saying to yourself, "You mean you can't always diagnose the seizure from the EEG?" The answer is yes! Some people have normal EEGs when they are not having seizures; other people may exhibit some abnormality on the EEG but not have seizures.

Many different things can be mistaken for seizures. In all children, fainting spells are, for example, sometimes mistaken for seizures. And children with autism often have behaviors such as unusual movements or periods of staring that are easy to mistake for seizures. They may be frightened or have very unusual responses to things that the rest of us take for granted. Even if the child has had one seizure, keep in mind that he may not have another. The decision about how extensively you need to investigate the possible seizure is something you and your doctor should discuss.

OBSERVING A SEIZURE

When observing a seizure, it is better to be a good and careful observer rather than attempt to be a doctor. That is, describe it, but do not attempt to classify it. What was the child doing before the seizure happened? What did she do during the seizure? How long did it last and what happened afterward?

When a seizure happens, people tend to become very anxious and disorganized. It is helpful if you stay calm. You should help turn the child onto her side. Do not restrain her in an attempt to stop the seizure. Do not force any water, food, or anything else into the person's mouth. Contrary to popular belief, people with seizures do not "swallow their tongues," and trying to put something in the mouth often ends up causing other damage. During a generalized tonic–clonic seizure, help the person lie down. Be sure that there are no objects in the area that could injure her. During an absence seizure, you should be aware that the seizure has happened. During a complex partial seizure, do not stop or restrain the person unless you really have to. Seizures are usually over very quickly. Let the child resume normal activities as soon as it seems reasonable.

When seizures continue for longer than about 30 minutes or happen very frequently, the situation known as **status epilepticus** may result. In this situation, the person is more or less continuously having seizures. Status epilepticus is a medical emergency. If the child's seizure lasts longer than usual or if he does not regain consciousness, obtain medical help immediately, as this situation is potentially life threatening.

FIRST AID FOR SEIZURES

- Try to prevent injury if the child falls.
- Turn the child to the side to prevent vomit from going into the lungs.
- **Do not** try to stop the movements of the seizure.
- **Do not** try to put something into the mouth.

TREATMENT OF SEIZURES

Typically, epilepsy or a seizure disorder is treated with special drugs. Occasionally, special dietary treatment or surgery may be indicated. Far and away the most common treatment for a seizure disorder, however, is drugs. There are many different drugs that treat epilepsy. Sometimes these are used alone, and sometimes they are used in combination, especially if the seizures prove difficult to control.

In considering the use of drugs, the first question you have to deal with is whether to treat immediately or wait. As with any other treatment, you and the child's doctor (and the child, if possible) should balance the potential risks and benefits of the treatment.

In general, there are two important considerations to weigh when thinking about drug treatment for seizures: the risk for and from more seizures and whether the benefits of using drugs will outweigh any possible risks from side effects.

The doctor will have information on the kind of seizure and the potential benefits and risks of the treatment, as well as of the seizures themselves. Clearly, recurrent seizures complicate the task of providing an intervention program, and it is important to consider the implications of treating the seizures on other parts of the child's life and treatment program. All the various medicines used to treat seizures have their own possible risks.

Risk of Recurrence

As previously discussed, often fever-related seizures in young children do not come back. Even if the child has had a single major nonfebrile seizure, it is possible that the seizure may not come back—particularly if the child's EEG is normal. Many neurologists will not treat seizures unless a patient has had more than one. However, some kinds of seizures, such as absence seizures, are notoriously easy to miss, and it is possible that by the time the child is diagnosed and goes to see the doctor, she may already have had many seizures. In this case, the doctor may recommend treatment right away.

Risks Versus Benefits of Drug Treatment

The overall goal of drug treatment is to control the seizure disorder with the fewest possible side effects and the least interference in the child's learning. In general, these medications are safe, but they have potentially important side effects. Accordingly, it is very important that the neurologist be involved on a continuous basis in monitoring the child's medication. Amounts of drugs used in treating epilepsy vary depending on the individual's body weight, the level of the drug in the bloodstream, and other drugs being taken. The risk of the drugs depends on the type of medicine and the dose, as well as how long the child is treated.

In order to look for side effects, the doctor will need to see the child periodically. He or she will do an exam, talk with you (and your child, if possible), and maybe order blood tests. Blood tests are used to determine levels of the medicine in the bloodstream, as well as to assess liver function and blood counts to be sure that the medication is not causing unwanted side effects.

Parents who have children with seizure disorders need to be familiar with the medications that are used to treat the seizures. They should know both the specific trade name as well as the generic name of the medication. They should know the amount that is administered. They should pay attention to the size, shape, and color of the pill and be careful to ask the pharmacist if it looks like the pill has been changed when they pick up refills from their pharmacy.

It is very important that drugs are taken as they are directed and that they are administered consistently. It may be helpful for parents to buy a pill container in which the pills can be arranged by part of the day or day of the week. When doses are missed, ask the doctor how, or whether, to make up the missed dose. Make sure that the doctor prescribing the medication knows exactly what other medicines the child is receiving. Also let him or her know about changes in the child, such as significant changes in weight, since these may affect the dose of medication needed. It is also important that you be aware of possible side effects of the medication. Usually, the doctor will have described these in some detail. Sometimes complications occur when medicines interact with each other—a good reason to always use the same pharmacy, since the pharmacist can also be on the lookout for any problems with taking more than one medicine. And, of course, always keep medications out of the reach of children!

If you know the child has seizures, you can also talk to the doctor about ways to try to prevent them, as much as possible. For example, since we know that fevers can make seizures more likely, you may want to be careful to use medicines to try to reduce a fever. Also, excessive tiredness, blinking lights, and other factors may tend to bring seizures on.

Medicines Used to Treat Seizures

A number of different kinds of medications (called **anticonvulsants**) are used to treat seizures. We summarize some of the more common medicines used here. Additional medicines are also used, so don't feel badly if the child is on a medicine not discussed here!

Always keep in mind that the dose has to be adjusted, with the goal of control of the seizures. Ideal control means the child has no further seizures. Sometimes this is not possible (the seizures cannot be fully controlled). Instead, you may be happy with a reduction in the frequency of seizures and willing to tolerate the occasional seizure without too many bad side effects from the medication. Usually, the dose of seizure medicines is adjusted depending on the level of the medicine in the blood, although some medications do not require this. Often, it takes a while (and various adjustments) to get this dose to where it should be. The amount of time it takes will vary depending on the medicine, but can range from a few days to several weeks. Depending on the situation and the medicine, the doctor will want to balance the gradual increases in dose with the blood level and the degree of seizure control. Sometimes a second medicine may be added if the first one is working somewhat but not providing as much seizure control as is wanted. The neurologist and primary care provider should always be your major source of information on medications for the child, but you can be an even more effective part of the treatment team if you yourself learn something about the medications.

Occasionally, children are truly allergic to a medicine and they get a mild, or sometimes serious, skin rash that can itself be dangerous, so be sure to keep a careful lookout and call your doctor if you see a skin rash (it is better to be safe than sorry). Other kinds of reactions can involve the blood cells and other organs in the body such as the liver. Your health care provider will do periodic blood tests to check for these reactions. Behavioral side effects can also be observed. These can include sleepiness and sedation, but children also sometimes become rather hyper and excited. In addition, some of these medicines have the potential for a negative impact on learning.

For each of the following medications, we give the brand name (if there is one) and the generic (or general) name. You can talk with the doctor and pharmacist about the pros/cons of brand and generic medicines—the latter are sometimes much cheaper, but may be absorbed differently. Also, the insurance may pay for only generic, so you may need to decide if it's worth paying for brand name out of pocket. Keep in mind that the information here is given for your general information and that this is no substitute for talking with the child's primary physician and neurologist about the child! First, we will discuss the oldest anticonvulsants and then the most commonly used ones. After that, we will list some of the more frequently used newer drugs.

Phenobarbital is used for all kinds of seizures except for the absence (petit mal) variety. This medicine has been around a long time and is one of the most well known (and cheapest) of the anticonvulsants. Because it takes a while for the body to break it down, often the child can take a single dose a day. The child can develop allergies to this medicine, which often first manifest as a skin rash. You absolutely should have this seen right away, as the medicine may have to be stopped. In recent years, phenobarbital has been used less often than in the past because of evidence that it can have a negative impact on learning and behavior, and because newer and better anticonvulsants have become available.

Phenytoin (Dilantin) has also been around for a long time. It is frequently used for both generalized tonic–clonic seizures and partial seizures. It has a number of different side effects. Allergies sometimes develop and can be quite serious; any child started on this medicine who develops a skin rash should be seen by his doctor right away. Other problems include an increase in body hair, overgrowth of the gums, anemia, poor coordination, and nausea/vomiting. Behavioral difficulties can include slurred speech and confusion. Rarely, severe reactions develop in the liver or bone marrow. An unusual jerking of the eye (nystagmus) is often an early sign that the blood level is too high. Because of the problems with gum overgrowth, good dental care is very important. The overgrown gums can become a significant cosmetic problem and sometimes have to be removed surgically by the dentist.

Carbamazepine (Tegretol) is often used for generalized tonic-clonic and for partial seizures. It is frequently prescribed because it has fewer side effects than many other anticonvulsants. Because of the way the body adjusts to this medicine, it is usually started gradually. Unlike phenobarbital, which you may be able to give the child just once a day, Tegretol often has to be taken several times a day.

There are several side effects that suggest the drug level is too high. These include double vision or dizziness (often this goes away, but consult the doctor if this develops and especially if it keeps up). Difficulties in walking, unsteadiness, and sleepiness can also suggest a high drug level. Reducing the drug level (in consultation with the doctor) will take care of these problems. Sometimes blood levels need to be done because some children with autism will not be able to recognize or describe the early side effects to people.

Potential difficulties include allergic reactions and a decrease in the white blood cell count. The decrease in the white blood cell count has to be monitored. Very rarely, a severe reaction in the bone marrow occurs (aplastic anemia). Liver function also has to be monitored. As with some of the other anticonvulsants, taking Tegretol with certain other medicines has the potential for causing problems. For example, this medicine interacts with a fairly commonly used antibiotic (erythromycin). A few of the other medicines that can at times cause problem interactions are some antifungal drugs, some prescription antihistamines, some antacids, oral contraceptives, and even some other anti-convulsants. This makes it important that the doctor prescribing any seizure medicine knows all the medicines the child is receiving. Let the neurologist know if the pediatrician has given the child an antibiotic, and make sure the pediatrician knows what drugs the neurologist has prescribed. Also, be sure to use the same pharmacist/pharmacy for all the child's medicines, as the pharmacist can then also be alert to any potential for problem interactions.

Oxcarbazepine (Trileptal) is used for treatment of partial seizures. As with many other anticonvulsant medications, you have to have blood tests to look for side effects (in this case, loss of sodium from the body). Allergic skin rashes also need to be looked for. When stopping this medicine, it is important to taper off it gradually. As with many other antiseizure medicines, there may be effects on thinking and movement. An advantage of this medicine is that you can take it less frequently. It is now used quite frequently for treatment of partial seizures.

Valproic acid (Depakene/Depakote) is used in treating many different kinds of seizures (tonic–clonic, absence, and myoclonic, as well as complex partial seizures). It can take several weeks for the medicine to begin to work. Behavioral difficulties are not very common. In fact, you'll see in Chapter 15 that this medicine is sometimes used as a "mood stabilizer." There is the potential for severe liver problems (this is rare, but obviously of concern due to its seriousness). It can also adversely affect the pancreas or decrease the platelet count. The child will need periodic blood work if he is on Depakene/Depakote. This medicine also may affect the way the body breaks down other drugs, thereby changing levels of other anticonvulsants or medicines the child is on. Sometimes children have nausea and vomiting or indigestion. Younger children may have some trouble with loss of appetite, and older children may gain weight.

Ethosuximide (Zarontin) is most frequently used in treating absence (petit mal) seizures. It does not work for other kinds of seizures. Various allergies to the medication can develop, although these are not common. Generally, behavioral side effects seem to be minimal. Nightmares can develop on this medication.

Gabapentin (Neurontin) is used to treat partial seizures and frequently is prescribed along with another anticonvulsant. It may be used alone to treat a type of seizure known as benign rolandic epilepsy. Behavior changes may occur as a side effect. This drug must be stopped slowly; otherwise, it may cause an increase in seizures.

Lamotrigine (Lamictal) can treat a wide range of seizure types. Usually, it is tried when either Depakene or Tegretol has failed to stop the seizures, or in situations where these medications are contraindicated. For children with an unusual seizure type known as Lennox–Gastaut syndrome, Lamictal may be the first drug used. The most important side effect to watch for with Lamictal is a rash. This can be quite serious.

Topiramate (Topamax), like Lamictal, is frequently used when other medications, such as Depakene and Tegretol, have not worked by themselves. It can be given alone or in combination with other anticonvulsants. It is used to treat both tonic–clonic seizures and partial seizures. It may be avoided at times because of behavioral or cognitive side effects. Blood electrolytes and liver and kidney function need to be monitored when children are taking this medication. Blurred vision or eye pain can be signs of worrisome side effects.

Levetiracetam (Keppra) is usually used along with other anticonvulsants to treat partial seizures, but has been used for generalized seizures.

Zonisamide (Zonegran) is used along with other anticonvulsants to treat partial seizures. There can be serious allergic reactions to this medication. Blood counts and liver function must be monitored.

Benzodiazepines are a group of medicines that have antiseizure properties. These include such well-known medicines as diazepam (Valium), lorazepam (Ativan), and clonazepam (Klonopin) and cloazepam (Tranxene). Some of these medicines, such as Valium and Ativan, are shorter acting and are used to treat uncontrollable seizures (status epilepticus). The longer acting medicines, such as Tranxene and Klonopin, are used sometimes in nonemergency situations. They can be useful for many different types of seizures. Unfortunately, the behavioral side effects often limit their usefulness in children. These side effects can take the form of hyperactivity and excitability on the one hand and sleepiness and sedation on the other! These drugs most frequently are added to other seizure medicines in an attempt to get better control of seizures.

Other Treatments for Seizures

Dietary Treatments for Seizures   For hundreds of years it has been known that fasting seemed to make seizures less common in people with epilepsy. As this was studied, it became clear that you could also achieve the same effect not by fasting but by consuming a high-fat diet with very little sugar or starch. What happens in the body is that without sugar to digest, the body forms chemicals called ketones, which appear in the urine. The diet is called *ketogenic* because it generates these ketones. The idea is to give just enough protein and fat to allow for growth, but with as little sugar and carbohydrate as possible. Although we still don't know exactly how this works, we do know that it can help control seizures but takes a lot of supervision. You *must* do this diet in consultation with a supervising physician!

The **ketogenic diet** often is used after multiple medicines have been tried and seizure control has still not been achieved. Given the stringency of the diet, it requires very careful supervision from people who know what they are doing. The diet is not easy to do, and not everyone responds with a reduction in seizures. You might consider talking with the neurologist about the diet, particularly if the child has not done well after trials of several different medicines.

Surgery and Seizure Disorders   Rarely, surgery to remove part of the brain is used in the treatment of epilepsy. Usually, this surgery is done with adults rather than children and then usually only as a last resort. The exceptions would be if it is possible to identify and precisely pinpoint a specific area of the brain that starts the seizures (particularly if this is an area that is easy to get to and can likely be taken out without causing further problems). Another example would be if seizures are being caused by a tumor or cyst that likely won't be as responsive to medicines.

Vagus nerve stimulation is something that is used in some children who continue to have seizures even after multiple medications, and possibly diets, have been tried without success. This involves implanting a device that includes a small battery pack with a wire going from it to the vagus nerve in the neck. These are implanted surgically into the child. Stimulation of the nerve can be either preset at a regular interval or initiated during a seizure and may shorten or stop seizures. Again, this is a very specialized technique and would be done only after medications have failed.

Alternative Treatments for Seizure Disorder   We discuss alterative treatments approaches in general in Chapter 18, but do want to say a bit in this chapter about complementary/alternative medicine approaches to seizures. Various treatments have been used, ranging from massage to biofeedback, Oriental medicine, and so forth. These can (in general) be used in addition to traditional therapies but do not substitute for the traditional therapies. For example, we know that in reasonable doses vitamins are not harmful, but vitamins do not really treat seizure disorders except in the very rare case of severe vitamin deficiency.

CONTINUING CARE AND SAFETY CONCERNS

It is important that all people with seizures be evaluated periodically. This includes monitoring seizure control and the dose of the medicine, and looking for side effects. Once the child has achieved good seizure control, you may not need to bring him in to the doctor as frequently. Still, it is important to be in periodic contact with the doctor, since things like changes in size of the child may require changes in the dose of medicine. For some children, it is possible to gradually discontinue seizure medicines (under supervision) over time to determine whether they still need them.

Most children, adolescents, and adults with seizures can engage in normal physical activities. At times, you may have to limit certain kinds of activities with the potential for danger if your child loses consciousness or has an impairment in consciousness. As with other things, the risks of participating in activities have to be measured against their possible benefit. It is important to take simple, common sense precautions. For example, the child can engage in sports such as swimming, but it's important to have a life preserver and lifeguards readily available.

Talk with the doctor as well about MedicAlert bracelets, which can say that the child has a seizure disorder. This is probably most important if the child is spending time around people who won't know about her seizure disorder.

What Causes Seizures?

There are many different causes for a seizure disorder and epilepsy. For example, babies who are born with congenital infections, were exposed to certain medications in the uterus, or have had birth injuries and lack of oxygen to the brain may be at increased risk for epilepsy. Other causes include strokes, brain infections after birth, brain tumors, and injuries to the head. Many times, however, a specific cause can't be determined even after the individual is extensively evaluated. These are called *idiopathic seizures*—a fancy word to say that we don't know the cause!

In autism, it is likely that the same thing that caused the autism causes the epilepsy. Some disorders such as phenylketonuria (PKU) and tuberous sclerosis (see Chapter 1) are sometimes seen in autism and may themselves be associated with seizures. There is also some suggestion that if a parent has epilepsy, there may be an increased risk for the child. Similarly, if both parents have epilepsy, the risk increases. In autism, the risk for seizure disorder increases with lower levels of cognitive ability. That is, children with more severe intellectual disability are more likely to have seizures.

Summary

In this chapter, we talked about some aspects of seizures and their treatment. Children with autism are at higher risk for seizures than other children. Sometimes the onset of a seizure disorder is very obvious. Other times, it may be difficult to notice. Do not hesitate to bring up any concerns about changes in the child's behavior and level of alertness with the child's doctor, since seizures can develop at any time.

Many effective treatments for seizure disorders are now available. If you are not satisfied with the care the child is receiving for his seizures, do not hesitate to look for a doctor who can help you achieve reasonable control of the seizures.

■ READING LIST

Bazil, C. W. (2004). *Living well with epilepsy and other seizure disorders: An expert explains what you really need to know.* New York: Collins Living.

Blackburn, L. B. (2003). *Growing up with epilepsy: A practical guide for parents.* New York: Demos Medical.

Cooper, J. E. (1975). Epilepsy in a longitudinal survey of 5,000 children. *British Medical Journal, 1,* 1020–1022.

Devinsky, O. (2007). *Epilepsy: Patient and family guide* (3rd ed.). New York: Demos Medical.

Deykin, E. Y., & MacMahon, B. (1979). The incidence of seizures among children with autistic symptoms. *American Journal of Psychiatry, 136*(10), 1310–1312.

Freeman, J., Vining, E. P. J., & Pillas, D. J. (2002). *Seizures and epilepsy in childhood: A guide.* Baltimore: Johns Hopkins University Press.

Gosselin, K. (2001). *Taking seizure disorders to school: A story about epilepsy* (2nd ed.). Plainview, NY: JayJo Books.

Hollins, S., Bernal, J., & Thacker, A. (1999). *Getting on with epilepsy.* London: St. George's Hospital Medical School and Gaskell.

Kutscher, M. L. (2006). *Children with seizures: A guide for parents, teachers, and other professionals.* London: Jessica Kingsley.

Lears, L. (2002). *Becky the brave: A story about epilepsy.* Morton Grove, IL: Albert Whitman & Company.

Minshew, N. J., Sweeney, J. A., & Bauman, M. L. (2005). Neurological aspects of autism. In F. R. Volkmar, R. Paul, A. Klin, & D. Cohen (Eds.), *Handbook of autism and pervasive developmental disorders* (3rd ed. , pp. 453–472). Hoboken, NJ: Wiley.

Montouris, G. D., & Pellock, J. M. (2007). *Epilepsy on our terms: Stories by children with seizures and their parents.* New York: Oxford University Press.

Rapin, I., & Katzman, R. (1998). Neurobiology of autism. *Annals of Neurology, 43*(1), 7–14.

Tuchman, R., & Rapin, I. (2002). Epilepsy in autism. *Lancet Neurology, 1*(6), 352–358.

Volkmar, F. R., & Nelson, D. S. (1990). Seizure disorders in autism. *Journal of the Amercian Academy of Child & Adolescent Psychiatry, 29*(1), 127–129.

Wilner, A. N. (2007). *Epilepsy: 199 answers: A doctor responds to his patients' questions* (3rd ed.). New York: Demos Medical.

■ QUESTIONS AND ANSWERS

1. **My daughter has a seizure disorder, and we have now twice had the experience of being called from the emergency department, where she was taken by school staff after a seizure. The seizures take the form of staring spells and are not long lasting, and I think the school is overreacting. What can we do about this?**

   It sounds like the school is being a bit overly cautious. Discuss this with them as well as with your child's doctor. See if it might be possible for school staff to call you and have you decide, maybe in consultation with your regular doctor, when a trip to the emergency department is best. It is possible that your child could be seen in the doctor's office instead or might just be able to rest in the school health room for a while before returning to class. If her type of seizure never causes any problems other than staring spells, you may be able to arrange for her to go back to class after the seizure.

2. **A friend told me that all children with autism eventually have seizures. Is this true?**

No, about 20% or so of children with autism develop seizures. Children with Rett's and childhood disintegrative disorder (CDD) also have an increased chance of developing seizures. Seizures are less common in Asperger's and pervasive developmental disorder not otherwise specified (PDD-NOS). For children with autism, there is an increased risk of developing seizures throughout childhood and adolescence—even into young adulthood. Even if your child had an EEG that was normal at one point, he may still, unfortunately, develop seizures later. But clearly, most children with autism don't develop seizures.

3. **My 16-year-old son is a pretty high functioning child with autism. He just had his first seizure, but at age 5 he had a normal EEG. How commonly does this happen?**

The risk for developing seizures is increased through adolescence, and this does happen with some frequency. Unfortunately, having a normal EEG at one point does *not* mean that the EEG will always be normal. Treating the seizures is important at whatever age they develop!

4. **Our 10-year-old has recently developed seizures. His teacher at school tells us that it is possible to treat these behaviorally without medication. Is this true?**

It might be helpful to have your doctor (or your neurologist) talk with the teacher to be absolutely sure the teacher understands what is being talked about and has good information. While an isolated fever-related seizure might not be medicated, it would be very unusual not to try medications for recurrent seizures that are not related to fevers. While behavioral treatments are wonderfully helpful for some problems that children with autism have, they shouldn't be used to treat seizures! You may want to check with the teacher first to be sure you understand exactly what he or she meant.

5. **My child had a number of different EEG tests and one of them was positive. Should we be treating him as if he had epilepsy?**

You will need to speak with the neurologist about the differing results and see if there is any clinical correlation between how the child was acting and what the EEG showed at the different times.

CHAPTER 13

Dealing With Regression

In this chapter, we discuss the phenomenon of loss of developmental skills. Fortunately, this doesn't happen to most children with an autism spectrum disorder (ASD) but does with some, including all children with Rett's disorder and childhood disintegrative disorder (CDD). We review what is known about **regression** and discuss some issues that are important to keep in mind if the child's behavior significantly deteriorates. This chapter won't be relevant for every reader. If it is not something you need to know about, skip it! However, if you have a child who has experienced a major loss in developmental skills, please read on.

REGRESSION IN AUTISM

When he first described autism, Leo Kanner mentioned that he thought autism was congenital, that is, that children were born with it. Subsequently, it has become clear that approximately 20% of children who are eventually diagnosed with autism seem to be relatively normal at birth and in the early months—or sometimes years—of life but then are reported by their parents to lose skills and develop autism. This number is probably an overestimate of the number who actually show dramatic regression.

Children reported to regress fall into several distinct groups:

- Sometimes there is indeed a dramatic loss of skills and the development of what looks like autism. This occasionally occurs in children over age 2 who have had perfectly normal language, in which case a special diagnostic category, childhood disintegrative disorder (CDD), is used; this is discussed in detail later in this chapter.

- Sometimes regression happens in association with Rett's disorder (another topic discussed later in the chapter).

- Sometimes regression is reported in the first year of life, before the child has really acquired language. For example, a child may become progressively less socially related at 8 or 9 months (in this case, an autism diagnosis would be made).

- In some cases, even though parents of a child with autism report a regression, careful discussion with them will uncover a previously undetected abnormality. For example, parents may report a regression in their child's behavior at 18 months, but then it turns out that their child hadn't ever used words and may have been lagging behind even before they started worrying about his development. Some researchers have studied home videotapes, such as those of first birthday parties. Sometimes differences in development of these children can be observed. This would suggest that these children probably had autism earlier on but it was hard for parents to notice for whatever reason and wasn't recognized for a while.

- Finally, some children with autism may seem to lose skills in adolescence, particularly if they develop seizures (see Chapters 9 and 12).

Sometimes when we talk with parents in some detail, we discover that what parents are really talking about when they use the word *regression* is not so much a regression as a "stagnation." That is, the issue really is that the child's development hasn't progressed, rather than that it regressed. Occasionally, a child will have a couple of words or possible words and then not develop more words or do so only very slowly. It is sometimes not clear whether the child really had a good grasp of the words or was simply playing with making sounds as many babies do.

LANGUAGE REGRESSION AND SEIZURES

Recently, reports on television have suggested that some children diagnosed with autism may actually have a rare form of aphasia (language loss) associated with epilepsy. This is called **Landau-Kleffner syndrome** (**LKS**, also known as "acquired aphasia with epilepsy" or "epileptic aphasia"), which usually describes a condition in which epilepsy and language loss occur together (or very close together). Children with LKS develop normally for some years and acquire the ability to speak but then lose their speech (become *aphasic*, in medical terminology) and develop seizures (either thing could happen first).

Usually, LKS occurs in somewhat "older" children (after age 3), with variable degrees of recovery occurring. The EEG in these children shows a characteristic pattern that neurologists can look for.

Because young children with autism sometimes acquire speech skills and then seem to lose them, some professionals have gotten the idea that treating such children as if they had Landau-Kleffner Syndrome (i.e., with seizure medicines) might improve their speech. This idea has received a lot of attention and has led some doctors to quickly treat any child who has developmental problems associated with language loss with powerful anti-seizure medicines. As is often the case when things are not studied in great detail, a fair amount of ambiguity has occurred. For example, some doctors will treat any child with language loss, even if they don't show EEG abnormalities!

At present, there are not good data to suggest that children with autism who do not clearly have seizures should be treated with antiseizure medicines. These medicines have a range of side effects that make their use controversial when no clear benefit may ensue.

Other parents report a relatively "late onset" of autism, and may not have become worried until the child was age 24 months. Here, the issue may be less one of regression and more the parents' growing awareness of their toddler's social difficulties and oddities. These children often have said first words on time and end up being higher functioning children with autism or pervasive developmental disorder not otherwise specified (PDD-NOS). Finally, sometimes it does appear that the child was developing reasonably normally and may have had several words, but then did regress. These cases are probably a relatively small fraction of all cases where some concerns about regression are raised.

Although there has been great interest in regression in autism, the studies done have not always shown much in the way of differences between these cases and other cases of autism. That is, there aren't many proven differences in symptoms or outcomes in children with autism who are reported to regress versus those who don't—at least so far. This turns out to be a complicated topic. This is particularly true when you take into account that children who are recognized earliest probably are the ones who have the greatest cognitive handicap. In addition, it is important to realize that all the various complexities in defining regression may complicate the research that has been done. For example, one researcher may take a parent's word that his child regressed, whereas another might seek corroboration from something like a videotape. Although it seems kind of arbitrary, and indeed it is, these differences may make a major difference in how we understand the importance of regression. (See Table 13.1.)

At present, treatments for children with autism who have had a regression are no different than for other children with autism—unless a medical condition is found to explain the deterioration (see Table 13.2). With the exception of unrecognized seizure activity, the chances of finding an underlying condition are quite low, however. Still, the study of possible differences in these children remains an important area for research.

TABLE 13.1   REGRESSION IN AUTISM SPECTRUM DISORDER—
SUBTYPES

Type	Features
Childhood disintegrative disorder*	Normal development until at least age 2 years (usually 3 or 4 years) with dramatic loss of skills and development of autistic behaviors.
Rett's disorder*	Normal development early on but there is a decrease in the rate of head growth, loss of purposeful hand movements, and other characteristic symptoms.
Subtypes of autism with Reported Regression*	
Developmental stagnation	Child seems to develop reasonably normally but then development slows down.
Late onset - higher functioning	Child talks on time but social and behavioral oddities more apparent after age 2 years
Regressive or "setback" autism	Child has several words and then loses them; development and behavior regresses

*Official diagnoses; note that although autism is a recognized diagnosis, the various subtypes of "regressive autism" are not.

CHILDHOOD DISINTEGRATIVE DISORDER (CDD)

As discussed in Chapter 1, CDD is a rare condition in which a child develops normally for several years—usually 3 to 4 years, but sometimes even longer—and then has a very marked loss of skills and comes to look "classically" autistic. By definition, the child must have spoken on time and used language appropriately (speaking in sentences) before the regression, which, by definition, must be after age 2 years. It is probable that at least some children diagnosed with autism who apparently regressed at a fairly early age and are now diagnosed with autism may represent the very early cases of CDD, but the current approach to diagnosis requires at least 2 years of normal development for a diagnosis of CDD.

TABLE 13.2   MEDICAL CONDITIONS CAUSING DETERIORATION

Selected Disorders Associated With Loss of Developmental Skills*

Infections (HIV, measles, CMV)	Mitochondrial deficits (e.g., Leigh disease)
Hypothyroidism	Subacute sclerosing panencephalitis
Neurolipidosis	Metachromatic leukodystrophy
Addison–Schilder disease	Seizures
Angleman Syndrome	Gangliosidoses
Lipofuscinosis	Aminoacidopathies (e.g., PKU)

*For an exhaustive list, see Dyken, P., & Krawiecki N (1983). Neurodegenerative diseases of infancy and childhood. *Annals of Neurology, 13,* 351–364.

Over the past century, slightly more than 100 cases of CDD have been identified. You will see terms such as *disintegrative psychosis* or maybe *Heller's syndrome* used to refer to it in older papers (Theodore Heller was the man who first described the condition back in 1908). The psychosis idea was clearly a mistake; the term was used because people thought that almost every serious mental disorder was "psychosis." Today, we use the term *psychosis* much more strictly for disorders in which there is a loss of reality testing, and it doesn't really apply to conditions on the autism spectrum.

CDD was added to the *Diagnostic and Statistical Manual of Mental Disorders* (DSM) in 1994. There was some controversy about including CDD in the DSM for several reasons. One was that people thought that perhaps CDD always results from some medical condition—that it is essentially like a childhood onset of Alzheimer's disease. Interestingly, however, despite very careful medical evaluations (discussed later), usually no specific medical cause for CDD is identified; this doesn't mean you shouldn't look, though. CDD probably arises as a result of the operation of some factor or factors in development. For example, some gene or genes might turn off or on in some unexpected way and disrupt development and lead to the development of CDD.

Another concern about adding CDD to the DSM was the idea that parents were perhaps mistaken that the child had been developing normally for the first several years. One of the advantages of home videotapes is that we can often now document the early normal development of children with CDD, showing that parents indeed are correct that their children certainly looked normal. The data on outcome of CDD further support its inclusion as a separate diagnosis.

Onset

The onset of CDD is much later than that for autism. The usual age of onset is between 3 and 5 years. Occasionally, the condition begins somewhat later in childhood, though always before age 10. The onset of this condition can be relatively sudden—over days to weeks—or it can be more drawn out—over weeks to months. Occasionally, the child becomes more anxious or agitated at the onset of CDD. He becomes less interested in the environment and starts to lose skills in multiple areas. Although he previously had talked normally, he loses the ability to speak entirely or can now say only an occasional single word. He loses interest in other people, including parents and siblings, and becomes socially withdrawn. Sometimes, if he had the ability to use the bathroom independently, he loses this skill and may again end up in diapers. Figure 13.1 summarizes the different ages of onset of autism and CDD.

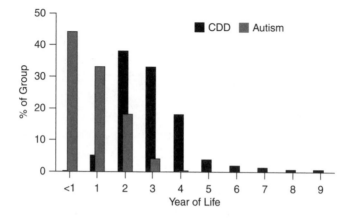

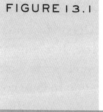
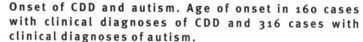

FIGURE 13.1   **Onset of CDD and autism. Age of onset in 160 cases with clinical diagnoses of CDD and 316 cases with clinical diagnoses of autism.**

Reprinted, with permission, from Volkmar, F., Koenig, K., & State, M. Childhood disintegrative disorder (2005). In F. Volkmar, R. Paul, A. Klin, & D. Cohen (Eds.), *Handbook of autism* (3rd ed., vol. 1, p. 73). Hoboken, NJ: Wiley.

Not surprisingly, given the dramatic nature of this regression, parents are desperate. Usually, they take their child for very extensive medical evaluations. Parents often presume—as did most professionals, at least until recently—that some underlying medical condition is responsible for the child's regression. However, this seems not to be the case. Most children are given very extensive medical evaluations, and no specific cause for the condition can be pinpointed. This does not, of course, mean that one does not exist. However, it does suggest that we by no means understand the vast majority of cases of this rare and perplexing condition.

Clinical Features of CDD

The clinical features of a disorder (the things a doctor can observe) in CDD are summarized in Table 13.3. Overall, more boys than girls appear to be affected—about four boys for every girl. It is likely that some girls with Rett's disorder

TABLE 13.3	CLINICAL FEATURES OF CHILDHOOD DISINTEGRATIVE DISORDER
Speech deterioration/loss	100%
Social disturbance	99%
Stereotyped mannerisms and resistance to change	88%
Overactivity	77%
Anxiety/affective symptoms	71%
Deterioration in self-help skills	83%

were incorrectly thought to have CDD in the past. Although CDD is clearly rare, it is unclear exactly how common the condition is since cases have probably often been incorrectly diagnosed. The condition is probably about 100 times less common than autism.

Medical Evaluations

Typically, parents become worried—usually very worried—quickly once their child starts to lose skills. Often, the child's primary doctor will be concerned. He or she may do some basic tests, such as screening tests of blood and urine for disorders of metabolism. Looking for medical causes of regression is sufficiently specialized that the primary health care provider will want to get some outside help, and will send the child for more specialized evaluations. These might include consultation with a pediatric neurologist or specialist in genetics, since many of the medical conditions associated with loss of skills are the result of neurological illness such as seizures or genetic problems. In coordination with the health care provider, the specialists will conduct a careful search for any genetic or neurological conditions that might explain the regression. These include a range of disorders, all of which are quite rare. A number of laboratory tests can be done to look for many of these conditions.

TESTS FOR MEDICAL CONDITIONS WHEN DEVELOPMENT DETERIORATES

Type of Test	What Is Being Looked For
EEG (brain wave)	Seizure activity (see Chapter 12) may lead to loss of developmental skills; some types of seizures are associated with loss of language.
Blood tests	Used to check for low (or high) levels of chemicals and other substances in the blood, for example, low thyroid (hypothyroidism), signs of infection, or amino acids.
Urine tests	High levels of certain chemicals may be present in the urine in some disorders such as those that prevent the body from properly using amino acids.
Brain scans (CT/MRI)	Can reveal changes in the brain seen in some disorders, these may be general (throughout the brain) or localized to specific parts of the brain.
X-rays	Deformities in the bones are seen in some conditions.
Other tests	In addition to standard physical or neurological examinations, other tests, including examination of the eyes, of hearing, of the skin, and other systems may be needed.

Sometimes development deteriorates following the onset of a recognized (or sometimes unrecognized) seizure disorder. Neurological examination and electroencephalogram (EEG) should therefore definitely be performed. Rates of EEG abnormalities and seizure disorders in CDD are probably about the same as in autism.[1] Some degree of loss of skills may also follow the onset of other medical conditions, such as meningitis. In these instances, CDD would be diagnosed only if the characteristic symptoms that are so strongly suggestive of autism were present—that is, social and other abilities would need to be even more impaired than general development.

Most of the time, even after extensive testing, nothing specific is found. Even if a medical cause is found, the diagnosis of CDD is made. However, other aspects of treatment may change or there may be important information for the family, for example, about inherited conditions.

Outcome and Interventions

In about three-fourths of children with CDD, behavior and development deteriorate but then stabilize at some lower level. No additional deterioration then occurs, but gains are often frustratingly small. These children almost universally have some degree of intellectual deficiency. In other children, particularly when loss of skills is associated with some other identifiable medical condition, deterioration is progressive. Sometimes after the regression, some degree of recovery then occurs—for example, a child who had become mute regains the ability to say single words. In a handful of cases, children have made a major recovery after the deterioration. Unfortunately, the outlook for children with CDD is generally worse than for children with autism, although a few children have made dramatic improvement. Except when deterioration is progressive, life expectancy apparently is normal. When deterioration is progressive, life span depends on the associated medical problem.

As a practical matter, the behavioral and educational interventions for CDD are the same as for autism. These techniques include special education, behavioral treatments, and drug therapy. The goals are, as in autism, to select appropriate goals and services and then help the child benefit from services. Unfortunately, even when children with CDD receive the best possible services, they are more likely than children with autism to require residential programs. At present, no drug treatments are available to treat the underlying cause of CDD, but drug treatments (see Chapter 15) can help deal with problem behaviors. When seizure disorders are present, drug treatments can also be helpful (see Chapter 12).

---

[1]See Chapter 12 for information about seizures in general and page 408 for information about the relatively rare syndrome of acquired aphasia (language loss) with epilepsy.

RETT'S DISORDER

As discussed in Chapter 1, Rett's disorder is one of the more recently described autism spectrum conditions. Dr. Andreas Rett reported on this condition in 1966 after seeing two girls with the unusual hand wringing movements of the disorder in his waiting room; he then collected and reported on a series of cases. In 1985, Dr. Bengt Hagberg and colleagues published clinical criteria for classical Rett's syndrome and in 2001 the gene responsible for Rett's was discovered.

Early on, there was much confusion about the possibility that Rett's disorder was a form of autism. As time went on, however, it became clear that, although some "autistic-like" features are present early in life, they tend to diminish as the child grows a bit older. In addition, the course of Rett's disorder is very different from that of autism. Rett's disorder was included in the PDD category of the DSM in 1994 primarily because there is some potential for confusion with autism, particularly early in life, and because it was felt that it was important to include Rett's somewhere and PDD seemed the best fit.

The discovery of the gene made it clear that the many different causes that had been previously put forth were incorrect. It is now known that most cases of Rett's disorder are caused by abnormalities known as mutations in the **MECP2** gene on the X chromosome, one of the two sex chromosomes that everyone has. We will discuss the genetics of Rett's later in the chapter.

Originally, the condition was thought to be confined to girls. Since then, boys who have the disorder—or at least have the gene for Rett's disorder—have been seen, although not very frequently. Probably, fetuses that are male and carry the gene are more likely to spontaneously abort before birth or to have profound medical difficulties early on in life. Rett's is a rare disorder, affecting only one in every 10,000 to 15,000 live female births. The disorder has been described as having four stages, which are detailed in Table 13.4.

In Rett's disorder, typically the pregnancy, labor, and delivery are not unusual, and the child's very early development also seems to be fine. After some months or even a year or more of what seems to be normal development, things seem to slow down. This has been termed *developmental stagnation*. The child may also lose interest in the environment, and this has often led to a suspicion that the child is autistic. The doctor may notice that head and body growth are slowing down. Often, these changes are difficult to notice at first. Once development slows down, it may stabilize for a time before motor difficulties are observed (see the next section).

Clinical Features

Unusual behaviors and medical problems frequently associated with Rett's include:

- Very unusual hand washing/wringing sterotypies (the child looks as if she is constantly washing her hands).

TABLE 13.4   **STAGES OF RETT'S DISORDER**

Stage	Clinical Features
1. Early Onset	This stage usually begins between 6 and 18 months of age. There may be decreased eye contact and loss of interest in the child's environment. Some motor skills may be delayed. Changes in hand movements and decreased head growth start but all of these features may be so subtle that they are not recognized during this stage. This stage can last from a few months to over a year.
2. Rapid Deterioration	This stage starts between ages 1 and 4 years and is usually much shorter than Stage 1, lasting for only weeks to months. The decreased head growth which is characteristic of Rett's is often recognized at this stage although it may have started earlier. Some features that resemble autism develop at this time. These include loss of language and decreased social interaction. Some of the features that people associate with Rett's disorder also develop in this stage. These include characteristic hand movements such as wringing and washing movements. Sleep problems as well as gait problems also develop in this stage.
3. Plateau	This stage starts between 2 and 10 years of age. Seizures, intellectual disability and further motor problems develop. Breathing problems such as hyperventilation, breath holding spells and apnea can start also. Some of the more autistic-like features may lessen. Many girls may stay in this stage for the rest of their lives.
4. Late Motor Deterioration	Eye contact may improve but significant motor problems limit the ability to move around independently and scoliosis (curvature of the spine) can become a significant problem. Seizures may decrease.

Adapted, with permission, from Van Acker, R., Loncola, J., & Van Acker, E. (2005). Rett's syndrome. In F. R. Volkmar, R. Paul, A. Klin, & D. Cohen (Eds.), *Handbook of autism and pervasive developmental disorders* (3rd ed., p. 133). Hoboken, NJ: Wiley.

- A loss of purposeful hand movements (the child has increasing difficulty using her hands for self-care, for drawing, etc.).
- **Ataxia** (motor difficulties), such as in walking (if the child has learned to walk, she may become much more unstable on her feet).
- Breathing problems may develop (breath-holding spells and disorganized breathing patterns may be seen).
- Seizures may develop (often starting in the preschool years).
- **Scoliosis** (curvature of the spine) may develop.
- Eating and growth problems are fairly common, and constipation can be severe.
- **Bruxism** (teeth grinding) can be a problem.

Severe intellectual deficiency develops. Social skills are, on balance, somewhat less severely affected than in autism, although the severe intellectual deficiency contributes to problems in social interaction and communication (the motor difficulties also contribute to both).

Genetic Issues

Now that the gene for Rett's disorder has been found, a girl who is suspected of having it should see a clinical geneticist and be tested. The MECP2 gene, which is abnormal in Rett's, is known to contain instructions for making a protein in the brain that is needed for normal brain development. The details of how and what is involved are under investigation. Severity seems to relate to several factors, including how much of the difficulty is expressed in the brain (this has to do with the way the defective gene is expressed on one of the two X chromosomes) and how extensively the gene is damaged. It is hoped that a better understanding of the function of these proteins will lead to a more general understanding of what has gone wrong in Rett's and someday lead to possible treatments for the disorder. Most cases of the abnormal gene in Rett's occur spontaneously; that is, it is not inherited from a parent; some cases that appear to run in families have been reported; this is another reason to do testing. This is an area where knowledge is advancing rapidly, and if Rett's is suspected, consultation with an experienced specialist is needed.

Development and Symptoms

Children with Rett's disorder present some special challenges for medical care. They have multiple problems, mentioned above, that involve treatment from a range of specialists. As a result, it becomes even more important that the child's primary physician be centrally involved in coordinating care. Medical problems include seizures (in 75–80% of cases)—most commonly, generalized tonic-clonic and partial seizures, with other types less frequently observed. Often, abnormalities on the EEG are seen before seizures develop. Treatment of seizures depends on the type of seizure (as discussed in Chapter 12). Some children with Rett's disorder are very sensitive to seizure medicines and may need careful monitoring. Sometimes seizures decrease in adolescence. Occasionally, children with Rett's have other behaviors (staring spells) that mimic seizures but do not represent actual seizures; if these are not seizures, they do not require drug treatment.

Breathing problems can include:

- Hyperventilation (breathing rapidly) and apnea (stopping breathing)
- Breath holding and disorganized breathing (sometimes the child will actually pass out; there is some potential for mistaking these for seizures)
- Swallowing air (aerophagia) and then regurgitating it (like burping)

The reasons for these behaviors are not known. They can present serious medical problems. These behaviors do *not* usually respond to behavioral interventions and should not be thought of as attention seeking! The efforts of respiratory therapists are sometimes needed. Apnea monitors and other special equipment may be needed.

Movement problems are often seen in children with Rett's disorder, and usually the services of multiple specialists in both school and medical settings are needed. These may include occupational and physical therapists, as well as orthopedists—medical specialists in the muscular and skeletal system. Ongoing therapy has the potential to improve mobility. Given the up-and-down pattern of regression, it is important that this intervention continue over time—even when the child is having some loss of skills. As for other conditions, it is important that treatment be very individualized. **Hypotonia** (a general decrease in muscle tone) along with **ataxia** (uncoordinated movements) and **apraxia** (unsteadiness) may be some of the earliest motor manifestations in the disorder. These problems lead to difficulties with walking and other problems in movement; children often walk with an unusual, unsteady gait. As time goes on, difficulties with stability of the trunk further contribute to movement problems.

It is important to encourage and maintain the ability to walk independently and stay active as long as possible. Some children lose the ability to walk, and this can lead to other complications, such as contractures (permanent tightening of muscle or tendon causing deformity) and bedsores. Various techniques can be used to help with walking. Some of these are methods also used with children with cerebral palsy or adults after a stroke. These might involve balancing activities, learning to shift weight, and so forth. Some children also respond well to swinging and to vestibular stimulation (bouncing movement, etc.). Sometimes problems with the feet contribute to walking difficulties and need to be addressed as well. It is also important to realize that the child may be somewhat resistant to exercise or therapy activities and may also be slow to respond. Unfortunately, difficulties with hand movements and purposeful hand control can complicate the use of aids such as walkers.

The unusual hand movements in Rett's disorder can take various forms. These are often seen as hand washing or hand wringing but can also include hand-to-mouth movements (e.g., pulling on the tongue). Often, these movements change over time. Younger children may make quick, fairly simple hand movements. As children grow older, the movements may become more complex and then eventually less complicated. These movements often seem to increase when the child is stressed or upset; they may disappear, briefly, when the child is doing something. The movements do not otherwise seem to be particularly stimulated in either direction by the environment. Medications have not been particularly helpful in dealing with these movements. Occasionally, other techniques such as hand splints have been tried, but results are not always consistent. Assistive technology methods can be used to help increase functional movement of the hands.

As time goes on, children with Rett's may develop difficulty with spasticity (increased muscle tone). This can affect different muscle groups and varies in severity. Sometimes it causes very significant contractures. It may also contribute to some of the difficulties with deformities of the spinal column. Various activities, sometimes including pool-based hydrotherapy, may be helpful in preventing or delaying these problems. The scoliosis and kyphosis (hunchback) can further contribute to difficulties in walking and movement. Various exercises and physical therapy can be helpful. Special wheelchairs and other chairs that support the back and produce good posture may be needed.

Outcome and Interventions

Like children with other developmental disabilities, children with Rett's disorder should receive special education services individually tailored to their needs. They will likely need the help of many professionals, including physical therapists, occupational therapists, speech–language pathologists, respiratory therapists, and orthopedic physicians.

Although some of the usual principles of behavior modification and special education can be used, it is important to realize that the hand movements that interfere with learning are involuntary behaviors not under the conscious control of the child. That is, you can't talk the child out of them, and punishment won't work either. Behavioral methods can be used, along with occupational therapy and physical therapy procedures to help increase or maintain functional skills, such as in eating. Whenever possible, communication skills and basic self-care skills should be encouraged. Medications for seizures are often needed and medications for behavior problems are sometimes used.

Unfortunately, adults with Rett's disorder are quite disabled. Their ability to move, walk, and control hand movement independently is often limited. Although assessment can be difficult, many function in the severely impaired range on cognitive testing. It is worth remembering, however, that Rett's disorder is a fairly new diagnosis. As more researchers become interested in studying the disorder, there is hope that increased understanding will lead to more effective treatments. Mouse models have been developed since the gene was discovered, and they hopefully will make it easier to investigate possible treatments. Recent studies in these animal models suggest that some of the deficits may be reversed if the function of the gene can be restored. This is an exciting finding that has promise for future therapies. One of the challenges is being able to specifically target those nerve cells that need it. For more information about Rett's disorder and new developments on the horizon, contact the International Rett Syndrome Association, listed in the Resource Guide.

SUMMARY

In this chapter, we briefly reviewed some of the autism spectrum disorders in which behavior and development deteriorates. This kind of regression most often occurs in children with CDD or Rett's disorder. A small number of children with "classic" autism also seem to have this pattern—most often before the age of 2 years. In general, regression is not expected in older children with autism, Asperger's disorder, or PDD-NOS.

Sometimes when children with autism are reported to have regressed, it really is more often a case of "developmental stagnation." That is, the child is not making as much progress as predicted, but he is not usually losing skills.

Keep in mind that some children with autism may seem to lose skills in adolescence, as discussed in Chapter 9. This change is *not* the same kind of regression we are talking about in this chapter.

■ READING LIST

Amir, R. E., Van den Veyver, I. B., Wan, M., Tran, C. Q., Francke, U., Zoghbi, H. Y. (1990). Rett syndrome is caused by mutations in X-linked MeCP2, encoding methyl-CpG-binding protein 2. *Nature Genetics, 23*, 185–8.

Catalano, R. A. (1998). *When autism strikes: Families cope with childhood disintegrative disorder.* New York: Perseus.

Chahrour, M., & Zoghbi, H. Y. (2007). The story of Rett syndrome: From clinic to neurobiology. *Neuron, 56*(3), 422–437.

Hagberg, B. A., & Skjeldal, O. H. (1994). Rett variants: A suggested model for inclusion criteria. *Pediatric Neurology, 11*(1), 5–11.

Hansen, R. L., Ozonoff, S., Krakowiak, P., Angkustsiri, K., Jones, C., Deprey, L. J., et al. (2008). Regression in autism: Prevalence and associated factors in the CHARGE Study. *Ambulatory Pediatrics, 8*(1), 25–31.

Lainhart, J. E., Ozonoff, S., Coon, H., Krasny, L., Dinh, E., Nice, J., et al. (2002). Autism, regression, and the broader autism phenotype. *American Journal of Medical Genetics, 113*(3), 231–237.

Lewis, J., & Wilson, D. (1998). *Pathways to learning in Rett syndrome.* London: David Fulton.

Lord, C., Shulman, C., & DiLavore, P. (2004). Regression and word loss in autistic spectrum disorders. *Journal of Child Psychology and Psychiatry, 45*(5): 936–955.

Parker, J., & Parker, P. (Eds.). (2002). *The official parent's sourcebook on Rett's syndrome.* San Diego, CA: Icon Health.

Schulze, C. (1996). *When snow turns to rain: One family's struggle to solve the riddle of autism.* Bethesda, MD: Woodbine House.

Siperstein, R., & Volkmar, F. (2004). Brief report: Parental reporting of regression in children with pervasive developmental disorders. *Journal of Autism and Developmental Disorders, 34*(6), 731–734.

Van Acker, R., Loncola, J., & Van Acker, E. (2005). Rett's syndrome. In F. R. Volkmar, R. Paul, A. Klin, & D. Cohen (Eds.), *Handbook of autism and pervasive developmental disorders* (3rd ed., pp. 126–164). Hoboken, NJ: Wiley.

Volkmar, F., Koenig, K., & State, M. (2005). Childhood disintegrative disorder. In F. R. Volkmar, R. Paul, A. Klin, & D. Cohen (Eds.), *Handbook of autism and pervasive developmental disorders* (3rd ed. , pp. 70–87). Hoboken, NJ: Wiley.

Volkmar, F. R., & Rutter, M. (1995). Childhood disintegrative disorder: Results of the DSM-IV autism field trial. *Journal of the American Academy of Child and Adolescent Psychiatry, 34*(8), 1092–1095.

Werner, E., & Dawson, G. (2005). Validation of the phenomenon of autistic regression using home videotapes. *Archives of General Psychiatry, 62*(8), 889–895.

Zoghbi, H. (1988). Genetic aspects of Rett syndrome. *Journal of Child Neurology, 3* (Suppl), S76S78.

■ WEB SITES

www.med.yale.edu/chldstdy/autism/cdd.html
www.ninds.nih.gov/disorders/rett/rett.htm
www.rettsyndrome.org/

■ QUESTIONS AND ANSWERS

1. **Can Rett's disorder coexist with autism?**

    No. By definition, the two disorders are distinctive. There is a relatively brief "autistic-like" phase in Rett's (usually in the preschool years), but after that, the conditions are quite different. Although children with Rett's do have impaired social and communication skills, these are not of the same type seen in autism.

2. **What is the relationship between Rett's disorder and childhood disintegrative disorder?**

    The main, obvious relationship is that in both conditions there is some deterioration in the child's development and behavior. It is not at all clear that there is much of a relationship past this obvious one, though. Children with Rett's disorder are almost always girls. The regression often starts very early in life and has a characteristic course, with slowing down of head growth, loss of purposeful hand movements, and development of unusual "hand washing" stereotypies. In CDD, the period of normal development is usually longer and the child has, by definition, progressed to the point of speech before the onset of a dramatic regression. Boys seem much more likely than girls to have CDD. The course of CDD seems much different than that in Rett's disorder as well. Usually, children with CDD look like they have very severe "classic" autism and do not have the problems in movement or breathing that children with Rett's syndrome exhibit.

A gene has been discovered that causes most of cases of Rett's syndrome. Genes that might cause CDD have not yet been identified.

3. **My 12-year-old with autism developed seizures, which are now being treated, but I think his language is not what it once was. Could this be because of the seizures? They seem well controlled.**

We don't always understand why some older children with autism either lose skills or sometimes stagnate for a while. As he followed children over time, Leo Kanner observed that in adolescence some children made gains and others didn't do as well (see Chapter 12 on seizures and Chapter 9 on adolescence). Sometimes this has to do with developing seizures, and often we can't be sure if it is the seizures that cause the problem or maybe even if the medicine used to control the seizures has some negative effect on the child's learning. This is the kind of issue you should discuss with the neurologist and the child's pediatrician. The goal is to control the seizures but not to overly medicate the child—which itself may interfere with learning!

CHAPTER 14

Dealing With Behavior Problems

Behavioral difficulties in autism and related conditions can take many forms and can be uncommon or very frequent. Common behavior can include repetitive movements such as hand mannerisms, finger/hand flapping, or complicated whole-body movements such as rocking. Sometimes challenging behaviors may take other forms such as major tantrums or self-injurious behaviors like head banging. The child may pursue very unusual interests; for example, she may line up toys or dolls rather than play with them. Behavioral problems also tend to change over time, often becoming most problematic in the early and middle teenage years. Sometimes behaviors persist over time, but what was slightly problematic behavior in a 3-year-old can become much more so in a larger 13-year-old!

In this chapter, we discuss some of the behavioral problems and emotional difficulties seen in autism spectrum disorders (ASDs). Keep in mind that, when the problem is affecting a particular child, you'll need to work with people who know the child very well. Also keep in mind that we're discussing the entire range of difficulties that can be seen, but an individual may not have many or even any of these problems! When considering any treatment, you must always weigh the potential benefits against the risks of treatment. Several excellent resources for parents are now available on behavioral treatments and are listed in the reading list at the end of this chapter.

For purposes of this chapter, we group problem behaviors and emotional problems into several broad categories that include the most common kinds of behaviors you might see within each category. Then we discuss some general aspects of interventions. Near the end of the chapter, we also talk about behavior problems related to mental health conditions—an issue usually most relevant to more cognitively able individuals on the autism spectrum. Specific medications and aspects of drug treatment are discussed in the next chapter.

In an ideal world, there would be a simple one-to-one correspondence between a behavioral or emotional difficulty and a treatment. Unfortunately, things are a lot more complicated than this in the real world. First, it may be difficult to apply the usual diagnostic categories, particularly in a more impaired child with an ASD. (This is a general problem for all children with significant disabilities.) Second, people sometimes do not recognize the other difficulties/disorders that are present, or mistakenly assume that having autism somehow protects you from other problems. That is, the diagnosis of autism or Asperger's disorder overshadows an awareness of other difficulties like anxiety or depression. As we talk about later in this chapter, these issues complicate decisions about how best to treat behavioral difficulties—particularly in children who have significant communication problems. Even the most cognitively able children can have "meltdowns" and other difficulties, and sometimes it is hard for people to get a handle on these as well.

COMMON BEHAVIORAL/MOOD PROBLEMS IN AUTISM SPECTRUM CONDITIONS	
Type of Behaviors	**Specific Examples**
Stereotyped behaviors	Body rocking
	Hand/finger flicking
	Other repetitive behaviors
Self-injury and aggression	Injury to self or others; property destruction
Problems with rigidity and perseveration	Resistance to change
	Perseveration, compulsiveness
	Unusual interests
Overactivity and problems with attention	High activity levels
	Difficulties with attention
	Impulsivity
	Running/Bolting
Mood problems	Depression
	Anxiety
	Bipolar disorders

As mentioned, children with ASDs often have many different problems. For example, problems with attention may go along with problems with stereotyped (apparently purposeless and repetitive) behaviors. It is important to decide which problems are the ones to focus on, as well as what the benefits and potential risks of the treatment are. Sometimes the same problem behavior is the product of several different factors. However, sometimes the fact that the child has several different problems will be very important in selecting a treatment. As a practical matter, problem behaviors often seem to travel in groups! For simplicity's sake, we usually refer to "the child," but what we have to say is relevant to adolescents and adults as well.

BEHAVIORAL INTERVENTIONS—A BRIEF INTRODUCTION

Behavioral and educational interventions are usually the first line of treatment for behavioral difficulties. A whole body of work on understanding and treating behavioral difficulties using assessment and intervention principles from **applied behavior analysis (ABA)** provides a very helpful framework for dealing with behavioral difficulties. The assumptions of ABA are that, like other children, those with an ASD learn through experience. Accordingly, the events that precede behavioral difficulties (the antecedents) and those that follow them (the consequences) are important. The antecedents are the things that set off the behavior in the first place. For example, if you ask the child to stop body rocking and put away her toys and this leads to a tantrum, you have a pretty good idea that the child does not want to stop her body rocking or put away her toys. If the response to the tantrum is to let the child continue to body rock, you've given a pretty strong message (the consequence) that the child doesn't need to listen to you!

There are many different approaches to dealing with behavior problems; the reading list at the end of this chapter and the additional readings at the end of the book provide some basic information. Because parents (and sometimes teachers) find themselves coping with a lot of things at the same time, it is not always easy to step back and get the "big picture" on behavior problems. There are some general principles to keep in mind. First don't pay attention to the child only when he is behaving badly. If you want to encourage positive behavior, then be sure to acknowledge and praise it specifically! Put another way, one of the "tricks" of dealing with problem behaviors is also to have a vision of the kinds of positive behavior you want to have replace them.

Generally, one of the most important steps is to see if you can observe regularities in the problem behaviors—for example, does the behavior happen only at a certain time or place or following a certain activity? Look at what goes before and what follows the behavior—is the behavior being (unintentionally) rewarded (reinforced)? This assessment approach is sometimes referred to as doing an ABC analysis—that is, analysis of Antecedent–Behavior–Consequence.

Keep in mind that you want to reinforce good behavior. To do this, be sure to praise such behavior quickly and specifically when it happens. In many ways, the solution to the problem of bad behavior is to get the child to increase good behaviors that will replace the problem behaviors. Planning ahead is helpful; if you know a situation will be stressful or a problem for the child, have a plan in advance. It is always easier to prevent problems than to have to react to them during a crisis. Keep in mind that when you are trying to eliminate or reduce a problem behavior, you ought to have something you want to happen instead.

Be a careful observer of your child. Often, you'll be able to notice subtle behaviors that may be clues that she is going to have difficulties. Use these warning signs to head off problem behaviors, for example, by giving the child something else to do or giving the child a better strategy to use for communicating his needs (e.g., picture exchange; see Chapter 6). When you do need to set limits or have consequences, be clear, be specific, and then follow through. Again, being prepared is a big part of the battle! If you have a plan in place, you can implement it rather than feeling confused and overwhelmed. If, for example, the child has trouble at the grocery store, you should make a specific plan before you go. First, you probably should do everything possible to make initial visits a success such as making initial visits very brief and going in to get the child's favorite food. The idea, for children who have problems with change, is to introduce change gradually and to build on success. As time goes on, you can use a shopping list (if need be with photographs, visual cues, or actual labels from cans/cartons) that the child can help you complete. If the child has behavioral difficulties, tell her in advance what will happen if she engages in the problem behavior: "Jenny, there is no screaming in the grocery store; if you scream, we'll have to leave and can't get ice cream."

It may help to take notes and/or develop a chart where you can list the ABC's of problem behaviors: antecedents, the behavior itself, and the consequences. Often, as you pay more attention, you'll start to notice important clues and patterns—for example, that the behavior happens only in one place or at one time of the day.

Also take a careful look at the environment. Sometimes what seem to be simple adjustments in the child's environment (e.g., moving from a more disorganized and disorganizing environment to a simpler, structured one) can make for a major change in her behavior. Children with ASDs respond well to structure, predictability, and consistency, and it is important to be sure that the environment is not contributing to the child's problems. We'll give an example of a situation where the environment was contributing to a problem behavior at the end of this chapter.

In addition, pay attention to the functions of the behavior. If the child is using some behavior to get attention, then try planned ignoring. That is, don't acknowledge what the child is doing inappropriately but *do* pay attention when she starts doing something you want her to do. You might even try time-outs. Be sure to pair this with lavish and appropriate praise when the child is behaving well. If the child has trouble with the word *no* (as most children do), be careful not to reinforce tantrums or other inappropriate behaviors. Sometimes parents unintentionally encourage this behavior by doing exactly what the child wants. It is important to become adept at "catching" the child doing the right thing—if only for a moment—so you can praise that rather than punish "bad" behavior.

Sometimes problems will arise because the child is trying to avoid work or other activities. Unfortunately, if you give in, this sends a strong message to the child about how to get out of work! Try, instead, to get her to engage for a short time in the activity, then praise her and let her do something else for a while. Also try to model and encourage good, straightforward communication.

Some sensory behaviors (see Chapter 16) can be addressed by helping the child find more appropriate ways to engage in the behavior. The child's occupational therapist (OT) may be helpful to you here. For example, if the child has trouble with prolonged body rocking, you might start by trying to contain the behavior to a certain place (e.g., a rocking chair) with set amounts of time for rocking alternated with periods of time for work. (The work times can be made progressively longer!)

Many times, children who have major communication difficulties use problem behaviors as an inappropriate way of communicating. To try to minimize communication difficulties in dealing with problem behaviors, keep your communications clear and simple. Be sure the child is paying attention when you communicate with her. Be exact and specific about what you want. Try to give her appropriate ways for communicating her needs and wants, for example, using a "Help" card to ask for help rather than screaming. Helping children learn to communicate—at whatever level they can—feelings of frustration, anxiety, and so forth is important. The child's speech–language pathologist should be able to suggest strategies or communication methods to help with this and may be able to collaborate with the school psychologist or a behavior specialist on ways to do this.

COMMON MISTAKES IN DEALING WITH BEHAVIOR PROBLEMS

MAKING LANGUAGE TOO COMPLICATED

When children or adolescents seem upset, there is often an understandable desire on the part of teachers and parents to be sympathetic, polite, and caring. This is indeed understandable but often results in the language used with the child being overly complicated. It is more helpful to be short, simple, and directive. More complex language is difficult to follow and may only make the child feel more frustrated.

FOCUSING ONLY ON THE NEGATIVE

If you want the child to stop doing something, then be prepared to give some alternatives.

TIME PRESSURE

Sometimes there is a sense of wanting a difficult activity to be over and, as a result, teacher and parents (and sometimes student) try to move things along very quickly. For individuals on the autism spectrum, giving sufficient time lets them "take it easy" and helps the individual plan and respond more effectively.

SARCASM, IRONY, OR COMPLEX HUMOR

Individuals on the autism spectrum can have wonderful senses of humor. That being said, it is common for them to truly be made fun of, to misunderstand attempts at humor as criticism, and be confused by multiple conflicting cues. Keep jokes and humor to a minimum. Be on the alert for more able children and adolescents to be confused by humor and explicitly target working on humor as a goal in their program.

AMBIGUITY

Lack of clarity often leads to trouble. Keep in mind that imprecision may lead to confusion. This is particularly common when tasks don't have obvious start/stop points. For example, when asked to clean a rectangular table with a dusting cloth, the person with autism may keep cleaning and cleaning and cleaning—there is no obvious start and stop. In a situation of this kind, build in a start and stop; this is totally artificial but can be very helpful. For example, teach that in cleaning a table you start from the top left-hand corner and work until you are at the bottom right corner— and then you're done!

INCONSISTENCY

Introduce change in a planful and sensible way when it is needed. Children on the autism spectrum often have trouble in dealing with the unexpected. Inconsistency leads to anxiety and disorganization. Try, as much as possible, to use the child's interest in consistency to help him organize himself at home and in the classroom.

UNINTENTIONALLY REWARDING UNDESIRED BEHAVIOR

Often, minimally problematic behaviors can be made much worse by excessive attention from parents and teachers.

As always, keep the big picture in mind. It is often easy to say what you don't want the child to do, but it is essential that you teach the child what you want her to do. The child's classroom teacher, school psychologist, speech–language pathologist, and OT or physical therapist (PT) all have valuable perspectives and may be able to give good advice to parents and each other. Sometimes the assistance of a behavior specialist is needed. Unfortunately, children with ASDs are all sufficiently different from each other that one really needs to tailor the intervention to the child. Having an outside specialist can be a great help in this process, particularly if the behavior is challenging. A large body of work on behavioral approaches now exists and can help parents and teachers in their efforts to encourage positive behavioral change.

DRUG INTERVENTIONS—A BRIEF DISCUSSION

Although behavioral and educational interventions are typically tried first, medications also play an important role in helping children with behavioral difficulties. Sometimes behavioral interventions alone don't do the trick. Other times there may be a real emergency (such as when a child is seriously injuring herself by head banging). For still other situations—for example, depression—medicines may be the first line of treatment. Medicines and behavioral procedures can be used together— often very effectively. We discuss this issue in much more detail in the next chapter.

There are several times in the life of a child with autism when medications are more likely to be considered. Generally, very young children are least likely to receive medications. Usually, their behavioral difficulties are pretty minimal, and it is much easier to physically manage an out-of-control 2-year-old than a 12-year-old. The year or so before children enter puberty is often a time when behavioral difficulties arise. We are not sure why this is, although the various changes they experience in their bodies and changes in hormone levels probably are part of the picture.

For some children, particularly higher functioning children, the advent of adolescence also means that the child is more aware of being different, in some important ways, from other children. They may be able to talk about feeling anxious and may also talk about feelings of depression and sometimes serious symptoms of depression. Fortunately, we have fairly effective treatments for depression—both drug and behavioral treatments. Even more important, the desire to fit in really spurs remarkable growth in some children.

TYPES OF BEHAVIORAL AND EMOTIONAL DIFFICULTIES

Behavioral and emotional difficulties in autism and related conditions can take many different forms, but these generally fall into several, sometimes overlapping, categories.

Occasionally, the individual exhibits so many difficulties that it is hard to sort out exactly what is going on. This is particularly true if—as is understandable for a parent or teacher—you are so closely involved that it is hard to get a sense of the "big picture." This is one of the reasons that an outside consultant (a behavioral psychologist or behavior specialist) can be helpful. These individuals have the great advantage of being able to "step back a bit" and look at the entire picture.

Stereotyped Behaviors and Agitation

These apparently purposeless, repetitive movements are common in young children with autism and related conditions (although not as common in Asperger's disorder). They often seem to emerge around ages 2 to 3 (see Chapter 7). These can include body rocking, finger flicking, toe walking, body rocking, and other complex, whole-body movements. As discussed in Chapter 13, other kinds of unusual movements are seen in Rett's disorder—for example, hand washing or hand wringing, as well as some other very odd behaviors such as pulling at the tongue. Stereotyped movements may also be referred to as self-stimulatory movements (although this sometimes leads to confusion with masturbation, which is a somewhat different problem; see Chapter 9).

Stereotyped movements are often associated with other behavior problems such as self-injury or sometimes with aggression (particularly if you attempt to interrupt the movements). They also are often associated with behavioral rigidity and difficulties with change. Some degree of agitation or general tendency toward being upset and "on edge" is also often seen; you can feel as if the child is about to explode at any second.

Sometimes infants and very young children who go on to have typical development engage in some body rocking, occasionally even head banging, sometimes while asleep. For these children, the problem usually goes away on its own in the first couple years of life. Many of us know typical children and adolescents who engage in self-stimulatory movements such as moving their leg rapidly while taking a test. These seem to have an anxiety-reducing function, but are not as all-encompassing as those seen in autism, and they go away once the stressful situation is over.

In contrast to the stereotyped movements seen in ASDs, the unusual movements or tics of Tourette's disorder are different in several ways. Tics tend to occur in bouts, tend to involve the head and neck—particularly early on—and the child doesn't seem to enjoy engaging in them. Thus, they tend not to involve the hands or finger flicking or the whirling/twirling more frequent in ASDs. Movement problems may also be seen in other disorders (e.g., sometimes following infections), and occasionally it can be difficult to disentangle the nature of the movements. This is one of the reasons it is good to have a specialist such as an experienced psychiatrist or neurologist involved if the child is making seemingly purposeless movements.

For children with autism and related disorders, some unusual interests and fascinations often come before the more typical stereotyped behaviors. These interests can include lights (and light switches), twirling and spinning objects (such as fans and tops), and fascination with the smell, taste, or feel of things. The child may begin to engage in some form of visual self-stimulation—for example, looking at things out of the corner of her eye or bringing materials up to the corner of her eye. Sometimes the development of an unusual attachment—such as to a ball of string or unusual objects—may come before the more typical stereotyped movements.

Repetitive, stereotyped movements vary over both the short and long term. Often, they seem to increase after about age 3 and then may increase in frequency or intensity (or both) again around 5 or 6 years of age. For some children, they may then subside only to return in force around the onset of puberty—often some months before. These behaviors can show up at times when the child is bored or stressed, as well as overstimulated or anxious. They may also seem to serve as a preferred mode of activity for the child, almost like relaxation. Sometimes these behaviors shade off into more compulsive and ritualistic behaviors (which we discuss shortly).

Parents and teachers often ask us when we would intervene with these behaviors and often are eager to try medications. These behaviors are often more difficult for parents to manage effectively when the child is in more public settings, and parents—and particularly siblings—are often quite distressed by these behaviors. Teachers may find that the behaviors interfere with engaging the child in the educational program. Fortunately, although these behaviors are difficult to entirely eliminate, many children can be helped to decrease them. The decision to pursue treatment should include consideration of whether the behavior really interferes with the child's or the family's life or the classroom in some important way. Low levels of such behavior are often easier to live with, and parents and others can work to confine the behaviors to certain places or contexts. Occasionally, giving the child the opportunity to engage in these behaviors can itself even be used as a reward for appropriate behavior. With occasional exceptions (e.g., when the behavior is putting the child in some danger), we would not generally recommend medications as a first step.

There are many different behaviorally based approaches for dealing with these behaviors. A whole body of work in behavioral psychology has focused on reducing levels of such behaviors by viewing them as learned behaviors. That is, they are not necessarily so much part and parcel of autism but, rather, responses that the child learns to help her deal with her environment. Many of the effective treatments developed have used this perspective—for example, to see when the behaviors occur, what sets them off, what keeps them going, and so forth. Having understood something about the functions of these behaviors, steps can then be taken to reduce them. For example, if a child has problems with finger flicking or spinning objects, giving her something else to do with her hands may reduce the behavior. Analysis of the environment may reveal that it is too stimulating and that the child is overloaded with information. By giving the child a less stimulating environment, levels of these behaviors may be reduced.

It is also clear that movement and vigorous physical activity can help reduce stereotyped behaviors. Children who engage in high levels of spinning or twirling can benefit from regular exercise. Even getting the child up for short periods in the classroom engaging in vigorous movement such as stretching, jumping, or bouncing can help. Sometimes one of the problems with more inclusive classroom settings is that opportunities for physical movement and vigorous activity are limited to gym and recess (places where children with autism often need the most supervision and where they may not get as much exercise as other children). In addition, children are generally encouraged to stay seated in the regular classroom setting. If movement seems to help, some modification in the program to allow for breaks for movement and other physical activity can be useful. Often, the OT can be very useful in consulting with parents and the classroom teacher about possible activities to try.

Occasionally, children engage in auditory self-stimulation, for example, by spending long periods of time humming or making noises. Again, this sometimes happens when the child is overly stimulated (particularly by noises and sounds), and a look at the environment may help clarify what is going on. For children who are overly responsive to sounds, various devices are available, ranging from simple earplugs to music devices (a portable CD player or MP3 player) and those that produce "white noise" or certain sounds (such as the sound of the ocean or of rain falling).

Some drug treatments are also effective in helping reduce levels of these behaviors. These are discussed in detail in the next chapter and include the major tranquilizers and some other agents. When a major change occurs in the child's behavior, you should also ask the pediatrician to rule out medical reasons. Sometimes behavior problems increase as a child is becoming sick or when she is unable to communicate that she is ill or in pain.

Aggression and Self-Injury

These behaviors involve either self-inflicted injury or injury to others and are among the most difficult and problematic behaviors for parents, teachers, and professionals to deal with. Fortunately, this problem is not that common, and, even when it occurs, there are a number of potential interventions. **Aggression** and/or **self-injury** tend to occur along with other problems (such as stereo-typed movements, rigidity, or perseveration).

Self-injury can take many different forms, including head banging, pinching oneself, pulling out hair, poking the eye, biting the hand, and so forth. Aggression against others may include biting, scratching, or hitting. Behavior that is destructive to property is also often associated with this category of difficulties. Self-injurious behavior can be extremely distressing for parents to see. It is not common until school age but occasionally it occurs in younger children with autism.

The sudden onset of self-injurious behavior, particularly head banging, should prompt a trip to the pediatrician, since such behavior may be a way for a child who does not have words to communicate about her physical pain. Infected ears are particularly likely culprits in younger children; in adolescents who are nonverbal and who start head banging for the first time, dental problems such as impacted wisdom teeth are sometimes to blame. (This is another important reason for the child to have regular dental care!) Children who start to poke their eye may have some physical problem or occasionally even a visual difficulty that they can't complain about in words.

Aggression toward others is often (but not always) "provoked" in some way. For example, the child is interrupted or asked to do something more challenging. Because of the unusual interests and preoccupations, it may be hard to know what sets off these behaviors. Similarly, the unusual ways that the person who is verbal talks may sometimes make it difficult to understand what gets the behavior going. Like self-injury, aggression can be a major problem for parents as well as teachers and school staff. It may take the form of biting, hitting, kicking, scratching, or head butting.

Again a careful analysis of what seems to set off the behavior is very important. For example, is it a response to frustration or an escape behavior or the child's way of saying, "No, I don't want to do this"? In analyzing the behavior, it is also important to look at the context in which the behavior occurs. For example, is it only at school? Only with some care providers? Only during some activities or situations? Only at certain times of the day? Often, this information gives important clues as to why the behavior may be happening and what you can do about it. Turn yourself into a reporter or a detective and ask the basic "wh" questions—who, what, where, when, and why. The parents of one 8-year-old boy with autism called one of us complaining that their child needed medication to decrease his aggression. Discussion with the parents made it clear that this was a new behavior for the boy. The aggression had started when the child's bus route and driver had been changed. The new route (itself a potential problem) was much longer, there was no longer a bus monitor, and there was a new student on board who screamed during the bus ride. The child, who was very sensitive to loud sounds and greatly annoyed by the screaming student, reacted by trying to bite him. In this case, some modifications in the bus arrangements and giving the boy an MP3 player to listen to resulted in a quick change in the behavior.

As our example illustrates and as with other behavioral difficulties, a good analysis of potential causes and consequences of the behavior is very important. Did the head banging or self-injury start after the child entered a new classroom or after some aspect of her program was changed? Does the self-injury occur only during "downtimes"? Is it related to levels of environmental stimulation (either too much or too little)? Some children head bang only at night, while others will engage in this behavior only in very specific situations. For other children it may be a more general problem seen in many different situations and contexts.

For situations where the behavior is potentially very dangerous, medications may be used much more quickly. For example, occasionally children with autism will bite themselves to the point of causing significant injury and may need medications. Even when medications are used, it is important to try to understand what sets off, and keeps up, the behavior. In such cases, a comprehensive functional assessment is essential in part of the treatment planning process.

Aggression against others is usually seen in very specific situations. These include when the child is frustrated and unable to communicate, when favored routines are violated, or when someone attempts to interfere with the child's behavior. Transitions and times of change are often a time when children are very anxious and easily provoked. Many people have made the observation that such behaviors may represent a very basic (and sometimes difficult-to-understand) communication, that is, that the child is overwhelmed and unable to cope. What provokes the behavior may be hard to understand—something as seemingly simple as a small change in routine may lead to major troubles.

Communication difficulties may make it hard for children with autism to tell people how they feel or when they are being pushed too much. This can happen even with older children who can communicate. For example, a 10-year-old boy with Asperger's disorder went to his PE class in school without his usual paraprofessional (a stressful situation now made worse), where the children were running sprints and timing themselves using a stopwatch. The substitute was a regular gym teacher, totally new to the child, who gave him a stopwatch (which he did not know how to operate) and told him to run as fast as he could. The boy put in a great effort, but at the finish line discovered that the stopwatch hadn't worked because he hadn't realized you had to start it. The coach said something like, "Hey, dummy, why'd you stop?" and then refused to let him run again. The boy threw the stopwatch on the ground, breaking it, and the coach came up to restrain the boy, only to get smacked in the face. The school threatened to expel the youngster for aggression since he should have "used his words" and not hit the teacher. In this case, the multiple difficulties included the stressful situation, the lack of his usual supporter, a lack of any instruction on how to operate the stopwatch, an unsympathetic coach who was anxiety provoking, and a boy who was really trying his hardest to cope. In fact, the aggression toward the coach would not have happened at all had the coach "used his words" at any of a number of points with the boy!

Some children with autism also have problems with destroying property. Again, many different solutions are available, depending on the circumstance and function of the behavior. You should *not* feel as if you have to turn the home or classroom into Stalag 17! Rather, explore different options, talk with other parents and teachers, and, if need be, talk to professionals who can provide suggestions. Again, the help of someone who can stand back a bit and see the big picture may be helpful. One child we know loved tearing up clothes, books, and furniture. His parents coped with this in several ways, but most importantly realized that by giving him his own (more-or-less indestructible) room, as well as plenty of physical exercise, they could greatly reduce his destructive behavior.

Some of the same medicines used for treating stereotyped behaviors can be used for treating aggression. Again, behavioral methods are, generally, the first things to try, and again, the exception has to do with dangerous behaviors. As with other behaviors, it is important to do an analysis of the behavior to understand when it occurs, what makes it better or worse, how it changes over time, and so forth.

Rigidity and Perseverative Behaviors

Unusual interests, ritualistic and compulsive behaviors, and problems with transitions are frequent in children with ASDs. These behaviors can take many forms. For example, a child may be preoccupied with turning lights on and off, or opening and closing doors, or feeling water run out of faucets. Some children may hoard objects or place them in very specific ways/places (and become upset if anyone changes them).

Although sometimes hard to measure, these behaviors can be particular sources of difficulty for higher functioning children. For example, children with Asperger's syndrome can spend inordinate amounts of time pursuing more facts in relation to their topic of interest. Typical kinds of interests in Asperger's include time, geology, astronomy, dinosaurs, and snakes. Some of the more unusual interests we've seen have included deep fat fryers, telegraph pole line insulators, disasters, and the names (of spouses and children) and dates of birth and home addresses of every member of Congress!

Sometimes lower functioning children with autism who otherwise seem to have very short attention spans can spend seemingly endless time on their particular fixation. Regardless of the child's level of functioning, these special interests are a problem if the child spends so much time on them that they actually interfere with her functioning in other areas.

Related problems are the "resistance to change" and "insistence on sameness" first described by Leo Kanner back in 1943. These problems often are combined with the restricted interests, since, in some ways, they are two sides of the same coin. That is, by being so fixated on a particular object or topic, the child also avoids being exposed to new situations and learning new things. Teaching staff and parents may find themselves going to great lengths not to provoke the child by keeping her from pursuing her interests, and, as a result, the child's learning may suffer.

In younger and lower functioning children, insistence on sameness can take various forms. For example, the child may insist that you always take the same route to school, or that you always wear the same clothes to church, or that on Monday night you always have pizza. Sometimes it seems almost as if the child learns a thing once—the first time—and then cannot tolerate any change. Older and higher functioning children may rely on a set of very specific social routines. For example, one young man one of us knows always opens any conversation with a question from the quiz show *Jeopardy!* This is (kind of) okay for someone who knows him, but does cause trouble for those who don't when he opens a conversation with, "Monica Lewinsky and the category is politics"!

The difficulties that children with autism have in dealing with change really speak to their problems with information processing as well as their tendency to learn things in whole chunks (what psychologists call "gestalt learning") rather than breaking things down into bits (see Chapter 5). As long as things stay exactly the same, the child doesn't have to deal with the complexity posed by change. This problem also speaks to the difficulties children with autism have in getting the big picture of social interaction. That is, social interaction presents many significant obstacles if you have trouble dealing with any change, since meaning is always changing, depending on who is talking and what he is talking about. Furthermore, the multiple competing cues in interaction (tone of voice, facial expression, gesture, and content of words), which provide important meaning for the rest of us, are potential sources of confusion and disorganization for children with ASD.

Sometimes, particularly for higher functioning children, special interests and preoccupations can be put to good use. For example, a child with Asperger's disorder who was interested in astronomy led the discussion of space and planets in his fifth-grade class. Similarly, another child who was interested in chess was able to work as a chess teacher for his peers. Unfortunately, finding a good use for special interests is not usually so easily done.

Various strategies can be used to help deal with resistance to change. For children who do not have much spoken language, visual schedules can be quite helpful. As we mentioned previously, a small camera and notebook or cards can be used to help the child see what came before, what is happening now, and what is happening in the future. These visual schedules can be placed on refrigerators at home or on bulletin boards in the classroom, and the student's attention can periodically be drawn to them. A growing literature on the use of these visual schedules now exists (see the reading list). A second strategy entails helping the child tolerate change through a more gradual process. Again, an entire body of work based on learning theory can be used to introduce change gradually. You can try "planned change" or "planned surprises"—have times when you give the child the choice among three secret surprises—these can be put on the back of an index card. The child gets to pick one, not knowing what it is—of course, in the beginning make all the choices ones the child will like. Help the child work with time and organization skills (see also Chapter 6). Depending on the child's level of ability, these can range from use of simple visual supports to lists (for children who can read) and organizers and more sophisticated computer/software devices. Another approach is to make the behavior more functional—that is, by helping the child use her interest in a more normal or typical way. The idea is that by helping the child learn to use her behavior in more productive ways, she can be helped to be more functional in daily life.

Other strategies are available for verbal individuals and are especially effective for children with Asperger's syndrome. These can include use of:

- Scripts and verbal routines (basically a "canned" set of verbalized guidelines a child can use to talk herself through specific situations)
- Social Stories (prewritten stories a child can review to help her practice and rehearse strategies for dealing with potentially problematic situations (see Chapter 6)
- Provided "rules" (e.g., you must always ask before you take something) that are simple, functional, and can be written down for children who read

Behavioral approaches can be helpful with more able children as well. For example, many higher functioning individuals have difficulty dealing with novelty—which makes them anxious. In addition they may have trouble both in recognizing that something is new and in realizing that they are anxious. Explicit teaching and counseling can be quite helpful for these children.

A related issue has to do with compulsive and ritualistic behaviors. The child may have to go through a set series of actions or behaviors when engaging in some activity. One high-functioning man with autism we know will, for example, walk 3 miles out of his way every day as he walks to work to pick up his (same) lunch at a corner market because that market is the one he happened to go to on his first day on the job. A young adult woman with autism we know is very preoccupied with keeping all her clothes neat—every single item has a place in her room and heaven help anyone who tries to interfere with this!

Some ritualistic or compulsive behaviors have some similarity to those seen in **obsessive–compulsive disorder (OCD)**, a condition where people are troubled by obsessions (things they can't stop thinking about, such as the thought that they are bad, or the need to do something) and compulsions (the need to do an activity over and over, such as washing the hands because you are afraid they are dirty). Some degree of obsessiveness and compulsiveness is perfectly normal. It is not normal, however, if the child is washing her hands for 50 minutes at a time (often to the point where they are bleeding) or is so troubled by doing something bad that she is essentially immobilized.

The similarities of more typical OCD-type behaviors to some of these seen in autism (the rigidity and tendency to repeat things) are very interesting, and some of the drug treatments for these behaviors are similar for OCD and autism. A major point of difference is that often children (or adolescents and adults) with OCD will tell you that they *don't like* having to engage in the behaviors. In contrast, individuals with ASDs often find their compulsive behaviors are not distressing—if anything, they are things the child *likes* to do.

Various medications may be helpful with this set of problems (see Chapter 15). The most frequently used medications are the selective serotonin reuptake inhibitors (SSRIs). The particular advantage of these medications is that they target both the rigidity and compulsiveness as well as the anxiety involved in dealing with change. Sometimes these behaviors respond to other medications as well.

ATTENTION AND OVERACTIVITY

Problems with attention and overactivity **(hyperactivity)** are fairly common in children with ASDs. These problems may include difficulties with listening, disorganization, high levels of activity, and impulsiveness. The child may be restless and on the go more or less all the time. Difficulties with not listening and impulsive behavior can be the source of much trouble, such as bolting into the street. For children with emerging language or no language, it is important to realize that at least some of the difficulties may relate to difficulties with language and communication. That is, if you have language, you can use it to help organize yourself, but if you don't, you will tend to be disorganized.

For higher functioning children with pervasive developmental disorder not otherwise specified (PDD-NOS), autism, and Asperger's syndrome who have language, the attentional problems (and to some extent hyperactivity) may suggest attention deficit hyperactivity disorder (ADHD), a commonly recognized syndrome in otherwise typically developing children of school age. The question as to whether to formally diagnose ADHD in children with ASDs remains somewhat controversial. One reason is that—at least for some children—language problems, learning issues, and difficulties with organization and lack of good judgment seem more part and parcel of the ASD. We know, for example, that children with language problems are also likely to have attentional problems. Particularly if attentional problems are confined to the school setting, it is important to look at the curriculum to be sure it is appropriately matched to the student's needs.

One of the first questions to ask is whether the child's difficulties with activity and attention are seen in all situations or only at school. If they occur only at school, it is then worth asking if these difficulties are seen in every class or setting or only in some. If only in school and only in some settings, it would be worth paying careful attention to what is going on. Ask questions such as:

- Are the language (or social–communication) demands for the child too high?
- Is the academic material over his head?
- Can the classroom environment be modified to help the child be more organized?
- Can visual support or augmentative communication systems or other strategies be used to help the child have a more predictable learning environment? For example can a review of a schedule or preteaching be helpful?
- Does the child start the day doing well and then seem to "lose it" as time goes on? (If so, fatigue may be a factor.)
- Do different approaches seem to be helpful (giving the child periods for activity interspersed with school work)?
- What rewards motivate the child? What will the child work for?

If the problems with attention and/or overactivity seem to be happening in all parts of the child's life, some of the same considerations will apply. For instance, there should be a functional assessment and consideration of measures (such as visual cues) to help the child be more organized. For the more able child with Asperger's or high functioning autism/PDD, other organizational aids may be helpful. A behavioral program may be helpful in both school and home settings, with consistent record keeping and attention to the child's behavior coupled with a system of rewards and positive supports. This effort should involve both parents and teachers so that the system can be applied consistently across the child's day.

A number of different treatments have been used over the years to help children with attentional problems. The most commonly used medicines (in all children) are the stimulants (amphetamines, methylphenidate). Some children, particularly more "classically autistic" children, may respond to these medicines by becoming *more* disorganized and active. (This does not always happen, and even when it does, the medicine is out of the system fairly quickly!). Other medicines are sometimes used as well and are discussed in the next chapter.

MENTAL HEALTH ISSUES AND BEHAVIOR PROBLEMS

Sometimes, particularly for more verbal and cognitively able individuals, behavior problems are seen but in the context of what appear to be additional mental health problems. The behaviors of the child with Asperger's who is highly anxious or depressed, or the more able student with autism who is rigid and compulsive can be suggestive of OCD. The phenomenon of having more than one disorder at a time is called *comorbidity*—a fancy term to basically say you have two problems, not just one. This issue comes up with reference to thinking about both behavioral problems and medications (and we talk about this again in the next chapter with special reference to drug treatments). In thinking about behavior problems, this issue of comorbidity has special importance when we think that behavior problems are coming about because of some other difficulties with anxiety or attention or depression. There can be issues of assessment and diagnosis with more cognitively able individuals with autism; these are magnified even further when the person doesn't talk much or at all. For example, how would you know the person is feeling depressed or that their blowups come when they feel the most anxious? Even when the child does talk, when do you decide when he is feeling depressed about school crosses the boundary from an understandable response to a clinical disorder? And finally, some problems come more frequently at some times; for example, clinical depression tends to be seen more in adolescents and adults, while anxiety and attention problems are usually first seen in younger children.

Several books have now appeared that focus on issues of dual diagnosis. One book attempts to modify the traditional diagnostic guidebook (the *Diagnostic and Statistical Manual of Mental Disorders* [DSM]) to make it more appropriate to individuals with cognitive challenge/intellectual disability (Fletcher, Loschen, Stavrakaki, & First, 2007). In contrast other works (e.g., Ghaziuddin 2005) focus more specifically on mental health issues in individuals on the autism spectrum.

It makes sense that many of the same treatments (behavioral, counseling, and drug treatments) might work for emotional problems in individuals with ASDs at least as well as they work for other problems. Unfortunately, until recently, this area has been a relatively neglected topic for research. Several different issues probably worked to delay work in this area, an important historical one being the tendency, in the 1950s, to (1) blame parents for causing their child's autism and (2) then recommending long-term intensive psychotherapy for the child (and parents) to "fix" the underlying parent-caused problem (Riddle, 1987). This approach was discredited in the 1970s, and, partly as a result, the entire issue of psychotherapy for individuals on the autism spectrum was relatively neglected.

Fortunately, this situation is beginning to change. Within the field of autism, particularly as individuals have become older, it is clear that many people can profit from very focused, counseling-type psychotherapies (Volkmar et al. 1999). Often, the explicit verbal teaching and focused problem solving so helpful to students with Asperger's (Myles, 2003) verges into psychotherapy. The boundaries of teaching, counseling, and psychotherapy can be blurry, but these approaches can sometimes be very, very helpful to students with behavior problems. There are some excellent papers that address some of these issues (Atwood, 2003; Bauminger, 2002). These address the behavioral difficulties, social problems, and difficulties with mood and anxiety so often found, particularly in older children and adolescents.

Within the psychotherapy field itself there have been some important advances. One approach, called *cognitive behavior therapy* (CBT), is grounded in findings from research in both cognitive and behavioral psychology. CBT refers to a range of different treatments used for a number of different problems, including mood and anxiety disorders. Some of these approaches focus more on the cognitive side, while others focus more on the behavioral side of things. These approaches have a number of advantages over older psychotherapies in that they tend to be brief and time limited. They may be done on an individual or group basis, and some have been adapted for people to do on their own. For example, the objective may be to help the individual understand why he or she becomes anxious and how anxiety can be identified and dealt with in more appropriate ways. In some ways, as you might imagine, the teaching aspects (the cognitive part) of CBT can be very helpful for people on the autism spectrum, and, at the same time, the focus on behavior is also very helpful.

These approaches can be used to address various problems common in individuals on the autism spectrum, including mood and anxiety problems, recurrent thoughts, and obsessive features; and social problems, including coping with social relationships, making friends, and so forth (Atwood, 2003; Bauminger, 2007; Bauminger, Shulman, & Agam, 2004; Sze & Wood, 2007).

There now have been some scientifically well controlled studies showing that this method works well in helping children cope with and reduce levels of anxiety (e.g., Wood et al., 2009).

What are the limitations of these methods? It is important to realize that one of the reasons why psychotherapy (and, by extension, many forms of counseling) got a "bad rep" in the autism world was the early focus on blaming parents and attempting to cure the child with autism. Even now, when our perspectives have changed dramatically, there is some potential for people to overly focus on some condition as causing/explaining/excusing bad behavior. The excusing part is a particular source of disagreement with schools. Sometimes there is, of course, truth in the observation that the child acted out because he was stressed or anxious or depressed. However, other children without ASDs also become anxious and depressed and stressed. So, as is often the case, the truth lies somewhere between the two extremes. For many children, an explicit focus on problem behavior will lead parents and teachers to a straightforward behavioral assessment and intervention. However, particularly for more able students, a broader view of the troubles may lead to other kinds of intervention. When CBT or other talking-type therapies are explored, it is important that teachers and parents (and the individual) *not* lose sight of the behavioral difficulties. Also, it is important for therapists to keep in mind that usual short-term intervention models—for example, the individual comes to a group for 6 to 10 weeks and then is finished—may be less applicable. In our experience (and one of us has seen a handful of folks, off and on, for several decades), a model where people on the autism spectrum tap into services when they need them may be most appropriate.

CASE EXAMPLES

Here are three case examples of how behavioral techniques could be used effectively in dealing with "bolting" (see Chapter 11 for a more general discussion of safety issues) and a third case using CBT.

Case 1: Willy

Willy was a 9-year-old boy with autism. He had some words, but generally his expressive speech was rather limited. He understood language to a greater degree than he actually used it. Cognitive testing with him had consistently shown that he was functioning overall in the moderate range of intellectual disability, with a full-scale intelligence quotient (IQ) of about 50, although his nonverbal abilities were higher (close to 70). The problem with bolting/running out of the classroom had started in the fall as Willy was enrolled in a new classroom setting. He previously had not had many behavior problems. As part of the

understandable attempt to provide him with greater access to peers, he was being mainstreamed for the mornings (for the most part), spending most of his
afternoon in special education and/or getting his various specials. Staffing in the
morning included a regular education teacher along with a paraprofessional
(mostly for Willy, but also for one other student with special needs). The special
education teacher consulted to the regular ed teacher, but only periodically. The
bolting was almost entirely confined to the morning setting. The regular ed
teacher had tried several things, including trying to reason with Willy, and then,
at the suggestion of the speech pathologist, giving him a written schedule and
making some other accommodations for him. Despite these changes, by the
middle of October, he was running/bolting about 15 times a day on average. A
behaviorally trained psychologist was asked to consult and spent some time observing Willy at various points during his day and spent time in his various classroom settings. She also spoke to Willy's parents, who were as mystified as his
regular ed teacher since Willy did not generally have a problem with bolting/
running at home.

The psychologist noticed two different factors that seemed to contribute to
the behavioral difficulties. She recommended two different interventions, but
did this in stages. The first recommendation (see Figure 14.1) occurred on day
5. The psychologist in her previous 4 days of observation realized that the bolt-
ing/running business had turned into a fairly exciting and dramatic game for
Willy. He would carefully wait for his moment, then bolt, precipitating yelling/
screaming/general upset. He was smiling a good part of the time and seemed to
enjoy the run-and-chase activities.

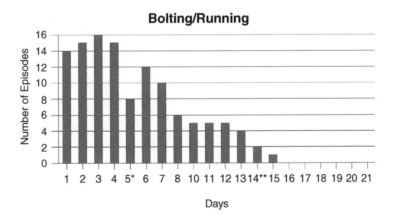

FIGURE 14.1   Behavioral data from Willy, a boy with ''bolting.''
Data are presented for consecutive school days; *and
** indicate changes in behavior procedures. See text
for explanation.

The psychologist arranged for the school guard to be available in the immediate area (but outside the classroom on day 5) and had arranged with him to be on the alert for Willy and to calmly and matter-of-factly escort him back to class. The teacher and paraprofessional were instructed when Willy bolted to *not* engage in the run-and-chase game but to generally ignore this behavior. The system was in place for alerting the school guard, who indeed would meet Willy in the hall and redirect him back to the classroom.

On the first day this was instituted as a procedure, the bolting decreased. For the next 2 days, it appeared that Willy was testing the limits, but by day 8 it did appear that the behavior had been markedly reduced but still persisted at lower levels. At this point, the psychologist introduced her second change (day 14). In keeping track of episodes, she realized that these were now almost always confined to a situation (reading group) when Willy was most challenged. Accordingly, she arranged for Willy to spend this time in a quiet area away from the main group, where he worked with his paraprofessional for most of the time, rejoining the class only at the end. Willy's bolting quickly dropped to zero.

Case 2: Johnny

Johnny was a 6-year-old with Asperger's who had begun attending a new primary school. He was quite verbal but also very socially disabled. Although motorically clumsy, he was fascinated with the furnace and the basement of his school (which is where the furnace was located). He quickly developed a habit of sneaking away (whenever the teacher's back was turned). After a search, he was invariably found in the furnace room in the basement. Attempts to reason with him were not successful. The custodian, whose room was next to the furnace, was considerably annoyed by all the trouble Johnny created.

In this case the psychologist's recommendation was to try to use, to the extent possible, Johnny's motivations and interest in a positive way. Accordingly, a token reward system was instituted. When he stayed through an entire class without sneaking away, he received a red poker chip. When he had six chips (and there were six classes during the day), he was able, at the end of the day, to have a prearranged 10-minute meeting with the janitor (Mr. Bob) at the furnace area, who would demonstrate different aspects of the furnace, talk about furnaces, and so on. This turned out to be highly motivating for Johnny, and, somewhat paradoxically, Mr. Bob developed a real friendship with him (after all, they shared an interest in the furnace). The predictability meant that the janitor's life was not constantly disrupted and, in the end, Mr. Bob became a real advocate for Johnny at school and served as his "safe address;" when things got tough for Johnny, he could always ask for a pass to see Mr. Bob, who would ask him what was going on and have him return to his classroom. At the end of the day, Mr. Bob would check with the teacher to be sure she or he knew about Johnny's trouble.

In this instance it was possible to rapidly address the problem behavior. More importantly, what seemed like a simple subsequent step (having Mr. Bob serve as Johnny's safe address in school) was actually a fairly sophisticated technique. Rather than losing it (for reasons he often was unaware of), Johnny was encouraged to substitute a more appropriate behavior (seeking his adult friend), which prevented/disrupted blowups and got a sympathetic adult involved in the process of monitoring Johnny's behavior.

Case 3: Carla

Carla was a 12-year-old girl with Asperger's disorder. She had (for many years) a preoccupation with small creatures—now focused on the various kinds of protozoans. Her nonverbal problem-solving skills were in the average range, while her verbal skills were in the superior range. Her social skills were more like those of a typically developing 4-year-old. She had a strong desire to have friends but rather limited abilities to make and actually keep friends. Her anxiety was a major problem for her—any kind of pressure (a test, assignment, upcoming school special event) would be the source of tremendous anxiety, and behavioral upset regularly followed. Her parents began to dread "special" days in school because they knew she would be highly anxious and extremely difficult in the day or two before the event.

The school psychologist recommended a local clinical psychologist who was interested in CBT. He worked with Carla on a regular basis for a preplanned 10 sessions. During the therapy, the two of them worked on a set of very specific issues that they outlined together in the first two sessions. This included stress identification and stress management, learned relaxation techniques, increased awareness of the experience of anxiety, and a series of homeworks/practices in which Carla was able to focus on using specific strategies to reduce anxiety. This effort met with considerable success in reducing acute anxiety levels, although both Carla and the therapist realized it had done little to work on her desire for more friends in her peer group. They agreed to continue individual work focused on this issue, and Carla began to attend a social skills group.

In this case, a more cognitively able child could use some of the strategies provided by CBT to focus on acquiring specific problem-solving skills and strategies. As is sometimes the case, having helped her become more able to cope with her anxiety, Carla was then aware of other issues, particularly peer relationships, and she and her family chose to pursue further focused work on this topic.

SUMMARY

In this chapter, we described some of the more common behavior problems that children with ASDs exhibit. Again, we emphasize that many children with autism do *not* have these problems. Sometimes problems come up at certain times in life or in certain situations (the start of a new school, adolescence), and sometimes they go away on their own. It is important to realize that behavioral interventions can be very effective. Occasionally, problem behaviors are unwittingly encouraged by teachers or parents. It is important that parents and teachers be aware of their own impact on the child and the potential—for good or ill—of significant effects of their behavior on the child.

Thinking about interventions requires a careful look at the entire situation, including the child's environment and a detailed analysis of when, where, and why the behaviors seem to be occurring. The good news is that many problem behaviors can be managed effectively.

■ READING LIST

Atwood, T. (2003). Frameworks for behavioral intervention. *Child & Adolescent Psychiatric Clinics of North America, 12*, 65–86.

Atwood, T. (2004). *Exploring feelings: Cognitive behavior therapy to manage anxiety.* Arlington, TX: Future Horizons.

Bailey, J., & Bruch, M. (2006). *How to think like a behavior analyst.* Mahwah, NJ: Erlbaum.

Bauminger, N. (2002). The facilitation of social-emotional understanding and social interaction in high-functioning children with autism: Intervention outcomes. *Journal of Autism and Developmental Disorders, 32*(4), 283–298.

Bauminger, N. (2007). Brief report: group social-multimodal intervention for HFASD. *Journal of Autism and Developmental Disorders, 37*(8), 1605–1615.

Bauminger, N., & Shulman, C., & Agam, G. (2004). The link between perceptions of self and of social relationships in high-functioning children with autism. *Journal of Developmental and Physical Disabilities, 16*(2), 193–214.

Bregman, J. D., & Zager, D., & Gerdtz, J. (2005). *Behavioral interventions.* In F. R. Volkmar, R. Paul, A. Klin, & D. Cohen (Eds.), *Handbook of autism and pervasive developmental disorders* (3rd ed. , vol. 2; pp. 897–924). Hoboken, NJ: Wiley.

Buron, K. D., & Myles, B. S. (2004). *When my autism gets too big! A relaxation book for children with autism spectrum disorders.* Shawnee Mission, KS: Autism Asperger.

Cardon, T. A. (2004). *Let's talk emotions: Helping children with social cognitive deficits including AS, HFA, and NVLD learn to understand and express empathy and emotions.* Shawnee Mission, KS: Autism Asperger.

Clements, J., & Zarkowska, E. (2000). *Behavioural concerns and autism spectrum disorders: Explanations and strategies for change.* London: Jessica Kingsley.

Cooper, J. O., Heron, T. E., & Heward, W. L. (2007). *Applied behavior analysis* (2nd ed). Upper Saddle River, NJ: Prentice Hall.

Dubin, N. (2009). *Asperger Syndrome and anxiety: A guide to successful stress management.* London: Jessica Kingsley.

Evans, K., & Dubowski, J. (2001). *Art therapy with children on the autistic spectrum: Beyond words*. London: Jessica Kingsley.

Fletcher, R., Loschen, E., Stavrakaki, C., & First, M. (2007). *Diagnostic manual-intellectual disability (DM-ID): A textbook of diagnosis of mental disorders in persons with intellectual disability*. Kingston, NY: NADD Press.

Fouse, B., & Wheeler, M. (1997). *A treasure chest of behavioral strategies for individuals with autism*. Arlington, TX: Future Horizons.

Gaus, V. O. (2007). *Cognitive-behavioral therapy for adult Asperger syndrome*. New York: Guilford Press.

Ghaziuddin, M. (2005). *Mental health aspects of autism and Asperger syndrome*. London: Jessica Kingsley.

Glasberg, B. A. (2006). *Functional behavior assessment for people with autism: Making sense of seemingly senseless behavior*. Bethesda, MD: Woodbine House.

Grandin, T., & Barron, S. (2005). *The unwritten rules of social relationships: Decoding social mysteries through the unique perspectives of autism*. Arlington, TX: Future Horizons.

Harpur, J. Lawlor, M., & Fitzgerald, M. (2006). *Succeeding with interventions for Asperger syndrome adolescents: A guide to communication and socialization in interaction therapy*. London: Jessica Kingsley.

Hodgdon, L. (1999). *Solving behavior problems in autism: Improving communication with visual strategies*. Troy, MI: QuirkRoberts.

Huebner, D. (2006). *What to do when you worry too much: A kid's guide to overcoming anxiety*. Washington, DC: Magination Press.

Jacobsen, P. (2003). *Asperger syndrome and psychotherapy: Understanding Asperger perspectives*. London: Jessica Kingsley.

Kearney, A. J. (2007). *Understanding applied behavior analysis: An introduction to ABA for parents, teachers, and other professionals*. London: Jessica Kingsley.

Leaf, R., McEachin, J. & Harsh, J. D. (1999). *A work in progress: Behavior management strategies & a curriculum for intensive behavioral treatment of autism*. New York: DRL Books.

Leaf, R., Taubman, M., & McEachin, J. (2008). *It's time for school! Building quality ABA educational programs for students with autism spectrum disorders*. New York: DRL Books.

Luiselli, J. K., Russo, D. C., Christian, W. P., & Wilczynski, S. M. (2008). *Effective practices for children with autism: Educational and behavior support interventions that work*. New York: Oxford University Press.

Maurice, C. M., Green, G., & Luce, S. L. (Eds.). (1996). *Behavioral intervention for young children with autism: A manual for parents and professionals*. Austin, TX: Pro-Ed.

Miller-Kuhaneck, H. (2004). *Autism: A comprehensive occupational therapy approach* (2nd ed.). Bethesda, MD: American Occupational Therapy Association.

Moyes, R. A. (2002) *Addressing the challenging behavior of children with high functioning autism/ asperger syndrome in the classroom*. London: Jessica Kingsley.

Myles, B. S. (2001). *Asperger syndrome and sensory issues: Practical solutions for making sense of the world*. Shawnee Mission, KS: Autism Asperger.

Myles, B. S. (2003). Behavioral forms of stress management for individuals with Asperger syndrome. *Child and Adolescent Psychiatric Clinics of North America, 12*(1), 123–141.

Myles, B. S., Adreon, D., & Gitilitz, D. (2006). *Simple strategies that work! Helpful hints for all educators of students with Asperger syndrome, high-functioning autism, and related disabilities.* Shawnee Mission, KS: Autism Asperger.

Myles, B. S., & Southwick, J. (2005). *Asperger syndrome and difficult moments: Practical solutions for tantrums, rage and meltdowns.* Shawnee Mission, KS: Autism Asperger.

Myles, B. S., Trautman, M. L., & Schelvan, R. L. (2004). *The hidden curriculum: Practical solutions for understanding unstated rules in social situations.* Shawnee Mission, KS: Autism Asperger.

O'Donohue, W. T., & Fisher, J. E. (2009). *General principles and empirically supported techniques of cognitive behavior therapy.* Hoboken, NJ: Wiley.

O'Neill, R. E., Horner, R. H., Albin, R. Q., Storey, K., & Sprague, J. R. (1997). *Functional assessment and program development for problem behavior: A practical handbook.* Pacific Grove, CA: Brooks/Cole.

Paxton, K., & Estay, I. A. (2007). *Counseling people on the autism spectrum: A practical manual.* London: Jessica Kingsley.

Powers, M. D. (2005). *Behavioral assessment of individuals with autism: A functional ecological approach.* In F. R. Volkmar, R. Paul, A. Klin, & D. J. Cohen (Eds.), *Handbook of autism and pervasive developmental disorders* (3rd ed., vol. 2; pp. 817–830). Hoboken, NJ: Wiley.

Prior, M. (Ed.). (2003). *Learning and behavior problems in Asperger syndrome.* New York: Guilford Press.

Richman, S. (2001). *Raising a child with autism: A guide to applied behavior analysis for parents.* London: Jessica Kingsley.

Richman, S. (2006). *Encouraging appropriate behavior for children on the autism spectrum: Frequently asked questions.* London: Jessica Kingsley.

Riddle, M. A. (1987). *Individual and parental psychotherapy in autism.* In D. J. Cohen & A. Donnellan (Eds.), *Handbook of autism and pervasive developmental disorders* (1st ed.; pp. 528–544). New York: Wiley.

Savner, J., & Myles, B. S. (2000). *Making visual supports work in the home and community: Strategies for individuals with autism and Asperger syndrome.* Shawnee Mission, KS: Autism Asperger.

Schopler, E. (Ed.). (1995). *Parent survival manual: A guide to crisis resolution in autism and related developmental disorders.* New York: Plenum Press.

Schopler, E., & Mesibov, G. (1994). *Behavioral issues in autism.* New York: Plenum Press.

Sze, K. M., & Wood, J. J. (2007). Cognitive behavioral treatment of comorbid anxiety disorders and social difficulties in children with high-functioning autism: A case report. *Journal of Contemporary Psychotherapy, 37*(3), 133–143.

Tinsley, M., & Hendrick, S. (2007). *Asperger's syndrome and alcohol: Drinking to cope.* London: Jessica Kingsley.

Volkmar, F., Cook, E. H. Jr., Pomeroy, J., Realmuto, G., Tanguay, P., & the Work Group on Quality Issues. (1999). Practice parameters for the assessment and treatment of children, adolescents, and adults with autism and other pervasive developmental disorders. American Academy of Child and Adolescent Psychiatry Working Group on Quality Issues. *Journal of the American Academy of Child and Adolescent Psychiatry, 38*(12), 32S–54S.

Weiss, M. J., & McBride, K. (2008). *Practical solutions for educating children with high-functioning autism and Asperger syndrome.* Shawnee Mission, KS: Autism Asperger.

Wood, J. J., Drahota, A., Sze, K., Har, K., Chiu, A., Langer, D. A., et al. (2009). Cognitive behavioral therapy for anxiety in children with autism spectrum disorders: A randomized controlled trial. *Journal of Child Psychology and Psychiatry, 50*(3), 224–234.

■ QUESTIONS AND ANSWERS

1. **We have a child with autism who has had severe self-injury. We want to find a specialist who can work with us and the school. What kind of doctor are we looking for?**

   Various specialists might be helpful. These include behavioral psychologists and behavioral specialists as well as adult and child psychiatrists, adult and child neurologists, and developmental and behavioral pediatricians. You should look for someone who has experience in dealing with these problems. Your primary care doctor may be able to give you names of people. Other good sources of information include school staff and other parents.

2. **My child has recently started slapping the side of his jaw. He has never done this before and only slaps one spot. What should I do?**

   You might want to see your doctor and your dentist to check his ears and his teeth. The new onset of self-injurious behavior should usually prompt a doctor visit, particularly in a child who is not able to communicate well with words.

3. **A 10-year-old boy with autism has developed some significant behavior problems in my classroom. He is mainstreamed for most subjects with pull-out time for special services. He gets agitated and increasingly upset just before it is time for the class to move on to gym (he goes to a special adaptive PE class). Should we let him skip gym?**

   You have already made a crucially important observation—you can predict when the trouble starts! Now the thing to do is ask yourself the basic who, what, where, when, and then why to think about what you want to do. If the boy is verbal, you can start by talking to him about this. Depending on what you learn, you may decide to use any of several different strategies. It may be that he is trying to avoid the special PE class for some reason—then the issue is to find out why. Or it may be that he is upset that he is not joining the rest of the class for regular PE; if so, maybe he could join with some supports for at least part of the time to start with. Or maybe it is just because the literal transition from one classroom to another is difficult; if this is so, thinking about having him go a minute or so before the class is over (when the hallways aren't so busy and confusing) might be appropriate. All of these are just some ideas—what you do depends on carefully thinking about the situation. Probably the one thing we would *not* recommend is skipping PE; children with autism have better behavior when they exercise regularly and because of their social difficulties often don't get enough exercise to begin with.

4. **My 8-year-old daughter has a thing about doors—she loves to open and close them. In the past she did the same thing with light switches, turning them on and off. I know this doesn't sound like a big problem, but it drives me and my husband crazy sometimes!**

The problems with social development in autism also lead to major problems in play. The kinds of behavior you described (repeated doing and undoing) are more typical of younger (typically developing) toddlers, who enjoy doing and undoing things, for example opening and closing things, and stacking blocks and knocking them down. For children on the autism spectrum, these interests become entwined in the tendency to insist on sameness and don't go on, like those of the typically developing child, to be replaced with more symbolic and imaginative play.

There are several things you can try. First, see if you daughter can be interested in simple play materials with doors or light switches, for example, a little dollhouse or even a special toy you make with some little doors on it. Look in a toy store for simple cause–effect toys (the child does something and immediately something happens). If you can get your daughter interested in a dollhouse, you can then try to start building in more pretend play with you and with other children. A behavior consultant may be able to suggest some things; for example, you can try to control her interest in doors by using 5 minutes of this activity as a reward for having a good lesson. The idea is to have you gain some control over the behavior so it is not so dominating. Another possibility is to have her be in charge of the doors at home or school; for example, she can be the official doorkeeper, opening the door only when someone knocks.

5. **My 6-year-old son used to have a real problem with spinning things or sometimes flicking things back and forth in front of his eyes. This seemed to have disappeared around age 4, but now that he is going to school, it has started up again. He is now in an inclusion classroom for most of the day. This seems to come up only in the classroom, but the teacher says the other kids really notice it. What should we do?**

It is always helpful to ask yourself *why* a behavior is coming up. It is possible that your child is overstimulated in the classroom and, as a result, is resorting to some other (although odd) behaviors that make him feel more comfortable and in control. Take a look at the classroom setting; you can also think about ways of reducing sensory or information overload (see Chapter 5) if the class is too stimulating. Another option is to have the other students be more proactive in helping your child learn more appropriate social skills (see Chapter 6). Peers can be very good at both modeling more appropriate behaviors and giving the child on the autism spectrum something to do!

6. **My 8-year-old son with autism was doing relatively well with partial mainstreaming last year. This year he is fully included and his behavior seems to have deteriorated. It always seems like he is on edge and "ready to blow." For the first time in years, we are getting negative reports of his behavior in the classroom, particularly around transitions from one room to another. Should we rethink the mainstreaming?**

   It may be helpful to request a functional behavioral analysis (in which a behavioral psychologist or trained special educator analyzes what exactly sets off and follows the problem behavior). There are many benefits to mainstreaming; that being said, it is not uncommon for children on the autism spectrum to start having difficulties if the academic level of the class is at a much higher level than they understand; that is, the child becomes frustrated and behavior deteriorates. This may happen in only one class (e.g., spelling) and not others. Or it may happen only in some situations, for example, when the child feels like his space is being invaded. Or—and this may be true for your child—it may be that the actual moving around (from one room to another) is the source of the problem. A behavioral psychologist can help identify the cause of the difficulty and help you and school staff put a plan in place to deal with it.

7. **My 16-year-old son with Asperger's has horrible problems in dealing with novelty. Is there anything you can suggest to help him deal with this?**

   You have already done an important part of the work in identifying the source of the problem (novelty). You also mention that he has Asperger's, and so we assume he is more cognitively able. If this is indeed true, several possibilities come to mind.

   First, you can work to help him recognize when he is in new situations—he may be having trouble realizing this and get anxious, and then have behavioral troubles, before any recognition on his part of what is going on. Help him recognize and articulate ways he can (1) tell that he is in a new situation and (2) recognize signs of anxiety (increase in heart rate, feelings of anxiety, sweaty palms, etc.). Once you have done this, you can then start to think about ways to give explicit coping strategies. For some individuals, the awareness that they are in a novel situation may be helpful. Sometimes it is helpful to teach ways to then apply specific strategies; for example, I can tell myself I'm anxious in new situations and take steps A, B, and C to deal with it. Another approach is to use cognitive behavior therapy procedures (e.g., teaching relaxation techniques). Several good resources are provided in the reading list.

CHAPTER 15

Considering Medications for Behavior Problems

Unfortunately, at the present time, there is no medication that can cure a child of autism. However, medications are playing a growing and promising role in treating some of the behaviors that often go along with autism. For some children, drugs can help reduce difficulties with anxiety, moodiness, irritability, hyperactivity, or stereotyped behaviors. Decreasing these problem behaviors can often help children be more amenable to educational and other interventions.

In this chapter, we will be talking about some of the medicines more frequently used in treating challenging behaviors in individuals with autism spectrum disorders. A discussion of *all* the medicines would fill this book (and has filled several others listed in the reading list at the end of the chapter). Keep in mind that the health care provider may want to recommend a drug that we don't discuss here, and that can be just fine. As we've mentioned repeatedly, there is no substitute for working with an experienced health care provider.

MENTAL HEALTH ISSUES IN AUTISM

In the past, many people thought that having a chronic condition like autism (or any developmental disorder) almost seemed to "protect" the individual from other disorders; in fact, this is not at all true. We know, for example, that people with mild intellectual disability/mental retardation who don't have autism do have much higher rates of other mental health disorders—in fact, four to five times higher than in the general population. This tendency *not* to see other problems when they are present in people with disabilities like autism has a special name: **diagnostic overshadowing**. We have now come to realize that having a problem like autism makes it even more likely that the person will have other difficulties, for example, problems with anxiety or depression. There is a special term for this as well—comorbidity, which means having more than one disorder at a time. There are many problems in disentangling the complicated effects autism has on behavior and emotional problems, that is, in deciding whether the difficulty is really part of having autism or is something separate. There are also marked differences around the world in how these problems are thought of. In the United States, there has been a tendency to equate symptoms with disorder; that is, if a child with autism has trouble with feeling moody or sad, he often will be diagnosed with a form of depression. In some cases, this is much less clear-cut. This is even more the case when the individual with an autism spectrum disorder (ASD) has trouble communicating. As a result, it is sometimes hard to know when a symptom or symptoms really become another disorder. We do know that there are higher-than-expected rates of both anxiety and mood problems in family members of people with autism.

In younger children and those with less language, some of the most frequent presenting problems have to do with irritability, tantrums, and sometimes self-injury. Sometimes these problems also seem related to difficulties in focusing on activities and in having trouble tolerating change. It remains unclear how we ought to best think about these problems but some medications can be very helpful (and so can behavioral treatments). For older and more able individuals (who communicate with words), issues with depression and anxiety and, sometimes, trouble with change and rigid behavior patterns become more predominant.

Clearly, all of us experience changes in our mood during the course of the day, as well as over longer periods. Some of us have periods when we feel low and depressed for long periods of time. Clinical depression is defined by symptoms such as lack of energy, loss of appetite, feeling "down" all the time, and so forth. Others of us have more difficulties with anxiety, including anxiety about certain events or situations or sometimes more general, free-floating anxiety. Individuals with ASD (and particularly adolescents and young adults) seem to have an increased risk for depression. This is particularly true among higher functioning individuals (with autism, Asperger's, or pervasive developmental disorder not otherwise specified [PDD-NOS]) who may, as time goes on, have an increasing sense of being isolated and missing out on many things their typically developing peers enjoy. Research also suggests that there may be a genetic basis for some increased vulnerability for depression and anxiety problems in the families of children with ASD.

More verbal children may talk about feeling depressed or express negative thoughts about themselves. Occasionally (and this can be tricky to sort out), children may feel irritable rather than depressed. To complicate things further, some children seem to get more agitated and upset when depressed. Not surprisingly, depression can be difficult to diagnose in younger children with developmental problems and in older children who have significant communication problems.

Occasionally, children with ASD have periods of depression and then go back to "normal" before becoming somewhat high and "hyper." It has been suggested that perhaps they have bipolar disorder. This is what used to be known as manic-depressive illness and now is called bipolar disorer. It is characterized by pronounced mood swings. Often, the individual experiences periods of depression followed by "normal" periods and then periods of elation and **grandiosity** with rapid speech, giving the impression that she is on a "natural high." The final word is not yet in on whether some children with ASD are more likely to have bipolar disorder, although marked swings in mood combined with major changes in behavior suggest that this might be considered. It is always important to look at the big picture, since, for example, some of the medicines used to treat depression can cause children to be agitated if they actually have bipolar disorder, not depression.

Recurrent difficulties with anxiety can also be seen in children with ASD. These may include free-floating, high levels of anxiety (sometimes related to difficulties with change), as well as more specific anxiety problems (anxiety in social situations or anxiety around specific things or activities, such as fear of cats or dogs). Sometimes the problem is with panic attacks—that is, the child becomes profoundly anxious and fearful and his heart races. Children with better language skills may be able to talk about some of the symptoms of anxiety, but even when children do not have good language, you may be able to see that they "look anxious." Sometimes the difficulties with anxiety lead to other problems, such as self-injury, aggression, or stereotyped movements.

Some researchers have suggested that anxiety may be part and parcel of the autism spectrum disorders. Others suggest that it may come about as a result of repeated frustration and negative experiences. We certainly know that higher functioning children with ASDs complain about feeling socially isolated and victimized. If you have trouble processing social information (itself the hallmark of autism spectrum disorders) you almost certainly will seem anxious. Indeed, some work from our group indicates that in some situations maybe 90% of the social–affective information in interaction is lost to the child on the autism spectrum. Clearly, a growing awareness of difficulties in dealing with peers and social situations may lead to a vicious cycle in which anxiety increases and makes it more likely that the child won't join in with peers.

For typically developing children, counseling, psychotherapy, and play therapy can often be helpful. This is sometimes true for children with ASDs, although usually the therapist has to be more structured in their interaction with the person than would be typical and also has to be more problem focused (that is, more like a teacher in some respects). Various behavioral techniques can also be used, particularly for anxiety difficulties. These include teaching the child how to relax through methods such as biofeedback, visual imagery, and relaxation training. If you decide to pursue any of these interventions, you would be well advised to find a psychologist or other professional who has had a fair amount of experience with the technique and who ideally has also had experience working with children with autism. There are effective behavioral treatments for anxiety and depression (see Chapter 14). There are also a number of interventions to put into place relative to teaching social and coping skills that may also help (see Chapter 6).

Fortunately, depression is usually quite treatable with medication and sometimes with counseling or with both. A number of effective drug treatments for depression are available. These include the more traditional antidepressants as well as the more recently developed **selective serotonin reuptake inhibitors (SSRIs)**. Keep in mind that it may take some time for these medicines to reach an effective level, and you may not see an improvement for some weeks. These medicines need to be appropriately monitored, including for side effects.

There are also various medications that can be used to help deal with anxiety problems. These include the minor tranquilizers and buspirone, the SSRIs, and some of the alpha-adrenergic agonist medications (like clonidine). Careful monitoring is again important. Side effects can include a kind of behavioral disinhibition—that is, the child becomes *more* agitated, not less.

For children with mood swings, various medications are available. These are often referred to as mood stabilizers. The dose of these medications often can be monitored and adjusted based on drug levels in the blood.

When to Use a Medication

In Chapter 14, we discussed the various kinds of behavioral and emotional difficulties common in children with autism and related conditions and discussed some of the problems that behavioral interventions can help with. In this chapter, we consider how medicines are sometimes used in treatment. In thinking about whether to try medication to help the child, there are several things you should consider:

- Are there alternatives to medication, and have these been given a (good) try?

- Are there any physical problems or changes in the child's life that may have contributed to the problem?

- How serious is the problem; for example, does it jeopardize the child's education, or does it put him or others at risk of harm?

- Is it possible that addressing the problem may improve the child's feelings or adjustment to his intervention program?

- When did the behavior/problem start?

- How long does it last?

- How severe is it?

- What makes it worse (or better)?

- Does it happen in some places and not others?

- Is this a long-standing problem or worsening of a long-standing problem, or is it really a new problem?

- Is the problem getting better or worse?

- How is it changing over time?

As discussed in Chapter 14, a careful behavioral assessment may be very worthwhile. There is no reason that medications can't be used with behavioral interventions (in some ways, these often work quite well together). *But* keep in mind that once you start doing multiple things at the same time, it gets more and more difficult to understand why someone might get better, that is, it is hard to know which intervention (or combination) is responsible for the improvement.

Depending on the specifics of the situation, it may make the most sense to try behavioral interventions first and then move to medications if these are not successful or only *partly* successful. Exceptions would be for problems that are more serious, such as those that pose some risk of serious physical injury to the child or others. For example, an adolescent girl who engages in dangerous self-injurious behavior might well be appropriately treated with medication even to the point of slight **sedation**. In weighing the risks and benefits of the medication, the risks of slight sedation might well be worth the benefit of preventing serious self-injury. However, drug interventions may be less effective than behavioral ones for infrequent behaviors that are less intense and that seem to come up only in certain places or at certain times.

Often, children with ASDs have more than one emotional or behavioral problem. In such cases, it is sometimes possible to choose a medication that may target both problems. But, in many cases, it may be necessary to choose one target problem at a time to focus on because the effects of the medication may be relatively narrower.

It's important to realize that all drugs have potential side effects, and, in general, drugs should not be the first thing you try in treating behavior problems. When medications are used, they are usually best combined with behavioral and educational approaches to produce more lasting benefit. The use of medications always requires a careful balancing act between risk and benefit and a consideration of all the causes of the behavioral difficulties.

The variety of medications used to treat children with autism and related conditions is growing. Some medications have been used more frequently and have been carefully studied in a scientific way so we know a fair amount about them. For other medications, the information available is based on a small number of children treated with the medication, children treated "nonblindly" or involving only one or a few cases. In the following discussion, it is important to realize that knowledge is constantly increasing; that we are providing you with some general information; and that, in considering medications, it will always be important to review the child's specific needs with his care provider.

RULING OUT PAIN AS A CAUSE

Sometimes behavioral troubles arise because a child is in pain. This is most common in children with limited communication skills. For example, a child who previously had not had self-injurious behavior might one day start to hit the side of his head. Before beginning medications to control his self-injurious behavior, it would be important for his physician to look in his ears and mouth to be sure that an ear infection, sore throat, or some other medical problem has not triggered the self-injury. See Chapter 10 for more information about determining whether the child is in pain.

Medication Fads and Off-Label Uses

Often, when a new medicine is first proposed for autism, there is great enthusiasm for it. Usually, early reports make it appear to be helpful in many if not most cases, with few, if any, side effects. An example of such a medication was fenfluramine, which initially, according to a few case reports, seemed to produce significant and dramatic improvements in children with autism. Unfortunately, this turned out not to be the case over time. In general, it is better not to jump on the bandwagon when a new drug treatment first receives attention, but instead use medications that have a proven track record in autism. For new medications, it may make sense to wait until the results of well-conducted clinical trials are available.

Medications on the market are approved by the Food and Drug Administration (FDA; www.fda.gov) for a specific purpose: depression, anxiety, schizophrenia. Once a medication is on the market, health care providers can use it for purposes other than those for which it was approved. The term *off-label use* refers to the practice of using the drug for a condition outside of the approved use. In other words, once a drug has been approved by the FDA, it is up to the people who prescribe medications to use good judgment in prescribing. Off-label use of medicines is very common—possibly 50% or more of medicines used in pediatrics are given for off-label uses. This is a real problem in pediatrics in general, and in autism in particular, and reflects several different problems—difficulties in doing research in children, particular difficulties in doing research with children with disabilities, and a lack of incentives and/or requirements for testing medications in these populations. Thus, given the lack of research on medications for children with autism, it is often the case that the medicines being used are "off label." In contrast to off-label uses, in 2006 the FDA approved the use of risperidone for the treatment of tantrums, aggression, and self-injury in children with autism. However, many of the drugs commonly given to children with autism for behavioral and emotional problems may not have been studied or approved by the FDA for use in children with autism (or in any children, for that matter).

The doctor may discuss the complexities of all this with you, but you should realize that "off-label" use of medications is quite common—really the rule, rather than the exception. Discussion with the care provider should focus on matching the target problem with the medication.

RESEARCH ON MEDICATIONS

DOUBLE-BLIND, PLACEBO-CONTROLLED STUDIES

Groups of individuals are studied with careful attention to scientific controls, such as randomly dividing individuals into groups. One group (the control group) might receive a placebo or nonactive substance, while the other group might receive the active medication. Neither the child, parents, nor doctor giving the medicine know what group the child is in, hence the term *double-blind*). There are many advantages to this kind of study.

- The data that are collected can be analyzed free from the potential bias that goes with an unblinded study.

- In the variation on this method called the *crossover design*, children might be treated with a placebo for some weeks and then started on the active medicine or vice versa, giving all participants the opportunity to try the treatment being studied.

- Limitations: Although controlled studies are the most effective ways for giving us good information, they are the most costly to do.

OPEN-LABEL STUDIES

In these studies, the treatment is administered to many people, and everyone involved knows what medication is being studied, hence the term *open-label*.

This kind of study has some advantages, particularly when a medicine is first being used.

- Groups of individuals are studied (more powerful than studying just a few people).
- The study may provide information about who does and doesn't respond and what the side effects are.
- Limitations arise because the study is open (or technically what is termed *nonblinded*), so things like the placebo effect can cloud the results. Placebo effects can be substantial; for example, sometimes up to 20% or 30% of patients will improve on placebo.

CASE REPORTS

These are written accounts of individual patients' responses to a treatment; sometimes results are collected and reported with objective, scientific rigor, but sometimes the report may be more casual or even biased, whether intentionally or unintentionally.

- Studies of this kind often provide the first clues that a drug may be effective for a problem.
- They are severely limited by:
  - Concerns about whether the children studied actually had the disorder (e.g., autism) to begin with
  - The possibility that lack of a good control group/condition and the "placebo effect" may make the medicine look more effective than it will be in subsequent studies
  - The possibility that gains made may not last

What Is the Placebo Effect?

The **placebo effect** refers to the many important benefits of being involved in research, whether or not the child is receiving the treatment being studied or a **placebo** (inactive medication). These effects all can make a major change (for the better) in the child. The first question to ask is why children get better on placebo. There are several answers to this question:

- Research involves high levels of clinician, parent, and teacher involvement, and more attention and interest may help the child improve.
- Every effort is made to provide high-quality care during a study.
- Symptoms change over time (often, people try something new, such as volunteering for a research study, when things are at their worst and the only way for things to change at that point is for them to get better).

- The effects of expecting a change for the better can be important; for example, expectations for improvement change how a parent or teacher observes and interacts with the child.

Developing a Treatment Plan

If you plan to pursue drug treatment for the child's behavioral or emotional problems, you should work with a physician or other health care provider who is knowledgeable about the use of these medicines (and their side effects). This provider (who may be a psychiatrist or child psychiatrist or sometimes a pediatrician or neurologist, or **nurse practitioner**) will want to meet with you and the child. During this meeting, the doctor, or sometimes another health care provider, will take a history of the problem as well as a more general history of the child. This will typically include the child's birth and developmental history, results of any previous evaluation, the child's medical history, previous drugs used (if any), and the child's response, as well as any relevant family history. This history may be important, because conditions such as depression and other mood disorders can run in families. Any history of unusual responses to medication, drug allergies, and similar information will also be reviewed. The doctor will want to spend some time with the child and may want to see the child in his classroom or talk with school staff (obviously, with permission from the parents).

The doctor will tell you about the pros and cons of various options and develop a treatment plan. Depending on the kinds of medicines that are being discussed, some baseline lab tests (e.g., of the blood or urine) might be obtained. Before beginning some medicines, the doctor might want the child to have an electrocardiogram (ECG). For other medicines, periodic blood tests might be needed to monitor the level of the medication or to look for possible negative side effects. If the doctor prescribes medication for the child, he or she should tell you:

- The name or names of the medication
- What the expected benefit is
- What the possible adverse effects and risks are
- How the medicine is monitored and the dose is adjusted
- When you should see a change, and what to do when you see a change

Some clinicians may ask you to sign something to document, for the record, what you have actually discussed. If appropriate, the child (particularly if an adolescent or young adult) should be involved in this discussion.

The child's primary care physician should always be kept informed about the child's medication(s). This is important because it is this person who knows the child's medical history best. In some cases, you may see a specialist some distance away for a consultation, but the local primary care provider may be willing to prescribe the medications as long as the specialist is available for backup. Depending on the nature of the child's problems and other aspects of the situation, it may also be advisable to inform school staff such as the classroom teacher and school nurse that the child is receiving medicine. This is mandatory if the child is to receive medicines during the day at school. Schools may have their own requirements about documenting medicine, and the staff may be helpful in documenting how well the medicine is working and in observing side effects.

Understanding Potential Side Effects

All drugs have at least some potential adverse effects. This is true for medications as simple as aspirin! Sometimes side effects are related to dose and are more likely at higher doses. Other times, side effects may occur regardless of the dose, as is the case with true allergies to medications. Side effects vary from medicine to medicine. Sometimes side effects can be something that may help; for example, some medicine might have some sedative side effect that might help with getting to sleep. Technically, the term *adverse effects* is more frequently used to refer only to side effects that are unwanted. In the discussion of medicines later in this chapter, we mention some of the main side effects seen with different groups of medicines. A child may not have any of these side effects. However, the child may have some side effects we don't list. Sometimes side effects are seen right away; other times, they can take a while to develop. Some side effects might be seen early on but then tend to go away with time.

All of this means that when parents discuss medicine for behavioral or emotional problems with the doctor, they should be sure to get a good sense of the more common possible side effects, as well as the rare but more worrisome side effects. Based on the side effects reported to the doctor, she or he may want to change the dose, switch to a new medicine, or even add a medicine that will help with the side effects or further strengthen a positive response.

DO'S AND DON'TS FOR PARENTS

Parents play an integral role in working with the prescribing clinician to ensure their child is benefiting from medication and receiving the optimal dose. Here are some do's and don'ts to pay attention to, whenever the child starts taking a new medication.

DO:

- Have a detailed discussion with the doctor prescribing the medication about exactly what you can expect: the possible benefits and risks, how long it might take to see results, how the doctor will monitor the medicine, how often you will see the doctor.

- Ask why the doctor favors one medicine over another and what form the medicine is in (pills, capsule, liquid).

- Make sure you understand when to administer the medication and what to do if the child misses a dose.

- Ask if there are reasons to call the doctor right away and how you can get hold of him or her if there is an emergency.

- Ask how you can help determine whether the medication is helping the child. Is there specific information you (or the school) can collect? What kind of information should you track, and how often should you record it? How can you best record this information and get it to the doctor?

- Be sure the child's primary health care provider is "in the loop" and knows why the medicine is being prescribed and what the side effects might be.

- Ask the primary care provider if you need any blood tests or other medical tests before you start the medication. Remember, your child may be much more comfortable having blood taken in a familiar office than a strange place.

- Use the same pharmacy for all the child's prescriptions. This helps ensure that the pharmacist will notify you and the doctor if there is any potential for medicines to interact with each other.

- Let the doctor and pharmacist know if the child is taking vitamin supplements, herbal treatments, or any other nonprescription remedies that could affect the way medication works.

- Be a careful observer of the child; often, you'll notice changes before other people do.

DON'T:

- Pretend to be a doctor—ask for help if you need it.

- Stop the medication without asking the doctor first. Many medicines must be slowly discontinued (tapered) and not stopped abruptly.

- Give up too quickly. Some medicines can take weeks or months to work.

- Stop behavioral or educational interventions when you begin a new medication.

- Try to do a lot of new things at the same time as beginning a new medicine. This complicates figuring out what accounts for any improvement.

MEDICATIONS USED IN AUTISM AND RELATED CONDITIONS

The following sections provide some basic information on the major classes or groups of medication sometimes used in treating the behavioral difficulties of children with autism and other pervasive developmental disorders. In each section, there is a short description of what we know about how the medication works and what it seems most useful for. The most common adverse effects of the medications are discussed, and we give some examples of medications in this group. Please remember that this is a selective and not an exhaustive list of medications. Also keep in mind that we provide only a short description of some of the more common side effects and that many others are possible. If you are considering a trial of medications, you need to have a detailed discussion of the potential benefits and risks as they apply to the child. That is, the discussion should take into account all the information relevant to the child such as his medical history, family history, previous response to medications, and so forth.

The reading list at the end of the chapter provides some reference to fairly detailed books on medications written for parents, teachers, and other nonphysicians. You may want to look at these. Some excellent books (written specifically for medical professionals) are also available, and some of these are included in the reading list as well. Given that this is an area where, fortunately, more research is going on now, parents and others may wish to check online resources like PubMed (www.pubmed.gov) as well.

With a few notable exceptions (discussed later), most of the information available to us on medications for treating behavior problems is, unfortunately, rather limited. Mostly, we are relying on case reports and studies of series of cases rather than on well-controlled, double-blind studies. Fortunately, more research is now being done on these medicines, and new knowledge will be coming out at an increasingly rapid pace. Although the information we provide here is up to date at the time of our writing, keep in mind that new studies are always being conducted and information may change—another reason to work with a professional who keeps up with new developments.

Major Tranquilizers (Antipsychotic Medications)

The medications most often prescribed to treat behavior problems in autism are called *major tranquilizers*. These medicines were some of the first medicines developed 50 years ago in psychiatry specifically for treating schizophrenia, hence the name *antipsychotic*. There is more research on them than on other classes of drugs. Some newer, second-generation antipsychotics in this group have been developed in recent years and lack some of the side effects of the older medicines in this group. These medicines are often used when children have significant problems with self-injury, stereotyped behaviors, aggression, and irritability. They are sometimes used for children with high levels of activity or behavioral rigidity.

The antipsychotics seem to have a major effect on the brain systems that involve dopamine, one of the messengers **(neurotransmitters)** between nerve cells. To varying degrees, these medications act in some way to block the effects of **dopamine** in the brain. They also have effects on other chemical systems in the brain. These various effects account for the desired—or positive—effects, as well as the adverse effects of medication. The brain chemical dopamine appears to be involved in some way in certain behavior problems in autism, for example, the self-injurious behavior and stereotyped or purposeless repetitive movements. Sometimes low doses of antipsychotics effectively increase the attention span of children with autism and help them to learn more effectively. This is not usually why antipsychotics are prescribed for children with autism. But it is an example of how side effects can actually be a good thing once in a while.

Usually, the dose is started at a very low level and gradually increased. The effects of the medicine can be relatively rapid. Occasionally, a higher dose may be used to start. This is mostly done in emergency situations.

We'll start our discussion with the newer of these medications; these are the ones most commonly used today. Then we'll discuss some of the older medications in this group; these are now less commonly used.

Second-Generation Antipsychotics   Second-generation antipsychotics (see Table 15.1) are a relatively new group of medicines, which have attracted much attention because of their greatly reduced risk of a side effect called *tardive dyskinesia*. This term literally means a slow to develop movement disorder and is a side effect that occurred more frequently with the first generation of drugs. These newer medicines, sometimes called *atypical antipsychotics*, also seem to be more effective in helping with the social withdrawal and lack of motivation in adults with schizophrenia (which may or may not have much to do with the social problems in autism). Additionally, these medicines seem to help with agitation, temper tantrums, aggressiveness, self-injury, high activity levels, and impulsivity—the same problems that the older "first-generation" **neuroleptics** were used for. One large, double-blind, placebo-controlled study of these medications has shown them to be effective in children with autism.

TABLE 15.1	SELECTED SECOND-GENERATION (ATYPICAL ANTIPSYCHOTICS)	
Generic Name	**Brand Name**	**Typical Range of Dose**
Risperidone	Risperdal	0.5–3.0 mg/day
Qetiapine	Seroquel	50–300 mg/day
Olanzapine	Zyprexa	5–100 mg/day
Ziprasidone	Geodon	20–100 mg/day
Aripiprazole	Abilify	2–15 mg/day

Note: Dose ranges are approximate; other medications are available in this category.
Potential side effects include weight gain (varies with medicine), sedation, movement problems, and possibly diabetes, among others.

The atypical neuroleptics are largely replacing the older, first-generation medications, in part because of the lower risk of serious side effects. Still, there is a variety of side effects, which can include sedation, movement problems, weight gain (with the possible exception of ziprasidone), changes in the ECG, and possibly diabetes.

One of the first drugs in this group, clozapine, can have some major side effects, including reducing the white blood count. Consequently, it is not used as frequently as the others and has not been as intensively studied in autism.

Another of these medicines, risperidone, has been very well studied and is now approved by the FDA for the treatment of aggression, tantrums, and self-injury of children with autism ages 5 to 17 years. One of the studies that contributed to approval of risperidone was a trial by the Research Units on Pediatric Psychopharmacology (RUPP) Autism Network. In this study, children with autism and serious behavioral problems were randomly assigned to an 8-week double-blind trial of either risperidone or placebo. The children in the risperidone group had a large and significant reduction in these serious behaviors and were more likely to be rated as much or very much improved by clinicians who did not know whether the child was on the active medicine or placebo. There were some minor side effects of risperidone (fatigue, drooling, drowsiness), most of which passed quickly. The major side effect was weight gain (2.7 kg or almost 6 pounds on average).

In a second part of the study, children were followed over time in an open-label study (i.e., there was no longer any attempt to keep up the double-blind part of the study). Children who responded well to risperidone continued to do so at a low to medium dose level. After 6 months, children were then randomly assigned to a discontinuation trial (some children stayed on the active medicine; others gradually switched over to placebo). As with the first phase of the study, the discontinuation was double-blinded. Only a few children tapered off the medicine successfully; most had the return of behavioral difficulties and went back on the risperidone. The response to risperidone in this study was larger than the response to the first-generation antipsychotics in older studies. Although there were many fewer side effects overall, weight gain emerged as a common problem. It is worth noting that sometimes weight gain can be substantial, and it may not be easy for a child to lose the extra weight even after the medicine is stopped.

There have been studies of other atypical antipsychotics as well, although they have not been as well studied as risperidone. In particular, olanzapine has shown some potential to reduce irritability, aggressiveness, overactivity, and obsessiveness in open trials. Weight gain seems to be an even bigger problem with olanzapine. Some parents don't mind the weight gain (particularly if their child is on the thin side). However, substantial weight gain can be a problem for many children with autism, who may not get enough exercise anyway.

First-Generation Antipsychotics   Because these medicines have been around longer, they are often called *first-generation antipsychotics*. These medicines are often used for treatment of severe behavioral difficulties such as aggression and self-injury, as well as agitation and stereotyped movements. Some of these medicines have been studied in controlled, double-blind trials in autism. A few trials have followed children for several months. Improvements have been documented in such areas as agitation, withdrawal, and self-stimulatory movement. Many children respond well to these medicines.

In general, children should be prescribed the lowest possible dose of these medications, as some of the side effects occur more often at higher doses. (See the section on side effects later in the chapter.) These medications are more likely to make the child feel drowsy or sleepy (some cause more sedation than others). Sometimes sedation is mistakenly viewed as a positive response. That is, the child is no longer making much trouble. However, the child may also not be doing much learning!

There are a number of medicines in this group. Haloperidol (Haldol) is one of the more potent members of this group and is the most well studied in children with autism. It can be effective in reducing high levels of activity, agitation, and stereotyped or self-injurious behavior. Studies of Haldol have demonstrated that it works quite well in children affected with moderate to severe autism. Significant behavioral improvement may occur at relatively low doses. Side effects are observed but are not usually common at low doses. It is usually started at a low dose and gradually increased. When effective, usually there are periodic attempts to lower the dose of medication. It is important that such drug "holidays" be planned to ensure that children receive the lowest effective dose of medication. At very low doses, haloperidol is not usually very sedating, but at higher doses, it can be.

Another medicine sometimes used in treating children with autism is chlorpromazine (Thorazine). Thorazine is a low-potency antipsychotic; that is, a higher dose needs to be taken to achieve the same effects as with a high-potency medication such as Haldol. For example, about 100 mg of Thorazine equals about 1 mg of Haldol in terms of effectiveness. It's important to realize that the differences in **potency** in this and other groups of medications can make it difficult for anyone other than a professional to evaluate how high or low a dose of medication actually is. Thorazine is much more sedating than Haldol. This can be a benefit for some children; however, sedation is often a problem, but sometimes this can be avoided by giving a larger dose before bedtime, when it may help the child get to sleep.

In between Haldol and Thorazine, there are a number of other medications (see Table 15.2). These tend to be intermediate in terms of potency and their side effect profile. Some of these medicines come as capsules or tablets and some

TABLE 15.2   **SELECTED FIRST-GENERATION ANTIPSYCHOTIC MEDICATIONS**

Generic Name	Brand Name	Typical Range of Dose
Haloperidol	Haldol	0.5–3 mg/day[a]
Thiothixene	Navane	1–20 mg/day
Chlorpromazine	Thorazine	50–400 mg/day[b]

Note: Dose ranges are approximate. Liquid forms (which may be easier to give and provide a range of dosing options) are also often available. Many similar drugs are available. Possible side effects include sedation, movement problems, restlessness, allergic reactions, and dry mouth, among others.

[a]Least sedating and most potent but with the most motor side effects.
[b]Most sedating and less potent with fewer motor side effects.

are available in liquid form; this can be important if the child has trouble taking pills.

Adverse Effects Side effects of antipsychotics include a group of neurological abnormalities. These symptoms can include stiffness in arms or legs, shaking of the fingers or hands, restlessness (akathisia), stiffness of the neck, and unusual movements of the head and eyes. These problems often appear in the first weeks or with dose increase. These neurological adverse effects are called dystonias (muscle stiffness), and dyskinesia (disordered movements). These can sometimes also be seen when the medicine is discontinued or reduced (withdrawal dyskinesia).

The restlessness and some of the motor movements associated with these medications can be treated with other medications such as benztropine (Cogentine) or diphenhydramine (Benadryl), which can be given along with the major tranquilizer. Some doctors use these additional medicines almost routinely to try to prevent any of the acute movement problems.

Sometimes, a movement problem called **tardive dyskinesia** occurs. This movement disorder usually develops after months or even years of treatment, but sometimes more quickly. It takes the form of various involuntary movements of the body extremities; neck; or the face, mouth, and tongue, and may be associated with what appear to be grunts or **tics**. This condition can be confusing because at times it resembles the kinds of motor mannerisms frequently seen in autism. It is important to note that reducing the dose of medication may seem to make the tardive dyskinesia even worse.

Because tardive dyskinesia is sometimes reversible, doctors should screen for it when they begin treatment with antipsychotics and as they follow a child who is treated over time. That way, if there are early signs suggesting tardive dyskinesia, the medicine can be stopped. There are specific rating scales that doctors and nurses can use to monitor the unusual movements sometimes associated with these medications.

Occasionally, when a medication is discontinued or reduced, withdrawal dyskinesias occur; that is, the child begins to exhibit some unusual movements. These usually persist for only a few weeks but may be disturbing to parents and children. Adolescents and adults appear to be more likely to have these than young children. The risk of withdrawal dyskinesia increases if the medication is stopped abruptly rather than being slowly tapered.

Other side effects sometimes observed in first-generation antipsychotics include true allergic reactions (not just motor side effects), which can cause serious medical problems. True allergic reactions can include breathing problems, hives, and other skin symptoms, and are a serious medical problem. Sometimes parents will say that their child had an "allergy" to a medicine when what they really mean is that he or she didn't do well with it or had some other side effects (not really allergy). It is important for parents not to call other types of side effects *allergies*. Sometimes you can inadvertently confuse a doctor by telling her the child had an allergy to a medicine when you really mean he had a side effect of some kind, and not a true allergic reaction.

As a group, these medicines tend to have some of the same side effects as "cold pills," such as dry mouth, constipation, and so forth. Because these drugs are metabolized in the liver and other parts of the body blood tests are periodically used to monitor liver, kidney, and other functions. In addition, many of these medicines in this group have a tendency to increase the likelihood of seizures in children with epilepsy (Chapter 12). Thus, their use should be considered carefully in a child with a seizure disorder. Furthermore, many of these medications can cause some degree of weight gain. Finally, individuals taking these medications (especially in high doses) need to be careful not to become too hot. A rare condition (malignant hyperthermia) can occur in children whose temperature increases dramatically. Children on these medications should be encouraged to drink a lot of fluids, particularly in the summer.

Again, it's important to keep in mind that adverse effects are often dose related; that is, they are more likely with higher doses of medicine, but sometimes they can occur at low doses.

Medications for Attentional Problems

Stimulant medications are very widely used in the United States for treatment of **attention deficit hyperactivity disorder (ADHD)**. It appears that these medicines work by increasing levels of a brain messenger chemical called **dopamine**. (Note that this is different from antipsychotics, which block dopamine in the brain.) Stimulants help the child to focus, attend, and be less restless. These medicines are very effective in individuals with ADHD; probably helping about 75% of those diagnosed with the disorder (see Table 15.3). There are also some

TABLE 15.3   SELECTED MEDICATIONS FOR TREATMENT OF ADHD

Generic Name	Brand Name	Typical Range of Dose
Methyphenidate	Ritalin	Regular tablets 15–60 mg/day
	Metadate	Extended-release tablets
	Concerta	Extended-release tablets
Dextroamphetamine	Dexedrine	10–40 mg/day
Amphetamine mixture	Adderall	10–40 mg/day
	Adderall XR	Extended release tablets
Atomoxetine	Strattera	1–3 mg/day

Note that dose is adjusted based on child's size and clinical response. Except for Strattera, the medications listed are stimulants and controlled substances. Side effects vary with agent and can include activation (restless and increased activity/irritability), poor growth, and hallucinations.

nonstimulant medications used to treat attentional problems although the stimulants are still the most widely used.

There are many different types of stimulant medications. They differ from each other in some ways. For instance, some are longer acting than others, and some tend to be associated with different side effects. Side effects of these medicines in children with ADHD include irritability, occasional worsening of hyperactivity, sleep problems, and decreased appetite. Occasionally, children have problems with dizziness and sometimes seem to become more moody or agitated. Children taking these medications sometimes develop tics (rapid, repetitive movements often involving the head and neck and upper body), or, if they have very mild tics, these can get worse. Other side effects can include other habit problems (picking their skin) or, more rarely, hallucinations.

Stimulant medications are among the more commonly used in children with ASDs for the same reason they are used in children with ADHD: to help increase attention and decrease hyperactivity and decrease impulsivity.

Until recently, there were few studies of stimulant medications in children with ASDs. The few studies that were done included only small numbers of children. As is often the case, results of these small studies don't agree simply because the samples were not comparable. The RUPP Autism Network completed a large-scale trial using three different doses of methylphenidate (Ritalin) and placebo. The trial used a so-called crossover design so that each child took the low dose, the medium dose, the high dose, and placebo in alternating weeks. The medication was disguised to make sure that each dose and placebo was blinded. Parents and teachers scored the behavior every week. The results showed that each active dose was better than placebo. But only about 50% of the children showed improvement. This rate of positive response is much lower than the positive response rate in the 75% of children with ADHD but not autism. The adverse events were similar to what we see in children with ADHD, but these adverse events were more common in the children with ASDs. The RUPP group looked closely in order to identify which subjects were more likely to show a positive response. There is some evidence that children with normal or near normal intelligence quotient (IQ) are more likely to show a positive response. But no other subgroups (e.g. autism, Asperger's, or PDD-NOS) were more or less likely to show a positive response to methylphenidate. Although stimulant medication can help to reduce hyperactivity and improve attention, these medications may not help other problems, such as anxiety, depression, or compulsive routines or rigidities. Then the question of adding a second medicine to deal with those problems may come up (we'll return to this topic toward the end of this chapter).

When stimulant medications do work, they should be monitored over time. Given the medications' potential to decrease appetite, the pediatrician will want to monitor the child's height and weight every 4 to 6 months or so. If there are problems with growth and weight gain, you can try lowering the dose, using drug holidays, or switching to a different class of medicine. Medications such as atomoxetine (Strattera) or guanfacine (Tenex) can also be used to treat hyperactivity. As the child grows older (and if the medicine is still needed), the dose can be adjusted. It is also important to make sure the child still really needs the medication by occasionally having a drug holiday—planned periods off medication to reevaluate the benefit. These trials off medication should be done in close collaboration with the primary care provider or mental health clinician.

Antidepressants and Selective Serotonin Reuptake Inhibitors

Antidepressants and the chemically related SSRIs were originally developed for the treatment of depression and/or obsessive–compulsive disorders (OCDs). There are several antidepressant medications on the market (see Table 15.4). These medications differ according to the brain chemical systems they affect. The most common type is the so-called selective serotonin reuptake inhibitors (SSRIs), which prevent (inhibit) the reabsorption (reuptake) of serotonin after it is produced in the brain, thereby increasing the level of serotonin in the brain. SSRIs are quite selective in how they act on serotonin; that is, they have little, if any, effect on other brain chemical systems such as norephinephrine and dopamine. There is also one medicine in the group (clomipramine [Anafranil]) that is less selective but still a potent reuptake inhibitor of serotonin (technically an SRI rather than an SSRI). Because SSRIs are used more frequently, we'll discuss them first.

SSRIs have attracted much interest for autism based on the assumption that these medicines could be useful in treating the prominent behavioral rigidity, ritualistic behaviors, and rituals commonly seen in autism spectrum conditions.

TABLE 15.4   **SELECTED ANTIDEPRESSANTS AND SEROTONIN REUPTAKE INHIBITOR MEDICATIONS**

Generic Name	Brand Name	Typical Range of Dose	Purpose
Clomipramine	Anafranil	25–200 mg/day[a]	Depression/OCD
Fluoxetine	Prozac Serafem	5–20 mg/day[b]	Depression/OCD
Citalopram	Celexa	10–40 mg/day[c]	Depression/OCD
Fluvoxamine	Luvos	50–200 mg/day[c]	Depression/OCD
Paroxetine	Paxil	10–50 mg/day[c]	Depression/OCD
Sertraline	Zoloft	50–200 mg/day[c]	Depression/OCD
Venlafaxine	Effexor	150–300 mg/day[c]	Depression
Bupropion	Wellbutrin	150–300 mg/day[c]	Depression
Mirtazaphine	Remeron	7.5–15 mg/day[c]	Depression

Note: Dose ranges are approximate. Approval for specific ages varies. Many other medicines are available in this category. Beneficial effects may take a period of time (weeks) to develop. Liquid forms (which may be easier to give and provide a range of dosing options) are available for some of these medications. Some medications also have long-acting forms. Needs for ECG and blood tests vary. Side effects vary with medication and can include activation (restless and increased activity/irritability), dry mouth, constipation, and heart (cardiac) effects.
[a]Traditional antidepressants.
[b]Selective serotonin reuptake inhibitors.
[c]Newer antidepressant/SSRI with different chemical structure than the older medicines.

A number of studies, not always well controlled, have looked at how well the SSRIs work in autism. In general, these early studies have been encouraging, with many individuals responding positively, but research is still in the early phases. One complication is that—for some reason we don't understand—there seems to be a lot of variability in how individuals with autism respond. Some children respond well to a lower dose than a slightly higher dose; others to one of these medicines but not another. It does seem that adolescents and children who are nearing adolescence respond better than younger children.

Although initial studies and clinical experience showed some promise for SSRIs on these outcomes, more recent studies have not been so positive. The earlier studies were small and the clinical target(s) for the medicine not always so clear. A recent federally funded study with a large sample of children (5 to 17 years of age) was conducted at six different medical centers. One of the SSRIs was studied in terms of its effects on repetitive behaviors and other symptoms. In this placebo-controlled study, after 16 weeks the group treated with the SSRI was no better than the placebo group but did have more adverse effects: sleep problems, overactivity, talkativeness, and impulsivity (this combination of adverse effects is often called *activation* and is sometimes seen with SSRI treatment). The results of this study have challenged the widespread use of SSRIs, although, clearly, other conditions such as depression or clear-cut OCD might be improved.

If the child is prescribed an SSRI, you will need to work fairly closely with a psychiatrist or other health care provider. First, because of the variable response in children with ASDs, the first SSRI you try may not be the most effective one. Second, it takes a relatively long time (weeks) to get the dose to a reasonable level and determine how effective the medication is for the child. When stopping these medications, they should generally be gradually tapered. This is because some children may have a kind of withdrawal reaction to stopping too quickly, which can include nausea and vomiting, abdominal pain, headache, and other reactions. Before starting either SSRIs or antidepressants, the child should have a medical history and physical exam. As noted earlier, treatment with clomipramine requires an ECG before and during treatments, as well as blood tests for drug levels. The antidepressant bupropion (sold as Welbutrin, Zyban, and Budeprion) should not be used in individuals with epilepsy (seizure disorder).

Another important consideration with the use of the drugs is the possibility of drug interaction. This can happen several different ways. For example, fluoxetine **(Prozac)** and citalopram can slow down the metabolism of other medications; this can actually result in an increase in levels of medicines (e.g., risperidone, and may increase the likelihood of adverse effects). To deal with this possibility, clinicians usually move even more slowly than usual if combining medications. Other antidepressants, notably clomipramine, are vulnerable to drug interaction. Because high levels of clomipramine can be toxic, it is important to be very careful. Commonly used medications such as erythromycin or even grapefruit juice can retard the metabolism of clomipramine and cause levels to rise. The important point is that all the prescribing care providers need to be aware of the medicines the individual is taking and to warn about possible drug interactions.

Mood Stabilizers

As you would expect from the name, the medications in this group all help to level out or stabilize mood disorders. The classic example of a mood disorder is something called manic-depressive illness or bipolar disorder. Individuals with **bipolar disorder** have major swings in mood. For instance, they may have periods (weeks to months) of serious depression followed by periods of having a normal mood and then by periods of elation and mania. The adult forms of the mood disorders are more straightforward to diagnose than the forms seen in children. In children, irritability, overactivity, and aggressive behaviors may signal a mood disorder or reflect severe disruptive behavior. The up-and-down cycle of mood disorders can be a bit more difficult to see in children.

There has been some speculation that mood disorders may be increased in children and adolescents with PDD. These issues are somewhat controversial, given that, for example, irritability and overactivity are often seen in children with PDD.

TABLE 15.5	SELECTED MOOD STABILIZERS
Generic Name	**Brand Name**
Divalproex	Depakote
Valproic acid	Depakane
Carbamazepine	Tegretol
Oxcarbamazepine	Trilepta
Lithium compounds	Eskalith
	Lithobid
	Lithone

Note: All these medicines require careful monitoring for side effects, including changes in the blood count, liver, thyroid, and kidneys. Dose of these medicines depends on blood level and side effects. Side effects can include sedation, changes in blood count, liver problems, and thyroid or kidney problems. Potential side effects for these and other medications should be carefully reviewed with the doctor who prescribes the medicine.

In strictly diagnosed autism, the general response to mood stabilizers is not usually positive. However, these medications may be helpful if the child has symptoms suggesting that an additional diagnosis of bipolar disorder or other mood disorder is justified, particularly if there is a family history of mood disorders. Children with cyclical patterns of mood problems and irritability associated with insomnia and overactivity may also be candidates for mood stabilizers. We have seen a few patients who have responded positively to mood stabilizers. These children had clear evidence of cyclicity in behaviors (swings from good weeks to weeks when the child's behavior was more out of control), and often there was a member of the immediate family who also had a mood disorder.

Medications used to treat mood disorders (see Table 15.5) include lithium and some of the same medicines used to treat seizures (anticonvulsants). The precise way these medicines work is not known. Lithium is probably the most well known of the mood stabilizers used with adults, although anticonvulsants are more frequently used now and are more likely to be used in children.

There are some studies of anticonvulsants for mood problems in children with autism, but these are mostly reports of single or a few cases and tend not to be of the most rigorous quality. More research is clearly needed. Some of the medicines used to deal with cycles in mood associated with overactivity and insomnia include carbamazepine and valproate (valproic acid), and also sometimes lamotrigine. In children with ASDs, problems that have reportedly improved on such mood stabilizers include mood problems, impulsivity, and aggression.

When anticonvulsants are used as mood stabilizers, levels of medicine are monitored through regular blood tests, to be sure that both an effective or therapeutic level of the medicine is reached and the level does not get too high. Typically, a child is put on a medicine for several days, before the first blood level is taken. The blood level is usually taken about 12 hours after the last dose (usually first thing in the morning before the child takes the morning medication).

Various medical tests are usually done before starting treatment with mood stabilizers. Depending on the medication, these may include tests of the kidney and thyroid (particularly if lithium has been prescribed), as well as tests of the liver and blood counts for some of the other medicines.

Side effects of mood stabilizers can include sedation, changes in the blood count, and liver toxicity. Lithium can affect thyroid and kidney function and lead to a fair amount of weight gain over time. (Because of concerns about lithium's side effects, it is used less often than some of the other mood stabilizers but can still be used for children with major mood problems.) The doctor should discuss all the potential side effects with you.

Medicines to Reduce Anxiety

All of us have experienced **anxiety**. Anxiety can serve a useful function, such as reminding us of dangerous or risky situations. Sometimes, however, anxiety becomes a problem that needs treatment, for example, if someone is immobilized by chronic anxiety or has panic attacks or specific fears that make it difficult to function in the day-to-day world.

Children with ASDs also can have problems with anxiety. Sometimes this seems similar to the kinds of anxiety that others of us experience in confronting frightening or stressful situations. Other times, the anxiety in autism is highly unusual and may be more related to difficulties in dealing with new situations or certain problem situations.

The medicines used in treating anxiety problems for typically developing children, adolescents, and adults can sometimes be successfully used in treating serious anxiety problems in children with autism spectrum conditions. However, as we will discuss shortly, there has not been much research on using these medicines in autism. In addition, sometimes the same medicines that seem to help the rest of us relax can make children with autism worse, that is, more agitated and disorganized.

Several different groups of medicine can be used to reduce anxiety (see Table 15.6). Some of them may be familiar to you because you or someone else in the family has used them for anxiety (e.g., lorazepam [Ativan]). Others in this group may be less familiar. We'll discuss each group briefly.

Benzodiazepines The benzodiazepines have been widely used in adults and typically developing children to help deal with anxiety specific to situations, for example, before the person goes for dental work. However, these medicines have not been well studied in children, and even less so for children with ASDs,

TABLE 15.6   SELECTED ANTIANXIETY MEDICATIONS

Generic Name	Brand Name	Typical Range of Dose
Benzodiazepines:		
Lorazepam	Ativan	0.5–2 mg/day
Clonazepam	Klonopin	0.25–2 mg/day
Beta blockers:		
Propranolol	Inderal	10–120 mg/day
Nadolol	Corgard	20–200 mg/day

Note: Dose ranges are approximate. Approval for specific ages varies. Other medicines are also available. Side effects include sedation and agitation. Beta blockers should be carefully monitored and should not be stopped abruptly. They also may make asthma worse.

but they can be useful at times. Common benzodiazepines include diazepam (Valium) and (lorazepam) Ativan.

Occasionally, children including those with developmental problems become somewhat more agitated on these medicines (this is called *paradoxical agitation*). If, for example, the dentist suggests that you try one of these medications to help calm the child during a dental procedure, you may want to try a test dose at home first to judge the child's response. There are some alternatives for sedation when these medicines don't work. For instance, occasional Benadryl works well in some children. You can also discuss other alternatives with the health care provider.

The benzodiazepines are habit forming and should not be used in an open-ended way. However, if these medications do work for the child, they can be valuable when used on an occasional basis for situations you know will make the child very anxious. They should not be mixed with alcohol, since they each can make the effects of the other stronger. As when trying any new medicine, discuss with the doctor and/or pharmacist the other medicines the child is taking.

Beta Blockers   Another group of medicines called **beta blockers** are sometimes used for children with autism and related conditions. These medicines were originally used as blood pressure medicines, but are now also used to deal with anxiety and irritability. There have been some open-label studies and case reports of beta blockers in the treatment of anxiety, but good double-blind studies are not available.

These medicines have a number of potential side effects, and it is important to weigh the pros and cons seriously before starting them. Side effects can include low blood pressure and problems with heart rate. These medicines can also make asthma worse. You have to be careful to take the medicine as prescribed and taper when the child is through with it. In general, these medicines have to be taken chronically (all the time) to work.

Alpha-Adrenergic Agonists   Another group of medicines that were first used to lower blood pressure are sometimes used to treat behavioral problems. These medicines, called **alpha-adrenergic agonists**, work through a different system than beta blockers and can help in the treatment of tics (unusual, recurrent impulsiveness and distractible movements). For some children, they can also improve problems with overactivity. They are sometimes recommended for children with autism, particularly for children who are hyperactive and impulsive. The data on using these drugs for ASDs are limited, but they are commonly used in children with other conditions such as Tourette's syndrome and ADHD.

Clonidine (Catapres) has been used to treat tics as well as attention problems; a similar medicine is guanfacine (Tenex). The medicines are given in divided doses by mouth. (Clonidine also comes in a patch formulation.)

Because these medicines are also used to control blood pressure, they can lower blood pressure (hypotension) and heart rates. Occasionally, children may develop what is called *orthostatic hypotension*, or low blood pressure when standing up, which can cause dizziness. In addition, these medications can cause sedation, either at the start or over the long term. If sedation is a problem, the medication can be given mostly at night to help with sleep. Some children may fall asleep without difficulty, but may wake up during the night. This can usually be handled by adjusting the dose. It is particularly important that they be given as prescribed and tapered off slowly if they are discontinued. (Blood pressure can rapidly increase if these medicines are stopped too quickly.) Sometimes tolerance to the medicine seems to develop.

Opiate Blockers   There has been some speculation that some of the self-injurious behaviors in autism may be designed to induce the release of opiate-like compounds in the brain. The theory runs like this: Perhaps when individuals hit themselves or engage in other self-injurious behaviors, they generate a kind of natural "high" (similar to a "runner's high") because their bodies are producing a kind of internal opiate (like opium). If so, perhaps the same medicines that are used to block the effects of externally produced opiate (i.e., opiate drugs, such as heroin) might also serve to undercut this effect and thus eliminate or reduce the behavior. Another theory is that individuals with autism have a very high pain threshold and that self-injury is a form of self-stimulation. A small number of studies have raised the possibility that individuals with autism have higher natural levels of endorphins (the opiate-like compounds the body naturally produces). If so, it could be that self-injury is, paradoxically, an attempt by the child to make himself feel better.

Two different drugs that are ordinarily used to help people with opiate drug overdose problems have been used in children with ASDs: naloxone (Narcan) and naltrexone (Trexan). Since naloxone has to be given intravenouly, naltrexone has been more extensively studied in autism. Studies were conducted starting in the late 1980s and continuing through the past 10 years. Initial studies tended to be small case reports. As often is the case early on, initial results were encouraging. Unfortunately, double-blind studies have not shown the same positive picture. Now most of the apparent benefit appears to be in reducing hyperactivity. (Again, this is a reminder of why it is so important to conduct double-blind studies.) There is some suggestion that this group of medicines may cause worsened troubles in children with Rett's disorder. Side effects of these medicines include, notably, nausea and vomiting. At the moment, these medicines do not seem to have major usefulness in children with autism.

Combining Medications

Children with ASDs often end up being given more than one medicine for their emotional or behavioral problems. This practice, referred to as *polypharmacy*, is a complicated one. Sometimes two medicines are given because one is controlling side effects of the other. Sometimes a second medicine is added after a first one seems to work a bit but not as much as is wanted. Occasionally, taking two medicines together may mean that a lower dose of each can be used. Sometimes one medicine, which acts more quickly, may be given while a longer-acting medicine is being introduced. Sometimes the doctor will feel that two conditions are really present and consider using two medications to treat them. (We have discussed comorbidity on page 454.) These are just some of the possible reasons for giving more than one medicine at a time.

Unfortunately, there are a number of potential problems with taking multiple medicines. One is in sorting out which medicine is doing what; in other words, how can you tell which medicine is being most helpful? In addition, there is always a trade-off when using more than one medicine. For example, there may be more potential for side effects and more hassle in giving more than one medicine. Furthermore, the potential for drug interaction clearly increases, and it is important that the pharmacist and regular health care provider are aware of all the medicines the child is taking. Finally, some combinations of medicine clearly don't work and might be more risky than taking one medicine.

Occasionally, we have seen children with autism on many different medicines at the same time (the record is about 10) with the idea that each medicine is treating a different thing—anxiety, depression, attention, and so forth. In these situations, the child's behavior often deteriorates and it is impossible to figure out why and what to change. In general, with some exceptions, it probably makes sense to start with one medicine.

If the child's doctor discusses adding a second medicine, you should feel like you understand why he or she is recommending this. If things start to get very complicated and you are giving the child many different medicines, it may be time to step back and think about getting another opinion.

Summary

Although many gaps remain, our knowledge of drug treatments in autism and related disorders has increased dramatically in recent years. Although no medicine has, as yet, been shown to really improve the core difficulties of autism, medicines have been shown to help with some of the very problematic symptoms associated with autism. Medicines can be very effective in dealing with agitation, hyperactivity, anxiety, aggression, depression, and some aspects of obsessions and compulsions.

In thinking about medications for behavioral problems, always weigh the pros (potential benefits) and cons (potential side effects and problems). You should think about drug treatments if problems are quite severe, if they limit the child's opportunities to participate in his educational program or community activities, or if they negatively affect his quality of life (or the quality of the family's life). The medical professionals working with you should take a look at the "big picture" and help you get a good sense of the pros and cons involved. For some medicines, side effects are pretty minimal, and, depending on the situation, you might consider using these medicines for a problem that is less severe or interfering. For more serious behavioral problems that warrant more potent medication, you may want to track the behavior for a period of time in order to gauge severity and to help determine if the medication is actually making a difference.

The doctor you work with should be in touch with the child's regular medical care provider, and, potentially, with school staff as well. It can be extremely helpful for school staff to collect data when a new drug (or any intervention) is tried to see whether there is a difference in behavior at school. The doctor you are working with may also want to use some rating scales or checklists as a way of monitoring the medicine (including potential side effects).

One of the exciting, but as yet unrealized possibilities is that in the future, as we discover more about what really causes autism, we may be able to develop much better treatments that target the core difficulties. In the meantime, we now have a number of medicines that can often be helpful.

■ READING LIST

Blumer, J. L. (1999). Off-label uses of drugs in children. *Pediatrics, 104*(3), 598–602.
Connor, D. F., & Meltzer, B. M. (2006). *Pediatric psychopharmacology—fast facts.* New York: Norton.

Dulcan, M. K. (2006). *Helping parents, youth, and teachers understand medications for behavioral and emotional problems: A resource book on medication information handouts* (3rd ed.). Washington, DC: American Psychiatric Press.

Green, W. H. (2006). *Child and adolescent clinical psychopharmacology.* Philadelphia: Lippincott.

Kennedy, D. (2002). *The ADHD autism connection.* Colorado Springs, CO: Random House.

King, B., Hollander, E., Sikich, L., Marcaken, J., Scahill, L,et al. (2009) Lack of efficacy of citalopram in children with autism spectrum disorders and high levels of repetitive behavior. *Archives of General Psychiatry, 66*(6) 583–590.

Kutcher, S.(Ed.) (2002). *Practical child and adolescent psychopharmacology.* Cambridge, UK: Cambridge University Press.

Martin, A., Scahill, L., Charney, D. S., & Leckman, J. F. (2003). *Pediatric psychopharmacology.* Oxford, UK: Oxford University Press.

McCracken, J. T., McGough, J., Shah, B., Cronin, P., Hong, D., Aman, M. G., et al. (2002). Risperidone in children with autism and serious behavioral problems. *New England Journal of Medicine, 347*(5), 314–321.

Posey, D. J., Erickson, C. A., Stigler, K. A. & McDougle, C. J. (2006). The use of selective serotonin reuptake inhibitors in autism and related disorders. *Journal of Child and Adolescent Psychopharmacology, 16*, 181–186.

Research Units in Pediatric Psychopharmacology (RUPP). (2002). Risperidone in children with autism and serious behavioral problems. *New England Journal of Medicine, 347*, 314–321.

Tinsley, M., & Hendrickx, S. (2008). *Asperger syndrome and alcohol: Drinking to cope?* Philadelphia, PA: Jessica Kingsley.

Towbin, K. E. (2003). Strategies for pharmacologic treatment of high functioning autism and Asperger syndrome. *Child and Adolescent Psychiatric Clinics of North America, 12*, 23–45.

Tsai, L. K. (2001). *Taking the mystery out of medication in autism/Asperger syndrome: A guide for parents and non-medical professionals.* Arlington, TX: Future Horizons.

Volkmar, F.R. (in press). Commentary on Citalopram treatment in children with autism spectrum disorder and high levels of repetitive behavior. *Archives of General Psychiatry, 66*(6), 581–582.

Werry, J. S., & Aman, M. G. (1999). *Practioner's guide to psychoactive drugs for children and adolescents* (2nd ed.). New York: Plenum Press.

Wilens, T. E. (2008). *Straight talk about psychiatric medications for kids* (3rd ed.). New York: Guilford Press.

■ QUESTIONS AND ANSWERS

1. **My 3-year-old has just been diagnosed with autism. Does he need medications now to help with his disruptive behavior? Will he ever need medications?**

   In general, we try not to give medications to very young children because behavioral interventions have more potential payoffs and fewer side effects. By the time children are entering school (and sometimes sooner) medications can help deal with specific symptoms and problem behaviors, but they still don't substitute for a good behavioral and educational program. Whether your son will *ever* need medications is hard to know. Many children do not; others do. The reasons why children would need medications vary a lot. Part of what you should consider is how much the disruptive behavior interferes with family life and school. Some parents are willing to try medications that may help with certain behaviors, whereas other parents feel that they or their child can learn to live with the behaviors.

2. **My 15-year-old daughter has PDD-NOS and horrible problems dealing with new situations—to the point that she gets almost paralyzed. Are there any medications that might help?**

There are several medicines that might help. Some of the SSRIs have shown positive effects in typically developing children with anxiety. But these medications have been less well studied in youths with ASDs.

3. **Our 8-year-old son has fragile X syndrome and autism. I've been told that children with fragile X syndrome always need stimulant medications to help them focus. Is this true?**

Many, but not all, children with fragile X syndrome have attention problems, so a decision on medication needs to be made relative to the child in particular. Stimulants can help with attention problems, hyperactivity, and impulsivity. Occasionally, stimulants make children a bit more irritable and may affect sleep. Also, stimulants sometimes decrease the appetite. This can be more of a problem for younger children who have not stopped growing, although the impact is usually very small. As with all medications, you need to balance the benefits and risks.

4. **Our 8-year-old son has had many behavioral difficulties over the years. He has had many different diagnostic labels and recently has been on a number of different medicines for his behavior. His behavior has deteriorated dramatically. He is now on five different medicines, and it seems like we are juggling them all the time. We are at our wits' end. What can we do?**

Think about admitting the child to a hospital (pediatric or child psychiatry service) where the diagnostic and medication issues can be carefully evaluated. One of the problems of using many different medicines is that it gets hard to figure out what medicine is doing what.

5. **We have a 15-year-old with Asperger's syndrome. He has done pretty well on an SSRI, but now our doctor wants to add a small dose of something he called an "atypical antipsychotic" because our son has gotten more irritable. Does this make sense?**

Of all the various medication combinations that people use, this is one of the more common. Often, children respond well to an SSRI initially, but as time goes on they seem to have a bit more trouble. Sometimes changing the dose of the medicine can help. For example, it may be worth reviewing the original purpose for the SSRI and consider a trial off. In other cases, it is helpful to increase the dose of the SSRI. Sometimes switching to a different SSRI may do the trick. Other times, particularly when new symptoms such as irritability arise, the doctor may think about adding one of the newer atypical antipsychotics, which normally have fewer side effects. It is possible that in addition to their effect on the behavior, they also may augment, or increase, the effect of the SSRI. That is, the SSRI may work even better.

CHAPTER 16

Managing Sensory Issues

O ur senses provide us with important information about our environment. Touch, smell, taste, hearing, sight, and sensations of balance, body position, and movement provide us with important cues such as whether something will taste good or whether something could be dangerous. Most of us learn fairly quickly what sensations we need to pay attention to and which ones we can ignore. For most of us, extraneous stimulation—for example, the slight flicker of a fluorescent light—is something we can quickly learn to ignore. For most children, hearing (especially what people say to you) and vision become the most important senses, particularly for communicating and learning about the world. For children with developmental challenges, particularly children with difficulties on the autism spectrum, the other senses may be just as relevant, if not more so. As a result, they may seem to overreact to some sensory stimuli and may have trouble filtering out other, less important stimuli—a tendency that can lead, in some cases, to higher levels of arousal and/or feelings of anxiety. Given the potential impact of this tendency on the child's ability to learn and socially engage, such sensory issues should be considered in planning intervention. In this chapter, we talk about sensory issues in autism spectrum disorders. We'll discuss hearing and vision (and screening for problems in hearing and sight), as well as some aspects of unusual sensitivities and sensory problems that children with autism spectrum disorders (ASDs) often have. As with other topics, please keep in mind that there are many individual differences. The child you know with autism or a related condition may not have *any* of these problems, although some children have many of them. It clearly is important to make sure that the child is hearing and seeing well so that he can take full benefit of his educational program.

SENSORY DIFFERENCES IN AUTISM

Unusual sensory features in autism were reported by Leo Kanner in his first description of autism. Many children with autism have some unusual sensory responses and interests, for example, being over- or undersensitive to the extraneous environment. What seems extraneous to most of us (typically developing) folks may not be so to the child with autism or ASD. While the social world seems much less relevant to them, the nonsocial environment may loom very large. Often, there seems to be a paradoxical combination of too much sensitivity (some sounds that you might not even notice will drive the child to distraction) and undersensitivity (the same child may not respond to his own name when it is called). Some children with autism are preoccupied with lights or patterns. Sometimes they bring things very close to their eyes and move them back and forth. Children with autism may also be preoccupied with the feel or texture of things or other sensory properties. For example, rather than play with the figures in a dollhouse and make up stories about them, they might repeatedly feel the wooden dollhouse furniture, spin the furniture around, or stack the pieces in a pile.

We don't know why all these unusual sensory issues develop in children with ASDs. It is likely that these problems are intimately related to other problems in development, particularly social development and attentional abilities. We do know, however, that they can make life more difficult for the child, family, and teachers. Sometimes unusual sensory experiences pose problems at home or school, for example, by diverting the individual's attention from what is most relevant (maybe the teacher or a lesson) and onto what is much less relevant (the light switch or the sound of the air conditioner or texture of the carpet on the floor). These behaviors also appear to peers to be very unusual and can result in isolation of the individual. At other times, unusual sensory sensitivities may be unpleasant for the person and their reactions may seem very odd indeed to onlookers as she becomes overly preoccupied with what, to the onlooker, seems a very minor detail!

Various theories have tried to account for these problems, but with only limited success. It is not clear whether the problems have to do with too much (or too little) processing, with anxiety, with difficulties in dealing with change, or with basic aspects of information processing and attention—although probably all of these are involved in some degree. The social problems so characteristic of autism and ASDs also likely contribute, that is, probably, most of us learn very early in life from other people what is, and isn't, so important to focus on. Similarly most of us learn early in life to ask for help, one way or the other, when we need to cope with sensory stimuli or sensory overload, for example, by turning to parents or caregivers. As we'll discuss later in this chapter, tests of hearing and vision in children with autism usually show normal sensory abilities, but it is interesting that some children who have visual impairments or deafness (but not autism) will show some unusual sensitivities and behaviors similar to those seen in autism.

Sometimes unusual responses to sensations are one of the first warning signs of autism. For example, a parent may notice that her infant won't respond to her voice consistently but becomes very upset if the vacuum cleaner is running. For some children, unusual sensory problems become more dramatic with age. Other unusual sensory behaviors may include preoccupation with moving objects (fans) or staring at the hand/fingers, or sometimes children will dangle string in front of their eyes. Leo Kanner viewed these behaviors as an attempt for the child to "maintain sameness" and avoid new experience—yet another challenge for learning from the world.

For individuals with more language, sensory issues/problems may diminish over time—probably, in large part, because language helps them cope more effectively and thus makes them less likely to be disorganized by the environment. For these children, some important ways for the child to self-regulate may develop; for example, self-talk may function as a way of coping. Many higher functioning individuals (with autism or Asperger's disorder) do report unusual sensory experiences and may be bothered by things that the typically developing person wouldn't notice. For example, in some of the work done at Yale on eye tracking, we have had very able people with ASDs watch clips from movies, and through the use of a special infrared camera and various computers, we can see what exactly the person is focused on in viewing a scene. In one instance, a person with an ASD was watching a scene from the classic movie *Who's Afraid of Virginia Woolf*, and as Richard Burton and Elizabeth Taylor were passionately kissing, the person with autism was focused on a light switch in the background!

EATING AND FEEDING ISSUES

Children with autism and related disorders can have a number of problems with eating and food. These often include:

- Unusual food preferences and sensitivities, which can lead to a restricted diet
- Pica (eating nonnutritive substances such as dirt or string)

In this section, we'll consider some of these problems and potential solutions. Again, keep in mind that this is a general discussion with general suggestions and that when specific advice is needed various professionals can be of help; these include **speech–language pathologists (SLPs), occupational therapists (OTs)**, and **dietitians**, as well as experienced teachers and parents.

Unusual Food Preferences and Sensitivities

Children with autism or other pervasive developmental disorders (PDDs) may have unusual eating habits. Some have pronounced likes and dislikes when it comes to food. Sometimes these habits keep the child from having a good diet. Some children are extremely sensitive to certain food textures or tastes or smells. Some children may eat only certain kinds of food (e.g., foods that are soft and mushy). Other children may resist new foods or may not tolerate foods of certain temperatures. Sometimes children eat the same foods over and over again. We've seen children who would eat only white food, who would eat only cold food, who would eat only French fries, and certain fast foods.

The attempt to introduce new foods at mealtimes can lead to temper tantrums and other difficulties. Occasionally, these escalate to the point that the child becomes malnourished, although this is unusual. These food preferences are not always easy to understand. They may be part of the difficulties children have in dealing with change or related to oversensitivity to smells and tastes.

Many parents of children with autism report some food sensitivities starting more or less from the moment that solid foods are introduced. It is interesting, however, that we've seen only a handful of children with autism who failed to gain weight appropriately as infants (sometimes called *failure to thrive*). When problems start early, they often seem to get worse as the child becomes a bit older, so it is worth trying to help the child when these problems first develop.

To some extent the unusual food preferences of some children with ASDs may be understood as having some resemblance to problems seen in typically developing toddlers where struggles over food are very common. The endless reminders from your mother to eat your peas or broccoli may come to mind! These problems are, however, often much more marked and severe in children with autism. Several things help the typically developing child cope—for example, being motivated to imitate the models provided by family members eating a range of foods or enjoying praise from parents for trying new foods. Unfortunately, children with ASDs often feel less social motivation and desire for praise. In addition to heightened sensitivities regarding food, rigidity and difficulties with change further complicate the attempt to introduce new foods into the diets of children with autism. These problems can be even more complicated when parents are also pursuing dietary interventions (see Chapter 18) that further restrict what the child can eat. It is possible to restrict the diet so much that a young child who otherwise responds to very few things other than food will no longer have that as an option.

THE ROLE OF DIETITIANS

Registered dietitians and dietetics technicians have had specific training in diet and nutrition. If your doctor suggests a consultation with the dietitian, he or she will talk with you, observe the child, and look at her medical records. The dietitian may be able to identify specific nutritional problems and can evaluate the child's need for special vitamins, minerals, or other diet changes. He or she will also consider any special issues related to the child's appetite, food preferences, medical history, and nutritional needs.

The dietitian can help you design a better diet for the child and may also work on increasing independence in feeding and dietary skills. This can sometimes be done in conjunction with the child's behavioral program. The dietitian may work with other professionals, including the child's doctor, SLP, or occupational therapist. Information on diet and accredited dietetic professionals is provided on the American Dietetic Association's web site (www.eatright.org).

Dealing with unusual food preferences is not easy. Strategies for coping with this problem are quite varied. One approach is to attempt very *gradual* change—very, very gradually introducing new foods. This might work well, for example, for a child who eats only white foods, where you could gradually begin to introduce color into the food. Blenders and food processors can be a real help in this regard. Sometimes unpopular foods can be hidden in other blenderized foods; this may make the texture more tolerable as well. Depending on the child's preferences, it may be possible to add to foods she does like. For example, if she will drink milkshakes, you can try adding different kinds of foods to the shake.

For some children, varying the way in which the food is presented may be the trick. Sometimes freezing pureed vegetables into popsicles may make them more interesting. Or a child who would never eat cooked peas might respond if they were presented in frozen form. Other children might be willing to try dried peas. The usual rule of thumb is to try gradually introducing new foods. Even though it is a hassle, keep at it, since otherwise the tendency is often for the child to become even more rigid.

Sometimes children are delighted to try foods that they have been involved in preparing. This approach can also have payoffs if you need to plan school lunches or snacks. You can try a visual approach to help involve her in cooking. For example, make up a set of index cards with photos illustrating how to prepare spaghetti. Put them in order in a notebook or on a ring. (Photos might show the child getting the spaghetti box out of your cupboard, getting the pot out, and putting water in it, etc.) For children who can read, the printed words may be sufficient or the pictures may be gradually eliminated over time. For some children, eating what they have helped prepare is very helpful.

Parents can also try involving the child in grocery shopping to try to spark an interest in new foods. Parents can consult with the child's school staff about ways to make this a positive learning experience. For example, you can make a visual shopping list ahead of time. Use a digital or instant camera and make photographs of the actual items the child will need in the store. You can put these onto a shopping list using Velcro tabs. This special list can help the child shop with you in the store. You can start with very simple foods and gradually increase the complexity as time goes on. This is a wonderful way to make grocery shopping a positive learning experience for the child and help her take pride in her abilities. Over time, other skills can also be involved, such as counting money, quantities, and so on. You also help encourage adaptive behaviors and important community and daily living skills.

Various behavioral approaches can also be used to help the child learn to tolerate a greater range of foods, such as those suggested by an occupational therapist or SLP. Often, a gradual, step-by-step approach is used with carefully selected rewards for more appropriate eating. The specific plan is individualized depending on the child's needs and problems. Praise, time-limited meals, ignoring food refusals, and more frequent "mini-meals" (with limited snacks in between) can all be used in various combinations. As with everything else, it is important to weigh the pros and cons of the various approaches. Children whose limited diets put their growth and development at risk are the ones who will need the most intensive intervention programs.

Various professionals can be helpful to you in dealing with the food preference problem. Behavioral psychologists may help you design a plan for gradually introducing new foods and expanding the child's range of foods. Especially if the child eats a very narrow range of food, it may be worth meeting with a dietitian to review the child's diet and think about ways to supplement it. Often, it is the texture rather than the taste of food that seems to be a problem. SLPs or occupational therapists may be able to work with you in developing ways to help the child be able to tolerate a greater range of textures or help with other aspects of the "presentation" of foods.

Eating Nonfood Substances (Pica)

Some children with ASDs have a different problem; they have a tendency to eat things that are not food (this is technically called pica). This may include dirt, paint chips, string, or anything they find on the floor. Other children will chew on materials and/or keep them in their mouths without swallowing them (or sometimes swallowing them by mistake). These behaviors can lead to various medical problems, including bowel obstruction and increased risk of poisoning. Various strategies can be used for dealing with inappropriate eating and mouthing behaviors. The choice of strategy depends on the age and cognitive level of the child and on the specific behavior that is at issue. Some children like the experience of moving their mouth and/or chewing. If this is the case, you can try several different things, including crunchy foods or foods with interesting textures, gum, and so forth (be aware that there is potential for adding a lot of sugar to the child's diet, so search for reduced-sugar or sugar-free chewing substitutes). The SLP or occupational therapist may have suggestions for nontoxic things the child could chew. Sometimes chewing is a reflection of overstimulation, and reducing the level of environmental stimulation may help. At other times, the use of an electric toothbrush (sometimes several times a day) can provide oral simulation (this also has the advantage of promoting clean teeth!).

Various professionals may also be helpful in reducing pica. The SLP or occupational therapist may help you think about new ways to cope with the problem and give the child alternative behaviors. A psychologist or physician with experience in developmental disabilities may also be helpful in suggesting behavioral interventions to try. Sometimes you can find a substitute or alternative behavior such as eating ice chips (with or without flavor). Sometimes your reactions to the behavior may be an important part of what keeps it going. You may need to learn to ignore the behavior if it is not endangering the child's health, while simultaneously providing plenty of praise and attention for more appropriate behavior.

Hearing Problems

The most common sensory sensitivities reported among children with ASDs are probably those that involve sensitivity to sounds and noises. This can take the form of seeming either undersensitive or oversensitive. Often, the parents' initial concern may be that their child is deaf because of his apparent lack of sensitivity to some sounds. At the same time, the child may seem to respond exquisitely to some sounds from the inanimate (nonsocial) environment such as sirens, planes, or the rustle of a candy wrapper.

Deafness occasionally is associated with autism. As we mentioned in Chapter 10, children can sometimes have some degree of temporary hearing loss due to recurrent ear infections leading to fluid in the middle ear. On the opposite side of the coin, sometimes children with deafness may initially look somewhat autistic, but they improve markedly when provided with assistance devices such as hearing aids or implants, or when taught to use communication programs such as sign language.

Assessment of Hearing Ability

Good hearing is a prerequisite to developing the ability to speak. And it is also important in the development of good social skills. Accordingly, hearing testing is typically conducted in very young children when autism or related problems are suspected and when a child has delayed speech and language skills. It is particularly important if the child seems to respond to no or very few sounds.

Apart from genetic testing for fragile X, hearing testing is the additional medical test that is almost always important in autism. Many states are starting to require that a hearing test be done on all newborns before they are discharged from the hospital. This early screening will be very helpful in picking up **congenital** hearing problems. Your pediatrician or family doctor may be able to assess the child's hearing in his or her office. If not, you will be referred to an **audiologist**, an individual trained and licensed to assess hearing impairment. If possible, the audiologist should be experienced in working with children with developmental problems.

Types of Hearing Loss

There are different kinds of hearing loss. **Conductive hearing loss** occurs when there are difficulties in the transmission of the sound as it enters the ear canal through the middle ear and the small bones in the middle ear. This type of hearing loss in children is usually the result of fluid in the middle ear following recurrent infection or allergies. Impacted wax in the ear canal can also cause conductive hearing loss. Your pediatrician can usually remove the wax. One problem with conductive hearing loss is that only certain sounds may be heard due to the way different levels of fluid affect the way the eardrum responds to different sound frequencies. At different times, different sounds may be muffled or distorted in different ways by the fluid. Obviously, when specific speech sounds do not sound the same from day to day, it can be very confusing—especially for children who are just learning language. Conductive hearing loss is usually reversible.

A **sensorineural hearing loss** occurs less often. It results from a problem in the transmission of sound further along in the pathway between the middle ear and the brain and indicates that there has been damage to the inner ear or to the **auditory** nerve. There are many possible causes of sensorineural hearing loss. This type of hearing loss may run in the family, either as the sole problem or associated with certain genetic disorders that also cause other difficulties (such as heart problems). It can be associated with some in utero infections, very high bilirubin levels in the newborn, bacterial meningitis, and the use of certain antibiotics. This kind of hearing loss is generally permanent and does not improve with age.

Some children may have a **mixed hearing loss** involving both conductive and sensorineural hearing loss. Children with autism can have any of these types of hearing loss.

Problems With Sound Sensitivities

If the child has normal hearing and exhibits sensitivities to sounds, there are several things to do. At school, a minimally distracting and less noisy environment may well help. Some school buildings and classrooms seem almost perversely designed to complicate life for the child with an ASD. Concrete block construction and linoleum floors all contribute to an "echo chamber" effect. Sometimes simple steps can be taken to reduce auditory "clutter" in the classroom. For example, if the classroom is carpeted or if the bottoms of chairs are modified to make less noise, this may help reduce the overall sound level. Seating the child near the teacher and away from sources of noise (e.g., air conditioners) also may be helpful. Closing doors when possible will reduce noise. For some individuals the use of earphones to block out extraneous noises may help. Other things that have been tried include special amplifiers that amplify speech sounds for the child (similar to hearing aids) to help the child focus on the sounds that are most important (i.e., the speech of the teacher or peers). FM sound systems may help some children cope with an intrusive auditory (i.e., noisy) environment. It can be helpful for the child to learn to let the teacher know when sound levels are too much or he or she is feeling overwhelmed by sounds. Some alternative treatments also focus on reducing sound sensitivity (see Chapter 18), but research support for these is somewhat limited.

For some children, the sounds (and unpredictability) of things like fire alarms can lead to tremendous anxiety and behavioral difficulties. As discussed in Chapter 11, safety procedures are important and the teacher can work with the child in advance using pictures or stories to help prepare the child for the inevitable fire drill. Again, when possible, the emphasis should be on helping the child learn to self-regulate; thus, if the child is very sensitive to noise, the story can have him pull out a pair of headphones to muffle the noise as he is leaving the room or, for a verbal child, having a specific script he can "run through" to reassure himself may be helpful. Having a practice run-through may also be a good thing to try; we've even had firefighters who could help with this. Often, the practice will make it easier for the child when a real fire drill happens. This is something teachers should work on as part of basic safety teaching (see Chapter 11).

Other accommodations for the child who is very sensitive to sounds in the classroom can include use of earplugs (with or without the option of music). For the child who tends to be less responsive to auditory **input**, it is important that teachers and parents try to err on the side of speaking loudly, that is, exaggerating their voice to help the child focus.

VISUAL PROBLEMS

For many children with autism, some aspects of visual skills represent an area of strength (e.g., visual spatial skills of the type used in putting together puzzles). However, unusual visual preferences may also be seen. Some children will spend long periods of time engaged in visual stereotypies (such as flicking a string back and forth in front of their eyes) or may be interested in unusual visual aspects of materials (focusing on minor details of a toy). These visual abnormalities are often related to other behavioral difficulties (motor mannerisms or odd movements) and problems in self-regulation. In addition, many children with ASDs have striking difficulties with social gaze, that is, in making eye contact while talking with others. It may seem (and may be) that the child is attempting to avoid new experiences by engaging in some repetitive activities.

Children born with visual problems sometimes exhibit unusual body movements that may be mistaken for those seen in autism. Obviously, normal vision is important for development and learning. If you suspect that the child is not seeing clearly, you should speak with your doctor.

Assessment of Vision

Visual testing that requires the child's cooperation and understanding on the part of the child may be hard to perform in children with ASDs.

Most typical children can cooperate with vision screening by the age of 3 or 4 years. There are special picture charts that have been developed for children who are not yet reading. They use figures such as a house, an umbrella, or a circle. Children are asked to say which one of these is being pointed to by the examiner instead of naming letters as with the regular adult eye chart. A nonverbal child can be given a card with pictures of the objects on it and be asked to point to the one shown on the eye chart.

If there are significant concerns about vision and if the primary care provider can't test the child's vision, he or she will probably refer the child to an **ophthalmologist** (doctor who specializes in eye problems) or a pediatric ophthalmologist (who specializes in children's eye problems).

Solutions for Vision Problems

If the child does need glasses, it may be difficult to get her to keep them on. For some children, it may be helpful to get bands that go around the head to help the glasses stay on. It is probably worth the extra expense to buy a lifetime warranty when you purchase the glasses. At least that way you can get them repaired or replaced for free if they are broken or lost.

If the child has **strabismus** or **amblyopia**, the eye doctor may recommend that one of the eyes be patched part of the time. An alternative to patching is the use of eye drops. They are put in the better eye to blur the vision in that eye instead of patching it. This forces the child to use the poorer eye. While not easy, for some autistic children the drops may be easier than trying to keep a patch in place.

In the classroom, accommodations for the child who is easily overstimulated visually can include reducing the amounts of visual stimulation. For example, the child might work in a carrel or other area where visual distractions are reduced. For other students, visual stimulation may be used as a reward, for example, computerized screen savers, lava lamps, or other materials with slow but continuing movement. Be careful that, if these are used, they don't serve as too much of a distraction but are used as rewards and for times of relaxation.

Other Sensory Problems

In addition to having problems with the senses of vision and hearing, children with autism can be over- or undersensitive to other types of sensations, including touch, movement, smell, and taste. Again, we do not know why these sensitivities are so common in autism. There are many different theories. Below are a few examples of ways that sensory problems may manifest themselves in a child with autism:

- *Movement sensitivities.* Some children enjoy twirling themselves around; others hate it. Many children like the feeling of swinging in an outdoor swing or hammock. Some children will walk in unusual ways, for example, on their toes; others may have a peculiar gait. For individuals with movement sensitivities, opportunities for physical exercise (which has been shown to decrease stereotyped movements) is helpful. Swinging and rocking and similar activities may help children with issues in the area of **vestibular** stimulation.

- *Tactile (touch) responsivity.* Some children with autism have **tactile defensiveness**. That is, they cannot tolerate touching or being touched by things that are a certain texture, consistency, temperature, and so on. For example, some children will find the feeling of certain kinds of cloth intolerable or won't be able to wear clothes with any labels in them (the labels being a source of constant annoyance to them). They may find the seasonal change of clothes difficult, for example, going from long sleeves and pants to short sleeves and short pants. Other children can't stand to have their hair combed or their face washed. Some will seem less than normally sensitive to temperature change and won't mind being cold in winter or hot in summer. Solutions include removing labels from clothes and being careful to note what types of cloth/clothing children are sensitive to. You can also give access to sensory activities the child may enjoy, for example, a ball or object they can squeeze, materials that have interesting textures, and so forth to distract them from irritating changes. For some children, wearing tight clothes or weighted vests may help them have a better sense of their body.

- *Smell and taste sensitivities.* Sometimes these unusual sensitivities extend to food so certain textures, tastes, smells, or colors of food are avoided. A few children will respond dramatically to smells that the rest of us would generally not have a problem with. In the classroom, be attentive to things that may be a distraction, for example, if teachers or aides apply perfumes/colognes/after shaves. If the child has problems with the level of conflicting smells at lunchtime, one option might be for the child to eat in a different area. Some students may be interested in things with characteristic odors, for example, candies with strong scents or markers that smell. For children who seem to have a strong need to chew, use of gums and chewy foods may help.

Unusual sensitivities to light, touch, and balance (technically what is referred to as **proprioception** or the sense of one's body in space) may be closely related to self-stimulatory behaviors. For example, the younger child with autism might want to flick a string in front of his eyes, while an older child might want to spin or body rock (both behaviors that stimulate the balance system of the body). Behavioral interventions (Chapter 14) and sometimes medications (Chapter 15) may be helpful as well.

Assessment of Sensory Difficulties

Various professionals are often involved in assessing sensory difficulties. As mentioned earlier, tests of vision and hearing should be a standard part of the assessment of any child with an ASD. Dietitians and SLPs may be involved for problems with smell and taste sensitivities and the resulting issues with feeding. Usually, occupational and physical therapists are involved in dealing with unusual sensory responses—particularly those involving the child's ability to feel and have a sense of his body; these professionals can also work well as part of the treatment team at school in developing functional abilities across the school day, thus making the child more available for learning. We talked about some issues in motor and sensory assessments earlier in this book (Chapter 3).

As a general rule, physical therapists are most involved in assessing **gross motor** skills, balance, posture, and movement; occupational therapists may be involved in assessing fine motor movements, self-care, sensory and regulatory capacities, and other adaptive skills. There are a few tests of motor abilities and sensory responsiveness; often, an evaluation will focus a lot on real-world situations and the kinds of responses that cause the child trouble.

Areas evaluated by occupational therapists often include eye–hand coordination, spatial awareness, quality of movements of the hand and body, muscle tone, and **sensory integration** abilities (see below). Usually, there will be a strong focus on functional skills needed by the child in day-to-day activities. Particularly for younger children, there may also be a focus on play (ability to imitate).

SOLUTIONS FOR OTHER SENSORY PROBLEMS

Occupational therapists can draw on a wonderful range of materials to try to help the child. For example, drawing materials might include chalk, paint, special pens and pencils, and markers—with the idea being to try to find materials that will interest the child or that provide special help for a child with unusual sensitivities. Children who have trouble touching or holding things (tactile defensiveness) may be helped by being introduced to a range of new materials—clay, Play-Doh, sand, shaving cream, bubbles. Difficulties with motor planning can be addressed by breaking down tasks into subparts and working on them. Eye–hand coordination can be worked on with ball play. For children who have trouble having a good sense of their bodies, materials like a weighted vest might be used to help them stay focused on a task. Specially adapted materials like chairs and tables may also be helpful. Children who spend excessive time spinning or rocking can be helped by providing opportunities for swinging/rocking during movement breaks. Occupational therapists can also work on learning readiness skills, that is, organizing the child's sensory experiences to help secure attention and promote active engagement and learning.

Occupational therapists can also work quite well with other professionals, such as SLPs, on specific issues such as difficulties with the mouth and eating. Physical therapists tend to focus on body movement and posture problems. They work on the bigger muscle groups in the body and focus on problem areas like balance, stability of the body, muscle strength, and flexibility. Various tests of motor abilities are available. Activities might include swinging or jumping, walking on a balance beam, and other balancing activities. The physical therapist will typically work with you and the classroom teacher to be sure that everyone is working toward the same end.

SENSORY INTEGRATION THERAPY

Sensory integration refers to the process by which we take in, sort out, and organize information from our senses and then use the information to understand and respond to the entire situation. For example, waking disoriented in the dark on your first morning of vacation, you may be aware that the mattress beneath you is unusually hard and that there is a soft rumbling sound outside the window and a faint whiff of salt in the air. Putting all these sensory clues together, you remember that you are staying at a bed-and-breakfast by the sea.

Sensory integration (SI) therapy was developed by A. Jean Ayres, an occupational therapist, with the goal of helping people with sensory problems better integrate their sensations. It is based on the observation that children with autism and other developmental disabilities often have unusual sensitivities or responses. The hope is that helping the child learn to be more tolerant of different sensory experiences will lead to gains in the child's developmental functioning.

A basic idea behind SI therapy is that repeated experience with the environment will help the child develop better abilities to cope with potentially distracting sensory experiences. Goals include decreasing sensitivity to bothersome sensations, increasing the child's awareness of times when the environment is becoming overwhelming, and helping the child learn techniques for calming herself. The treatment may include a "sensory diet" designed to provide the child with a range of materials addressing the child's sensory needs. Massage, stimulation of the sense of balance, joint compression, or a weighted vest might be used. Brushing (using a soft brush) on the arms, legs, and back may be combined with other techniques. Some aspects of the intervention can be adapted to include more complicated problem solving for higher functioning individuals, for example, in helping the person be aware of their perceptions and dealing with overstimulation. You may find a range of therapists trained in SI techniques, including occupational therapists, physical therapists, and SLPs.

The theoretical basis for sensory integration is not very strong. However, many of the techniques used attract the interest of the child and may help her deal with difficult aspects of the environment that are difficult for them. Particularly when done as part of a broader intervention program, the methods may be helpful in some ways. Children may attend better, sleep better, and have lower activity levels. Evidence for cognitive gains is not, however, very strong.

SUMMARY

Children with ASDs often have unusual sensitivities or responses to the environment. These problems can take the form of over- or underresponsiveness to the environment or can include a mix of both; these can pose difficulties for the child and can complicate the task of providing a good educational program. These sensitivities can also limit opportunities for activities in the community, since unusual preoccupations and sensitivities can also complicate peer interaction. Occupational therapists and other professionals can help you and the child learn to better cope with his sensitivities; there are also medications that can help with some self-stimulatory behaviors linked to sensory sensitivities.

Food sensitivities and eating issues can also be problems. Some children may have limited food preferences, and still others may eat nonfood substances. If food problems are really substantial, a dietitian, nutritionist, or another professional (occupational therapist or SLP) may be needed.

In addition to understanding the unusual sensory responses, it is important to be sure that the child has normal hearing and vision. Obviously, if the child is having a hearing or vision problem, it is important to try to correct this as a major aspect of the intervention program. For individuals with unusual sensitivities to the environment, a number of different steps can be taken, depending on the situation, to make the person more comfortable and better able to learn.

■ READING LIST

Anderson, L., & Emomons, P. G. (2005). *Understanding sensory dysfunction: Learning and development and sensory dysfunction in autism spectrum disorders, ADHD, learning disabilities, and bipolar disorders*. London: Jessica Kingsley.

Baranek, G. T., Boyd, B. A., Poe, M. D., David, F. J., & Watson, L. R. (2007, July). Hyperresponsive sensory patterns in young children with autism, developmental delay, and typical development. *American Journal on Mental Retardation, 112*(4), 233–245.

Baranek, G. T., David, F. J., Poe, M. D., Stone, W. L., & Watson, L. R. (2006). Sensory Experiences Questionnaire: Discriminating sensory features in young children with autism, developmental delays, and typical development. *Journal of Child Psychology and Psychiatry, 47*(6), 591–601.

Baranek, G. T., Parham, D. L., & Bodfish, J. W. (2005). *Sensory and motor features in autism: Assessment and intervention*. In F. R. Volkmar, R. Paul, A. Klin, & D. Cohen (Eds.), *Handbook of autism and pervasive developmental disorders* (3rd ed. , pp. 831–862). Hoboken, NJ: Wiley.

Bogdashina, O. (2003). *Sensory perceptual issues in autism and Asperger syndrome: Different sensory experiences, different perceptual worlds*. London: Jessica Kingsley.

Fowler, S. (2008). *Multisensory rooms and environments*. London: Jessica Kinglsey.

Heflin, L. J. & Alaimo, D. F. (2007). *Students with autism spectrum disorders: Effective instructional practices*. Upper Saddle River, NJ: Pearson.

Klin, A., Jones, W., Schultz, R., Volkmar, F., & Cohen, D. (2002). Visual fixation patterns during viewing of naturalistic social situations as predictors of social competence in individuals with autism. *Archives of General Psychiatry, 59*(9), 809–816.

Kranowitz, C. S. (1995). *101 activities for kids in tight spaces: At the doctor's office, on car, train, and plane trips, home sick in bed*. New York: St. Martin's Press.

Kranowitz, C. S., Sava, D. I., Haber, E., Balzer-Martin, L., & Szklut, S. (2001). *Answers to questions teachers ask about sensory integration* (2nd ed.). Las Vegas, NV: Sensory Resources.

Legge, B. (2008). *Can't Eat, Won't Eat. Dietary Difficulties and Autistic Spectrum Disorders.* London: Jessica Kingsley

Myles, B. S., Cook, K. T., Miller, N. E., Rinner, L., & Robbins, L. A. (2001). *Asperger syndrome and sensory issues: Practical solutions for making sense of the world.* Shawnee Mission, KS: Autism Asperger.

Myles, B. S., Hagiwara, T., Dunn, W., Rinner, L., Reese, M., Huggins, A., et al. (2004). Sensory issues in children with Asperger syndrome and autism. *Education and Training in Developmental Disabilities, 39*(4), 283–290.

Rogers, S. J., Hepburn, S., & Wehner, E. (2003). Parent reports of sensory symptoms in toddlers with autism and those with other developmental disorders. *Journal of Autism and Developmental Disorders, 33*(6), 631–642.

Rogers, S. J., & Ozonoff, S. (2005). What do we know about sensory dysfunction in autism? A critical review of the empirical evidence. *Journal of Child Psychology and Psychiatry, 46* (12), 1255–1268.

■ QUESTIONS AND ANSWERS

1. **A child with autism is included in my first-grade classroom. Particularly during some activities, he gets very involved in visual self-stimulation at school. This seems to happen during art, recess, and gym. I've heard from our consultant that this behavior may reflect overstimulation, but these seem to be the times most students are more relaxed. This child will look at his fingers and flick them back and forth. Sometimes he looks at things out of the corner of his eye. All these things seem very odd. What can be done about this?**

   The behaviors you describe are fairly common in autism, and your consultant is correct that often they reflect overstimulation (it can also happen for children who are understimulated!). The main feature that all the times you mention have in common is that they are probably less structured and more "free-form" and more social. What may seem like a relaxing situation to you may be making the child with autism more anxious. Take a look at the classroom during these times. How included is the child? Are there more distractions than usual? See if giving the child a specific agenda/visual schedule or prompts helps. It may be that giving special activities (one on one or small group) during these periods may be helpful.

2. **My daughter loves to put all kinds of things into her mouth. This includes dirt and stuff she has picked right up off the floor. What can I do about this?**

In the first place, be sure the environment is lead free and have your daughter's lead level tested. Talk to the school psychologist, speech pathologist, occupational therapist, or behavior specialist. Often, these are the same people who will be working on the problem at school. If your daughter has a strong need to chew, try providing something safe to chew (avoid things that stick to the teeth and cause cavities, though—notably, fruit sticks are bad!). Sometimes crunchy foods or access to materials that can be chewed without swallowing will help. Occasionally, children respond well to activities that include blowing or sucking.

3. **My 9-year-old son likes to body rock a lot. This makes him seem very odd. What can I do about it?**

    Sometimes giving the child more opportunities for physical activity during the day can help. This can include running and other, more strenuous activities but could also include use of a rocking chair or swing. Sometimes using seats that have a degree of "give" (large therapy balls or cushions) can help with this. You can talk with your occupational therapist about other ideas.

4. **A 22-year-old woman with autism has come to work in our restaurant with a full-time supporter. I notice that she hums a lot, particularly when we get busy at lunchtime. We'd like to keep her as an employee but wonder why she does this and if there is any way to control it?**

    You mention that this is worse in one setting—likely a time when things are most busy and noisy in your restaurant. Talk with her supporter. Our suspicion is that she is overwhelmed with auditory input at the busy times and may be attempting to compensate by producing her own sound. If reducing the sound level is not an option, think about giving her a small portable music player so that she can play her own music. Even just wearing the earplugs or listening to white noise may help.

CHAPTER 17

Managing Sleep and Sleep Problems

Needs for sleep vary considerably over children's development, although those of parents stay the same! Autism and related disorders pose many challenges for parents and family members; of these many challenges, problems in sleep are among some of the most difficult to cope with. There are several reasons why sleep problems can be such a problem:

- Parents, who are often already stressed, can become chronically tired and even frustrated by their child's late bedtimes and frequent awakenings during the night.

- The child who does not get a good night's sleep may have more trouble during the day with problem behaviors and with learning.

- Poor nighttime sleeping may result in changes in sleep patterns (such as daytime napping) that can disrupt the family and interfere with school and behavioral interventions.

In this chapter, we talk about some of the problems that children with autism and autism spectrum disorders (ASDs) have with sleep and discuss some of the reasons why these problems exist. We also review some potential resources and solutions. Keep in mind, however, that compared to other troubles, sleep problems can be more difficult than most to deal with, and you may need some special help to cope with them. More than half of children with autism will, at some point, have problems with sleep that last over a month and are distressing to them or their parents.

TYPICAL SLEEP PATTERNS

In understanding sleep problems, it helps to know a little bit about sleep and how our sleep patterns evolve in childhood. Infants spend much of their time asleep and their level of awareness seems to vary along a continuum from deep sleep to light sleep to drowsiness to alertness. During the first month or so of life, the typical baby will sleep about two-thirds of the time. Regular patterns of sleeping and wakefulness are not yet established, but during much of this time the infant is having rapid eye movement (REM) sleep—parents can see the baby's eyes move even while she is asleep! This is the part of sleep when dreaming occurs. As time goes on, the various stages of alertness and sleep become more and more clearly defined. These changes in sleep patterns also reflect other changes, such as in brain wave patterns, and seem to go along with the increasing maturity of the brain.

Throughout life, there is a pattern of cycling between deeper and lighter stages of sleep during the night, with awakenings being much more likely to occur during lighter stages of sleep. Children who are considered "good sleepers" may awaken briefly but immediately go back to sleep on their own during these periods. Children with problematic sleep often end up staying awake during these transition times and require parental intervention to fall back to sleep. The lighter stages of sleep appear every 50 to 90 minutes (depending on the age of the child). In addition to this pattern of cycling, a pattern of daytime/ nighttime awakening/sleep also becomes established. A full-term baby will spend about half his sleep time in REM sleep. This percentage gradually decreases with age so that by age 5, only about 20% of a child's sleep is spent this way. During the first several months, there is not usually a pattern of different daytime and nighttime sleeping, but at around 4 months this starts to shift for most babies. Around this time, the baby will start to move toward a pattern of doing more sleeping at night, although he still will be asleep during much of the day. The age at which sleeping through the night occurs on a regular basis is quite variable. Most babies will sleep for a 6- to 8-hour stretch by 6 months. Some will do this as early as 3 to 4 months of age, and, unfortunately for parents, some much later than 6 months. Between 6 and 15 months, most children start to sleep 10 to 12 hours at night. There will also be regular daytime naps.

Problems with sleeping are fairly common in typically developing toddlers; about one-third of infants and young children have some kind of sleep problem. These may include reluctance to go to bed and get to sleep, waking during the night, and waking too early in the morning. Generally, such sleep problems get better with age, and some physicians will tell parents the "tincture of time" treatment is indicated, that is, that the child will outgrow the problem. For typically developing children, a pattern of daytime–nighttime sleeping like an adult's will usually be quite well established, with only a small group still having problems by the middle childhood ages. Unfortunately, this often is not true for children with autism and related difficulties.

> ## COMMON CAUSES OF SLEEP DISORDERS
>
> - Lack of consistent bedtime routine
> - Lack of exercise
> - New medical problems or illnesses
> - Side effects of medications

SLEEP IN AUTISM

For many children with autism and related conditions, the development of more typical sleep patterns can take much longer. Studies suggest that somewhere between 40% and 80% or so of children with autism either have or have had sleep problems. Sometimes parents will tell us that sleep has never been a problem. Other times parents will tell us that their child slept pretty well as an infant, but then sleep seemed to get more disorganized. For example, as a toddler, she might have started to wake during the night and climb into her parents' bed or demand attention. Also, it seems that many children with autism may not sleep through the night on a regular basis until much later in life. They may stay up late and sometimes cause troubles for themselves and their parents as they wander about the house at night. Sometimes the problem is that they wake up early. Or they may be highly dependent on quite specific and precise bedtime routines, which sometimes get more and more complicated over time, with any violation of the routine leading to a rough night.

Many parents are up for a good part of the night waiting until the child finally goes to sleep so that they can go to bed. As parents become more tired and stressed, they may have more difficulty coping with their child (and other parts of their lives) in the daytime, which may further contribute to the child's troubles.

There is a small but growing body of research on this important problem. It can, however, be difficult to understand all the studies, since often there are major differences in the ways the investigators approached the problem or because they studied only very small groups of children, so we don't have a good sense of how "typical" the population of very atypical children really is. Most importantly, very few studies have followed the same children over time; these longitudinal studies would be very important in helping us understand how sleep problems change over time. There is also not as much information about sleep problems in children with Asperger's and other ASDs as there is for those with classical autism. As a result, there is, unfortunately, no unanimous agreement among researchers on the true nature of the sleep troubles in autism. For example, some researchers suggest that it is younger children with autism who are most likely to have sleep problems. Others suggest that the issue has less to do with age and more with the child's overall level of development. Still others suggest that differences are not strongly related to either the child's age or developmental level! Some argue that perhaps parents of children with special needs may be more sensitive to sleep problems, although recent data suggest that, if anything, sleep problems are much more common in children with ASD.

In one study from California, it was found that a bit more than 50% of parents of school-aged children with ASDs reported sleep problems. This was confirmed by use of **sleep diaries** (records parents kept of the child's sleep), as well as a questionnaire. This number is consistent with reports from other researchers. The problems parents noted included difficulties in getting their child to sleep as well as frequent awakenings in their child. In this study, there were some age-related changes in sleep. For example, younger children who did not have sleep problems slept longer than older children who did not have sleep problems. However, in the children who had sleep problems, these age-related changes were not seen nearly as strongly. In this study, it was also true that parents of children with sleep problems were, as we might expect, more likely to feel stressed and hassled than parents of children who were "good" sleepers. It also seemed that, if anything, parents probably underreported sleep problems, most likely because they were used to them! Unfortunately, we don't know how representative the group of children in this study was, but it is clear that sleep problems are very common.

We don't know all the reasons why sleep patterns don't become well organized for many children with autism and other developmental disabilities. There have been many theories and speculations, but relatively little research has been done. There likely are very complicated relationships between the developmental problems and a lack of sleep, which tends to cycle on itself by causing chronic tiredness and further sleep difficulties. Lack of physical exercise, which typically developing children get through social play at a young age, may also contribute. Some investigators have suggested that some of the brain problems that are responsible for the autism in the first place may disrupt the child's sleep. For example, perhaps problems with brain chemistry that affect the neurotransmitters or hormone levels may be responsible for some of the sleep disturbances. Basic problems in the day–night cycle may also be involved. One reassuring fact for parents is that while children with ASDs are more likely than typically developing children to have sleep problems, the types of sleep problems they have are the same.

SUGGESTIONS FOR HOW TO SOLVE SLEEP DISORDERS

- Keep a sleep diary for 1 to 2 weeks to help understand the problem.
- Make sure the child is tired by increasing exercise; decreasing daytime sleeping; or changing type, dose, or timing of medications.
- Avoid foods, drinks, or activities that overstimulate the child at bedtime.
- Work toward having the child fall asleep on his own at the beginning of the night.

DEALING WITH SLEEP PROBLEMS—SOME GENERAL ADVICE

Fortunately, there are a number of steps you can take to help the child have and maintain a more reasonable sleep cycle. Keeping a sleep diary for at least a week to give detailed accounting of the times, routines, and problems you are encountering can be very helpful. Sometimes parents themselves are so sleep deprived that they don't always remember all of the details of the sleep problems. The doctor may be better at making suggestions once he or she sees a detailed description of the problems you are facing.

One of the simple things to try first, as with other behavior problems in autism, is to try to capitalize on the child's desire for structure and consistency. That is, try to use the child's desire for routine and predictability to help establish a reasonable sleep pattern. This means having a bedtime routine that is followed consistently. Approximately 15 to 30 minutes for the entire routine seems to work well. You should also be consistent in the choice of the predetermined bedtime—the goal of the bedtime routine. The bedtime routine should include whatever activities and preparations you and the child can use in getting set for bed. A review of the day's events, a relaxing bath, and a story or other favorite (but quiet) activity in the bed all may help. The use of visual schedules or stories specifically focused on bedtime may also be helpful here. You can make a bedtime book or a story board with pictures that outlines the bedtime routine and then turn over a picture as each bedtime activity is completed. Be sure to avoid any activities or foods that the child would find very stimulating at this time of day. Too much exercise just before bedtime may make it harder for the child to fall asleep. Also, avoid all drinks or food with caffeine for at least 6 hours before bedtime.

As with other activities, always think about building in some slight variations to the usual routine, since children with autism may tend to become very rigid about everything involved in the ritual of going to sleep. Try, when you can, to vary things a bit to be sure the child has some flexibility when things can't always be the same. You may, for example, want to have a couple of different books the child can look at with you before going to sleep. If the child has a favorite object he sleeps with, it is okay to use it every night (but then be careful because you'll need to have it!). While a routine may help the child get to sleep, you don't want to be stuck with too rigid or involved a bedtime routine that takes forever to get just right. Ideally, after the routine is over, you will leave the room with the child awake in bed falling asleep on his own.

Keep in mind that while the goal is to help the child get to sleep at a reasonable hour, what you can actually control is only that the child is in bed on time. If the child stays up for a while but is quiet in her bedroom, that may be perfectly fine. Try not to teach the child to be dependent on you for falling and staying asleep. For many parents, the most burdensome part of sleeping difficulties is coping with the child's need for the parent(s) every night as part of his bedtime routine. When children have this need and have difficulties falling asleep, parents can quickly find themselves sleep deprived. Some parents will end up sleeping with their child, although then the child's tendency to wake up frequently may make it difficult for the parent to get a good night's sleep (not to mention complicating relationships with the spouse). Also, if the child's bedtime routine requires that you are with him to actually fall asleep, it is more likely that when he wakes up at night he is going to want you there to help him get back to sleep.

Give the child the chance to get to sleep on her own and don't "hover" around her. Praise and rewards can be used—again, not necessarily for sleep but for quiet time in the bedroom. If the child needs a bottle or glass of water next to the bed, that is fine. However, be careful not to get into the habit of giving the child a snack, since this can unintentionally reinforce getting up!

Pay attention to the environment in the bedroom. Is it one that will help the child get to sleep (and stay asleep) or is it one that will "jazz" him up and make getting to sleep even more difficult? Try not to have the child play on the bed at other times of the day; rather, reserve it for sleep. Some children are very sensitive to sounds, and the sound of the furnace coming on may, for example, be a source of annoyance to him. Occasionally, parents tell us that working to quiet the various noises in the house (dishwasher, laundry, etc.) helps. Other parents buy a "white noise" machine or similar device to hide or mask other noises that bother their child; there are many variations available, some with a choice of sounds like rain, waves at the beach, and so on. Determining the right amount of light can also be crucial. Some children cannot sleep with too much light in the room or hall. Others need the light for reassurance. This may vary with the child's age.

Whatever else you do, do not make the mistake of encouraging problematic sleep patterns, for example, by letting the child miss school because she had a "bad night." This is a surefire ticket to disaster as the problem starts to build and cycles on itself and the child becomes even more likely to stay up at night and sleep in the daytime. When you are tired and stressed and dealing with a tired child, it can be very easy for you to unintentionally reinforce the behavior that is causing trouble in the first place!

Pay attention to the child's schedule of daily activities. Excessive sleep (naps) during the day can cause trouble with nighttime sleep. If this is a problem, try to restrict nap times or shorten them. Be very sure that the child has enough physical activity during the day. In addition to its many benefits for health (and often for socialization), regular exercise will help the child feel tired when the end of the day comes. It can be worth it to hire an active, energetic teenager whose job is to engage the child in some vigorous physical activity before dinner! However, be sure not to have too much exercise too close to bedtime or it may prevent sleeping at that time. Try, as much as you can, to help the child establish a regular pattern or cycle of sleep and waking that is as much like yours as possible.

Dealing With Specific Sleep Problems

Difficulty Getting to Sleep

One of the biggest sleep problems that parents face is getting their child to sleep in the first place. Some people spend hours trying to get their child to sleep, while others stay up much later than they like. There are several different strategies that can be used to deal with this problem. We will discuss a few of these here. If the child has sleep problems that don't respond to these suggestions, look at the reading list at the end of the chapter for additional resources (your doctor and other parents can often be good sources of additional information as well).

As mentioned earlier, one of the most important places to start in trying to improve the child's sleep habits is to set a specific schedule for the bedtime routine, including when it will start, what activities will be involved, and when the child must be in bed. The idea here is to use the tendency of children with autism to be a bit rigid in helping you set a regular and predictable routine that the child will want to follow. Even with a good, consistent schedule, many children won't go easily to bed. Many are used to their parent(s) being with them until they fall asleep. Some people recommend gradually distancing yourself from the child in his room. For example, if the child is used to having a parent lie on his bed until he falls asleep, you can start by sitting beside him on the side of the bed instead of lying down. If that works for a few nights, you can start sitting at the end of the bed. Eventually, you can work your way to a chair in the room and then into the hall (but where the child can still see you), and eventually out of view altogether. This method does not work for all children, but has the advantage of not causing much distress.

Another popular method for reducing the child's reliance on you is called "graduated extinction" by some sleep experts. This involves putting the child into bed by herself and letting her cry for a short, previously set amount of time. Usually, this is less than 10 minutes. After that, you go back into the room to reassure the child that you are near and to assure yourself that the child is okay. You shouldn't pick the child up or turn on the lights or start to play, but just quickly check on her and leave. You can gradually increase the amount of time you let the child cry before you check on her. This method allows the child to learn how to settle herself down to sleep. Some children will start sleeping on their own within a few days to weeks. It does not work for all children and parents. One of the problems is that many parents cannot stand to see (or hear) their child being upset. It might also be a problem if the child is extremely hard to calm down once she gets upset and starts banging her head.

Another method that is less likely to upset the child is referred to as *bedtime fading*. In this method, you determine what time the child always seems to get so tired he finally falls asleep. This is usually quite a long time after the originally planned bedtime, say 1AM. But once you determine this time, you start to put the child to bed an hour or so later than the time he will fall asleep quickly. Then you gradually move the bedtime back to the originally desired time. Usually, you move it back about 15 minutes every few days until you get to the desired time.

Difficulty With Nighttime Awakenings

Many children go to sleep well but wake up during the night and then don't go back to sleep easily or quickly. If the child can fall asleep on her own at the beginning of the night, she is more likely to get back to sleep on her own if she wakes up during the night. Studies of typically developing children show that they frequently wake up briefly during the night as they transition through the different stages of sleep. The children we call "good sleepers" (who sleep through the night) are the ones who settle back to sleep on their own during the night without needing their parents. If the bedtime routine involves the parent holding the child, or lying next to her in bed, singing to her, or providing something to drink, the same interventions are frequently needed when the child awakens at night. If a child gets into bed awake and falls asleep without the parent there, she has a much better chance of getting back to sleep alone during the night.

Sometimes you have to use methods such as graduated extinction (described earlier) to get the child back to sleep in the middle of the night. Some children with ASDs who wake up during the night may engage in body rocking or other kinds of stereotyped movements. If the movement helps the child get back to sleep and doesn't otherwise cause trouble, you probably won't need to interfere with it. Other behaviors may need more specific intervention. For example, some children engage in head banging, which we talk about later in the chapter. Sometimes behaviors like head banging can be made worse by paying a lot of attention to them. At other times the behavior will be sufficiently serious that you have to pay attention to it. In these complicated situations, it is very helpful to get some outside advice and perspectives. Both the child's health care providers and other professionals such as psychologists or occupational therapists may be helpful. Other habits, such as teeth grinding, may also need special interventions.

Early or Late Awakenings

Sometimes noises or too much light will awaken the child earlier than you want. If these environmental factors are contributing to early awakening, they are easy enough to change. For example, put up shades or curtains to keep the room dark. You can also try putting the child to bed a bit later in hopes that he may sleep longer, although this does not always work. Sometimes the thing to do is help the child learn to play quietly on his own in his bedroom until the household is up. As time goes on, the child can have a list of early morning activities to engage in that will help him transition more easily into the day.

Some children have trouble getting up in the morning. Sometimes this is part of a more complicated set of difficulties (such as going to sleep too late). It is important to realize that one of the important goals for the child is to have a fairly normal sleep–wake cycle. We've seen children who are basically up during the night and asleep during the day—a situation that helps neither parents nor child get a good night's sleep! No one can take advantage of their educational program when they are sleep deprived. With the occasional, understandable exception, you do not want the child to sleep too late in the morning.

If the child has trouble getting up, then look at ways that you might help her wake up in the morning in a lower key way—a tape recorder set to come on with a favorite song or CD, letting a favorite pet into the room to wake the child up, and so forth. Again, having a plan with a clear goal and set of graduated steps can be helpful.

Wandering During the Night

Nighttime wandering refers to children who get up and roam (wander) about the house. It is one thing if the child gets up only to go to the bathroom or get a drink; it is much more difficult if the child is getting into trouble, for example, by leaving the house or engaging in behaviors that might be dangerous. If the child has problems with wandering at night, you can think about some modifications to the environment to ensure his safety. Possible solutions include:

- Use strategically placed baby monitors. By strategically placed, we mean putting these just outside the child's bedroom so you don't have to listen to every noise that the child makes at night but will know when he decides to venture outside the room.

- You may need a gate at the door to keep a younger child from wandering outside the room (and possibly hurting himself).

- If the older child can get over a baby gate, you may do well with a Dutch door (one with a top and bottom half), where you can lock the bottom half but keep the top part open.

If the child tries to get out of the house, you'll clearly need to take more extensive precautions, such as double locking the front and back doors with a key that you keep hidden near the door or having an alarm that goes off if the door is opened (see Chapter 11 for more on keeping the house safe).

Nighttime Bedwetting (Enuresis)

Bedwetting during sleep (nocturnal **enuresis**) is seen in many typically developing children, particularly boys who are otherwise dry in the daytime. This problem tends to get much better as children get older, although it persists into adolescence for a few children. Among typical children, those who are very deep sleepers are more likely to be the ones with enuresis.

Many children with autism/pervasive developmental disorder (PDD) have a prolonged period of toilet training, although for others, toilet training goes fairly close to schedule (see Chapter 15). Some children become toilet trained during the day but then wet themselves at night. Sometimes they have never had a period of being consistently dry through the night and other times they are able to be dry for a period of time (typically a month or longer) but then lose this ability and start to wet again.

For typically developing children, nighttime bedwetting can be a major problem. Depending on the child's developmental level, this may or may not be distressing to the child (but can still be quite distressing to parents). Before trying any of the solutions in this section, consult the doctor. Also, keep in mind that the goal is to be sure not to disrupt any progress the child has already made in getting to sleep!

Studies of children in special sleep laboratories suggest that most of the time bedwetting happens early in the morning. Usually, there is no specific physical cause for the bedwetting. Limiting fluids in the evenings usually does not help children stay dry at night. (Obviously, if the child is drinking a tremendous amount, that may be a problem.) Sometimes children who had previously been dry at night start bedwetting after experiencing some upsetting event. Sometimes this event is quite understandable, for example, the birth of a new brother or sister or a move from one house to another. But sometimes the responses of children with ASDs are very different from those of other children, and it may be hard to understand exactly what has gotten the child upset or stressed. If the bedwetting is a new symptom, you should check with the doctor about getting a urine culture, just to be sure that the bedwetting is not due to a urinary tract infection.

Both behavioral and drug treatments are available for bedwetting that occurs once daytime toilet training had been established. A hormone called desmopressin (DDAVP) helps many children and can be taken at bedtime as a chewable pill. It requires a prescription from the doctor. It works only while you take it, and the bedwetting problem will continue until the child outgrows it. Some other drugs have been used for short times for older children and can be very effective; as with any medication, the potential risks of the medicine should, as always, be balanced against the potential benefits.

Behavioral methods have commonly used a technique referred to as the **bell and pad**, in which the child sleeps on a special pad that sounds an alarm when she wets the bed. This is supposed to wake the child up, and, over time, she should learn to stay dry. Unfortunately, sometimes other people in the house wake up, but the child with the bedwetting problem sleeps through the alarm.

Over time, most children do become dry. If you reach a point where the hassles involved in changing wet sheets every morning are too much for you, keep the option of using large-size "pull-ups" in mind, until the child is consistently dry in the morning.

Nightmares and Night Terrors

Occasionally, verbal children with autism will complain of nightmares, often associated with specific fears. Nightmares tend to happen in the later part of the night and the child may remember some part of the bad dream. Nightmares may also occur when children are sick. Usually, going to the child and reassuring him that he was just dreaming is sufficient. If the child has repeated nightmares, however, it may be worthy trying to understand more about it. For example, if the child is chronically having frightening dreams about school, find out if anything unusual is going on at school.

Night terrors (also called sleep terrors) are different from nightmares. These tend to happen in the first part of the night's sleep. The child arouses but does not awaken completely, seems to be in a panic, and may not be able to explain what has happened. Unlike with nightmares, the child will have little memory of any content of night terrors. Sometimes night terrors are associated with sleep-walking (somnambulism). If the child seems to be having night terrors, be sure to discuss this with the doctor. Very rarely, the symptoms of temporal lobe seizures (see Chapter 12) may be similar.

If you keep a log of the night terrors, you may discover that they happen at about the same time each night. Sometimes waking the child up briefly about a half-hour before the night terror is expected and then allowing her to fall back to sleep will decrease the chance of having a night terror.

The most important thing to know about sleep terrors and sleepwalking is that it is important to keep the child safe. You can use a baby monitor or alarm system to alert you if the child is up and wandering. Sometimes drug treatment is indicated, but only if the problem is severe.

Head Banging and Body Rocking

Some typically developing children (roughly around 5%) will bang their heads or body on the crib or bed. This usually starts in very young children (under a year). Body rocking before the child falls asleep is also seen. In typically develop-ing children, these behaviors tend to disappear on their own, sometimes fairly quickly, but at other times they may go on for several years. These movements are likely pleasurable to the child and are a form of self-soothing around the occasionally anxiety-provoking transition to sleep.

Children with autism and related disorders also sometimes head bang or body rock at night. These behaviors may, however, persist in children with autism for a longer period of time and may become part of the child's nighttime sleeping ritual. Often, these movements are not a major problem, but sometimes the be-havior may escalate over time and pose a threat to the child.

If the child has these behaviors, keep several things in mind. First, make sure the child is safe. Putting pillows or pads around the bed may help. Second, ask yourself if anything seemed to set the behavior off. Did you move to a new house? Was there a change in the child's behavior during the day? Is she having pain anywhere; for example, are new teeth coming in? If you can figure out what set the behavior off, you may be able to think about some potential solu-tions. Third, consider whether the child might be using head banging for some reason, such as to communicate frustration or to get attention. For example, does the child stop head banging when you come into the room? Does she stop if you can identify something she wants? Behaviors like head banging can be very effective at getting parental attention, and this, in turn, may reinforce the child's behavior.

There are some things that people suggest to try to help with these problems, but unfortunately, they don't always work. Try putting a clock with a loud "tick-tock" in the room. Sometimes the rhythm of the sound of the clock will soothe the child. Or try other forms of rhythmical sounds, such as a sound generator to mimic the sound of the beach or of rain falling. Some parents have used a metronome.

If there are serious concerns about injury, parents will need to take additional steps to ensure the child's safety. If the pillows/cushion approach hasn't worked, you can try taking the bed out of the room and putting the mattress on the floor. (This may be particularly helpful if body rocking is the main problem.) The bed-time fading method described earlier of putting the child to bed so late that he is so tired he falls asleep without head banging or rocking may be helpful. Very occasionally, parents have to resort to having their child wear a helmet or some other protective gear in order to avoid head injury. If you are concerned about the child's safety at night, consult a behavior specialist for suggestions.

Teeth Grinding

Like head banging and body rocking, grinding of the teeth **(bruxism)** is fairly common in typically developing children. In fact, as many as 10% or so of typically developing younger children may grind their teeth. In typically developing children, the problem tends to go away over time, doesn't cause trouble for the teeth, and usually does not need any special treatment.

In children with ASDs, teeth grinding can be more persistent and thus cause more trouble. As with bedtime body rocking, occasionally teeth grinding seems to be stress related; see if you can find any connection to potentially stressful events in the child's life. At other times, it may be more self-stimulatory. Sometimes teeth grinding is more of a problem for parents than for the child, but it can cause dental problems, and a dentist or other specialist may need to be involved if it persists.

MEDICAL ISSUES AND MEDICATIONS

Keep in mind that some medical problems, as well as some medicines and foods or drinks that have caffeine, give people problems with sleep. If, for example, the child is drinking many sodas with caffeine in them, you may want to switch to caffeine free.

If the child has been sleeping well but suddenly starts having sleeping troubles, it is worth asking yourself whether he is getting sick or is uncomfortable. This is a complicated issue, particularly for children who are not yet able to use words well to communicate. Some children who have gas or intestinal pain may have trouble sleeping. Has the child been started on a new medicine that might be upsetting his stomach? Other medical problems such as ear infections or urinary tract (bladder) infections or gastrointestinal problems (like reflux) may also disrupt sleep. Ask the child's doctor if any physical problems might be causing trouble. For example, sometimes breathing problems cause sleep difficulties. This may be related to very enlarged tonsils and adenoids, for example, or sometimes to allergies. Being very overweight can also cause some sleep problems. Notice if the sleep problems seem to come and go, for example, with the change of season. Ask yourself if there are any regularities to the child's sleep troubles. Some children seem to have more trouble in winter; others in summer. Any such regularities might help you understand what may be going on. For example, if the child has sleeping difficulties only in winter after you turn on the furnace, it might be worth checking for allergies to dust mites that commonly live in air ducts and get stirred up again once the furnace is switched on.

If the child receives medications, ask the doctor or pharmacist whether these might be affecting sleep. Medicine the child is given for other reasons might also help with sleep problems if they tend to make her drowsy. If so, you can ask whether these medicines could be given at nighttime. These medicines include some of those given for behavior problems (see Chapter 14) and some given for other reasons, such as allergies or seizures.

Parents often ask us about medicines that might help their child with autism go to sleep. These, unfortunately, work with variable success. Medicines for sleep problems are best used as a last resort, for example, at a time when you know you are likely to have trouble (on a vacation or when a parent is away) or to deal with an expected situation or crisis. You should be aware that these are, at best, a temporary solution. There are various medicines that can be used. These include a range of different medicines, and the doctor would be the best person to speak to about this possibility.

A commonly used nonprescription medication for temporary relief is diphenhydramine (Benadryl). It is an antihistamine that often makes people a bit drowsy (sometimes that is enough). There are also many prescription medicines to help people sleep. These include other antihistamines, barbiturates and other sedatives, and medicines such as diazepam (Valium) and the related group of medicines called the benzodiazepines (see Chapter 15). These sometimes help children with autism, for periods of time, although some children get "hyper" on them. One of the problems with these medicines is that if you take them on a regular basis, the body gets used to them and you must take a larger dose over time.

Melatonin has received a great deal of publicity in recent years as a "natural" cure for sleep problems. It makes people sleepy and also helps to reset their sleep cycles. It is a hormone that is secreted normally by a part of the brain called the pineal gland. The body puts out more melatonin as it gets darker outside. There is some research on the use of melatonin to help with sleep problems in children with various disabilities. A few reports mention its use in autism. None of these are large, well-designed studies. The doses given vary over the different studies, and none of the studies look at the possible side effects of long-term use. All this being said, some studies report success. Doses mentioned most frequently are between 1 and 3 mg a half-hour before bedtime, although some authors recommend an even smaller dose and others a larger dose. Melatonin is not a prescription drug and is sold widely in health food stores. Keep in mind that because it is not a prescription drug, it is not regulated by the Food and Drug Administration (FDA). Be sure to discuss the use of melatonin with the child's health care provider before trying it.

If the child has significant sleep problems, the doctor may want to refer you to someone who specializes in the use of medicines in the treatment of autism, as sometimes the process of finding the right medicine can be tricky. Occasionally, children with autism will have the opposite reaction to what is expected (or what is called *paradoxical reaction*) when given a medicine for help with sleep. As a result, it is usually a very good idea to try the medicine at home once or twice before you use it elsewhere (to be sure that it seems to work well). As with any medicine, there are risks and potential benefits, and you should discuss these with the doctor before trying the medicine.

When All Else Fails

When you feel you have done a reasonable job in trying to deal with sleep problems but they still occur, ask the doctor about other resources that may be available. There are a number of professionals who may be able to help, including psychologists and physicians who are interested in autism and related conditions, as well as specialists in sleep problems. Many major medical centers have sleep disorder clinics that may be a resource for you. Also consult some of the reading material found in the reading list for this chapter.

SUMMARY

In this chapter, we discussed some of the most common sleep problems in children with autism and related disorders. Some children with autism have difficulty falling asleep, others with staying asleep, and yet others with waking up early in the morning. Since insufficient sleep at night can add to the child's learning and behavioral problems during the day and also impair parents' own coping abilities, you should never just accept sleep problems as an inevitable part of autism. Various methods can be useful in helping the child achieve and maintain a good sleep pattern.

READING LIST

Andersen, I. M., Kaczmarska, J., McGrew, S. G., & Malow, B. A. (2008, May). Melatonin for insomnia in children with autism spectrum disorders. *Journal of Child Neurology, 23* (5), 482–485.

Durand, V. M. (1998). *Sleep better! A guide to improving sleep for children with special needs.* Baltimore: Brookes.

Durand, V. M. (2008). *When children don't sleep well: Interventions for pediatric sleep disorders, parent workbook.* New York: Oxford University Press.

Ferber, R. (1985). *Solve your child's sleep problems.* New York: Simon & Schuster.

Ferber, R. (2006). Solve your child's sleep problems: New, revised, and expanded edition (Rev. ed.). New York: Simon & Schuster.

Johnson, K. P., & Malow, B. A.(March 2008). Sleep in children with autism spectrum disorders. *Current Neurology and Neuroscience Reports, 8*(2), 155–161.

Johnson, K. P., & Malow, B. A. (Oct., 2008). Assessment and pharmacological treatment of sleep disturbance in autism. *Child and Adolescent Psychiatric Clinics of North America, 17,* 773–785.

Pantley, E., & Sears, W. (2002). *The no-cry sleep solution: Gentle ways to help your baby sleep through the night.* Columbus, OH: McGraw-Hill.

Polimeni, M. A., Richdale, A. L., & Francis, A. J. (April, 2005). A survey of sleep problems in autism, Asperger's disorder and typically developing children. *Journal of Intellectual Disability Research, 49*(Pt 4), 260–268.

Weiskop, S., Richdale, A., & Matthews, J. (February, 2005). Behavioural treatment to reduce sleep problems in children with autism or fragile X syndrome. *Developmental Medicine and Child Neurology, 47*(2), 94–104.

Weissbluth, M. (2005). *Healthy sleep habits, happy child.* New York: Ballantine Books.

QUESTIONS AND ANSWERS

1. **My son seemed to be sleeping fine but then we went away on vacation and he was so excited he stayed up most of the night. Now he seems to have day and night mixed up—he is sleeping most of the day and up at night. What can I do about this?**

   It sounds like you already have a pretty good sense of the problem—somehow his sleep cycle has gotten mixed up. You should try to keep him awake during the day, not letting him have naps, and be sure that he is good and tired by the time that bedtime comes. In the beginning, try to keep him up late enough that he'll fall asleep quickly, and then gradually try to move it back to a more reasonable hour.

2. **My child is toilet trained during the day but still has accidents sometimes at night. What can I do about this?**

There are several things you can do. First, look to see if there is any pattern or regularity to when the nighttime wetting occurs. Is it every night? Is it on nights when he has gone to bed early? Is a trip to the toilet part of the nighttime routine? Is the child drinking excessively in the evening? Discuss this with the doctor. If there seems to be no particular pattern, there are several things you can try; both behavioral intervention and medications can often be helpful.

3. **We have a 12-year-old with Asperger's disorder. He was just started on long-acting stimulant medications to help with his attention. It has helped with that, but he is now having a lot of trouble sleeping at night. Could this be because of the medicine?**

Yes, it could. You may want to talk with the doctor who is prescribing the medicine to see if you could change either the dose or the time you give it. A shorter acting medicine might be better for your son.

CHAPTER 18

Considering Complementary and Alternative Treatments

It is not surprising that many different treatments have been tried for a condition like autism—indeed, almost every treatment you can think of has been tried over the years. In this chapter, we focus on some of the treatments that are often referred to as *alternative* treatments (undertaken instead of more conventional treatments) or as *complementary* treatments (treatments undertaken in combination with more traditional treatments). Another way to refer to this group of treatments is as *nonestablished*; that is, the research showing that the treatment actually works is either minimal or nonexistent. Sometimes there is a fine line between established and nonestablished treatments; occasionally, as research is done, treatments move between alternative and mainstream. At other times, as we discuss, treatments that start out looking very promising don't pan out the way they are expected. The reading list at the end of the book has a list of references including some Internet resources as well as books and scientific papers that may be of interest to you.

> ### COMPLEMENTARY AND ALTERNATIVE THERAPIES
>
> **Alternative Treatment: INSTEAD of usual or proven treatment**
> **Complementary Treatment: IN ADDITION to proven treatments**

Complementary and alternative medicine (CAM) methods are frequently used, and it is important that both parents and teachers have some information about them. We emphasize that by presenting this information, we want parents and teachers to have information and make informed choices about treatment. By discussing these treatments we are not, of course, endorsing them. We emphasize that deciding what treatments are established and which are not sometimes is difficult. Often things become clearer over time as research is done. Sometimes treatments that have no basis in scientific proof persist. Parents and teachers hear about many different kinds of treatments; Many parents, particularly parents of younger children, investigate alternative treatments. Schools sometimes may be asked to accommodate these treatments in various ways. In this chapter, we discuss some of the more common of these treatments and outline some of the ways to think about them relative to a specific child. Unfortunately, you have to educate yourself a bit in the way science works. This includes understanding the role of peer review, the importance of replication, and understanding what kinds of studies give the best evidence.

UNDERSTANDING HOW SCIENCE WORKS

Science works to evaluate treatment in several different ways. Often, a researcher has an idea or educated guess about something (known as a **hypothesis**) and then sets about to scientifically prove that it is or isn't true. There may or may not be a theory to explain *why* the guess is made. Often, if the treatment looks promising or an observation is interesting, other scientists will try to develop such a theory. Sometimes it is an interesting observation that leads to a major treatment, for example, Alexander Fleming's discovering that penicillin mold slowed the growth of bacteria. What is important in research is that the investigator use the scientific method.

This includes careful description of what the guess or hypothesis is (treatment X will help children with autism learn), a careful description of how the researcher goes about trying to research this (the number of children studied, the nature of their problems, how the treatment was done, etc.). If the results look to be good—and this is defined scientifically by what is called **statistical significance**, usually taken as less than a 1 in 20 chance (or what scientifically is termed a *probability* of less than 5% chance) that what was observed was not an accident—the investigator will then write up the paper and send it out for peer review. A journal editor will assign the paper, which often has the author(s)' name(s) disguised to get feedback. She or he may then accept the paper for publication, reject it, or ask the author to try to modify it to meet any concerns that the scientific reviewers have. Once the paper actually appears in print (or, these days, online), other groups may try to replicate the finding, that is, to see if they can reproduce it. This is important because sometimes things just happen by chance; if a treatment works in New Haven, it should work in San Diego. Some of these issues are summarized in Table 18.1.

In thinking about treatments parents and teachers should try, as much as possible, to give more consideration to treatments that have gone through this process of peer review. This will mean that the study was conducted in a careful way and reported about in a reputable, scientific, reviewed journal. The goal of peer

TABLE 18.1	THE SCIENTIFIC METHOD

Step 1: Asking a question. Typically a researcher notices something and asks a question about it; for example, why does this happen? Or why does this happen now? Or what makes this happen? The researcher might notice that children with autism in school seem more focused after a period of exercise.

Step 2: Literature review. The researcher then looks in the literature to see if other people have noticed the same thing or asked a similar question.

Step 3: Formulate a hypothesis. This is a statement that is to be proven; for example, 30 minutes of exercise before math class will increase attention during class.

Step 4: Experimental design. Now the researcher will develop a study to address the question. In the example of exercise and attention, the researcher might propose a study with two groups of children, some of whom have exercise before math class and others who don't. As part of the design of the study, the researcher would have to think about various factors that might impact the results; for example, will the teachers be aware of the study goals? The researcher also would need to develop a measure (or probably several measures) of what *attention* means in math class. This might be done by systematic observation or by having the children wear small gadgets that record how much they move around. Having some form of scientific control is important, since even just doing something may have an impact. There are many other steps involved here as well; the researcher needs to be sure his measure will be accurate and reliable across children; if people are involved, there are special requirements for informed consent to be met.

Step 5: Data collection and analysis. At this step, the researcher actually conducts the study. Once the data are collected, they are analyzed to see if there are truly differences based on the intervention. Statistical methods are used to see if results are "statistically significant," that is, whether they are more likely to have happened than by chance alone.

Step 6: Preparing a report or paper. The researcher would typically next develop a scientific paper to present the results. Usually, scientific papers include a short summary (abstract) and then a review of the literature, the methods used, the results, and a discussion of what the results mean along with a reference section that lists the research and information the investigator relied on in doing the study.

Step 7: Peer review. The paper is then submitted to a journal, where an editor usually sends it out for peer review; that is, other researchers have a chance to comment on the paper, make suggestions, and tell both the author and editor what they think. These comments are usually done in an anonymous fashion (to help people be very honest). The editor can then reject the paper, ask the author to make revisions, or accept the paper for publication.

Step 8: Replication. Once a finding has been reported, other groups of investigators will attempt to see if they can make the same finding. The replication process is important, particularly for treatment research.

review is not to ban discussion, but rather to inject some element of quality control into what gets published. Many studies that are done never appear in peer-reviewed journals; for example, too few children may have been studied or the peer reviewers had questions about the methods or the ways the results were analyzed or presented.

In this age of instant information, there are many other ways that information may appear or claims may be made about a treatment. For example, someone may say that they presented a paper at a scientific meeting; these are *not* usually peer reviewed. Similarly, you may also hear in the paper or on television about some new treatment; these are almost always *not* peer reviewed.

Even if a treatment is reported in a peer-reviewed journal, you should still evaluate the report carefully. It is important to look at the question being asked, the theory behind the research, the quality of the research study itself, the number of individuals being studied, and the claims made based on the findings. The issues involved in evaluating research vary to some extent depending on the kind of study being done. For some purposes, even very small groups of children can be meaningfully studied. You can, for example, use information on even one child's behavior before and after an intervention and get useful information, if you do this in a careful, scientific way. However, most studies look at larger groups of children (not just an individual child). In general, the larger the groups studied, the more confidence we can have in the results. (It is harder to demonstrate statistical significance with small groups.)

It is also important to look carefully at exactly who is being studied and what measures the researcher has used to ensure that his research is as strong as possible. For example, in the best kinds of studies, there is some attempt to control for the important effects of just being in a study (the placebo effect). The placebo effect refers to all the changes that tend to occur when people are involved in something new. Because this novelty and participation in a study tends to make things better by itself, we want to be sure that what we are testing (a new drug or treatment) works even *better* than the placebo effect. This may involve using a control group (some of the children get treatment A and others do not, or get treatment B instead). Likewise, to avoid the possibility that unintentional bias might distort the results, children might be assigned randomly to treatment groups. Careful attention to issues of diagnosis and assessment is also important. All these precautions make good research difficult but very important to do.

PLACEBO EFFECT

What Is the Placebo Effect?

The placebo effect refers to the many important benefits and effects of being involved in research—these all can make a major change (for the better) in the child.

Why Do Children Get Better on Placebo?

- Research involves high levels of clinician, parent, and teacher involvement.
- Every effort is made to provide high-quality care during a study.
- Symptoms change over time (often people try something new when things are at their worst and the only way for things to change is to get better).
- More attention and interest may benefit the child.

> - The effects of expecting a change for the better can be very important (they can, for example, change how a parent or teacher observes and interacts with the child).

The fact that a report about a treatment is published in a peer-reviewed journal does not necessarily mean that it is really true. Studies always have to be repeated. Sometimes fluke results are observed, and we may be misled into thinking a treatment works when it really doesn't. Also, journals vary in quality—some are more prestigious than others, although even prestigious journals can make mistakes. It is also important to realize that sometimes the first reports of effective treatments are the most positive and that, over time, one gets a better sense of how well the treatment will work. This reflects several different things, including the greater enthusiasm associated with initial treatment studies. For example, although **applied behavior analysis (ABA)** therapy is clearly helpful, it is the case that the earliest reports of its benefits were more dramatically positive than later ones. This often speaks to a combination of factors, including tremendous initial enthusiasm on the part of the investigators and careful adherence to the treatment methods. Often in the real world, treatments may be more difficult to implement. The issue of treatment fidelity is important and also is an issue in CAM treatments; that is, how are practitioners of the treatment trained or certified?

MEDIA AND THE INTERNET AS SOURCES OF INFORMATION

Mark Twain (Figure 18.1) supposedly once said that there are three kinds of stories: stories that are true, stories that are false, and stories you read in the newspapers! You should always keep this saying in mind when you hear reports on the television or radio or in magazines and newspapers. Most newspeople try to be responsible. However, given that the nature of the news business is to sell a product, you might expect that media professionals would be most interested in flamboyant and exciting stories. It is less exciting, for example, to talk about how several years of patient behavioral work with groups of young children with autism makes a difference than it is to report that a new medicine or other intervention "cures" a single child (who may or may not have had autism in the first place). It is also important to realize that stories reporting that "treatment X does not help autism" are also (usually) not of much interest. This is one reason that there is what scientists call a *bias* for only positive case reports to be published. One of the easiest things in the world is to make extravagant claims, which are likely to seem the most exciting and therefore perhaps more newsworthy!

FIGURE 18.1   **Mark Twain**

Source: Courtesy of the Mark Twain House & Museum, Hartford, CT.

We are constantly amazed at how often judgment goes out the window when people hear a sensationalized news account or TV story. We know one set of parents who are stockbrokers, and, understandably, do a very careful job of researching any stock they are about to buy or recommend to their clients. Yet they are perfectly happy to believe anything they hear about the latest treatments in autism and have indeed tried almost all of them!

TYPES OF SCIENTIFIC STUDIES	
Kinds of Evidence	**Strengths and Limitations**
Case report/anecdote	Easy to understand, results may either not be real or apply to only one child, no scientific control
Single case studies	Easier to organize, see the child on and off. Treatment, frequently used in behavioral studies; need to replicate in additional children
Randomized controlled trial	Very good scientific confidence in results, because subjects are randomly assigned, you can be more confident of the results; hard to organize and fund

Double-blind, placebo-controlled study	Most rigorous kind of study, neither parents nor the people evaluating the child know when he is receiving the active treatment (e.g., medication); has ability to show treatment is more than a placebo response; very hard to organize

Evaluating claims for treatments discussed on the Internet is even more challenging. The Internet presents some wonderful opportunities for exchange of information as well as many potential pitfalls. It can help parents connect with each other and with professionals and keep up with current research. One of the great beauties of the Internet is that it is a very free medium—people can say what they want. This is also one of the great problems, since what people say may not always be true. Many of the same considerations we have talked about in understanding claims for treatments apply here—but even more so. There are some, and probably will eventually be more, sources on the Internet that rely on peer review or on another process of quality control, but at present it is usually very hard to know how to make sense out of the various claims made. If you were to believe all the many reports of "cures" for autism, you'd think we wouldn't have any more children with autism—unfortunately, this is not the case!

There are several questions to ask yourself when you are trying to evaluate newspaper, television, or other media stories. First of all, is the story about a single case or a group of children? Is the story about a scientific paper that has appeared in a reputable journal, or is it the claim of someone working more or less outside the usual scientific framework? What claim(s) are being made, and do these make much sense? If something sounds too good to be true, it probably is. A number of television programs and even some otherwise responsible newspapers have chosen particular treatments to highlight and publicize. This happened, for example, with facilitated communication, and, more recently, with secretin.

EVALUATING INTERNET RESOURCES

- Who is responsible for the information? What qualifications does this person or organization have? Who sponsors the site? Government agencies, universities and medical schools, public agencies, and peer-reviewed journals tend to have the most objective sites.

- Has there been some form of peer review, or is what is presented a matter of opinion?

- Are there references or links to credible scientific organizations, papers, and books?

- Does what is said make sense? Who is the treatment supposed to work for and not work for?

- Does anyone make money on the treatment? Be very careful of any sites that tell you to send money immediately. Give yourself time to check things out.

THINKING ABOUT COMPLEMENTARY AND ALTERNATIVE TREATMENTS

If you are exploring possible alternative or other less conventional treatments for your child, here are some questions to keep in mind:

1. **Do the claims make sense?**
   What are the claims being made? Usually, the more dramatic and flamboyant they are, the less likely they are to be true. Is there some attempt at providing a scientific explanation for the treatment? If so, does it make much sense? This can be one of the hardest things for nonprofessionals to figure out. You should use the same amount of caution and good sense you would use in making a major investment, since you will be investing your own and your child's time and, often, your own money.

2. **What is the evidence?**
   If advocates for the treatment claim they have evidence in favor of the treatment, ask to see copies of this evidence. Be very wary if:
   - You are told that it is "going to be published."
   - You are simply given a list of testimonials.
   - You are told that the people doing the treatment are too busy curing autism (or don't have the time or money) to show that the treatment works.

   When you hear testimonials about successful treatments, ask exactly what was done and why. Often, you'll find that proponents of the treatment tried many different things and treatments kind of "rolled into" each other; this makes it hard to understand which of the treatments, if any, was responsible for the change.

   If the data supporting the treatment is based on reports of cases, you should be aware that case reports are sometimes the most difficult kind of evidence to interpret. This is so for any number of reasons. Perhaps the child did not have autism in the first place, or perhaps the researcher was not as objective as he should have been, or maybe the child would have done well no matter what. Find out if there have been any attempts to have an independent assessment of the child or treatment.

3. **Who was involved in the study?**

   Sometimes claims are made for treatments when it is not clear that the children studied really had autism in the first place. Other times, the treatment proposed may be applicable only to a very small subgroup of children with autism. Also keep in mind that a handful of children with autism spectrum disorders (ASDs) do well—pretty much no matter what. This is why controlled studies with groups of children are so important.

   There are other problems as well. Autism is a chronic condition, and, as with any chronic problem, there will be ups and downs over time— periods when the child does better and periods when she does worse. Parents are more likely to seek out treatments when their child is having more trouble, but then the tendency, as the pendulum swings over time, is for the child to get better, and this may have nothing to do with the treatment. Remember, too, that simply the wish and expectation that the child will "get better" may color our objectivity (the placebo effect).

4. **How reputable is the publisher of the study?**

   Another source of confusion for parents has to with other kinds of printed information, for example, book chapters, newsletters, or pamphlets. Chapters in books usually have been the subject of some editing, but only rarely are they really peer reviewed. You can usually do some research on authors, however, and find out whether they have been published in peer-reviewed journals or are associated with reputable universities or organizations. Evaluating newsletters, pamphlets, and similar publications can be even more problematic, and you should be wary of a possible hidden or not-so-hidden agenda. You should always use good common sense in interpreting what you read. Your child's physician may be a good sounding board if you run across an article.

   Keep in mind that even with papers published in peer-reviewed journals, more work remains to be done. It is important to be sure that the work can be replicated and then the implications for future research need to be undersood. Science slowly accumulates knowledge based not only on what we know but also on what mistakes have been made. You can ask your doctor or school professionals if you are not sure a journal is really seen as a serious scientific journal.

Warning Signs for Complementary and Alternative Treatments

There are some important warning signs that suggest that a treatment should be avoided. If you were told that a new kitchen appliance slices, dices, makes ice, mops the floor, and does the dishes, you would be skeptical. The same rule applies here: If the treatment is supposed to treat all aspects of autism or cure everyone, it is not very likely it works. Pay particular attention to the costs of the treatment, both the obvious cost in dollars and the hidden costs such as your time and that of your child. Also be wary if treatment proponents explain that when it doesn't work, it is because the parents or other people did not do it "quite right." There is the potential to find yourself in a Catch-22 situation in which you may be blamed if the treatment does not work!

EVALUATING NEW THERAPIES

- What is the quality of the evidence? Word-of-mouth, case report, or a more controlled scientific study? Watch out for claims not based on solid, scientific information.

- Has a paper on the work been published in a peer-reviewed journal? If not, why not? If so, what is the quality of the science in the paper? (Your doctor, school professionals, and consultants may be able to help you get a good sense of this.) If people tell you a treatment can't be "scientifically proven" to work, take them at their word and drop it!

- Has the finding been replicated? If not, be wary.

- Can the treatment be proven wrong? (If it can't, it is a matter of faith, not science!) It is perfectly fine, of course, to have faith and to hope for good things to happen. This is not, of course, a matter for science or scientific investigation.

- What are the costs (financial and time) of the treatment? Be careful of treatments where you have a lot of up-front costs! Also, be very wary if treatments consume a lot of your child's time (and often yours as well) when other treatments such as educational and behavioral intervention have already been shown to work.

- Who is the treatment designed to help? Treatments usually won't work for everyone. A claim that every single child is helped should arouse skepticism.

- What is the treatment supposed to do? Is there a theory behind the treatment? Is the theory a scientifically reputable one? (Again, this can be hard for parents to judge; your child's doctor and teachers can be helpful here.)

- Who doesn't the treatment work for? No treatment works the same for everyone.

- What is the evidence that it works (and how was this measured)?

- What are the side effects? All treatments have side effects. Are the potential side effects worth the potential benefits?

- How are people trained to do the treatment? Is there some way to be sure that the training was adequate?

If you are a parent or teacher of a child with autism, you will hear a lot about these treatments. You also will see treatments come and often go. We can understand what motivates parents to want to undertake these treatments but, again, emphasize that in talking about them here we are not necessarily recommending them. (Sometimes you'll see that we recommend against them!) What we do encourage you to do is be an informed and sensible consumer for your child. Always find out what the potential risks as well as promised benefits are.

Even when treatments seem pretty safe or innocuous, there may be some hidden dangers. For example, sometimes parents pursue a nonestablished treatment to the extent that the child's education suffers. We now have a lot of evidence that educational interventions make a very big difference indeed for children with ASDs. Occasionally, the danger has to do more with depleting the family's resources—for example, when large amounts of your time and money are involved.

COMPLEMENTARY AND ALTERNATIVE TREATMENTS FOR CHILDREN WITH AUTISM

This is a free country, and we believe that parents are entitled (within reason) to make choices about the treatment of their child. By the same token, we feel that physicians and other professionals should be open to innovative treatments. However, we also believe that all of us should expect that treatments of any kind should be capable of validation—that is, that we ought to be able to show that they work. In the sections that follow, we provide short summaries of some of the more widely discussed complementary and alternative treatments for children with autism and discuss what evidence there is about their effectiveness.

Sensory Treatments

Children with autism frequently seem to have more trouble processing sensations. As a result, quite a few treatments aimed at improving how children deal with sensory input have been proposed. Some of these treatments are also advocated for children with other disorders, such as learning disabilities.

Auditory Training Individuals with autism often exhibit unusual sensitivities to some sounds and do not seem to pay enough attention to other sounds. Proponents of auditory training methods believe that these differences lead to distortion in perception and thus in the child's development and behavior. A program of therapy (costing hundreds or, more typically, thousands of dollars) is then devised to correct, at least in theory, these distortions. Several different versions of auditory therapy exist. The most common forms are based on the idea that first you identify the sound frequencies that a children is overly sensitive (or not sensitive enough) to, and then train her to better tolerate these sounds.

Most of the supporting evidence for auditory training and auditory treatments is based on testimonials and thus on case reports that are difficult to evaluate. The treatment got a lot of publicity in the lay press some years ago. One early study reported positive outcomes of treatment but did not include a control group, and the reported behavior changes were based on parent report only (and the parents were very aware of their children's treatment). Better studies that use more careful scientific controls have not been able to show that this therapy is effective. Nonetheless, many practitioners are willing, again for a fee, to use these methods.

There are other treatments that emphasize listening. Some are designed to improve auditory processing—that is, how the brain interprets and makes sense of sounds. Often, these therapies focus on helping children process the sounds produced in speech or on helping children understand the connection between written and spoken language (phonics). Sometimes these problems are thought to be the result of what are termed *central auditory processing* problems. The theory is that even though hearing is normal, the child has trouble processing language and more complex auditory information, which results in, among other things, problems with reading and spelling. There is some work on how this alleged condition might be diagnosed and treated, for example, by improving listening to material, improving auditory memory, and assisting listening skills. The basic idea behind the concept remains controversial because there seem to be problems with the definition and theory of the problem and with how the various approaches suggested for improving such skills really differ from other approaches to improving listening and attention.

Visual Therapies   Visual problems can further handicap a child who already has a disability. Clearly we want to maximize the child's potential in every area where we can, and any loss of vision is something to be concerned about. This is particularly important since the visual modality is often an effective mode of providing intervention for children with autism, so visual problems can interfere with your child's progress in other areas. What you hear can be very transient (human speech), but what you see (written signs/icons/words) tends to be much more permanent. Indeed, various books have been written on using visual aids in teaching children with autism and in helping to deal with behavior problems (several of these are listed in the reading list at the end of the chapter).

Fortunately, visual problems are not all that frequent in autism. There are, of course, some exceptions, but children with autism do not usually have obvious visual problems, and they are often good visual learners. If your child needs glasses because she is farsighted or nearsighted or has some other eye problem, of course, you should pursue treatment. Other visual therapies have been proposed and are sometimes suggested for children with autism. More commonly, these therapies are used for crossed eyes or other eye movement problems, but some practitioners, often optometrists, will suggest them for children with learning problems. Sometimes these treatments and exercises are suggested as a way of reducing the need for prescription glasses, but occasionally they are suggested for children with autism, for example, special colored lenses are suggested theoretically to reduce eyestrain and increase reading speed.

Typically, your child is seen for an evaluation and then for follow-up therapy. Often, special kinds of glasses—such as with colored filters or prisms—may be suggested, with the idea that they might filter out the frequencies in the light spectrum that your child is sensitive to. Many children with autism do not like to wear glasses and may be very resistant to them. Other kinds of vision therapies may involve rapid eye movement training with the goal of helping the child better process visual information.

It is clear that vision therapy is, at best, an indirect treatment, since the goal is to help the child be better able to learn. A substantial body of rigorous scientific evidence for these treatments is presently lacking in autism. There is not good evidence, however, that visual therapies are helpful in autism.

Learning-Focused Therapies

Several other programs exist that emphasize the combination of auditory and visual (and other) processing abilities in tasks like reading. Often, these programs build on older systems of intervention, some of which have been well studied in children with dyslexia (but usually not in autism). One of the oldest of these is the Orton–Gilliam method, which was developed in the 1930s and emphasizes integration of auditory, visual, and tactile cues in a phonics-based approach to reading. Modern approaches include Letterland, which attempts to provide a more meaningful context to phonics.

Another program emphasizing improved listening and attending skills is Fast-ForWord, a computer-based program administered by professionals specifically trained in the method. FastForWord emphasizes specific exercises, games, and other activities that are thought to help the child understand spoken language and/or help her to more readily understand the relationship between spoken and written language. Again, there is an important kernel of truth here, since we know that many children with autism, in particular, have much stronger interest in written letters and numbers than in spoken ones. The activities proposed may have to do with helping the child "transfer" information—for example, to identify a sound by naming the musical instrument that produces it or to draw a picture of an object named. Other activities are designed to help children better hear the component sounds of words. Goals may also have to do with improving discrimination, auditory memory, and the sequencing of material. Some of these techniques have been used for children with other kinds of learning problems. Children can be enrolled over the Internet or receive training from a practitioner.

There are several scientific papers published on FastForWord. But the data on these studies have not been made widely available to other investigators, and others need to be able to replicate the work independently. Other issues include the length of time the child is meant to be involved in the program and the lack of specific data on the response of children with autism. Some of the techniques proposed for improving listening, and particularly language listening, skills may be helpful, but there remains a need for well-done research to evaluate these methods in various centers and to look at how much any gains made are generalized into the real world. That is, do the therapies result in changes in real-world settings?

The Lindamood–Bell intervention is concerned with sounding out words and comprehending language. Variants of this approach focus on math and other skills.

Motor and Body Manipulation Treatments

A number of therapies focus on motor, or sometimes sensory-motor skills. Individuals with autism often have trouble dealing with some situations and these interventions are designed to help them cope more effectively with upsetting situations. One of the more common of these approaches is called sensory integration (SI) therapy, which was first developed by Jean Ayers over 30 years ago. Techniques from this approach are frequently used by occupational therapists to help the child develop greater awareness of his or her body and to tolerate different kinds of sensory input. Frequently, various tests or assessments will be done to demonstrate areas where the child has difficulty. A related approach aims to increase the child's sensory problems through brushing of the body (this is usually one bit of an entire program of interventions). While these approaches are very commonly used, the amount of research on them is, unfortunately, very small.

A number of other programs focus on motor or sensory–motor skills. Again, many of these were first developed for children with dyslexia or other learning problems. The Miller method aims to help the child build a sense of bodily awareness and then use this awareness to build other skills. One aspect of this approach is the use of various platforms that force the child to balance and solve problems. Controlled studies are lacking, and most of the support for this method comes from case studies and testimonials.

Over the years, a number of different therapies that involve some kind of manipulation of the body have sprung up. There have been claims for "nerve realignment" (on the basis of manipulation of the back), as well as for various other therapies that involve the child's "relearning" skills correctly—for example, by teaching the child to walk in the proper way. These therapies have no independent verification, and it is a "far stretch" to believe that some of them could possibly work.

In recent years, one of the more popular of these "body" therapies, at least in some areas of the United States, has involved holding. The holding therapy approaches come out of the view of a famous ethologist (scientist who studies animal behavior) named Nikolaas Tinbergen. The idea of this treatment is that you can help children with autism to connect with others by holding onto them until they realize that they are connected with other people (the ones doing the holding). This typically involves sessions where one holds the child (who struggles initially at being held) until she stops fighting the holding. As you might imagine, many children with autism do *not* like to be held, so fights can ensue over the holding. Watching these sessions can be upsetting.

Again, there is no good scientific information that suggests that holding therapy does anything for children with ASDs other than upsetting them (at least initially). One of the problems with this and other therapies is that if the child does not get better, it is possible that the parents (who usually are doing the holding) may be blamed for doing it incorrectly.

One treatment in the past, called patterning, had to do with children "relearning" skills. It was based on work with children who had suffered brain injuries, and the idea was that the child needed to relearn tasks in correct ways and sequences. This treatment required considerable time and effort on the part of families and others, and systematic research failed to show benefit.

Other body therapies have been proposed as well. For example, at least one study has shown some improvement in imitation and social skills in young children with autism who received massage therapy several times a week as compared to children who were only held (see reading list). There are also several studies that have shown that regular aerobic exercise for children with autism results in lower levels of some maladaptive behaviors (see reading list).

You may hear about a range of other treatments, including cranial–sacral therapy, Feldenkrais, reflexology, and similar treatments. These treatments often involve light pressure, massage, or sometimes work on body movements. Although each of these has its own theory, there is no solid scientific data that these treatments are of help in autism. These treatments may, however, be of benefit for another reason: reducing the individual's anxiety level. Indeed, many nonspecific activities that involve relaxation may help children with behavior problems.

Diet and Nutritional Interventions

Vitamins and Other Supplements   Nutrition is as important for children with autism as it is for other children. Sometimes the diet of a child with an

ASD is complicated because of marked food preferences. Occasionally, children with autism, like other children, have trouble with certain kinds of foods, such as lactose, and have to avoid them. Other children may be put on special diets to help control seizures. Children with autism may also be more likely to eat nonfood items such as dirt, clay, or paper. Obviously, addressing these nutritional issues can help children with autism lead healthier lives. Some people go further, however, and claim that various modifications in diet can lead to improvements in behavior, communication skills, or even cognitive functioning.

Unfortunately, although there is much interest in the effects of diet on autism, the quality of the scientific information available to address such claims are not very good, and high-quality studies are lacking. Usually, the claims for dietary treatments invoke any of several factors to account for the difficulties that children with ASDs have. These may include food sensitivities, such as to artificial food dyes or to wheat- and gluten-containing products, or allergies to some food or other substance. Occasionally, very complex diets are suggested—sometimes after a prolonged period of fasting, which can be somewhat dangerous!

Most of the evidence in favor of these claims is based on single case reports or, at times, grouped case reports. (Remember, in these types of reports, it may be the increased attention to the child and her behavior that results in the observed changes, rather than the diet itself.) Controlled scientific studies with groups of cases are not yet widely available. Many different types of dietary treatments have been proposed. We can discuss only some of them here. For each of these diets, we provide a brief summary of the basic idea of the diet and what is involved. These are also summarized briefly in Table 18.2.

TABLE 18.2   COMPLEMENTARY AND ALTERNATIVE DIETARY/ NUTRITIONAL TREATMENTS IN AUTISM—AN OVERVIEW

Treatment	Rational/What Is Involved
Vitamin/mineral supplements	Autism is presumed to respond to high doses of vitamins/minerals. These are then given as supplements. There can be problems at times with very high doses of vitamins.
Anti-yeast diets	Autism is thought to be caused by yeast infection. The goal of this diet is to decrease consumption of foods that contain yeast or are fermented or aged.
Gluten-free–casein-free diet	Sensitivities to gluten (found in wheat and grains) and/or casein (found in milk) are presumed to lead to behavioral and other problems in autism. The diet requires elimination of milk/dairy and wheat products.
Feingold diet	This diet was originally developed for treatment of attention difficulties and hyperactivity (ADHD). It presumes that artificial additives in food cause these problems in children. The diet therefore eliminates these resulting in an essentially all organic diet.

Feingold Diet   This diet was quite popular about 30 years ago. The idea (proposed by Dr. Ben Feingold) was that artificial additives (food colorings, preservatives, and artificial flavors and other ingredients) caused attentional difficulties and hyperactivity. The original diet proposed eliminating all nonnatural ingredients, and, of itself, was not particularly risky in terms of the child's health. A few parents of children with ASDs investigate the diet because their child also has difficulties with hyperactivity. There have been some attempts to combine the Feingold diet with the gluten-free–casein-free diet (see below). There is some serious scientific work on this diet, and the results are mixed; most apply to children with attention deficit disorder, not autism.

Gluten-Free–Casein-Free (GFCF) Diet   Some children and adults in the general population are sensitive to **casein** (a protein found in milk) or gluten (a protein found in wheat, rye, barley, and other grain products) or both. These individuals need to be on special diets to prevent damage to their intestines and to avoid **malnutrition** and growth problems (see Chapter 10). Some people believe that many children with ASDs have these sensitivities and that they can lead to some of the behavioral and other problems seen in autism. At present, however, there is no solid evidence to suggest that sensitivities to casein or gluten are any more common in children with ASDs than in other children.

For this diet, you basically eliminate milk products (the casein part of the diet) and substitute soy milk, tofu, and other non-milk-containing foods. Because gluten is found in wheat, other grains, and many food additives, it can be harder to eliminate. Usually, people will use corn, rice, and other substitutes, or buy commercially available gluten-free products. There are some special cookbooks that can help parents make GFCF food more appetizing for their children.

Advocates of this diet have differing recommendations regarding the length of time you are supposed to try it to determine whether it helps (a couple of months seems to be the most frequent recommendation). The advocates for this diet also have different views about whether your child needs to stay on the diet permanently.

The evidence for the GFCF diet is largely case reports and anecdotes. Often, this diet is tried in combination with other interventions, complicating the task of figuring out exactly why changes might be observed. If you want to try this diet, discuss it with your doctor and perhaps with a nutritionist or dietitian. Your doctor may suggest blood tests (and even more specialized tests) to see if your child is really allergic to milk (see Chapter 10). If you give the diet a reasonable period of time to work and it doesn't, then be prepared to abandon it. There is possibly a slight risk of inadequate nutrition with this (and other specialized) diets, so discuss the issue with your health care provider and also find out whether he thinks your child may need vitamins to supplement her regular food intake.

Anti-Yeast Diets   The idea behind this diet is that yeast (which is called *Candida* in scientific language) causes an infection, which, in turn, causes autism. Children on this diet try to stay away from foods that contain yeast (e.g., baked goods), as well as foods that are fermented (e.g., soy sauce) or aged in some way (e.g., cheeses). Sugar is also to be avoided. Since you are supposed to avoid baked goods, this diet is also a gluten-free diet.

Although claims have been made for dramatic cures using this diet, scientific support is lacking. The evidence supporting the idea of "yeast overgrowth" in children with autism is unproven.

Omega-3 (Fish Oil)   This group of what are called *fatty acids* is important for normal growth and development. This, and related, fatty acids are involved in several important processes in the body. Taking more of these may have some role in preventing heart problems and possibly some other disorders (such as cancer) as well. There are some (although generally slight) risks in taking too much. There has been some interest in whether these might be used in disorders like attention deficit hyperactivity disorder (ADHD) and bipolar disorder. The evidence in autism is limited.

Vitamin and Mineral Treatments   Vitamins are organic (carbon-containing) chemicals that the body needs in small amounts for important biological processes. Minerals are inorganic (do not contain carbon) chemicals such as calcium, iron, iodine, which are also needed for some functions in the body. Other chemicals (such as lead and mercury) are not needed by the body and are actually toxic.

Over the past 100 to 200 years, a number of diseases linked to vitamin or mineral deficiencies were identified and largely eliminated as a result of better attention to diet and vitamin supplementation. There is no doubt that using vitamins to prevent or treat vitamin deficiency diseases is extremely effective. However, in addition to the routine use of vitamins, it has been proposed that autism (and some other disorders, including attentional disorders and learning disability) might be treated by **"mega"dose vitamins**. This is one aspect of the Defeat Autism Now (DAN) protocol.

As with many treatments, there are reasons that, at least on the surface, megavitamin therapies might seem to make sense. Perhaps the main reason is that it is clear that in vitamin deficiency states, learning (and many other aspects of life) can be severely affected. There have been some studies on the topic—including studies of megadose vitamins in autism. Unfortunately, these studies have had a number of basic problems. For example, many are based on case reports, or, if large numbers of individuals are included, the study does not include appropriate controls. More rigorous scientific studies have generally failed to find good evidence for the use of megavitamins to treat autism or other developmental disorders.

The issue of exactly which vitamins to supplement has been a source of some disagreement. One of the problems, unfortunately, is that often a vitamin cocktail is used (typically including vitamin B_6 and magnesium), which makes things even more complicated to understand. Although it is possible that a small subgroup of children with autism might respond to vitamins, the data supporting this are very limited. For children with fragile X syndrome (which is sometimes associated with autism), there has been some work on supplementing **folic acid** (which is known to be deficient) with, perhaps, some positive change in a few patients.

At usual doses, most vitamins pose relatively little risk to children. However, the use of these agents can be associated with problems. For example, very high doses of certain vitamins can cause liver damage. Very high doses of vitamin B_6 can cause nerve damage as well as ulcers and seizures. High doses of folic acid can cause irritability.

The information on minerals in autism is also quite limited. Clearly, the body needs some minerals such as iron for the formation of red blood cells, and children may sometimes develop iron deficiency anemia. A recent television program highlighted the possible role of copper or zinc in autism, but based on rather little evidence. There are also some **homeopathic** and **naturopathic** physicians who recommend supplementing the diet with very small amounts of minerals in the belief that such supplementation may produce behavioral or developmental change. Some years ago, a mother who believed in such supplementation told one of us she was giving her child arsenic! Having visions of having to call in the police, it then emerged that this was part of a "natural" treatment program and probably involved less arsenic than most of us get every day!

Again, there is no good evidence that individuals with autism who have adequate diets and do not have medical problems (such as anemia) need additional mineral or vitamin supplementation. If your child eats a very restricted diet, you might want to consult a dietitian to make sure she is getting enough of all needed nutrients. In addition, your doctor can do blood tests and other tests to check for vitamin deficiencies and anemia. Information on dietary and vitamin treatments is summarized in Table 18.2 (page 534).

Dietary Interventions—A Summary   At present, there really is not very good scientific data to suggest that these diets actually work. Furthermore, these diets can be a real hassle for parents, teachers, and the child. However, these diets are (generally speaking) relatively safe. While we have personally not seen many children we were convinced were really helped, we also have not seen many children who were made worse, either. (Usually, if a treatment works for some children, it won't work for all and may make some worse). On very, very rare occasions, we have heard of children who suffered as a result of these diets, sometimes because the family became so fixated on the diet that they failed to pay attention to the interventions (like educational intervention) that we know *do* work. On occasion, we also have run across children who were quite low functioning and whose diet was so restricted that there were, in essence no food-based rewards that could be used in behavioral programs for them. Finally, we have heard of children who developed nutritional problems as a result of markedly restricted diets; there are now several studies suggesting that this sometimes happens.

Clearly, if a child has lactose intolerance, switching off of milk may help her feel better, and, as a result, behave better. In general, dietary treatments probably don't pose much of a risk to children although, occasionally, families can go overboard on diets, and, rarely, the child's health educational program may suffer as a result.

DRUG TREATMENTS AND MEDICAL PROCEDURES

As discussed in Chapter 15, various medications are used by psychiatrists and other physicians in order to improve some of the behaviors that often go along with ASD, including anxiety, attentional difficulties, behavioral rigidity, and other problems. Although not all parents and professionals agree with the use of these medications in children, they are not considered alternative or controversial treatments when studies have shown that these medications are often effective in improving behavior. There are also many drug treatments for ASD that *are* controversial because there is no good data proving that they work. Some of the most commonly advocated are described below.

Secretin

Secretin is a hormone in the gut and is used in diagnostic testing for certain diseases of the digestive system. Interest in secretin started some years ago, with news and television reports of a dramatic "cure" based on the report of three cases in a relatively obscure medical journal. A black market sprang up for secretin, on the theory that maybe there was something wrong with the digestive system in children with autism. Because secretin had to be administered intravenously, it was somewhat more cumbersome to give than other medicines. Also, it was not clear at the time how safe it was—much less how effective it was. However, the tremendous interest in this agent led to a series of much more rigorous scientific studies.

All of these more careful scientific studies have so far failed to show significant improvement in autism following secretin treatment. (References for these studies are included in the reading list at the end of the book.) The studies have included both single and multiple doses of secretin using various scientifically controlled methods. Several hundred children have now been studied, and secretin has not been shown to work in improving the symptoms of autism.

All of us, of course, wish that secretin had been shown to improve the functioning of children with autism. Sadly, it does not. The tremendous hype over secretin does, however, point to some of the problems for parents in evaluating new treatments, particularly very new treatments where there is a lot of excitement without, necessarily, much solid scientific data. As discussed earlier, single case studies tend to be published only when they are positive, and, because these studies are not controlled, it is essential to rely on studies that use more rigorous scientific methods.

The experience with secretin also points out the problem in relying on the news media for medical information. The original and exciting story that secretin *might* have some benefit (also sometimes blown horribly out of proportion by claims of cures and major improvement) got a lot more attention than the subsequent, much more painstakingly done, scientific studies that have *not* shown it to help. As one of us has said in another context, "What makes an effective television program may not, of course, be the same as what makes good science."[1] Most of the time in medicine and science, like life, important findings emerge in a slow, step-by-step, fashion as scientists build on each other's work, improving and refining it. Secretin is an example of a treatment where "too good to be true," unfortunately, seems to apply.

Anticonvulsants and Steroids

There is a clear role for use of anticonvulsant medications in treating children with seizure disorders. There is much more controversy about using these medicines to treat children with autism spectrum disorders who may (or may not) have an abnormal brain wave test (electroencephalogram [EEG]) but who do *not* clearly have seizures. Another approach has advocated use of powerful steroid medicines to treat presumed immune problems. Often, these drugs are tried in children who have had some form of "regression," but data to support the use of these medicines mostly consists of case reports and results of more rigorous, controlled trials is presently lacking. The medicines, like all medicines, can have serious side effects. Sometimes they "activate" the child—that is, they make her seem more "hyper" or energetic. This may give the impression that the child has suddenly made developmental gains—but these gains are lost over time as the child's system

---

[1] F. R. Volkmar (1999). Editorial: Lessons from secretin. *New England Journal of Medicine*, 341, 1842–1844.

becomes used to the medication. Parents who have themselves been on steroids may know exactly what we are talking about here!

At present, there are not good data to support the use of anticonvulsants or steroids for an abnormal EEG in the absence of a clear seizure disorder. You can talk with your child's neurologist about this in more detail.

Drug Treatments for Infections

One group of alternative therapies holds that autism results from infections (either from bacteria, viruses, or yeast) and that treatment of the underlying infection should lead to improvement in the child's symptoms. Yeast infections probably have gotten the most notice. Many women have chronic but very, very mild yeast infections, and someone suggested that maybe mothers of children with autism were more likely to have such infections that had never been recognized. This led a number of doctors to try medicines, such as nystatin, to treat yeast infections in children with autism.

Somewhat surprisingly, many of the advocates of this treatment are not particularly concerned about whether or not the mother can be shown to have a yeast infection. (This can be tested for in both mothers and their children.) Also, they are not bothered by the fact that many women who have mild yeast infections have children who are perfectly fine. Potential side effects of the treatment include stomach upset and, rarely, allergic reactions. There again is no good data suggesting that this treatment works in autism.

Another recent therapy has entailed the use of high-potency antibiotics (with the presumption that autism arises as a result of some form of infection). There are no good data at present to support this idea. As with other medicines, antibiotics can have serious side effects.

Intravenous Immunoglobulin Infusion

Some people have thought that perhaps autism might represent an immune problem, particularly an autoimmune problem (where the body develops some adverse reaction to something within itself). Some fairly straightforward blood tests are available to look for the more frequent autoimmune disorders. At least one of these disorders has been associated with the development of movement problems in children, but has not been shown to be more common in children with ASD.

Some parents (and physicians) have explored various ways to treat what are presumed to be autoimmune problems in autism. These include antibiotics (mentioned earlier) as well as intravenous immunoglobulin G (IVIG), which is a blood product, so there is some risk for infection. There have also been reports of stroke following IVIG. At the time we are writing this, data to support the use of IVIG are not available.

Chelation

Although the body needs some kinds of minerals to grow and develop, there are a few chemicals such as lead, mercury, and cadmium (what chemists call the heavy metals) that are not needed. In fact, these chemicals can cause trouble when they are taken in. For example, the bad effects of high lead levels on children's development is well known. These effects can include attention and learning problems, as well as much more serious neurological problems when the child has very high lead levels. As a result (as discussed in Chapter 7), children are screened for high lead levels so that they (and maybe their environment) can be treated if this is found.

When children are objectively shown to have high levels of minerals such as lead, chelation therapy might be medically necessary. This therapy involves administering medicine that is designed to bind with (stick to) the heavy metal and take it out of the body, by way of the kidney. In the absence of demonstrated, documented high lead levels, however, there is no reason to conduct chelation therapy (which has potentially serious risks itself).

Plasmapheresis

Another approach to removal of suspected toxins is plasmapheresis. In this medical procedure, plasma is separated from the rest of the blood. Then the plasma is discarded and the remaining blood is returned to the body along with a plasma replacement. There are legitimate medical uses for this approach in some conditions, but not in autism. There are the usual risks that are involved with IVs, as well as the potential for serious (and potentially life-threatening) reactions.

Hyperbaric Oxygen Therapy

If you remember some of the older television shows or movies, you may recall the special chambers used to treat "the bends" as a result of divers coming to the surface of the ocean too rapidly. Hyperbaric oxygen chambers are used for several medical purposes; for example, they can help wounds heal if there is poor circulation or they can be used to treat carbon monoxide poisoning. In this treatment, the individual is placed in a special pressurized chamber and breathes oxygen (or air with more than usual amounts of oxygen). There have been claims that this procedure can be used for children with various developmental disabilities, but data are lacking. Controlled studies of this treatment are needed. There are also some potentially important medical risks (e.g., seizures).

COMMUNICATION AND AUDITORY INTERVENTIONS

Facilitated Communication

Facilitated communication (FC) is an unusual treatment in that it has now been clearly shown not to work. This is rather an accomplishment, since it usually is much easier to show that a treatment works rather than that it doesn't. Although most parents of young children with ASDs may not hear much about FC, parents of older children may be familiar with it. We mention it here for several reasons. In many ways it illustrates some of the dangers associated with what seem like relatively safe treatments. It also illustrates some of the basic questions you should ask about very unusual treatments.

FC got its start in Australia, where it was originally proposed to help children with significant motor problems communicate. This intervention involved having a "facilitator" hold the hand of the child with his or her index finger pointed out, steadying the hand. In this way, the child could allegedly type out words/sentences on a computer keyboard or communicate by picking out letters of the alphabet—for example, on a board or other communication device. The individual who started to work with children with autism in Australia claimed that they could communicate very effectively and at *much* higher levels using this method.

This claim was a bit perplexing for several reasons. In the first place, unlike children with cerebral palsy or serious motor problems, children with autism usually do not have difficulties using their hands. Second, the kinds of communication that were alleged to come from the child were amazing and at a much, much higher and more sophisticated level than would be expected given either the child's verbal abilities or intelligence quotient (IQ).

This technique took a while to catch on in the United States, but was eventually popularized by a small group of special educators who went on to claim that it could be used for children with other kinds of problems, such as mental retardation, as well. It was believed that children with autism were actually very highly intelligent and that the FC was a way to release them from the difficulties that they had in communication. Indeed, it was thought that with no apparent training or education, these children—including children who had never talked—could communicate in very sophisticated ways and could demonstrate the ability to read and write (sometimes in several different languages—again, with no formal training). Interestingly, many brighter (and verbal) children with autism were said to be able to facilitate more effectively than they could talk, leading to the notion that you often had to ignore what the child actually said and really pay attention only to the FC. One of us had the experience of seeing a number of children using FC who were, among other things, allegedly asking for changes in their medication based on what they had "read" in the *New England Journal of Medicine*.

One of the first ominous warning signs about FC was that it was quickly apparent that the people doing the facilitating were often reluctant to have the method validated. For example, it was clear that very often the child who was allegedly communicating was not even looking at the keyboard. (Those of you who type can try to do this and will see that it is very difficult for even a good typist to do without occasionally glancing at the keyboard.) Sometimes the claim was made that attempting to "test" the child would ruin her trust in the facilitator (again, somewhat odd, given that we know that children with autism often have a hard time in forming relationships anyway).

This was not a difficult method to test once people could be persuaded to cooperate. For example, you could set up a situation where the child saw one thing and the facilitator another, then ask (supposedly) the child what she saw. Of course, what got typed was what the facilitator saw. Other studies looked at how well different facilitators did with different children. Again, the kinds of "communications" produced had more to do with the facilitator than the child. Many, many studies quickly demonstrated that there was no validity to this method.

Perhaps you are wondering what difference it makes anyway. Unfortunately, even for a treatment like this, there were a number of very real dangers. First of all, children's programs were turned upside down, more or less overnight, as people pulled the children out of special education and other intervention services to enroll them in classes where their "true" level could be accommodated. Sometimes doctors were asked to prescribe medications on the basis of the alleged communication; some mental health workers even had group therapy sessions using FC! Most worrisome, however, was the potential for abuse of parents. Since many facilitators were not consciously aware of what they were doing, sometimes very bad messages emerged from the "facilitation." Often, these messages disparaged the parents—sometimes even claims of sexual or physical abuse were made, and some parents were reported to protective services on this basis! In the end, this "treatment" seemed to have more to do with the kind of mass hysteria depicted in plays like *The Crucible*.

OTHER COMPLEMENTARY AND ALTERNATIVE APPROACHES

Options Method

The options method grew out of the experience of two parents in dealing with their child with autism. In a series of books, Barry Kaufman describes how he and his wife spent long periods of time trying to follow their son's lead and reconnect with him. This method is expensive due to the training required and the amount of time expended. Some aspects of its philosophy are also controversial (the suggestion, for example, that a good part of the cause of autism is psychological). There are no solid scientific data to back it up, although the Kaufman's claim that their son recovered from his autism, and indeed he is listed as the co-author of one of the books.

Art, Music, and Related Therapies

These therapies (which could also sometimes be just as usefully thought of as pleasant activities) are concerned with helping people be more able to express themselves through any of a number of modalities—art, music, drama, and so forth. Art therapists have training counseling as well as in art therapy. Music therapists use simple, or more complicated, musical activities for a similar purpose. As with art therapy there are training programs available. Similar approaches are based on dance or movement associated with music. The literature supporting these activities as treatments is mostly anecdotal (case reports). Certainly with a gifted therapist who is able to adjust his or her techniques and materials to the level of the student, these activities can be highly enjoyable and expand the lives of children on the autism spectrum. Indeed engagement in activities like music lessons has potential for being a good activity for children with ASD particularly if the teacher is sensitive to the child's special needs; some methods, notably the Suzuki method, are very developmental in nature and easily adapted to individuals with disabilities (i.e., they start simply, are highly structured, and gradually build up in terms of complexity).

In this regard, it is important to note that activities can be therapeutic without necessarily needing to be thought of as "therapies." For example, many disabled children love art or music. Some of them enjoy lessons, as do typically developing children. If your child is interested in these activities, it is worth encouraging them. For the musically interested child, the Suzuki approach has many advantages: It is highly respectful of the child, emphasizes a developmental approach, can readily be accommodated to individuals with various levels of disability, and is largely one on one—thus minimizing social demands.

Animals and Pet Therapy

Children (and adults) with autism can have pets for the same reasons the rest of us do. Pets can be wonderful companions and can encourage independence and increase motivation. Sometimes animals are used for special activities; for example, there may be a dog or cat that lives in a group home or residential facility. Other animals may be present specifically to provide support to an individual with a disability. We have seen some truly amazing helper dogs; in at least one instance, in a life-threatening situation for a less cognitively able boy with autism who tended to wander, his dog faithfully went with him—yelping for help the entire time! Animals offer many advantages over people, since they are less complicated, but still have social and other needs. Obviously, many factors go into the decision to have a pet, particularly if the pet is a special helper pet. These include consideration of the needs of the pet and individual(s) living with it. Again, much of the literature in this area is anecdotal and testimonial.

Horses provide a special example of animal/pet therapy. Hippotherapy has been widely used for children with movement problems as one part of a therapeutic program that encourages better motor and postural control. It is not concerned as much with riding as with the child's ability to adapt to the horse. Therapeutic riding is concerned with actual riding ability. There is a small amount of research work on hippotherapy. Some work has also been done with dolphins.

Other Therapies

Although this chapter may seem fairly long, we have covered only some of the main complementary and alternative treatments you will hear about. Other approaches based on "energy fields" verge out of the range of the scientifically testable. Other approaches, like yoga or relaxation training, may have good benefits for people without having special applicability to autism. Other treatments we have not covered include aromatherapy, acupuncture (although some work is now being done with it), homeopathic treatments, and so on. The reading list provides information on a range of these treatments.

SUMMARY

Sometimes a fine line exists between accepted and unconventional treatments. Unfortunately, despite much interest, less conventional treatments generally have very little, if any, solid scientific basis and it is difficult for parents to get good information about them (although the reading list provides several comprehensive guides).

Anytime parents think about any treatment, it is important that the parent be a well-informed consumer. Parents can seek out other parents, as well as professionals, to talk with. Be aware of hidden as well as the more obvious costs. Be particularly concerned about therapies in which there is direct, or even indirect, potential for harm to your child. Occasionally, we have seen parents devote many months or years to the pursuit of "the cure" through some unconventional treatment program. This is a particular problem when parents engage in these unproven treatments at the expense of their child's education, particularly in the first years of life when some children make the greatest gains with proven therapies.

In general, parents and teachers should be appropriately skeptical of highly dramatic accounts of "cures" and "miracles" in television and newspaper stories. If you decide to undertake a treatment, you should know what the evidence is for the treatment, how long it will last, and what the potential good—and bad—effects of the treatment may be. It is important to realize that all children (including those with autism) change over time. Do not mistake the changes that occur naturally for those that might seem to result from nonconventional treatments.

■ READING LIST

Arnold, G. L., Hyman, S. L., Mooney, R. A., & Kirby, R. S. (2003). Plasma amino acids profiles in children with autism: potential risk of nutritional deficiencies. *Journal of Autism and Developmental Disorders, 33*(4), 449–454.

Chez, M. G., Buchanan, C. P., Bagan, B. T., Hammer, M. S., McCarthy, K. S., Ovrutskaya, I., et al. (2000). Secretin and autism: A two-part clinical investigation. *Journal of Autism and Developmental Disorders, 30,* 87–94.

Committee on Children With Disabilities. (2001). American Academy of Pediatrics: Counseling families who choose complementary and alternative medicine for their child with chronic illness or disability. *Pediatrics, 107*(3), 598–601.

Coniglio, S. J., Lewis, J. D., Lang, C., Burns, T. G., Subhani-Siddique, R., Weintraub, A., et al. (2001). A randomized, double-blind, placebo-controlled trial of single-dose intravenous secretin as treatment for children with autism. *Journal of Pediatrics, 138,* 649–655.

Dawson, G., & Watling, R. (2000). Interventions to facilitate auditory, visual, and motor integration in autism: A review of the evidence. *Journal of Autism and Developmental Disorders, 30,* 415–421.

Dunn-Geier, J., Ho, H. H., Auersperg, E., Doyle, D., Eaves, L., Matsuba, C., et al. (2000). Effect of secretin on children with autism: A randomized controlled trial. *Developmental Medicine and Child Neurology, 42,* 796–802.

Elder, J. H., Shankar, M., Shuster, J., Theriaque, D., Burns, S., & Sherrill, L. (2006). The gluten-free, casein-free diet in autism: Results of a preliminary double blind clinical trial. *Journal of Autism and Developmental Disorders, 36,* 413–420.

Escalona, A., Field, T., Singer-Strunch, R., Cullen, C., & Hartshorn, K. Brief report: Improvements in behavior of children with autism following massage therapy. *Journal of Autism and Developmental Disorders, 31,* 513–516.

Findling, R. L., Maxwell, K., Scotese-Wojtila, L., Huang, J., Yamashita, T., & Wiznitzer, M. (1997). High-dose pyridoxine and magnesium administration in children with autistic disorder: An absence of salutary effects in a double blind, placebo-controlled study. *Journal of Autism and Developmental Disorders, 27,* 467–478.

Finn, P., Bothe, A. K., & Bramlett, R. E. (2005). Science and pseudoscience in communication disorders: Criteria and applications. *American Journal of Speech–Language Pathology, 14,* 172–186.

Gerlach, E. (1998). *Autism treatment guide* (Rev. ed.). Eugene, OR: Four Leaf Press.

Hansen, R. L., & Ozonoff, S. (2003). Alternative theories: Assessment and therapy options. In S. Ozonoff, S. J. Rogers, and R. L. Hendren,(Eds.), *Autism spectrum disorders: A research review for practitioners.* Washington, DC: American Psychiatric Press.

Hanson, E., Kalish, L. A., et al. (2007). Use of complementary and alternative medicine among children diagnosed with autism spectrum disorder. *Journal of Autism and Developmental Disorders, 37*(4), 628–636.

Harrington, J., Rosen, L., Garnecho, A., Patrick, P. (2006). Parental perceptions and use of complementary and alternative medicine practices for children with autistic spectrum disorders in private practice. *Journal of Developmental and Behavioral Pediatrics, 27*(2): S156-S161.

Honda, H., Shimizu, Y., & Rutter, M. (2005). No effect of MMR withdrawal on the incidence of autism: A total population study. *Journal of Child Psychology and Psychiatry, 46,* 572–579.

Horvath, K., Stefanatos, G., Sokolski, K. N., Wachtel, R., Nabors, L., & Tildon, J.T. (1998). Improved social and language skills after secretin administration in patients with autistic spectrum disorders. *Journal of the Association for Academic Minority Physicians, 9,* 9–15.

Hyman, S. L., & Levy, S. E. (2000). Autistic spectrum disorders: When traditional medicine is not enough. *Contemporary Pediatrics, 17*(10), 101–116.

Hyman, S. L., & Levy, S. E. (2005). Introduction: Novel therapies in developmental disabilities—hope, reason, and evidence. *Mental Retardation and Developmental Disabilities Research Reviews, 11*(2), 107–109.

Institute of Medicine. (2004). *Immunization safety review: Vaccines and autism.* Washington, DC: National Academies Press.

Jacobson, J., Foxx, R., & Mulick, J. (2004). *Controversial therapies for developmental disabilities: Fad, fashion, and science in professional practice.* Mahwah, NJ: Erlbaum.

Joint Commission Resources. (2000). A practical system for evidence grading. *Joint Commission Journal on Quality Improvement, 26,* 700–712.

Kane, K. (2006, January 6). Death of 5-year-old boy linked to controversial chelation therapy. *Pittsburgh Post Gazette.* Retrieved January 30, 2006, from www.post-gazette .com/pg/06006/633541.stm.

Kay, S., & Vyse, S. (2005). Helping parents separate the wheat from the chaff: Putting autism treatments to the test. In J. W. Jacobson & R. M. Foxx (Eds.), *Fads, dubious and improbable treatments for developmental disabilities* (pp. 265–277). Mahwah, NJ: Erlbaum.

Lawler, C. P., Croen, L. A., Grether, J. K., & Van de Water, J. (2004). Identifying environmental contributions to autism: Provacative clues and false leads. *Mental Retardation and Developmental Disabilities Research Reviews, 10,* 292–302.

Levy, S. E., & Hyman, S. L. (2003). Use of complementary and alternative treatments for children with autism spectrum disorders is increasing. *Pediatric Annals, 32,* 685–691.

Levy, S. E., & Hyman, S. L. (2005). Novel treatments for autistic spectrum disorders. *Mental Retardation and Developmental Disabilities Research Reviews, 11,* 131–142.

Levy, S. E., Mandell, D. S., Merhar, S., Ittenbach, R. F., & Pinto-Martin, J. A. (2003). Use of complementary and alternative medicine among children recently diagnosed with autistic spectrum disorder. *Journal of Developmental and Behavioral Pediatrics, 24,* 418–423.

Marohn, S. (2002). *The natural medicine guide to autism.* Charlottesville, VA: Hampton Roads.

Millward, C., Ferriter, M., Calver, S., & Connell-Jones, G. (2004). Gluten and casein-free diets for autistic spectrum disorder. *Cochrane Database of Systematic Reviews, 3,* 1–14.

Mostert, M. P. (2001). Facilitated communication since 1995: A review of published studies. *Journal of Autism and Developmental Disorders, 31,* 287–313.

Mukhopadhyay, T. R. (2003). *The mind tree: A miraculous boy breaks the silence of autism.* New York: Arcade.

Newsom, C., & Hovanitz, C. A. (2005). The nature and value of empirically validated interventions. In J. W. Jacobson & R. M. Foxx (Eds.), *Fads, dubious and improbable treatments for developmental disabilities* (pp. 31–44). Mahwah, NJ: Erlbaum.

Owley, T., McMahon, W., Cook, E. H., Laulhere, T. M., South, M., Mays, L. Z., et al. (2001). Multi-site, double-blind, placebo-controlled trial of porcine secretin in autism. *Journal of the American Academy of Child and Adolescent Psychiatry, 40,* 1293–1299.

Park, R. (2000). *Voodoo science: The road from foolishness to fraud.* Oxford, UK: Oxford University Press.

Politi, P., Cena, H., Comelli, M., Marrone, G., Allegri, C., Emanuele, E., et al. (2008). Behavioral effects of omega-3 fatty acid supplementation in young adults with severe autism: an open label study. *Archives of Medical Research, 39*(7), 682–685.

Rawstron, J. A., Burley, C. D., & Eldeer, M. J. (2005). A systematic review of the applicability and efficacy of eye exercises. *Journal of Pediatric Ophthalmology and Strabismus, 42,* 82–88.

Reiten, D. J. (1987). Nutrition and developmental disabilities: Issues in chronic care. In E. Schopler & G. B. Mesibov (Eds.), *Neurobiological issues in autism* (pp. 373–388). New York: Plenum Press.

Roberts, W., Weaver, L., Brian, J., Bryson, S., Emelianova, S., Griffiths, A. M., MacKinnon, B., et al. (2001). Repeated doses of porcine secretin in the treatment of autism: A randomized, placebo-controlled trial. *Pediatrics, 107,* E71.

Rogers, S. J., & Ozonoff, S. (2005). What do we know about sensory dysfunction in autism? A critical review of the empirical evidence. *Journal of Child Psychology and Psychiatry, 46,* 1255–1268.

Sandler, A. D., & Bodfish, J. W. (2000). Placebo effects in autism: Lessons from secretin. *Journal of Developmental and Behavioral Pediatrics, 21,* 347–350.

Sandler, A. D., Sutton, K. A., DeWeese, J., Girardi, M. A., Sheppard, V., & Bodfish, J. W. (1999). Lack of benefit of a single dose of synthetic human secretin in the treatment of autism and pervasive developmental disorder. *New England Journal of Medicine, 341,* 1801–1806.

Shapiro, A. K., & Shapiro, E. (1997). *The powerful placebo.* Baltimore: Johns Hopkins University Press.

Smith, T. (1993). Autism. In T. Giles (Ed.), *Effective psychotherapies* (pp. 107–133). New York: Plenum Press.

Smith, T., & Antolovich, M. (2000). Parental perceptions of supplemental interventions received by young children with autism in intensive behavior analytic treatment. *Behavioral Interventions, 15,* 83–97.

Smith, T., Mruzek, D., & Mozingo, D. (2005). Sensory integrative therapy. In J. W. Jacobson & R. M. Foxx (Eds.), *Fads, dubious and improbable treatments for developmental disabilities* (pp. 331–350). Mahwah, NJ: Erlbaum.

Smith, T., Scahill, L., Dawson, G., Guthrie, D., Lord, C., Odom, S., et al. (2007). Designing research studies of psychosocial interventions in autism. *Journal of Autism and Developmental Disorders, 37,* 354–366.

Smith, T., & Wick, J. (2008). Controversial treatments. In K. Chawarska, A. Klin, & F. Volkmar (Eds.), *Autism spectrum disorders in infants and toddlers: Diagnosis, assessment, and treatment* (pp. 243–273). New York: Guilford Press.

Tolbert, L., Haigler, T., Waits, M. M., & Dennis, T. (1993). Brief report: Lack of response in an autistic population to a low dose clinical trial of pyridoxine plus magnesium. *Journal of Autism and Developmental Disabilities, 23,* 193–199.

Volkmar, F. R. (1999). Editorial—lessons from secretin. *New England Journal of Medicine, 341,* 1842–1844.

Volkmar, F., Cook, E. H.Jr., Pomeroy, J., Realmuto, G., Tanguay, P., & the Work Group on Quality Issues. (1999). Practice parameters for the assessment and treatment of children, adolescents, and adults with autism and other pervasive developmental disorders. American Academy of Child and Adolescent Psychiatry Working Group on Quality Issues [published erratum appears in *J Am Acad Child Adolesc Psychiatry* 2000 Jul; 39(7), 938]. *Journal of the American Academy of Child and Adolescent Psychiatry, 38*(12 Suppl), 32S–54S.

Watling, R., Deitz, J., Kanny, E. M., & McLaughlin, J. F. (1999). Current practice of occupational therapy for children with autism. *American Journal of Occupational Therapy, 53,* 489–497.

■ QUESTIONS AND ANSWERS

1. **We have heard of a therapy in Europe that involves injecting sheep brain to cure autism. Have you heard of this?**

   This is a therapy that is not very common, but we have heard of it. There is no evidence at all that this makes any sense whatsoever. On top of that, we do know that one of the ways that "mad cow" disease is passed on is through cattle eating by-products of other animals. Your child could also have an allergic reaction to the sheep brain injections.

2. **What is the "caveman diet"?**

   The idea behind the caveman diet is to go back to the kinds of food humans ate 100,000 years ago! In this diet you eat meat, fruit, nuts, vegetables, and so forth. If you were to follow this diet, you'd be avoiding sugar, dairy, and grains (like wheat), so this is also a form of the gluten-free–casein-free diet.

3. **We took our 4-year-old to the optometrist, who suggested that prism glasses would help her. Unfortunately, we can't get her to wear these. What can we do?**

   There is not good evidence that this works for children with autism (claims for it are mostly made on the basis of word of mouth and individual experience rather than good scientific data). If your child won't wear them, we'd say bag it. If you have any concerns that visual problems may be contributing to your child's behaviors, take her to an ophthalmologist who has experience in working with children with special needs.

4. **Does nerve realignment work in autism?**

   We presume you mean something like cranial sacral and similar therapies. There is no evidence that body manipulation therapy makes any real difference in the way that nerves and the brain work (in anybody, let alone in children with autism). Massage and similar treatment may make the child feel better, but this is not the same thing as saying that the nerves are "realigned." There is also no evidence that nerves in children with autism are out of alignment to begin with!

5. **Is my 18-year-old too old for auditory training?**

There is not good evidence that this therapy works, although there is a small amount of published information on it. Ask what the experience of other parents has been with this. We doubt that it will hurt but it is unlikely to help (although you will hear of cases where parents feel it has indeed made a major difference!).

6. **Every time I turn around, it seems like someone has come up with a new miracle treatment for autism. If a fantastic new treatment comes along that will really help my child, I want him to have it as soon as possible, but it gets tiresome, always having to sort out the hype from the facts whenever there's a new treatment. What's the best, most reliable way to know whether a new treatment is worth investigating for my child?**

Unfortunately, you are correct; every few months it seems someone has a new claim for a cure! If only this were so—we'd be delighted to be put out of business! In terms of evaluating new treatments, in the first place, use common sense. Get some information on what is claimed, find out if there is any really solid scientific evidence to back up the claims made. As we discuss in this chapter, be very wary about people who make extravagant claims but are "too busy" to go to the trouble of doing serious scientific research. The professionals who work with your child (your doctor, teachers and specialists at school) can be good sources of information on new treatments.

CHAPTER 19

Managing Sibling and Family Issues

L ike all parents those of children with autism have, of course, always wanted to maximize the potential of their child. Over time, there have been major changes in the ways in which, and degree to which, educators and others have welcomed family involvement. As discussed in Chapter 1, in the first years after autism was described, parents were sometimes blamed for causing autism and schools could, and did, refuse to educate children with autism. Things are now very, very different.

A large, and growing, body of research and clinical work has strongly supported the importance of active family involvement as one essential part of developing effective intervention programs for individuals with autism spectrum disorders (ASDs). As we emphasized in previous chapters, parents are the natural and rightful primary advocates for their child. Furthermore, in contrast to teachers and classmates, family members "stay the course" and are involved throughout the life of the person with an ASD. Siblings, in particular, have an important role in helping children with ASDs make developmental gains and learn essential skills. In this chapter, we discuss some of the issues involved for families. This includes the role of parents and other family members, the special issues that having a brother or sister with an ASD pose for siblings, and how parents and family members can effectively communicate both with each other and with people outside the family. As the reading list indicates, there are now a number of resources on this topic, and we urge parents to make good use of them. In this chapter, we talk about some of the issues that parents, siblings, and members of the extended family may deal with relative to a child, brother/sister, grandchild, or niece/nephew with autism or a related disorder.

STRESSES AND SUPPORTS

Many different issues determine the particular stresses, challenges, and accomplishments that the individual family faces. Having worked with thousands of families over the years has made it clear to us that the first and most important set of considerations are the strengths and vulnerabilities of the individual and family. Some of the strengths and vulnerabilities are obvious; others much less so. For example, obvious areas of strengths include higher levels of cognitive and communicative ability in the individual with autism, good educational programs, and greater resources available to parents and families. Somewhat less obvious resources include potential supports from extended family and friends, community resources, parental (and family) ability to cope, and willingness to tackle problems. Areas of vulnerability are also more and sometimes less obvious. Children with lower levels of cognitive ability and limited communication skills are more challenging for parents, siblings, and schools to cope with. School supports can be variable, ranging from great to marginally adequate or poor. Parents with few resources—be they educational, financial, or family supports—also have more difficulty in coping.

Parents may, for their own reasons, be less able—either individually or as a couple—to cope with the special needs of the individual with an ASD. Sometimes one parent is much more able than the other to tackle these issues; this creates its own tensions and stresses that we discuss shortly. Finally, sometimes it is important to emphasize that every family is unique—things that might be horribly difficult for one family to deal with turn out to be much easier for other families.

There are some obvious stresses for the couple and the marriage. Some you can prepare for, and others you can't. The process of getting a diagnosis itself can be stressful. Often weeks, or sometimes months or years, go by between the time you suspect there is a problem and the time when you get a diagnosis. All the many different feelings people have—denial, the sense of things being unfair, trying not to think or talk about it—all can surface at this time. Sometimes the initial experience is one of shock and helplessness. There can be anger at the person who first raised a concern or issue, for example, the pediatrician or day care provider or a grandparent. Occasionally, there are feelings of guilt, that is, that maybe you are secretly responsible for the child's difficulty. Some parents have an experience of severe loss and grief for the idealized child that they didn't get (and that all of us want). Sometimes anger may turn into feelings of resentment. It is important to realize that all these reactions are normal as long as a parent doesn't get stuck in them and not move on to more effective patterns of coping. One of the important aspects of getting more information is the increased awareness of the increasing range of supports available. We've discussed some of these supports in other parts of the book. Other supports, specifically designed for parents of young children, are available as well (e.g., Brereton and Tonge, 2009).

Paradoxically, some of the things that might seem to be (and are) potential areas of strength can also be stresses for families. So, for example, the combination of normal, often beautiful, physical appearance and some areas of strength or ability can easily lead the unknowing observer to assume the child is developing normally and that problem behaviors are a result of poor parenting of a difficult child. This can be particularly an issue for younger children where behavioral outbursts are fairly common in the typically developing population. The combination of social and language delays often contributes to the severity of behavioral difficulties. The naive observer often blames parents for having a child who is "out of control."

Transitions in school programs are almost inevitable in this day and age and are relatively predictable as stressful times. To the extent possible, of course, parents and educators should take as many steps as possible to make transitions flow smoothly. The kinds of transitions include the move from a preschool program to a more school-based program, the transition from primary to middle or junior high school, the transition to high school, and then the transition to adulthood. As we discussed in Chapter 4, there are some times when the law specifies transition planning, notably in moving from early intervention to school-based programs and again in high school. Planning at other times is, of course, very helpful. The individualized education plan (IEP) process should serve to help smooth transitions along. As part of the transition planning, the child's ability to deal with change should be thoughtfully considered, for example, touring a new school, meeting new teachers, having a picture book to show new classmates, and so forth. Even with the best of planning, transition can be stressful, but some planning will mitigate these problems.

Behavioral challenges can be very difficult to cope with. Difficulties in generalization can lead to unexpected problems. Sometimes the child adamantly refuses to engage in a behavior that parents know perfectly well he or she is capable of—often because some small (to typically developing people) issue has fundamentally changed the perception of the situation on the part of the child with an ASD. This often leaves parents and teachers feeling that children are intentionally exhibiting behavior problems which Marcus and colleagues, 2005, refer to as the "can't versus won't" dilemma. Misperceptions on the part of parents can lead to confrontation, anger and anxiety, and more problem behaviors. In addition, of course, behaviors can be truly very challenging.

Unusual patterns of communication pose other challenges. Lack of ready access to social communication and conversation makes it hard for parents and teachers to have immediate access to the child's experience. Language from parents/teachers may be difficult for the child to process. Often, when situations become tense, language from parents/teachers becomes even more complicated—further contributing to behavioral problems (see Chapter 14). A lack of feedback from the child can be problematic, again reflecting basic problems in processing. Unusual, idiosyncratic, or otherwise atypical language may pose other problems.

Behavioral and communication problems can be a source of distress and embarrassment to parents and, particularly, to siblings. This can lead to a vicious cycle, resulting in isolation of the child and family. For example, if the child with an ASD is disruptive at church or synagogue, parents may be less willing to bring the child, and the child and a parent remain at home, preventing the child from learning to behave more appropriately; the parent who stays at home is potentially angry and resentful and further isolated from potential supports. Behavioral difficulties can become a source of great stress for the family so that even a simple visit to the grocery store or park becomes fraught with anxiety. Parents, sometimes rightly, see themselves as being viewed by other parents as having an out-of-control child.

As children begin to receive more services, particularly from multiple service providers, aspects of time management can be challenging. Parents may be engaged in multiple treatments and working with one or more physicians, a speech pathologist, an occupational or physical therapist, applied behavior analysis (ABA) specialists, and others. Often, parents end up fulfilling an integrative function in working to help the entire team to communicate well with each other. While the overall goal, and often end result, may be good, it does come at a price in terms of the parents' personal, and sometimes work, life.

Parents are also often asked to choose from among a sometimes dizzying array of possible therapies—some of which have empirical support and others of which don't. Parents of younger children seem, in particular, to be likely to engage in alternative and/or complementary treatments, each with its own set of demands in terms of resources like time and money. Sometimes the sense of being active and doing something gives a parent a sense of accomplishment, but sometimes there is a price to be paid down the road, particularly if the child's progress is not as much as was hoped.

SUPPORT FROM EDUCATORS AND OTHERS

Educators and health and mental health professionals can be a great support to families with a child on the autism spectrum. As Marcus, Kunce, & Schopler (2005) have summarized, this support can take a number of different forms:[1]

- *Educational supports.* Provide parents and family members with relevant information about the child and his or her needs.

---

[1]Adapted with permission, from Table 42.1 in Marcus, L. M. Junce, L. J., & Schopler, E. (2005). Working with families. In F. Volkmar, A. Klin, R. Paul, & D. J. Cohen (Eds.), *Handbook of autism and pervasive developmental disorders* (3rd ed.; pp. 1062–1063). Hoboken, NJ: Wiley.

- *Parental–family involvement.* May involve work with parents learning to support the child's learning, for example, in generalization of skills from school to home and community settings.

- *Behavioral supports.* Parents and other family members can learn to apply behavioral approaches in encouraging desired behaviors and discouraging problem behaviors.

- *Social skills supports.* Parents and siblings can learn to help children have more positive family relationships and engage in more sophisticated interpersonal behaviors and play skills.

- *Learning-cognitive supports.* Parents and other family members can systematically encourage problem-solving skills, self-monitoring, and other approaches that facilitate learning.

- *Emotional-affective supports.* Parents and siblings can learn to encourage more sophisticated and integrated emotional responses, develop more appropriate communication of feelings, and develop more sophisticated coping strategies.

- *Instrumental supports.* Professionals can help parents and family members access services available in communities, including parent support networks, babysitters and respite services, financial supports, and so forth.

- *Advocacy.* Parents can learn to be more effective as advocates for their children in schools and other settings.

AGE-RELATED STRESSES

As noted previously, getting a diagnosis itself can be stressful. The anxieties and uncertainties related to young children with ASDs pose a number of problems. For parents of younger children who need constant supervision, fatigue can be a big problem. This is often particularly a problem for mothers who tend to have more of the day-to-day parenting burden. This problem can be a major issue with younger children and children who are more active, especially when they are very young and not yet in school full time during the day. Basic safety concerns (see Chapter 11) can loom large for these parents, and they know that any period where the child isn't supervised can lead to a dangerous situation. For other families, sleeping problems can be a very major issue. As we discuss in Chapter 17, sleep problems are relatively common for children with ASDs. They can impact the entire family, with many ripple effects for parents and siblings who don't and can't get a good night's sleep. The child with an ASD who insists on sleeping in the parents' bed creates other issues, including the impact on the parents' marital relationship. It is very important that this not happen and that parents have time for each other and their marriage.

For parents of school-aged children, behavioral difficulties have often decreased and parents have become better at coping with problem behaviors. Stresses for parents of children in this age group include those related to working with school districts, working on generalization of skills from school to home and community settings, and helping siblings cope with the brother or sister with an ASD (we talk more about siblings shortly). In contrast to preschool settings, there is typically less involvement of parents when children are of school age. There may be issues about academic progress, behavioral interventions, special supports, and inclusive settings (see Chapter 8) that all need some degree of parent involvement. Parents of children with IEPs must, of course, remain involved in the educational planning process. Parents have a very special role in helping to ensure generalization across settings.

Adolescence and young adulthood bring all the usual challenges associated with this age and more. As noted in Chapter 9, some children make gains while others seem to lose ground during this time. It is during this period that the possibilities for life after high school become much clearer. Parents understandably become more anxious during this time as they consider the child's longer term prospects. Some adolescents develop problems like seizures (see Chapter 12) and all the stresses associated with chronic medical conditions. Issues around sexual feelings and behavior may also be problematic. As adolescents become young adults, other issues/problems may surface around living arrangements, employment, postsecondary education, and the like. For some individuals, parents may need to think about longer term care and arrangements for the child after they're gone.

MARITAL ISSUES

Of all the potential supports parents have available to them, usually the most important resource is each other. Parents have an obvious stake in having their children do well. They also have to support each other as well as other children and members of the extended family and friends. Although fathers are much more involved in the lives of children than was true in the past decades, it often is mothers who spend much of their time on the "front line" in dealing with the child with an ASD. The father is frequently called in when the mother needs backup. Often, parents take somewhat different paths in dealing with their feelings about a child with a disability of any kind. Sometimes the mother spends more time during the day with the child and may be more aware of how things are in the real world, while the father, who spends less time with the child, may take longer to come to grips with the realities of his child's disabilities. At other times, the reverse is true. We occasionally see one parent in deep denial of the child's having *any* problem while the other parent is unrealistically glum about the child's future.

Respect the fact that a spouse can take more, or less, time to come to terms with the child's special needs. Also keep in mind that parents can genuinely experience children in different ways. Many different factors affect how easily parents cope. Sometimes a mother or father will have had a brother or sister with a problem or know someone else who did. This early experience, even when it isn't terribly relevant, may be the first thing the parent thinks of. The most important thing spouses can do for each other is to be sure to talk about their experience and their feelings. A commitment to ongoing communication is also important in dealing with siblings (as we discuss shortly) as well as with family and friends.

Parents have different ways of coping. Some move into getting information. Others become more depressed or angry. Others throw themselves into their occupation. Occasionally, parents deny the reality of the child's problem. For others, there are opportunities to enjoy and take pleasure in the child's successes. Problems are most likely to arise when parents are constantly denying their own emotions—this will mean that they can't effectively communicate with their spouse and often the emotion then leaks out in other, sometimes very inappropriate, ways. Although spouses should respect the fact that their partner can take different time and different routes in dealing with the problems, it can be an issue if parents are in very different stages of the process. One parent may have been upset, angry, and grieved and moved on to coping with thinking about a program, while the other parent is deeply denying that any problem exists at all. In situations where the difficulties are so severe as to compromise effective communication, particularly communication about the child and ways to intervene, it may be worth seeking some help. This can come from more formal therapy-type people: physicians, social workers, psychologists. Sometimes it may come from friends, ministers, relatives, priests, rabbis, or other parents.

Parents should become very effective in looking for supports. This can take various forms. Some levels of support come from attending parent groups and networking with parents; this information is often more helpful in knowing about programs, doctors, and other factors that are relevant to your child's care and school life. It can also sometimes be helpful just attending parent meetings and hearing that other people have gone through similar things. Just as important, parents should avail themselves of family resources—a niece or nephew who can be trusted to babysit or an aunt or uncle who may be willing to stay with the child for a weekend. Grandparents can be even more effective as caregivers and babysitters, particularly for younger children. Friends from work, as well as networking through churches, synagogues, and other groups, also offer natural supports. It is important to have an explicit focus on maintaining a life as a couple and to be able to "recharge" before you face the next set of issues. Parents can take pleasure in their children's accomplishments, sometimes with a much greater sense of pleasure and gratitude than parents of typically developing children because they know how hard the child worked.

Developing a sense of humor won't hurt either. Parents have endless stories to tell. We recall one parent who came up to us at a conference to tell us how well her teenage son was doing. He had gotten very interested in social skills development and was indeed doing much better, although he had to learn to sort out some of the language he learned from the typical peers. His mother laughingly reported how he had come across one of his old teachers in a shopping mall and run up to greet her, saying loudly, "Hi, Mrs. Smith. I am so happy to see you. How ya doing, you old whore!"

SINGLE-PARENT FAMILIES AND DIVORCE

Single parents raising a child with an ASD face the same stresses as other parents, although without the potential benefit of having someone to share the responsibilities and experiences with. Sometimes a marriage that was already in trouble is pushed over the edge by the addition of a child with a disability. Sometimes single mothers will chose to have a child without being married. It can be very helpful to single parents to have someone to talk with: a family member, friend, therapist, or social worker.

In situations of divorce, it is important that both parents to be in good communication with each other with regard to their children. This can be difficult when the process of divorce has been a bitter one. Some of the worst situations in our experience occur when an angry and bitter marital relationship continues during and after an angry and bitter divorce; often, the child or children suffer the brunt of the parents' mutual fury with each other. Fortunately, this is not common. Increasingly, parents realize they need to support each other—even when they are not married—in the challenging task of raising a child with special needs. Good and clear communication can be helpful. When feelings from the divorce or unresolved issues from the marriage interfere in this, it may be worth getting professional help.

GRANDPARENTS AND FAMILY MEMBERS

Grandparents, aunts, uncles, and other family members can be an invaluable resource and source of support for parents and children with ASDs. Grandparents, in particular, have a complicated set of issues to deal with. They want to support their own children, but they have to balance this with a need to support their grandchild. As with parents, grandparents and, to some extent, other family members may go through a complicated set of feelings and reactions to the news that a grandchild or family member has an ASD. As with parents, this can include anger and denial, followed sometimes by guilt or a temptation to blame. Feelings of mourning for the idealized child that all of us want may be prominent. Usually, grandparents are a step or two behind parents in accepting the diagnosis when a child has an ASD. As is true for parents, having good and continuing communication is important. In some ways, one of the benefits of our electronic age is the potential for staying in close touch even when living some distance away from each other.

TALKING WITH FRIENDS

There are some challenges in talking with friends about a child's problems. In the early stages, parents are often in some degree of denial or want to minimize the difficulties. The fact that, in general, children with autism are attractive and don't appear to have difficulties can hide difficulties from casual observers. Having friends the same age as parents may mean that friends are having typically developing children, and it may be hard for the parents of the child with autism to be with these friends and their children—at least initially. As a result, parents can feel somewhat cut off and isolated from friends in the early stages of dealing with a child's difficulties.

Parents should not be surprised to find that they end up being closer with some friends than others. Parents also will discover that some friends will have to take their own good time in dealing with the child's difficulties. Whenever possible, it is good to try to maintain relationships rather than lose them. This can occasionally be a challenge in dealing with friends who have little awareness of the process parents go through.

SIBLINGS

Siblings have unique relationships with each other. In contrast to relations with other children, those with siblings are lifelong. They are continuous and not episodic. Unlike many child relationships, siblings (with the exception of twins) are of different ages. As with parents, siblings have a myriad of ways of dealing with a brother or sister with some difficulty. Parents of very young children with an older sibling with a disability may find it hard to explain the problems to the younger child. In other instances, an older sibling may notice something different about a younger brother or sister with an ASD and ask parents why the child behaves in some unusual way or has some odd response to the environment.

What are the best ways for parents to deal with talking to siblings about the brother's or sister's difficulties? In general, providing appropriate information is the best way to go. This means neither overwhelming the child nor giving insufficient information. Fortunately, children are very good, in general, at asking questions. Keep things at the child's level. Children may wonder if they have somehow caused the sibling's trouble. They may be angry at the time the sibling with special needs takes and may talk about their feelings of resentment or anger. It is important to give the typically developing child an outlet for his or her feelings and to encourage communication. For young children, this often happens during play. Other times, when parents and children are together, there may be natural times to start a discussion; for example, seeing someone behave oddly on a television program may give an opening for a discussion of why a brother or sister behaves oddly at times.

For older children, other kinds of support can be helpful. This can include provision of information, including the many excellent books now available for siblings (see the box below for a list of some of these books). Sibling support groups also can be a good opportunity for brothers and sisters to talk about their feelings.

BOOKS FOR SIBLINGS

FOR YOUNGER CHILDREN

Amenta, C. A. (1992). *Russell is extra special: A book about autism for children*. New York: Magination Press.

Bodenheimer, C. (1979). *Everybody is a person: A book for brothers and sisters of autistic kids*. Syracuse, NY: Jowonio/The Learning Place.

Cassette, M. (2006). *My sister Katie: My 6 year old's view on her sister's autism*. Central Milton Keynes, UK: Authorhouse.

Cook, J., & Hartman, C. (2008). *My mouth is a volcano!* Chattanooga, TN: National Center for Youth Issues.

Donlon, L. (2007). *The other kid: A draw it out guidebook for kids dealing with a special needs sibling*. Coral Springs, FL: Llumina Press.

Donlon, L. (2008). *El otro niño: Una guia para niños que tienen un hermano o una hermana especial* (Spanish Edition). Bethpage, NY: Llumina.

Dwight, L. (2005). *Brothers and sisters*. New York: Star Bright Books.

Gold, P. (1976). Please don't say hello. New York: Human Sciences Press.

Gorrod, L., & Carger, B. (2003). *My brother is different—a book for young children who have a brother or sister with autism*. London: Natonal Autism Society.

Lears, L. (1998). *Ian's walk: A story about autism*. Morton Grove, IL: Albert Whitman & Company.

Meyer, D., & Gallagher, D. (2005). *The sibling slam book: What it's really like to have a brother or sister with special needs*. Bethesda, MD: Woodbine House.

Meyer, D., & Pillo, C. (1997). *Views from our shoes: Growing up with a brother or sister with special needs*. Bethesda, MD: Woodbine House.

Parker, R. (1974). *He's your brother*. Nashville, TN: Thomas Nelson.

Peralta, S. (2002). *All about my brother*. Shawnee Mission, KS: Autism Asperger.

Phalon, A. C. (2005). *Me, my brother, and autism*. Charleston, SC: BookSurge.

Spence, E. (1977). *The devil hole*. New York: Lothrop, Lee, and Shepard.

Thompson, M. (1996). *Andy and his yellow frisbee*. Bethesda, MD: Woodbine House.

Werlin, N. (1994). *Are you alone on purpose?* New York: Houghton Mifflin.

For Older Children, Adolescents, and Adults

Band, E., & Hect, E. (2001). *Autism through a sister's eye*. Arlington, TX: Future Horizons.

Barnill, A. C. (2007). *At home in the land of Oz: Autism, my sister, and me*. London: Jessica Kingsley.

Bleach, F. (2002). *Everybody is different*. Shawnee Mission, KS: Autism Asperger.

Cook, J., & Hartman, C. (2008). *My mouth is a volcano!* Chattanooga, TN: National Center for Youth Issues.

Donlon, L. (2007). *The other kid: A draw it out guidebook for kids dealing with a special needs sibling*. Coral Springs, FL: Llumina Press.

Feiges, L. S., & Weiss, M. J. (2004). *Sibling stories: Reflections on life with a brother or sister on the autism spectrum*. Shawnee Mission, KS: Autism Asperger.

Hale, N. (2004). *Oh brother! Growing up with a special needs sibling*. New York: Magination Press.

Hoopmann, K. (2001). *Blue bottle mystery: An Asperger adventure*. Philadelphia: Jessica Kingsley.

Hoopmann, K. (2001). *Of mice and aliens: An Asperger adventure*. Philadelphia: Jessica Kingsley.

Hoopmann, K. (2002). *Lisa and the lacemaker: An Asperger adventure*. Philadelphia: Jessica Kingsley.

Hoopmann, K. (2003). *Haze*. Philadelphia: Jessica Kingsley.

Keating-Velasco, J. L. (2007). *A is for autism, F is for friend: A kid's book for making friends with a child who has autism*. Shawnee Mission, KS: Autism Asperger.

Shally, C., & Herrnington, D. (2007) *Since we're friends: An autism picture book*. Shawnee Mission, KS: Awaken Specialty Press.

Thompson, M. (1996). *Andy and his yellow frisbee*. Bethesda, MD: Woodbine House.

There are a number of potential stresses for siblings. The behavior of the child with an ASD may be an embarrassment. The sibling may be a target of aggression from the child with ASD. The brother or sister with an ASD may seem to take up too much of the parents' time, with much of the family life revolving around them. The child who is typically developing may notice and be worried about parental reactions or may become overly responsible and assume a caretaking role himself. There may be tremendous frustration around not being able to relate normally to the brother or sister with an ASD. Sometimes siblings may worry about their long-term responsibility for care. As with other things, the experience of having a sibling with a disability may serve as a positive or a negative experience in the life of the typically developing child. The box below summarizes one sibling's experience of his older brother with severe autism.

ONE SIBLING'S EXPERIENCE OF AUTISM

My brother was diagnosed as autistic in 1974 . . . as a "classic case" of childhood autism. He was $3\frac{1}{2}$ years old. I was a year younger. . . . From that early age, I was consumed by a self-imposed sense of responsibility for my brother's safety and well-being. . . . I began trying to figure my brother out. I was wrought with questions. What does he want? What does he feel? Why does he not seem to love me? My brother had a complete inability to understand social conventions, matched by my inability to understand him. . . . He refused to make eye contact with me or anyone else for that matter. I learned to not take offense at it. . . . He broke anything and everything he could get his hands on. . . . He had pica and ate Play-Doh, among other things. . . . He ate staples. I learned to berate him without guilt because I drew the line at his health and well-being. . . . My brother emerged as one of my greatest teachers—through whom I learned responsibility, accountability, patience, stamina, self-discipline, and unconditional love. . . . My brother lived at home and attended a day school. From the beginning, my parents had made a conscious decision to keep him with the family during a time when the norm was to gravitate toward institutionalization. . . . This decision proved to be the single most significant force affecting my upbringing—one with long-lasting implications. I have always agreed with the decision for as long as I recall. . . . Family trips were a vacation from the everyday life at home, but never from the responsibility surrounding the care of my brother. He was a full-time job. At 9 years old . . . Disney World was exciting but not fun to me. I remember constantly looking over my shoulder to make sure my brother was following. . . . I had heard stories of autistic children getting lost in crowds and recovered by police. . . . My saddest moments revolved around my brother's disinterest in most activities and the rest of the family's lack of involvement as a result. My happiest times were when we found a ride that my brother would enjoy—a ride that we could get on together. . . . Eventually, I left for college. Siblings who do plan to leave home to pursue higher learning generally fall into one of two schools of thought. Many attend relatively close to home for the obvious purpose of being near the family and the subsequent ability to continue helping the autistic sibling. . . . The second mind-set takes an opposite approach . . . by attending school far away . . . I chose the first option. Our plans for maintaining the direct connection with my brother were changed dramatically when my family was transferred halfway across the country in August, due to my father's work. . . . I missed my brother tremendously. At the same time, though, I realized something that I had never felt before. I no longer looked over my shoulder after several months when out shopping or walking through large crowds. I was able to walk freely without the pressing fear of losing my brother. I also seemed to have much more time on my hands. There was no pressing feeling of need to occupy my brother with learning or activities. I never mentioned this to any of my friends at school. I assumed they would not have understood. I was probably right. . . . As I contemplated career decisions years before, I always viewed them within the context of my brother's future. How would I be able to help him best in the years to come? . . . I have been fortunate to know that neither one of my parents ever assumed that I would be completely responsible for my brother's well-being. That in itself removes an otherwise immense pressure. It has been my unspoken desire to oversee my brother's future. Why would I not do that as an adult, when I had already assumed that responsibility as a 4-year-old?

Adapted and reprinted, with permission, from Konidaris, J. B. (2005). A sibling's perspective on autism. In F. Volkmar, A. Klin, R. Paul, & D. Cohen, (Eds.), *Handbook of autism and pervasive developmental disorders* (Chapter 50, pp. 1265–1275). Hoboken, NJ: Wiley.

Older children may do quite a bit of the child rearing. Girls may do this more than boys, but that is certainly not always the case. Children who are close in age frequently feel closer to each other than those with greater age differences, but there can also be more competition between them because of the closeness in age. They may feel that it's harder to stand out as their own person when they are very close in age, or they may feel a special bond that others in the family don't have because of this closeness. Parents can take a number of steps to help brothers and sisters cope effectively.

Harris and Glasberg (2003) have produced an excellent book on siblings of children with autism that summarizes many of the steps parents can take to help siblings. Parents should try to look at the world through the normal sibling's eyes. For younger children, there can be confusion about what caused the autism in the first place. Children should be encouraged to ask questions and talk about their experience. Probably the most frequent mistake parents make is in *not* talking enough to siblings about their experience. Whatever else is true, the sibling will have many questions, emotions, and reactions to the brother or sister with autism. Parents, and to some extent other family members, friends, and teachers, should be prepared to deal with their questions in a sensible way. In this context, sensible means (1) adjusting your answer to the level of understanding of the child asking the question, (2) being open to having any questions asked, (3) modeling a willingness to talk, and (4) (explicitly or implicitly) conveying the message to the typically developing sibling that parents have a relationship with, and time for, them as well as for the child with an ASD. For example, a younger child may not understand the nature of autism. If it is presented as "Jimmy has a disease," the typically developing younger child may wonder if she can catch it from Jimmy. Or did she have it and pass it on to Jimmy? Keeping the explanation simple and appropriate is important. Don't, for example, overwhelm children with information they don't need to know. Also look at the 'big picture"—by this, we mean all children will know of other people with disabilities of many different varieties. This can range from a grandparent who has had a stroke and trouble talking to a father who is nearsighted and wears glasses, or an aunt who uses a cane because of a leg injury. Once children start looking, they will realize that many of us have disabilities of various types and all of us have things we are stronger at and things we are weaker at. The response to the question of why my sister acts a certain way can be very different for a 3-year-old versus an 8-year-old versus a 16-year-old. The 3-year-old may just want to know why his older sister doesn't talk to him. The 8-year-old may want to know why she behaves in odd ways. The 16-year-old may be interested in the biological basis of autism.

The age of the child with the ASD and the types of services she needs, and whether she is receiving them at home or outside the home, clearly also will have an impact on her siblings. A program at home that requires many hours of the parents' time will limit the time left for the parent to spend with a sibling. If the child requires many different services outside the home, such as speech and occupational therapy, this may also cut into time available for other siblings. Relatives other than the parents or friends or neighbors may volunteer to take care of the typical children for some of the time. Depending on the age of the sibling, he may or may not understand why the parent is away or busy so much. Even an older child who understands the needs of the child with an ASD may still resent the amount of time the parent is unavailable to him.

For typically developing siblings, the unusual behaviors and social–communication problems may be sources of frustration and embarrassment. Help the sibling to understand more about what the person with autism can and can't do and to understand that sometimes behavior is out of the person's control. Also, convey a strong message that you are there for the sibling as much as for the child with autism.

How parents cope with the diagnosis of an ASD in their child will also have an impact on how the siblings react. How the parents explain the diagnosis to the siblings, if they do explain it at all initially, will set the tone for how the siblings react. Some will feel free to ask questions, while others may realize that they should avoid any discussion for fear of upsetting their parents or grandparents or other family members. The impact of the stress in the family on the parents' relationship with each other may determine the overall level of stress in the household. What siblings are told may influence what they feel comfortable saying to their peers in the neighborhood, at school, and at home. Problems will vary over time. Some siblings will cope easily for long periods of time and then have some very particular problem, for example, the child who has done very well but suddenly, in adolescence, doesn't want to have potential girlfriends meet his older brother. Others will be fairly comfortable in talking to their friends about a brother's or sister's problems. By their own actions, parents play an important role in helping the typically developing sibling develop successful strategies for coping.

Other issues arise over time as siblings get older. Who will care for the sibling with an ASD as their parents get older and cannot manage it all on their own? What impact will this have on a future spouse of theirs? Will the sibling with an ASD come to live with them? Will they be able to manage as well as their parents have done? Who will provide the financial support that is needed over the years? And perhaps most concerning of all, will they have a child of their own with an ASD? These are all legitimate questions, some of which we can address now and some of which we'll be able to better address over the next several years (see Chapters 1 and 2).

Clearly, talking to siblings in an age-appropriate manner can be enormously helpful. Sometimes meeting with other siblings of children with ASDs can be of benefit. There are now more and more groups providing sibling support, some specifically for siblings of children and adults with ASDs, and some for siblings of children and adults with other chronic disorders with and without intellectual disabilities. We have listed a few web sites and a few books on these topics at the end of the book. The Sibling Support Network (www.siblingsupport.com) has been around for many years and has been very helpful for many people of different ages.

FAMILY ENGAGEMENT, GENERALIZATION, AND LIFE IN THE COMMUNITY

Children with ASDs have major problems in learning, particularly learning that involves **generalization** of skills across settings (see Chapter 6). This can be a major problem over the long term, even for the most cognitively able children. Over the past 2 decades, there has been a growing appreciation on the part of educators and other professionals of the important role that parents, siblings, and others can have in addressing this problem for the child with an ASD. Parents and siblings can be with the child in church, the grocery store, and in the park. The focus at home and in the community should not be concerned so much with teaching cognitive and other skills but in helping the child learn to apply these skills at home and in the community. The conversational skills taught by the speech pathologist should be generalized to daily life. This process can and should start when the child is very young, but it is often when the child enters elementary school that this becomes even more of an issue. Part of the issue at this time stems from increased demands for personal independence and self-sufficiency and expectations for growing social sophistication. Part of it also can come when, as is often the case, the degree of communication between home and school lessens.

Accordingly, it is important for parents to remain appropriately attentive to the child's school program. Notes or e-mail from the teacher, log books or diaries, homework assignments, and other means can be used to ensure good communication. Parents should also realize that work at home on activities involved in daily living and adaptive skills (see Chapter 6) is something they should encourage and monitor. While parents may, at times, be frustrated by the child's difficulties learning what seems, to the parents, relatively simple social or cognitive tasks, they may be pleased to discover how readily some daily living skills can be taught. As we discuss in Chapter 6, a range of supports can be used to this end—designed with the child's special needs in mind. These can range from work on functional routines using visual supports to help with written schedules, organizers, and so forth. The book by Anderson, Jablonski, Knapp, & Thomeer (2007) in the reading list has some helpful suggestions.

As with other children, parents should also think about helping their child be involved in community-based activities. This can naturally include things like groups affiliated with churches or temples. Children may be enrolled in music or art classes. For music, the Suzuki method is particularly good, since it is strongly developmental, rule governed, and highly respectful of the child. For other children, music or art therapy may be helpful. Sports and leisure time activities should take into account the child's needs and vulnerabilities. Team sports can be more challenging than more "solitary" or "dyadic" activities; for example, swimming or tennis probably is often a better choice than baseball or soccer. Even getting the child to participate in family hikes and other activities that involve some exercise can be helpful; indeed, exercise has been shown to be associated with improved behavior in several studies. The reading list provides some books concerned with leisure activities, some of which can be enjoyed by all members of the family. Leisure activities also involve opportunities for socialization and often for practicing other daily living skills.

Teachers and school staff may be helpful in suggesting potential extracurricular activities at school. These individuals often will be able to give helpful suggestions about teaching specific skills or working on certain problems. In this regard, it is important to note that information should flow in both directions; for example, if parents want to report a successful weekend outing or new interest, the teacher should be eager to get the information. It is important to keep in mind that experiences can be therapeutic (in the broader sense) without being "therapy" (in the narrower sense).

Summary

In this chapter, we talked about the impact that having a child with autism can have on parents and families. Having a child with autism can put stresses on the marriage and family. This is true for having typically developing children as well, but children on the autism spectrum have additional challenges and so do parents and family members. Concerns about long-term outcome, planning for the future, and dealing with behavioral issues can all pose stresses. Parents sometimes worry about the risk of having another child on the spectrum.

At the same time, parents and family members can and should take genuine pleasure in the accomplishments of the child with an ASD. It is important that parents feel positive about their ability to parent the child with an ASD along with their other children. It is important that siblings not feel left out or neglected. They will have their own reactions to a brother or sister with an ASD, and these may change over time. There is not a single right way to be an effective parent. From the point of view of both the couple and family, it is important to carve out time for each other and the family and still be a good parent to a child with an ASD.

Families should feel free to use other supports whenever they can. These supports can include relatives and friends. Other parents and parent and sibling support groups can provide useful information and ways to connect with other people having similar experiences and facing similar problems. Teachers and school personnel may be other sources of valuable information and support.

Siblings will have different feelings and experiences. Even as young children, they may well pick up on the fact that a brother or sister is different. Parents should be honest about these differences without overwhelming the sibling with too much information. Parents should also be aware that siblings can have different reactions over time, including negative ones. By the time children are in school, the typically developing brother or sister may develop any of (or many of) a number of reactions, ranging from trying to deny the reality of the brother's or sister's problems to becoming caretakers of the child, to being resentful of the sibling who receives more attention. As with other things, children are often guided by their parents (even when they protest that they are not), so if parents can model openness, tolerance, and a willingness to communicate, things will tend to go best over the long haul.

The challenges and problems families face will change over time, depending on the specifics of the situation and family and age and level of the child with an ASD. Families will work best when parents can have good communication with each other and with family members.

■ READING LIST

Adams, S. (2009). *A book about what autism can be like.* London: Jessica Kingsley.

Anderson, S. R., Jablonski, A. L., Knapp, V. M., & Thomeer, M. L. (2007). *Self-help skills for people with autism: A systematic teaching approach.* Bethesda, MD: Woodbine House.

Andron, L. (Ed.). (2001). *Our journey through high functioning autism & Asperger syndrome: A roadmap.* Philadelphia: Jessica Kingsley.

Bauer, A. (2005). *A wild ride up the cupboards.* New York: Scribner.

Bolick, T. (2004). *Asperger syndrome and young children: Building skills for the real world.* Gloucester, MA: Fair Winds Press.

Bondy, A., & Frost, L. (2008). *Autism 24/7: A family guide to learning at home and in the community.* Bethesda, MD: Woodbine House.

Boyd, B. (2003). *Parenting a child with Asperger syndrome.* London: Jessica Kingsley.

Brereton, A.V. & Tonge, B. (2009) *Pre-schoolers with autism: An education and skills training programme for parents - manual for parents.* London: Jessica Kingsley.

Brill, M. T. (2001). *Keys to parenting the child with autism* (2nd ed.). Hauppauge, NY: Barron's Educational Series.

Calinescu, M. (2009). *Matthew's enigma: A father's portrait of his autistic son.* Bloomington, IN: Indiana University Press.

Cohen, J. (2002). *The asperger parent: How to raise a child with asperger syndrome and maintain your sense of humor.* Shawnee Mission, KS: Autism Asperger.

Coulter, D. (Producer/Director). (2004). *Asperger syndrome for dad: Becoming an even better father to your child with Asperger syndrome* [DVD]. Winston Salem, NC: Coulter Video. www.coultervideo.com, 336-794-0298.

Coulter, D. (Producer/Director). (2007). *Understanding brothers and sisters with Asperger syndrome* [DVD]. Winston Salem, NC: Coulter Video. www.coultervideo.com

Coulter, D. (Producer/Director). (2007). *Understanding brothers and sisters on the autism spectrum* [DVD]. Winston Salem, NC: Coulter Video.

Coyne, P. (1999). *Developing leisure time skills for persons with autism: A practical approach for home, school and community.* Arlington, TX: Future Horizons.

Coyne, P. (2004). *Supporting individuals with autism spectrum disorder in recreation.* Champaign, IL: Sagamore.

Dillon, K. (1995). *Living with autism: The parents stories.* Boone, NC: Parkway.

Durand, V. M., & Hieneman, M. (2008). *Helping parents with challenging children: Positive family intervention—facilitator guide.* Oxford: Oxford University Press.

Elder, J. (2005). *Different like me: My book of autism heroes.* London: Jessica Kingsley.

Exkorn, K. (2005). *The autism sourcebook: Everything you need to know about diagnosis, treatment, coping, and healing.* New York: Regan Books.

Fawcett, H., & Baskin, A. (2006). *More than a mom: Living a full and balanced life when your child has special needs.* Bethesda, MD: Woodbine House.

Frender, S., Schiffmiller, R. (2007). *Brotherly feelings: Me, my emotions, and my brother with Asperger's Syndrome.* London: Jessica Kingsley.

Haddon, M. (2003). *The curious incident of the dog in the nighttime.* New York: Doubleday.

Harris, S. L. (1994). *Siblings of children with autism: A guide for families.* Bethesda, MD: Woodbine House.

Harris, S. L., & Glasberg, B. A. (2003). *Siblings of children with autism: A guide for families* (2nd ed). Bethesda, MD: Woodbine House.

Johnson, J., & Van Rensselaer, A. (2008). *Families of adults with autism: Stories and advice for the next generation.* London: Jessica Kingsley.

Kelly, A. B., Garnett, M. S., Attwood, T., & Peterson, C. (2008). Autism spectrum symptomatology in children: The impact of family and peer relationships. *Journal of Abnormal Child Psychology, 36,*1069–1081.

Konidaris, J. B. (2005). *A sibling's perspective on autism.* In F. R. Volkmar, R. Paul, A. Klin, & D. Cohen, (Eds.), *Handbook of autism and pervasive developmental disorders* (3rd ed., pp. 1265–1275). New York: Wiley.

Kranowitz, C. S. (1995). *101 activities for kids in tight spaces.* New York: St. Martin's Press.

Larson, E. M. (2006). *I am utterly unique: Celebrating the strengths of children with Asperger syndrome and high-functioning autism.* Shawnee Mission, KS: Autism Asperger.

Leventhal-Belfer, L., & Coe, C. (2004). *Asperger syndrome in young children.* London: Jessica Kingsley.

Lobato, D. J. (1990). *Brothers, sisters, and special needs: Information and activities for helping young siblings of children with chronic illnesses and developmental disabilities.* Foreword by Eunice Kennedy Shriver. Baltimore: Brookes.

Luchsinger, D. F. (2007). *Playing by the rules: A story about autism.* Bethesda, MD: Woodbine House.

Marcus, L. J., Kunce, L. J., & Schopler, E. (2005). Working with families. In F. R. Volkmar, R. Paul, A. Klin, & D. Cohen, (Eds.), *Handbook of autism and pervasive developmental disorders,* (3rd ed., pp. 1055–1086). New York: Wiley.

Marshak, L. E., & Prezant, F. B. (2007). *Married with special-needs children: A couples' guide to keeping connected.* Bethesda, MD: Woodbine House.

Martin, E. P. (1999). *Dear Charlie, a grandfather's love letter: A guide for living your life with autism.* Arlington, TX: Future Horizons.

Meyer, D., & Vadasy, P. (1996). *Living with a brother or sister with special needs: A book for sibs* (2nd ed.). Seattle, WA: University of Washington Press.

Miller, N., & Sammons, C. (1999). *Everybody's different: Understanding and changing our reactions to disabilities.* Baltimore: Brookes.

Moor, J. (2008). *Playing, laughing and learning with children on the autism spectrum: A practical resource of play ideas for parents and carers* (2nd ed). London: Jessica Kingsley.

Moore, C. (2006). *George & Sam: Two boys, one family, and autism.* New York: St. Martin's Press.

Nadworth, J. W., & Haddad, C. R. (2007). *The special needs planning guide: How to prepare for every stage of your child's life.* Baltimore, MD: Brookes.

Naseef, R. A. (2001). *Special children, challenged parents: The struggles and rewards of raising a child with a disability.* Baltimore: Brookes.

Newman, S. (2002). *Small steps forward: Using games and activities to help your preschool child with special needs.* London: Jessica Kingsley.

O'Brien, M., & Daggett, J. A. (2006). *Beyond the autism diagnosis: A professional's guide to helping families.* Baltimore: Brookes.

Ozonoff, S., Dawson, G., & McPartland, J. (2002). *A parent's guide to asperger syndrome and high-functioning autism.* New York: Guilford Press.

Richman, S. (2001). *Raising a child with autism: A guide to applied behavior analysis for parents.* London: Jessica Kingsley.

Schopler, E. (1995). *Parent survival manual: A guide to crisis resolution in autism and related developmental disorders.* New York: Plenum Press.

Senator, S. (2005). *Making peace with autism: One family's story of struggle, discovery, and unexpected gifts.* Boston: Trumpeter.

Sicile-Kira, C. (2006). *Adolescents on the autism spectrum: A parent's guide to the cognitive, social, physical, and transition needs of teenagers with autism spectrum disorders.* New York: Penguin.

Siegel, B., & Silverstein, S. (1994). *What about me? Growing up with a developmentally disabled sibling.* Cambridge, MA: Perseus.

Sohn, A., & Grayson, C. (2005). *Parenting your asperger child: Individualized solutions for teaching your child practical skills.* New York: Perigee Trade.

Sonders, S. A. (2003). *Giggle time—establishing the social connection: A program to develop the communication skills of children with autism, Asperger syndrome and PDD.* London: Jessica Kingsley.

Spilsbury, L. (2001). *What does it mean to have autism.* Chicago: Heinemann Library.

Stewart, K. (2002). *Helping a child with nonverbal learning disorder or asperger's syndrome: A parent's guide.* Oakland, CA: New Harbinger Publications, Inc.

Tammet, D. (2006). *Born on a blue day: Inside the extraordinary mind of an autistic savant.* New York: Free Press.

Twoy, R., Connolly, P. M., & Novak, J. M. (2007). Coping strategies used by parents of children with autism. *Journal of the American Academy of Nurse Practitioners, 19*(5), 251–260.

Vicker, B., & Lieberman, L. A. (2007). *Sharing information about your child with autism spectrum disorder.* Shawnee Mission, KS: Autism Asperger.

Welton, J. (2003). *Can I tell you about Asperger syndrome? A guide for friends and family.* Philadelphia: Jessica Kingsley.

Wheatley, T. (2005). *My sad is all gone: A family's triumph over violent autism.* Lancaster, OH: Lucky Press.

Whiteman, N. J. (2007). *Building a joyful life with your child who has special needs.* London: Jessica Kingsley.

Zysk, V., Notbohm, E. (2004). *1001 great ideas for teaching and raising children with autism spectrum disorders.* Arlington, TX: Future Horizons.

■ QUESTIONS AND ANSWERS

1. **Our $2\frac{1}{2}$-year-old son was just diagnosed with autism. What is the best way to talk to friends about this?**

   It used to be the case that people had never heard about autism; that has now changed dramatically. That being said, what people understand may either be incorrect or, more typically, very general. So, for example, they may have watched the movie *Rain Man* and assume that any child with autism is like the man portrayed in the movie. In general, it works best if you are straightforward with people and tell them as much as you want them to know. This can range from a very simple description of autism as a biological disorder that impacts on social skills, communication, and behavior, to a more complicated explanation, or you can refer them to any of the many different resources now available. Friends can be a great support; if they offer, let them help out in whatever ways you can. Keep in mind that people do have misconceptions about autism, and sometimes it takes people a while to digest things—so don't assume that an initial reaction of puzzlement or confusion on the part of friends will last.

2. **My son and daughter-in-law just got word that their 4-year-old has Asperger's disorder. We want to do something to help them out (we live in a different state). Should we send them money? Should we set up a trust fund for the child?**

   Probably the most important thing you can do is stay involved and be supportive. Talk to them about what their needs are. Sometimes it may be for something extra that money can help with—more babysitting time for the parents, additional services for the child, or something else. Be careful when you think about a trust fund; talk with a lawyer (see Chapter 9), for many different reasons, to be sure this is a good idea. Also, you didn't mention if you have other grandchildren. If so, be careful that you don't single out only one grandchild for support; that can lead other children/ grandchildren to feel resentful over time.

3. **We have a school-aged child with autism. He has done well with intervention and is now largely mainstreamed. My brother, who is a bit of a geek, is always sending me information from the Internet about how to "cure" my son. I'm starting to find that I resent this. Can I just tell him to stop?**

   You didn't mention how close or far away your brother lives. It sounds like he is well meaning, but his efforts are a bit annoying. If he lives far away, invite him for a visit so he can see how well your son is doing. Also, think about getting them in touch with each other; it may be more helpful if he can make a relationship with your son, and the Internet can be very good for children on the autism spectrum if they can manage the typing and computer.

4. **Our son gives us tremendous fits during mealtimes. It seems like the entire family has to revolve around getting him to the table to sit down with the rest of us.**

   There are a lot of specifics it would be good to know in terms or providing advice. Talk with your child's teacher or the behavior specialist/ psychologist at school and see if they have any tips or strategies.

Depending on your state, there may be a behavioral psychologist who works with the department of disabilities that can even come to your home to do an assessment and make recommendations. There are also some excellent resources for parents (see Chapter 14) in dealing with behavior problems. Depending on the circumstances, you might want to try to use routines, a careful analysis of the antecedents and consequences of the behaviors, sensory issues that contribute to meal disruption, visual schedules, stories, and so forth. The book by Durand and Hieneman in the reading list at the end of this chapter is another good resource.

5. **My husband would like to get our 8-year-old son with Asperger's involved in sports, but he just doesn't seem interested. We both worry he is going to turn into a couch potato—he likes to play on the computer or watch TV and that is it. What can we do to get him more involved? We'd like to do some things as a family.**

Leisure-time activities can be hard for children on the autism spectrum. Team sports involve a very large social–communication component. Also, they tend to be fast paced and require "multitasking." Finally, some children, particularly those with Asperger's, can have motor coordination issues. There are a couple of things you can do. First, there are some resources in the reading list that may be of interest (see the books by Coyne, for example). Second, think about sports that are more solitary and/or have a strong progressive component. Some of the martial arts things are, for example, very strictly rule governed, the child can progress at his or her own pace and there is a teacher to work with and keep an eye on things. Other possibilities include swimming. Some children will enjoy outdoor activities like hiking (an easy one for the whole family) or running or skiing.

6. **My wife and I always seem to be fighting about what to do with our 6-year-old daughter with autism. She can't sleep by herself, so either one of us is in sleeping with her or she is in bed with us. Neither one of us gets a good night's sleep and, of course, we're never able to be by ourselves.**

Sleep problems (see Chapter 17) can be some of the most difficult ones to deal with. They contribute to family tensions in a host of ways, including disrupted sleep for others and negative impact on marital relationships. Take a look at Chapter 17 for some tips on dealing with sleep issues. The two of you should do a couple of things as well. First, try to find some time for yourselves by yourselves—get a friend or relative to stay with your daughter overnight. Second, develop a coherent plan that you can both agree on to deal with the sleep problems; they will only get worse if you don't help your daughter develop better sleep habits now.

7. **Our 12-year-old son seems to be increasingly resentful about his younger sister with ASD. He wants to avoid spending time with us as a family—particularly in public. This seems a bit paradoxical to us since, if anything, her behavior has gotten a lot better. We've tried to get him to talk about this, but he is not willing to do it.**

   The responses of siblings can vary a lot over time, depending on a number of different things. It is possible that he is worried you won't want to hear it if he complains about his sister or that he doesn't want to burden you. It is possible that there is something very specific or something very general that is bothering him. Sometimes the offhand comment or question of a friend can get children into a bad mood. Or he may be worried that he will have to assume her care when he is grown up. Or he may have his own, very complicated, feelings about his sister and have trouble expressing them even to himself. In a situation like this, it might be worthwhile to think about some other forum where he could, at least potentially, talk about what is going on. This might be with a trusted family friend or with a counselor of some kind, or it could involve his going to a sibling group.

8. **My son is about to turn 18 and we wanted to name him as the executor of our will and as the person responsible for his younger sibling with autism. How much should we tell him about all this?**

   You should tell him everything he needs to know. He should understand exactly what you are asking and what the expectations are. Include him in any meeting with the attorney. Also, we assume/hope that this is part of a long-term, continuing discussion. Sometimes parents just assume a sibling will assume a role like this for a disabled brother or sister, but then they don't ask. Sometimes this leads to very unfortunate events, for example, if the sibling doesn't want to take on this role or feels unequal to it.

9. **We dread taking our daughter with autism on vacation because she is so difficult. To some extent this is true even of just going out to a restaurant—we're always on edge waiting for all hell to break loose. Is there anything we can do about this?**

   Your question suggests, at least by implication, that some of the trouble may have to do with difficulties tolerating change and the unexpected. Unfortunately, for some families vacations can turn into nightmares. The goal then is to try to help the child feel comfortable, or as comfortable as possible, in the new setting. Depending on the child's level of language ability and cognitive understanding, there are a number of steps to take.

You can put together picture books in advance, or sometimes even videos, that will help the child get a sense of what the place is going to be like. Have the child help put together a visual or written schedule and list of activities that she may enjoy doing. Some places, for example, some amusement parks and Disney World, make special accommodations for individuals with disabilities. Giving the child something to do when waiting or while traveling is also a good idea—there are some good resources in the reading list, for example, the ones by Kranowitz and by Zysk and Notbohm are good resources for activities. You can also think about ways to keep the child busy, for example, if she can use a digital camera to be the official photographer of the vacation (be a bit careful as this can take on a life of its own). Be sure everyone going is "on the same page" if it comes to dealing with problem situations. Sometimes you can find a familiar caretaker or family member who will come with and relieve parents of some of the burden.

Resources Lists: Books and Websites

Batshaw, M. L. (Ed.). (2001). *When your child has a disability: The complete sourcebook of daily and medical care.* Baltimore: Brookes.

Bowe, F. G. (2000). *Birth to five: Early childhood special education.* Albany, NY: Delmar Thomson Learning.

Doyle, B. T., & Iland, E. D. (2004). *Autism spectrum disorders from A to Z: Assessment, diagnosis . . . & more! Arlington,* TX: Future Horizons.

Exkorn, K. (2005). *The autism sourcebook: Everything you need to know about diagnosis, treatment, coping, and healing.* New York: Regan Books.

Iovannone, R., Dunlap, G., Huber, H., & Kincaid, D. (2003). Effective educational practices for students with autism spectrum disorders. *Focus on Autism and Other Developmental Disabilities, 18*(3), 150–165.

Kluth, P. (2003). *You're going to love this kid.* Baltimore: Brookes.

Legge, B. (2002). *Can't eat, won't eat: Dietary difficulties and autistic spectrum disorders.* London: Jessica Kingsley.

Lovaas, O. I., & Smith, T. (2003). *Early and intensive behavioral intervention in autism.* In A. E. Kazdin and J. R. Weisz (Eds.), *Evidence-based psychotherapies for children and adolescents,* (pp. 325–340). New York: Guilford Press.

Luecking, R. G. (2009). *The way to work: How to facilitate work experiences for youth in transition.* Baltimore: Brookes.

Matson, J. L. (Ed.). (1994). *Autism in children and adults: Etiology, assessment, and intervention.* Pacific Grove, CA: Brooks/Cole.

Strong, C. J., & North, K. H. (1996). *The magic of stories.* Eau Claire, WI: Thinking Publications.

Thompson, T. (2008). *Dr. Thompson's straight talk on autism.* Baltimore: Brookes.

Volkmar, F. R., Klin, A., Paul, R., Cohen, D. J. (Eds.). (2005). *Handbook of autism and pervasive developmental disorders,* 3rd ed . Hoboken, NJ: Wiley.

Whalen, C. (2009). *Real life, real progress for children with autism spectrum disorders: Strategies for successful generalization in natural environments.* Baltimore: Brookes.

WEBSITES

American Academy of Child and Adolescent Psychiatry: www.aacap.org.
American Academy of Family Doctors: www.aafp.org.

American Academy of Pediatrics: www.aap.org.

American Dental Association: www.ada.org.

American Dietetic Association: www.eatright.org.

American Occupational Therapy Association: www.aota.org.

American Speech-Language-Hearing Association (ASHA): www.asha.org.

Asperger Syndrome Coalition of the United States: www.asperger.org.

Asperger's Syndrome Education Network (ASPEN): www.aspennj.org.

Autism Society of American: www.autism-society.org.

Autism Speaks: www.autismpeaks.org.

Autism Science Foundation: www.autismsciencefoundation.org.

Epilepsy Foundation of America: www.efa.org.

Families for Early Autism Treatment (FEAT): www.Feat.org.

Friends of Autistic People: www.autisticadults.com.

International Rett Syndrome Association: www.rettsyndrome.org.

The International Society for Autism Research (INSAR): www.autism-insar.org.

Learning Disabilities Association of America: www.ldantl.org.

MedicAlert Foundation International: www.medicalert.org.

MEDLINEplus: www.medlineplus.gov.

More Advanced Autistic People: www.maapservices.org.

National Autism Society (United Kingdom): www.nas.org.uk.

National Fragile X Foundation: www.nfxf.org.

National Institutes of Health Autism Research Network: www.autismresearchnetwork.org/
AN/.

Nonverbal Learning Disabilities online (NLDline): www.nldline.com.

Nonverbal Learning Disorders Association: www.nlda.org.

PubMed: www.ncbi.nlm.nih.gov/pubmed.

Rethink Autism: www.rethinkautism.com.

Tuberous Sclerosis Alliance: www.tsalliance.org.

Yale Child Study Center Autism Program: www.autism.fm.

STATE-SPECIFIC RESOURCES

AK, ID, MT, OR & WA: Northwest Autism Foundation: www.autismnwaf.org/.

AL: Alabama Autism Society: www.autism-alabama.org/.

AR: Arkansas Autism Group: www.arkansasautism.org/.

AZ: Arizona Autism Support: www.arizonaautismsupport.org; Northern Arizona Chapter
of the Autism Society of America: www.nazasa.org/.

CA: California Autism Society: www.calautism.org/; Autism Society of California: www
.autismsocietyca.org/.

CO: Autism Society of Colorado: www.autismcolorado.org/.

CT: Connecticut Birth to Three Foundation: www.birth23.com; Connecticut Autism Resource Center: www.ct-asrc.org/; Autism Society of Connecticut: www.autismsocie
tyofct.org/.

DC: Talk about Curing Autism: www.talkaboutcuringautism.org.

DE: Autism Society of Delaware: www.delautism.org/; Lower Delaware Autism Foundation: www.ldaf.org.

FL: Autism Society of Florida: www.autismfl.com/; Central Florida Autism Institute: www
.cfaii.com/; Florida Autism Center of Excellence: www.faceprogram.org/.

GA: ASA-Georgia Chapter: www.asaga.com/; North Georgia Autism Center: www.north georgiaautismcenter.com/.

HI: Autism Society of Hawaii: www.autismhawaii.org/.

IA: Autism Society of Iowa: www.autismia.org.

IL: Illinois Autism Project: www.theautismprogram.org/; Autism Society of Illinois: www.autismillinois.org.

IN: Autism Society of Indiana: www.inautism.org.

KS: Kansas Chapter of Autism Society of America: www.kansasautism.org/.

KY: Autism Society of Kentuckiana: www.ask-lou.org/; Kentucky Autism Awareness: www.kyautismawareness.com/.

LA: Northeast Louisiana Autism Foundation: www.autismnela.org/.

MA: Massachusetts Community Autism Resources: www.community-autism-resources.org/.

MD: ASA-Maryland Chapter: www.maryland-autism.org.

ME: Autism Society of Maine: www.asmonline.org/; Maine Autism Society: www.maineautism.com.

MI: Autism Society of Michigan: www.autism-mi.org/.

MN: Minnesota Autism Center: www.mnautism.org/; Autism Society of Minnesota, www.ausm.org.

MO: Missouri Autism Coalition: www.missouriautism.org/; Missouri Parents for Effective Autism Treatment: www.mo-feat.org.

MS: Together Enhancing Autism Awareness in Mississippi: www.teaam.org.

NC: Autism Society of North Carolina: www.autismsociety-nc.org; TEACCH: www.teacch.com.

ND: Autism Society of North Dakota: www.AutismND.org.

NE: Autism Society of Nebraska: www.autismnebraska.org/.

NH: Autism Society of New Hampshire: www.autism-society-nh.org/.

NJ: New Jersey Center for Autism Outreach: www.njcosac.org/; New Jersey Autism Council: www.njautismcouncil.org/.

NM: New Mexico Autism Society: www.nmautismsociety.org/.

NV: Autism Coalition of Nevada: http://www.aconv.org/.

NY: Families for Autistic Children: www.nyfac.org/; Central New York Chapter of the Autism Society of America: www.cnyasa.org/.

OH: Ohio Autism Project: www.autismohio.org/; Ohio Center for Autism and Low Incidence: www.ocali.org/.

OK: Oklahoma Autism Alliance: www.okautism.org/; Autism Society of Central Oklahoma: www.asofok.org/.

PA: Pennsylvania Association of Autism Resources: http://par.net/.

RI: The Autism Project of Rhode Island: www.theautismproject.org/; Rhode Island Autism Family Network: www.riautism.org.

SC: South Carolina Autism Society: www.scautism.org/; Carolina Autism Project: www.carolinaautism.org/; South Carolina Early Autism Project: www.sceap.com/.

SD: University of South Dakota Autism Program: www.usd.edu/cd/autism/.

TN: Middle Tennessee Autism Society: www.autismmidtenn.org/; Vanderbilt University Treatment and Research for Autism: www.triad.vanderbilt.edu/.

TX: Texas Autism Advocacy: www.texasautismadvocacy.org/; Ziggurat Group Autism Services: www.texasautism.com/.

UT: Utah Registry of Autism and Developmental Disabilities: http://health.utah.gov/autism/; Utah Autism Foundation: www.utahautismfoundation.org/.

VA: Commonwealth Autism Services: www.autismva.org/; Virginia Peninsula Autism Program: www.peninsulautism.org/.

VT: Vermont Autism Task Force: www.autismtaskforce.com/; Autism Society of Vermont: www.autism-info.org/; Parent to Parent in Vermont: www.partoparvt.org.

WI: Wisconsin Society for Autism: www.asw4autism.org/; Wisconsin Early Autism Project: www.wiautism.com/.

WV: West Virginia Autism Society: www.wvautism.org/.

WY: N/A.

BOOK AND JOURNAL PUBLISHERS AND VENDORS WITH MAJOR AUTISM AND AUTISM SPECTRUM LISTINGS

Autism Asperger Publishing Company: www.asperger.net.

Brookes Publishing Company: www.brookespublishing.com.

Future Horizons, Inc: www.futurehorizons-autism.com.

Jessica Kingsley Publishing: www.jkp.com/.

John Wiley & Sons Publishing: www.wiley.com.

Springer Publishing Co. (Journal of Autism and Developmental Disorders): www.springer pub.com.

Woodbine House: www.woodbinehouse.com.

Diagnostic Descriptions and Criteria for Autism and Related Pervasive Developmental Disorders from *International Classification of Diseases,* 10th Edition (World Health Organization, Geneva, Switzerland, 2003; Reprinted with Permission)

Childhood autism (F84.0)

A. Abnormal or impaired development is evident before the age of 3 years in at least one of the following areas:
   1. receptive or expressive language as used in social communication;
   2. the development of selective social attachments or of reciprocal social interaction;
   3. functional or symbolic play.

B. A total of at least six symptoms from (1), (2), and (3) must be present, with at least two from (1) and at least one from each of (2) and (3).
   1. Qualitative impairments in social interaction are manifest in at least two of the following areas:

a. failure adequately to use eye-to-eye gaze, facial expression, body postures, and gestures to regulate social interaction;

b. failure to develop (in a manner appropriate to mental age, and despite ample opportunities) peer relationships that involve a mutual sharing of interests, activities, and emotions;

c. lack of socio-emotional reciprocity as shown by an impaired or deviant response to other people's emotions; or lack of modulation of behavior according to social context; or a weak integration of social, emotional, and communicative behaviors;

d. lack of spontaneous seeking to share enjoyment, interests, or achievements with other people (e.g., a lack of showing, bringing, or pointing out to other people objects of interest to the individual).

2. Qualitative abnormalities in communication as manifest in at least one of the following areas:

a. delay in, or total lack of, development of spoken language that is not accompanied by an attempt to compensate through the use of gestures or mime as an alternative mode of communication (often preceded by a lack of communicative babbling);

b. relative failure to initiate or sustain conversational interchange (at whatever level of language skill is present), in which there is reciprocal responsiveness to the communications of the other person;

c. stereotyped and repetitive use of language or idiosyncratic use of words or phrases;

d. lack of varied spontaneous make-believe play or (when young) social imitative play.

3. Restricted, repetitive, and stereotyped patterns of behavior, interests, and activities are manifested in at least one of the following:

a. an encompassing preoccupation with one or more stereotyped and restricted patterns of interest that are abnormal in content or focus; or one or more interests that are abnormal in their intensity and circumscribed nature, though not in their content or focus;

b. apparently compulsive adherence to specific, nonfunctional routines or rituals;

c. stereotyped and repetitive motor mannerisms that involve either hand or finger flapping or twisting or complex whole-body movements;

    d.   preoccupations with part-objects or nonfunctional elements of play materials (such as their odor, the feel of their surface, or the noise or vibration they generate).

C.   The clinical picture is not attributable to the other varieties of pervasive developmental disorders; specific development disorder of receptive language (F80.2) with secondary socio-emotional problems, reactive attachment disorder (F94.1), or disinhibited attachment disorder (F94.2); mental retardation (F70–F72) with some associated emotional or behavioral disorders; schizophrenia (F20) of unusually early onset; and Rett's syndrome (F84.12).

F84.1 Atypical autism

A.   Abnormal or impaired development is evident at or after the age of 3 years (criteria as for autism except for age of manifestation).

B.   There are qualitative abnormalities in reciprocal social interaction or in communication; or restricted, repetitive, and stereotyped patterns of behavior, interests, and activities. (Criteria as for autism except that it is unnecessary to meet the criteria for number of areas of abnormality).

C.   The disorder does not meet the diagnostic criteria for autism (F84.0). Autism may be atypical in either age of onset (F84.10) or symptomatology (F84.11); the two types are differentiated with a fifth character for research purposes. Syndromes that are typical in both respects should be coded F84.12.

F84.10 Atypicality in age of onset

A.   The disorder does not meet criterion A for autism (F84.0); that is, abnormal or impaired development is evident only at or after age 3 years.

B.   The disorder meets criteria B and C for autism (F84.0).

F84.11 Atypicality in symptomatology

A.   The disorder meets criterion A for autism (F84.0); that is, abnormal or impaired development is evident before age 3 years.

B.   There are qualitative abnormalities in reciprocal social interactions or in communication, or restricted, repetitive, and stereotyped patterns of behavior, interests, and activities. (Criteria as for autism except that it is unnecessary to meet the criteria for number of areas of abnormality.)

C. The disorder meets criterion C for autism (F84.0).

D. The disorder does not fully meet criterion B for autism (F84.0).

F84.12 Atypicality in both age of onset and symptomatology

A. The disorder does not meet criterion A for autism (F84.0); that is, abnormal or impaired development is evident only at or after age 3 years.

B. There are qualitative abnormalities in reciprocal social interactions or in communication, or restricted, repetitive, and stereotyped patterns of behavior, interests, and activities. (Criteria as for autism except that it is unnecessary to meet the criteria for number of areas of abnormality.)

C. The disorder meets criterion C for autism (F84.0).

D. The disorder does not fully meet criterion B for autism (F84.0).

F84.2 Rett's syndrome

A. Apparently normal prenatal and perinatal period and apparently normal psychomotor development through the first six months and normal head circumference at birth.

B. Deceleration of head growth between five months and four years and loss of acquired purposeful hand skills between 6 and 30 months of age that is associated with concurrent communication dysfunction and impaired social interactions and appearance of poorly coordinated/unstable gait and/or trunk movements.

C. Development of severely impaired expressive and receptive language, together with severe psychomotor retardation.

D. Stereotyped midline hand movements (such as hand wringing or washing) with an onset at or after the time that purposeful hand movements are lost.

F84.3 Other childhood disintegrative disorder

A. An apparently normal development up to the age of at least 2 years. The presence of normal age-appropriate skills in communication, social relationships, play, and adaptive behaviour at age 2 years or later is required for diagnosis.

B. A definite loss of previously acquired skills at about the time of onset of the disorder. The diagnosis requires a clinically significant loss of skills (and not just a failure to use them in certain situations) in at least two out of the following areas:

1. expressive or receptive language;
2. play;
3. social skills or adaptive behavior;
4. bowel or bladder control;
5. motor skills.

C. Qualitatively abnormal social functioning, manifest in at least two of the following areas:
   1. qualitative abnormalities in reciprocal social interaction (of the type defined for autism);
   2. qualitative abnormalities in communication (of the type defined for autism);
   3. restricted, repetitive, and stereotyped patterns of behavior, interests, and activities including motor stereotypies and mannerisms;
   4. a general loss of interest in objects and in the environment.

D. The disorder is not attributable to the other varieties of pervasive developmental disorder; acquired aphasia with epilepsy (F80.6); elective mutism (F94.0); schizophrenia (F20–F29); Rett's syndrome (F84.2).

F84.5 Asperger's syndrome

A. A lack of any clinically significant general delay in spoken or receptive language or cognitive development. Diagnosis requires that single words should have developed by 2 years of age or earlier and that communicative phrases be used by 3 years of age or earlier. Self-help skills, adaptive behavior, and curiosity about the environment during the first 3 years should be at a level consistent with normal intellectual development. However, motor milestones may be somewhat delayed and motor clumsiness is usual (although not a necessary diagnostic feature). Isolated special skills, often related to abnormal preoccupations, are common, but are not required for diagnosis.

B. Qualitative abnormalities in reciprocal social interaction (criteria as for autism).

C. An unusually intense circumscribed interest or restricted, repetitive, and stereotyped patterns of behavior, interests, and activities (criteria as for autism; however, it would be less usual for these to include either motor mannerisms or preoccupations with part- objects or non-functional elements of play materials).

D. The disorder is not attributable to the other varieties of pervasive developmental disorder; schizotypal disorder (F21); simple schizophrenia

(F20.6); reactive and disinhibited attachment disorder of childhood (F94.1 and .2); obsessional personality disorder (F60.5); obsessive-compulsive disorder (F42).

F84.8 Other pervasive developmental disorders

F84.9 Pervasive developmental disorder, unspecified

This is a residual diagnostic category that should be used for disorders that fit the general description for pervasive developmental disorders but in which a lack of adequate information, or contradictory findings, means that the criteria for any of the other F84 codes cannot be met.

Glossary

ABA *See* Applied behavior analysis.

Absence seizure Previously known as a petit mal seizure; a type of generalized seizure that involves very brief loss of consciousness, frequently only a few seconds. There is staring and it may include eye fluttering or mild facial twitching. The child "tunes in" and "tunes out."

Accommodation An adaptation of the environment, format, or situation made to suit the needs of those participating.

Achievement tests Unlike IQ tests, achievement tests are less concerned with how able the person is and more with how they have used their ability to learn, for example, as applied in math or reading. In addition to standard scores, percentiles, and age equivalent scores, these tests also often give grade equivalent scores. These tests are often given in schools—they may be given to groups of children. Under the No Child Left Behind laws, tests of this kind have gotten more attention.

ADA *See* Americans With Disabilities Act.

Adaptive behavior (functioning) The ability to adjust to new environments, tasks, objects, and people, and to apply new skills to those situations.

ADD *See* Attention deficit disorder.

ADHD *See* Attention deficit hyperactivity disorder.

ADHD medication Medication used to treat ADHD. Most of these medications are stimulants.

Age-equivalent score It compares the individual's ability to what would be typical for a person of a specific age. For example, an age-equivalent score of 5 years 2 months might be computed based on a child's ability. The meaning of age-equivalent scores clearly varies depending on the child's age (the same 5 year 2 month score would mean very different things if the child were 5 or 10 years of age).

Akinetic seizure *See* Atonic seizure.

Allergy A hypersensitivity to a specific substance that results in the immune system's trying to defend the body against the substance, triggering adverse symptoms such as runny nose or itchy eyes, skin rashes, and at times more serious reactions such as trouble breathing or drop in blood pressure.

Alpha-adrenergic agonist Medications first used to treat high blood pressure, but used in autism to treat hyperactivity and irritability.

---

*Specific drug names can be found in the index, only classes of drugs are described in the glossary. For example, you will find **Prozac** in the index and **Selective Serotonin Reuptake Inhibitor** in the glossary.

Designations used by companies to distinguish their products are often claimed as trademarks. In all instances where John Wiley & Sons, Inc. is aware of a claim, the product names appear in initial capital or all capital letters. Readers, however, should contact the appropriate companies for more complete information regarding trademarks and registration.

Also used to treat ADHD and Tourette's syndrome.

Amblyopia   A term used to refer to poor vision an eye that is otherwise apparently normal physically. This term is sometimes used interchangeably with "lazy eye" although that term is more commonly used for strabismus.

Americans With Disabilities Act   The comprehensive civil rights law passed in 1990 that prohibits discrimination against people with disabilities in employment, public service, public accommodation, and telecommunications.

Amniocentesis   Test by which amniotic fluid is removed from around the fetus in order to test for genetic disorders such as fragile X and Down syndrome.

Antianxiety medication   Medication to treat anxiety problems.

Anticonvulsant   Medication used to treat *seizures* (convulsions).

Antidepressants   Medications to treat depression, anxiety, OCD, and other conditions.

Antihistamine   The type of drug most often used for treating allergies.

Antipsychotics   Medications to treat psychotic disorders in adults and repetitive movements and repetitive behaviors in autism. Includes both typical (first generation) and atypical (second generation) antipsychotics.

Anxiety   A feeling of unease, dread, fear or "nervousness," which can be accompanied by physical symptoms such as increased heart rate or sweating. Some degree of anxiety may be normal (e.g., in new situations), but when anxiety is irrational, excessive, or causes distress or impairment, it can be part of an anxiety disorder.

Anxiety disorders   Psychiatric illnesses characterized by high levels of anxiety that cause distress or impairment to the individual. Types of anxiety disorders include phobias (fear of some specific thing), generalized anxiety disorder, panic disorder, and post-traumatic stress disorder.

Applied behavior analysis (ABA)   A behavioral science that uses research-based, highly structured teaching procedures to develop skills in individuals. An emphasis is placed on modifying behavior in a precisely measurable manner using repeated trials. *See also* Discrete Trial Teaching; Behavior Management Plan.

Apraxia   Difficulty or inability in planning and sequencing movements.

Asperger's disorder   A *pervasive developmental disorder* characterized by serious social disability but good early language skills, often associated with motor difficulties and intense special interests.

Asperger Syndrome Diagnostic Scale (ASDA)   Diagnostic test for Asperger's.

Assessment   The process used to determine a child's strengths and weaknesses. Includes testing and observations performed by a variety of professionals, including special educators, psychiatrists, psychologists, speech–language pathologists, and the like. Also called *evaluation*.

"At risk of experiencing developmental delay"   The term applied to children under the age of 3 who have not been formally diagnosed with a specific condition. This heading may render them eligible for *special education* services.

Ataxia   Difficulty coordinating movements of the body, as in walking.

Atonic seizure   A type of generalized seizure in which there is a sudden loss of muscle tone. Also known as Akinetic seizure.

Attention   The ability to focus on and sustain concentration on a task. *See also* Attention span.

Attention deficit disorder (ADD)   A term sometimes used for a condition that does not include the *hyperactivity* found in *ADHD*.

Attention deficit/hyperactivity disorder (ADHD)   A condition characterized by distractibility, restlessness, short *attention span*, impulsivity, and *hyperactivity*.

Attention deficit hyperactivity disorder medication   Medication used to treat ADHD. Most are stimulants.

Attention span The amount of time one is able to concentrate on a task.

Atypical antipsychotic medication Second-generation antipsychotic medication.

Audiologist A health care professional who diagnoses and treats hearing and balance problems.

Auditory Relating to the ability to hear.

Auditory integration training (AIT) Treatment, involving sound, for sensory problems in autism, such as hypersensitivity to sound.

Auditory memory Recalling what is heard.

Aura A sensation of some type, visual, motor, sensoty or other psychological experience that precedes some types of *seizures*.

Autism A form of *pervasive developmental disorder* characterized by difficulties in social interaction and *language* acquisition and use, as well as odd or unusual mannerisms, behaviors, and habits.

Autism Behavior Checklist (ABC) Screening instrument for autism.

Autism Diagnostic Interview–Revised (ADI-R) Diagnostic/assessment instrument for autism.

Autism Diagnostic Observation Schedule (ADOS) Diagnostic/assessment instrument for autism.

Autistic disorder The "official" term for autism used in the *Diagnostic and Statistical Manual of Mental Disorders*.

Autism Society of America A parent organization, founded in 1965 dedicated to improving the lives of everyone affected by autism.

Autistic spectrum disorder Another term sometimes used for pervasive developmental disorders.

Aversive An unpleasant stimulus used after an undesirable behavior to try to prevent the behavior in the future.

Babbling Early sounds made by babies that involve adding consonants to vowels, for example, "dada"or "baba."

Behavior management plan A plan designed to modify or reshape the behavior of an individual with *disabilities* that addresses existing behavior, *interventions*, support, and goals.

Behavior modification Use of positive and negative reinforcements to change behavior.

Benzodiazepines A class of medications that treat both seizures and anxiety.

Best Buddies An organization formed to enhance the lives of people with intellectual disabilities by helping them form relationships with peers without intellectual disabilities.

Beta blocker A class of medication initially used to treat cardiac (heart) problems but also used to treatment some forms of anxiety.

Bipolar disorder The condition, formerly known as manic depression, in which an individual experiences periods of *depression* alternating with periods of elation (mania).

Bruxism Grinding the teeth.

Candida albicans A common fungus that can cause infections.

Cardiac Related to the heart.

Case manager A person who coordinates services for individuals with *disabilities*. *See also* Service coordinator.

Case reports Accounts of individual patients' responses to treatment; sometimes used as proof that a treatment works, but more properly regarded as an indication that the treatment may merit more formal research.

Casein A protein substance found in cow's milk and in products derived from cow's milk.

CDD *See* Childhood disintegrative disorder.

Celiac disease A disorder that causes sensitivity to *gluten* in food and results in damage

Designations used by companies to distinguish their products are often claimed as trademarks. In all instances where John Wiley & Sons, Inc. is aware of a claim, the product names appear in initial capital or all capital letters. Readers, however, should contact the appropriate companies for more complete information regarding trademarks and registration.

to the lining of the small intestine if a gluten-free diet is not followed.

Cerebellum A region of the brain involved with integration of sensory perception, co-ordination, and motor control.

Cerebral cortex The structure within the brain that plays an important role in memory, attention, perceptual awareness, thought, language, and consciousness.

Cerebral palsy A disability caused by brain damage before, at, or after birth. Body movements and coordination are affected and vary, depending on which parts of the brain have been damaged.

Checklist for Autism in Toddlers (CHAT) Screening instrument for autism.

Childhood Asperger Syndrome Test (CAST) Diagnostic test for Asperger's.

Childhood autism *See* Autistic disorder.

Childhood Autism Rating Scale (CARS) Diagnostic/assessment instrument for autism.

Childhood disintegrative disorder (CDD) A rare form of *pervasive developmental disorder* in which a child, who has developed typically in early childhood, begins to display *autistic-like* characteristics. By definition, development is normal until age 2 years. The usual time of onset is between ages 3 and 4 years.

Childhood schizophrenia A psychiatric disorder, probably with multiple causes. Symptoms include disturbances in form and content of thought, perception, emotions, sense of self, relationship to the external world, and other behaviors. Childhood schizophrenia is very rare. Schizophrenia becomes more common in adolescence.

Chorionic villus sampling (CVS) Removal of a piece of the placenta (chorionic villi) in early pregnancy to screen for genetic disorders, such as fragile X and Down syndrome. It can be performed earlier than amniocentesis.

Chromosomes Threadlike structures made of DNA in the nucleus of cells, which contain the *genes*. Unless they have a chromosomal disorder such as Down syndrome, people have 23 pairs of chromosomes in their cells.

Chronic Long-lasting or permanent.

Circle of Friends Peer-based social skills groups.

Clinical Evaluation of Language Fundamentals, 4th edition (CELF-4) Test of language/communication skills.

Cognition The ability to know and understand the environment and to solve problems.

Comorbid Related to two or more disorders occurring in the same individual.

Competitive employment Jobs for people with disabilities in a setting with those without disabilities and for competitive pay.

Complementary and alternative medicine (CAM) A diverse group of medical and healthcare practices and products that are not considered part of established, conventional medicine.

Complex partial seizure A type of partial seizure starting in one area of the brain which causes jerking or unusual movement in one part of the body and eventually results in loss of consciousness.

Comprehensive Assessment of Spoken Language (CASL) Test of language/communication skills.

Computed tomography (CT) scan A diagnostic procedure in which a computerized picture of cross-sections of the body is created by passing x-rays through the area that is being studied at various angles.

Conductive hearing loss Hearing loss that results from a blockage in the middle ear (such as from fluid), which prevents or reduces transmission of sound to the inner ear.

Congenital Present at birth.

Constipation Infrequent or hard stools.

Contraception Pregnancy prevention.

Convulsion Seizure.

Criterion-referenced tests Tests of this kind are *not* used to compare people to each other; rather, the comparison is to a specific criterion or standard. Taking a test to get a driver's license is a criterion-referenced test. For educational purposes, tests of this kind can be used to show that a student has demonstrated mastery of material, that is, before moving on to a different grade or more advanced work.

Daily living skills   Skills needed for everyday life, e.g., shopping, using the phone, dressing appropriately for weather, self-care skills.

Department of Vocational Rehabilitation (DVR)   Departments in each state required by the Vocational Rehabilitation Act of 1973 to correct the problems of discrimination against people with disabilities.

Depression   Mental disorder in which a person can have pervasive low moods, low self-esteem and loss of pleasure or interest in normally enjoyable activities.

Development   The process of growth and learning during which a child acquires skills and abilities.

Developmental delay   In children birth to 18, *development* that is significantly slower than average.

Developmental disability   A condition originating before the age of 18 that may be expected to continue indefinitely and that impairs or delays *development*. Such conditions include *autism*, *pervasive developmental disorders*, and *intellectual disability*.

Developmental evaluation   *See* Assessment.

Developmental milestone   A goal that functions as a measurement of progress in development over time, for example, rolling over from back to front or speaking in two-word phrases.

Developmental scales   Checklists to compare a child's development with others of the same age.

Developmental test   A test of developmental status.

Diagnostic and Statistical Manual of Mental Disorders (DSM-IV)   A manual published by the American Psychiatric Association that defines and describes the diagnostic criteria for mental disorders and provides systematic descriptions of them.

Dietitian   A professional with expertise in food and nutrition; registered dietitians have completed an internship and passed a national exam.

Differential Ability Scales, 2nd Edition (DAS-II)   Test of intelligence.

Disability   A term used to describe a delay in physical or cognitive *development*. The older term *handicap* is also sometimes used.

Discrete trial teaching   An instructional technique that is part of *applied behavior analysis*. This technique involves four steps: (1) presenting a *cue* or *stimulus* to the learner; (2) obtaining the learner's response; (3) providing a positive consequence (reinforcer) or correction; and (4) a brief 3- to 5-second break until the next teaching trial is provided. *See* Applied behavior analysis.

Dopamine   One of the *neurotransmitters* in the brain that plays a major role in regulating movement.

Down syndrome   A congenital disorder caused by the presence of an extra copy of the 21st chromosome; it is usually associated with some degree of mental retardation, low muscle tone, speech and language delay, and sometimes autistic-like behaviors.

DSM-IV   *See Diagnostic and Statistical Manual of Mental Disorders* (DSM-IV).

Due process hearing   Hearing to decide whether an individualized education plan meets the requirements of the Individuals With Disabilities Education Act.

Designations used by companies to distinguish their products are often claimed as trademarks. In all instances where John Wiley & Sons, Inc. is aware of a claim, the product names appear in initial capital or all capital letters. Readers, however, should contact the appropriate companies for more complete information regarding trademarks and registration.

Early intervention   Services provided to infants and young children before they become eligible for school-based services.

Echolalia   A parrot-like repetition of phrases or words just heard (immediate echolalia) or heard hours, days, weeks, or even months before (delayed echolalia).

EEG   *See* Electroencephalogram.

Electroencephalogram (EEG)   A test which records electrical activity produced by the firing of neurons in the brain. Used to diagnose *seizures*.

Engagement   The ability to remain focused and interactive with (or responsive to) a person or object.

Enuresis   Bedwetting. This can happen either in the day or at night—the latter is more frequent.

Epidemiology   All of the elements that contribute to the occurrence of a disease in specific peoples or areas of the world.

Epilepsy   A recurrent condition in which abnormal electrical discharges in the brain cause *seizures*.

Equal Employment Opportunity Commision (EEOC)   Enforces federal laws that prohibit job discrimination.

Estate planning   The process of planning for passing along one's assets to others (often one's children).

Etiology   The study of the cause of something- in medicine usually of a disease.

Evaluation   *See* Assessment.

Evaluation of Sensory Processing (ESP)   Test of sensory processing.

Expressive language   The use of words to communicate.

Expressive One Word Picture Vocabulary Test (EOWPVT)   Test of expressive vocabulary.

Extended school year (ESY)   Special education services beyond the usual school year. This is specified in the Individuals With Disabilities Education Act. Eligibility is determined by a child's IEP.

Extinction   A reinforcer used in behavior modification to weaken a negative behavior. The behavior is weakened by no longer experiencing a positive condition related to it.

Eye–hand coordination   Ability to coordinate these visual and motor systems as needed to perform many daily tasks such as dressing, eating, and writing.

Family physician   A physician who sees both adult and child patients.

Febrile seizure   A seizure that occurs as a result of a fever.

Fine motor   Use of fingers for fine muscle movement.

Formal complaint   A written complaint against an alleged violation of the requirements of the Individuals With Disabilities Education Act.

Fragile X syndrome   A condition caused by a *mutation* in the *genetic* information on the X *chromosome*. (The X chromosome is one of the two so-called sex chromosomes; children with two X chromosomes are girls, and those with an X and a Y chromosome are boys.) Fragile X often causes mental retardation or learning disabilities, language difficulties, and distinctive physical characteristics.

Free appropriate public education (FAPE)   A right under federal law for children in the U.S. All programs and schools that receive federal funding must provide appropriate education to those with disabilities.

Functional behavior analysis   Observation by a trained specialist directed toward understanding the antecedents and consequences of behavior.

Functional life skills   Skills needed in daily living, social, and work settings.

Functional MRI (fMRI)   A type of MRI (magnetic brain scan) that evaluates brain activity during specific tasks.

Genes   The microscopic sequences of DNA found on the *chromosomes*, which determine which traits an individual inherits from his parents.

Genetic Inherited.

Genetic disorder Any disorder that is inherited.

Geneticist A professional who evaluates people for genetic disorders and may provide counseling and information about these disorders.

Generalization Transferring a skill taught in one place or with one person to other places and people.

Generalized seizure A seizure that affects both sides of the brain at the same time. The category includes tonic–clonic, absence, and akinetic seizures.

Gestalt processing A tendency to process material in its entirety rather than seeing composite parts (often an aspect of learning style in individuals with autism).

Gilliam Asperger's Disorder Scale (GADS) Diagnostic test for Asperger's.

Gilliam Autism Rating Scales, 2nd edition Diagnostic/assessment instrument for autism.

Gluten A protein found in wheat, rye, and barley.

Grade-equivalent score: A score from an achievement test that expresses the students performance in grade year and months, e.g., a score of 4.6 would be the typical score that a child in the 4th grade and 6th month of the academic year would receive.

Grandiosity A feeling that one is more powerful or important than one really is; sometimes a symptom of *bipolar disorder.*

Grand mal seizure An older term for a generalized seizure.

Gross motor Related to the use of the large muscles of the body, such as those of the back, legs, and arms.

Guardian A person appointed by law to manage the legal, medical, and/or financial affairs of someone else.

Hand flapping Stereotyped motor mannerism involving repeated flapping of the hand.

Head circumference The distance around the larger part of the head, typically measured by pediatricians routinely early in life and often increased in toddlers with autism.

Heller's syndrome An alternate (older) name for childhood disintegrative disorder.

Hepatitis An inflammation of the liver.

Hives An itchy rash, usually caused by an allergic reaction.

Hyperactivity A nervous system–based difficulty that makes it hard for a person to control *motor* (muscle) behavior. It is characterized by frequent movement, rapidly switching from one activity to another, or having difficulty remaining seated or controlling restless movements.

Hyperlexia A precocious, often isolated, ability to read single words. A frequent phenomenon in autism the ability to "decode" written language may be much greater than actual understanding of what is read.

Hypotonia Low (reduced) muscle tone; muscles feel "floppier" than usual, and it takes more effort to initiate movement and maintain posture.

ICD The *International Classification of Diseases,* the manual used in place of the DSM in countries other than the United States for diagnosing mental disorders.

IDEA *See* Individuals with Disabilities Education Act.

Identification The determination that a child should be *evaluated* as a possible candidate for *special education* services.

Idiosyncratic language Language use that is unique to the individual, often reflecting their own experience; may be hard to understand for people unfamiliar with the individual who is speaking; for example, a

Designations used by companies to distinguish their products are often claimed as trademarks. In all instances where John Wiley & Sons, Inc. is aware of a claim, the product names appear in initial capital or all capital letters. Readers, however, should contact the appropriate companies for more complete information regarding trademarks and registration.

child with autism might yell "stop that child" when he is upset because the first time he was upset he ran from his mother in a crowded department store and she yelled this phrase at him.

IEP *See* Individualized education plan.

IFSP *See* Individualized family service plan.

Imitation The ability to observe the actions of others and to copy them in one's own actions. Also known as *modeling.*

Immunization The process of inducing protection against an infectious disease, either by administering a *vaccine* or by contracting the disease and then developing a natural immunity to it.

Impulsivity Behavior characterized by acting without thinking through the consequences of actions.

Inclusion Placing children with *disabilities* in the same schools and classrooms with children who are developing typically. The environment includes the special supports and services necessary for educational success.

Independent living The ability for an adult with disabilities to live in the community without supervision.

Individualized education plan (IEP) The written plan that specifies the special education and other services (such as occupational or speech therapy) the school has agreed to provide a child with *disabilities* who is eligible under the Individuals With Disabilities Education Act; for children ages 3 to 21.

Individualized family service plan (IFSP) The written plan that specifies the education and *related services* to be provided to children eligible for *early intervention* under the Individuals With Disabilities Education Act and their families; for children birth to age 3.

Individualized plan for employment (IPE) Plan for services needed to help individuals reach their work goals.

Individuals With Disabilities Education Act (IDEA) A federal law originally passed in 1975 and subsequently amended that requires states to provide a *"free appropriate public education* in the *least restrictive environment"* to children with *disabilities.* This is the major special education law in the United States.

Infantile autism *See* Autistic disorder.

Insistence on sameness A tendency in many people with *autism* to become upset when familiar routines or environments are changed and, conversely, to prefer things to remain the same.

Instrument A set of questions or activities administered to evaluate functioning; a test.

Integration *See* Inclusion.

Intellectual disability Significantly subaverage intellectual and adaptive functioning; also referred to as mental retardation.

Intelligence The ability to learn, think, and use knowledge to deal with problems.

Intelligence quotient (IQ) A numerical measurement of intellectual capacity that compares a person's chronological age to his or her "mental age," as shown on *standardized tests.*

Intelligence test These norm-referenced tests are usually administered individually by a psychologist who is very familiar with the test and the rules for giving and scoring it. Tests of intelligence sample various cognitive skills and are concerned with establishing how able the individual is to solve various kinds of problems. Typically, intelligence tests include various tasks that sample abilities that require more or less language and may look at issues like problem solving, memory, and so forth.

Internist A physician who specializes in internal medicine or the diagnosis and nonsurgical treatment of illnesses in adults.

Interpretive A meeting in which parents and teachers discuss a child's evaluation.

Intervention Action taken to improve a child's potential for success in compensating for a delay or deficit in their physical, emotional, or mental functioning.

IQ *See* Intelligence quotient.

Joint attention The activity of engaging with others in watching activities/materials/events. This can typically be demonstrated readily in normally developing infants; for example, when something interesting or unusual happens, the child will look at it, then turn to the parent to evaluate his or her reaction, then turn back to look.

Kaufmann Assessment Battery for Children (KABC-II) Test of intelligence.

Ketogenic diet A diet that is high in fat and very low in protein and carbohydrates that is sometimes effective in controlling seizures.

Krug Asperger Disorder Index (KADI) Diagnostic test for Asperger's.

Landau–Kleffner syndrome (LKS) A disorder that has some similarities to CDD, in which a child loses the ability to understand and use spoken language (after previously having normal abilities) and usually experiences seizures. Children with LKS may regain all or some of their language skills over time and become seizure free.

Language A system of symbols (spoken, written, signed) used to communicate. *See* Expressive language; Receptive language.

Least restrictive environment The Individuals with Disabilities Education Act requires that children requiring special education services must be taught as much as possible with children without disabilities.

Leiter International Performance Scale-Revised (Leiter-R) Nonverbal test of intelligence.

Limbic system The part of the brain having to do with emotions.

Local Education Agency (LEA) Agency at the local level that provides educational services.

Magnetic resonance imaging (MRI) A computerized diagnostic procedure that involves creating cross-sectional images of the body or its organs by exposing the patient to a magnetic field.

Mainstreaming *See* Inclusion.

Malnutrition Nutritional intake that is insufficient to promote or maintain growth and *development*.

Mannerisms Repetitive, seemingly purposeless movements or sounds; sterotyped behavior.

Mediation Way to resolve a formal complaint between parents and the school required under the Individuals With Disabilities Education Act. This can be used instead of going through a due process hearing.

Medicaid A joint state and federal program that offers medical assistance to people in need.

Medicare A federal program, not based on financial need, that provides payments for medical care to people who are receiving Social Security payments.

Megadose vitamin therapy Using vitamins in dosages that are at levels higher than the recommended daily allowance.

Mental age Age equivalent score on a test of intelligence.

Mental retardation (MR) Now frequently referred to as *intellectual disability*.

Mercury A heavy, silver metal, liquid at room temperature; in the past, used in some preservatives for *vaccines*.

MMR The abbreviation for the measles, mumps, and rubella vaccine.

Modeling *See* Imitation.

Modified Checklist for Autism in Toddlers (M-CHAT) Screening instrument for Autism.

Mood disorder Disorder in which a person's emotional mood is disturbed.

Designations used by companies to distinguish their products are often claimed as trademarks. In all instances where John Wiley & Sons, Inc. is aware of a claim, the product names appear in initial capital or all capital letters. Readers, however, should contact the appropriate companies for more complete information regarding trademarks and registration.

Mood stabilizers   Medications to treat mood disorders.

Monotonic voice   A style of speech which lacks inflection/prosody, sometimes referred to as *robot-like* speech.

Motor   Relating to the ability to use muscles to move oneself.

Motor planning   Preparing and carrying out a physical task.

Mullen Scales of Early Learning   Developmental Test.

Muscle tone   The degree of stretch or relaxation in a resting muscle. *See also* hypotonia.

Mutation   A change or alteration in *genetic* information.

Myoclonic seizure   A generalized *seizure* that produces brief, involuntary jerking of muscles and may also cause loss of consciousness.

Naturopathic   Referring to "natural" treatment with sunshine, water, or other naturally occurring agents; without drugs.

Negative reinforcer   A reinforcing stimulus that, when removed, serves to decrease the likelihood that the response it produced will continue.

Neurologist   A physician specializing in medical problems associated with the nervous system.

Neuroleptic   A tranquilizing drug.

Neuropsychological tests   Tests of this kind are usually focused on a particular process such as memory, attention, or particular kinds of problem solving.

Neurotransmitter   A chemical substance in the brain that allows the transmission of impulses from one nerve cell to another. Abnormal levels of neurotransmitters may result in difficulties with mood, attention, impulse control, and the like. *See* Dopamine; Norepinephrine; Serotonin.

Nonverbal learning disability   A pattern of strengths and weaknesses that includes better verbal abilities than nonverbal abilities.

Norepinephrine   A neurotransmitter and a hormone synthesized from dopamine that plays a role in maintaining blood pressure and also in regulating mood and attention.

Norm-referenced tests   Tests that compare an individual's score against a group of people selected to be representative of the general population. Scores derived from tests of this kind can be presented in various ways, including percentiles, standard scores, and age-equivalent scores. Typically, test results are distributed along what is called the bell-shaped curve (or what is technically called the *normal distribution*). The ability to compare scores across people of the same, and different, ages is a strength of this approach. Considerable care has to go into exactly how the test is designed and administered; any deviation from the rules makes the scores difficult to interpret.

Nurse practitioner   A registered nurse who has additional training in medical practices or therapies.

Obesity   Body weight that is much greater than what is healthy. In adults, having a Body Mass Index (BMI) of greater than 30 is considered obese. In children, the BMI that indicates obesity varies with the age and height.

Obsessive–compulsive disorder (OCD)   An anxiety disorder involving recurrent thoughts (obsessions) or behaviors (compulsions), causing distress to the individual.

Occupational therapist (OT)   A therapist who specializes in improving the *development* of *fine motor* and adaptive skills.

Ophthalmologist   A physician who specializes in diagnosing and treating eye and vision problems; ophthalmologists can perform surgery and prescribe medications, as well as prescribe corrective lenses.

Options approach   Alternative treatment described in the book *Son Rise*.

Oral–motor   Use of the muscles of the tongue, lips, and jaw.

OT   *See* Occupational therapist.

Otitis media   An infection of the middle ear.

Otolaryngologist   A physician specializing in the ear, nose, and throat; an ENT.

Paradoxical reaction The opposite reaction than would typically be expected.

PDD *See* Pervasive developmental disorder.

PDD-NOS *See* Pervasive developmental disorder not otherwise specified.

Peabody Developmental Motor Scales (PDMS) Test of motor skills.

Peabody Picture Vocabulary Test, 4th edition (PPVT-4) Test of repetitive vocabulary.

Pediatric neurologist A specialist in disorders of the nervous system in children.

Pediatrician A physician who specializes in the care of infants, children, and adolescents.

Percentile scores Presents a score based on what percentage of scores are lower; for example, an 85th percentile score means the person scored higher than 85% of the people who take the test.

Perseveration Getting stuck on an activity, spending an inappropriate amount of time doing and redoing the same thing.

Pervasive developmental disorder (PDD) An umbrella category in the *DSM* for a range of conditions, including *autistic disorder, Asperger's disorder, PDD-NOS, Rett's disorder,* and *childhood disintegrative disorder,* that can include symptoms such as difficulties with communication and social skills, unusual interests or habits, and *insistence on sameness.* The term may be used synonymously with *autism spectrum disorder.*

Pervasive developmental disorder not otherwise specified (PDD-NOS) A *pervasive developmental disorder* that includes most characteristics of *autistic disorder* but not enough to meet the specific diagnostic criteria for *autistic disorder.*

Pervasive Developmental Disorder Screening Test-II (PDD ST-II) Screening instrument for autism.

Pervasive lack of relatedness A condition characterized by an individual's extreme difficulty relating to objects or people in a typical or appropriate fashion.

Petit mal seizure *See* Absence seizure.

Phenylketonuria This condition (often refered to as PKU) is an inherited disorder of metabolism that can be sucessfully treated with dietary intervention. This condition is usually screened for at birth. If untreated it leads to significant intellectual disability.

Phonetics The system of speech sounds of any language.

Physical therapist (PT) A therapist who specializes in improving the development of *gross motor* skills.

Pica The eating of nonfood substances.

PKU *See* phenylketonuria.

Placebo A "dummy" medication or treatment used as a control in testing another medication or treatment in order to see whether the "real" treatment is more effective than no treatment.

Placebo effect The tendency of patients who are receiving a placebo to feel better or to be perceived as doing better when they are participating in a new treatment or study.

Placement The selection of a special education program for a child who requires one.

Placenta Organ inside the uterus in which the fetus develops.

Play therapy A diagnostic and treatment method sometimes used by child psychologists in which the child is encouraged to play or draw as a means of expressing his thoughts or feelings.

Polypharmacy Giving multiple medications often for what are believed to be various different conditions.

Positive reinforcement Providing a pleasant consequence after a behavior in order to maintain or increase the frequency of that behavior.

Designations used by companies to distinguish their products are often claimed as trademarks. In all instances where John Wiley & Sons, Inc. is aware of a claim, the product names appear in initial capital or all capital letters. Readers, however, should contact the appropriate companies for more complete information regarding trademarks and registration.

Postictal period Following a seizure, the period when the person is somewhat confused or disoriented as the brain recovers from the seizure.

Potency Strength, as of a medication.

Pragmatics The use of language for social communication.

Preschool Language Scale–4 (PLS-4) Test of language/communication skills.

Prevocational skills Skills needed before a job is possible.

Prognosis Long-term outcome.

Projective and personality tests These tests may be paper and pencil (self or parent report) or, in the case of some tests, are individually administered by a psychologist based on a person's responses to stimuli. Tests of personality may include scores related to levels of depression, anxiety, or problem behavior. Projective tests, like the Rorschach inkblot test, allow the individual to give a response to a very unstructured stimulus; tests of this kind may be used to look for unusual patterns of thinking or experience.

Prompt Input such as physical guidance or a verbal or visual reminder that encourages an individual to perform a movement or activity.

Prompt dependence When an individual requires a *prompt* in order to perform a taught task or behavior.

Proprioception The body's innate sense of its position in space.

Prosody The musical aspect of language, often distorted or markedly diminished in individuals with autism. It has various parts, including register (loudness), pitch, inflection, and so forth. Lack of prosody may be manifest in monotonic (one tone) (robot-like) speech.

Psychiatrist A medical doctor who diagnoses and treats mental illness; in contrast to a psychologist, he or she may prescribe medications in treatment.

Psychoeducational Profile–Revised (PEP-R) Diagnostic/Assessment instrument for autism.

Psychologist A professional who specializes in the study of human behavior and treatment of behavioral disorders.

Psychomotor seizure *See* Complex partial seizure.

Psychosis A mental disorder that alters an individual's understanding of reality, and may include delusions, hallucinations, or disturbed thought processes.

Psychotropic Medications that alter brain function. Pyschotropic drugs are often used in the treatment of mental illness and sometimes for certain *autistic* behaviors.

PT *See* Physical therapist.

Puberty The process of physical change that occur in adolescence making sexual reproduction possible and resulting in various other sexual charateristics.

Public Law 94-142 The Education of All Handicapped Children Act of 1975 that has been revised and is now known as the Individuals With Disabilities Education Act (IDEA).

Qualified Medicare beneficiary program Free Medicare supplement programs for qualified persons.

Reactive attachment disorder A disorder that develops in infants and young children as the result of emotional or physical neglect or abuse; children with the disorder have social skills delays and difficulty bonding with others.

Reasonable accommodation Required modifications to enable a child to participate in school.

Receptive language The ability to understand spoken and written communication as well as gestures.

Redirection Shifting of a child's focus from one task to another.

Reflex An involuntary, unlearned response to a stimulus.

Register The technical term that speech pathologists use to refer to voice volume.

Regression The loss of skill or ability.

Rehabilitation Act of 1973 Prohibits discrimination against anyone on the basis of disability.

Reinforcement Any consequence that increases the likelihood of the future occurrence of a behavior. A consequence is either presented or withheld in an effort to prompt the desired response.

Related services Services that enable a child to benefit from *special education*. Related services include speech–language, occupational, and physical therapies, as well as transportation.

Reliability When used relative to testing this term has various meanings but usually refers to how consistent the test is when used by various evaluators.

Repetitive speech Also called *echolalia. See also* Perseveration.

Residential services Living arrangements away from home but with supervision.

Resource room Separate classrooms for special education outside the mainstream classroom.

Respite care Care away from home, often providing relief for the usual caretakers.

Rett's disorder A rare *pervasive developmental disorder* that affects mostly females; is characterized by typical early development; and, later, a pervasive loss of social, cognitive, and physical skills. Some improvement in these areas may take place in late childhood. Many children with Rett's disorder develop *seizure* disorders.

Reynell Developmental Language Scales, U.S. edition Test of language/communication skills.

Rigidity Inflexibility of behavior; needing things to happen a very specific way in order for them to "feel right" to the child.

Rubella German measles; a disease that causes a mild rash in adults but that can lead to birth defects if a woman contracts it while pregnant.

Rumination Regurgitating food and chewing it again.

Savant Person with extraordinary skills, usually in an isolated area.

A Scale to Assist the Diagnosis of Autism and Asperger's Disorder in Adults (RAADS) Diagnostic test for Asperger's.

Schizophrenia *See* Childhood schizophrenia.

Scoliosis Abnormal curvature of the spine.

Screening test A test given to groups of children intended to determine which children need further *evaluation*.

Screening Tool for Assessment of Autism in 2-year-olds (STAT) Screening instrument for autism.

Secretin A gut hormone recently used as an alternative treatment in autism.

Section 504 Provides accommodations for people with disabilities under the Rehabilitation Act.

Sedation The process of reducing anxiety, nervousness, or wakefulness; may or may not involve loss of consciousness.

Seizure A sudden change in behavior, consciousness, or sensation caused by a change in brain activity.

Selective mutism A disorder characterized by failure to speak in specific situations despite speaking in other situations.

Selective norepinephrine reuptake inhibitor Type of medication used to treat ADHD. It is not a stimulant.

Selective serotonin reuptake inhibitor (SSRI) A type of medication used for treating depression or anxiety that works by preventing *serotonin* produced in the brain from being reabsorbed quickly, thus increasing the amount of serotonin available in the brain.

Designations used by companies to distinguish their products are often claimed as trademarks. In all instances where John Wiley & Sons, Inc. is aware of a claim, the product names appear in initial capital or all capital letters. Readers, however, should contact the appropriate companies for more complete information regarding trademarks and registration.

Self-help skills   Daily living skills needed to live independently.

Self-injury   Aggression directed against the individual, e.g., because of head banging.

Self-stimulation   The act of providing physical, visual, or auditory stimulation for oneself; rocking back and forth and *hand flapping* are examples.

Sensory-motor skills   Skills in infants and young children involving perception and action; these become the basis of subsequent cognitive and other skills.

Sensorineural hearing loss   Hearing loss caused by damage to the inner ear or to the auditory nerve, which transmits sounds to the brain.

Sensory   Relating to the senses.

Sensory Experiences Questionnaire (SEQ)   Test of sensory processing.

Sensory integration   The ability to receive *input* from the senses, to organize it into a meaningful message, and to act on it.

Sensory Profile   Test of sensory processing.

Serotonin   A neurotransmitter that is believed to play a role in mood regulation and sleep; levels of serotonin may be deficient in children who have depression or anxiety.

Service coordinator   The individual designated to oversee the education and *related services* for a child with *disabilities* and the services provided to his or her family. *See also* Case manager.

Sheltered employment   Employment of someone with a disability in a non-competitive, supportive environment with supervision.

Side effect   An effect which results unintentionally from the administration of medication; manifestations of side effects from medication vary from person to person.

Simple partial seizure   A type of partial seizure in which consciousness may be impaired. The features depend on the part of the brain that is involved. There may be involuntary jerking of muscles or tingling sensations or other features.

SLP   *See* Speech–language pathologist.

Social Communication Questionnaire (SCQ)   Screening instrument for autism.

Social Responsiveness Scale (SRS)   Diagnostic/screening instrument for autism.

Social Security Administration (SSA)   The federal agency that administers both *SSI* and *SSDI*.

Social Security Disability Insurance (SSDI)   Money that has been funneled into the Social Security system through payroll deductions on earnings. Workers who are disabled are entitled to these benefits. People who are born with a disability or become disabled before the age of 22 may collect SSDI under a parent's account if the parent is retired, disabled, or deceased.

Social skills   Learned abilities such as sharing, turn taking, asserting one's independence, and forming attachments, which allow one to effectively interact with others.

Social Stories   A social skills intervention strategy that teaches self-awareness, self-calming, and self-management skills.

Social worker   A professional who aids and counsels others to function within society; he or she may help to secure services such as counseling, financial assistance, or respite care.

Special education   Specialized instruction to address a student's unique educational *disabilities* as determined by an *evaluation*. Instruction must be precisely matched to the child's educational needs and adapted to his or her learning style.

Speech–language pathologist   A therapist who works to evaluate and improve speech and *language* skills, as well as to improve *oral motor* abilities.

SSA   *See* Social Security Administration.

SSDI   *See* Social Security Disability Insurance.

SSI   *See* Supplemental Security Income.

SSRI   *See* Selective serotonin reuptake inhibitor.

Standard deviation A measurement of the degree to which a given test score differs from the mean (average) score. On many IQ tests, for example, the majority of children score within 15 points above to 15 points below the mean score of 100, so one standard deviation is considered to be 15 points.

Standard score A test score based on the normal distribution curve (the *bell curve*). In tests scored with standard scores, 100 usually is considered exactly average, with scores from 85 to 115 considered to be in the average range.

Standardized test A test that is administered in exactly the same way each time and that is designed so that results can be compared with the performance of other individuals who have taken the test.

Stanford Binet Intelligence Scale (SBS-V) Test of intelligence.

Status epilepticus A life-threatening condition in which *seizures* continue without a break for more than 30 minutes and the child remains unconscious.

Stereotypic behavior Purposeless, repetitive movements or behaviors such as hand flapping.

Stereotypy *See* Stereotypic behavior.

Stimulant A type of medication used to treat ADHD.

Stimulus A physical object or environmental event that may trigger a response or have an effect on the behavior of a person. Some stimuli are internal (earache pain), while others are external (a smile from a loved one).

Substantial gainful activity SGA is used to decide if a person has a disability. This is used to determine eligibility for Social Security Disability Income and Supplemental Security Income.

Subthreshold A difference that is so slight that it is not detected by standard tests, but may cause some difficulties for the individual.

Supplemental Security Income (SSI) A program of payments available for eligible people who are disabled, blind, or elderly. SSI is based on financial need, not on past earnings.

Supported employment Employment in a community setting but with support.

Sustained release A long-lasting form of medication in which small amounts of the medication are released over time rather than releasing all of the medication immediately upon ingestion.

Syndrome A group of symptoms or traits that, occurring together, are characteristic of a particular disorder.

Syntax Rules of language.

Tactile Relating to touch.

Tactile defensiveness Oversensitivity or aversion to touch.

Tardive dyskinesia A condition characterized by involuntary jerky movements of the mouth, tongue, lips, and trunk. Some medications prescribed for behavior control may contribute to the development of this condition.

Task analysis Systematic and careful review of all the actions involved in a task.

Temporal lobe seizure *See* Complex partial seizure.

Test of Language Competence (TLC) Test of language/communication skills.

Test of Visual Motor Integration (VMI) Test of visual-motor skills.

Thimerosal An ethyl mercury–based substance formerly used to preserve some vaccines such as the *MMR*.

Designations used by companies to distinguish their products are often claimed as trademarks. In all instances where John Wiley & Sons, Inc. is aware of a claim, the product names appear in initial capital or all capital letters. Readers, however, should contact the appropriate companies for more complete information regarding trademarks and registration.

Tics   Involuntary, purposeless movements or sounds that occur, for example, in *Tourette's syndrome*. Tics are usually distressing to a child who has them, in contrast to *sterotypic behavior*, which children with autism find pleasurable or neutral.

Toddler Infant Motor Evaluation (TIME)   Test of motor skills.

Tonic–clonic seizure   A generalized seizure with two phases: a tonic phase, in which the body stiffens and the child loses consciousness; and a clonic phase, in which the muscles alternatingly jerk and relax.

Tourette's syndrome   A *developmental disability* characterized by vocal and motor movement *tics* that change in severity and nature over time.

Transition   The period between the end of one activity and the start of another.

Transition plan   Planning for major transitions, most notably between Birth-to-Three services and school-aged servicies, and again in adolescence.

Tricyclic antidepressant   A type of antidepressant medication.

Tuberous sclerosis   A congenital disorder in which benign tubers develop in the skin, organs, and brain, and which sometimes includes *seizures, autism,* and/or *mental retardation.*

Uniform Transfers to Minors Act (UTMA)   A law pertaining to gifts to minors. The gifts become the property of the minors at either 18 or 21, depending on the state.

Vaccine   A solution that is administered orally or as an injection in order to help the body create defenses against a specific disease. Vaccines contain bacteria or viruses (or parts of them) that ordinarily cause disease, but have been altered so that they won't cause an infection.

Validity   When used relative to testing, this term typically refers to the notion that the test is indeed measuring what it is supposed to.

Vestibular   Pertaining to the *sensory* system located in the inner ear that allows the body to maintain balance and enjoyably participate in movement such as swinging and roughhousing.

Vineland Adaptive Behavior Scales   Test of adaptive skills.

Visual–motor   Related to the use of the eyes to process and then motoricaly respond in tasks, e.g., putting a puzzle piece into a puzzle or a key into a keyhole.

Vocational rehabilitation   Employment program for people with disabilities.

Voice synthesizer   Technology that allows a computer to say what someone types.

Wechsler Intelligence Scales   Test of intelligence.

Work activity center   Provides opportunities for independence and individual growth for people with disabilities.

Index